THE
APOCRYPHAL
NEW TESTAMENT

Being the apocryphal gospels,
acts, epistles, and apocalypses

with other narratives and fragments translated by

Montague Rhodes James
Litt.D., F.B.A., F.S.A.

*Provost of Eton; sometime Provost
of King's College, Cambridge*

the apocryphile press
BERKELEY, CA
www.apocryphile.org

apocryphile press
BERKELEY, CA

Apocryphile Press
1700 Shattuck Ave #81
Berkeley, CA 94709
www.apocryphile.org

First published in 1924 by the Clarendon Press, Oxford, UK.
Apocryphile Press Edition, 2004.

Reprinted by permission of Oxford University Press, London.
For sale in the USA only. Sales prohibited in the UK.

ISBN 9781955821483

Also in this series:
The Apocrypha and Pseudepigrapha of the Old Testament,
Volume One: Apocrypha
The Apocrypha and Pseudepigrapha of the Old Testament,
Volume Two: Pseudepigrapha
The Apostolic Fathers
Apocrypha: The Compact King James Version
The Lost Books of the Bible & The Forgotten Books of Eden

CONTENTS

PREFACE

IT is a matter of common knowledge that there exist
such things as Apocryphal Gospels, Acts, Epistles, Revelations—in fact apocryphal representatives of every one of
the classes of writings which form the New Testament.
Bible dictionaries, encyclopaedias, manuals, and text-books
have made the fact familiar. Moreover, without much
trouble it is possible for the less incurious to get hold of
translations of a good many of these books. But I do not
think I am speaking inaccurately when I say that there is
at present no one book in existence which will supply the
English reader—or for that matter any reader, of Latin,
Greek, or Oriental languages—with a comprehensive view
of all that is meant by the phrase, 'the apocryphal literature
of the New Testament'.

The object of the present volume is to give that comprehensive view. It contains fresh versions of all the really
important texts, and full summaries, with extracts, of those
which do not need to be translated word for word. Further,
it attempts to put the reader in possession of the results of
the very fruitful researches of the last generation. In those
thirty years a great mass of material has been added to the
available stock, and, what is not less important, there has
been a sifting of what is early from what is late, and an
order and chronology of the writings, which is not likely to
be seriously disturbed, has been settled.

From the historical and the literary point of view, then,
it is worth while to present the apocryphal literature of the
New Testament afresh; but it is also worth while from the
religious point of view. People may still be heard to say,
'After all, these Apocryphal Gospels and Acts, as you call
them, are just as interesting as the old ones. It was only
by accident or caprice that they were not put into the New
Testament'. The best answer to such loose talk has always
been, and is now, to produce the writings and let them tell
their own story. It will very quickly be seen that there is

no question of any one's having excluded them from the
New Testament: they have done that for themselves.

Interesting as they are—and I will try to show later why
they are interesting—they do not achieve either of the two
principal purposes for which they were written, the instilling
of true religion and the conveyance of true history.

As religious books they were meant to reinforce the existing
stock of Christian beliefs: either by revealing new doctrines
—usually differing from those which held the field; or by
interpreting old ones—again, usually in a fresh sense; or by
extolling some special virtue, as chastity or temperance;
or by enforcing belief in certain doctrines or events, e. g. the
Virgin birth, the resurrection of Christ, the second coming,
the future state—by the production of evidence which, if
true, should be irrefragable. For all these purposes the
highest authority is claimed by the writings; they are the
work, they tell us, of eyewitnesses of the events, or they
report the utterances of the Lord himself. As books of
history they aim at supplementing the scanty data (as they
seemed) of the Gospels and Acts, and in this they resemble
many of the Jewish Midrashim and apocrypha. Like these,
they sometimes bear testimony to the currency of a tradition
which has other and better evidence to support it, as when
the Acts of John assume John's residence at Ephesus, and
the Acts of Peter and Paul the martyrdom of those apostles
at Rome.

But, as I have said, they fail of their purpose. Among
the prayers and discourses of the apostles in the spurious
Acts some utterances may be found which are remarkable
and even beautiful: not a few of the stories are notable
and imaginative, and have been consecrated and made
familiar to us by the genius of mediaeval artists. But the
authors do not speak with the voices of Paul or of John, or
with the quiet simplicity of the three first Gospels. It is
not unfair to say that when they attempt the former tone,
they are theatrical, and when they essay the latter, they are
jejune. In short, the result of anything like an attentive
study of the literature, in bulk and in detail, is an added
respect for the sense of the Church Catholic, and for the
wisdom of the scholars of Alexandria, Antioch, and Rome :
assuredly in this case they were tried money-changers, who
proved all things and held fast that which was good. Many

a book, like the venerable Gospel according to the Hebrews and the Preaching of Peter, which we should dearly have liked to possess for the light they would throw on primitive Christian history, has perished as a consequence of their unfavourable verdict, and we regret the loss—no one more keenly than myself: but with the verdict that consigned them first to obscurity and then to destruction I cannot quarrel.

But, it may be said, if these writings are good neither as books of history, nor of religion, nor even as literature, why spend time and labour on giving them a vogue which on your own showing they do not deserve? Partly, of course, in order to enable others to form a judgement on them; but that is not the whole case. The truth is that they must not be regarded only from the point of view which they claim for themselves. In almost every other aspect they have a great and enduring interest.

If they are not good sources of history in one sense, they are in another. They record the imaginations, hopes, and fears of the men who wrote them; they show what was acceptable to the unlearned Christians of the first ages, what interested them, what they admired, what ideals of conduct they cherished for this life, what they thought they would find in the next. As folk-lore and romance, again, they are precious ; and to the lover and student of mediaeval literature and art they reveal the source of no inconsiderable part of his material and the solution of many a puzzle. They have, indeed, exercised an influence (wholly disproportionate to their intrinsic merits) so great and so widespread, that no one who cares about the history of Christian thought and Christian art can possibly afford to neglect them.

The remainder of this Preface will be devoted to the explanation of several matters : the word apocryphal and my use of it : the misleading character of the last ' Apocryphal New Testament ' and the fallacies which dominate it : the contents of the present one : and, lastly, some notice of the writings which are not included in it.

First as to the title—the *Apocryphal New Testament*.

The words apocrypha and apocryphal, particularly the latter, have come to mean, oftener than not, in common speech, that which is spurious or untrue. They do not mean

that in themselves, nor did they in the minds of those who
first applied them to books. They began by being terms of
dignity and respect: they have degenerated into terms of
something like abuse. An apocryphal book was—originally
—one too sacred and *secret* to be in every one's hands: it
must be reserved for the initiate, the inner circle of believers.
But, in order to enlist respect, such books were almost
always issued under venerable names which they had no
true right to bear. We hear of apocryphal books of Adam,
Moses, and so forth. The pretence was that these had
lately been brought to light, after ages of concealment by
pious disciples. I do not intend to write a history of the
gradual degradation of the words: I need only say that the
falsity of the attributions was soon recognized: and so (to
pass over three centuries of transition), in the parlance of
Jerome, who has influenced posterity more than any one
else in this matter, apocryphal means spurious, false, to be
rejected and, probably, disliked.

The application of the word Apocrypha to that Appendix
to the Old Testament which we have in our Bibles is a new
departure, due to the reformers of the sixteenth century,
and it is not consistent either with the original sense of the
word or with Jerome's usage of it, for that Appendix contains
no books of secret lore (unless 2 Esdras be so reckoned),
but several books which are not spurious, besides some that
are. There is, then, some confusion here, and the existence
of that confusion has led scholars in recent years to use the
long word *pseudepigraphic* (= falsely entitled) when they
wish to describe a really spurious book, as distinct from
those contained in our 'Apocrypha'.

But, though all the writings in the present collection could
be called pseudepigrapha, the old word apocrypha is good
enough for my purpose, and I employ it here in the sense
of false and spurious, even when I am dealing with writings
which may contain ancient and truthful elements. This
book, then, I call the *Apocryphal New Testament*.

It is not the first of its name. Just over a hundred years
ago, in 1820, an *Apocryphal New Testament* was issued by
William Hone, best remembered as the author of the *Every-
day Book*, the *Year Book*, the *Table Book*, *Ancient Mysteries
Explained*.

Hone's book has long held the field: it is constantly being

reprinted, and it has enjoyed a popularity which is in truth
far beyond its deserts. For it is a misleading and an unoriginal book.

Misleading, because all its externals suggest that it is
a supplement to the New Testament. Printed in double
columns, with all the books divided into chapters and
verses, with a summary prefixed to each chapter in italic
type, with head-lines of the same character on every page,
with an 'Order of Books' beginning 'Mary hath Chapters 8',
it presents the familiar aspect of the English Bible to any
one who opens it. Misleading, again, because about half
the volume is occupied by the writings of the Apostolic
Fathers—the Epistles of Clement of Rome, Barnabas,
Ignatius, and Polycarp, and the Shepherd of Hermas—
which are not apocryphal. Misleading also in a more serious
way, because title-page and preface tell us that it contains
the writings which were 'not included in the New Testament
by its compilers' when it was first 'collected into a volume'.

Unoriginal, because the whole contents of the book
except the prefaces are borrowed bodily from two books
about a hundred years older than Hone's. All the apocryphal
writings are taken—I think without any acknowledgement
—from Jeremiah Jones's *New and Full Method of Settling
the Canonical Authority of the New Testament*, published in
1736, while the version of the Apostolic Fathers is that
of Archbishop Wake—whose footnotes, by the way, recording various readings of the manuscripts in Greek and Latin,
have suffered sadly at the hands of Hone's, and subse-
quent, compositors.

It is, in fact, to speak frankly, a very bad book; and
I should be justified in criticizing its composition and
particularly its prefaces much more sharply than I do.
Only I cannot forget that it was the first book on the New
Testament Apocrypha which fell into my hands, and that
it then exercised a fascination which has never lost its hold
upon me. I feel, therefore, that if I could consign it to
a more or less honourable grave by providing a better
substitute for it, I should in some sort be paying a debt of
gratitude and at the same time doing a service to the reading
public.

I have said, and I think proved, that Hone's is a quite
unoriginal book: I have also said that it is misleading in

several ways, but this latter assertion I have not as yet
sufficiently supported.   In doing so, I shall attempt to
present a truth as well as expose an error.
   The key-note of the book, the animus of it, comes out in
the phrase which I have quoted from its title-page, and
which speaks of writings 'not included in the New Testament
by its compilers'.   The words call up a picture of a number
of men—probably bishops in mitres—seated round a table
piled with rolls and books.   One pile is labelled 'Gospels ,
another 'Epistles', and so on.   The members of this com-
mittee examine each volume with more or less care: most
of them are put aside with gestures of disapproval.   Finally
a small selection is made, and entrusted to the chairman,
who draws up a careful list of its contents, and subsequently,
no doubt, hands it over to a publisher with a proper au-
thorization.   In due time the New Testament 'collected
into a volume' is disseminated throughout the Christian
world.   I really believe that something not very unlike this
fable is fairly deducible from Hone's prefaces.
   The fallacy which dominates it is the notion that the
writings which comprise our New Testament were 'collected
into a volume' at a given moment by a definite act of the
authorities of the Church.   Those who have read any
modern elementary account of the formation of the Canon
are aware that the processes of inclusion and exclusion were
gradual: that by the end of the second century we find the
Four Gospels in a secure position, and Irenaeus arguing
from the analogy of nature that there could be no more and
no fewer than four: that the Pauline Epistles are already
formed into a collection: that the authority of the Acts is
not doubted.   Doubt, indeed, really attaches only to some
of the lesser Epistles, and the Revelation: and the grounds
of doubt are various, the Revelation, for instance, being
disliked for its teaching about the millennium or its obscurity,
and some of the minor Epistles failing to find recognition
from their shortness and relative unimportance.   Exceptional
(within the Church) is the attitude of a party (so obscure is
its history that we are not sure whether it was a group of
people or a single writer) who in the second century rejected
the Johannine writings in bulk.
   The details of all this must be sought in professed histories
of the Canon: only the most general statements can find

a place here. The point is this, that when Hone or any one else speaks in terms which suggest that our New Testament is the result of a selection made by a council of the Church or any similar body, from among a number of competing books which might just as well have been included in it as not, he is very much astray.

Yet, as is usually the case, there is a grain of truth underlying the fallacy. There were a few books which attained a measure of recognition and eventually lost it.

Let us say that the best external test of the canonicity of a writing is, whether or not it was read in the public worship of Christian congregations which were in communion with the generality of other Christian congregations. We know that there were such congregations, or churches, all over the ancient world, and that there were others which were not in communion with these, but could be labelled as adherents of some teacher whose doctrine differed from that of the majority—were he Marcion, Valentinus, Montanus, or any other.

Now what books do we find, outside those of the New Testament, which we can be sure were so used by what we will call normal or Catholic Christians? The best evidence we can get, apart from definite statements by early writers (of which there are not many), is that of our oldest manuscripts of the complete Bible, made for public use. One of these, the Codex Sinaiticus, of the fourth century, adds to our books the Epistle of Barnabas and the Shepherd of Hermas. Another, the Codex Alexandrinus, of the fifth century, adds the Epistle of Clement of Rome to the Corinthians, and what is called his Second Epistle, which is really a sermon by another person unknown. We are definitely told that the First Epistle was read in many churches.

Then (turning to some facts we gather from other sources) the 'Muratorian fragment' (late in the second century?) tells us that the Revelation of Peter was received, not unanimously, at Rome: and a fifth-century Church historian, Sozomen, records that in his time it was read annually on Good Friday in some churches in Palestine.

A manuscript at Constantinople, which perhaps was copied from a supplement to a large Bible, gives us, together with the Epistles of Clement, Barnabas, Ignatius, and

Polycarp, another writing called the Teaching (Didache) of the Apostles. This book Eusebius, in the fourth century, classes among those that were not certainly spurious or certainly canonical, but disputed. We cannot say that it was used publicly by any Church.

A list of Biblical books in a sixth-century manuscript of the Epistles (Codex Claromontanus, Paris) includes among Biblical books, Barnabas, Hermas, the Revelation of Peter, and the Acts of Paul. But it is impossible to maintain that these Acts enjoyed a reputation equal to that of the other books.[1]

So our list is a very short one. We may fairly say that the only books which had a real chance of being included in the Canon of the New Testament were the Epistles of Clement and Barnabas, the Revelation of Peter, and the Shepherd of Hermas; for I do not think we need reckon in the Didache or the Acts of Paul. And we may be thankful that the Church at large finally declared against them; for the first Epistle of Clement is the only one of them which we should have found tolerable now.

There was, then, a serious claim for the recognition of four or five books. But when we have said this much, we have by no means exhausted the list of writings for which the same claim was made and was not so seriously entertained: books which in larger or smaller circles were placed on a level with those of our Canon, but were regarded by the Church at large as the Book of Mormon or the writings of Mrs. Mary Baker G. Eddy are now. Outside the ranks of these, too, there is an immense crowd of smaller writings which claim, indeed, to supplement the Bible in one way or another, but of which it is difficult to say that any one was ever looked upon as 'Scripture'. Such are many of the lesser Passion-narratives, or again those of the Death of the Virgin. Documents of this kind may be said to shade off gradually into the category of the Lives of the Saints.

Of all these classes is the present collection composed. A brief survey of the arrangement will make this clear.

I have placed first the remains of the oldest books, mainly

[1] One writing of the fifth century uses them, and cannot be proved to use the Canonical Acts ; but it is an exception, and an eccentric one in itself—a book called the *Supper* of (pseudo-)Cyprian, a cento of Bible tags, made perhaps for use in schools.

the Secondary Gospels, of none of which do we possess a complete text, and of one only, the Gospel of Peter, so much as a few pages. With these I have put a selection of the most important *Agrapha* (a rather clumsy name for the non-Biblical sayings of, and traditions about, our Lord). Notices of lost heretical books, and lists of apocrypha, are collected in the same section.

These fragments are followed by the complete texts, among which what have been called Gospels come first: and first among them is a group of Infancy Gospels and stories of the birth of the Virgin. Two of them, the Book of James (or Protevangelium), and the Gospel of Thomas, are second-century books. The first we have with comparatively slight alterations; the second has been drastically expurgated. The short prefatory notices prefixed to the several books give, I hope, enough details to guide the reader.

The later texts are summarized, not translated word for word. This plan I have adopted in order to avoid repetition, and to place the more important books in relief. The reader loses nothing by it, and is spared a vast deal of verbiage.

Of the Ministry we have no apocryphal narratives, except some rather late Coptic fragments, which I have classed with the Passion stories.

The Passion Gospels or narratives which are really important are two: the fragment of the Gospel of Peter, and the Acts of Pilate (Gospel of Nicodemus). The first is of the second century (about A. D. 150), the other of the fourth. There are old elements, perhaps, in the Report of Pilate. This, and the mass of later texts which deal with the Passion and Resurrection are, as before, summarized.

To these I append what is now called the Gospel of Bartholomew, probably a late *réchauffé* of a second-century book, a summary of a Coptic Book of Bartholomew, and a version of an heretical book attributed to John.

Between Gospels and Acts I place the famous legend of the Death and Assumption of the Virgin, translating the two leading narratives, and summarizing the rest. I cannot regard any of the texts as older than the fourth century, but the nucleus of the story may be—I think must be—at least as old as the third.

Of the Acts it will be useful to say a little more here:

The series was begun by the man who called himself Leucius
—that being the name (traditional or invented) of a companion and disciple of St. John. 'Leucius' writes the Acts
of JOHN not later than the middle of the second century,
taking the Canonical Acts as his model, but infusing into
his work more romantic elements. His presentation of
the Person of our Lord, and his use of Gnostic terminology,
cannot in my mind be reconciled with the view that he
was an orthodox Christian. A generation later, a priest of
Asia Minor writes the Acts of PAUL, with the object of
doing honour to the apostle. His authorship of the book
is detected, his book is regarded as an imposture, and he
is degraded from his office. So Tertullian tells us,[1] placing
the event in his own time.

This writer also takes St. Luke's Acts for his model.
There is little imitation of Leucius, but enough to show
that he knew the Acts of John. Next, not later than
A. D. 200, come the Acts of PETER: orthodox, as are those
of Paul, but written by a very close imitator of Leucius.,
So servile, indeed, is his imitation, that I have tried before
now to prove that he *was* Leucius. I am, however, no
longer of that opinion. This author was an Asiatic, probably:
at any rate he knew very little about Rome.

The Acts of ANDREW and of THOMAS both belong to
the third century. It is contended (I must refer the reader
to the notice prefixed to THOMAS) that the latter were
composed in Syriac. Imitation of Leucius is very apparent
in both books; but while ANDREW may be regarded at
a pinch as orthodox, THOMAS certainly oversteps the line.

These five books were collected into a *corpus*, probably
by the Manichaean sect. These, the disciples of Mani,
who blended Christianity with the old Magian religion
of Persia, teaching that the powers of Good and Evil were
coeternal, and that the material world was of the Evil
side, welcomed these books, in which asceticism is constantly

---

[1] A difficulty as to date has to be noted. Jerome, who repeats
Tertullian's story, adds something to it (we know not on what authority),
namely, the detail that the priest was convicted 'in the presence of
John' ('apud Ioannem'). This is not possible historically, but the words
stand for something. My conjecture that we ought to read 'at Iconium'
('apud Iconium') has met with some approval, and I believe it may be
right. It certainly agrees with all else that we know of the provenance
of these Acts.

superexalted, and marriage condemned (at least by Leucius) as an institution of the devil. In the fourth century, the Manichaeans upheld these as the true Acts of the Apostles, and most likely rejected the Canonical Acts in their favour. Photius, the learned patriarch of Constantinople at the end of the ninth century, read all five books as the work of Leucius, whose name had by that time come to be attached to the whole. But it is to be kept in mind that though they all came to be lumped together as the work of one heretical author, they are by five different writers, and three out of the five are, speaking somewhat generously, orthodox.

They were followed by a host of legends of the apostles, of which enough is said in the body of this book.

The Epistles are few. The famous correspondence of Christ with Abgarus is probably of the third century, the dull Epistle to the Laodiceans may be of the second, the letters of Paul and Seneca, equally poor, are not older than the fourth. But the Epistle of the Apostles, now first appearing in English, is dated by its editor at about A. D. 160, and the 'Third Epistle to the Corinthians' (which is part of the Acts of Paul) is also of that date.

The Apocalypses are headed by that of Peter, which I would assign to the first quarter of the second century. It has distinct resemblances in language and in matter to the Second Epistle of Peter. For instance, that book alone among the canonical scriptures speaks of the destruction of the world by fire; and this is prominent in the Apocalypse of Peter. For the first time, all the remains we have of this early book are brought together.

The Apocalypse of Paul follows. Though only of the fourth century, it is extremely interesting as a direct descendant of *Peter*, and as the parent of innumerable later visions of the next world.

That of Thomas—of uncertain date—appears (in a very ragged guise, it is true) for the first time in English. For the Virgin's Apocalypse and that of Stephen (a very doubtful item) summaries are enough. I have excluded, as not sufficiently interesting, the late Apocalypse of John which Tischendorf prints.

In translating my texts I have employed a style meant to remind the reader of the Authorized Version of the Bible.

In introducing them I have not attempted to record every
mention of them which is to be found in Church writers.
Where the date and character of a book is sufficiently
established, it is not important to know that Augustine
or even Eusebius names it. It is only when such writers
tell us something that we do not learn from other sources
that I quote them. And I have reduced the explanatory
notes, the mention of previous editions, and the record
of various readings, to an absolute minimum. In so doing
I have followed the example set in Hennecke's recent (1904)
German collection of New Testament Apocrypha. The
first volume of that excellent work contains only introductions and texts: the notes on language, text, and interpretation fill a second volume as large as the first. But
it is for the specialist that this second volume is meant:
the first is intended for the general reader, and it is for
him that my work also is designed.

Numerous as are the texts which appear here, the collection is not an absolutely complete *corpus* of the apocryphal
literature of the New Testament. Several whole groups
of writings do not find a place in it: I hope, for sufficient
reasons. Of these some notice must now be given.
    The first class of books which I have found it impossible
to include is that of the Gnostic Apocrypha. We have
a considerable mass of this literature, all in Coptic. As
a rule it is safe to assume that the Coptic is a version from
Greek: but in the case of some of these books it may
possibly be the original language.
    The oldest of the extant Gnostic treatises have not yet
been published. They are contained in a manuscript of the
fifth century at Berlin, which is almost complete. The first
of them is a Gospel of Mary, in which the risen Saviour
instructs the apostles, and Mary then describes a vision in
which she was shown the progress of the 'gnostic' (enlightened) soul through the seven planetary spheres.
    The second is an apocryphon of John, which we know to
be earlier than A.D. 180, since Irenaeus used it for his
account of a particular school of Gnostics, in Book I, 29–31,
of his refutation of heresies. It begins with a dialogue
between John and a Pharisee, but quickly merges into
Gnostic technicalities.

The third is a Wisdom of Jesus Christ: revelations made after the resurrection to the Twelve and to seven holy women, on a mountain in Galilee.

The last thing in the manuscript is an episode from the Acts of Peter, which has been published and will be found in its proper place among the Acts.

A manuscript, probably of the fifth century, in the British Museum, called Codex Askewianus from a former owner Askew, contains a bulky work, or works (for not all the treatises of which it is composed are of one date) known as the *Pistis Sophia* (Faith(ful) Wisdom) from the spiritual being of that name with whose progress through the universe it is largely concerned. This also is in the form of revelations given to the apostles and holy women after the resurrection. It is of the third century, has been more than once edited, and has been translated into English.

A very mutilated papyrus manuscript in the Bodleian Library, brought from Egypt by the famous traveller Bruce, and called the Codex Brucianus, contains two Gnostic treatises. One is the Two Books of Jeû (a spiritual being), the other, which is older, has lost its title. These are somewhat earlier in date than the *Pistis Sophia*. The whole manuscript has been finely edited by C. Schmidt.

While the *Pistis Sophia* is just readable, the Books of Jeû are not. The revelations they contain are conveyed in mystic diagrams, and numbers, and meaningless collections of letters, and it requires a vast deal of historical imagination and sympathy to put oneself in the place of anybody who could tolerate, let alone reverence, the dreary stuff.

A second large group of books omitted here consists of those which deal with Church order and with liturgy.

The earliest of these is the Teaching of the Apostles or Didache already mentioned, discovered about forty years ago and repeatedly edited and translated since.

Ultimately this short book was incorporated into a large work, the *Apostolic Constitutions,* in eight books, compiled by an Arian of Palestine in the fourth century. These eight books are compounded, with additions, out of the *Didascalia* (extant in Syriac and partly in Latin, and of the third century), which underlie Books I–VI of the *Constitutions*: the *Didache* and other early material (Book VII): the *Church Order* of Hippolytus, and additions by the compiler (Book

VIII). With these eight books should be reckoned the *Canons of the Apostles*, in the form of a code of rules.

All these books are occupied with prescribing rules for Church government, and for the order of divine service; and books of the same kind, purporting to emanate from the apostles and (very usually) to be recorded by Clement, were current all over Eastern Christendom: we have them in Syriac, Arabic, Coptic, Ethiopic. One, called the *Apostolic Church Order*, is couched in a series of speeches each pronounced by an apostle. This we have in Greek. Another notable member of the group is the Testament of the Lord (Syriac) which is a fairly recent discovery. It differs from the rest in beginning with an apocalyptic portion—a prophecy uttered by Christ—part of which is embodied in *another* Testament of the Lord which is prefixed, in the Ethiopic version, to the Epistle of the Apostles.

The attribution of many of these books to the Lord or the apostles is a very transparent fiction: one hardly knows how seriously the writers themselves expected or wished it to be taken. The same is true of the numerous Liturgies (i. e. Communion offices) which are current under the names of apostles.

A third group is known as the Clementine literature. We have, in Greek, Latin, and Syriac, a work in two forms. The setting is derived from secular romance; it is the ancient theme of the members of a family parted from one another by a series of accidents for many years, and in the end reunited: in this case it is Clement's family. His parents, his brothers, and himself are brought together by the agency of St. Peter. This setting is filled in, and indeed completely overlaid, by the matter which conveys the real purpose of the book, namely, the discourses of Peter; partly his debates with Simon Magus, and partly his unopposed expositions of doctrine.

The body of doctrine thus set forth is not orthodox. It is, in fact, eccentric. At one time it was contended that these books were precious monuments of a condition of the Church in primitive times, when the Twelve were in opposition to Paul; it being doubtless the case that Simon Magus in these books is to some extent Paul under a mask. But it is now recognized that the books are not only rather late in date (not earlier than the end of the third or beginning of the fourth century), but also that they do not represent the views of a large school of thought, but of a small and obscure sect.

The Greek form of the romance consists of twenty so-called Homilies—the Clementine *Homilies*. The Latin is a version of another form, expurgated and translated by Rufinus in the fourth century. It is in ten books, and is called the Clementine *Recognitions*. The Syriac, never yet translated, mingles the two forms together.

There are Epitomes and other off-shoots of this literature much later in date, which need not detain us. But with this same Clement's name are associated certain Revelations made to him by Peter which deserve a passing notice. Of these, again, there are several forms, extant in Syriac, Arabic, and Ethiopic, and not yet discriminated nor edited fully. Some of them treat of the whole history of the world from its creation to its end, with prophecies of such late events as the rise and progress of Islam. In one of the Ethiopic recensions the old Apocalypse of Peter was found embedded. Others are wholly devoted to ordinances for Church government.

A fourth group should perhaps just be mentioned, the works ascribed to Dionysius the Areopagite, Paul's Athenian convert. They consist of treatises on mystical theology, and letters: there is also a long Epistle to Timothy on the deaths of Peter and Paul. None of these are older than the fifth century. The theological treatises have had a great influence on Christian speculation: but they need a great deal of exposition by a specialist to make them intelligible.

Mention of a good many later books will be found under various heads in the body of this work. The names of a few which have escaped other notice may be given here.

There are Lives of St. John Baptist, by Mark, and by a supposed disciple, Eurippus, which have been edited by F. Nau in the *Patrologia Orientalis* with a French version.

An account of the death of Zacharias, and his being raised in order to be baptized by Christ, along with John, exists in Slavonic, and was translated by Berendts (*Zacharias-Apokryphen*). I have summarized it in my *Lost Apocrypha of the Old Testament*.

A document called the 'Priesthood of Jesus' is given by the twelfth-century lexicographer Suidas, s. v. *Jesus*. It

was rendered into Latin by Robert Grosseteste, Bishop of
Lincoln, in the thirteenth century. It is a late production,
telling how Jesus was appointed to fill a vacancy in the priesthood; how his pedigree had to be investigated, and how
the Virgin was summoned (Joseph being dead) and gave
an account of the Conception. All this purports to be
taken from the Jewish archives.

A long book, a discussion of Christianity at the Persian
court, contains a narrative of signs and wonders which
took place in a Persian temple at the birth of Christ, and
started the Magi on their journey. It was last edited by
Bratke in *Texte und Untersuchungen*.

A Dispute between Christ and the Devil exists in Greek.
Vassiliev prints two forms of it in his *Anecdota Graeco-
Byzantina*. It has some slight affinities with the Gospel of
Bartholomew, but it is very late and not very interesting.

A Revelation of Lazarus describing the torments of Hell
is perhaps the latest of the apocryphal Apocalypses. I have
only seen it in Old French. It occurs in the 'Calendrier des
Bergers', is described by Nisard in his *Histoire de la littérature
populaire*, and is also to be found, illustrated by paintings
of the early part of the sixteenth century, at the west end
of the cathedral of Albi.

All Rabbinic and Mohammedan traditions about Jesus
are excluded: among the latter is the very lengthy Gospel
of Barnabas (well edited by Canon Ragg in 1907) which
is a forgery of the fifteenth century at earliest, written in
Italian by a renegade from Christianity to Islam.

It is, I hope, obvious that I ought not to have included
in an apocryphal *New* Testament the Christian or Christian-
ized books which bear the names of *Old* Testament worthies;
but I shall be right in recording that there are such books:
notably the *Vision* (perhaps the whole book known as the
Ascension) *of Isaiah* ; the two first (and two last) chapters
of 4 Esdras (2 Esdras of our Apocrypha); the *Apocalypses
of Elijah, Daniel*, and *Zephaniah*: two books of *Baruch*:
an *Apocalypse of Esdras* edited by Tischendorf, and another,
in Latin, printed by Mercati: the *Apocalypse of Sedrach*:
probably the lost apocryphal *Ezekiel*: the *Testaments of
Abraham, Isaac, Jacob*, and *Job*: and not a few more.
Under this heading, too, may be placed many portions of
the *Sibylline Oracles* and the lost *Prophecy of Hystaspes*.

Again I may refer readers to my *Lost Apocrypha of the Old Testament.*

I have not even now enumerated all the writings, printed and unprinted, fragmentary or complete, which might be considered by some one to have a claim to appear in an Apocryphal New Testament. I have rather aimed at showing what manner of books those are which I have set aside, and at suggesting the reasons why they do not figure in this volume.

I am greatly indebted to Professor C. H. Turner, F.B.A., who has been so good as to read through the proofs of this book, and to call my attention to a number of doubtful points : he must not be held responsible for the errors which survive. To the Bishop of Ripon, who last year suggested to me the desirability of providing a substitute for Hone's *Apocryphal New Testament*, and who has also read through many of the sheets, my cordial thanks are likewise offered ; and to Professor F. C. Burkitt, D.D., F.B.A., for his valuable note on a passage of the Acts of Thomas.[1]

ETON, *August* 1923.

[1] See p. 378.

NOTE ON FIFTH IMPRESSION

IN this impression two Appendixes have been added by Dr. J. W. B. Barns in which are translated (1) the text published by [Sir] Harold Idris Bell and T. C. Skeat in *Fragments of an Unknown Gospel* and in *The New Gospel Fragments* (both 1935), and (2) some new portions of the *Acts of Paul* of which the most important is the Hamburg Greek papyrus edited by Schmidt and Schubart as ΠΡΑΞΕΙΣ ΠΑΥΛΟΥ (1936).

SELECT BIBLIOGRAPHY

References to less important works will be found in the body of the book. Antiquated publications are omitted.

COLLECTIONS OF TEXTS

FABRICIUS, JO. ALBERT. Codex Apocryphus Novi Testamenti. 8vo. 3 vols. in 2. Hamburg, 1719, 1743.
The first really good book: still indispensable.
THILO, JO. CAR. Codex Apocryphus N. T. Vol. I (all published). Leipzig, 1832.
Excellent commentaries.
TISCHENDORF, CONST. Evangelia Apocrypha. Ed. 2. 1876.
—— (Acta Apostolorum Apocrypha. 1851. Superseded: see below.)
—— Apocalypses Apocryphae. 1866. (Apoc. of Paul. Assumption of the Virgin.)
HENNECKE, EDGAR (and others). Neutestamentliche Apokryphen. 1904. Introductions and translations.
—— Handbuch zu den NTlichen Apokryphen. 1904. Commentaries and notes.
BELL, H. I., and SKEAT, T. C., Fragments of an Unknown Gospel; text also in The New Gospel Fragments. Both London, British Museum, 1935.
PREUSCHEN, E. Antilegomena. Giessen, 1901.
EVELYN WHITE, H. G. The Sayings of Jesus from Oxyrhynchus. Cambridge, 1920.
RESCH, A. Agrapha, 1889, &c. ⎫
ROPES, J. H. Die Sprüche Jesu. 1896. ⎬ Both in Texte und
(Select Agrapha.) ⎭ Untersuchungen.

GOSPELS

AMANN, E. Le Protévangile de Jacques et ses remaniements latins. 1910. In Les Apocryphes du N. T., Bousquet and Amann. Full commentary.
MICHEL, C., and PEETERS, P. Évangiles apocryphes I. 1911. (Protev. and History of Joseph.)
—— Évangiles apocryphes II. 1914. (Syriac, Arabic, and Armenian Infancy-Gospels): in Textes et Documents, Hemmer and Lejay.
SWETE, H. B. Gospel of Peter. Macmillan, 1893.
BONWETSCH, N. Die apokryphen Fragen des Bartholomäus. Göttinger Nachr., Philos.-Philol. Kl. 1897. (Greek and Slavonic).
WILMART, DOM A., and TISSERANT, E. Fragments grecs et latins de l'Évangile de Barthélemy. Revue Biblique, 1913.
MORICCA, U. Un nuovo testo dell' Evangelo di Bartolommeo. (The complete Latin version.) Ibid. 1921-2.

ROBINSON, FORBES. Coptic Apocryphal Gospels. Cambridge, 1896.
  In Texts and Studies.
REVILLOUT, E. Apocryphes coptes. In Patrologia Orientalis, Graffin
  and Nau. II. fasc. 2, IX. fasc. 2.
LACAU, P. Fragments d'Apocryphes coptes. Mém. de l'Inst. Archéol.
  du Caire. 1904.
BUDGE, SIR E. A. WALLIS. Coptic Apocrypha.
—— Coptic Martyrdoms.
—— Miscellaneous Texts.
  British Museum, 1913, 1914, 1915. (Containing the Book of
  Bartholomew, Apoc. of Paul, &c.)

ABGARUS AND VERONICA LEGENDS

DOBSCHÜTZ, E. VON. Christusbilder, 1899. (Texte u. Untersuchungen.)

ASSUMPTION OF THE VIRGIN

(TISCHENDORF, C. Apocalypses Apocr., above.)
WRIGHT, W. Contributions to the Apocryphal Literature of the N.T.
  1865.
LEWIS, MRS. A. S. Apocrypha Arabica. (Studia Sinaitica XI.)
  Cambridge, 1902.
BUDGE, SIR E. A. W. History of the B.V.M., &c. 1899. In Luzac's
  Semitic Text and Transl. Series.

ACTS

LIPSIUS, R. A. Die apokryphen Apostelgeschichten, 1883. Supple-
  ment, 1890. (4 vols.) Studies of the literature.
(TISCHENDORF, C. Acta Apost. Apocr., 1851, is superseded by)
LIPSIUS, R. A., and BONNET, MAX. Acta Apostolorum Apocrypha.
  I. Peter, Paul and Thecla, Thaddaeus. 1891.
  II. 1. (Bonnet.) Andrew, Bartholomew, John, Matthew. 1898.
  II. 2. Philip, Thomas, Barnabas. 1903.
ZAHN, TH. Acta Joannis. Erlangen, 1880.
  (The complete text of Prochorus.)
SCHMIDT, C. Acta Pauli. 1904. The Coptic text, &c.
—— Die alten Petrusakten. 1903. In Texte und Untersuchungen.
  Has the Coptic fragment, and an important study of the whole
  subject.
—— and SCHUBART, W. ΠΡΑΞΕΙΣ ΠΑΥΛΟΥ. 1936. New portions of the
  Greek text.
VOUAUX, L. Les Actes de Paul et ses lettres apocryphes. 1913.
—— Les Actes de Pierre. 1922.
  Both in Les Apocryphes du N. T.
FLAMION, J. Les Actes apocryphes de l'Apôtre André. Louvain, 1911.
  A study of these Acts.
WRIGHT, W. Apocryphal Acts of the Apostles (Syriac). 2 vols.
  Text and translation. 1871.
BUDGE, SIR E. A. W. Contendings of the Apostles (Ethiopic). 2 vols.
  Text and translation. 1901.
LEWIS, MRS. A. S. The Mythological Acts of the Apostles (Arabic)
  Horae Semiticae IV. Cambridge, 1904.

EPISTLES.

DOBSCHÜTZ, E. VON. Christusbilder, 1899. (*Above.*)
VOUAUX, L. Actes de Paul, *above.*
GUERRIER, L. Testament de N.-S. en Galilée. (Epistle of the Apostles, Ethiopic.) In Patrologia Orientalis IX, fasc. 3. 1913.
SCHMIDT, C. Gespräche Jesu mit seinen Jüngern, &c. (Epistle of the Apostles.) In Texte u. Unters. 1919.

APOCALYPSES

JAMES, M. R. A new text of the Apocalypse of Peter. Journal of Theol. Studies, 1910–11.
—— Apocrypha Anecdota I (Texts and Studies). Cambridge, 1893. (Apoc. of Paul, Latin, and of the Virgin.)

WRITINGS NOT INCLUDED

SCHMIDT, C. Koptisch-gnostische Schriften I. (Pistis Sophia, Books of Jeû.) 1905.
SCHWARTZE AND PETERMANN's earlier edition of the Pistis Sophia has a Latin version.
The Teaching of the Apostles (Didache), ed. Harnack 1886, Funk 1887, &c.
The Apostolic Church Order. Ed. Bickell, Geschichte des Kirchenrechts, 1843.
The Didascalia. Bunsen, Analecta Ante-Nicaena. 1854.
—— Gibson, Mrs. Horae Semiticae I. 1903.
—— Hauler, E. Fragmenta Veronensia. 1900.
The Apostolic Constitutions. Ed. F. X. Funk, 1905.
The Testament of our Lord. Cooper and Maclean, 1902.
Clementine Literature. Homilies. Lagarde, 1865.
—— Recognitions. Gersdorf, 1838.
English translations of some of the above will be found in T. & T. Clark's Ante-Nicene Christian Library.
Lives of John Baptist. Ed. F. Nau. Patrologia Orientalis IV, fasc. 5.
Gospel of Barnabas. Ed. L. and L. Ragg. Oxford, 1907.
Sibylline Oracles. J. Geffcken. Berlin, 1902.

FRAGMENTS OF EARLY GOSPELS, ETC.

THE GOSPEL ACCORDING TO THE HEBREWS

THIS is on a different level from all the other books we have to deal with. It was a divergent yet not heretical form of our Gospel according to St. Matthew. Even to sketch the controversies which have raged about it is impracticable here. What may be regarded as established is that it existed in either Hebrew or Aramaic, and was used by a Jewish Christian sect who were known as Nazaraeans (Nazarenes), and that it resembled our *Matthew* closely enough to have been regarded as the original Hebrew of that Gospel. I believe few, if any, would now contend that it *was* that original. It is generally, and I believe rightly, looked upon as a secondary document. What was the extent of the additions to or omissions from *Matthew* we do not know: but two considerations must be mentioned bearing on this: (1) The Stichometry of Nicephorus assigns it 2,200 lines, 300 less than *Matthew*. This figure, if correct, means that a good deal was left out. (2) If the Oxyrhynchus Sayings (see *post*) are really, as competent scholars think, extracts from it, we must suppose a large quantity of additional matter: for we have but two rather brief fragments of that collection of sayings, and eight out of thirteen sayings are either not represented in the canonical text, or differ widely therefrom.

Jerome, who is our chief source of knowledge about this Gospel, says that he had made a Greek and a Latin version of it. The statement is wholly rejected by some, and by others thought to be an exaggeration. It is very difficult to accept it as it stands. Perhaps, as Lagrange suggests, the truth may be that Jerome took notes of the text in Greek and Latin. Schmidtke, it should be added, has tried to show that all Jerome's quotations from it are borrowed from an earlier writer, Apollinaris; but there is no positive evidence for this.

If the Oxyrhynchus Sayings do come from *Hebrews*, they seem to imply the existence of a Greek version before Jerome's time. This is also implied by the entry in the Stichometry.

I will translate the fragments as they appear in the most recent study on the subject, that of the Rev. Père Lagrange in the *Revue Biblique*, 1922.

He begins by giving the fragments quoted by Epiphanius from what is properly called the Gospel of the Ebionites. Then he gives those of our Gospel, arranging them in the chronological order of the writers and the works in which they are found. This entails some little repetition, but is otherwise historically interesting, and sound.

IRENAEUS *against Heresies*, i. 26. 2. But *the Ebionites* use only that Gospel which is according to Matthew, and repudiate the Apostle Paul, calling him an apostate from the Law.

B

iii. 11. 7. For the Ebionites, who use only that Gospel which .
is according to Matthew, are convicted out of that very book as
not holding right views about the Lord.

The Ebionites mentioned here are a more primitive sect than those of
whom Epiphanius speaks. See below.

CLEMENT OF ALEXANDRIA (*Stromateis*), i. 9. 45. Even (*or* also)
in the Gospel according to the Hebrews is written *the saying*, 'he
that wondereth shall reign, and he that reigneth shall rest'.

id. (*Strom.*) v. 14. 96. For those words have the same force as
these: He shall not cease from seeking until he find, and having
found, he will be amazed, and having been amazed will reign,
and having reigned will rest.

This is identical with one of the Sayings from Oxyrhynchus: see
below.

ORIGEN *on John*, ii. 12. And if any accept the Gospel according
to the Hebrews, where the Saviour himself saith, 'Even now did
my mother the Holy Spirit take me by one of mine hairs, and
carried me away unto the great mountain Thabor', he will be
perplexed, &c. . . .

On Jeremiah, homily xv. 4. And if any one receive that *saying*,
'Even now my mother the Holy Spirit took me and carried me
up unto the great mountain Thabor', and the rest. . . .

The description of the Holy Spirit as 'my mother' is due to the
fact that the Hebrew word for spirit is of the feminine gender. The
saying, it is generally thought, refers to the Temptation.

EUSEBIUS, *Eccl. Hist.* iii. 39. 17, speaking of the early writer
Papias, says : He has also set forth (*or* expounded) another story,
about a woman accused of many sins before the Lord, which the
Gospel according to the Hebrews also contains.

It is the obvious, and general, view that this story was that of the
woman taken in adultery, which, as is well known, forms no part of
the true text of St. John's Gospel, though it is inserted by most manuscripts at the beginning of the eighth chapter. A few manuscripts
place it in St. Luke's Gospel. The description suggests that Papias's
story, with its mention of *many* sins, differed from ours in detail.

id. iv. 22. 8. Hegesippus made use in his *Memoirs* of the
Gospel according to the Hebrews.

id. iii. 25. 5 (in his list of *antilegomena*, writings whose canonicity
was disputed): And among them some have placed the Gospel
according to the Hebrews which is the especial delight of those
of the Hebrews who have accepted Christ.

iii. 27. 4. (The Ebionites repudiated Paul) and used only the
Gospel called according to the Hebrews, making but slight account
of the others.

Theophany, iv. 12 (preserved in Syriac). As we have found
somewhere in the Gospel which the Jews have in the Hebrew

tongue, where it is said: I choose for myself them that are good (or well pleasing) : the good are they whom my Father which in heaven giveth (or hath given) me.

ibid. (A passage preserved in Greek also.) But since the Gospel written in Hebrew characters which has reached our hands turns the threat not against the man who hid *the talent*, but against him who had lived riotously (for it told of three servants, one who devoured his master's substance with harlots and flute-girls, another who multiplied it by trading, and another who hid the talent; and made the one to be accepted, another only rebuked, and another to be shut up in prison), the question occurs to me whether in Matthew, after the conclusion of the speech against the man who did nothing, the threat that follows may refer, not to him, but by *epanalepsis* (i. e. taking up a former subject again) be said of the first, who ate and drank with the drunken.

EPIPHANIUS, *Heresy* xxix. 9. 4 (Nazoraeans). They have the Gospel according to Matthew quite complete, in Hebrew: for this *Gospel* is certainly still preserved among them as it was first written, in Hebrew letters. I do not know if they have even removed the genealogy from Abraham to Christ.

Their Gospel was 'quite complete' as distinguished from the Ebionite Gospel, which was mutilated.

STICHOMETRY OF NICEPHORUS (of uncertain date, but much older than the ninth-century chronicle to which it is attached).

Antilegomena of the New Testament:

Apocalypse of John, Apocalypse of Peter, Epistle of Barnabas, and

Gospel according to the Hebrews, 2,200 lines (300 lines less than the canonical Matthew).

JEROME. He is our principal authority in this matter.

On Ephesians, v. 4. As also we read in the Hebrew Gospel: 'And never, saith he, be ye joyful, save when ye behold your brother with love.'

On Micah, vii. 6. (The quotation about the Holy Spirit given above under Origen. Jerome quotes it again several times, not always in full.)

Of illustrious men, 2 (on James the Lord's brother).

Also the Gospel called according to the Hebrews, lately translated by me into Greek and Latin speech, which Origen often uses, tells, after the resurrection of the Saviour: 'Now the Lord, when he had given the linen cloth unto the servant of the priest, went unto James and appeared to him (for James had sworn that he would not eat bread from that hour wherein he had drunk the Lord's cup until he should see him risen again from among them that sleep)', and again after a little, 'Bring ye, saith the Lord, a table and bread', and immediately it is added, 'He took bread and blessed and brake and gave it unto James the Just and said unto him: My brother, eat thy bread, for the Son of Man is risen from among them that sleep '.

This is a famous passage. One interesting clause is apt to escape notice, about the giving of the shroud to the servant of the (high) priest, which implies that the priests must have been apprised of the resurrection as soon as the apostles. Was the servant of the priest Malchus? Presumably the servant was at the sepulchre : if so, it was being guarded by the Jews as well as the Roman soldiers (as in the Gospel of Peter).

ibid. 3. Further, the Hebrew itself (*or* original) is preserved to this day in the library at Caesarea which was collected with such care by the martyr Pamphilus. I also had an opportunity of copying it afforded me by the Nazarenes who use the book, at Beroea, a city of Syria.

This Beroea is Aleppo. In later years Jerome ceased to regard this Hebrew Gospel as the original Matthew.

ibid. 16. Of the Epistle of Ignatius 'to Polycarp' (*really to* Smyrna). In it he also inserts a testimony about the person of Christ, from the Gospel which was lately translated by me; his words are: But I both saw him (*this is wrongly quoted*) in the flesh after the resurrection, and believe that he is *in the flesh*: and when he came to Peter and those who were with Peter, he said to them: Lo, feel me and see that I am not a bodiless spirit (demon). And forthwith they touched him and believed.

Ignatius, to the Smyrnaeans, iii. 1, really says: For I know, and I believe that he is in the flesh even after his resurrection.

Another citation of these words of Christ is given by Origen as from the Doctrine of Peter: see p. 18.

On Matt. ii. Bethlehem of Judaea. This is a mistake of the scribes: for I think it was originally expressed by the Evangelist as we read in the Hebrew, 'of Judah', not Judaea.

On Matt. vi. 11 (the Lord's prayer).

In the Gospel called according to the Hebrews for 'super-substantial' bread I found *mahar*, which means 'of the morrow', so that the sense is: Our bread of the morrow, that is, of the future, give us this day.

The word supersubstantial is meant to render literally the difficult word *epiousios* which we translate 'daily'.

On Ps. cxxxv. In the Hebrew Gospel according to Matthew it is thus: Our bread of the morrow give us this day ; that is, 'the bread which thou wilt give us in thy kingdom, give us this day'.

On Matt. xii. 13. In the Gospel which the Nazarenes and Ebionites use (which I have lately translated into Greek from the Hebrew, and which is called by many (*or* most) people the original of Matthew), this man who has the withered hand is described as a mason, who prays for help in such words as these: 'I was a mason seeking a livelihood with my hands: I pray thee, Jesu, to restore me mine health, that I may not beg meanly for my food.'

The mention of the Ebionites here is gratuitous. Jerome nowhere else speaks of them as using the Gospel, and everything goes to show that, in his time, they did not.

Letter to Damasus (20) on Matt. xxi. 9. Matthew, who wrote his Gospel in the Hebrew speech, put it thus: Osanna barrama, i. e. Osanna in the highest.

On Matt. xxiii. 35. In the Gospel which the Nazarenes use, for 'son of Barachias' I find 'of Joiada' written.

This reading avoids an historical difficulty, and is doubtless secondary.

On Matt. xxvii. 16. This *Barabbas*, in the Gospel entitled (written) according to the Hebrews, is interpreted 'son of their master' (teacher).

By 'interpreted', says Lagrange, it is not meant that the Gospel translated the name, but that it used a form of it which suggested the meaning—Bar-rabban.

On Matt. xxvii. 51. In the Gospel I so often mention we read that a lintel of the temple of immense size was broken and divided.

Letter to Hedibia (ep. 120) 8. But in the Gospel that is written in Hebrew letters we read, not that the veil of the temple was rent, but that a lintel of the temple of wondrous size fell.

This was probably a change made under the influence of Isa. vi. 4, 'the posts of the door moved at the voice of him that cried'.

On Isa. xi. 2. (The Spirit of the Lord shall rest upon him) not partially as in the case of other holy men: but, according to the Gospel written in the Hebrew speech, which the Nazarenes read, 'There shall descend upon him the whole fount of the Holy Spirit'. . . . In the Gospel I mentioned above, I find this written: And it came to pass when the Lord was come up out of the water, the whole fount of the Holy Spirit descended and rested upon him, and said unto him: My son, in all the prophets was I waiting for thee that thou shouldst come, and I might rest in thee. For thou art my rest, thou art my first begotten son, that reignest for ever.

On Isa. xi. 9, My mother the Holy Spirit.

On Isa., preface to bk. xviii. For when the Apostles thought him to be a spirit, or, in the words of the Gospel which is of the Hebrews which the Nazarenes are wont to read, 'a bodiless demon', he said to them (Luke xxiv. 38).

On Ezek. xvi. 13. My mother, the Holy Spirit.

On Ezek. xviii. 7. And in the Gospel according to the Hebrews which the Nazarenes are accustomed to read, it is placed among the greatest sins 'if a man have grieved the spirit of his brother'.

Dialogue against Pelagius, iii. 2. In the Gospel according to the Hebrews which is indeed in the Chaldaean and Syrian speech but is written in Hebrew letters, which the Nazarenes use to this day, *called* 'according to the apostles', or, as most term it, 'according to Matthew', which also is to be seen in the library of Caesarea, the story tells: Behold, the mother of the Lord and his brethren said unto him: John Baptist baptizeth unto the remission of sins; let us go and be baptized of him. But he said unto them: Wherein (what) have I sinned, that I should go and be baptized of him? unless peradventure this very thing that I have said is *a sin of* ignorance.

ibid. And in the same book: If thy brother (saith he) have sinned by a word and made thee amends, seven times in a day receive thou him. Simon his disciple said unto him: Seven times in a day? The Lord answered and said unto him: Yea, I say unto thee, unto seventy times seven times. For in the prophets also, after they were anointed by the Holy Spirit, the word of sin was found.

'Word of sin' is Hebraistic for 'somewhat of sin': similarly 'sinned by a word' means 'sinned in anything'.

Latin version of Origen on Matthew (now called Pseudo-Origen).

It is written in a certain Gospel which is called according to the Hebrews (if at least any one care to accept it, not as authoritative, but to throw light on the question before us):

The second of the rich men (*it saith*) said unto him: Master, what good thing can I do and live? He said unto him: O man, fulfil (do) the law and the prophets.

He answered him: I have *kept them.* He said unto him: Go, sell all that thou ownest, and distribute it unto the poor, and come, follow me. But the rich man began to scratch his head, and it pleased him not. And the Lord said unto him: How sayest thou: I have kept the law and the prophets? For it is written in the law: Thou shalt love thy neighbour as thyself, and lo, many of thy brethren, sons of Abraham, are clad in filth, dying for hunger, and thine house is full of many good things, and nought at all goeth out of it unto them.

And he turned and said unto Simon his disciple who was sitting by him: Simon, son of Joanna, it is easier for a camel to enter in by a needle's eye than for a rich man *to enter* into the kingdom of heaven.

It is probable that this extract was found by the translator of Origen's commentary in some work of Jerome. It seems to be agreed that it was not in Origen's own commentary.

Some manuscripts of the Gospels have marginal notes recording readings of 'the Jewish' Gospel, by which our Gospel is evidently meant. Some of these were published by Tischendorf, others more recently by Schmidtke. According to the latter these notes were originally made between 370 and 500 by some one who did his work at Jerusalem.

Matt. iv. 5. The Jewish *copy* has not 'unto the holy city' but 'in Jerusalem'.

Matt. v. 22. The word 'without cause' is not inserted in some copies, nor in the Jewish.

Matt. vii. 5. The Jewish has here: If ye be in my bosom and do not the will of my Father which is in heaven, out of my bosom will I cast you away.

(The 'Second Epistle of Clement', iv. 5, has: The Lord said: If ye be with me gathered together in my bosom and do not my commandments, I will cast you away and say unto you: Depart from me; I know you not whence ye are, ye workers of wickedness.)

Matt. x. 16. The Jewish *has* '(wise) more than serpents' instead of 'as serpents'.

Matt. xi. 12. (The kingdom of heaven suffereth violence.) The Jewish has: 'is ravished (*or* plundered).'

Matt. xi. 25. (I thank thee (*lit.* confess unto thee), O Father.) The Jewish: 'I give thee thanks.'

Matt. xii. 40ᵇ. The Jewish has not: three days and three nights (in the heart of the earth).

Matt. xv. 5. The Jewish: Corban by which ye shall be profited by us.

Probably it is meant that the verse ran: But ye say to your father and mother: Corban, &c.

Matt. xvi. 2, 3. Omitted by 'the Jewish' (as by many extant manuscripts).

Matt. xvi. 17. The Jewish: (Simon) son of John.

Matt. xviii. 22. The Jewish has, immediately after the seventy times seven: For in the prophets, after they were anointed with the Holy Spirit, there was found in them a word (matter) of sin.

This shows the identity of 'the Jewish' with Jerome's gospel.

Matt. xxvi. 74. The Jewish: and he denied and swore and cursed.

Matt. xxvii. 65. The Jewish: And he delivered unto them armed men, that they might sit over against the cave and keep it day and night.

A commentary on Isaiah (liii. 12) by Haimo of Auxerre (c. 850) has this apropos of the word 'Father forgive them':

For, as is contained in the Gospel of the Nazarenes, at this word of the Lord many thousands of Jews that stood round about the Cross believed.

A marginal note (thirteenth century) on a copy of the versified Bible called the Aurora (by Petrus de Riga), in a manuscript at the Fitzwilliam Museum, Cambridge (one of a number of remarkable notes) is:

At the cleansing of the Temple:

In the books of the Gospels which the Nazarenes use it is read that rays issued from his eyes whereby they were terrified and put to flight.

Jerome *on Matt.* xxi. 12 says that the people whom Jesus drove out did not resist him: 'For a certain fiery and starry *light* shone (radiated) from his eyes and the majesty of Godhead gleamed in his face.'

When I published the note, I took it that it was a reminiscence of Jerome's words: *ray* and *radiate* occur in both. But Dr. Zahn was of opinion that it might really represent something in the old Gospel: so I include it, though with hesitation.

One other mention of this Gospel has to be added.

In Budge's *Miscellaneous Coptic Texts* is a Discourse on Mary by Cyril of Jerusalem. Cyril (Pseudo-Cyril) relates that he had to send for a monk of Maiôma of Gaza who was teaching false doctrine. Called on for an account of his belief the monk (p. 637, Eng. trans.) said: It is written in the *Gospel* to the Hebrews that when Christ wished to come upon the earth to men, the Good Father called a mighty power in the heavens which was called Michael, and committed Christ to the care thereof. And the power came down into the world and it was called Mary, and *Christ* was in her womb seven months. Afterwards she gave birth to him, and he increased in stature, and he chose the apostles, . . . 'was crucified, and taken up by the Father'. Cyril asked: Where in the Four Gospels is it said that the holy Virgin Mary the mother of God is a force? The monk said: In the *Gospel* to the Hebrews. Then, said Cyril, there are five Gospels? Where is the fifth? The monk said: It is *the Gospel* that was written to the Hebrews. (Cyril convinced him of his error and it was burned the books. No more is told of the Gospel, which, whatever it may have been, was certainly not the book we have been dealing with, but a writing of pronouncedly heretical (Docetic?) views. The last sentence of the monk's account of Christ, which I did not quote in full just now, is perhaps worth recording.) 'After they had raised him up on the cross, the Father took him up into heaven unto himself.' This, with its omission of all mention of the resurrection, might be construed as heretical: on the other hand, it may be merely a case of extreme compression of the narrative.

THE GOSPEL OF THE EBIONITES

All our knowledge of this is derived from Epiphanius, and he uses very confusing language about it (as about many other things). The passages are as follows : all occur in his work against Heresies—no. xxx.

And they (the Ebionites) receive the Gospel according to Matthew. For this they too, like the followers of Cerinthus and Merinthus, use to the exclusion of others. And they call it according to the Hebrews, as the truth is, that Matthew alone of New Testament writers made his exposition and preaching of the Gospel in Hebrew and in Hebrew letters.

Epiphanius goes on to say that he had heard of Hebrew versions of *John* and *Acts* kept privately in the treasuries (Geniza ?) at Tiberias, and continues :

In the Gospel they have, called according to Matthew, but not wholly complete, but falsified and mutilated (they call it the Hebrew *Gospel*), it is contained that 'There was a certain man named Jesus, and he was about thirty years old, who chose us. And coming unto Capernaum he entered into the house of Simon who was surnamed Peter, and opened his mouth and said: As I passed by the lake of Tiberias, I chose John and James the sons of Zebedee, and Simon and Andrew and ⟨Philip and Bartholomew, James *the son* of Alphaeus and Thomas⟩ Thaddaeus and Simon the Zealot and Judas the Iscariot: and thee, Matthew, as thou satest at the receipt of custom I called, and thou followedst me. You therefore I will to be twelve apostles for a testimony unto (of) Israel.

And:
John was baptizing, and there went out unto him Pharisees and were baptized, and all Jerusalem. And John had raiment of camel's hair and a leathern girdle about his loins: and his meat (it saith) was wild honey, whereof the taste is the *taste* of manna, as a cake *dipped* in oil. That, forsooth, they may pervert the word of truth into a lie and for locusts put a cake *dipped* in honey (*sic*).

These Ebionites were vegetarians and objected to the idea of eating locusts. A locust in Greek is *akris*, and the word they used for cake is *enkris*, so the change is slight. We shall meet with this tendency again.

And the beginning of their Gospel says that : It came to pass in the days of Herod the king of Judaea ⟨when Caiaphas was high priest⟩ that there came ⟨a certain man⟩ John ⟨by name⟩, baptizing with the baptism of repentance in the river Jordan, who was said to be of the lineage of Aaron the priest, child of Zacharias and Elisabeth, and all went out unto him.

The borrowing from St. Luke is very evident here. He goes on: And after a good deal more it continues that:

After the people were baptized, Jesus also came and was baptized by John; and as he came up from the water, the heavens were opened, and he saw the Holy Ghost in the likeness of a dove that descended and entered into him : and a voice from heaven saying: Thou art my beloved Son, in thee I am well pleased: and again: This day have I begotten thee. And straightway there shone about the place a great light. Which when John saw (it saith) he saith unto him: Who art thou, Lord? and again *there was* a voice from heaven saying unto him: This is my beloved Son in whom I am well pleased. And then (it saith) John fell down before him and said: I beseech thee, Lord, baptize thou me. But he prevented him saying: Suffer it (*or* let it go): for thus it behoveth that all things should be fulfilled.

And on this account they say that Jesus was begotten of the
seed of a man, and was chosen; and so by the choice *of God* he
was called the Son of God from the Christ that came into him
from above in the likeness of a dove. And they deny that he
was begotten of God the Father, but say that he was created,
as one of the archangels, yet greater, and that he is Lord of
angels and of all things made by the Almighty, and that
he came and taught, as the Gospel (so called) current among
them contains, that, 'I came to destroy the sacrifices, and
if ye cease not from sacrificing, the wrath *of God* will not cease
from you'.

(With reference to the Passover and the evasion of the idea that Jesus
partook of flesh :)

They have changed the saying, as is plain to all from the
combination of phrases, and have made the disciples say: Where
wilt thou that we make ready for thee to eat the Passover? and
him, forsooth, say: Have I desired with desire to eat this flesh
of the Passover with you?

These fragments show clearly that the Gospel was designed to support a particular set of views. They enable us also to distinguish it
from the Gospel according to the Hebrews, for, among other things,
the accounts of the Baptism in the two are quite different. Epiphanius
is only confusing the issue when he talks of it as the Hebrew Gospel—
or rather, the Ebionites may be guilty of the confusion, for he attributes
the name to them.

The Gospel according to the Twelve, or 'of the Twelve', mentioned
by Origen (Ambrose and Jerome) is identified by Zahn with the
Ebionite Gospel. He makes a good case for the identification. If the
two are not identical, it can only be said that we know nothing of the
Gospel according to the Twelve.

Revillout, indeed, claims the title for certain Coptic fragments of
narratives of the Passion which are described in their proper place in
this collection: but no one has been found to follow his lead.

THE GOSPEL ACCORDING TO THE EGYPTIANS

Origen, in his first Homily on Luke, speaks of those who 'took in
hand' or 'attempted' to write gospels (as Luke says in his prologue).
These, he says, came to the task rashly, without the needful gifts of
grace, unlike Matthew, Mark, John, and Luke himself. Such were
those who composed the Gospel which is written 'according to the
Egyptians' and the Gospel entitled 'of the Twelve'.

Apart from this there are but few mentions of the book. A series
of passages from Clement of Alexandria is our chief source of knowledge.
They are as follows:

CLEM. ALEX. *Strom.* iii. 9. 64.

Whence it is with reason that after the Word had told about
the End, Salome saith: Until when shall men *continue to* die?

(Now the Scripture speaks of man in two senses, the one that is seen, and the soul: and again, of him that is in a state of salvation, and him that is not: and sin is called the death of the soul) and it is advisedly that the Lord makes answer: So long as women bear *children*.

66. And why do not they who walk by anything rather than the true rule of the Gospel go on to quote the rest of that which was said to Salome: for when she had said, 'I have done well, then, in not bearing *children*?' (as if childbearing were not the right thing to accept) the Lord answers and says: Every plant eat thou, but that which hath bitterness eat not.

iii. 13. 92. When Salome inquired when the things concerning which she asked should be known, the Lord said: When ye have trampled on the garment of shame, and when the two become one and the male with the female *is* neither male nor female. In the first place, then, we have not this saying in the four Gospels that have been delivered to us, but in that according to the Egyptians.

(The so-called Second Epistle of Clement has this, in a slightly different form, c. xii. 2:

For the Lord himself being asked by some one when his kingdom should come, said: When the two shall be one, and the outside (that which is without) as the inside (that which is within), and the male with the female neither male nor female.)

There are allusions to the saying in the Apocryphal Acts, see pp. 335, 429, 450.

iii. 6. 45. The Lord said to Salome when she inquired: How long shall death prevail? 'As long as ye women bear *children*', not because life is an ill, and the creation evil: but as showing the sequence of nature: for in all cases birth is followed by decay.

Excerpts from Theodotus, 67. And when the Saviour says to Salome that there shall be death as long as women bear *children*, he did not say it as abusing birth, for that is necessary for the salvation of believers.

Strom. iii. 9. 63. But those who set themselves against God's creation because of continence, which has a fair-sounding name, quote also those words which were spoken to Salome, of which I made mention before. They are contained, I think (*or* I take it) in the Gospel according to the Egyptians. For they say that 'the Saviour himself said: I came to destroy the works of the female'. By *female* he means lust: by *works*, birth and decay.

HIPPOLYTUS *against Heresies*, v. 7. (The Naassenes) say that the soul is very hard to find and to perceive; for it does not continue in the same fashion or shape or in one emotion so that one can either describe it or comprehend it in essence. And they have these various changes *of the soul*, set forth in the Gospel entitled according to the Egyptians.

EPIPHANIUS, *Heresy* lxii. 2 (Sabellians). Their whole deceit (error) and the strength of it they draw from some apocryphal books, especially from what is called the Egyptian Gospel, to which some have given that name. For in it many suchlike things are recorded (*or* attributed) as from the person of the Saviour, *said* in a corner, purporting that he showed his disciples that the same person was Father, Son, and Holy Spirit.

All this goes to show that this Gospel was a secondary work with a distinct doctrinal tendency. It resembles the later Gnostic books such as the *Pistis Sophia* in assigning an important rôle in the dialogues with Christ to the female disciples.

GOSPEL OF PHILIP

One mention and citation of this occurs in Epiphanius, *Heresy* xxvi. 13. Speaking of the ' Gnostics ' of Egypt in his time (fourth century) he says :

They produce a Gospel forged in the name of Philip the holy disciple, which says:

The Lord revealed unto me what the soul must say as it goeth up into heaven, and how it must answer each of the Powers above. 'I have taken knowledge (it saith) of myself, and have gathered myself together out of every quarter and have not begotten (sown) children unto the Ruler, but have rooted out his roots and gathered together the members that were scattered abroad. And I know thee who thou art, for I (it saith) am of them that are from above.'

A very leading Gnostic doctrine was that the soul contained sparks of the Divine, which were dispersed about among the world of matter, and must be collected, destined as they were some day to be removed out of the influence of matter and taken up into the higher world. This is enunciated here.

In the *Pistis Sophia* Philip is one of the disciples who are specially ordered to write the revelations uttered by Christ.

GOSPEL OR TRADITIONS OF MATTHIAS

Origen *on Luke* (*Hom.* 1) says that he knows of a Gospel according to Matthias. Ambrose and Jerome, it seems, repeat his statement. Eusebius also mentions the book: none of these give more than the bare name. In the Gelasian Decree it is condemned, which need not mean that it was known to the condemner. It also occurs in the Greek 'List of the Sixty Books'.

It is possible that this book was identical with the Traditions of Matthias, a writing of which Clement of Alexandria speaks in the following passages:

Strom. ii. 9. 45. The beginning (of truth) is to wonder at things, as Plato says in the *Theaetetus*, and Matthias in the

Traditions, advising us: Wonder thou at the things that are before thee: making this the first step to further knowledge.

iii. 4. 26. (The Gnostics) say that Matthias also taught thus: that we should fight with the flesh and abuse it, not yielding to it at all for licentious pleasure, but should make the soul grow by faith and knowledge.

vii. 13. 82. They say that in the Traditions Matthias the apostle said that on every occasion, if the neighbour of a chosen one sin, the chosen one hath sinned: for had he behaved himself as the word enjoins, the neighbour also would have been ashamed of his way of life, so as not to sin.

This, too, is thought by Zahn to be traceable to the same source:

Strom. iv. 6. 35. It is said that Zacchaeus (or, as some say, Matthias), the chief publican, when he had heard the Lord, who condescended to come to him, said: Behold, the half of my goods I give in alms, Lord: and if I have defrauded any man of ought, I restore it fourfold. Whereupon also the Saviour said: The Son of man is come to-day and hath found that which was lost.

Hippolytus tells us that the heretics Basilides and Isidorus (his son) asserted that Matthias had spoken unto them certain secret words which he had heard from the Saviour, being taught by him apart.

GOSPEL OF PETER

The two fragments which we possess of the text of this book will be found among the Passion narratives and the Apocalypses respectively. Here I place the notices of it that are found in the Church writers. There are but three.

ORIGEN *on Matthew*, x. 17. (They of Nazareth thought that Jesus) was the son of Joseph and Mary: but the brothers of Jesus some (founding on a tradition of the Gospel entitled according to Peter or of the Book of James) say were sons of Joseph by a former wife who had lived with him before Mary.

The Book of James is the so-called Protevangelium, given below.

EUSEBIUS, *Eccl. Hist.* vi. 12, treating of Serapion, bishop of Antioch about A.D. 190, says:

There is another treatise composed by him about the Gospel called 'according to Peter', which he drew up to expose the false statements contained in it, for the benefit of some members of the church at Rhossus, who by the means of the aforesaid book had succumbed to unorthodox doctrines. Of this it will be well to adduce some passages in which he states his view of the book, writing thus:

For we, brethren, accept Peter and the other apostles as *we would* Christ, but, as experienced men, we repudiate what is falsely written under their name, knowing that we have not had any such things delivered to us. For I, when I was with you, supposed that all of you adhered to the right faith, and, not having gone through the Gospel which they produced under the name of Peter, I said: If this is all that seems to cause you scruples, let it be read. But now that I have learned from what has been told me, that somewhat of heresy was nesting in their mind (*lit.* their mind had its lair in a certain heresy), I will take care to come to you again: so, brethren, expect me soon.

But you, who have comprehended of what manner of heresy Marcion (*Gr.* Marcianus) was, and how he contradicted himself, not understanding what he uttered, will learn *the truth* from what has been written to you (in this treatise).

For we have been enabled to borrow this very Gospel from others who used it, namely, the successors of those who were its authors (*lit.* began it) whom we call Docetae (Seemers)—for most of their notions belong to that school—and to go through it, and to find that most of it is of the right teaching (word) of the Saviour, but some things are adventitious; a list of which we have drawn up for you.

EUSEBIUS (iii. 3. 2) also names the Gospel (with the Acts, Apocalypse, and Preaching of Peter) as a writing not handed down among the 'Catholic' Scriptures, and not used as testimony by ancient or modern church writers. (This, as regards the Apocalypse and Preaching, is an exaggeration.)

THEODORET (*of heretical Fables*, ii. 2) says: 'The Nazaraeans are Jews who know Christ as a righteous man, and use the Gospel called "according to Peter".' (What we know of the Gospel and of the Nazarenes forbids us to give credence to this statement.)

GOSPEL OF THOMAS

The Infancy Gospel current under the name of Thomas is also given below. The ancient testimonies, as in the case of *Peter*, are placed here. We are not absolutely certain that our Gospel of Thomas is a form of the older one, though the one quotation we have of the latter coincides curiously with the subject of the former. I have, myself, very little doubt that our Gospel is the skeleton of the old one— the stories retained and the unorthodox discourses cut out.[1]

ORIGEN says (*Hom. 1 on Luke*): There is also current the Gospel according to Thomas.

[1] Indian influence has been suggested as a factor in these stories, and tales of the childhood of Krishna and of Buddha have been cited, which have a colourable resemblance to some of those in the Gospel. The thesis is not proved, but I have sometimes thought that the name given to Thomas in the Latin version, 'Ismaelite', might be the

HIPPOLYTUS *against Heresies*, v. 7. The Naassenes speak of a nature of man at once hidden and manifesting itself, which they say is within man, and is the kingdom of heaven that is sought after: and they deliver this concerning it, expressly, in the Gospel entitled according to Thomas, in these words: He that seeketh me will find me in children from seven years old *and upwards*: for there am I manifested, who am hidden in the fourteenth age (aeon).

Our Gospel of Thomas tells of the acts of Jesus at five, six, and eight years of age: the naming of the age may originally have been significant. The fragment seems to indicate that the years from seven to fourteen were a period of mystic importance.

CYRIL OF JERUSALEM (A.D. 348) speaks of this book as a Manichaean production. Very likely the Manichaeans used it, but it was older than their sect. He says (*Catech.* iv. 36):

And of the New Testament *read* the four Gospels only. The others are apocryphal (pseudepigraphic) and harmful. The Manichaeans also wrote a Gospel according to Thomas, which, though coloured with the fragrance of a gospel-name, corrupts the souls of the simpler.

ib. vi. 31. Let no one read the Gospel according to Thomas, for it is not by one of the twelve apostles, but by one of the three wicked disciples of Manes.

Eusebius names it among undoubtedly spurious books.

The Stichometry of Nicephorus assigns it 1,300 lines.

IRENAEUS (i. 13. 1) says that the Marcosian sect support their doctrines by a vast number of apocryphal writings. 'They adduce, too, this false invention, that when the Lord as a child was learning the alphabet, and his teacher said, as the custom is: Say Alpha; he answered: Alpha. But when the teacher bade him say Beta, the Lord answered: First tell thou me what Alpha is, and then will I tell thee what Beta is. And this they interpret as meaning that he alone knew the unknown *mystery*, which he manifested in the form of Alpha.'

It seems probable from Irenaeus's language that the Marcosians took

original reading, and that if so, it might be interpreted as suggesting a connexion with the further East.

The case stands thus. The Greek text A calls the writer 'Thomas the Israelite *the Philosopher*'. Greek B, 'the holy apostle Thomas'. Latin, 'Thomas the Israelite (*or* Ismaelite) the apostle of the Lord'. 'Israelite' is a curious and pointless designation, if the apostle is meant, and a very easy corruption of Ismaelite. 'Philosopher' is a strikingly unusual description. The combination of Ismaelite and Philosopher would serve to convey the idea of an Eastern sage.

From a somewhat different point of view, it is not to be forgotten that Thomas the apostle was connected with India by a tradition probably a good deal older than the Acts of Thomas.

this from an apocryphal writing. I have not much doubt that that was the Gospel of Thomas. The story occurs in text A, c. vi, and in all Infancy Gospels in some form. It is also told shortly in the Epistle of the Apostles, c. 4 : see p. 486.

THE PREACHING OF PETER

Again our principal source of knowledge is Clement of Alexandria, who makes a series of quotations from it.

CLEMENT OF ALEXANDRIA, *Strom.* i. 29. 182. And in the Preaching of Peter you may find the Lord called 'Law and Word'.

Twice again he quotes this phrase.

vi. 5. 89. But that the most approved of the Greeks do not know God by *direct* knowledge, but indirectly, Peter says in his Preaching: Know ye then that there is one God who made the beginning of all things and hath power over their end; and: The invisible who seeth all things, uncontainable, who containeth all, having need of nought, of whom all things stand in need and for whose sake they exist, incomprehensible, perpetual, incorruptible, uncreated, who made all things by the word of his power. . . . that is, the Son.[1]

Then he goes on : This God worship ye, not after the manner of the Greeks . . . showing that we and the good (approved) Greeks worship the same God, though not according to *perfect* knowledge for they had not learned the tradition of the Son. 'Do not', he says, 'worship'—he does not say 'the God whom the Greeks worship', but 'not after the manner of the Greeks': he would change the method of worship of God, not proclaim another God. What, then, is meant by 'not after the manner of the Greeks'? Peter himself will explain, for he continues: Carried away by ignorance and not knowing God as we do, according to the perfect knowledge, *but* shaping those things over which he gave them power, for their use, *even* wood and stones, brass and iron, gold and silver (forgetting) their material and *proper* use, they set up things subservient to their existence and worship them; and what things God hath given them for food, the fowls of the air and the creatures that swim in the sea and creep upon the earth, wild beasts and fourfooted cattle of the field, weasels too and mice, cats and dogs and apes ; yea, their own eatables do they sacrifice as offerings to eatable *gods,* and offering dead things to the dead

---

[1] In vi. 7. 58 he repeats a clause of this:

For there is in very deed one God, who made the beginning of all things: meaning his first begotten Son; thus Peter writes, understanding rightly the words: In the beginning God created the heaven and the earth.

The words *In the beginning* were interpreted as meaning ' By the Son '.

as to gods, they show ingratitude to God, by these practices denying that he exists. . . . He will continue again in this fashion: Neither worship ye him as do the Jews, for they, who suppose that they alone know God, do not know him, serving angels and archangels, the month and the moon: and if no moon be seen, they do not celebrate what is called the first sabbath, nor keep the new moon, nor the days of unleavened bread, nor the feast (of tabernacles?), nor the great day (of atonement).

Then he adds the finale (colophon) of what is required: So then do ye, learning in a holy and righteous sort that which we deliver unto you, observe it, worshipping God through Christ in a new way. For we have found in the Scriptures, how the Lord saith: Behold, I make with you a new covenant, not as the covenant with your fathers in mount Horeb. He hath made a new one with us: for the *ways* of the Greeks and Jews are old, but we are they that worship him in a new way in a third generation (*or* race), *even* Christians.[1]

Shortly after this he cites Paul 'in addition to the Preaching of Peter' as referring to the Sibyl and Hystaspes. The passage is given below as a possible fragment of the Acts of Paul.

After his quotation from Paul, Clement continues:

Therefore Peter says that the Lord said to the apostles: If then any of Israel will repent, to believe in God through my name, his sins shall be forgiven him: (and) after twelve years go ye out into the world, lest any say: We did not hear.

In the next chapter (vi. 6) he has:

For example, in the Preaching of Peter the Lord says: I chose out you twelve, judging you to be disciples worthy of me, whom the Lord willed, and thinking you faithful apostles; sending you unto the world to preach the Gospel to men throughout the world, that they should know that there is one God; to declare by faith in me [the Christ] what shall be, that they that have heard and believed may be saved, and that they which have not believed may hear and bear witness, not having any defence *so as* to say 'We did not hear'.

---

[1] ORIGEN *on John*, xiii. 17, has part of the above passages:
It is too much to set forth now the quotations of Heracleon taken from the book entitled The Preaching of Peter and dwell on them, inquiring about the book whether it is genuine or spurious or compounded *of both elements*: so we willingly postpone that, and only note that according to him (Heracleon) Peter taught that we must not worship as do the Greeks, receiving the things of matter, and serving stocks and stones: nor worship God as do the Jews, since they, who suppose that they alone know God, are ignorant of him, and serve angels and the month and the moon.

After a few lines :

And to all reasonable souls it hath been said above: Whatsoever things any of you did in ignorance, not knowing God clearly, all his sins shall be forgiven him.

vi. 15. 128.   Peter in the Preaching, speaking of the apostles, says: But we having opened the books of the prophets which we had, found, sometimes expressed by parables, sometimes by riddles, and sometimes directly (authentically) and in so many words naming Jesus Christ, both his coming and his death and the cross and all the other torments which the Jews inflicted on him, and his resurrection and assumption into the heavens before Jerusalem was founded (*MS.* judged), even all these things as they had been written, what he must suffer and what shall be after him. When, therefore, we took knowledge of these things, we believed in God through that which had been written of him.

And a little after he adds that the prophecies came by Divine providence, in these terms: For we know that God commanded them in very deed, and without the Scripture we say nothing.

The character of the heathen worship, with its mention of weasels, cats, &c., and the fact that our authorities are all Alexandrine, point to the Egyptian origin and currency of the Preaching. We see also that it was an orthodox book. Origen even faces the possibility of its being genuine in whole or in part. The earliest of the Greek apologists for Christianity whose work we have, Aristides, takes a very similar line to the Preaching, and is thought to have used it.

A Syriac Preaching of Simon Cephas in the city of Rome (to be found in Cureton's *Syriac Documents*) has nothing in common with our book. Its gist is, briefly, this: A great assembly gathers to hear Peter. He speaks to them of the life and death of Jesus, and the call of the apostles, exhorts them to shun idolatry: reverts to the signs at the crucifixion, and the report of Pilate to Caesar and the senate, and warns them against Simon Magus. We then have the incident of the dead man raised by Peter after Simon had failed. Peter's episcopate of twenty-five years, his martyrdom and that of Paul, Nero's death, and a famine which ensued after many years, are shortly told.

In the Clementine Recognitions, &c., a great deal is said about books of Preachings of Peter: but these are to a great extent imaginary, and, if ever they existed, must have belonged to the same peculiar school of thought as the rest of that literature.

There are certain other fragments of a 'Teaching of Peter' which may be another name for the Preaching. Opinion is divided. Probably the first, from Origen, is from the Preaching. The others are of a different complexion.

ORIGEN *on First Principles* i, prologue 8. But if any would produce to us from that book which is called The Doctrine of Peter, *the passage* where the Saviour is represented as saying (*lit.* seems to say) to the disciples: I am not a bodiless spirit (demon): he must be answered in the first place that that book is not reckoned among the books of the church: (and then) it must be shown that the writing is neither by Peter nor by any one else who was inspired by the spirit of God.

The quotation agrees with one from the Gospel according to the Hebrews. See p. 4.

GREGORY OF NAZIANZUS, *ep.* 16. 'A soul in trouble is near unto God', saith Peter somewhere—a marvellous utterance.

(JOHN OF DAMASCUS), *Sacred Parallels*, A. 12:

Of Peter: Wretched that I am, I remembered not that God seeth the mind and observeth the voice of the soul. Allying myself with sin, I said unto myself: God is merciful, and will bear with thee: and because I was not immediately smitten, I ceased not, but rather despised pardon, and exhausted the long-suffering of God.

ibid. From the Teaching of Peter: Rich is he that hath mercy on many, and he that, imitating God, giveth of that he hath. For God hath given all things unto all, of his own creatures. Understand then, ye rich, that ye ought to minister, for ye have received more than ye yourselves need. Learn that others lack the things ye have in superfluity. Be ashamed to keep things that belong to others. Imitate the fairness (equality) of God, and no man will be poor.

OECUMENIUS *on James*, v. 16. And that happens to us which blessed Peter says: One building and one pulling down! they gain nought but their labour.

LOST HERETICAL BOOKS

Three such are quoted or described by Epiphanius which may be properly reckoned as New Testament Apocrypha. I exclude the Gospel of Eve and such books as the prophecies of Parchor and other mythical persons, and the book of Elxai.

First is a book called the Birth of Mary.

EPIPHANIUS, *Heresy* xxvi. 12.

(The Gnostics have a book which they call the Birth (*or* Descent) of Mary, in which are horrible and deadly things.) For they say that the reason of Zacharias being slain in the Temple was this, because, say they, he saw a vision and in his fear, as he was about to tell the vision, his mouth was stopped. For, say they, he saw at the hour of incense, as he was burning incense, a man standing there who had the form of an ass. And when he went out, they say, and would have said: Woe unto you! what (*or* whom) do ye worship? he that was seen of him within the Temple shut his mouth, that he might not be able to speak. And when his mouth was opened, so that he could speak, then he revealed it to them and they slew him. And thus, say they, died

Zacharias. For on this account the priest was commanded by the lawgiver himself to wear bells, that when he enters in to do his priestly office, he whom they worship may hear the sound of the bells and hide himself, that the likeness of his shape may not be detected.

This is the vulgarest expression of the hatred of the Old Covenant of which Marcion was the noblest exponent. I need not dwell here upon the prevalence of the belief among heathens that Jews and Christians worshipped a deity in the form of an ass. The Palatine *graffito* of the crucified figure with an ass's head will occur to many readers.

Another Gospel (?) of similar tendency was that which was used by the nameless 'Adversary of the Law and the Prophets' whom Augustine refutes, and from which the following is quoted:

The apostles having asked the Lord what they were to think about the Jewish prophets, who were thought in the past to have foretold his coming, he was troubled that they even yet had such thoughts, and answered: Ye have given up (let go) the living one who is before your eyes, and talk idly of the dead.

EPIPHANIUS in *Her.* xxvi. 8 quotes the Lesser Questions of Mary: but I must be excused from repeating the passage.

In *Her.* xxx. 16 he tells of a book used by the Ebionites called the Ascents of James:

Certain supposititious Ascents, and Discourses, so called, do they produce in the Ascents of James, representing him as speaking against the Temple and the sacrifices, and the fire on the altar; and many other things full of empty sound. And there, too, they are not ashamed to indict Paul, with forged discourses *full* of the malice and error of their false apostles: calling him a man of Tarsus (which he confesses and does not deny), but asserting that he came of the Greeks; taking their occasion from the place, because of the words truthfully spoken by him: I am a man of Tarsus, a citizen of no mean city; they then say that he was a Greek, the child of a Greek mother and a Greek father, and that he went up to Jerusalem and remained there some time, and desired to take the daughter of the *high* priest to wife, and on that account became a proselyte and was circumcised, and when he failed to secure the maiden he was enraged, and wrote against circumcision and against the sabbath and the Law.

The book, as Lightfoot (*Galatians*, 330, n. 2) says, 'was so called doubtless as describing the *ascents* of James up the Temple stairs, whence he harangued the people'. Relics of it may probably be discerned in the latter chapters of the first book of the Clementine Recognitions. Lightfoot also suggests, very ingeniously (l.c. 367, n. 1), that the account of the death of James, quoted by Eusebius from Hegesippus, in which James is cast down from the pinnacle of the Temple, 'was the grand *finale* of these ascents'. In the Recognitions he addresses the people from the Temple steps, and is thrown down and left for dead by the enemy (Paul); in Hegesippus he speaks from the pinnacle, 'is hurled from the still loftier station, and this time his death is made sure'. It is an attractive conjecture.

Epiphanius mentions some other heretical apocrypha: a Gospel of Judas Iscariot (Irenaeus also speaks of this) and an heretical Ascension (Anabaticon) of Paul, used by the Caianites or Cainites. They are mere names to us.

We also hear of 'Gospels' of heresiarchs—Basilides, Valentinus, and others: but these we cannot think of as real Gospels. They are—if they are not mere ghost-books—the treatises in which these teachers set forth their views, and they were nicknamed Gospels. The Gospel of Marcion is of a different class: it was an edition of Luke, from which all that went counter to Marcion's views was removed. He made a similar text of the Pauline Epistles.

From a Latin writer, Orosius, comes our only fragment of another heretical apocryphon, the *Memoria* (? Memoirs) of the Apostles. It was current among the Priscillianists who had their head-quarters in Spain in the fourth century. It was evidently a dualist book, no doubt Manichaean in origin.

OROSIUS, *Admonition of the errors of the Priscillianists and Origenists.* Priscillian delivered that the names of the Patriarchs are members (parts) of the soul: for that Ruben was in the head, Levi in the heart, Juda in the heart, Benjamin in the thighs, and the like. In the members of the body, on the other hand, the heavenly signs are arranged, viz. the Ram in the head, the Bull in the neck, the Twins in the arms, the Crab in the heart, &c. He would have it understood that the darkness is eternal, and that out of it the ruler of this world came forth. He confirms this from a book called the Memoria of the Apostles, where the Saviour is represented as being questioned privately by the disciples, and explaining that in the parable of the Gospel which says: *A sower went forth to sow his seed*, the sower was not good: asserting, that had he been good, he would not have been careless, nor cast the seed by the wayside or on stony places or untilled ground: willing it to be understood that this (the ruler of the world?) was the sower, who scattered the souls he had caught into various bodies, as he pleased. In the same book much is said of the principle of moist things, and the principle of fire : he would have it understood that all good things happen in this world, not by the power of God, but by contrivance (art).

(The cause of rain is then expounded in a manner best not repeated.)

In the Gelasian Decree 'Of Books to be received and not to be received' are the titles of many Apocryphal books. The date and source of this Decree are matters of dispute, but it cannot be later than the sixth century. Many of the titles that occur in it are derived from the works of Church writers, especially Jerome: the books had not been seen by the author of the Decree.

Its list of New Testament Apocrypha is remarkable alike for omissions and insertions. It runs thus:

The Itinerary under the name of the apostle Peter which is called of Saint Clement, nine books.

(= the Clementine Recognitions: in *ten* books.)

Acts under the name of Andrew the apostle.

,,   ,,   Thomas   ,,
,,   ,,   Peter   ,,
,,   ,,   Philip   ,,

(These will be found in their place in this collection.)

Gospel under the name of Matthias (see p. 12).

,,   ,,   Barnabas.

(Both the above occur in the Greek list of the Sixty Books, but the existence of a Gospel of Barnabas is most doubtful. The extant book under that name (ed. Ragg, 1907) is in Italian, a forgery of the late fifteenth or sixteenth century, by a renegade from Christianity to Islam.)

Gospel under the name of James the Less.

(Probably the Protevangelium: but a lesson on the Circumcision of Christ (printed by Bannister in *Journal of Theol. Studies*, 1908, p. 417), in a fragment of a tenth-century service book in an Irish hand, is headed: Lesson of the Gospel according to James *son* of Alphaeus. It is hardly worth translating.)

Gospel under the name of Peter the Apostle (fragments exist).

Gospel under the name of Thomas which the Manichaeans use (extant).

Gospel under the name of Bartholomew (extant).

Gospels under the name of Andrew (non-existent: a confusion with the Acts).

Gospels which Lucianus falsified.

,,   Hesychius   ,,

(These are recensions of the text of the canonical gospels, of which we know little.)

Book concerning the Infancy of the Saviour (Pseudo-Matthew's Gospel).

Book concerning the birth of the Saviour, and Mary, or the midwife (the same as the last, or the Protevangelium).

The book called of the Shepherd (of Hermas).

All the books which Leucius the disciple of the devil made.

(Leucius is really the name attached to the Acts of John only : the entry is quite a vague one).

The book called the Foundation.

,,   ,,   Treasure.

(Writings attributed to Manes, founder of the Manichaean sect.)

I omit, in what follows, the titles of Old Testament Apocrypha and patristic writings.

The book called the Acts of Thecla and Paul (an episode from the Acts of Paul, current separately).

The Revelation called of Paul (extant).

     ,,   ,,   Thomas (extant).

     ,,   ,,   Stephen (see under Apocalypses).

The book called the Passing of Saint Mary (probably Pseudo-Melito's narrative).

The book called the Lots of the Apostles (a system of divination).

The book called *Lusa apostolorum* (an unexplained title).

The book called Canons of the Apostles (extant, but not given in this collection).

Epistle of Jesus to Abgarus. Epistle of Abgarus to Jesus (extant).

I may append to this the portions of the leading Greek lists of biblical books which mention New Testament Apocrypha.

a. The List of the Sixty Books

It is as old as the seventh century. The Sixty Books are those of the Bible. Then follow lists of those 'outside the sixty' (nine) and of 'such as are Apocryphal'.

Nos. 1–14 of these are Old Testament.

    15. History of James (= Protevangelium).

    16. Apocalypse of Peter.

    17. Travels and Teachings of the Apostles (the Apocryphal Acts in general).

    18. Epistle of Barnabas.

    19. Acts of Paul.

    20. Apocalypse of Paul.

    21. Teaching (Didascalia) of Clement (Apostolic Constitutions).

    22. Teaching of Ignatius (= his letters).

    23. Teaching of Polycarp (= his letter).

    24. Gospel according to Barnabas (see p. 22).

    25. Gospel according to Matthias (see p. 12).

b. Stichometry of Nicephorus

Thought to have been drawn up in Jerusalem: *possibly* as old as the fourth century: appended ultimately to the ninth-century Chronography of Nicephorus.

Such of the New Testament books as are disputed.

1. Apocalypse of John	lines	1,400
2. Apocalypse of Peter	,,	300
3. Epistle of Barnabas	,,	1,360
4. Gospel according to the Hebrews	,,	2,200

Such of the New Testament as are Apocryphal.

1. Travels of Paul (= Acts)	lines	3,600
2. Travels of Peter	,,	2,750

    3. Travels of John (= Acts)   lines 2,600
    4. Travels of Thomas   ,, 1,600
    5. Gospel according to Thomas   ,, 1300
    6. Teaching (Didache) of the Apostles   ,,   200
    7. Of Clement (two Epistles)   ,, 2,600
    8. Of Ignatius, Polycarp, and Hermas.

    c. The Synopsis of Scripture ' of Athanasius '.

Extant in but one manuscript, at Eton. In the list of Old Testament
Apocrypha it is identical with the last, only it does not give the number
of lines. In the New Testament list it is confused, calling the obviously
apocryphal books 'disputed' only, and omitting the real 'antilegomena'.
Thus :

Of the New Testament again these are disputed. Travels of
Peter, Travels of John, Travels of Thomas, Gospel according to
Thomas, Teaching of the Apostles, Clementine *writings*: out of
which the truer and inspired portions have been selected and
paraphrased.

FRAGMENTS OF GOSPELS, ETC.

PRESERVED IN MANUSCRIPTS DISCOVERED IN RECENT YEARS

A. GREEK FRAGMENTS (See also Appendix I)

1. THE FAYOUM GOSPEL-FRAGMENT

THIS is a piece of papyrus of the third (?) century, in the Archduke Rainer's collection of papyri at Vienna: first published in 1885. There have been many attempts (as in all these cases) at restoring the missing words and letters. The first line remains quite doubtful. What may be regarded as certain is:

all ye in this
night shall be offended according to
the scripture: I will smite the shepherd and the
sheep shall be scattered. And when Peter
said: Even if all, not I, the Lord
{ said: The cock shall twice crow and thou
{ said: Before the cock crow twice to-day
{ first shalt thrice deny me
{ thou shalt thrice deny me.

It is not certain that this is a fragment of a Gospel: it may be, and is by many held to be, a somewhat abridged quotation made by a preacher or commentator. It omits, for instance, the clause: After I am risen I will go before you into Galilee. If the preacher or expositor wished to emphasize Peter's denial, he might easily pass over these words. On the other hand the first editor of it, and others, have thought that the omission was a mark of early date.

The word for *crow* is literally *cry cuckoo*.

2. THE OXYRHYNCHUS SAYINGS OF JESUS

These are on two papyri found at Oxyrhynchus by Messrs. Grenfell and Hunt in excavations carried out for the Graeco-Roman branch of the Egypt Exploration Fund.

The first was found in 1897: it is a leaf of a papyrus *book*, of the third century. It is numbered, apparently, '11'. The second was found in 1903: it is a piece of a papyrus *roll*, also of the third century, but a little later in date than the other. It has a title or prologue.

Both are mutilated. The latest editor, Professor H. G. Evelyn White (*The Sayings of Jesus from Oxyrhynchus*, Cambridge, 1920), has shown good cause for believing both fragments to belong to the same collection of Sayings. He makes the second precede the first (as I said, it has a title), and believes that the Sayings are extracts from the Gospel according to the Hebrews. I shall follow his order in

translating the Sayings: but I must refrain from quoting all his very
ingenious restorations.   As a rule I shall only give the practically
certain supplements.

Oxyrhynchus Papyrus 654.

Prologue. These are the (. . .) words which Jesus that liveth
and (. . .) spake to (. . .) and to Thomas. And
he said: (Whosoever heareth) these words shall not taste
(of death).

i. Let not him that seeketh cease (seeking till he) find, and
when he findeth (he shall marvel, and) having marvelled
he shall reign, and (having reigned) he shall rest.

(Quoted by Clement of Alexandria as from the Gospel according to
the Hebrews : see p. 2.)

ii. (. . .) saith (Who are they that) draw us (. . .
. . .) the kingdom that is in heaven
(. . . .) the fowls of the heaven
whatsoever is under the earth
the fish of the sea. (These are they
that draw) you; and the kingdom (of heaven) is
within you: (and whosoever) knoweth (. . .)
shall find it (. . .) know yourselves
(. . .) ye are (. . .) of the
Father (. . .) ye shall know yourselves to be in (. . .). And ye are
the city (?) (of God   (*See below for suggested restorations.*)

iii. A man shall not hesitate (
having found?) to ask of (
concerning the place of (
for (ye shall find?) that many (first shall be last and)
the last first and they shall (

iv. Jesus saith (
before thy face and (that which is hidden)
from thee shall be revealed (to thee: for there is nothing)
hid that shall not be manifested
and buried that (shall not be found *or* raised up)

v.   his disciples) question him (and)
say: How shall we fast (and how shall we
) and how (shall we
) and what shall we observe (
). Jesus saith (
) Do not do (
) of the truth (
) hidden (
) blessed is he (

Oxyrhynchus Papyrus 1.

vi. And then shalt thou see clearly to cast out the mote which
is in thy brother's eye.

vii. Jesus saith: If ye fast not from the world ye shall not find the kingdom of God, and if ye keep not Sabbath for the whole week, ye shall not see the Father.

viii. Jesus saith: I stood in the midst of the world, and in flesh appeared I unto them: and I found all men drunken, and none did I find thirsting among them and my soul is afflicted for the sons of men, because they are blind in their heart and see not . . .

(bottom of the column gone)

ix, col. 2.						poverty

x. (Jesus saith) Wheresoever there are (two, they are not without) God: and where there is one alone I say I am with him. Lift up the stone and there shalt thou find me: cleave the wood, and I am there.

xi. Jesus saith: A prophet is not acceptable in his own country, nor doth a physician do cures upon them that know him.

xii. Jesus saith: A city built upon the top of an high mountain and established can neither fall nor be hidden.

xiii. Jesus saith: Thou hearest with(in) thy (one) ear (but the other thou hast closed). . . .

. . . .

It is not practicable to give the numerous attempts at restoration which have been made. For these I refer the reader to Evelyn White's excellent edition. But by way of a specimen I will give Evelyn White's and Lagrange's suggestions for Saying II, which is one of the most puzzling of them all. Lagrange's appeared in the *Revue Biblique*, 1922, p. 432.

Evelyn White would restore thus:

Judas) saith: (Who then
are they that draw us, (and when shall come
the kingdom that is in heaven? (Jesus saith:)
The fowls of the heaven (and of the beasts what
-ever is beneath the earth (or upon the earth, and)
the fishes of the sea, (these are they that
draw you: and the kingdom (of heaven)
is within you: (and whosoever) knoweth (himself)
shall find (it: and having found it)
ye shall know yourselves, (that) ye are (sons and heirs)
of the Father the (Almighty, and)
shall know yourselves (that ye are) in (God and God in you).
And ye are the (City of God).

Judas the interrogator is 'not Iscariot'.

Lagrange:

(Judas) saith: (Who then
are they that draw us (unto heaven above, if
the kingdom (is) in heaven? (Jesus saith)
The fowls of the heaven, (the beasts and if

5 there be anything beneath the earth (or upon the earth, and
the fishes of the sea (are they that) draw you (unto God)
and the kingdom (of heaven)
is within you (and whosoever) knoweth (God)
shall find it: (for if ye know him)
10 ye shall know yourselves (and shall know that) ye are (sons)
of the Father that is (perfect: and likewise)
ye shall know yourselves (to be citizens in heaven).
And ye are the city (of God) or (that which affrighteth Satan).

He gives an alternative for lines 8–10:

is within you (and whosoever) knoweth (himself)
shall find it. (Take pains therefore)
to know yourselves, &c.

FRAGMENT OF A GOSPEL

Oxyrhynchus Papyrus 655. This is a broken leaf of a papyrus roll of
the third century. Very little of the second column—only the
beginnings of words—remains.

(Take no thought)
from morning until evening
nor from evening
to morning, either for
your food, what ye
shall eat, nor for your
raiment, what ye shall
put on. Much better
are ye than the lilies
which do not card
nor spin . . .
having one gar-
ment, what . . . and
ye, who can add
unto your stat-
ure? He shall give
you your rai-
ment. His disciples
say unto him
When wilt thou
be manifest unto us and when
shall we see thee? He saith:
When ye have put off your raiment and
are not ashamed.

(Cf. the Gospel according to the Egyptians.)

Col. 2. The sense of the lower part only can be made out with
certainty.

He said The key of knowledge have ye hidden:
yourselves ye entered not in, and to them that were
coming in ye opened not
.   .   .   .   .   (after two lines)
harmless as doves.
The other little pieces of the leaf give no sense.

FRAGMENT OF ANOTHER GOSPEL

Oxyrhynchus Papyri, Part V, 1908.
A leaf of a parchment book of the third century, almost complete.
first, before he doeth wrong he excuseth himself (*or* falleth into
error). But take ye heed lest haply ye also suffer like things
with them. For not only among the living do evildoers among
men receive (retribution), but they endure also a punishment
and great torment.[1]
And he took them with him and led them to the cleansing-place
itself (*or* holy place) and walked in the Temple. And there came
near a Pharisee, an high priest, Levi (?) by name, and met them
and said unto the Saviour: Who hath given thee leave to tread
this holy place and to look upon these holy vessels, without
thy first bathing thyself, and without thy disciples having washed
their feet, but unclean *as thou art* hast thou walked in this Temple,
which is a clean place, wherein no man walketh but one that
hath bathed himself and changed his clothes, nor presumeth
to look upon these holy vessels?
And straightway (the Saviour) stood with his disciples and
answered him: Art thou then clean, that art here in the Temple?
He said unto him: I am clean, for I have bathed myself in the
pool of David, and when I had gone down *into it* by the one ladder
(stair), I came up by the other: and I have put on white and
clean raiment, and then did I come, and have looked upon
these holy vessels. The Saviour answered him and said: Woe
unto you, ye blind, that see not! Thou hast bathed thyself in
these waters that are poured forth, into which, night and day,
dogs and swine are cast: and after thou hadst washed thyself
didst scour thine outer skin, which the harlots also and flute-
girls anoint and bathe and scour and beautify to (arouse) desire
in men,[2] but within it is (*or* they are) filled with scorpions and

[1] The above is mainly Zahn's rendering. Swete's is: 'beforehand
he useth every device to injure first (unlike the righteous, who—see
Wisdom xviii. 2—do not retaliate when they are injured first). . . . For
evildoers do not receive retribution among animals only (animals that do
harm are punished here and now) but *hereafter* also undergo torment,' &c.
[2] I am reminded of an addition in the Septuagint to the text of
1 Kings xxii. 38 : They washed (*Ahab's*) chariot at the fountain of
Samaria: and the *swine and the dogs* licked up the blood, and the
harlots washed themselves in the blood, according to the word of the
Lord which he spake.

all evil. But I and my disciples, of whom thou sayest, that
we are not washed, have been washed in living waters which
came down from (God out of heaven). But woe unto them that
(*wash the outside, but within are unclean,* is Dr. Swete's suggested
supplement).

The writer seems to show gross ignorance of Jewish matters in
assuming that swine could be suffered in the neighbourhood of the
Temple, and in other ways. Yet some have defended him on this score.
We have no clue to the identity of the book from which the fragment comes. If it were not that Jesus is here spoken of as 'the
Saviour', not 'the Lord', I should suggest the Gospel of Peter. 'Saviour'
is the common word in the Gnostic literature. The Gospel of the
Egyptians is an obvious possibility: but all is uncertain. At least,
the leaf is *not* from the Gospel according to the Hebrews : and it
approaches the style of the Synoptists more nearly than do the next
fragments.

B. COPTIC

1. A fragmentary papyrus of the fourth or fifth century at Strasburg,
edited by A. Jacoby in 1900. I follow the rendering in Hennecke's
Apokr. d. N.T., which seems better than Jacoby's.

[*front*] that he may be known by his (hospitality to strangers)
and be praised for his fruit: for . . .
. . . Amen. Give me now thy (strength) O Father, that (they)
with me may endure the world. Amen. (I have) received the
crown (*or* sceptre) of the kingdom.

.   .   .   .

I am become king through thee, Father. Thou wilt subject
all things unto me. (Amen.) Through whom shall (the last)
enemy be destroyed? Through (Christ). Through whom shall
the sting of death be (destroyed)? (Through the) only-begotten.
Amen.
Unto whom belongeth the dominion? (Unto the Son.) Amen.

.   .   .   .

[*back*] Now when he had ended all the (song of praise to his
Father?) he turned himself to us and said (unto us): The hour
is come when I shall be taken from you.
The spirit (is) willing, but the flesh is weak : (stay) and watch
with me.
But we the apostles wept, saying:

.   .   .   .

He answered and said unto us: Fear not (because of) the
destruction (of the body) but (fear) much more . . . the power
of (darkness). Remember all (that I) have said unto you: (If)
they have persecuted me, (they will) persecute you also. . . .
(Ye) rejoice because I (have overcome the world).

.   .   .   .

Another fragment of the same.

[*front*] (that I) may reveal unto you all my glory and show you all your strength and the mystery of your apostleship. . . .

[*back*] Our eyes penetrated through all places. We beheld the glory of his Godhead and all the glory of his dominion. He clothed us with the power of (our) apostleship.

We gain little from this. The scene is evidently the garden of Gethsemane. Our Lord utters a hymn to the Father: a faint resemblance to that in the Acts of John is perceptible. In it are clear reminiscences of 1 Cor. xv. Further reminiscences of St. John's Gospel occur just after this. The second fragment implies a vision of the glorified Christ seen by the apostles. The writing of which these are fragments cannot have been a very early production. The apostles speak in the first person plural: but we need not infer that the book was *a* Gospel or *the* Gospel according to the Twelve (though this is Revillout's view). As in other cases (e.g. the Gospel of Peter) a single apostle would most likely have figured as the author in some other part of it.

2. Bound up with the fifth-century manuscript which contains the *Pistis Sophia* is a slightly later leaf on which is the end of a book that may have been a Gospel. It has echoes of the last twelve verses of St. Mark.

the righteous man. They went forth by threes to the four regions of the heaven and preached the gospel of the kingdom in the whole world, Christ working with them by the word of strengthening and the signs and wonders which accompanied them. And so have men learned of the kingdom of God in all the earth and in the whole world of Israel for a testimony for all nations that are from the rising of the sun unto the going down thereof.

3.[1] Similarly the remains of the ancient manuscript of the Acts of Paul include a single leaf of a Gospel narrative:

   . . . the works . . .
they wondered greatly and pondered
in their hearts. He said unto them:
Why marvel ye that I raise
the dead, or that I make the lame
to go, or that I cleanse the lepers
or raise up the sick, or that I have
healed the palsied and the possessed,
or that I have parted a few
loaves and satisfied many, or that I
have walked on the sea or that I
have commanded the winds? If ye
believe this and are convinced,
then are ye great. For verily I say

[1] See Appendix II.

unto you: If ye say unto this mountain
Lift thyself and be cast into the sea
without having doubted in your soul,
it shall happen unto you . . .
as one of them was convinced
whose name was Simon, and who
said: O Lord verily great are
the works which thou doest. For
we have never heard, nor have we seen
[2nd page]   ever a man that hath raised
the dead, save thee.
The Lord said unto him: Ye shall
pray for the works, which I myself shall do
. . . But the other works will I
do straightway. For these I do
for the sake of (?) a momentary salvation in time, in these places where
they are, that they may believe on him who
hath sent me. Simon said unto him:
O Lord, command me, that I may
speak. He said unto him: Speak, Peter.
For from that day he did
call them by name. He said:
What then is this work which is greater than these
. . . except the raising of the dead
and the feeding of such a multitude?
The Lord said unto him: There is somewhat that is greater
than this, and blessed are they, that have believed
with their whole heart. But Philip
lifted up his voice in wrath
saying: What manner of
thing is this, that thou wilt teach us?
But he said unto him: Thou

This again is not very instructive. The burden of it is, 'Greater
works than these will I do'. There is nothing in it which goes outside
the sphere of the canonical Gospels, save Philip's anger. We shall see
that in the Acts of Philip his proneness to wrath is emphasized.

AGRAPHA

By this curious name, which means 'unwritten things', it is usual to designate sayings and traditions of Christ which are not recorded in our Gospels, and are not capable of being traced to their source. But collectors of them—especially Resch—have swept into their net all manner of fragments which do not come under the original definition.

Many of these appear in other parts of this volume: but there is a residue for which a place must be found here.

I distinguish two classes. First, those which are found as additions to the text of our Gospels, in manuscripts of the Gospels; second, those which are quoted by other writers.

A

1. At Matt. xx. 28, Codex Bezae (D of the Gospels, at Cambridge) and some Latin and Syriac authorities add: But ye seek (*or* seek ye) to increase from smallness and from the greater to become less. And when ye go in and are invited to dine, do not recline in the prominent place lest haply one more illustrious than thou come in, and he that bade thee to dinner say to thee: Go yet lower down; and thou shalt be put to shame. But if thou recline in the lesser place, and a lesser man come in, he that bade thee to dinner will say to thee: Get thee yet higher up; and this will be profitable to thee.

Cf. Luke xiv. 8–10.

2. At Luke vi. 4, Codex Bezae has: On the same day, seeing one working on the sabbath, he said unto him: Man, if indeed thou knowest what thou doest, thou art blessed: but if thou knowest not, thou art cursed, and a transgressor of the law.

3. At Matt. iii. 17, the fourth-century Latin Codex Vercellensis has: And when he was being baptized, a very great light shone round about from the water, so that all that had come thither feared.

The Codex Sangermanensis (g^1) has: And when Jesus was being baptized, a great light shone from the water, so that all that were gathered together feared.

The same addition is found in many early writers. Justin Martyr (*Dialogue with Trypho*, 88) says, 'a fire was kindled in Jordan'. Ephraem Syrus (fourth century) has, 'a light rising over the water'. See also the Gospel of the Ebionites.

4. At Mark xvi. 3, after the words 'roll away the stone from the door of the sepulchre', the early Codex Bobiensis *k* (at Turin) has: But suddenly at the third hour of the day (*or* by day)

there came darkness throughout all the globe of the earth; and angels came down from the heavens, and rising in the glory (brightness) of the living God they went up together with him, and immediately there was light. Then the *women* drew near to the sepulchre and saw that the stone was rolled away: for it was very great.

Compare the account of the resurrection in the Gospel of Peter.

5.   *The 'Freer-logion'.*

At Mark xvi. 14, W, a fifth-century uncial Greek manuscript of Mark discovered in recent years in Egypt, and purchased by Mr. Freer of Detroit, has: (Afterward he appeared unto the eleven as they sat at meat and upbraided them with their unbelief and hardness of heart, because they believed not them which had seen him after he was risen) and they made excuse (defended themselves), saying: This age of wickedness and unbelief is under Satan who, by means of unclean spirits, permitteth not *men* to apprehend the true power of God: therefore do thou now reveal thy righteousness. They, *then*, said *these things* unto Christ. And Christ said unto them: The limit of the years of the power of Satan is fulfilled: but other fearful things draw near even *upon them* for whom, because they had sinned, I was delivered unto death that they may return unto the truth and sin no more: that they may inherit the spiritual and incorruptible glory of righteousness which is in heaven. But go ye into all the world, &c.

Part of this remarkable addition was already known through St. Jerome, who in the *Dialogue against Pelagius*, ii. 15, says that it was found in some copies, and especially Greek manuscripts. He has: And they excused themselves (*lit.* made satisfaction) saying: This age of iniquity and unbelief is under Satan who (which) by unclean spirits suffereth not the true power of God to be perceived: therefore now forthwith reveal thou thy righteousness.

Dr. Swete observes: 'It seems probable that almost from the beginning there were two recensions (of the Last Twelve Verses) of which one contained our passage and the other did not, and that the latter for some reason was commonly preferred.' ... 'The style of the addition does not differ markedly from the language of the rest of the Appendix.'

It is hardly necessary, perhaps, to observe that the Last Twelve Verses of St. Mark and the story of the woman taken in adultery (John vii. 53–viii. 11) form no part of the original text of the Gospels.

To discuss other small additions or supposed additions to the text would take us into the sphere of textual criticism.

B

Of sayings, &c., preserved in other sources the following are the most important:

1. It is more blessed to give than to receive.

Quoted by Paul at Miletus, Acts xx. 35.

2. Wherein I find you, there will I judge you.

Quoted by Justin Martyr (*Dialogue with Trypho*, 47), by Clement of Alexandria, and by many others; one writer attributes it to the prophet Ezekiel.

3. Ask ye for the greater things, and the small shall be added unto you: and ask for the heavenly things, and the earthly shall be added unto you.

Origen (*on prayer*, 2) quotes both parts of this saying; Clement of Alexandria (*Strom.* i. 24. 158) the first part only.

4. Be ye approved (*or* tried) money-changers (bankers).

Quoted by Clement of Alexandria (*Strom.* i. 28. 177) and many others. Paul's words in 1 Thess. v. 21, 'Prove all things, hold fast that which is good', are really a comment on the saying, and show its meaning.

5. The 'Second Epistle of Clement', v. 2–4 has: For the Lord saith: Ye shall be as lambs in the midst of wolves. And Peter answering saith unto him: If then the wolves tear the lambs in pieces? Jesus said unto Peter: Let not the lambs fear the wolves, after they are dead. And do not ye fear them that kill you, and can do nothing unto you, but fear him who, after ye are dead, hath power over soul and body, to cast *them* into the hell of fire.

6. CLEMENT OF ALEXANDRIA, *Excerpts from Theodotus*, 2 : As the Valentinians say . . . on this account the Saviour saith: Be thou saved (*or* Save thyself, thou) and thy soul.

7. TERTULLIAN *on Baptism*, 20. The disciples were tempted because they fell asleep, so that they forsook the Lord when he was taken, and even he who abode with him and used the sword, so that he even denied thrice: for the saying had gone before, that: No man that is not tempted shall obtain the kingdom of heaven.

Didascalia, ii. 8. The scripture saith: A man that is not tempted is not approved.

8. ORIGEN *on Jeremiah*, hom. 3. 3 (Latin). I have read somewhere that the Saviour said—and I question whether some one has assumed the person of the Saviour, or called the words to memory, or whether it be true that is said—but *at any rate* the Saviour himself says: He that is near me is near the fire. He that is far from me is far from the kingdom.

DIDYMUS *on Ps.* lxxxviii. 8, quotes the same in Greek.

9. In the *Apostolic Church Order* is this curious passage. Peter said: We have gone too fast in making ordinances: let us signify accurately concerning the offering of the body and the blood.

John said: Ye have forgotten, brethren, when the Teacher asked for the bread and the cup, and blessed them, saying: This is my body and my blood, that he permitted not these *women* to be (stand) with us. Martha said: *It was* because of

Mary, because he saw her smiling. Mary said: I laughed not yet (or I laughed no more): for he said unto us before that: That which is weak shall be saved by means of that which is strong. (So the Greek and Latin texts. The Syriac, which seems better, has:) I did not verily laugh, but I remembered the words of our Lord, and was glad: for ye know that he said unto us aforetime, when he taught us, that, &c.

10. CLEMENT OF ALEXANDRIA, *Strom.* v. 10. 63. For the prophet saith: Who shall understand a parable of the Lord save he that is wise and knowledgeable and loveth his Lord? For it is given to few to contain all things: for it is not as grudging (saith he) that the Lord commanded in a certain Gospel: My secret (mystery) for me and for the sons of mine house.

Clementine Homilies, xix. 20. For we remember our Lord and Teacher, how he charged us saying: Ye shall keep my secrets (mysteries) for me and for the sons of mine house.

The source of the words is Isa. xxiv. 16 (Greek).

11. JUSTIN, *Dialogue with Trypho*, 35. For he said: Many shall come in my name clad outwardly with sheep skins, but within they are ravening wolves. And: There shall be divisions (schisms) and heresies.

12. *Acts of Philip*, 34. For the Lord said unto me: If ye make not that which is below in you to be above, and the left hand things to be right, ye shall not enter into my kingdom.

Linus, *Martyrdom of Peter*, 17. The Lord said in a mystery: If ye make not the left hand as the right and the right as the left, and the things that are above as those that are below, and the things that are before as those that are behind, ye shall not know the kingdom of God.

13. IRENAEUS *against Heresies*, v. 33. 3. As the elders remember, which saw John the Lord's disciple, that they heard from him how the Lord taught concerning those times, and said: The days shall come wherein vines shall grow each having ten thousand branches, and on one branch ten thousand shoots, and on every shoot ten thousand clusters, and in every cluster ten thousand grapes, and every grape when it is pressed shall yield five and twenty measures (*metrētes*) of wine. And when any of the saints taketh hold of one of the clusters, another will cry out: I am a better cluster, take me, through me bless thou the Lord. Likewise also *he said* that a grain of wheat shall bring forth ten thousand ears, and every ear shall have ten thousand grains, and every grain *shall yield* five double pounds of white clean flour; and all other fruits and seeds and plants according to the agreement that followeth with them (*sc.* in the same proportion): and all animals using those foods which are got from the earth shall be peaceable and in concord one with

another, subject unto men with all obedience. These things Papias also, a hearer of John, and an associate of Polycarp, an ancient man, testifies in writing in the fourth of his books—for he wrote five. And he adds, saying: But these things are credible unto believers. And, he says, when Judas the traitor believed not, and asked: How then shall these growths be accomplished by the Lord? the Lord said: They shall see who shall come thereto.

HIPPOLYTUS *on Daniel*, 4. 60. So when the Lord was telling the disciples about the future kingdom of the saints, how glorious and wonderful it should be, Judas was struck by his words, and said: Who then shall see these things? And the Lord said: These things shall they see who are worthy.

In the Jewish Apocalypse of Baruch (xxix. 5) is a passage describing the Messianic kingdom in similar terms: and other Rabbinic parallels are not uncommon. The words in Baruch are:

The earth also will yield its fruit ten thousand fold, and on one vine there will be a thousand branches, and each branch will produce a thousand clusters, and each cluster will produce a thousand grapes, and each grape will produce a cor of wine.

The Papias text is somewhat fuller.

One more parallel may be quoted, from one of the writings which I have omitted from the collection. In an Encomium on John the Baptist attributed—absurdly—to Chrysostom (Budge, *Coptic Apocrypha*, 1913, p. 348), an Apocalypse by James the Lord's brother is quoted (pretended to have been found in a library at Jerusalem).

(The Saviour tells the apostles of the glories of John Baptist, who lives in the third heaven and ferries those who honour him on earth in a golden boat over the river of fire. He then takes the apostles to Paradise, and Thomas asks him how much fruit the trees bear.)

The Saviour said: I will hide nothing from you about the things concerning which ye have questioned me. As regardeth the vine, concerning the fruit of which ye have asked, there are ten thousand bunches of grapes upon it, and each bunch will produce six metrites (the same word as in Irenaeus) *of wine*. As regards the palm-trees in Paradise, each cluster yieldeth ten thousand dates, and each cluster is as long as a man is high. So likewise is it in the matter of the fig-trees: each shoot produceth ten thousand figs, and if three men were to partake of one fig, each of them would be satisfied. On each ear of the wheat which is in Paradise there are ten thousand grains, and each grain produceth six measures of flour. And the cedars also are on the same scale: each tree produceth ten thousand *cones* and is of a very great height. And the apple-tree and the thourakion-tree are of the same height; there are ten thousand apples on each shoot, and if three men were to partake of one apple, each of them would be satisfied.

INFANCY GOSPELS

UNDER this heading I have put together the narratives of the birth of the Virgin, and birth and childhood of our Lord.

The texts which may be called 'original' are two, the Book of James (Protevangelium), and the Gospel of Thomas.

The Book of James we have largely in its original form. The Gospel of Thomas seems to be the skeleton of the original, the stories retained, the speeches, which conveyed the doctrinal teaching of the book, almost entirely removed. It is in fact an expurgated edition.

All the other texts are variants and embroideries upon these: some contain details which probably are derived from the original text of the Gospel of Thomas.

BOOK OF JAMES, OR PROTEVANGELIUM

The latter of these names is a modern one: it was given to the book by Guillaume Postel, who in the sixteenth century introduced it to Europe.

Origen mentions the Book of James (and the Gospel of Peter) as stating that the 'brethren of the Lord' were sons of Joseph by a former wife. This is the first mention of it, and shows us that the book is as old as the second century. To collect later references to it is unnecessary.

It is generally agreed that the story of the death of Zacharias (chs. xxii–xxiv) does not properly belong to the text. Origen and other early writers give a different account of the cause of his death: it was, they say, because, after the Nativity, he still allowed Mary to take her place among the virgins in the Temple.

Difficulty is also caused by the sudden introduction of Joseph as the narrator in ch. xviii. 2 sqq. We cannot be sure whether this means that a fragment of a 'Joseph-apocryphon' has been introduced at this point; or, if so, how far it extends. We are sure, from a sentence of Clement of Alexandria,[1] that some story of a midwife being present at the Nativity was current in the second century.

We have the book in the original Greek and in several oriental versions, the oldest of which is the Syriac. But, oddly enough, there is no Latin version. The matter is found in an expanded and altered form in the 'Gospel of Pseudo-Matthew', but we have yet to find an old Latin translation of the present text. Such a thing seems to have existed, for a book identifiable with ours is condemned in the Gelasian Decree.

In the early chapters the Old Testament is extensively drawn upon, and imitated; but the author is not familiar with Jewish life or usages.

The best recent edition of this book is a French one, by Amann. There is as yet no really critical edition of the text, in which all manu-

---

[1] *Strom.* vii. 93, 'for after she had brought forth some say that she was attended by a midwife, and was found to be a virgin'.

scripts and versions are made use of. I follow Tischendorf's in the main.

I. 1 In the histories of the twelve tribes of Israel *it is written that* there was *one* Ioacim, exceeding rich: and he offered his gifts twofold, saying: That which is of my superfluity shall be for the whole people, and that which is for my forgiveness shall be for the Lord, for a propitiation unto me.

2 Now the great day of the Lord drew nigh and the children of Israel offered their gifts. And Reuben stood over against him saying: It is not lawful for thee to offer thy gifts first, forasmuch as thou hast gotten no seed in Israel. 3 And Ioacim was sore grieved, and went unto *the record of* the twelve tribes of the people, saying: I will look upon *the record of* the twelve tribes of Israel, whether I only have not gotten seed in Israel. And he searched, and found *concerning* all the righteous that they had raised up seed in Israel. And he remembered the patriarch Abraham, how in the last days God gave him a son, even Isaac. 4 And Ioacim was sore grieved, and showed not himself to his wife, but betook himself into the wilderness, and pitched his tent there, and fasted forty days and forty nights, saying within himself: I will not go down either for meat or for drink until the Lord my God visit me, and my prayer shall be unto me meat and drink.

II. 1 Now his wife Anna lamented with two lamentations, and bewailed herself with two bewailings, saying: I will bewail my widowhood, and I will bewail my childlessness.

2 And the great day of the Lord drew nigh, and Judith her handmaid said *unto her*: How long humblest thou thy soul? The great day of the Lord hath come, and it is not lawful for thee to mourn: but take this headband, which the mistress of *my* work gave me, and it is not lawful for me to put it on, forasmuch as I am an handmaid, and it hath a mark of royalty. And Anna said: Get thee from me. Lo! I have done nothing (*or* I will not do so) and the Lord hath greatly humbled me: peradventure one gave it to thee in subtilty, and thou art come to make me partaker in thy sin. And Judith said: How shall I curse thee, seeing the Lord hath shut up thy womb, to give thee no fruit in Israel?

3 And Anna was sore grieved [and mourned with a great mourning because she was reproached by all the tribes of Israel. And coming to herself she said: What shall I do? I will pray with weeping unto the Lord my God that he visit me]. And she put off her mourning garments and cleansed (*or* adorned) her head and put on her bridal garments: and about the ninth hour she went down into the garden to walk there. And she saw a laurel-tree and sat down underneath it and besought the Lord saying: O God of our fathers, bless me, and hearken unto my prayer, as thou didst bless the womb of Sarah, and gavest her a son, even Isaac.

III. 1 And looking up to the heaven she espied a nest of sparrows in the laurel-tree, and made a lamentation within herself, saying: Woe unto me, who begat me? And what womb brought me forth, for I am become a curse before the children of Israel, and I am reproached, and they have mocked me forth out of the temple of the Lord? 2 Woe unto me, unto what am I likened? I am not likened unto the fowls of the heaven, for even the fowls of the heaven are fruitful before thee, O Lord. Woe unto me, unto what am I likened? I am not likened unto the beasts of the earth, for even the beasts of the earth are fruitful before thee, O Lord. Woe unto me, unto what am I likened? I am not likened unto these waters, for even these waters are fruitful before thee, O Lord. 3 Woe unto me, unto what am I likened? I am not likened unto this earth, for even this earth bringeth forth her fruits in due season and blesseth thee, O Lord.

IV. 1 And behold an angel of the Lord appeared, saying unto her: Anna, Anna, the Lord hath hearkened unto thy prayer, and thou shalt conceive and bear, and thy seed shall be spoken of in the whole world. And Anna said: As the Lord my God liveth, if I bring forth either male or female, I will bring it for a gift unto the Lord my God, and it shall be ministering unto him all the days of its life.

2 And behold there came two messengers saying unto her: Behold Ioacim thy husband cometh with his flocks: for an angel of the Lord came down unto him saying: Ioacim, Ioacim, the Lord God hath hearkened unto thy prayer. Get thee down hence, for behold thy wife Anna hath conceived. 3 And Ioacim gat him down and called his herdsmen saying: Bring me hither ten lambs without blemish and without spot, and they shall be for the Lord my God; and bring me twelve tender calves, and they shall be for the priests and for the assembly of the elders; and an hundred kids for the whole people.

4 And behold Ioacim came with his flocks, and Anna stood at the gate and saw Ioacim coming, and ran and hung upon his neck, saying: Now know I that the Lord God hath greatly blessed me: for behold the widow is no more a widow, and she that was childless shall conceive. And Ioacim rested the first day in his house.

V. 1 And on the morrow he offered his gifts, saying in himself: If the Lord God be reconciled unto me, the plate *that is upon the forehead* of the priest will make it manifest unto me. And Ioacim offered his gifts and looked earnestly upon the plate of the priest when he went up unto the altar of the Lord, and he saw no sin in himself. And Ioacim said: Now know I that the Lord is become propitious unto me and hath forgiven all my sins. And he went down from the temple of the Lord justified, and went unto his house.

2 And her months were fulfilled, and in the ninth month Anna brought forth. And she said unto the midwife: What have I brought forth? And she said: A female. And Anna said: My soul is magnified this day, and she laid herself down. And when the days were fulfilled, Anna purified herself and gave suck to the child and called her name Mary.

VI. 1 And day by day the child waxed strong, and when she was six months old her mother stood her upon the ground to try if she would stand; and she walked seven steps and returned unto her bosom. And she caught her up, saying: As the Lord my God liveth, thou shalt walk no more upon this ground, until I bring thee into the temple of the Lord. And she made a sanctuary in her bedchamber and suffered nothing common or unclean to pass through it. And she called for the daughters of the Hebrews that were undefiled, and they carried her hither and thither.

2 And the first year of the child was *fulfilled*, and Ioacim made a great feast and bade the priests and the scribes and the assembly of the elders and the whole people of Israel. And Ioacim brought the child to the priests, and they blessed her, saying: O God of our fathers, bless this child and give her a name renowned for ever among all generations. And all the people said: So be it, so be it. Amen. And he brought her to the high priests, and they blessed her, saying: O God of the high places, look upon this child, and bless her with the last blessing which hath no successor.

3 And her mother caught her up into the sanctuary of her bedchamber and gave her suck. And Anna made a song unto the Lord God, saying:

I will sing an hymn unto the Lord my God, because he hath visited me and taken away from me the reproach of mine enemies, and the Lord hath given me a fruit of his righteousness, single *and* manifold before him. Who shall declare unto the sons of Reuben that Anna giveth suck? Hearken, hearken, ye twelve tribes of Israel, that Anna giveth suck. And she laid the child to rest in the bedchamber of her sanctuary, and went forth and ministered unto them. And when the feast was ended, they gat them down rejoicing, and glorifying the God of Israel.

VII. 1 And unto the child her months were added: and the child became two years old. And Ioacim said: Let us bring her up to the temple of the Lord that we may pay the promise which we promised; lest the Lord require it of us (*lit.* send unto us), and our gift become unacceptable. And Anna said: Let us wait until the third year, that the child may not long after her father or mother. And Ioacim said: Let us wait.

2 And the child became three years old, and Ioacim said: Call for the daughters of the Hebrews that are undefiled, and let them take every one a lamp, and let them be burning, that the child turn not backward and her heart be taken captive

away from the temple of the Lord. And they did so until they were gone up into the temple of the Lord.

And the priest received her and kissed her and blessed her and said: The Lord hath magnified thy name among all generations: in thee in the latter days shall the Lord make manifest his redemption unto the children of Israel. And he made her to sit upon the third step of the altar. And the Lord put grace upon her and she danced with her feet and all the house of Israel loved her.

VIII. 1 And her parents gat them down marvelling, and praising the Lord God because the child was not turned away backward. And Mary was in the temple of the Lord as a dove that is nurtured: and she received food from the hand of an angel.

2 And when she was twelve years old, there was a council of the priests, saying: Behold Mary is become twelve years old in the temple of the Lord. What then shall we do with her? lest she pollute the sanctuary of the Lord. And they said unto the high priest: Thou standest over the altar of the Lord. Enter in and pray concerning her: And whatsoever the Lord shall reveal to thee, that let us do.

3 And the high priest took the vestment with the twelve bells and went in unto the Holy of Holies and prayed concerning her. And lo, an angel of the Lord appeared saying unto him: Zacharias, Zacharias, go forth and assemble them that are widowers of the people, and let them bring every man a rod, and to whomsoever the Lord shall show a sign, his wife shall she be. And the heralds went forth over all the country round about Judaea, and the trumpet of the Lord sounded, and all men ran thereto.

IX. 1 And Joseph cast down his adze and ran to meet them, and when they were gathered together they went to the high priest and took their rods *with them*. And he took the rods of them all and went into the temple and prayed. And when he had finished the prayer he took the rods and went forth and gave them back to them: and there was no sign upon them. But Joseph received the last rod: and lo, a dove came forth of the rod and flew upon the head of Joseph. And the priest said unto Joseph: Unto thee hath it fallen to take the virgin of the Lord and keep her for thyself. 2 And Joseph refused, saying: I have sons, and I am an old man, but she is a girl: lest I became a laughing-stock to the children of Israel. And the priest said unto Joseph: Fear the Lord thy God, and remember what things God did unto Dathan and Abiram and Korah, how the earth clave and they were swallowed up because of their gainsaying. And now fear thou, Joseph, lest it be so in thine house. And Joseph was afraid, and took her to keep her for himself. And Joseph said unto Mary: Lo, I have received thee out of the temple of the Lord: and now do I leave thee in my house, and I go away to build my buildings and I will come *again* unto thee. The Lord shall watch over thee.

X. 1 Now there was a council of the priests, and they said: Let us make a veil for the temple of the Lord. And the priest said: Call unto me pure virgins of the tribe of David. And the officers departed and sought and found seven virgins. And the priests called to mind the child Mary, that she was of the tribe of David and was undefiled before God: and the officers went and fetched her. And they brought them into the temple of the Lord, and the priest said: Cast me lots, which *of you* shall weave the gold and the undefiled (the white) and the fine linen and the silk and the hyacinthine, and the scarlet and the true purple. And the lot of the true purple and the scarlet fell unto Mary, and she took them and went unto her house.

[And at that season Zacharias became dumb, and Samuel was in his stead until the time when Zacharias spake *again*.]

But Mary took the scarlet and began to spin it.

XI. 1 And she took the pitcher and went forth to fill it with water: and lo a voice saying: Hail, thou that art highly favoured; the Lord is with thee: blessed art thou among women.

And she looked about her upon the right hand and upon the left, to see whence this voice should be: and being filled with trembling she went to her house and set down the pitcher, and took the purple and sat down upon her seat and drew out the thread.

2 And behold an angel of the Lord stood before her saying: Fear not, Mary, for thou hast found grace before the Lord of all things, and thou shalt conceive of his word. And she, when she heard it, questioned in herself, saying: Shall I *verily* conceive of the living God, and bring forth after the manner of all women? And the angel of the Lord said: Not so, Mary, for a power of the Lord shall overshadow thee: wherefore also that holy thing which shall be born of thee shall be called the Son of the Highest. And thou shalt call his name Jesus: for he shall save his people from their sins. And Mary said: Behold the handmaid of the Lord is before him: be it unto me according to thy word.

XII. 1 And she made the purple and the scarlet and brought them unto the priest. And the priest blessed her and said: Mary, the Lord God hath magnified thy name, and thou shalt be blessed among all generations of the earth. 2 And Mary rejoiced and went away unto Elizabeth her kinswoman: and she knocked at the door. And Elizabeth when she heard it cast down the scarlet (*al.* the wool) and ran to the door and opened it, and when she saw Mary she blessed her and said: Whence is this to me that the mother of my Lord should come unto me? for behold that which is in me leaped and blessed thee. And Mary forgat the mysteries which Gabriel the archangel had told her, and she looked up unto the heaven and said: Who am I, Lord, that all the generations of the earth do bless me? 3 And she abode three months with Elizabeth, and day by day her womb grew: and

Mary was afraid and departed unto her house and hid herself from the children of Israel. Now she was sixteen years old when these mysteries came to pass.

XIII. 1 Now it was the sixth month with her, and behold Joseph came from his building, and he entered into his house and found her great with child. And he smote his face, and cast himself down upon the ground on sackcloth and wept bitterly, saying: With what countenance shall I look unto the Lord my God? and what prayer shall I make concerning this maiden? for I received her out of the temple of the Lord my God a virgin, and have not kept her safe. Who is he that hath ensnared me? Who hath done this evil in mine house and hath defiled the virgin? Is not the story of Adam repeated in me? for as at the hour of his giving thanks the serpent came and found Eve alone and deceived her, so hath it befallen me also. 2 And Joseph arose from off the sackcloth and called Mary and said unto her O thou that wast cared for by God, why hast thou done this? thou hast forgotten the Lord thy God. Why hast thou humbled thy soul, thou that wast nourished up in the Holy of Holies and didst receive food at the hand of an angel? 3 But she wept bitterly, saying: I am pure and I know not a man. And Joseph said unto her: Whence then is that which is in thy womb? and she said: As the Lord my God liveth, I know not whence it is come unto me.

XIV. 1 And Joseph was sore afraid and ceased from *speaking unto* her (*or* left her alone), and pondered what he should do with her. And Joseph said: If I hide her sin, I shall be found fighting against the law of the Lord: and if I manifest her unto the children of Israel, I fear lest that which is in her be the seed of an angel, and I shall be found delivering up innocent blood to the judgement of death. What then shall I do? I will let her go from me privily. And the night came upon him. 2 And behold an angel of the Lord appeared unto him in a dream, saying: Fear not this child, for that which is in her is of the Holy Ghost, and she shall bear a son and thou shalt call his name Jesus, for he shall save his people from their sins. And Joseph arose from sleep and glorified the God of Israel which had shown this favour unto her: and he watched over her.

XV. 1 Now Annas the scribe came unto him and said to him: Wherefore didst thou not appear in our assembly? and Joseph said unto him: I was weary with the journey, and I rested the first day. And *Annas* turned him about and saw Mary great with child. 2 And he went hastily to the priest and said unto him: Joseph, to whom thou bearest witness [that he is righteous] hath sinned grievously. And the priest said: Wherein? And he said: The virgin whom he received out of the temple of the Lord, he hath defiled her, and married her by stealth (*lit.* stolen her marriage), and hath not declared it to the children of Israel.

And the priest answered and said: Hath Joseph done this? And Annas the scribe said: Send officers, and thou shalt find the virgin great with child. And the officers went and found as he had said, and they brought her together with Joseph unto the place of judgement. 3 And the priest said: Mary, wherefore hast thou done this, and wherefore hast thou humbled thy soul and forgotten the Lord thy God, thou that wast nurtured in the Holy of Holies and didst receive food at the hand of an angel and didst hear *the* hymns and didst dance before *the Lord*, wherefore hast thou done this?

But she wept bitterly, saying: As the Lord my God liveth I am pure before him and I know not a man. 4 And the priest said unto Joseph: Wherefore hast thou done this? And Joseph said: As the Lord my God liveth I am pure as concerning her. And the priest said: Bear no false witness but speak the truth: thou hast married her by stealth and hast not declared it unto the children of Israel, and hast not bowed thine head under the mighty hand that thy seed should be blessed. And Joseph held his peace.

XVI. 1 And the priest said: Restore the virgin whom thou didst receive out of the temple of the Lord. And Joseph was full of weeping. And the priest said: I will give you to drink of the water of the conviction of the Lord, and it will make manifest your sins before your eyes. 2 And the priest took thereof and made Joseph drink and sent him into the hill-country. And he returned whole. He made Mary also drink and sent her into the hill-country. And she returned whole. And all the people marvelled, because sin appeared not in them. 3 And the priest said: If the Lord God hath not made your sin manifest, neither do I condemn you. And he let them go. And Joseph took Mary and departed unto his house rejoicing, and glorifying the God of Israel.

XVII. 1 Now there went out a decree from Augustus the king that all that were in Bethlehem of Judaea should be recorded. And Joseph said: I will record my sons: but this child, what shall I do with her? how shall I record her? as my wife? *nay,* I am ashamed. Or as my daughter? but all the children of Israel know that she is not my daughter. This day of the Lord shall do as the Lord willeth. 2 And he saddled the she-ass, and set her upon it, and his son led it and Joseph followed after. And they drew near (unto Bethlehem) within three miles: and Joseph turned himself about and saw her of a sad countenance and said within himself: Peradventure that which is within her paineth her. And again Joseph turned himself about and saw her laughing, and said unto her: Mary, what aileth thee that I see thy face at one time laughing and at another time sad? And Mary said unto Joseph: It is because I behold two peoples with mine eyes, the one weeping and lamenting and the other rejoicing and exulting.

3 And they came to the midst of the way, and Mary said unto him: Take me down from the ass, for that which is within me presseth me, to come forth. And he took her down from the ass and said unto her: Whither shall I take thee to hide thy shame? for the place is desert.

XVIII. 1 And he found a cave there and brought her into it, and set his sons by her: and he went forth and sought for a midwife of the Hebrews in the country of Bethlehem.

2 Now I Joseph was walking, and I walked not. And I looked up to the air and saw the air in amazement. And I looked up unto the pole of the heaven and saw it standing still, and the fowls of the heaven without motion. And I looked upon the earth and saw a dish set, and workmen lying *by it*, and their hands were in the dish: and they that were chewing chewed not, and they that were lifting *the food* lifted it not, and they that put it to their mouth put it not thereto, but the faces of all of them were looking upward. And behold there were sheep being driven, and they went not forward but stood still; and the shepherd lifted his hand to smite them with his staff, and his hand remained up. And I looked upon the stream of the river and saw the mouths of the kids upon *the water* and they drank not. And of a sudden all things moved onward in their course.

XIX. 1 And behold a woman coming down from the hill-country, and she said to me: Man, whither goest thou? And I said: I seek a midwife of the Hebrews. And she answered and said unto me: Art thou of Israel? And I said unto her: Yea. And she said: And who is she that bringeth forth in the cave? And I said: She that is betrothed unto me. And she said to me: Is she not thy wife? And I said to her: It is Mary that was nurtured up in the temple of the Lord: and I received her to wife by lot: and she is not my wife, but she hath conception by the Holy Ghost.

And the midwife said unto him: Is this the truth? And Joseph said unto her: Come hither and see. And the midwife went with him.

2 And they stood in the place of the cave: and behold a bright cloud overshadowing the cave. And the midwife said: My soul is magnified this day, because mine eyes have seen marvellous things: for salvation is born unto Israel. And immediately the cloud withdrew itself out of the cave, and a great light appeared in the cave so that our eyes could not endure it. And by little and little that light withdrew itself until the young child appeared: and it went and took the breast of its mother Mary.

And the midwife cried aloud and said: Great unto me to-day is this day, in that I have seen this new sight. 3 And the midwife went forth of the cave and Salome met her. And she said to her: Salome, Salome, a new sight have I to tell thee. A virgin hath brought forth, which her nature alloweth not. And Salome said:

As the Lord my God liveth, if I make not trial and prove her nature I will not believe that a virgin hath brought forth. XX. 1 And the midwife went in and said unto Mary: Order thyself, for *there is no small contention* arisen concerning thee.[1] And Salome made trial and cried out and said: Woe unto mine iniquity and mine unbelief, because I have tempted the living God, and lo, my hand falleth away from me in fire. And she bowed her knees unto the Lord, saying: O God of my fathers, remember that I am the seed of Abraham and Isaac and Jacob: make me not a public example unto the children of Israel, but restore me unto the poor, for thou knowest, Lord, that in thy name did I perform my cures, and did receive my hire of thee. 3 And lo, an angel of the Lord appeared, saying unto her: Salome, Salome, the Lord hath hearkened to thee: bring thine hand near unto the young child and take him up, and there shall be unto thee salvation and joy. 4 And Salome came near and took him up, saying: I will do him worship, for a great king is born unto Israel. And behold immediately Salome was healed: and she went forth of the cave justified. And lo, a voice saying: Salome, Salome, tell none of the marvels which thou hast seen, until the child enter into Jerusalem.

XXI. 1 And behold, Joseph made him ready to go forth into Judaea. And there came a great tumult in Bethlehem of Judaea; for there came wise men, saying: Where is he that is born king of the Jews? for we have seen his star in the east and are come to worship him. 2 And when Herod heard it he was troubled and sent officers unto the wise men. And he sent for the high priests and examined them, saying: How is it written concerning the Christ, where he is born? They say unto him: In Bethlehem of Judaea: for so it is written. And he let them go. And he examined the wise men, saying unto them: What sign saw ye concerning the king that is born? And the wise men said: We saw a very great star shining among those stars and dimming them so that the stars appeared not: and thereby knew we that a king was born unto Israel, and we came to worship him. And Herod said: Go and seek for him, and if ye find him, tell me, that I also may come and worship him. 3 And the wise men went forth. And lo, the star which they saw in the east went before them until they entered into the cave: and it stood over the head of the cave. And the wise men saw the young child with Mary his mother: and they brought out of their scrip gifts, gold and frankincense and myrrh. 4 And being warned by the angel that they should not enter into Judaea, they went into their own country by another way.

[1] The italicized words are from the LXX Greek version of Isa. vii, which we render, 'Is it a small thing for you to weary men?' Immediately after is the prophecy, 'Behold, a virgin shall conceive,' &c., which accounts for the employment of the phrase here.

XXII. 1 But when Herod perceived that he was mocked by the wise men, he was wroth, and sent murderers, saying unto them: Slay the children from two years old and under. 2 And when Mary heard that the children were being slain, she was afraid, and took the young child and wrapped him in swaddling clothes and laid him in an ox-manger.

3 But Elizabeth when she heard that they sought for John, took him and went up into the hill-country and looked about her where she should hide him: and there was no hiding-place. And Elizabeth groaned and said with a loud voice: O mountain of God, receive thou a mother with a child. For Elizabeth was not able to go up. And immediately the mountain clave asunder and took her in. And there was a light shining *alway* for them: for an angel of the Lord was with them, keeping watch over them.

XXIII. 1 Now Herod sought for John, and sent officers to Zacharias, saying: Where hast thou hidden thy son? And he answered and said unto them: I am a minister of God and attend continually upon the temple of the Lord: I know not where my son is. 2 And the officers departed and told Herod all these things. And Herod was wroth and said: His son is to be king over Israel. And he sent unto him again, saying: Say the truth: where is thy son? for thou knowest that thy blood is under my hand. And the officers departed and told him all these things. 3 And Zacharias said: I am a martyr of God if thou sheddest my blood: for my spirit the Lord shall receive, because thou sheddest innocent blood in the fore-court of the temple of the Lord.

And about the dawning of the day Zacharias was slain. And the children of Israel knew not that he was slain.

XXIV. 1 But the priests entered in at the hour of the salutation, and the blessing of Zacharias met them not according to the manner. And the priests stood waiting for Zacharias, to salute him with the prayer, and to glorify the Most High. 2 But as he delayed to come, they were all afraid: and one of them took courage and entered in: and he saw beside the altar congealed blood: and a voice saying: Zacharias hath been slain, and his blood shall not be wiped out until his avenger come. And when he heard that word he was afraid, and went forth and told the priests. 3 And they took courage and went in and saw that which was done: and the panels of the temple did wail: and they rent [1] *their clothes* from the top to the bottom. And his body they found not, but his blood they found turned into stone. And they feared, and went forth and told all the people that Zacharias was slain. And all the tribes of the people heard it, and they mourned for him and lamented him three days and three nights. And after the three days the priests took counsel whom they should set in his stead: and the lot came up upon Symeon. Now he it was which was warned by the Holy Ghost

[1] *al.* and (*the panels*) were split, &c. See Amos viii. 3 (lxx).

that he should not see death until he should see the Christ in the flesh.

XXV. 1 Now I, James, which wrote this history in Jerusalem, when there arose a tumult when Herod died, withdrew myself into the wilderness until the tumult ceased in Jerusalem. Glorifying the Lord God which gave me the gift, and the wisdom to write this history.

2 And grace shall be with those that fear our Lord Jesus Christ: to whom be glory for ever and ever. Amen.

GOSPEL OF THOMAS
GREEK TEXT A

The older testimonies about this book have been given already. I now present the three principal forms of it, as given by Tischendorf: two Greek texts, A and B, and one Latin.

The few Greek manuscripts are all late. The earliest authorities are a much abbreviated Syriac[1] version of which the manuscript is of the sixth century, and a Latin palimpsest at Vienna of the fifth or sixth century, which has never been deciphered in full.

The Latin version translated here is found in more manuscripts than the Greek; none of them, I think, is earlier than the thirteenth century.

The stories of Thomas the Israelite, the Philosopher, concerning the works of the Childhood of the Lord.

I. I, Thomas the Israelite, tell unto you, even all the brethren that are of the Gentiles, to make known unto you the works of the childhood of our Lord Jesus Christ and his mighty deeds, even all that he did when he was born in our land: whereof the beginning is thus:

II. 1 This little child Jesus when he was five years old was playing at the ford of a brook: and he gathered together the waters that flowed *there* into pools, and made them straightway clean, and commanded them by his word alone. 2 And having made soft clay, he fashioned thereof twelve sparrows. And it was the sabbath when he did these things (*or* made them). And there were also many other little children playing with him.

3 And a certain Jew when he saw what Jesus did, playing upon the sabbath day, departed straightway and told his father Joseph: Lo, thy child is at the brook, and he hath taken clay and fashioned twelve little birds, and hath polluted the sabbath day. 4 And Joseph came to the place and saw: and cried out to him, saying: Wherefore doest thou these things on the sabbath, which it is not lawful to do? But Jesus clapped his hands together and cried out to the sparrows and said to them: Go! and the sparrows took their flight and went away chirping. 5 And when the Jews saw it they were amazed, and departed and told their chief men that which they had seen Jesus do.

[1] Peeters is convinced that our Greek and Latin texts are all derived from Syriac.

III. 1 But the son of Annas the scribe was standing there with Joseph; and he took a branch of a willow and dispersed the waters which Jesus had gathered together. 2 And when Jesus saw what was done, he was wroth and said unto him: O evil, ungodly, and foolish one, what hurt did the pools and the waters do thee? behold, now also thou shalt be withered like a tree, and shalt not bear leaves, neither root, nor fruit. 3 And straightway that lad withered up wholly, but Jesus departed and went unto Joseph's house. But the parents of him that was withered took him up, bewailing his youth, and brought him to Joseph, and accused him 'for that thou hast such a child which doeth such deeds'.

IV. 1 After that again he went through the village, and a child ran and dashed against his shoulder. And Jesus was provoked and said unto him: Thou shalt not finish thy course (*lit.* go all thy way). And immediately he fell down and died. But certain when they saw what was done said: Whence was this young child born, for that every word of his is an accomplished work? And the parents of him that was dead came unto Joseph, and blamed him, saying: Thou that hast such a child canst not dwell with us in the village: or do thou teach him to bless and not to curse: for he slayeth our children.

V. 1 And Joseph called the young child apart and admonished him, saying: Wherefore doest thou such things, that these suffer and hate us and persecute us? But Jesus said: I know that these thy words are not thine: nevertheless for thy sake I will hold my peace: but they shall bear their punishment. And straightway they that accused him were smitten with blindness. 2 And they that saw it were sore afraid and perplexed, and said concerning him that every word which he spake, whether it were good or bad, was a deed, and became a marvel. And when they (he?) saw that Jesus had so done, Joseph arose and took hold upon his ear and wrung it sore. 3 And the young child was wroth and said unto him: It sufficeth thee (*or* them) to seek and not to find, and verily thou hast done unwisely: knowest thou not that I am thine? vex me not.

VI. 1 Now a certain teacher, Zacchaeus by name, stood there, and he heard in part when Jesus said these things to his father, and he marvelled greatly that being a young child he spake such matters. 2 And after a few days he came near unto Joseph and said unto him: Thou hast a wise child, and he hath understanding. Come, deliver him to me that he may learn letters. And I will teach him with the letters all knowledge, and that he salute all the elders and honour them as grandfathers and fathers, and love them of his own years. 3 And he told him all the letters from Alpha even to Omega clearly, with much questioning. But *Jesus* looked upon Zacchaeus the teacher and saith unto him: Thou that knowest not the Alpha according to its nature, how canst thou teach others the Beta? thou hypocrite, first, if thou knowest it, teach the Alpha, and then will we believe thee concerning the Beta. Then began he to confound the mouth of the teacher concerning the first letter, and he could not prevail to answer him. 4 And in the hearing of many the young child saith to Zacchaeus: Hear, O teacher, the ordinance of the first letter and pay heed to this, how that it hath [*what follows is really unintelligible in this and in all the parallel texts : a literal version would run somewhat thus :* how that it hath lines, and a middle mark, which thou seest, common to both, going apart; coming together, raised up on high, dancing (*a corrupt word*), of three signs, like in kind (*a corrupt word*), balanced, equal in measure]: thou hast the rules of the Alpha.

VII. 1 Now when Zacchaeus the teacher heard such and so many allegories of the first letter spoken by the young child, he was perplexed at his answer and his instruction being so great, and said to them that were there: Woe is me, wretch that I am, I am confounded: I have brought shame to myself by drawing to me this young child. 2 Take him away, therefore, I beseech thee, my brother Joseph: I cannot endure the severity of his look, I cannot once make clear my (*or* his) word. This young child is not earthly born: this is one that can tame even fire: belike this is one begotten before the making of the world. What belly bare this, what womb nurtured it? I know not. Woe is me, O my friend, he putteth me from my sense, I cannot follow his understanding. I have deceived myself, thrice wretched man that I am: I strove to get me a disciple and I am found to have a master. 3 I think, O my friends, upon my shame, for that being old I have been overcome by a young child; and I am even ready to faint and to die because of the boy, for I am not able at this present hour to look him in the face. And when all men say that I have been overcome by a little child, what have I to say? and what can I tell concerning the lines of the first letter whereof he spake to me? I am ignorant, O my friends, for neither beginning nor end of it (*or* him) do I know. 4 Wherefore I beseech thee, my brother Joseph, take him away unto thine house: for he is somewhat great, whether god or angel or what I should call him, I know not.

VIII. 1 And as the Jews were counselling Zacchaeus, the young child laughed greatly and said: Now let those bear fruit that were barren (*Gr.* that are thine) and let them see that were blind in heart. I am come from above that I may curse them, and call them to the things that are above, even as he commanded which hath sent me for your sakes. 2 And when the young child ceased speaking, immediately all they were made whole which had come under his curse. And no man after that durst provoke him, lest he should curse him, and he should be maimed.

IX. 1 Now after certain days Jesus was playing in the upper
story of a certain house, and one of the young children that
played with him fell down from the house and died. And the
other children when they saw it fled, and Jesus remained alone.
2 And the parents of him that was dead came and accused him
that he had cast him down. (And Jesus said: I did not cast
him down) but they reviled him still. 3 Then Jesus leaped down
from the roof and stood by the body of the child and cried with
a loud voice and said: Zeno (for so was his name called), arise
and tell me, did I cast thee down? And straightway he arose
and said: Nay, Lord, thou didst not cast me down, but didst
raise me up. And when they saw it they were amazed: and the
parents of the child glorified God for the sign which had come to
pass, and worshipped Jesus.

X. 1 After a few days, a certain young man was cleaving
wood in the neighbourhood (*MSS*. corner), and the axe fell and
cut in sunder the sole of his foot, and losing much blood he was
at the point to die. 2 And when there was a tumult and concourse, the young child Jesus also ran thither, and by force
passed through the multitude, and took hold upon the foot of
the young man that was smitten, and straightway it was healed.
And he said unto the young man: Arise now and cleave the wood,
and remember me. But when the multitude saw what was done
they worshipped the young child, saying: Verily the spirit of
God dwelleth in this young child.

XI. 1 Now when he was six years old, his mother sendeth
him to draw water and bear it into the house, and gave him a
pitcher: but in the press he struck it *against another* and the
pitcher was broken. 2 But Jesus spread out the garment which
was upon him and filled it with water and brought it to his
mother. And when his mother saw what was done she kissed
him; and she kept within herself the mysteries which she saw
him do.

XII. 1 Again, in the time of sowing the young child went forth
with his father to sow wheat in their land: and as his father sowed,
the young child Jesus sowed also one corn of wheat. 2 And he
reaped it and threshed it and made thereof an hundred measures
(cors): and he called all the poor of the village unto the threshing-
floor and gave them the wheat. And Joseph took the residue
of the wheat. And he was eight years old when he wrought
this sign.

XIII. 1 Now his father was a carpenter and made at that time
ploughs and yokes. And there was required of him a bed by a
certain rich man, that he should make it for him. And whereas
one beam, that which is called the shifting one, was too short,
and *Joseph* knew not what to do, the young child Jesus said to
his father Joseph: Lay down the two pieces of wood and make
them even at the end next unto thee (*MSS*. at the middle part).

And Joseph did as the young child said unto him. And Jesus stood at the other end and took hold upon the shorter beam and stretched it and made it equal with the other. And his father Joseph saw it and marvelled: and he embraced the young child and kissed him, saying: Happy am I for that God hath given me this young child.

XIV. 1 But when Joseph saw the understanding of the child, and his age, that it was coming to the full, he thought with himself again that he should not be ignorant of letters; and he took him and delivered him to another teacher. And the teacher said unto Joseph: First will I teach him the Greek letters, and after that the Hebrew. For the teacher knew the skill of the child and was afraid of him: notwithstanding he wrote the alphabet and *Jesus* pondered thereon a long time [1] and answered him not. 2 And Jesus said to him: If thou be indeed a teacher, and if thou knowest letters well, tell me the power of the Alpha, and then will I tell thee the power of the Beta. And the teacher was provoked and smote him on the head. And the young child was hurt and cursed him, and straightway he fainted and fell to the ground on his face. 3 And the child returned unto the house of Joseph: and Joseph was grieved and commanded his mother, *saying*: Let him not forth without the door, for all they die that provoke him to wrath.

XV. 1 And after some time yet another teacher which was a faithful friend of Joseph said to him: Bring the young child unto me to the school; peradventure I may be able by cockering him to teach him the letters. And Joseph said: If thou hast no fear, my brother, take him with thee. And he took him with him, in fear and much trouble of spirit, but the young child followed him gladly. 2 And going with boldness into the school he found a book lying upon the pulpit and he took it, and read not the letters that were therein, but opened his mouth and spake by the Holy Spirit, and taught the law to them that stood by. And a great multitude came together and stood there hearkening, and marvelled at the beauty of his teaching and the readiness of his words, in that being an infant he uttered such things. 3 But when Joseph heard it, he was afraid, and ran unto the school, thinking whether this teacher also were without skill (*or* smitten with infirmity): but the teacher said unto Joseph: Know, my brother, that I received this child for a disciple, but he is full of grace and wisdom; and now I beseech thee, brother, take him unto thine house. 4 And when the young child heard that, he smiled upon him and said: Forasmuch as thou hast said well, and hast borne right witness, for thy sake shall he also that was smitten be healed. And forthwith the other teacher was healed. And Joseph took the young child and departed unto his house.

XVI. 1 And Joseph sent his son James to bind fuel and carry

[1] Probably 'repeated it to him (Jesus) many times', as *Syr.*

it into his house. And the young child Jesus also followed him. And as James was gathering of faggots, a viper bit the hand of James. 2 And as he was sore afflicted and ready to perish, Jesus came near and breathed upon the bite, and straightway the pain ceased, and the serpent burst, and forthwith James continued whole.

XVII. 1 And after these things, in the neighbourhood of Joseph, a little child fell sick and died, and his mother wept sore. And Jesus heard that there was great mourning and trouble, and he ran quickly and found the child dead: and he touched his breast and said: I say unto thee, Child, die not, but live and be with thy mother. And straightway it looked up and laughed. And he said to the woman: Take him up and give him milk, and remember me. 2 And the multitude that stood by saw it and marvelled, and said: Of a truth this young child is either a god or an angel of God; for every word of his is a perfect work. And Jesus departed thence, and was playing with other children.

XVIII. 1 And after some time there was work of building. And there came a great tumult, and Jesus arose and went thither: and he saw a man lying dead, and took hold of his hand and said: Man, I say unto thee, arise and do thy work. And immediately he arose and worshipped him. 2 And when the multitude saw it, they were astonished, and said: This young child is from heaven: for he hath saved many souls from death, and hath power to save them all his life long.

XIX. 1 And when he was twelve years old his parents went according to the custom unto Jerusalem to the feast of the passover with their company: and after the passover they returned to go unto their house. And as they returned the child Jesus went back to Jerusalem; but his parents supposed that he was in their company. 2 And when they had gone a day's journey, they sought him among their kinsfolk, and when they found him not, they were troubled, and returned again to the city seeking him. And after the third day they found him in the temple sitting in the midst of the doctors and hearing and asking them *questions*. And all men paid heed to him and marvelled how that being a young child he put to silence the elders and teachers of the people, expounding the heads of the law and the parables of the prophets. 3 And his mother Mary came near and said unto him: Child, wherefore hast thou so done unto us? behold we have sought thee sorrowing. And Jesus said unto them: Why seek ye me? know ye not that I must be in my Father's house? 4 But the scribes and Pharisees said: Art thou the mother of this child? and she said: I am. And they said unto her: Blessed art thou among women, because God hath blessed the fruit of thy womb. For such glory and such excellence and wisdom we have neither seen nor heard at any time.

5 And Jesus arose and followed his mother and was subject unto his parents: but his mother kept *in mind* all that came to pass. And Jesus increased in wisdom and stature and grace. Unto him be glory for ever and ever. Amen.

GREEK TEXT B

The Writing of the holy Apostle Thomas concerning the conversation of the Lord in his childhood.

I. I, Thomas the Israelite, have thought it needful to make known unto all the brethren that are of the Gentiles the mighty works of childhood which our Lord Jesus Christ wrought when he was conversant in the body, and came unto the city of Nazareth in the fifth year of his age.

II. 1 On a certain day when there had fallen a shower of rain he went forth of the house where his mother was and played upon the ground where the waters were running: and he made pools, and the waters flowed down, and the pools were filled with water. Then saith he: I will that ye become clean and wholesome waters. And straightway they did so. 2 But a certain son of Annas the scribe passed by bearing a branch of willow, and he overthrew the pools with the branch, and the waters were poured out. And Jesus turned about and said unto him: O ungodly and disobedient one, what hurt have the pools done thee that thou hast emptied them? Thou shalt not finish thy course, and thou shalt be withered up even as the branch which thou hast in hand. 3 And he went on, and after a little he fell and gave up the ghost. And when the young children that played with him saw it, they marvelled and departed and told the father of him that was dead. And he ran and found the child dead, and went and accused Joseph.

III. 1 Now Jesus made of that clay twelve sparrows: and it was the sabbath day. And a child ran and told Joseph, saying: Behold, thy child playeth about the brook, and hath made sparrows of the clay, which is not lawful. 2 And he when he heard it went and said to the child: Wherefore doest thou so and profaneth the sabbath? But Jesus answered him not, but looked upon the sparrows and said: Go ye, take your flight, and remember me in your life. And at the word they took flight and went up into the air. And when Joseph saw it he was astonished.

IV. 1 And after certain days, as Jesus passed through the midst of the city, a certain child cast a stone at him and smote his shoulder. And Jesus said unto him: Thou shalt not finish thy course. And straightway he also fell down and died. And they that were there were amazed, saying: From whence is this child, that every word which he speaketh becometh a perfect

work? 2 But they also departed and accused Joseph, saying:
Thou wilt not be able to dwell with us in this city: but if thou
wilt, teach thy child to bless and not to curse: for verily he
slayeth our children: and every thing that he saith becometh
a perfect work.

V. And as Joseph sat upon his seat, the child stood before
him; and he took hold upon his ear and pinched it sore. But
Jesus looked upon him earnestly and said: It sufficeth thee.

VI. 1 And on the morrow he took him by the hand and led
him to a certain teacher, Zacchaeus by name. and said unto him:
Take this child, O master, and teach him letters. And the
other said: Deliver him unto me, my brother, and I will teach
him the scripture, and I will persuade him to bless all men and
not to curse them. 2 And when Jesus heard that he laughed
and said unto them: Ye speak that ye know, but I have knowledge more than you, for I am before the worlds. And I know
when the fathers of your fathers were begotten, and I know how
many are the years of your life. And *every* one that heard it
was amazed. 3 And again saith Jesus unto them: Marvel ye
because I said unto you that I know how many are the years
of your life? Of a truth I know when the world was created.
Behold, now ye believe me not: when ye shall see my cross,
then will ye believe that I speak truth. And they were astonied
when they heard all these things.

VII. 1 Now Zacchaeus wrote the alphabet in Hebrew, and
saith unto him: Alpha. And the young child said: Alpha.
And again the master said: Alpha, and the young child likewise.
Then again the third time the master said: Alpha. Then Jesus
looked upon the teacher and said: Thou that knowest not the
Alpha, how canst thou teach another the Beta? And the child
beginning at the Alpha said of his own accord the two and
twenty letters. 2 And thereafter saith he: Hear, O master,
the ordinance of the first letter, and know how many incomings
and lines it hath, and marks, common, going apart, and coming
together. And when Zacchaeus heard such designations of
the one letter he was amazed and had nothing to answer;
and turning about he said unto Joseph: My brother, this
child is of a truth not earthly born: take him away therefore
from me.

VIII. 1 And after these things one day Jesus was playing
with other boys upon the top of an house of two stories. And
one child was pushed down by another and thrown down to the
ground and died. And the boys which were playing with him,
when they saw it, fled, and Jesus was left alone standing upon
the roof whence the boy was thrown down. 2 And when the
parents of the boy that was dead heard of it they ran weeping,
and when they found the boy lying dead upon the earth and
Jesus standing alone, they supposed that the boy had been

thrown down by him, and they looked upon him and reviled him. 3 But Jesus, seeing that, leaped down straightway from the upper story and stood at the head of him that was dead and saith to him: Zeno, did I cast thee down? Arise and tell. For so was the boy called. And with the word the boy rose up and worshipped Jesus and said: Lord, thou didst not cast me down, but when I was dead thou didst make me alive.

IX. 1 And a few days after one of the neighbours was cleaving wood and did cut off the sole of his foot with the axe, and by loss of blood was at the point to die. 2 And much people ran together and Jesus came thither with them. 3 And he took hold on the foot of the young man that was smitten, and healed him forthwith, and saith unto him: Arise, cleave thy wood. And he arose and worshipped him, giving thanks, and cleft the wood. Likewise also all they that were there marvelled and gave thanks unto him.

X. Now when he was six years old, Mary his mother sent him to fetch water from the spring: and as he went his pitcher was broken. And he went to the spring and spread out his upper garment and drew water out of the spring and filled it and took it and brought back the water to his mother. And she, when she saw it, was amazed and embraced him and kissed him.

XI. 1 And when he came to the eighth year of his age Joseph was required by a certain rich man to build him a bed, for he was a carpenter. And he went forth into the field to gather wood, and Jesus also went with him. And he cut two beams of wood and wrought them with the axe, and set one beside the other and measured and found it too short; and when he saw that he was vexed and sought to find another. 2 But Jesus seeing it saith unto him: Set these two together so that the ends of both be even. And Joseph, though he was perplexed concerning this, what the child should mean, did that which was commanded. And he saith again unto him: Take firm hold of the short beam. And Joseph took hold on it, marvelling. Then Jesus also took hold of the other end and pulled the [other] end thereof and made it also equal to the other beam, and saith unto Joseph: Be no more vexed, but do thy work without hindrance. And he when he saw it was exceedingly amazed, and said within himself: Blessed am I for that God hath given me such a son. 3 And when they departed into the city Joseph told it to Mary, and she when she heard and saw the wonderful mighty works of her son rejoiced, glorifying him.

with the Father and the Holy Spirit now and for ever and world without end. Amen.

LATIN TEXT

Here beginneth a treatise of the Boyhood of Jesus according
to Thomas.

I. *How Mary and Joseph fled with him into Egypt.*

When there was a tumult because search was made by Herod
for our Lord Jesus Christ, that he might slay him, then said an
angel unto Joseph: Take Mary and her child and flee into Egypt
from the face of them that seek to slay him. Now Jesus was two
years old when he entered into Egypt.

And as he walked through a sown field he put forth his hand
and took of the ears and put them upon the fire and ground them
and began to eat. [And he gave such favour unto that field
that year by year when it was sown it yielded unto the lord of it
so many measures of wheat as the number of the grains which
he had taken from it.]

Now when they had entered into Egypt they took lodging in
the house of a certain widow, and abode in the same place one
year.

And Jesus became three years old. And seeing boys playing
he began to play with them. And he took a dried fish and put
it into a bason and commanded it to move to and fro, and it began
to move. And again he said to the fish: Cast out thy salt that
is in thee and go into the water. And it came to pass. But when
the neighbours saw what was done they told it to the widow
woman in whose house his mother Mary dwelt. And she when
she heard it hasted and cast them out of her house.

II. *How a Master cast him out of the city.*

1 And as Jesus walked with Mary his mother through the
midst of the market-place of the city, he looked about and saw
a master teaching his pupils. And behold twelve sparrows which
were quarrelling one with another fell from the wall into the lap
of the master who taught the boys. And when Jesus saw it he
laughed and stood still. 2 Now when that teacher saw him
laughing, he said to his pupils in great anger: Go, bring him
hither unto me. And when they had brought him, the master
took hold on his ear and said: What sawest thou that thou didst
laugh? And he said unto him: Master, see, my hand is full of
corn, and I shewed it unto them, and scattered the corn, which
they are carrying away † in danger †: for for this cause they fought
with one another that they might partake of the corn. 3 And
Jesus left not the place until it was accomplished.

And for this cause the master laboured to cast him out of the
city together with his mother.

III. *How Jesus came out of Egypt.*

1 And behold, an angel of the Lord met with Mary and said unto her: Take the child and return into the land of the Jews: for they are dead which sought his life. So Mary arose with Jesus, and they went into the city Nazareth, which is in the inheritance of his (her?) father. 2 But when Joseph departed out of Egypt after the death of Herod, he took *Jesus* into the wilderness until there was quiet in Jerusalem from them that sought the life of the child.

And he gave thanks to God for that he had given him understanding, and because he had found grace before the Lord God. Amen.

or, And Mary arose with Jesus, and they went unto the city of Capernaum which is of Tiberias, unto the inheritance of her father. 2 But when Joseph heard that Jesus was come out of Egypt after the death of Herod, he took him, &c.

or, After these things an angel of the Lord came unto Joseph and unto Mary the mother of Jesus and said unto them: Take the child, return into the land of Israel, for they are dead that sought the life of the child. And they arose and went to Nazareth where Joseph possessed the goods of his father. 2 And when Jesus was seven years old, there was quiet in the realm of Herod from all them that sought the life of the child. And they returned unto Bethlehem and abode there.

IV. *What Jesus did in the city of Nazareth.*

It is *a* glorious *work* for Thomas the Israelite (Ismaelite) the apostle of the Lord to tell of the works of Jesus after he came out of Egypt unto Nazareth. Hear (understand) therefore all of you, beloved brethren, the signs which the Lord Jesus did when he was in the city of Nazareth: as it is said in the first chapter.

1 Now when Jesus was five years old there was a great rain upon the earth, and the child Jesus walked about therein. And the rain was very terrible: and he gathered the water together into a pool and commanded with a word that it should become clear: and forthwith it did so.

2 Again, he took of the clay which came of that pool and made thereof to the number of twelve sparrows. Now it was the sabbath day when Jesus did this among the children of the Hebrews: and the children of the Hebrews went and said unto Joseph his father: Lo, thy son was playing with us and he took clay and made sparrows which it was not right to do upon the sabbath, and he hath broken it. And Joseph went to the child Jesus, and said unto him: Wherefore hast thou done this which it was not right to do on the sabbath? But Jesus spread forth (opened) his hands and commanded the sparrows, saying: Go forth into the height and fly: ye shall not meet death at any

man's hands. And they flew and began to cry out and praise almighty God. But when the Jews saw what was done they marvelled and departed, proclaiming the signs which Jesus did.

3 But a Pharisee which was with Jesus took a branch of an olive tree and began to empty the pool which Jesus had made. And when Jesus saw it he was vexed and said to him: O thou of Sodom, ungodly and ignorant, what hurt did the fountain of water do thee, which I made? Lo, thou shalt become like a dry tree which hath neither roots nor leaf nor fruit. And straightway he was dried up and fell to the earth and died: but his parents carried him away dead and reviled Joseph, saying: Behold what thy son hath done: teach thou him to pray and not to blaspheme.

V. How the people of the city were grieved against Joseph because of that which Jesus did.

1 And after some days as Jesus walked with Joseph through the city, there ran one of the children and smote Jesus on the arms: but Jesus said unto him: So finish thou thy course. And immediately he fell to the earth and died. But they when they saw this wonder, cried out saying: From whence cometh this child? And they said unto Joseph: It is not right that such a child should be among us. And he departed and took him with him. And they said to him: Depart out of this place; and if thou must be with us, teach him to pray and not to blaspheme: for our sons are put to death by him (lit. lose their senses). 2 And Joseph called Jesus and began to admonish him, saying: Wherefore blasphemest thou? They that dwell in this place conceive hatred against us. But Jesus said: I know that these words are not mine but thine: yet for thy sake I will hold my peace: but let them see (? bear) their own foolishness. And straightway they that spake against Jesus were made blind, and as they walked to and fro they said: Every word that cometh out of his mouth hath fulfilment. 3 And when Joseph saw what Jesus had done he took hold on him by his ear in anger: but Jesus was vexed and said unto Joseph: It sufficeth thee to see me and not to touch me. For thou knowest not who I am, which if thou knewest, thou wouldest not grieve me. And albeit I am with thee now, yet was I made before thee.

VI. How Jesus was treated by the Master.

1 There was therefore a man named Zacheus who heard all that Jesus said unto Joseph, and he marvelled in himself and said: I have never beheld such a child that spake so. And he came near unto Joseph and said to him: Thou hast a wise child: deliver him to me to learn letters, and when he is learned in the study of the letters, I will teach him reverently that he become not foolish. Joseph answered and said unto him: No man is

able to teach him but God only. Think you that this young child
will be the occasion unto us of little torment, my brother?
[*There should be mention of a cross in this sentence. Syriac has,*
Thinkest thou that he is worthy to receive a little cross? *See
below.*]
2 But when Jesus heard Joseph saying these things, he said
unto Zacheus: Verily, O master, all things that proceed out of
my mouth are true. And I am before all men, and I am Lord,
but ye are the children of strangers: for unto me is given the
glory of them (*or* of the worlds) but unto you nothing is given:
for I am before *all* worlds. And I know how many are the years
of thy life, and when thou shalt raise that standard (i. e. the
cross) whereof my father spake, *then shalt thou* understand that
all things that proceed out of my mouth are true.
3 But the Jews which stood by and heard the words which
Jesus spake, marvelled and said: *Now* have we seen such wonders
and heard such words from this child, as we have never heard
neither shall hear from any other man, neither from the chief
priests nor the doctors nor the Pharisees. 4 Jesus answered and
said unto them: Wherefore marvel ye? Do ye think it a thing
incredible that I have told you the truth? I know when ye were
born, and your fathers: and if I should say more unto you,
I know when the world was created, and who sent me unto you.
When the Jews heard the word which the child spake, they
were wroth because they were not able to answer *him.* And the
child turned himself about and rejoiced and said: I spake unto
you a proverb; but I know that ye are weak and know not any
thing.
5 Now that master said unto Joseph: Bring him unto me and
I will teach him letters. And Joseph took the child Jesus and
brought him to the house [of a certain master] where other
children also were taught. But the master began to teach him
the letters with sweet speech, and wrote for him the first line
which goeth from A unto T, and began to flatter him and to
teach him (*and commanded him to say the letters*:) but the child
held his peace. 6 Then that teacher smote the child on the head,
and when the child received the blow, he said unto him: I ought to
teach thee and not thou to teach me. I know the letters which
thou wouldest teach me, and I know that ye are unto me as vessels
out of which cometh nought but sound, and neither wisdom nor
salvation of the soul. And beginning the line he spake all the
letters from A even unto T fully with much quickness: and he
looked upon the master and said: But thou knowest not how to
interpret A and B: how wouldest thou teach others? Thou
hypocrite, if thou knowest and canst tell me concerning A, then
will I tell thee concerning B. But when the teacher began to
expound concerning the first letter, he was not able to give any
answer.

7 Then said Jesus unto Zacheus: Hearken unto me, O master, and understand the first letter. Give ear unto me, how that it hath two lines (*eight quite unintelligible descriptive phrases follow*). 8 Now when Zacheus saw that he so divided the first letter, he was confounded at such names, and at his teaching, and cried out and said: Woe is me, for I am confounded: I have hired shame unto myself by means of this child. And he said unto Joseph: I beseech thee earnestly, my brother, take him away from me: for I cannot look upon his face nor hear his mighty words. For this child is able to subdue the fire and to restrain the sea, for he was born before the worlds. What womb bare him or what manner of mother brought him up I know not. 10 O my friends, I am astray in my wits, I am mocked, wretched man that I am. I said that I had a disciple, but he is found to be my master. I cannot overcome my shame, for I am old, and I cannot find wherewithal to answer him, so that I am like to fall into heavy sickness and depart out of the world or go away from this city, for all men have seen my shame, that a child hath ensnared me. What can I answer any man, or what words can I speak, for he hath overcome me at the first letter! I am confounded, O ye my friends and acquaintances, and I can find neither first nor last to answer him. 11 And now I beseech thee, brother Joseph, remove him from me and take him unto thine house, for either he is a sorcerer or a god (Lord) or an angel, and what to say I know not.

12 And Jesus turned himself unto the Jews that were with Zacheus and said unto them: Now let all them that see not see, and let them understand which understand not, and let the deaf hear, and let them arise which have died by my means, and let me call them that are high unto that which is higher, even as he that sent me unto you hath commanded me. And when the child Jesus ceased speaking, all the afflicted were made whole, as many as had been afflicted at his word. And they durst not speak unto him.

VII. *How Jesus raised up a boy.*

1 Now on a day, when Jesus climbed up upon an house with the children, he began to play with them: but one of the boys fell down through the door out of the upper chamber and died straightway. And when the children saw it they fled all of them, but Jesus remained alone in the house. 2 And when the parents of the child which had died came they spake against Jesus saying: Of a truth thou madest him fall. But Jesus said: I never made him fall: nevertheless they accused him *still.* Jesus therefore came down from the house and stood over the dead child and cried with a loud voice, calling him by his name: Zeno, Zeno, arise and say if I made thee fall. And on a sudden

he arose and said: Nay, Lord. And when his parents saw this great miracle which Jesus did, they glorified God, and worshipped Jesus.

VIII. *How Jesus healed the foot of a boy.*

1 And after a few days a certain boy of that village was cleaving wood, and smote his foot. 2 And when much people came unto him, Jesus also came with them. And he touched the foot which was hurt, and forthwith it was made whole. And Jesus said unto him: Arise and cleave the wood and remember me. But when the multitude that were with him saw the signs which were done they worshipped Jesus and said: Of a truth we believe surely that thou art God.

IX. *How Jesus bare water in his cloak.*

1 And when Jesus was six years old, his mother sent him to draw water. And when Jesus was come unto the well there was much people there and they brake his pitcher. 2 But he took the cloak which he had upon him and filled it with water and brought it to Mary his mother. And when his mother saw the miracle that Jesus did she kissed him and said: Lord, hearken unto me and save my son.

X. *How Jesus sowed wheat.*

1 Now when it was seed-time, Joseph went forth to sow corn, and Jesus followed after him. And when Joseph began to sow, Jesus put forth his hand and took of the corn so much as he could hold in his hand, and scattered it. 2 Joseph therefore came at the time of harvest to reap his harvest. And Jesus also came and gathered the ears which he had sown, and they made an hundred measures of good corn: and he called the poor and the widows and fatherless and gave them the corn which he had gained, save that Joseph took a little thereof unto his house for a blessing [of Jesus].

XI. *How Jesus made a short beam even with a long one.*

1 And Jesus came to be eight years old. Now Joseph was a builder and wrought ploughs and yokes for oxen. And on a day a certain rich man said unto Joseph: Sir, make me a bed serviceable and comely. But Joseph was troubled because the beam which he had made ready for the work was short. 2 Jesus said unto him: Be not troubled, *but* take thou hold of this beam by the one end and I by the other, and let us draw it out. And so it came to pass, and forthwith *Joseph* found it serviceable for that which he desired. And he said unto Joseph: Behold, fashion that thou wilt. But Joseph when he saw what was done embraced him and said: Blessed am I for that God hath given me such a son.

XII. *How Jesus was delivered over to learn letters.*

1 And when Joseph saw that he had so great grace and that he
increased in stature, he thought to deliver him over to learn
letters. And he delivered him to another doctor that he should
teach him. Then said that doctor unto Joseph: What manner
of letters wouldest thou teach this child? Joseph answered and
said: Teach him first the letters of the Gentiles and after that
the Hebrew. Now the doctor knew that he was of an excellent
understanding, and received him gladly. And when he had
written for him the first line, that is to say A and B, he taught
him for the space of some hours: but Jesus held his peace and
answered nothing. 2 At the last Jesus said unto the master:
If thou be verily a master, and indeed knowest the letters, tell
me the power of A and I will tell thee the power of B. Then was
the master filled with indignation and smote him on the head.
But Jesus was wroth and cursed him, and on a sudden he fell
down and died. 3 But Jesus returned unto his own home. And
Joseph enjoined Mary his mother that she should not let him go
out of the court of the house.

XIII. *How he was delivered unto another master.*

1 After many days there came another doctor which was a friend
of Joseph and said unto him: Deliver him to me and I will teach
him letters with much gentleness. And Joseph said unto him:
If thou art able, take him and teach him, and it shall be done
gladly. And when the doctor received *Jesus*, he went with fear
and great †boldness† and took him rejoicing. 2 And when he was
come unto the house of the doctor, he found a book lying in that
place and took it and opened it, and read not those things which
were written therein, but opened his mouth and spake by the
Holy Ghost and taught the law: and all that stood by hearkened
attentively, and the teacher sat by him and heard him gladly
and entreated him to continue teaching. And much people
gathered together and heard all the holy doctrine which he taught
and the beloved words which proceeded out of his mouth,
marvelling that he being a little child spake such things.
3 But when Joseph heard, he was afraid and ran unto the
place where Jesus was; and the master said unto Joseph: Know,
my brother, that I received thy child to teach him and instruct
him, but he is filled with great grace and wisdom. *Therefore*
behold now, take him unto thy house with joy, because the grace
which he hath is given him of the Lord. 4 And when Jesus heard
the master speak thus he was joyful and said: Lo, now thou hast
well said, O master: for thy sake shall he rise again who was
dead. And Joseph took him unto his own home.

XIV. *How Jesus made James whole of the bite of a serpent.*

Now Joseph sent James to gather straw, and Jesus followed after him. And as James gathered straw, a viper bit him and he fell to the earth as dead by means of the venom. But when Jesus saw that, he breathed upon his wound and forthwith James was made whole, and the viper died.

XV. *How Jesus raised up a boy.*

After a few days a child that was his neighbour died, and his mother mourned for him sore; and when Jesus heard, he went and stood over the child, and smote him on the breast and said: Child, I say unto thee, die not, but live. And immediately the child arose: and Jesus said unto the mother of the child: Take up thy son and give him suck, and remember me. 2 But the multitudes when they saw that miracle said: Of a truth this child is from heaven; for now hath he set free many souls from death and hath saved all them that hoped in him.

[*A gap in all the Latin MSS. filled by the Greek text* A, *cap.* 19, 1–3 *Jesus and the doctors in the Temple.*]

3 The Scribes and Pharisees said unto Mary: Art thou the mother of this child? and Mary said: Of a truth I am. And they said unto her: Blessed art thou among women, because God hath blessed the fruit of thy womb in that he hath given thee a child so glorious : for so great gifts of wisdom we have never seen nor heard in any.

4 And Jesus arose and followed his mother. But Mary kept in her heart all the great signs which Jesus wrought among the people, in healing many that were sick.

And Jesus increased in stature and wisdom, and all that saw him glorified God the Father Almighty: Who is blessed for ever and ever. Amen.

All these things have I, Thomas the Israelite (Ismaelite), written and recorded for the Gentiles and for our brethren, and *likewise* many other things which Jesus did, which was born in the land of Juda. Behold, the house of Israel hath seen all these from the first even unto the last, even how great signs and wonders Jesus did among them, which were good exceedingly. And this is he which shall judge the world according to the will of his Father, immortal and invisible[1], as the holy Scripture declareth and as the prophets have testified of his works among all the peoples of Israel: for he is the Son of God throughout all the world. And unto him belongeth all glory and honour everlastingly, who liveth and reigneth God, world without end. Amen.

[1] The text is corrupt here : I have tried to mend it.

APPENDIX I

From the *Pistis Sophia.*

The Gnostic book called *Pistis Sophia* (see Introd.) contains a characteristic account of an incident of the Infancy. It may be compared with the Hymn of the Soul in the Acts of Thomas. The book in which it occurs is of the third century.

C. Schmidt's version, p. 77. Mary answered and said: . . . Thy Power prophesied through David: Grace and Truth are met together, Righteousness and Peace have kissed each other. Truth hath flourished out of the earth, and Righteousness hath looked down from heaven. Thus did thy Power prophesy once concerning thee. When thou wast little, before the Spirit came upon thee, the Spirit came from the height whilst thou wast in a vineyard with Joseph, and came unto me in mine house in thy likeness, and I knew it not, and I thought that it was thou. And the Spirit said unto me: Where is Jesus my brother, that I may meet with him? And when it spake thus unto me, I was in perplexity, and thought that it was a phantom *come* to tempt me. I took it therefore and bound it to the foot of the bed that was in mine house, until I should go forth unto thee and Joseph in the field and find you in the vineyard, where Joseph was staking the vineyard. It came to pass then, that when thou heardest me tell the matter unto Joseph, thou understoodest the matter, and didst rejoice, and say: Where is he, that I may behold him? otherwise I will tarry for him in this place. And it came to pass, when Joseph heard thee speak these words, he was troubled: and we went together and entered into the house and found the Spirit bound to the bed. And we looked upon thee and upon it, and found that thou wert like unto him: and he that was bound to the bed was loosed, and embraced thee and kissed thee, and thou also kissedst him, and ye became one.

Mary goes on to expound the application of the passage she had quoted from the Psalm.

APPENDIX II

I. *Miracle of the Dyer.*

In a Paris manuscript (gr. 239) of the Gospel of Thomas a fragment of this story is contained in Greek (Tisch., p. 148 n.). It occurs in no other Greek or Latin manuscript of Thomas. But in the Milan Ambrosian MS. L. 58 *sup.*, edited in facsimile by Ceriani for Gibson Craig (1873, *Canonical Histories and Apocryphal Legends*), it occurs in Latin on p. 12, being the first miracle after the Return from Egypt. It is also told in the Arabic Gospel, ch. 38, and, at great length, in the Armenian (ch. xxi, Peeters, p. 232–46). Thilo quotes a Mohammedan version (p. 150), and shows that the tale was current in Persia. There seems little doubt that it stood in the completer texts of the

Gospel of Thomas. It is found in the mediaeval French and English Histories of the Infancy, and doubtless in other vernacular versions. I give a rendering from the Milan MS.

It came to pass on a day that the blessed Virgin Mary went unto the house of a certain neighbour of hers which was of the craft of a dyer. And the child Jesus, her glorious son, followed her as is the wont of boys to follow their mothers. Now while the Virgin Mary spake with the man unto whom she had come, the child Jesus went unto the place wherein that man was wont to practise his trade, and found there divers vessels containing several dyes; and likewise he found divers cloths belonging to many men, which those men had given to be dyed. All the which cloths the child took and wrapped them together and sunk all of them in a vessel wherein was only a black dye.

Now when this thing which he had done came to the knowledge of that man, he began to be sore vexed and to complain greatly against the mother of Jesus. And he said to his mother: Alas! behold what thy son hath done: he hath brought all my labour to nought. But know thou this for certain, that the child shall not be let go by me till the damage that he hath done be made good. But the mother of Jesus when she heard these things from the man began to say unto her son: My beloved son, what hast thou done? wherefore hast thou done this? for I hoped that I should have great joy of thee: for I know how I had thee (=received thee?). But thou, whereas thou oughtest to make me glad in all things, as thou hast done alway, now contrariwise makest me sad. The child Jesus answered his mother ⟨and said: Wherein have I grieved thee?⟩. The blessed virgin said unto him: See, thou hast destroyed all the labour of this man. But Jesus said unto her: How have I destroyed it? His mother answered and said unto him: Because, whereas he had the cloths from many men to give to each one of their cloths a several dye, thou hast made of all of them a dye of one colour. Now, therefore, I must amend that which thou hast done. But the beautiful child Jesus when he heard that came near to the vessel wherein he had cast the cloths, and according to the will of the master he drew thereout every cloth dyed of a several colour and gave them unto the man.

And when that man saw it, together with the mother of the Lord, he glorified the child, and they had him in great admiration. But the virgin, the mother of the Lord, embraced her son in her arms and kissed him, and so being filled with great joy returned to her house with Christ her son.

II. *Miracle of the Children in the Oven.*

This does not occur in known Greek or Latin texts, but is in the Arabic Gospel (ch. 40), the Syriac *History* (Budge), and also in the French and English mediaeval versions (in which the children are changed into pigs). Most probably the occurrence in both East and West means that the story formed part of the text that lies behind all the versions. I quote Sir E. A. Wallis Budge's rendering of the Syriac (*History of the Virgin*, p. 76).

And it came to pass that Jesus went out one day and saw a company of children playing together, and he went after them, but they fled before him and went into a furnace (*al.* cellar). And Jesus came after them and stood by the door and said unto the women who were sitting there: Where are the children who came in here before me? And the women said unto Jesus: No children came here. Then Jesus said unto them: Then what are the beings that are inside the house? And the women said unto him: They are goats. And Jesus said unto them: Let the goats which are in the furnace go out to their shepherds. And there came forth from the furnace goats which leaped round about Jesus and skipped joyfully. And when the women had seen what had taken place, they wondered, and great fear laid hold upon them. Then the women rose up and did homage unto Jesus, and they made supplication unto him, saying: O Jesus, thou son of Mary, thou good shepherd of Israel, have compassion upon thine handmaidens; for thou didst come to heal and not to destroy. And Jesus answered and said unto them: Verily the children of Israel are like unto the black folk among the natives, for the black ones seize the outer side of the flock and harass their shepherd: even thus are the people of Israel. Then the women said unto him: Thy disciples could never hide themselves away from thee, and they could never harass thee, for they perform thy will and they fulfil thy commandments. [*Arab.* Lord, thou knowest all things and nothing is hid from thee. Now we pray thee and ask of thy goodness that thou wouldest restore unto these children thy servants their former state.] And Jesus gave the word of command and said unto the goats: Come, O ye children, my playfellows, and let us play together. And straightway whilst these women were looking on, they were changed from the similitude of goats and became children again. And they went after Jesus. And from that day the children were not able to flee from Jesus; and their parents admonished them saying: See that ye do everything that Jesus the son of Mary commandeth you to do.

III. *The Boy in the Tower.*

It is more doubtful whether this story belongs to the old stock. It occurs in the mediaeval vernaculars, and may probably be discovered in some Latin text at least. I quote one of the English metrical versions (MS. Harley 3954, ed. Horstmann, *Sammlung altenglischer Legenden*, 1878, p. 108). The spelling is slightly simplified.

l. 531.   A Rych man was in that cete (city)
That to Jhesu had envye,
Josep fader, Braudyn hyth he,
Ouer his sone he made maystrye.
He seyd: my sone, thou were me dere,
Now thou dost ayen my wylle
To ben with Jhesu, of hym to lere—
Thou were wel betre to ben stylle.

For hys loue thou xalt (shalt) be kept
In a tour of lym and stone,
Hys loue thou xalt abyin (rue), Josep,
Ne geynyt the no betre won.
To the xal noman komyn ne lep:
Ther myth thou cry & kalle alon
That noman of the xal takyn kep,
Ne for onys to her thi bon.
I suere by God adonay
Lyth ther thou xalt non haue:
Lud thou cry wellaway,
Non helpe geynyt the to craue.

Jhesu, that hath the thus shent
Out of presoun xal the not bryng
Be (By) no maner of sharment (charm)
That he kan of rede & synge.
Josep seyd anon ryth:
'Fader, thou myth done thi wyl.
Jhesu is ful of mekyl myth,
He wyl not suffre me to spyle.'
Josep left in that prisoun,
The dorys weryn lokyn faste;
Ther lay Josep al alon,
To hym kam Jhesu ryth in haste.

'Josep, felaw,' qwath Jhesu,
'For my loue thou lyst here,
Thou xalt se more of my vertu,
For so I wyl, my leue fere.'
Jhesu fond a lytyl bore (hole)
And bad Josep hys fynger take:
Heyl & sond as he was core
He kam out withoutyn wrake.
Euer with Jhesu he wold be;
Nothyng myth hym lette:
Euer was Jhesu hym so fre,
For hys felaw he hym fette.

In some versions the father, returning and finding the tower empty,
is struck blind. The names in the English version, Joseph and

Braudyn, are probably the versifier's invention. Both the *Infancies* printed by Horstmann contain many such names, which do not occur elsewhere.

Other miracles which find a place in the vernacular versions or in the *Vita Rhythmica* (see p. 82) are: Jesus slides on a sunbeam, and other boys attempting this fall and are hurt, and cured; he hangs his pitcher on a sunbeam, other boys' pitchers are (similarly) broken and mended; he brings bitter herbs to Mary and sweetens them by putting flour in the pot; a lion carries off a shepherd's boy and is made to bring him back; he finds a hunter killed by a snake and raises him; he cures one who had swallowed a viper in his sleep.

THE LIBER DE INFANTIA, OR GOSPEL OF PSEUDO-MATTHEW

I do not propose to include a full version of this book in the present collection. Influential as it was in the later mediaeval period, all or nearly all the contents have already been given in the Protevangelium and Gospel of Thomas. But a full account and analysis will not be out of place.

It is a Latin compilation, possibly as old as the eighth or ninth century, though no manuscript earlier than the eleventh has been hitherto brought to light. It was used by Hrosvita, Abbess of Gandersheim, in her poems in the tenth century.

The two main sources are the Protevangelium and the Gospel of Thomas, but some few episodes are not to be found in either. These will be pointed out in the analysis.

By way of introducing it to the world under good auspices the compiler (probably) provided it with credentials in the shape of pretended letters to and from St. Jerome. These are also commonly found prefixed to the 'Story of the Birth of Mary' of which something will be said later. But as Dr. Amann, following Tischendorf, rightly says, the letters apply better to our present text than to the other. They allude to the 'Infancy of Christ', and the *Birth of Mary* stops short at the Nativity.

The letters run as follows:

To their most beloved brother Jerome the presbyter, Cromatius and Heliodorus, bishops, send greeting in the Lord.

We have found in *certain* apocryphal books the birth of the Virgin Mary and the infancy of our Lord Jesus Christ. Wherein noticing many passages contrary to our faith, we judge that the whole should be rejected, lest on the pretext of Christ we should afford triumph to antichrist. So while we were considering the matter, there came to us the holy men Parmenius and Virinus, who told us that your holiness had found a Hebrew book written by the hand of the most blessed evangelist Matthew, in which both the birth of the Virgin mother and the infancy of our Saviour were recorded. And therefore we entreat your charity, through the same our Lord Jesus Christ, and beg you to give it from the Hebrew to Latin ears, not so much in order to ascertain the wonderful works of Christ as to counteract the guile of heretics, who in order to establish their evil teaching have mingled their own lies with the wholesome nativity of Christ, so to disguise the bitterness of death under the sweetness of life. It will therefore be of the purest charity on your part either to hearken to us as brothers who beseech you, or to pay to us, as bishops who beg for it, that debt of charity which you shall think fit. Farewell in the Lord, and pray for us.

To the holy and most blessed lords Cromatius and Heliodorus, bishops, Jerome the little servant of Christ sends greeting in the Lord.

He who digs in earth which conceals gold does not at once snatch whatever the ragged trench may throw up: but before the stroke of the iron he wields brings up the shining mass, he ever and anon pauses in turning over the turfs, and feeds himself with hope, while as yet he is not enriched with gain. It is a heavy task that you lay upon me when I am ordered by your blessedness to do what not even Saint Matthew the apostle and evangelist would have to be written openly. For had it not been somewhat secret, he would no doubt have added it to the Gospel which he published. But in fact he composed this book to be locked up in Hebrew letters, and so far refrained from publishing it that even now the book, written in Hebrew letters with his own hand, is kept by *certain* religious men who have received it from their predecessors through a long course of time. Now whereas they have never delivered this book to any one to be translated, but have revealed its contents (text) at various times, it has come about that the book, published by a disciple of Manichaeus named Leucius (who also composed the Acts of the Apostles in false words), has afforded matter not for edification but destruction, and has been proved in a synod to be such that the ears of the church should properly be closed to it.

Now let there be an end to the bites of barking critics, for we are not adding this book to the canonical scriptures, but are translating the writing of an apostle and evangelist to unmask the deceit of heresy: and in so doing we are alike obeying the command of pious bishops and blocking the way of impious heretics. It is, then, the love of Christ to which we are rendering service, in the belief that they will help us with their prayers who by means of our compliance have been able to attain *the knowledge of* the holy infancy of our Saviour.

A third letter, ostensibly from St. Jerome to the same bishops, is prefixed sometimes to the story of the Birth of Mary.

You ask me to write you my opinion of a book which some have concerning the Birth of Saint Mary. So I would have you know that much that is false is found in it. For a certain Seleucus (= Leucius *above*), who wrote the Passions of the Apostles, composed this book also. But just as he told the truth about their mighty deeds and the miracles done by them, but lied much concerning their doctrine, so here also he forged much that is untrue, of his own heart. On this account I shall be careful to translate it word for word as it is in the Hebrew, inasmuch as it appears that the holy evangelist Matthew composed this same book and prefixed it, concealed as it was in Hebrew letters, to his Gospel. The truth of this statement I leave to the author of the preface and the faith of the writer; for myself, while pronouncing it doubtful, I do not affirm that it is clearly false. This, however, I say boldly, that I believe none of the faithful will deny that, whether this story be true or invented by some one, great miracles preceded the holy birth of Mary, and yet greater ones followed upon it; and therefore this can be believed and read with intact faith and without peril to the soul, by those who believe that God is able to do such things. Finally, as far as my recollection serves me, following the sense, not the words, of the writer, and walking, now in the same path though not in the same footprints, now regaining the same road after some digressions, I shall so attempt (*or* temper) the style of the narrative, and shall not tell anything but what is either written therein or might reasonably have been written.

A document so full of contradictions can seldom have been put together! 'Seleucus composed the book—no, Matthew composed it ; I shall translate it word for word—no, I shall follow the sense, not the words ', and so forth.

Finally, some copies have a prologue attributing the writing not to Matthew but to James. Such a prologue was known to Hrosvita, who cites James as her authority. It is as follows:

I, James the son of Joseph, walking in the fear of God, have written all things that I saw with mine own eyes come to pass at the time of the birth of Saint Mary the virgin or of the Lord the Saviour: giving thanks to God who gave me understanding in the histories of his coming, showing forth the fulness *of time* unto the twelve tribes of Israel.

It is worthy of remark that the last sentence of this evidently late prologue contains the two expressions 'histories' and 'twelve tribes of Israel', which recall the opening words of the Protevangelium, but not of Ps.-Matthew. The clause 'giving thanks to God', &c., comes from Protev. xxv. 1.

ANALYSIS OF THE GOSPEL OF PSEUDO-MATTHEW

In chs. i–xvii the Protevangelium is used, and is in all likelihood the sole source: but there are many omissions and amplifications.

I begins. In those days there was a man in Jerusalem, Joachim by name, of the tribe of Juda.

His whole care was his flocks. He offered double offerings. He divided his substance into three parts, one for the poor, one for the pious, the third for himself. God increased his wealth. This charity he had practised since he was 15 years old. At 20 he married Anna, daughter of Ysachar of his own tribe; they lived twenty years childless.

II. Ruben rejects his offering. He goes to the mountains to his flocks for five months.

Anna has no news of him. She complains to God.

She sees a sparrow's nest, and laments her childlessness, and vows if she has a child to dedicate it in the temple. An angel comes and promises her a daughter. In fear and sorrow she throws herself on her bed for a whole day and night. She reproaches her maid (not named) for not coming to her. The maid answers her sharply and she weeps yet more.

III. A youth—an angel—comes to Joachim in the wilderness and promises him a daughter and predicts her glory. Joachim makes an offering: is urged by his servants to return. The angel comes again in a vision. They set off and journey thirty days.

The angel comes to Anna and bids her meet Joachim at the Golden Gate of the Temple, which she does.

IV. Mary is born. At three years old she is taken to the temple and walks up fifteen steps.

V. Anna's thanksgiving.

VI. Mary's beauty and chastity and wisdom and devoutness described at length. She is fed daily by angels.

VII. Abiathar the priest offers many gifts that Mary may marry his son. She refuses, saying that she has vowed perpetual virginity.

VIII. When she was 14, a council was held and Israel was summoned to the temple on the third day. The high priest addressed them and said that since Solomon's time there had always been noble virgins brought up in the temple and married when they were of age. But Mary had vowed virginity and it must be ascertained who should take charge of her. Those who had no wives were to bring rods. There was no sign, so Abiathar went in and prayed, and an angel pointed out that one very small rod had not been returned to its owner. This was Joseph's. The dove appeared. Joseph resisted, but was overcome: he stipulated that some virgins should accompany Mary. Rebecca, Sephora, Susanna, Abigea, and Zahel were chosen. They cast lots for the colours of the veil. Mary had the purple: the others were jealous and called her in sport 'Regina virginum'. An angel rebuked them and said it was a true prophecy. They were abashed and asked Mary to pray for them.

IX. Mary at the fountain addressed by an angel. On the next day as she wove he appeared again and completed the Annunciation.

X. Joseph returned from Capernaum and found Mary great with child. His lament. The virgins defended Mary, but Joseph lamented still.

XI. The angel reassured him, and he asked pardon of Mary.

XII. Rumour went forth, and Joseph and Mary were summoned by the priests. The water of jealousy administered by Abiathar. Joseph and Mary each went about the altar seven times and no sign appeared. All asked her pardon and took her home in triumph.

XIII. Caesar's decree. They went to Bethlehem. The two peoples—Jews and Gentiles—weeping and laughing. An angel made her dismount and enter a dark cave which began to shine. There Christ was born. Joseph was gone to find midwives and brought Zelomi and Salome. Zelomi believed, Salome was incredulous, and her hand withered and was healed by touching the swaddling cloth. The shepherds' vision. The star shone.

XIV. On the third day Mary left the cave and went to a stable and put the child in the manger, and the ox and ass adored him, fulfilling the prophecies of Isaiah and Habakkuk. There they stayed three days.

XV. On the sixth day they went to Bethlehem, kept the sabbath, and circumcised the child on the eighth day. The Presentation: Symeon and Anna.

XVI. After the second year came the magi: told as in the Gospel.

XVII. Massacre of the Innocents; the warning to flee into Egypt.

Here the use of the Protevangelium ends. It will be seen that it has been freely dealt with. Among the interesting things that have been left out is the standing still of all creation at the moment of the Birth. Nor is John the Baptist or Zacharias mentioned at all.

Chapters XVIII–XXIV deal with the Flight into Egypt and the sojourn there. They may or may not be translated from a written source: on the whole I think they are not. Some tell of fulfilments of prophecy, others may depend on local legend.

XVIII. They came to a cave and wished to rest there. Mary dismounted and sat with Jesus in her lap. There were three boys with Joseph and a girl with Mary. Suddenly a number of dragons came out of the cave, and all cried out in fear. Jesus got down from his mother's lap and stood before the dragons, which worshipped him. Thus was fulfilled the word, 'Praise the Lord out of the earth, ye dragons and all deeps'. Jesus walked before them and bade them hurt no one. Mary was alarmed for him, but he said, 'Fear not, neither conceive that I am a child, for I always was and am a perfect man, and it is necessary that all the beasts of the forest should grow tame before me.'

XIX. In like manner lions and leopards adored him and accompanied them, showed them the way, and bowed their heads to Jesus. At first Mary was afraid, but Jesus smiled on her and reassured her. The lions never injured their oxen and asses or the sheep they had brought from Judaea. Wolves, too, came and were harmless. Thus was fulfilled the word, 'The wolves shall feed with the lambs, the lion and ox shall eat straw together.' They had with them two oxen and a cart to carry their necessaries.

XX. On the third day Mary saw a palm and wished to rest under it. When she was seated there she saw fruit on it, and said to Joseph that she should like to have some. Joseph said he was surprised she should say that because the tree was so high: he himself was thinking more about water, of which they had very little left. Jesus sitting in Mary's lap with a joyful countenance bade the palm give his mother of its fruit. The tree bent as low as her feet and she gathered what she would. He bade it rise again, and give them of the water concealed below its roots. A spring came forth and all rejoiced and drank of it.

XXI. Next day when they left the place Jesus said to the palm: I give thee this privilege, that one of thy branches shall be taken by my angels and planted in my Father's garden. And henceforth all who win contests shall be told that they have won the palm of victory. An angel came and took a branch and flew away with it. All fell down in fear, but Jesus reassured them.

XXII. As they went, Joseph said that as it was hot they might go by the sea coast. But Jesus said he would shorten the way—and even as he spoke they began to see the hills and cities of Egypt. They arrived at Hermopolis and entered a city called Sotinen, and had to lodge in a temple where were 365 gods.

XXIII. When Mary and the Child entered, all the idols fell, and Isaiah's word was fulfilled. 'Behold the Lord shall come upon a light cloud and enter into Egypt, and all the gods made by the hand of the Egyptians shall be moved before his face.'

XXIV. Affrodosius, governor of the city, heard of it and came with all his host. The priests thought he would punish those who had destroyed the gods: but when he saw them fallen he adored the child and said to those present that 'unless this were the God of our gods they would not have fallen. If we

do not adore him, as they have done, we are in danger of such
destruction as fell upon Pharaoh who was drowned with all
his army.'

Then all the people of the city believed in the Lord through
Jesus Christ.

Here begins the second part—the Infancy proper of our Lord. The
source is the Gospel of Thomas : sometimes a better text of that work
than we have elsewhere is represented, but there is also a good deal of
late amplification.

XXV. The angel bade Joseph return to Judaea.

XXVI. When Jesus was in Galilee at the beginning of his
fourth year he was playing by the Jordan, and made seven pools.
A boy spoilt them, and was struck dead. The parents complained. Joseph asked Mary to admonish Jesus. She begged
him not to do such things, and he, not willing to grieve her, 'smote
the back side of the dead boy with his foot and bade him rise:
which he did, and Jesus went on with his pools'.

XXVII. He took clay from the pools and made twelve
sparrows, on the sabbath. A Jew saw it and spoke to Joseph,
who spoke to Jesus. Jesus clapped his hands and bade the
sparrows fly away. All marvelled, and some went and told the
chief priests and Pharisees.

XXVIII. The son of Annas the priest broke up the pools
with a stick, and Jesus with a word withered him up.

XXIX. Joseph was afraid and took Jesus home. On the way
a boy ran against Jesus and got on his shoulder, meaning to hurt
him. Jesus said: 'Mayest thou not return whole from the way
thou goest.' He fell dead. Complaints of the parents, as in
Thomas. Joseph to Jesus: 'Why doest thou such things? Many
are now complaining against thee and hate us on thy account,
and we suffer injuries through thee.' Jesus: 'No son is wise
whom his father hath not taught according to the knowledge of
this age, and the curse of his father hurteth no man save them
that do ill.' All reviled Jesus to Joseph and he was much afraid.
'Then Jesus took the dead boy by the ear and held him up by
it in the sight of all, and they saw Jesus speaking to him as a
father to his son. And his spirit returned unto him and he lived
again, and all marvelled.'

In *Thomas* Joseph takes Jesus by the ear. Our compiler found this
offensive and changed it. He also changed the speech of Jesus to Joseph
and made it wholly pointless as far as I can see.

XXX. Master Zachyas spoke reproachfully to Joseph : 'You
and Mary think more of your son than of the traditions of the
elders.' *Joseph*: But who can teach him? if you can do so, we
are very willing. Jesus overhearing said: What you say is well
for ordinary people: I have no earthly father. When I am lifted
up from the earth I will make all mention of your descent to

cease. I know when you were born and how long you have to live. All cried out in wonder: We have never heard the like. *Jesus*: Does this surprise you? I will tell you more. I have seen Abraham and spoken with him, and he has seen me. None could answer. *Jesus*: I have been among you with the children, and ye have not known me. I have spoken with you as with the wise and ye have not understood my voice, for ye are less than me, and of little faith.

XXXI. Zachyas said: Give him to me and I will take him to Levi who shall teach him letters. Levi bade him answer to Aleph: he was silent. Levi smote him with a rod of storax on the head. *Jesus*: Why smitest thou me? Know of a truth that he which is smitten teacheth the smiter more than he is taught of him. For I can teach thee the things that thou thyself sayest. But all these which speak and hear are blind like sounding brass or a tinkling cymbal wherein is no perception of those things that are signified by their sound. Further he said to Zachyas (?): Every letter from Aleph to Thau is discerned by the arrangement of it. Do thou then first say what Thau is, and I will tell thee what Aleph is. And again he said: They that know not Aleph, how can they tell Thau, hypocrites that they are? Say ye what Aleph is first and then will I believe you when ye say Beth. (I quote this to show how the text is conflated out of various earlier forms.) He said to the master: Let the master of the law say what the first letter is, or why it hath many triangles (eight adjectives follow). Levi was stupefied and then began to lament: Ought he to live on the earth? Nay, rather is he worthy to be hung on a great cross. He can put out fire and escape all torments by guile. I think he was born before the flood, before the deluge. What womb bare him? What mother gave him birth? What breasts suckled him? I fly before him, &c., &c.

Jesus smiled and said with command to all the children of Israel that stood and heard him: Let the unfruitful bear fruit, and the blind see, and the lame walk straight, and the poor enjoy good things, and the dead revive, and every one return into a restored state, and abide in him who is the root of life and of everlasting sweetness. All were healed who had fallen into evil infirmities. No one thereafter dared to say aught to him or hear aught of him.

(This speech is simplified from every trace of mystery.)

XXXII. At Nazareth the boy Zeno fell from the soler and was raised. Joseph, Mary, and Jesus went thence to Jericho.

XXXIII. Jesus' pitcher was broken by a child, and he brought water in his cloak.

XXXIV. He took a little corn out of his mother's barn and sowed it. When reaped it made three cors, which he gave away.

(Another manuscript has a form like that of the Latin *Thomas*.)

XXXV–XXXVI do not occur in *Thomas* nor in the manuscript just mentioned.

XXXV. There is a road from Jericho to Jordan, at the place where Israel crossed and the ark rested. Jesus, eight years old, went from Jericho to Jordan. On the way there was a vault (crypta), where was a lioness with whelps. He went in and sat there, and the whelps played about him: the older lions stood at a distance and adored him, wagging their tails. The people who saw it said that he or his parents must have sinned or he would not have delivered himself to the lions. Then he came forth and the lions went before him, and the whelps played before his feet. His parents and the people looked on. Jesus said: How much better than you are the beasts which know me and are tame, while men know me not.

XXXVI. Then he went over Jordan, whose waters were divided, with the lions: and told them in the hearing of all to go back home and hurt no one. And so they did.

XXXVII–XXXIX are again from *Thomas*.

XXXVII. A bed of six cubits was ordered of Joseph, and he told his lad to cut a beam of the right length, but he made it too short. Joseph was troubled. Jesus pulled it out to the right length.

(The change is made in order to free Joseph from the charge of stupidity.)

XXXVIII. He went to school the second time. 'Say Alpha.' *Jesus*: Tell thou me first what Beta is, and I will tell thee what Alpha is. The master smote him and died.

Joseph said to Mary: Know verily that my soul is sorrowful even unto death because of this boy. It may chance that any one may smite him in malice and he may die. Mary said: O man of God, believe not that this can happen, but believe surely that he who sent him to be born among men will keep him from all malice and in his name preserve him from evil.

XXXIX. For the third time they took him to school at the request of others, though they knew that it was not possible for a man to teach him. He entered the school, took the book from the master's hand, and taught—not what was written in it—like a torrent of water flowing from a living fountain. All marvelled, and the master adored him. Joseph ran thither in fear. The master said: You have given me no scholar but a teacher! Who can ascertain his words? Then was fulfilled the word: 'The river of God is full of water. Thou hast prepared their food, for thus is the preparation thereof.'

XL is not in *Thomas*.

XL. They removed to Capernaum. A rich man named Joseph fell ill and died. Jesus heard the mourning and said to Joseph: Why dost thou not do him a service since he is of thy name? *Joseph*: What can I do? *Jesus*: Take the kerchief that is on thy head and go and put it on his face and say: Christ save thee. He did so and said: Jesus save thee. The dead man was raised and asked who Jesus was.

XLI. They moved from Bethlehem to Capernaum (perhaps it should be vice versa). Joseph sent his eldest son James into the garden to gather herbs for pottage. Story of the viper as in *Thomas*.

XLII is a conclusion, not in *Thomas*.

When Joseph came to a feast with his sons James, Joseph, Juda, and Simeon, and his two daughters, Jesus and Mary came with her sister Mary of Cleophas, whom the Lord gave to her father Cleophas and her mother Anna because they had offered Mary the mother of Jesus to the Lord, and this other was given for their consolation and called by the same name. When they were together Jesus blessed and sanctified them, and was the first to eat and drink, for no one ventured even to sit down until he had done so, and all waited for him if he was not there. And his brethren watched him ever and feared him. And when he slept by day or by night the light of God shone always over him. To whom be all praise and glory, world without end. Amen.

The real importance of Pseudo-Matthew lies not so much in the stories which it preserves, as in the fact that it was the principal vehicle by which they were known to the Middle Ages and the principal source of inspiration to the artists and poets of the centuries from the twelfth to the fifteenth. It is upon this text that the many vernacular versions for the most part depend; and by this that the pictures of the Rejection of Joachim's offering, his meeting with Anne at the Golden Gate, the Presentation of the Virgin, the Repose in Egypt, and the few that we have of the Infancy Miracles, are inspired.

THE GOSPEL OF THE BIRTH OF MARY,

as it was called by Hone, demands but a short notice. It is attributed to St. Jerome and finds a place in the editions among the spurious works that bear his name. It has passed almost bodily into the Golden Legend of James de Voragine, and so has exercised an influence on art and literature. But in itself it is, compared even with Pseudo-Matthew, a very poor production; being no more than an amplification of the earlier chapters of that work in more elegant Latin, and with all the detail blurred and smoothed down. No source has been employed by the writer but Pseudo-Matthew and the canonical Gospels. A brief analysis may be given.

I. Mary was born at Nazareth. Her parents. Ioachim's charity.

II. At the dedication feast his offering is rejected by Isachar. He retires to his flocks.

III. The angel appears to him and bids him return to Anne;

IV. And to Anne and bids her meet him at the Golden Gate.

V. They meet. Mary is born.

VI. Her presentation in the Temple at three years old.

VII. Her life there. At 14 years old it is agreed to summon the single men.

VIII. Joseph's rod. He takes her home with seven other virgins.
IX. The Annunciation: mostly from the Gospels.
X. Joseph's perplexity: the angel reassures him: Christ is born.

THE ARABIC GOSPEL OF THE INFANCY

Our present text of this book depends in the main upon a single Arabic manuscript, now lost, which was used by Sike, the first editor, in 1697. There are now known to be other manuscripts at Rome and Florence, but they have not been fully collated. The greater part of the book, however, is also embodied in a Syriac History of the Virgin which was edited and translated by Sir E. A. Wallis Budge in 1899.

The Arabic Gospel is a late compilation, as has been shown most clearly by Father P. Peeters in his recent French edition (1914, Évangiles apocryphes, ii).

The book falls into several divisions:
I is a late note prefixed.
II–IX. The Nativity to the Flight into Egypt. The Protevangelium is the ultimate source of some parts of this.
X–XXV. Miracles in Egypt, some of which show influence of late local traditions.
XXVI–XXXV. Return to Nazareth. Miracles done there, which do not occur in other texts.
XXXVI–LIII. Further miracles, mostly derived from Thomas: ending with Jesus in the Temple.
LIV. Baptism of Jesus.
LV. Doxology.

A briefer analysis of this book will suffice than in the case of Pseudo-Matthew.

I. States that it is found in the book of Joseph the high-priest in the time of Christ, who some say is Caiaphas, that Jesus in the cradle proclaimed his Godhead.

II. The decree of Augustus in the year 300 (or 304) of the era of Alexander. The Birth in a cave. An old Hebrew woman comes as midwife. III. Her hands are withered (?) because of her unbelief, and she is healed. (There is a gap in the text.) IV. The Shepherds. The midwife praises God. V. The Circumcision. V, VI. The Presentation.

VII. The Magi. VIII. They bring back one of Jesus' swaddling cloths which is proof against fire, and is preserved with veneration. IX. The Flight.

X, XI. Arrival in Egypt. An idol announces the presence of a God, and falls. The demoniac son of a priest is healed. XII. Alarm of Joseph and Mary.

XIII. Robbers hear a noise of an approaching host and flee, leaving their captives. Joseph and Mary arrive, and the captives ask who is the king who is coming. Answer: 'He is coming on after us.'

XIV. A demoniac woman healed. XV. A dumb bride healed.
XVI. A woman oppressed by a demon-serpent relieved.
XVII. A leprous girl healed by water in which Jesus was
washed.
XVIII. A leprous child healed in like manner. XIX. A husband and wife released from a spell. XX, XXI. The brother of
two women, who had been changed into a mule, restored by
having Jesus placed on his back (Peeters points out the identity
of this miracle with one told of St. Macarius in the *Historia
Lausiaca* of Palladius). XXII. The leprous girl of XVII married
to the brother.
XXIII. The robbers Titus and Dumachus (the good and bad
thieves of the Crucifixion) capture them. Titus redeems them:
Jesus prophesies his end.[1]
XXIV. At Matarieh in Egypt a spring bursts forth and balm
originates from the sweat of Jesus. XXV. They lived three
years at Misr (Cairo) and saw Pharaoh. Many miracles were
done which are not written in the Gospel of the Infancy or in
the complete Gospel (probably the Canonical Gospels are meant).
These chapters are an Egyptian interpolation not earlier than
the twelfth century.
XXVI. Return to Nazareth. XXVII. At Bethlehem a sick
child healed. XXVIII. A child diseased in the eyes healed.
XXIX. Two women, mothers of children. One child dies, the
other, Cleopas, is healed. The mother of the dead throws Cleopas
first into an oven, then into a well: he is uninjured: she herself
falls into the well and is killed. XXX. One of two twin boys
healed—the Bartholomew of the Gospels. XXXI. A leprous

---

[1] The meeting with the good thief is told in other places: in the
B Recension (Greek) of the Acts of Pilate; and by Aelred of Rievaulx
(de Vita Eremitica ad Sororem, xlviii: printed with St. Augustine's
works, ed. Bened. I, App. 51: Migne P. L. xxxii). Aelred's form is thus:
Do not in thy meditation pass over the gifts of the Magi: nor leave
him without company when he flees into Egypt. Think that to be
true which is told, that he was captured by robbers in the way and
saved by the kindness of a youth. This was, they say, the son of the
chief of the robbers, and when he got possession of his prey, and found
the child on his mother's breast, such splendour of majesty appeared
in his lovely face that *the youth*, not doubting that he was more than
man, inflamed with love embraced him and said: O most blessed of
children, if ever there come a time for having mercy on me, then
remember me and forget not this hour.
This they say was the robber who was crucified on Christ's right
hand, and when the other blasphemed, said: Dost thou not fear God
(*and the rest*), and turning to the Lord and beholding him in that
majesty which he had seen in him as a child, and not forgetful of his
pact, said: Remember me when thou comest into thy kingdom. So
as an incentive of love I think it not useless to hold this belief, though
I would not rashly affirm its truth.

woman healed. XXXII. A leprous bride healed. XXXIII, XXXIV. A woman haunted by a dragon freed by one of Christ's swaddling cloths.   XXXV. Judas, a child possessed by the devil, smites Jesus, and the devil leaves him in the form of a dog.
XXXVI. Jesus (seven years old) makes figures of all sorts of animals of clay, and makes them walk, fly, and feed. XXXVII. The story of the Dyer Salem (see above). XXXVIII. Jesus lengthens or shortens beams which Joseph had cut wrongly: for he was not clever at his trade. XXXIX. A bed made for the king of Jerusalem pulled out to the right size. XL. The children in the oven (see above). XLI. In the month of Adar the boys make Jesus their king, and passers by have to stop and salute him. XLII. The parents of a child bitten by a snake come, and are stopped: Jesus goes with them to the snake's nest and makes it suck out the poison: it bursts: the child is healed: he was Simon Zelotes. XLIII. James bitten by the viper and healed. XLIV. Zeno falls from the house and is raised. XLV. Jesus brings water in his cloak.
XLVI. The pools and sparrows of clay. The son of Hanan spoils the pools and is palsied. XLVII. The child who ran against Jesus falls dead. XLVIII. Taught by Zacheus, who is confounded by his wisdom. XLIX. Taught by another master, who smites him and dies.
L. With the doctors at Jerusalem: questioned about the Law. LI. Questioned about astronomy. LII. And by a philosopher about philosophy: he answers all perfectly. LIII. Is found by Mary and Joseph. Returns with them. LIV. He lived in obscurity until his baptism. LV. Doxology.

The stories which this book has in common with *Thomas* are rather shortly told and do not help to solve difficulties in the older text. The long series of healings in Egypt and at Bethlehem is monotonous: for the most part the Virgin is the prominent figure in them. It is to her that the sufferers apply, and she gives them the water in which the child has been washed, or some of his linen, or allows them to touch him.

There is an echo of the story in ch. xli in a Western book, the *Vita Rhythmica* of the Virgin and Christ, a long Latin rhyming composition of the thirteenth century, edited by Vögtlin (Bibl. d. Litterar. Vereins in Stuttgart, no. 180, 1888). In ll. 2,564 sqq. it is said that the Egyptian boys crowned Jesus as king: and again in 2,612, after the return from Egypt, the boys made him their king and called him *domicellus*, 'young Lord'. The sources of this *Vita* are enumerated by the compiler, and are ostensibly Greek to a large extent—Germanus, Theophilus, Epiphanius, Ignatius are named, as well as the *Infantia Salvatoris*. With it should be read the Latin stories printed from a Giessen manuscript by O. Schade, Königsberg, 1876, *Narrationes de vita et conversatione B.V.M.* &c. They follow the text of the *Vita Rhythmica* closely.

THE ARMENIAN GOSPEL OF THE INFANCY

The only accessible edition of this is the excellent French one of P. Peeters in *Évangiles apocryphes*, ii, 1914 (*Textes et Documents*: Hemmer & Lejay). It is a very long text, occupying over 200 pages of print. Like the other secondary documents with which we have been dealing, it is ultimately dependent on the Protevangelium and the Gospel of Thomas, but the data of both are enormously amplified.

It comes into Armenian from Syriac, but the date of the Syriac book from which it was translated is open to question. An Infancy Gospel was brought into Armenia by Nestorian missionaries in 590. This cannot be the present text: on the other hand, an Armenian writer of the twelfth century mentions a book of the Infancy which may be ours.

I. 'Récit de Saint Jacques, frère du Seigneur.' Story of the birth of Mary. It begins abruptly with Joachim's retirement to the desert, and follows the Protevangelium with some omissions and many expansions. In III is a long digression about Zacharias. In IV the marriage: Joseph's protests are much lengthened. V has an immense dialogue between Gabriel and the Virgin. VI, another between the Virgin and Joseph. VII. The water of jealousy.

VIII. The decree of Augustus and the Nativity: the silence of creation is related. Joseph in his search for a midwife meets first Eve, who comes to see the promise of redemption fulfilled: then Salome, whose unbelief and cure are told of.

X. The Shepherds. XI. The Magi, Melkon, king of Persia, Gaspar, of India, Balthasar, of Arabia. This episode is very long. The Magi bring with them the testament which Adam delivered to Seth. XII. The Presentation. XIII. The Massacre of the Innocents.

XIV. The death of Zacharias and escape of John (*Protev.*).

XV. The Flight and Sojourn in Egypt. The fall of idols and temples is told at vast length. The Family dwell for a time with a prince called Eleazar (who appears under the name of Lazarus in Budge's Syriac *History*).

XVI. The beginning of the return. There is more destruction of temples and there are healings of children, and also the first of several scenes—protracted to great length—in which Jesus is accused of causing the death of a child and is summoned before a judge. Long dialogues take place, and finally the dead child is raised to exculpate Jesus; after which he sometimes dies again. XVIII. Continues these stories. XIX, XX. Jesus is sent at the suggestion of the King (of Bethlehem, Barjesus) to learn from Gamaliel, who is confounded by his wisdom: then follows the story of the throne made straight. XXI. The story of the dyer, Israel, at Tiberias. XXII. Another trial of Jesus. XXIII. Miracles (or tricks) wrought on children on a mountain. XXIV.

Cure of a leper at Emmaus, with a very long dialogue. **XXV.**
They go to Nazareth. Jesus arbitrates between two brothers,
Malachias and Micheas. **XXVI.** Cure of a man, Hiram. **XXVII.**
Cure of an old man, Balthasar: long dialogue. **XXVIII.** Jesus
arbitrates between two soldiers.

There is on the whole little of ancient flavour in the book, and it
does not seem to preserve any details, which are not to be found elsewhere, of the old tradition. The diffuseness of the expansions reminds
one of the Armenian version of 4 Esdras, which takes the most
unwarrantable liberties with the text.

HISTORY OF JOSEPH THE CARPENTER, OR DEATH OF JOSEPH

This is an Egyptian book, not earlier than the fourth century in
date, and very probably later: it exists in fragments in Sahidic,
complete in Bohairic (the dialects of Upper and Lower Egypt respectively), and complete also in Arabic. A Latin version made in the
fourteenth century from the Arabic exists, but has not been printed.

The object of the book is the glorification of St. Joseph and his
feast-day: his cult, so popular in the West, was long confined to Egypt.
The interest of it lies in a few reminiscences of earlier books, and in
the picturesque and highly Egyptian descriptions of death. The
lamentations of Joseph and his prayers find many parallels in the
literature of Christian Egypt, and especially in the Coptic accounts of
the death of the Virgin.

The order of the book is as follows (I use Forbes Robinson's and
Peeters's versions):

Proem: 'This is the going forth from the body of our father
Joseph the carpenter, the father of Christ according to flesh,
whose life was 111 years.' It was told by Christ to the apostles
on Mount Olivet, was written down by them, and laid up in the
library at Jerusalem. The day of the death was the 26th of the
month Epep.

I. Christ on Mount Olivet addresses the apostles: on the
certainty of death and the justice of God, &c.

II. Joseph was of Bethlehem: he was a carpenter, and married
and had four sons, Judas, Josetos (*Arab.* Justus), James, Simon,
and two daughters, Lysia (*Arab.* Asia) and Lydia. His wife died,
leaving James still young.

III. Mary was being brought up in the Temple till she was
twelve years old. The priests decided to give her to a husband.

IV. The lot fell on Joseph. Mary brought up James and was
called Mary of James. Two years passed.

V. 'I came and dwelt in her.' Joseph's perplexity. VI. Reassured by Gabriel.

VII. Decree of Caesar. The Birth 'by the tomb of Rachel'.
VIII. Herod sought to slay me. The Flight: Salome was with us. A year in Egypt.
IX. Return to Nazareth. Joseph worked at his trade.
X. His health and strength were unimpaired: he lived to be 111.
XI. Josetos and Symeon married. Joseph dwelt with James. I was subject to Mary and to him.
XII. Joseph's death drew nigh. He went to the temple and prayed at the altar.
XIII. His prayer to be saved from the terrors after death, 'the river of fire wherein all souls are purified before they see the glory of God'.
XIV. He returned to Nazareth and fell ill. The dates of his life: he was 40 when he married, and was married forty-nine years: a year alone after his wife's death. Two years with Mary before the Nativity.
XV. His strength gave way and he was troubled and uttered a lamentation (XVI) over all the parts of his body, for their several transgressions.
XVII. I went to him. His greeting and address: he told of his doubt about Mary, and of another incident (a fusion of two stories in *Thomas*). The Sahidic tells it thus: I remember also the day that the horned serpent bit the lad on his foot and he died. His relations were gathered unto thee, wishing to take thee and deliver thee to Herod the lawless. And I found thee (*Boh.* Thy mercy found him), and thy godhead laid hold of him and he lived; and when thou didst raise him up to his parents there was great joy to them. But I requested thee, O my beloved son, *saying*: Be quiet in all things: and I took hold of thy right ear and pulled it. Thou didst answer, saying unto me: Unless thou wert my father according to the flesh, surely I would have warned thee because thou didst pull my right ear. (The Bohairic has slight variants, and the Arabic softens the incident by saying, 'I took hold of thy hand'.)
XVIII. I wept. My mother asked if Joseph must die, and I told her that it must be so.
XIX. I sat at his head, Mary at his feet. I felt his heart and found that the soul was in his throat.
XX. Mary felt his feet and legs and found them cold as ice. The brethren and sisters were summoned. Lysia the eldest daughter ('who is the seller of purple', Sahidic: cf. Acts xvi. 14) lamented: so did all.
XXI. I looked at the south of the door and saw Death, and Amente following with their satellites 'decani' armed with fire. Joseph saw them and feared. I rebuked them and they fled. Death hid himself behind the door. I prayed.
XXII. Prayer for protection for the soul of Joseph 'until it cross the seven aeons of darkness'. 'Let the river of fire be as

water and the sea of demons cease vexing.' Address to the apostles on the terrors of death.

XXIII. When I had said Amen, my mother answering me in the language of the inhabitants of the heavens, Michael, Gabriel, and the choir of the angels came. Numbness and panting seized on Joseph. Death seeing me dared not enter. I arose and went outside and bade him go in and do his appointed work, but deal gently. Then Abbaton went in and took the soul, at sunrise on 26th Epep. Michael and Gabriel put the soul into a precious silken napkin and the angels took it away, singing. (The passage about Death (Abbaton) is only in Sahidic: the Bohairic shortens the section.)

XXIV. I sat down by the body and closed the eyes and mouth; and comforted Mary and the rest.

XXV. The people of Nazareth came and mourned till the ninth hour. Then I put all forth, anointed and washed the body. 'I prayed to my Father with heavenly prayers which I wrote with my own fingers on the tables of heaven before I took flesh in the holy Virgin Mary.' Angels came and shrouded the body.

XXVI. I blessed it from all corruption; pronounced blessings on all who celebrate his memory by good deeds or write the story of his death.

XXVII. The chief men of the place came to prepare the body, and found it already shrouded. The burial. I wept.

XXVIII. The lament of Jesus.

XXIX. The body was laid in the tomb beside Jacob his father.

XXX. We the apostles rejoiced to hear all this. We asked why Joseph should not have been exempted from death like Enoch and Elias.

XXXI. Jesus speaks of the inevitableness of death, and tells how Enoch and Elias still have to die, and are in trouble until their death is over. Antichrist will shed the blood of two men (*Arab.* four) like a cup of water, because of the reproaches they will heap upon him.

XXXII. We asked: Who are the two whom he will slay? Answer: Enoch and Elias. (*Arabic* has, 'Who are the Four whom he will slay? Answer: Enoch, Elias, Schila, and Tabitha.' Mr. W. E. Crum has shown that for Schila we ought to read Sibylla. This gives two men and two women. Nothing is known of stories in which the Sibyl is killed by Antichrist, but in the Coptic Apocalypse of Elias, Tabitha figures prominently, withstanding Antichrist and being slain by him.)

The book ends with a doxology of the apostles.

COPTIC LIVES, ETC., OF THE VIRGIN

There are a number of Lives, Panegyrics, Discourses, &c., in Coptic, complete and fragmentary, which tell the story of the Virgin's birth. In Forbes Robinson's *Coptic Apocryphal Gospels* are:

I. A Sahidic fragment of a homily, perhaps attributed to Evodius of Antioch, disciple of the apostles.

This tells of Joakim—formerly called Cleopas—and Anna, and of the way in which they were taunted by the men and women they met when they went to Jerusalem, because they had no children: and of their grief in consequence. Each then had a vision of a white dove: it came and sat on Joakim's head, and on Anna's bosom. Anna had another vision with a prediction of Mary's birth. Mary was born on the 15th of Hathor. Zacharias was warned by an angel to tell Anna and Joakim to dedicate Mary in three years' time.

II A. (Sahidic.) Mary is brought to the Temple and lives there, fed by angels. Her chastity and sobriety of attire are described in terms which recur in other panegyrics, especially that of Demetrius: see below.

II B. The Annunciation. Decree of Augustus. Nativity. Before it, Mary's face is radiant and then troubled, but her vision of two peoples is not mentioned. Joseph goes to find a midwife.

There seem to be only rather faint memories of the Protevangelium in these fragments.

In Budge's *Miscellaneous Coptic Texts*, 1915, are some which bear on this subject, viz.

1. p. 626. The Twentieth Discourse of Cyril of Jerusalem.

In this Mary is represented as saying to Cyril: 'I was a child promised to God, and my parents dedicated me to Him before I came into the world. My parents . . . were of the tribe of Judah and house of David. My father was Joakim, which is being interpreted Kleopa. My mother was Anna . . . who was usually called Mariham. I am Mary Magdalene because the name of the village wherein I was born was Magdalia. My name is Mary of Cleopa. I am Mary of James the son of Joseph the carpenter.'

p. 631. We are told that in the village of Magdalia dwelt a rich and devout man David. A vision told him that the Redeemer should come out of his family. His wife Sara bore him a child whom the father called Joakim, and the mother Cleopa. He married Anna, daughter of Aminadab, David's brother. They were childless. After many days they went to the Temple, prayed for a child, and promised to dedicate it to God. A voice came, saying that their prayer was heard. Mary was born, dedicated in the Temple at three years old, and brought up there till she was fifteen.

The reckless identification of the Virgin Mary with all the other Maries of the Gospels is characteristic of these Egyptian rhapsodies. In the Book of Bartholomew the appearance of Christ to Magdalene after the resurrection is turned into an appearance to his mother: and so too in another Coptic fragment on the Passion described later on.

2. Discourse by Demetrius of Antioch.

p. 653.   There was a man in Jerusalem whose name was Joakim and he had a wife whose name was Susanna (*sic.* elsewhere in the discourse it is Anna).   They were childless and prayed for a child.   A man of light appeared and promised them a daughter whom they were to dedicate to God.   She was born on 15th of Athor and dedicated.   The description of her habits is almost identical with that in fragment II A of Robinson. When she was twelve the priests decided to commit her to the care of a man.   The lot fell on Joseph.   She sat in his house and weaved the veil of the Temple.   Angels ministered to her in the form of doves or some other kind of holy bird.   'They flew about her in the place where she used to sit working at her handicraft, and they would alight upon the window of her room and they longed to hear her holy voice, which was sweet, and pretty, and holy.'   We then read of the Annunciation and the salutation of Gabriel—of great length—the Visitation, Decree of Caesar, journey to Bethlehem.   Joseph looked at Mary and saw her whole body shining, and that she was greatly moved, for the time of the birth drew nigh.   A great star appeared and excited much comment.   At dawn on the 29th of Khoiak, Mary asked Joseph to seek a woman to help her.   He found one on the roof of her house, and asked if she knew a midwife.   She said: 'Thou art Joseph the husband of Mary,' and came down, and put on her finest apparel.   Before they reached the caravanserai the child was born.   The woman's name was Salome.   When they entered the house they saw the Child in the manger and the ox and ass protecting him.   Salome worshipped him.   She was the first who recognized the Christ, and she followed him everywhere throughout his life.   'I wish very much that I might describe unto you fully the life of that woman and her acts and deeds . . .' but there is not time.[1]

The story is continued with some few non-Biblical details to the Flight into Egypt, on p. 682.   The killing of Zacharias is shortly told in agreement with the account in the Protevangelium.

3. The Discourse of Epiphanius.

This has very few points of contact with the Apocrypha.   It

[1] There is, however, a Coptic text not yet printed in full, which does tell the whole story of Salome, and simply transfers to her a great part of the legend of Thais or of Mary the niece of the hermit Abraham.

is mentioned that Mary was working when the Annunciation took place.

4. The Discourse of Cyril of Alexandria.

In this the care of Mary for her child, and her intercourse with him, is rather prettily described. 'She used to take hold of his hand and lead him along the roads, saying, "My sweet son, walk a little way", in the same manner as all other babes are taught to walk. And he, Jesus, the very God, followed after her untroubled. He clung to her with his little fingers, he stopped from time to time, and he hung on to the skirts of Mary his mother, he upon whom the whole universe hangeth. He would lift up his eyes to her face . . . and she would catch him up to herself and lift him up in her arms, and walk along with him.'

At p. 721 is essentially the same description of the Virgin's habits that we have found in Robinson, II A, and Demetrius.

These documents on the whole show great negligence in the use of ancient sources and great licence on the part of the writers; and I think this is rather characteristic of the Christian literature of Egypt. When we come to the Passion-narratives and the Acts and Apocalypses we shall encounter some striking instances of the taking of liberties with texts.

A MODERN INFANCY GOSPEL

By way of a curiosity, and to dispel illusions that may perhaps be entertained, I add a short note on a modern forgery, 'The childhood of Christ—translated from the Latin by Henry Copley Greene, with original text of the manuscript at the monastery of St. Wolfgang. New York: Scott-Thaw Co. London: Burns & Oates. 1904.' This is the form in which some readers may have met the book. The original is: 'L'Évangile de la jeunesse de Notre-Seigneur Jésus-Christ d'après S. Pierre.' Latin text and French version by Catulle Mendès: Paris, Armand Colin, 1894. All that we are told of the provenance of the Latin text is that it was 'found some years ago in the ancient abbey of St. Wolfgang in the Salzkammergut'. The opening words of the prologue attribute the work to St. Peter. It is a sentimentalized compilation from Protevangelium, Pseudo-Matthew, the Latin Thomas, and the Arabic Gospel. It claims to be at least mediaeval in date, but the claim is made null by the simple fact that the Latin contains many phrases from Sike's Latin version of the Arabic Gospel, which was written in 1697. Perhaps one specimen of the turn which is given to the original stories may be given. In the case of the boy who runs against Jesus, Jesus laments, saying, 'Non ploro quia malum mihi inflixum est, sed quia malum altero inflixurus sum. Euh! frater mi,' &c. He then puts his hand on the boy's forehead, saying, 'Quoniam pulsavisti, cade, et quoniam vitae in me currens offendisti, siste in morte'. (Because you have pushed me, fall; and because by running against me you have offended (or stumbled against) life, continue dead.) The boy dies and Jesus mourns for twelve days.

Presumably the Latin text as well as the French version may be regarded as the work of Catulle Mendès.

Three other modern forgeries about the Life of Christ I will just name—more to show my consciousness of their existence than because they are at all interesting. One is a life said to have been found in a Buddhist monastery in Tibet, and connected with the name of Notovich as discoverer or translator. The second is a ridiculous and disgusting American book called 'The Archko Volume'. The third is the Letter of Benan (an Egyptian physician), shown by Professor Carl Schmidt (*Der Benanbrief*, 1919) to have been forged by Ernst Edler von der Planitz. This, I believe, had a great vogue recently in Central Europe, but I have never heard of it in an English dress.

PASSION GOSPELS

GOSPEL OF PETER

THE early testimonies about this book have been set forth already. The present fragment was discovered in 1884 in a tomb at Akhmim in Egypt. The manuscript in which it is is a little book containing a portion of the Book of Enoch in Greek, this fragment on the Passion, and another, a description of Heaven and Hell, which is either (as I now think) a second fragment of the Gospel, or a piece of the Apocalypse of Peter. It will be given later under that head.

We have seen that the Gospel of Peter is quoted by writers of the latter end of the second century. It has been contended that Justin Martyr also used it soon after the middle of that century, but the evidence is not demonstrative. I believe it is not safe to date the book much earlier than A.D. 150.

It uses all four canonical Gospels, and is the earliest uncanonical account of the Passion that exists. It is not wholly orthodox: for it throws doubt on the reality of the Lord's sufferings, and by consequence upon the reality of his human body. In other words it is, as Serapion of Antioch indicated, of a Docetic character.

Another characteristic of it is its extremely anti-Jewish attitude. Blame is thrown on the Jews wherever possible, and Pilate is white-washed.

In this case I give, in Roman and Arabic figures respectively, a double division into sections and verses. The first is that of Armitage Robinson, the second that of Harnack.

FRAGMENT I

I. 1 But of the Jews no man washed his hands, neither *did* Herod nor any one of his judges: and whereas they would not 2 wash, Pilate rose up. And then Herod the king commanded that the Lord should be taken *into their hands*, saying unto them: All that I commanded you to do unto him, do ye.
II. 3 Now there stood there Joseph the friend of Pilate and of the Lord, and he, knowing that they were about to crucify him, came unto Pilate and begged the body of Jesus for

4 burial. And Pilate sending unto Herod, begged his body.
5 And Herod said: Brother Pilate, even if none had begged for him, we should have buried him, since also the sabbath dawneth; for it is written in the law that the sun should not set upon one that hath been slain (murdered).
III. 6 And he delivered him unto the people before the first day of (*or* on the day before the) unleavened bread, *even* their feast. And they having taken the Lord pushed him as they ran, and said: Let us hale the Son of God, now that
7 we have gotten authority over him. And they put on him a purple robe, and made him sit upon the seat of judgement,
8 saying: Give righteous judgement, thou King of Israel. And one of them brought a crown of thorns and set it upon the
9 Lord's head; and others stood and did spit in his eyes, and others buffeted his cheeks; and others did prick him with a reed, and some of them scourged him, saying: With this honour let us honour (*or* at this price let us value) the son of God.
IV. 10 And they brought two malefactors, and crucified the
11 Lord betwixt them. But he kept silence, as one feeling no pain. And when they set the cross upright, they wrote
12 thereon: This is the King of Israel. And they laid his garments before him, and divided them *among themselves* and
13 cast the lot upon them. But one of those malefactors reproached them, saying: We have thus suffered for the evils which we have done; but this man which hath become the
14 saviour of men, wherein hath he injured you? And they were wroth with him, and commanded that his legs should not be broken, that so he might die in torment.
V. 15 Now it was noonday, and darkness prevailed over all Judaea: and they were troubled and in an agony lest the sun should have set, for that he yet lived: *for* it is written for them that the sun should not set upon him that hath been
16 slain (murdered). And one of them said: Give ye him to drink gall with vinegar: and they mingled it and gave him
17 to drink: and they fulfilled all things and accomplished
18 their sins upon their own heads. And many went about with
19 lamps, supposing that it was night: and *some* fell. And the Lord cried out aloud saying: My power, *my* power, thou hast forsaken me. And when he had *so* said, he was taken up.
20 And in the same hour was the veil of the temple of Jerusalem rent in two.
VI. 21 And then they plucked the nails from the hands of the Lord and laid him upon the earth: and the whole earth was shaken, and there came a great fear *on all*.
22 Then the sun shone forth, and it was found to be the ninth
23 hour. And the Jews rejoiced, and gave his body unto Joseph to bury it, because he had beheld all the good things which

24 he did. And he took the Lord and washed him and wrapped
him in linen and brought him unto his own sepulchre, *which is*
called the Garden of Joseph.

VII. 25 Then the Jews and the elders and the priests, when
they perceived how great evil they had done themselves,
began to lament and to say: Woe unto our sins: the judgement
and the end of Jerusalem is drawn nigh.

26   But I with my fellows was in grief, and we were wounded
in our minds and would have hid ourselves; for we were
sought after by them as malefactors, and as thinking to set
27 the temple on fire. And beside all these things we were
fasting, and we sat mourning and weeping night and day
until the sabbath.

VIII. 28 But the scribes and Pharisees and elders gathered
one with another, for they had heard that all the people were
murmuring and beating their breasts, saying: If these very
great signs have come to pass at his death, behold how
29 righteous he was. *And* the elders were afraid and came unto
30 Pilate, entreating him and saying: Give us soldiers that we
(*or* they) may watch his sepulchre for three days, lest his
disciples come and steal him away and the people suppose
31 that he is risen from the dead, and do us hurt. And Pilate
gave them Petronius the centurion with soldiers to watch the
sepulchre; and *the* elders and scribes came with them unto
32 the tomb, and when they had rolled a great stone to keep
out (*al.* together with) the centurion and the soldiers, *then* all
33 that were there together set it upon the door of the tomb ; and
plastered thereon seven seals ; and they pitched a tent there
and kept watch.

IX. 34 And early in the morning as the sabbath dawned,
there came a multitude from Jerusalem and the region round
about to see the sepulchre that had been sealed.

35   Now in the night whereon the Lord's day dawned, as the
soldiers were keeping guard two by two in every watch,
36 there came a great sound in the heaven, and they saw the
heavens opened and two men descend thence, shining with
(*lit.* having) a great light, and drawing near unto the sepulchre.
37 And that stone which had been set on the door rolled away
of itself and went back to the side, and the sepulchre was

X. 38 opened and both of the young men entered in. When
therefore those soldiers saw *that,* they waked up the centurion and the elders (for they also were there keeping
39 watch); and while they were *yet* telling them the things
which they had seen, they saw again three men come out of
the sepulchre, and two of them sustaining the other (*lit.* the
40 one), and a cross following after them. And of the two *they
saw* that their heads reached unto heaven, but of him that
41 was led by them that it overpassed the heavens. And they

42 heard a voice out of the heavens saying: Hast thou (*or* Thou
   hast) preached unto them that sleep? And an answer was
   heard from the cross, *saying*: Yea.

XI. 43 Those men therefore took counsel one with another to
44 go and report these things unto Pilate. And while they yet
   thought thereabout, again the heavens were opened and a
45 man descended and entered into the tomb. And they that
   were with the centurion (*or* the centurion and they that were
   with him) when they saw that, hasted to go by night unto
   Pilate and left the sepulchre whereon they were keeping
   watch, and told all that they had seen, and were in great
   agony, saying: Of a truth he was the son of God.
46   Pilate answered and said: I am clear from the blood of
47 the son of God, but thus it seemed good unto you. Then
   all they came and besought him and exhorted him to charge
   the centurion and the soldiers to tell nothing of that they had
48 seen: For, said they, it is expedient for us to incur the
   greatest sin before God, rather than to (and not to) fall into
49 the hands of the people of the Jews and to be stoned. Pilate
   therefore charged the centurion and the soldiers that they
   should say nothing.

XII. 50 Now early on the Lord's day Mary Magdalene, a
   disciple (*fem.*) of the Lord—*which*, being afraid because of
   the Jews, for they were inflamed with anger, had not performed at the sepulchre of the Lord those things which
   women are accustomed to do unto them that die and are
51 beloved of them—took with her the *women her* friends and
52 came unto the tomb where he was laid. And they feared lest
   the Jews should see them, and said: Even if we were not
   able to weep and lament him on that day whereon he was
53 crucified, yet let us now do so at his tomb. But who will
   roll away for us the stone also that is set upon the door of
   the tomb, that we may enter in and sit beside him and perform
54 that which is due? for the stone was great, and we fear lest
   any man see us. And if we cannot do so, yet let us cast down
   at the door these things which we bring for a memorial of
   him, *and* we will weep and lament until we come unto our
   house.

XIII. 55 And they went and found the sepulchre open: and
   they drew near and looked in there, and saw there a young man
   sitting in the midst of the sepulchre, of a fair countenance
   and clad in very bright raiment, which said unto them:
56 Wherefore are ye come? whom seek ye? not him that was
   crucified? He is risen and is departed; but if ye believe it
   not, look in and see the place where he lay, that he is not *here*:
   for he is risen and is departed thither whence he was sent.
57 Then the women were affrighted and fled.

XIV. 58 Now it was the last day of unleavened bread, and

many were coming forth *of the city* and returning unto their
59 own homes because the feast was at an end. But we, the
twelve disciples of the Lord, were weeping and were in
sorrow, and each one being grieved for that which had befallen
60 departed unto his own house. But I, Simon Peter, and Andrew
my brother, took our nets and went unto the sea: and there
was with us Levi the son of Alphaeus, whom the Lord
(For Fragment II see Apocalypse of Peter.)

THE GOSPEL OF NICODEMUS, OR ACTS OF PILATE

We have as yet no true critical edition of this book: one is in preparation, by E. von Dobschütz, to be included in the Berlin corpus of
Greek Ante-Nicene Christian writers. A short statement of the
authorities available at this moment is therefore necessary.

Tischendorf in his *Evangelia Apocrypha* divides the whole writing
into two parts: (1) the story of the Passion; (2) the Descent into
Hell; and prints the following forms of each: six in all:

1. Part I, Recension A in Greek from eight manuscripts, and a Latin
translation of the Coptic version in the notes.
2. Part I, Recension B in Greek from three late manuscripts.
3. Part II (Descent into Hell) in Greek from three manuscripts.
4. Part I in Latin, using twelve manuscripts, and some old editions.
5. Part II in Latin (A) from four manuscripts.
6. Part II in Latin (B) from three manuscripts.

Tischendorf's must be described as an eclectic text not representing,
probably, any one single line of transmission: but it presents the book
in a readable, and doubtless, on the whole, correct form.

There are, besides the Latin, three ancient versions of Part I of
considerable importance, viz.:

Coptic, preserved in an early papyrus at Turin, and in some fragments at Paris. Last edited by Revillout in *Patrologia orientalis*, ix. 2.

Syriac, edited by Rahmani in *Studia Syriaca*, II.

Armenian, edited by F. C. Conybeare in *Studia Biblica*, IV (Oxford,
1896): he gives a Greek rendering of one manuscript and a Latin one
of another.

All of these conform to Tischendorf's Recension A of Part I : and
this must be regarded as the most original form of the *Acta* which we
have. Recension B is a late and diffuse working-over of the same
matter: it will not be translated here in full.

The first part of the book, containing the story of the Passion and
Resurrection, is not earlier than the fourth century. Its object in
the main is to furnish irrefragable testimony to the resurrection.
Attempts have been made to show that it is of early date—that it is,
for instance, the writing which Justin Martyr meant when in his
Apology he referred his heathen readers to the 'Acts' of Christ's trial
preserved among the archives of Rome. The truth of that matter is

that he simply assumed that such records must exist. False 'acts' of the trial were written in the Pagan interest under Maximin, and introduced into schools early in the fourth century. It is imagined by some that our book was a counterblast to these.

The account of the Descent into Hell (Part II) is an addition to the *Acta*. It does not appear in any Oriental version, and the Greek copies are rare. It is in Latin that it has chiefly flourished, and has been the parent of versions in every European language.

The central idea, the delivery of the righteous Fathers from Hades, is exceedingly ancient. Second-century writers are full of it. The embellishments, the dialogues of Satan with Hades, which are so dramatic, come in later, perhaps with the development of pulpit oratory among Christians. We find them in fourth-century homilies attributed to Eusebius of Emesa.

This second part used to be called Gnostic, but there is nothing unorthodox about it, save the choice of the names of the two men who are supposed to tell the story, viz. Leucius and Karinus. Leucius Charinus is the name given by church writers to the supposed author of the Apocryphal Acts of John, Paul, Peter, Andrew, and Thomas. In reality Leucius was the *soi-disant* author of the Acts of John only. His name was transferred to the other Acts in process of time, and also (sometimes disguised as Seleucus) to Gospels of the Infancy and narratives of the Assumption of the Virgin. With all these the original Leucius had nothing to do. When his name came to be attached to the Descent into Hell we do not yet know: nor do we know when the *Descent* was first appended to the Acts of Pilate. Not, I should conjecture, before the fifth century.

MEMORIALS OF OUR LORD JESUS CHRIST DONE IN THE TIME OF PONTIUS PILATE

PROLOGUE

(Absent from some manuscripts and versions).

I Ananias (Aeneas *Copt.*, Emaus *Latt.*), the Protector, of praetorian rank, learned in the law, did from the divine scriptures recognize our Lord Jesus Christ and came near to him by faith, and was accounted worthy of holy baptism: and I sought out the memorials that were made at that season in the time of our master Jesus Christ, which the Jews deposited with Pontius Pilate, and found the memorials in Hebrew (letters), and by the good pleasure of God I translated them into Greek (letters) for the informing of all them that call upon the name of our Lord Jesus Christ: in the reign of our Lord Flavius Theodosius, in the seventeenth year, and of Flavius Valentinianus the sixth, in the ninth indiction [corrupt : *Lat.* has the eighteenth year of Theodosius, when Valentinian was *proclaimed* Augustus, i. e. A. D. 425].

All ye therefore that read this and translate (*or* copy) it into other books, remember me and pray for me that God will be gracious unto me and be merciful unto my sins which I have sinned against him.

Peace be to them that read and that hear these things and to their servants. Amen.

In the fifteenth (*al.* nineteenth) year of the governance of Tiberius Caesar, emperor of the Romans, and of Herod, king of Galilee, in the nineteenth year of his rule, on the eighth of the Kalends of April, which is the 25th of March, in the consulate of Rufus and Rubellio, in the fourth year of the two hundred and second Olympiad, Joseph who is Caiaphas being high priest of the Jews:

These be the things which after the cross and passion of the Lord Nicodemus recorded [1] and delivered unto the high priest and the rest of the Jews: and the same Nicodemus set them forth in Hebrew (letters).

I

1 For the chief priests and scribes assembled in council, even Annas and Caiaphas and Somne (Senes) and Dothaim (Dothael, Dathaës, Datam) and Gamaliel, Judas, Levi and Nepthalim, Alexander and Jairus and the rest of the Jews, and came unto Pilate accusing Jesus for many deeds, saying: We know this man, that he is the son of Joseph the carpenter, begotten of Mary, and he saith that he is the Son of God and a king; moreover he doth pollute the sabbaths and he would destroy the law of our fathers.

Pilate saith: And what things are they that he doeth, and would destroy the law?

The Jews say: We have a law that we should not heal any man on the sabbath: but this man of his evil deeds hath healed the lame and the bent, the withered and the blind and the paralytic, the dumb and them that were possessed, on the sabbath day!

Pilate saith unto them: By what evil deeds?

They say unto him: He is a sorcerer, and by Beelzebub the prince of the devils he casteth out devils, and they are all subject unto him.

Pilate saith unto them: This is not to cast out devils by an unclean spirit, but by the god Asclepius.

2 The Jews say unto Pilate: We beseech thy majesty that he appear before thy judgement-seat and be heard. And Pilate called them unto him and said: Tell me, how can I that am a governor examine a king? They say unto him: We say not that he is a king, but he saith it of himself.

And Pilate called the messenger (*cursor*) and said unto him: Let Jesus be brought hither, *but* with gentleness. And the messenger went forth, and when he perceived Jesus he worshipped

---

[1] For 'recorded', &c., other manuscripts and Coptic and Latin have 'recorded those things that were done by the high priests and the Jews'.

him and took the kerchief that was on his hand and spread it upon the earth and saith unto him: Lord, walk hereon and enter in, for the governor calleth thee. And when the Jews saw what the messenger had done, they cried out against Pilate saying: Wherefore didst thou not summon him by an herald to enter in, but by a messenger? for the messenger when he saw him worshipped him and spread out his kerchief upon the ground and hath made him walk *upon it* like a king!

3 Then Pilate called for the messenger and said unto him: Wherefore hast thou done this, and hast spread thy kerchief upon the ground and made Jesus to walk upon it? The messenger saith unto him: Lord governor, when thou sentest me to Jerusalem unto Alexander, I saw *Jesus* sitting upon an ass, and the children of the Hebrews held branches in their hands and cried out, and others spread their garments beneath him, saying: Save now, thou that art in the highest: blessed is he that cometh in the name of the Lord.

4 The Jews cried out and said unto the messenger: The children of the Hebrews cried out in Hebrew: how then hast thou it in the Greek? The messenger saith to them: I did ask one of the Jews and said: What is it that they cry out in Hebrew? and he interpreted it unto me.

Pilate saith unto them: And how cried they in Hebrew? The Jews say unto him: Hosanna membrome barouchamma adonai. Pilate saith unto them: And the Hosanna and the rest, how is it interpreted? The Jews say unto him: Save now, thou that art in the highest: blessed is he that cometh in the name of the Lord. Pilate saith unto them: If you yourselves bear witness of the words which were said of the children, wherein hath the messenger sinned? and they held their peace.

The governor saith unto the messenger: Go forth and bring him in after what manner thou wilt. And the messenger went forth and did after the former manner and said unto Jesus: Lord, enter in: the governor calleth thee.

5 Now when Jesus entered in, and the ensigns were holding the standards, the images (busts) of the standards bowed and did reverence to Jesus. And when the Jews saw the carriage of the standards, how they bowed themselves and did reverence unto Jesus, they cried out above measure against the ensigns. But Pilate said unto the Jews: Marvel ye not that the images bowed themselves and did reverence unto Jesus? The Jews say unto Pilate: We saw how the ensigns made them to bow and did reverence to him. And the governor called for the ensigns and saith unto them: Wherefore did ye so? They say unto Pilate: We are Greeks and servers of temples, and how could we do him reverence? for indeed, whilst we held the images they bowed of themselves and did reverence unto him.

6 Then saith Pilate unto the rulers of the synagogue and the

elders of the people: Choose you out able and strong men and
let them hold the standards, and let us see if they bow of themselves. And the elders of the Jews took twelve men strong and
able and made them to hold the standards by sixes, and they
were set before the judgement-seat of the governor; and Pilate
said to the messenger: Take him out of the judgement hall
(*praetorium*) and bring him in again after what manner thou wilt.
And Jesus went out of the judgement hall, he and the messenger.
And Pilate called unto him them that before held the images,
and said unto them: I have sworn by the safety of Caesar that
if the standards bow not when Jesus entereth in, I will cut off
your heads.

And the governor commanded Jesus to enter in the second
time. And the messenger did after the former manner and
besought Jesus much that he would walk upon his kerchief; and
he walked upon it and entered in. And when he had entered, the
standards bowed themselves again and did reverence unto Jesus.

II

1 Now when Pilate saw it he was afraid, and sought to rise up
from the judgement-seat. And while he yet thought to rise up,
his wife sent unto him, saying: Have thou nothing to do with
this just man, for I have suffered many things because of him by
night. And Pilate called unto him all the Jews, and said unto
them: Ye know that my wife feareth God and favoureth rather
the customs of the Jews, with you? They say unto him: Yea,
we know it. Pilate saith unto them: Lo, my wife hath sent unto
me, saying: Have thou nothing to do with this just man: for I
have suffered many things because of him by night. But the Jews
answered and said unto Pilate: Said we not unto thee that he is
a sorcerer? behold, he hath sent a vision of a dream unto thy wife.

2 And Pilate called Jesus unto him and said to him: What
is it that these witness against thee? speakest thou nothing? But
Jesus said: If they had not had power they would have spoken
nothing; for every man hath power over his own mouth, to
speak good or evil: they shall see *to it*.

3 The elders of the Jews answered and said unto Jesus: What
shall we see? Firstly, that thou wast born of fornication;
secondly, that thy birth in Bethlehem was *the cause of* the slaying
of children; thirdly, that thy father Joseph and thy mother Mary
fled into Egypt because they had no confidence before the people.

4 Then said certain of them that stood by, devout men of
the Jews: We say not that he came of fornication; but we know
that Joseph was betrothed unto Mary, and he was not born of
fornication. Pilate saith unto those Jews which said that he
came of fornication: This your saying is not true, for there were
espousals, as these also say which are of your nation. Annas and
Caiaphas say unto Pilate: The whole multitude of us cry out

that he was born of fornication, and we are not believed: but these are proselytes and disciples of his. And Pilate called Annas and Caiaphas unto him and said to them: What be proselytes? They say unto him: They were born children of Greeks, and now are they become Jews. Then said they which said that he was not born of fornication, even Lazarus, Asterius, Antonius, Jacob, Amnes, Zenas, Samuel, Isaac, Phinees, Crispus, Agrippa, and Judas : We were not born proselytes (are not Greeks, *Copt.*), but we are children of Jews and we speak the truth ; for verily we were present at the espousals of Joseph and Mary.

5 And Pilate called unto him those twelve men which said that he was not born of fornication, and saith unto them: I adjure you by the safety of Caesar, are these things true which ye have said, that he was not born of fornication? They say unto Pilate: We have a law that we swear not, because it is sin: but let them swear by the safety of Caesar that it is not as we have said, and we will be guilty of death. Pilate saith to Annas and Caiaphas: Answer ye nothing to these things? Annas and Caiaphas say unto Pilate: These twelve men are believed *which say* that he was not born of fornication, *but* the whole multitude of us cry out that he was born of fornication, and is a sorcerer, and saith that he is the Son of God and a king, and we are not believed.

6 And Pilate commanded the whole multitude to go out, saving the twelve men which said that he was not born of fornication, and he commanded Jesus to be set apart: and Pilate saith unto them: For what cause do they desire to put him to death? They say unto Pilate: They have jealousy, because he healeth on the sabbath day. Pilate saith: For a good work do they desire to put him to death? They say unto him: Yea.

III

1 And Pilate was filled with indignation and went forth without the judgement hall and saith unto them: I call the Sun to witness that I find no fault in this man. The Jews answered and said to the governor: If this man were not a malefactor we would not have delivered him unto thee. And Pilate said: Take ye him and judge him according to your law. The Jews said unto Pilate: It is not lawful for us to put any man to death. Pilate said: Hath God forbidden you to slay, and allowed me?

2 And Pilate went in again into the judgement hall and called Jesus apart and said unto him: Art thou the King of the Jews? Jesus answered and said to Pilate: Sayest thou this thing of thyself, or did others tell it thee of me? Pilate answered Jesus: Am I also a Jew? thine own nation and the chief priests have delivered thee unto me: what hast thou done? Jesus answered: My kingdom is not of this world; for if my kingdom were of this

world, my servants would have striven that I should not be delivered to the Jews: but now is my kingdom not from hence. Pilate said unto him: Art thou a king, then? Jesus answered him: Thou sayest that I am a king; for for this cause was I born and am come, that every one that is of the truth should hear my voice. Pilate saith unto him: What is truth? Jesus saith unto him: Truth is of heaven. Pilate saith: Is there not truth upon earth? Jesus saith unto Pilate: Thou seest how that they which speak the truth are judged of them that have authority upon earth.

IV

1 And Pilate left Jesus in the judgement hall and went forth to the Jews and said unto them: I find no fault in him. The Jews say unto him: This man said: I am able to destroy this temple and in three days to build it up. Pilate saith: What temple? The Jews say: That which Solomon built in forty and six years, but which this man saith he will destroy and build it in three days. Pilate saith unto them: I am guiltless of the blood of this just man: see ye to it. The Jews say: His blood be upon us and on our children.

2 And Pilate called the elders and the priests and Levites unto him and said to them secretly: Do not so: for there is nothing worthy of death whereof ye have accused him, for your accusation is concerning healing and profaning of the sabbath. The elders and the priests and Levites say: If a man blaspheme against Caesar, is he worthy of death or no? Pilate saith: He is worthy of death. The Jews say unto Pilate: If a man be worthy of death if he blaspheme against Caesar, this man hath blasphemed against God.

3 Then the governor commanded all the Jews to go out from the judgement hall, and he called Jesus to him and saith unto him: What shall I do with thee? Jesus saith unto Pilate: *Do* as it hath been given thee. Pilate saith: How hath it been given? Jesus saith: Moses and the prophets did foretell concerning my death and rising again. Now the Jews inquired by stealth and heard, and they say unto Pilate: What needest thou to hear further of this blasphemy? Pilate saith unto the Jews: If this word be of blasphemy, take ye him for his blasphemy, and bring him into your synagogue and judge him according to your law. The Jews say unto Pilate: It is contained in our law, that if a man sin against a man, he is worthy to receive forty stripes save one: but he that blasphemeth against God, that he should be stoned with stoning.

4 Pilate saith unto them: Take ye him and avenge yourselves of him in what manner ye will. The Jews say unto Pilate: We will that he be crucified. Pilate saith : He deserveth not to be crucified.

5 Now as the governor looked round about upon the multitude of the Jews which stood by, he beheld many of the Jews weeping, and said : Not all the multitude desire that he should be put to death. The elder of the Jews said : To this end have the whole multitude of us come hither, that he should be put to death. Pilate saith to the Jews : Wherefore should he die ? The Jews said : Because he called himself the Son of God, and a king.

V

1 But a certain man, Nicodemus, a Jew, *came and* stood before the governor and said: I beseech thee, good (pious) *lord*, bid me speak a few words. Pilate saith: Say *on*. Nicodemus saith: I said unto the elders and the priests and Levites and unto all the multitude of the Jews in the synagogue: Wherefore contend ye with this man ? This man doeth many and wonderful signs, which no man hath done, neither will do: let him alone and contrive not any evil against him: if the signs which he doeth are of God, they will stand, but if they be of men, they will come to nought. For verily Moses, when he was sent of God into Egypt did many signs, which God commanded him to do before Pharaoh, king of Egypt; and there were there *certain* men, servants of Pharaoh, Jannes and Jambres, and they also did signs not a few, *of them* which Moses did, and the Egyptians held them as gods, even Jannes and Jambres: and whereas the signs which they did were not of God, they perished and those also that believed on them. And now let this man go, for he is not worthy of death.

2 The Jews say unto Nicodemus: Thou didst become his disciple and thou speakest on his behalf. Nicodemus saith unto them: Is the governor also become his disciple, that he speaketh on his behalf ? did not Caesar appoint him unto this dignity? And the Jews were raging and gnashing their teeth against Nicodemus. Pilate saith unto them: Wherefore gnash ye your teeth against him, whereas ye have heard the truth ? The Jews say unto Nicodemus: Mayest thou receive his truth and his portion. Nicodemus saith: Amen, Amen: may I receive it as ye have said.

VI

1 Now one of the Jews came forward [1] and besought the governor that he might speak a word. The governor saith: If thou wilt say aught, speak on. And the Jew said: Thirty and eight years lay I on a bed in suffering of pains, and at the coming of Jesus many that were possessed and laid with divers diseases

[1] 'Came forward', *lit.* 'leaped'. The word is said to be technically used for the coming forward of a witness.

were healed by him, and certain (faithful) young men took
pity on me and carried me with my bed and brought me unto
him; and when Jesus saw me he had compassion, and spake
a word unto me: Take up thy bed and walk. And I took up
my bed and walked. The Jews say unto Pilate: Ask of him what
day it was whereon he was healed? ⟨Pilate said unto him that
was healed of his sickness: Tell *me* truly what day it was whereon
he healed thee. *Copt. only.*⟩ He that was healed saith: On the
sabbath. The Jews say: Did we not inform thee so, that upon
the sabbath he healeth and casteth out devils?

2 And another Jew came forward and said: [1] I was born blind:
I heard words but I saw no man's face: and as Jesus passed by
I cried with a loud voice: Have mercy on me, O son of David.
And he took pity on me and put his hands upon mine eyes and
I received sight immediately.[2]

And another Jew came forward and said: I was bowed and
he made me straight with a word. And another said: I was
a leper, and he healed me with a word.

VII

And a certain woman named Bernice (Beronice *Copt.*, Veronica
Lat.) crying out from afar off said: I had an issue of blood and
I touched the hem of his garment, and the flowing of my blood
was stayed which I had twelve years. The Jews say: We have
a law that a woman shall not come to give testimony.

VIII

And certain others, even a multitude both of men and women,
cried out, saying: This man is a prophet and the devils are
subject unto him. Pilate saith to them which said: The devils
are subject unto him: Wherefore were not your teachers also
subject unto him? They say unto Pilate: We know not. Others
also said: He raised up Lazarus which was dead out of his tomb
after four days. And the governor was afraid and said unto all
the multitude of the Jews: Wherefore will ye shed innocent
blood?

IX

1 And he called unto him Nicodemus and those twelve men
which said that he was not born of fornication, and said unto
them: What shall I do, for there riseth sedition among the

[1] MS. J has, 'Another said with tears'.
[2] After the blind man, MS. J has, 'Another, a dumb man, said:
I was without speech and he touched my tongue and immediately
I was healed.'

people? They say unto him: We know not; let them see to it.
Again Pilate called for all the multitude of the Jews and saith:
Ye know that ye have a custom that at the feast of unleavened
bread *I* should release unto you a prisoner. Now I have a
prisoner under condemnation in the prison, a murderer, Barabbas
by name, and this Jesus also which standeth before you, in whom
I find no fault: Whom will ye that I release unto you? But
they cried out: Barabbas. Pilate saith: What shall I do then
with Jesus who is called Christ? The Jews say: Let him be
crucified. But certain of the Jews answered: Thou art not a
friend of Caesar's if thou let this man go; for he called himself
the Son of God and a king: thou wilt therefore have him for
king and not Caesar.

2 And Pilate was wroth and said unto the Jews: Your nation
is alway seditious and ye rebel against your benefactors. The
Jews say: Against what benefactors? Pilate saith: According
as I have heard, your God brought you out of Egypt out of hard
bondage, and led you safe through the sea as by dry land, and
in the wilderness he nourished you with manna and gave you
quails, and gave you water to drink out of a rock, and gave
unto you a law. And in all these things ye provoked your
God to anger, and sought out a molten calf, and angered your
God and he sought to slay you: and Moses made supplication
for you and ye were not put to death. And now ye do accuse
me that I hate the king (emperor). 3 And he rose up from the
judgment-seat and sought to go forth. And the Jews cried out,
saying: We know our king, even Caesar and not Jesus. For
indeed the wise men brought gifts from the east unto him as
unto a king, and when Herod heard from the wise men that
a king was born, he sought to slay him; and when his father
Joseph knew that, he took him and his mother and they fled
into Egypt. And when Herod heard it he destroyed the children
of the Hebrews that were born in Bethlehem.

4 And when Pilate heard these words he was afraid. And
Pilate silenced the multitude, because they cried *still*, and said
unto them: So, then, this is he whom Herod sought? The Jews
say: Yea, this is he. And Pilate took water and washed his
hands before the sun, saying: I am innocent of the blood of this
just man: see ye to it. Again the Jews cried out: His blood
be upon us and upon our children.

5 Then Pilate commanded the veil to be drawn before the
judgement-seat whereon he sat, and saith unto Jesus: Thy nation
hath convicted thee (accused thee) as *being* a king: therefore
have I decreed that thou shouldest first be scourged according to
the law of the pious emperors, and thereafter hanged upon the
cross in the garden wherein thou wast taken: and let Dysmas and
Gestas the two malefactors be crucified with thee.

X

1 And Jesus went forth of the judgement hall and the two malefactors with him. And when they were come to the place they stripped him of his garments and girt him with a linen cloth and put a crown of thorns about his head: likewise also they hanged up the two malefactors.[1] But Jesus said: Father, forgive them, for they know not what they do. And the soldiers divided his garments among them.

And the people stood looking upon him, and the chief priests and the rulers with them derided him, saying: He saved others, let him save himself: if he be the son of God [let him come down from the cross]. And the soldiers also mocked him, coming and offering him vinegar with gall; and they said: If thou be the King of the Jews, save thyself.

And Pilate after the sentence commanded his accusation to be written for a title in letters of Greek and Latin and Hebrew, according to the saying of the Jews: that he was the King of the Jews.

2 And one of the malefactors that were hanged [by name Gestas] spake unto him, saying: If thou be the Christ, save thyself, and us. But Dysmas answering rebuked him, saying: Dost thou not at all fear God, seeing thou art in the same condemnation? and we indeed justly, for we receive the due reward of our deeds; but this man hath done nothing amiss. And he said unto Jesus: Remember me, Lord, in thy kingdom. And Jesus said unto him: Verily, verily, I say unto thee, that to-day thou shalt be (art) with me in paradise.

XI

1 And it was about the sixth hour, and there was darkness over the land until the ninth hour, for the sun was darkened: and the veil of the temple was rent asunder in the midst. And Jesus called with a loud voice and said: Father, baddach ephkid rouel,[2] which is interpreted: Into thy hands I commend my spirit. And having thus said he gave up the ghost. And when the centurion saw what was done, he glorified God, saying: This man was righteous. And all the multitudes that had come

---

[1] Coptic, Latin, and others have, 'Dysmas on the right and Gestas on the left'. MS. J has, 'Gestas on the right and Dysmas on the left', and makes Gestas the penitent thief. There is some evidence supporting this in the original story: Dumachus in the Arabic gospel is the bad thief, Titus the good one. But the view that Dysmas was the good one has prevailed.

[2] A Coptic fragment has: 'Father, Abi (= my Father), Adach Ephkidrou, Adonai Aroa, Sabel, Louel, Eloeï, Elemas, Abakdanei (Eli, Eli, lama sabachthani), Orioth, Mioth, Ouaath, Soun, Perineth, Tothat. The prayer of the Saviour upon the cross concerning Adam.'

to the sight, when they beheld what was done smote their breasts and returned.

2 But the centurion reported unto the governor the things that had come to pass: and when the governor and his wife heard, they were sore vexed, and neither ate nor drank that day. And Pilate sent for the Jews and said unto them: Did ye see that which came to pass? But they said: There was an eclipse of the sun after the accustomed sort.

3 And his acquaintance had stood afar off, and the women which came with him from Galilee, beholding these things. But a certain man named Joseph, being a counsellor, of the city of Arimathaea, who also himself looked for the kingdom of God, this man went to Pilate and begged the body of Jesus. And he took it down and wrapped it in a clean linen cloth and laid it in a hewn sepulchre wherein was never man yet laid.

XII

1 Now when the Jews heard that Joseph had begged the body of Jesus, they sought for him and for the twelve men which said that Jesus was not born of fornication, and for Nicodemus and many others which had come forth before Pilate and declared his good works. But all they hid themselves, and Nicodemus only was seen of them, for he was a ruler of the Jews. And Nicodemus said unto them: How came ye into the synagogue? The Jews say unto him: How didst thou come into the synagogue? for thou art confederate with him, and his portion shall be with thee in the life to come. Nicodemus saith: Amen, Amen. Likewise Joseph also came forth and said unto them: Why is it that ye are vexed against me, for that I begged the body of Jesus? behold I have laid it in my new tomb, having wrapped it in clean linen, and I rolled a stone over the door of the cave. And ye have not dealt well with the just one, for ye repented not when ye had crucified him, but ye also pierced him with a spear.

But the Jews took hold on Joseph and commanded him to be put in safeguard until the first day of the week: and they said unto him: Know thou that the time alloweth us not to do anything against thee, because the sabbath dawneth: but know that thou shalt not obtain burial, but we will give thy flesh unto the fowls of the heaven. Joseph saith unto them: This is the word of Goliath the boastful which reproached the living God and the holy David. For God said by the prophet: Vengeance is mine, and I will recompense, saith the Lord. And now, lo, one that was uncircumcised, but circumcised in heart, took water and washed his hands before the sun, saying: I am innocent of the blood of this just person: see ye to it. And ye answered Pilate and said: His blood be upon us and upon our

children. And now I fear lest the wrath of the Lord come upon
you and upon your children, as ye have said. But when the
Jews heard these words they waxed bitter in soul, and caught
hold on Joseph and took him and shut him up in an house wherein
was no window, and guards were set at the door: and they sealed
the door of the place where Joseph was shut up.[1]

2 And upon the sabbath day the rulers of the synagogue and
the priests and the Levites made an ordinance that all men
should appear in the synagogue on the first day of the week.
And all the multitude rose up early and took council in the
synagogue by what death they should kill him. And when the
council was set they commanded him to be brought with great
dishonour. And when they had opened the door they found
him not. And all the people were beside themselves and
amazed, because they found the seals closed, and Caiaphas had
the key. And they durst not any more lay hands upon them
that had spoken in the behalf of Jesus before Pilate.

XIII

1 And while they yet sat in the synagogue and marvelled
because of Joseph, there came certain of the guard which the
Jews had asked of Pilate to keep the sepulchre of Jesus lest
peradventure his disciples should come and steal him away.
And they spake and declared unto the rulers of the synagogue
and the priests and the Levites that which had come to pass:
how that there was a great earthquake, and we saw an angel
descend from heaven, and he rolled away the stone from the
mouth of the cave, and sat upon it. And he did shine like snow
and like lightning, and we were sore afraid and lay as dead men.
And we heard the voice of the angel speaking with the women
which waited at the sepulchre, saying: Fear ye not: for I know
that ye seek Jesus which was crucified. He is not here: he is
risen, as he said. Come, see the place where the Lord lay, and
go quickly and say unto his disciples that he is risen from the
dead, and is in Galilee.

2 The Jews say: With what women spake he? They of the
guard say: We know not who they were. The Jews say: At
what hour was it? They of the guard say: At midnight. The
Jews say: And wherefore did ye not take the women? They of
the guard say: We were become as dead men through fear, and
we looked not to see the light of the day; how then could we
take them? The Jews say: As the Lord liveth, we believe you
not. They of the guard say unto the Jews: So many signs saw
ye in that man, and ye believed not, how then should ye believe
us? verily ye sware rightly 'as the Lord liveth', for he liveth

[1] MS. J alone adds: 'and sealed the door with the finger-ring of
Caiaphas.'

indeed. Again they of the guard say: We have heard that ye shut up him that begged the body of Jesus, and that ye sealed the door; and when ye had opened it ye found him not. Give ye therefore Joseph and we will give you Jesus. The Jews say: Joseph is departed unto his own city. They of the guard say unto the Jews: Jesus also is risen, as we have heard of the angel, and he is in Galilee.

3 And when the Jews heard these words they were sore afraid, saying: *Take heed* lest this report be heard and all men incline unto Jesus. And the Jews took counsel and laid down much money and gave it to the soldiers, saying: Say ye: While we slept his disciples came by night and stole him away. And if this come to the governor's hearing we will persuade him and secure you. And they took *the money* and did as they were instructed. [And this their saying was published abroad among all men. *Lat.*]

XIV

1 Now a certain priest *named* Phinees and Addas a teacher and Aggaeus (Ogias *Copt.*, Egias *Lat.*) a Levite came down from Galilee unto Jerusalem and told the rulers of the synagogue and the priests and the Levites, *saying*: We saw Jesus and his disciples sitting upon the mountain which is called Mamilch (Mambre or Malech *Lat.*, Mabrech *Copt.*), and he said unto his disciples: Go into all the world and preach unto every creature (the whole creation): he that believeth and is baptized shall be saved, but he that disbelieveth shall be condemned. [And these signs shall follow upon them that believe: in my name they shall cast out devils, they shall speak with new tongues, they shall take up serpents, and if they drink any deadly thing it shall not hurt them: they shall lay hands upon the sick and they shall recover.] And while Jesus yet spake unto his disciples we saw him taken up into heaven.

2 The elders and the priests and Levites say: Give glory to the God of Israel and make confession unto him: did ye indeed (*or* that ye did) hear and see those things which ye have told us? They that told them say: As the Lord God of our fathers Abraham, Isaac, and Jacob liveth, we did hear these things and we saw him taken up into heaven. The elders and the priests and the Levites say unto them: Came ye for this end, that ye might tell us, or came ye to pay your vows unto God? And they say: To pay our vows unto God. The elders and the chief priests and the Levites say unto them: If ye came to pay your vows unto God, to what purpose is this idle tale which ye have babbled before all the people? Phinees the priest and Addas the teacher and Aggaeus the Levite say unto the rulers of the synagogue

and priests and Levites: If these words which we have spoken and seen be sin, lo, we are before you: do unto us as seemeth good in your eyes. And they took the *book of the* law and adjured them that they should no more tell any man these words: and they gave them to eat and to drink, and put them out of the city: moreover they gave them money, and three men to go with them, and they set them on their way as far as Galilee, and they departed in peace.

3 Now when these men were departed into Galilee, the chief priests and the rulers of the synagogue and the elders gathered together in the synagogue, and shut the gate, and lamented with a great lamentation, saying: What is this sign which is come to pass in Israel? But Annas and Caiaphas said: Wherefore are ye troubled? why weep ye? Know ye not that his disciples gave much gold unto them that kept the sepulchre and taught them to say that an angel came down and rolled away the stone from the door of the sepulchre? But the priests and the elders said : Be it so, that his disciples did steal away his body ; but how is his soul entered into his body, and how abideth he in Galilee ? But they could not answer these things, and hardly in the end said : It is not lawful for us to believe the uncircumcised. [*Lat.* (and *Copt.*, and *Arm.*) : Ought we to believe the soldiers, that an angel came down from heaven and rolled away the stone from the door of the sepulchre ? but in truth his disciples gave . . . sepulchre. Know ye not that it is not lawful for Jews to believe any word of the uncircumcised, knowing that they who received much gold from us have spoken according as we taught them.]

XV

1 And Nicodemus rose up and stood before the council, saying: Ye say well. Know ye not, O people of the Lord, the men that came down out of Galilee, that they fear God and are men of substance, hating covetousness (a lie, *Lat.*), men of peace? And they have told you with an oath, *saying*: We saw Jesus upon the mount Mamilch with his disciples and that he taught them all things that ye heard of them, and, *say they*, we saw him taken up into heaven. And no man asked them in what manner he was taken up. For like as the book of the holy scriptures hath taught us that Elias also was taken up into heaven, and Eliseus cried out with a loud voice, and Elias cast his hairy cloak upon Eliseus, and Eliseus cast the cloak upon Jordan and passed over and went unto Jericho. And the sons of the prophets met him and said: Eliseus, where is thy lord Elias ? and he said that he was taken up into heaven. And they said unto Eliseus: Hath not a spirit caught him up and cast him upon one of the mountains ? but let us take our servants with us and seek after him. And they persuaded Eliseus and he went with them, and they

sought him three days and found him not: and they knew that he had been taken up. And now hearken unto me, and let us send into all the coasts (*al.* mountains) of Israel and see whether the Christ were not taken up by a spirit and cast upon one of the mountains. And this saying pleased them all: and they sent into all the coasts (mountains, *Lat.*) and sought Jesus and found him not. But they found Joseph in Arimathaea, and no man durst lay hands upon him.

2 And they told the elders and the priests and the Levites, *saying*: We went about throughout all the coasts of Israel, and we found not Jesus; but Joseph we found in Arimathaea.

And when they heard of Joseph they rejoiced and gave glory to the God of Israel. And the rulers of the synagogue and the priests and the Levites took counsel how they should meet with Joseph, and they took a volume of paper and wrote unto Joseph these words:

Peace be unto thee. We know that we have sinned against God and against thee, and we have prayed unto the God of Israel that thou shouldest vouchsafe to come unto thy fathers and unto thy children (*Lat.* But thou didst pray unto the God of Israel, and he delivered thee out of our hands. Now therefore vouchsafe, &c.) for we are all troubled, because when we opened the door we found thee not: and we know that we devised an evil counsel against thee, but the Lord helped thee. And the Lord himself made of none effect (scattered) our counsel against thee, O father Joseph, thou that art honourable among all the people.

3 And they chose out of all Israel seven men that were friends of Joseph, whom Joseph also himself accounted his friends, and the rulers of the synagogue and the priests and the Levites said unto them: See: if he receive our epistle and read it, know that he will come with you unto us: but if he read it not, know that he is vexed with us, and salute ye him in peace and return unto us. And they blessed the men and let them go.

And the men came unto Joseph and did him reverence, and said unto him: Peace be unto thee. And he said: Peace be unto you and unto all the people of Israel. And they gave him the book of the epistle, and Joseph received it and read it and embraced (*or* kissed) the epistle and blessed God and said: Blessed be the Lord God, which hath redeemed Israel from shedding innocent blood; and blessed be the Lord, which sent his angel and sheltered me under his wings. (And he kissed them) and set a table before them, and they did eat and drink and lay there.

4 And they rose up early and prayed: and Joseph saddled his she-ass and went with the men, and they came unto the holy city, *even* Jerusalem. And all the people came to meet Joseph and cried: Peace be to thine entering-in. And he said unto all the people: Peace be unto you, and all the people

kissed him. And the people prayed with Joseph, and they were
astonished at the sight of him.

And Nicodemus received him into his house and made a great
feast, and called Annas and Caiaphas and the elders and the
priests and the Levites unto his house. And they made merry,
eating and drinking with Joseph. And when they had sung an
hymn (*or* blessed God) every man went unto his house. But
Joseph abode in the house of Nicodemus.

5 And on the morrow, which was the preparation, the rulers
of the synagogue and the priests and the Levites rose up early
and came to the house of Nicodemus, and Nicodemus met them
and said: Peace be unto you. And they said : Peace be unto thee
and to Joseph and unto all thy house and to all the house of
Joseph. And he brought them into his house. And the whole
council was set, and Joseph sat between Annas and Caiaphas;
and no man durst speak unto him a word. And Joseph said:
Why is it that ye have called me? And they beckoned unto
Nicodemus that he should speak unto Joseph. And Nicodemus
opened his mouth and said unto Joseph: Father, thou knowest
that the reverend doctors and the priests and the Levites seek
to learn a matter of thee. And Joseph said: Inquire ye. And
Annas and Caiaphas took the *book of the* law and adjured Joseph,
saying: Give glory to the God of Israel and make confession
unto him: [for Achar, when he was adjured of the prophet Jesus
(Joshua), forsware not himself but declared unto him all things,
and hid not a word from him: thou therefore also hide not from
us so much as a word. And Joseph: I will not hide one word
from you.][1] And they said unto him: We were greatly vexed
because thou didst beg the body of Jesus and wrappedst it in
a clean linen cloth and didst lay him in a tomb. And for this
cause we put thee in safeguard in an house wherein was no
window, and we put keys and seals upon the doors, and guards
did keep the place wherein thou wast shut up. And on the
first day of the week we opened it and found thee not, and we
were sore troubled, and amazement fell upon all the people of
the Lord until yesterday. Now, therefore, declare unto us what
befell thee.

6 And Joseph said: On the preparation day about the tenth
hour ye did shut me up, and I continued there the whole sabbath.
And at midnight as I stood and prayed the house wherein ye
shut me up was taken up by the four corners, and I saw as it
were a flashing of light in mine eyes, and being filled with fear
I fell to the earth. And one took me by the hand and removed
me from the place whereon I had fallen; and moisture of water
was shed *on me* from my head unto my feet, and an odour of
ointment came about my nostrils. And he wiped my face and
kissed me and said unto me: Fear not, Joseph: open thine eyes

[1] om. *Latt., Arm.*

and see who it is that speaketh with thee. And I looked up and saw Jesus and I trembled, and supposed that it was a spirit: and I said the commandments: and he said them with me. And [as] [1] ye are not ignorant that a spirit, if it meet any man and hear the commandments, straightway fleeth. And when I perceived that he said them with me, I said unto him: Rabbi Elias? And he said unto me: I am not Elias. And I said unto him: Who art thou, Lord? And he said unto me: I am Jesus, whose body thou didst beg of Pilate, and didst clothe me in clean linen and cover my face with a napkin, and lay me in thy new cave and roll a great stone upon the door of the cave. And I said to him that spake with me: Show me the place where I laid thee. And he brought me and showed me the place where I laid him, and the linen cloth lay therein, and the napkin that was upon his face. And I knew that it was Jesus. And he took me by the hand and set me in the midst of mine house, the doors being shut, and laid me upon my bed and said unto me: Peace be unto thee. And he kissed me and said unto me: Until forty days *be ended* go not out of thine house: for behold I go unto my brethren into Galilee.

XVI

1 And when the rulers of the synagogue and the priests and the Levites heard these words of Joseph they became as dead men and fell to the ground, and they fasted until the ninth hour. And Nicodemus with Joseph comforted Annas and Caiaphas and the priests and the Levites, saying: Rise up and stand on your feet and taste bread and strengthen your souls, for to-morrow is the sabbath of the Lord. And they rose up and prayed unto God and did eat and drink, and departed every man to his house.

2 And on the sabbath the (*al.* our) teachers and the priests and Levites sat and questioned one another and said: What is this wrath that is come upon us? for we know his father and his mother. Levi the teacher saith: I know that his parents feared God and kept not back their vows and paid tithes three times a year. And when Jesus was born, his parents brought him up unto this place and gave sacrifices and burnt-offerings to God. And [when] the great teacher Symeon took him into his arms and said: Now lettest thou thy servant, Lord, depart in peace, for mine eyes have seen thy salvation which thou hast prepared before the face of all peoples, a light to lighten the Gentiles and the glory of thy people Israel. And Symeon blessed them and said unto Mary his mother: I give thee good tidings concerning this child. And Mary said: Good, my lord? And Symeon said to her: Good. Behold, he is set for the fall and rising again of many in Israel, and for a sign spoken against: and a sword shall

[1] om. *Latt.*

pierce through thine own heart also, that the thoughts of many hearts may be revealed.

3 They say unto Levi the teacher: How knowest thou these things? Levi saith unto them: Know ye not that from him I did learn the law? The council say unto him: We would see thy father. And they sent after his father, and asked of him, and he said to them: Why believed ye not my son? the blessed and righteous Symeon, he did teach him the law. The council saith: Rabbi Levi, is the word true which thou hast spoken? And he said: It is true.

Then the rulers of the synagogue and the priests and the Levites said among themselves: Come, let us send into Galilee unto the three men which came and told us of his teaching and his taking-up, and let them tell us how they saw him taken up. And this word pleased them all, and they sent the three men which before had gone with them into Galilee and said to them: Say unto Rabbi Addas and Rabbi Phineës and Rabbi Aggaeus: peace be to you and to all that are with you. Inasmuch as great questioning hath arisen in the council, we have sent unto you to call you unto this holy place of Jerusalem.

4 And the men went into Galilee and found them sitting and meditating upon the law, and saluted them in peace. And the men that were in Galilee said unto them that were come to them: Peace be upon all Israel. And they said: Peace be unto you. Again they said unto them: Wherefore are ye come? And they that were sent said: The council calleth you unto the holy city Jerusalem. And when the men heard that they were bidden by the council, they prayed to God and sat down to meat with the men and did eat and drink, and rose up and came in peace unto Jerusalem.

5 And on the morrow the council was set in the synagogue, and they examined them, saying: Did ye in very deed see Jesus sitting upon the mount Mamilch, as he taught his eleven disciples, and saw ye him taken up? And the men answered them and said: Even as we saw him taken up, even so did we tell it unto you.

6 Annas saith: Set them apart from one another, and let us see if their word agreeth. And they set them apart one from another, and they call Addas first and say unto him: How sawest thou Jesus taken up? Addas saith: While he yet sat upon the Mount Mamilch and taught his disciples, we saw a cloud that overshadowed him and his disciples: and the cloud carried him up into heaven, and his disciples lay (al. prayed, lying) on their faces upon the earth. And they called Phineës the priest, and questioned him also, saying: How sawest thou Jesus taken up? And he spake in like manner. And again they asked Aggaeus, and he also spake in like manner. And the council said: It is contained in the law of Moses: At the mouth of two or three shall every word be established.

Abuthem (Bouthem *Gr.*, Abudem *Lat.*, Abuden, Abuthen *Arm.*, om. *Copt.*) the teacher saith: It is written in the law: Enoch walked with God and is not, because God took him. Jaeirus the teacher said: Also we have heard of the death of the holy Moses, and have not seen him; for it is written in the law of the Lord: And Moses died at the mouth of the Lord, and no man knew of his sepulchre unto this day. And Rabbi Levi said: Wherefore was it that Rabbi Symeon said when he saw Jesus: Behold, this *child* is set for the fall and rising again of many in Israel and for a sign spoken against? And Rabbi Isaac said: It is written in the law: Behold I send my messenger before thy face, which shall go before thee to keep thee in every good way, for my name is named thereon.[1]

7 Then said Annas and Caiaphas: Ye have well said those things which are written in the law of Moses, that no man saw the death of Enoch, and no man hath named the death of Moses. But Jesus spake before Pilate, and *we know* that we saw him receive buffets and spittings upon his face, and that the soldiers put on him a crown of thorns, and that he was scourged and received condemnation from Pilate, and that he was crucified at *the place of* a skull and two thieves with him, and that they gave him vinegar to drink with gall, and that Longinus the soldier pierced his side with a spear, and that Joseph our honourable father begged his body, and that, as he saith, he rose again, and that (*lit.* as) the three teachers say : We saw him taken up into heaven, and that Rabbi Levi spake and testified to the things which were spoken by Rabbi Symeon, and that he said : Behold this *child* is set for the fall and rising again of many in Israel and for a sign spoken against.

And all the teachers said unto all the people of the Lord: If this hath come to pass from the Lord, and it is marvellous in our eyes, ye shall surely know, O house of Jacob, that it is written: Cursed is every one that hangeth upon a tree. And another scripture teacheth: The gods which made not the heaven and the earth shall perish.

And the priests and the Levites said one to another: If his memorial *endure* until the Sommos (*Copt.* Soum) which is called Jobel (i. e. the Jubilee), know ye that he will prevail for ever and raise up for himself a new people.

Then the rulers of the synagogue and the priests and the Levites admonished all Israel, saying: Cursed is that man who shall worship that which man's hand hath made, and cursed is the man who shall worship creatures beside the Creator. And all the people said: Amen, Amen.

And all the people sang an hymn unto the Lord and said: Blessed be the Lord who hath given rest unto the people of

[1] *Copt.* for my name is in thee. *Lat.* for I have brought the (a) new name thereof, (*or* his new name): *corrupt.*

Israel according to all that he spake. There hath not one word
fallen to the ground of all his good saying which he spake unto
his servant Moses. The Lord our God be with us as he was with
our fathers: let him not forsake us. And let him not destroy us
from turning our heart unto him, from walking in all his ways
and keeping his statutes and his judgements which he commanded
our fathers. And the Lord shall be King over all the earth in
that day. And there shall be one Lord and his name one, even
the Lord our King: he shall save us.

There is none like unto thee, O Lord. Great art thou, O Lord,
and great is thy name.

Heal us, O Lord, by thy power, and we shall be healed: save
us, Lord, and we shall be saved: for we are thy portion and
thine inheritance.

And the Lord will not forsake his people for his great name's
sake, for the Lord hath begun to make us to be his people.

And when they had all sung *this* hymn they departed every
man to his house, glorifying God. [For his is the glory, world
without end. Amen.]

There is a considerable divergence of the versions in the concluding
sections.

The Coptic agrees substantially with the Greek A as translated
above.

The Armenian β (rendered into Latin by Conybeare) has only two
clauses of the final hymn, thus:

Blessed be the Lord God who hath given rest unto all the
people of Israel according as he hath said. And let the Lord our
God be with us, as he was with our fathers.

And they went every man to his house praising God.

The Armenian α has (after ' the people said Amen (thrice) ').

And all the people sang an hymn unto the Lord and departed
every man to his house.

The Syriac ends at: the people said Amen (thrice).

The Latin, after 'a sign spoken against' has:

Then the teacher (Addas) said unto all the congregation:
If all the things which these have testified came to pass in
Jerusalem (*al.* Jesus), they are of God, and let them not be
marvellous in our eyes. The rulers of the synagogue and the
priests and the Levites said one to another: It is contained in
our law: His name shall be blessed for ever: his place shall
endure before the sun and his seat before the moon: and in him
shall all the tribes of the earth be blessed, and all nations shall
serve him: and kings shall come from afar worshipping and
magnifying him.

The Greek recension B, which abridges the latter part of the story
(after the Crucifixion) very extensively, has this for its last paragraph:

Then Annas and Caiaphas separated the three by one and

one, and questioned them in private singly. And they agreed, and the three of them told one tale. The chief priests answered and said: Our scripture saith that every word shall be established by two or three witnesses. Joseph therefore confessed that he tended him and buried him, with Nicodemus; and how it is true that he rose again.

This leads on to the opening words of Part II:

Joseph saith: And why marvel ye that Jesus is risen? &c.

The fact is that the two forms (Greek B and Latin) which have the Second Part—the Descent into Hell—attached to them, have been obliged on that account to modify the end of the First Part, so as to manage a plausible transition.

ACTS OF PILATE

PART I. RECENSION B OF THE GREEK

It has been said that this is a later working-over of the original text. No known copy of it is earlier than the fifteenth century, and the language in some of them is very mediaeval. A short review only of the principal additions to the story will be given here.

The title runs thus:

A narrative concerning the Passion of our Lord Jesus Christ and his holy Resurrection. Written by a Jew named Aeneas, which Nicodemus, a Roman toparch, translated out of the Hebrew tongue into the Roman speech.

In two copies there is this prologue:

After the kingdom of the Hebrews was dissolved, and four hundred years had gone by, and the Hebrews also were subject to the empire of the Romans, the Emperor of the Romans appointing them a king: afterward, when Tiberius Caesar wielded the sceptre of the Romans, in the eighteenth year of his reign, when he had appointed Herod king in Judaea, the son of that Herod who aforetime killed the children in Bethlehem: and when he had Pilate as governor in Jerusalem, and Annas and Caiaphas had the high-priesthood of Jerusalem; Nicodemus, a Roman toparch, called unto him a Jew named Aeneas, and sought to record the things that were done in Jerusalem in the days of Annas and Caiaphas concerning Christ: which also the Jew having done and delivered it to Nicodemus, he translated these things from the Hebrew writing into the Roman speech: and the matter of this history is thus:

(Where it will be noted that Nicodemus is no longer the Biblical personage, but a Roman official. Roman (Romaïc) speech means here not Latin but Greek, and the term is an indication of very late date.)

Cap. i begins:

When our Lord Jesus Christ had wrought many and great and unwonted wonders in Judaea, and for that cause was envied by the Hebrews: Pilate being governor in Jerusalem, and Annas and Caiaphas being high priests: there came certain of the Jews unto the same high priests, even Judas, Levi, Nephthalim, Alexander, Syrus, and many others, speaking against Christ; whom also those high priests sent to tell Pilate also these things.

The story follows the same lines as A, naturally, but with differences great and small; and the individual manuscripts often make large insertions.

Pilate gives his own mantle ($\mu\alpha\nu\delta\acute{\upsilon}\lambda\iota\sigma\nu$) to the messenger, whom one manuscript calls Rachaab.

The Hebrew words except Hosanna are eliminated: one manuscript then interpolates a notice of the call of the apostles and a great many of the miracles of the ministry, and brings the narrative down to the denial of Peter. Malchus, it says, was the one who buffeted Jesus.

Another manuscript, omitting all that has preceded, begins the story with the repentance of Judas. He brings the money back to the priests, and they abuse him at some length for his treachery. Then he casts down the money and leaves them.

And departing to his house to make a halter of rope to hang himself, he found his wife sitting and roasting a cock on a fire of coals or in a pan before eating it: and saith to her: Rise up, wife, and provide me a rope, for I would hang myself, as I deserve. But his wife said to him: Why sayest thou such things? And Judas saith to her: Know of a truth that I have wickedly betrayed my master Jesus to the evil-doers for Pilate to put him to death: but he will rise again on the third day, and woe unto us! And his wife said to him: Say not nor think not so: for as well as this cock that is roasting on the fire of coals can crow, just so well shall Jesus rise again, as thou sayest. And immediately at her word that cock spread his wings and crowed thrice. Then was Judas yet more convinced, and straightway made the halter of rope and hanged himself.

The rest of the story is as we know it.

This story of the cock has made its way into Latin and thence into many mediaeval vernacular legends. The Latin copies say that it is found 'in the books of the Greeks'.

In cap. ix the sending of Jesus to Herod is inserted: one of many harmonistic changes which this text makes, to include all that is told in the canonical Gospels.

In cap. x the Bearing of the Cross is greatly amplified. We have first of all Simon of Cyrene: 'They gave the cross unto him, not because they had compassion on Jesus and would lighten him of his burden, but desiring, as has been said, to kill him more quickly.' John followed with them, and then fled and went to the Mother of God (always called the Theotokos here) and told her. Her lament is given— and she and Martha and Mary Magdalene and Salome and the other women go to the place. John points out Jesus and the Virgin swoons and laments again. These lamentations are greatly expanded in one or other of the manuscripts. Dysmas is crucified on the right hand

and Gestas on the left. At the end of cap. x, where the words of the thieves are narrated, two of the three manuscripts used by Tischendorf insert the story of the meeting with Dysmas in Egypt. First we have the incident of the palm-tree bowing to give its fruit. Then the Holy Family meet Dysmas, who is struck with the beauty of Mary and of the child in her arms, adores them, and says, 'If God had a mother I would have said that thou art she'. He receives them into his house, and when he goes out hunting commends them to his wife's care. He has a leprous child who is always crying, and is healed by the water in which Jesus was washed. Dysmas hearing of this on his return is moved to do all he can to help Mary: and on the return from Egypt he aids them again, and Mary promises him a reward for his goodness. 'Therefore was he accounted worthy through the grace of the merciful God and his Mother . . . to bear witness upon the cross together with Christ.' [1]

In cap. xi the episode of Joseph's begging the body is expanded. The Virgin, in one copy, asks him to do this. In another he goes to Nicodemus, who will not accompany him to Pilate but is ready to help in the burial. There is a long address of Joseph to Pilate, every clause beginning with 'Give me this stranger'.

At the burial there is a final lamentation of the Virgin and one of Mary Magdalene, who says: 'Who shall make this known unto all the world? I will go alone to Rome unto Caesar: I will show him what evil Pilate hath done, consenting unto the wicked Jews.' This story of Mary Magdalene's going to Rome is one which appears in Byzantine chronicles and other late documents.

In cap. xii two of the copies mark a conclusion after the sealing of the tomb. In fact one of them actually ends here: the other has a doxology and colophon, but continues with xii. 2, 'When the Lord's day dawned the chief priests took counsel', &c.

The remaining chapters, xiii–xvi, are most drastically abridged, containing 147 lines of print as against 333 of recension A. The concluding paragraph has been translated above, and the text runs on, as is there shown, into Part II, the Descent into Hell. Among the variations from the A narrative, of which the object is not clear, is this, that the three witnesses of the Ascension are here called 'a priest named Phinees, a Levite named Aggaeus, and a soldier named Adas'.

ACTS OF PILATE
PART II. THE DESCENT INTO HELL

This writing, or the nucleus of it, the story of the Descent into Hell, was not originally part of the Acts of Pilate. It is—apart from its setting—probably an older document. When it was first attached to the Acts of Pilate is uncertain. The object of this prefatory note is to say that we have the text in three forms.

[1] See further on the Arabic Gospel, ch. xxiii, and note that the *Vita Rhythmica* (which draws on late Greek sources) has at l. 2234 a story of the Holy Family being captured by robbers, one of whom treats them kindly. Wounded robbers are healed by the water in which Jesus was washed.

1. Greek, only in late manuscripts of Recension B. Tischendorf used three.
2. Latin A, found in the majority, perhaps, of the Latin manuscripts. Be it noted that all the Latin manuscripts have both parts of the Acts of Pilate.
3. Latin B, rather an abridged text in the account of the Descent, differing in order of contents and in setting from A. But the opening section is far longer than either of the others.

There are no early versions except the Latin. The Coptic, Syriac, and Armenian contain Part I only.

The order of the story in the three recensions demands a note. Latin A and Greek go together. Latin B differs.

i. The two men (nameless in Greek) are found and induced to write their story.
ii. The story. A light shines in Hell. Adam, Esaias, Simeon speak (not in B). (In Greek, Abraham and Esaias.) John Baptist comes.
iii. Seth's story of the oil of mercy.
iv. Satan's dialogue with Hell.
v. First cry: Lift up the gates. David and Isaiah speak. Second cry. David speaks. Christ enters. (Greek, David speaks only once.)
vi. Address of Hell to Christ (not in B). Satan bound.
vii. Hell derides Satan.

viii. Christ greets Adam and takes all saints out of hell. David, Habacuc, Micheas speak (not in B). (Greek omits the prophecies.)
ix. They meet Enoch and Elias (not in B.).
x. They meet the thief.

xi. Conclusion.
xii. The two men vanish, &c.

i. The two men are found, write their story, and return to their tombs.
ii. The story. A light shines. A voice: Lift up the gates. Satan has the doors secured.

iii. Dialogue of Hell and Satan (A. iv).
iv. Seth's story.
v. Isaiah and John Baptist (A. ii).

vi. David and Jeremiah. Satan not allowed to leave hell.
vii. Cry: Lift up the gates. The good thief appears (A. x). Second cry.
viii. Doors broken. Christ enters. Satan bound.

ix. Christ greets Adam and Eve (not in A).
x. Sets up his cross in hell (not in A). Leaves hell. Conclusion.

In order to place the material fairly before readers it seems necessary to give all three texts. Here the Greek, which, like the rest of Recension B, is of late type, shall be relegated to the second place, and preference given to Latin A. The chapter- and verse-numberings are those of Tischendorf.

Latin A.

[Part I, cap. xvi, ends with words of the rulers of the synagogue, &c. All nations shall serve him, and kings shall come from afar worshipping and magnifying him. Part II, cap. i, runs on from this.]

I (XVII)

1 And Joseph arose and said unto Annas and Caiaphas: Truly and of right do ye marvel because ye have heard that Jesus hath been seen alive after death, and that he hath ascended into heaven. Nevertheless it is more marvellous that he rose not alone from the dead, but did raise up alive many other dead out

---

Greek. I (XVII)

[Part I ends in this text with words of the priests: Our scripture saith that every word shall be established at the mouths of two or three. Joseph therefore doth confess that he tended him and buried him, and how that it is true that he rose again.]

(Part II.) 1 Joseph saith: And why marvel ye that Jesus rose again. This is not marvellous: but this is marvellous, that he rose not alone, but raised up many other dead men which appeared

---

Latin B. I (XVII)

1 Then Rabbi Addas and Rabbi Fineës and Rabbi Egias, *even* the three men which had come out of Galilee testifying that they had seen Jesus taken up into heaven, arose in the midst of the multitude of the chief men of the Jews, and said before the priests and Levites which were assembled unto the council of the Lord: As we came from Galilee unto Jordan, there met us a great multitude of men in white garments who had died aforetime. Among whom we beheld Karinus and Leucius to be present with them; and they came near unto us, and we kissed one another, for they were beloved friends of ours, and asked them, *saying*: Tell us, friends and brethren, what is this soul and flesh? and who are these with whom ye go? and how are ye which were dead remaining in the body.

2 And they answered and said: We arose with Christ out of hell, and he raised us up from the dead. And hereby may ye know that the gates of death and darkness are destroyed, and the souls of the saints are taken out thence, and have ascended into heaven with Christ the Lord. But we also have been commanded by the Lord himself that for a set time we should walk the banks of Jordan and the mountains, yet not being seen of all men, neither speaking with all men, but only with those with whom it shall please him. And even now we should not have been able to speak unto you or to be seen of you unless we had been suffered by the Holy Ghost.

3 Now when all the multitude that were present in the council

Latin A.

of their sepulchres, and they have been seen of many in Jeru
salem. And now hearken unto me; for we all know the blessed
Simeon, the high priest which received the child Jesus in his hands
in the temple. And this Simeon had two sons, brothers in blood,
and we all were at their falling asleep and at their burial. Go therefore and look upon their sepulchres : for they are open, because
they have risen, and behold they are in the city of Arimathaea
dwelling together in prayer. And indeed men hear them crying
out, yet they speak with no man, but are silent as dead men.
But come, let us go unto them and with all honour and gentleness

Greek.

in Jerusalem unto many. And if ye know not the others, yet
Simeon at least, which received Jesus, and his two sons, whom
he hath raised up, these at least ye do know, for we buried them
but a little while ago: and now their sepulchres are seen to be
opened and empty, and they themselves are alive and dwelling
in Arimathaea. They sent therefore men, and found their sepulchres opened and empty. Joseph saith: Let us go unto Arimathaea
and find them.

Latin B.

heard these things they were stricken with fear and trembling,
and wondered, *saying,* Did these things truly come to pass which
these men of Galilee testify? Then Caiaphas and Annas said
unto the council: Now shall it be made plain concerning all the
things which these have testified, both first and last: if it shall
be found true that Karinus and Leucius do remain alive in the
body, and if we are able to behold them with our eyes, then that
is true in all points which these testify; and if we find them, they
will assure us of all things: but if not, ye shall know that all are
lying reports.

4 Then they took counsel quickly, and it pleased them to
choose out fit men fearing God, which knew when these men
had died and the sepulchre where they were buried, and should
inquire diligently and see if it were so as they had heard. There
went therefore to the place fifteen men which had been present
throughout at their falling asleep, and had stood on their feet in
the place where they were buried, and had seen their sepulchres.
And these came and found their sepulchres and many others
open, and found not any sign of the bones or the dust of them:
and they returned with all speed and reported the things which
they had seen.

5 Then was all their synagogue troubled with great sadness,
and they said one to another: What shall we do? Annas and
Caiaphas said: Let us send unto the place wherein we have

Latin A.

bring them unto us, and if we adjure them, perchance they will tell us concerning the mystery of their rising again.

2 When they heard these things, they all rejoiced. And Annas and Caiaphas, Nicodemus and Joseph and Gamaliel went and found them not in their sepulchre, but they went unto the city of Arimathaea, and found them there, kneeling on their knees and giving themselves unto prayer. And they kissed them, and with all reverence and in the fear of God they brought them to Jerusalem into the synagogue. And they shut the doors and took the law of the Lord and put it into their hands, and adjured them

Greek.

2 Then rose up the chief priests Annas and Caiaphas, and Joseph and Nicodemus and Gamaliel and others with them, and went unto Arimathaea and found the men of whom Joseph spake. So they did offer prayer, and saluted one another: then they came with them to Jerusalem; and they brought them into the synagogue and made fast the doors, and set the Old *Testament*

Latin B.

heard that they are, and dispatch unto them men of the nobler sort, beseeching and supplicating them: peradventure they will vouchsafe to come unto us. Then they sent unto them Nicodemus and Joseph and the three men, the Rabbis of Galilee which had seen them, entreating them that they would vouchsafe to come to them. And these went and walked about all the region of Jordan and of the mountains and found them not, and returned back again.

6 And behold on a sudden there appeared coming down from Mount Amalech a very great multitude, about twelve thousand men, which had risen with the Lord. And though *the men* recognized many in that place, they were not able to speak a word unto them because of their fear, and the vision of angels; and they stood afar off beholding them and hearkening to them, how they went singing and saying: The Lord is risen from the dead as he said: let us all rejoice and be glad, for he reigneth for ever.

Then they that had been sent were amazed and fell down upon the earth for fear: and they were warned by an angel of the Lord which raised them up from the earth, that they should seek out Karinus and Leucius in their own house.

7 They arose then and went to their house and found them giving themselves unto prayer: and entering in unto them they fell on their faces to the earth and greeted them, and arose and said: O ye friends of God, the whole multitude of the Jews hath sent us unto you, for they have heard that ye are risen from the

Latin A.

by the God Adonai and the God of Israel which spake unto our
fathers by the prophets, saying: Believe ye that it is Jesus
which raised you from the dead? Tell us how ye have arisen from
the dead.

3 And when Karinus and Leucius heard this adjuration, they
trembled in their body and groaned, being troubled in heart.
And looking up together unto heaven they made the seal of the
cross with their fingers upon their tongues, and forthwith they
spake both of them, saying: Give us each a volume of paper,

Greek.

of the Jews in the midst: and the high priests said unto them:
We would have you swear by the God of Israel and by Adonai,
and so speak the truth, how ye arose and who raised you from
the dead.

3 When the men that had arisen heard that, they made upon

Latin B.

dead, entreating and beseeching you to come unto them, that
we may all know the wonderful works of God which have been
wrought upon us (*or* you?) in our days. And they rose immediately by the bidding of God and went with them, and entered
into their synagogue. And when the chief of the priests saw them
they were greatly troubled and trembling took hold upon them:
and finally Annas and Caiaphas took the books of the law of God
and put them into their hands, and adjured them by the god
Heloi and the god Adonai and by the law and the prophets,
saying: Tell us how ye arose from the dead, and what are these
wonders which have been wrought in our days, even such as we
have never heard to be done at any time: for now all our bones
are confounded and dried up for fear, and the earth moveth itself
beneath our feet: for *verily* we have joined together all our hearts
to shed righteous and holy blood.

8 Then Karinus and Leucius beckoned to them with their
hands that they should give them a volume of paper, and ink:
and this they did because the Holy Ghost suffered them not to
speak with them. And they gave unto each of them paper, and
separated them one from the other in several chambers (cells).
And they, making with their fingers the sign of the cross of
Christ, began to write each his volume; and when they had
ended, they cried out as it were with one voice out of their several
chambers: Amen. And Karinus rose and gave his paper unto
Annas and Leucius unto Caiaphas, and they saluted one another
and went forth and returned unto their sepulchres.

9 Then Annas and Caiaphas opened the roll of paper and began
each of them to read to himself privily. But all the people took

Latin A.

and let us write that which we have seen and heard.　And they gave them unto them, and each of them sat down and wrote, saying:

II (XVIII)

1 O Lord Jesu Christ, the life and resurrection of the dead (*al.* resurrection of the dead and the life of the living), suffer us to speak of the mysteries of thy majesty which thou didst perform after thy death upon the cross, inasmuch as we have been adjured by thy Name.　For thou didst command us thy servants to tell no man the secrets of thy divine majesty which thou wroughtest in hell.

Now when we were set together with all our fathers in the deep, in obscurity of darkness, on a sudden there came a golden heat of the sun and a purple and royal light shining upon us.　And immediately the father of the whole race of men, together with all the patriarchs and prophets, rejoiced, saying: This light is

---

Greek.

their faces the sign of the cross, and said unto the chief priests: Give us paper and ink and pen.　So they brought these things. And they sat down and wrote thus:

II (XVIII)

1 O Lord Jesu Christ, the resurrection and the life of the world, give us grace that we may tell of thy resurrection and of thy marvellous works which thou didst in Hell (Hades).

We, then, were in hell together with all them that have fallen

---

Latin B.

it ill, and there was a cry from all of them: Read these writings unto us openly: and when they have been read, we will keep them, that this truth of God be not turned by blinding our eyes, unto deceit, by unclean and deceitful men.　And thereupon Annas and Caiaphas, being seized with trembling, delivered the roll of paper unto Rabbi Addas and Rabbi Fineës and Rabbi Egias, which had come from Galilee and declared that Jesus was taken up into heaven: and unto them all the multitude of the Jews gave credence that they should read this writing.　And they read the paper, wherein was contained this *that followeth*.

II (XVIII)

1 I Karinus.　O Lord Jesu Christ, son of the living God, suffer me to speak of thy marvellous works which thou didst in hell.

When therefore we were holden in hell in darkness and the shadow of death, suddenly there shone upon us a great light, and hell did tremble, and the gates of death.　And there was

Latin A.

the beginning (author) of everlasting light which did promise to send unto us his co-eternal light. And Esaias cried out and said: This is the light of the Father, even the Son of God, according as I prophesied when I lived upon the earth: The land of Zabulon and the land of Nephthalim beyond Jordan, of Galilee of the Gentiles, the people that walked in darkness have seen a great light, and they that dwell in the land of the shadow of death, upon them did the light shine. And now hath it come and shone upon us that sit in death.

2 And as we all rejoiced in the light which shined upon us, there came unto us our father Simeon, and he rejoicing said unto us: Glorify ye the Lord Jesus Christ, the Son of God; for I received him in my hands in the temple when he was born a child, and being moved of the Holy Ghost I made confession and said unto him: Now have mine eyes seen thy salvation which thou hast prepared before the face of all people, a light to lighten the Gentiles, and to be the glory of thy people Israel. And when they heard these things, the whole multitude of the saints rejoiced yet more.

Greek.

asleep since the beginning: and at the hour of midnight there rose upon those dark places as it were the light of the sun, and shined, and all we were enlightened and beheld one another. And straightway our father Abraham, together with the patriarchs and the prophets, were all at once filled with joy and said one to another: This light cometh of the great lightening. The prophet Esaias being there present said: This light is of the Father, and of the Son, and of the Holy Ghost: concerning which I prophesied when I was yet alive, saying: The land of Zabulon and the land of Nephthalim, the people that sat in darkness, hath seen a great light.

Latin B.

heard the voice of the Son of the most high Father, as it were the voice of a great thundering, and it proclaimed aloud and began: Draw back, O princes, your gates, remove your everlasting doors: Christ the Lord the king of glory approacheth to enter in.

2 Then came Satan the prince of death, fleeing in fear and saying to his ministers and unto the hells: O my ministers and all the hells, come together, and shut your gates, set in place the bars of iron, and fight boldly and withstand, that we that hold them be not made captive in bonds. Then were all his evil ministers troubled, and began to shut the gates of death with all

Latin A.

3 And after that there came one as it were a dweller in the wilderness, and he was inquired of by all: Who art thou? And he answered them and said: I am John, the voice and the prophet of the most High, which came before the face of his advent to prepare his ways, to give knowledge of salvation unto his people, for the remission of their sins. And when I saw him coming unto me, being moved of the Holy Ghost, I said: Behold the Lamb of God, behold him that taketh away the sins of the world. And I baptized him in the river of Jordan, and saw the Holy Ghost descending upon him in the likeness of a dove, and heard a voice out of heaven saying: This is my beloved Son, in whom I am well pleased. And now have I come before his face, and come down to declare unto you that he is at hand to visit us, even the dayspring, the Son of God, coming from on high unto us that sit in darkness and in the shadow of death.

Greek.

2 Then came there unto the midst another out of the wilderness, an anchorite (ascete), and the patriarchs said unto him : Who art thou? and he said: I am John, the end of the prophets, which made straight the ways of the Son of God, and preached repentance unto the people for the remission of sins.

And the Son of God came unto me, and when I saw him afar off I said unto the people: Behold the Lamb of God which taketh away the sins of the world. And with mine hands I baptized him in the river Jordan, and saw as it were a dove, and the Holy Ghost coming upon him, and I heard also the voice of God and the Father thus speaking: This is my beloved Son, in whom I am well pleased. And for this cause sent he me unto you also,

---

Latin B.

diligence, and by little to make fast the locks and the bars of iron, and to take fast in hand all their instruments, and to utter howlings with dreadful and hideous voice.

III (XIX)

1 Then said Satan unto Hell: Make thee ready to receive him whom I shall bring down unto thee. Thereupon did Hell make answer unto Satan thus: This voice was nothing else but the cry of the Son of the most high Father, that the earth and all the places of hell did so quake at it: wherefore I think that I and all my bonds are now wide open. But I adjure thee, O Satan, head of all evil, by thy might and mine own, bring him not unto me, lest when we would take him we be taken captive of him.

Latin A.   III (XIX)

1 And when father Adam that was first created heard this, even that Jesus was baptized in Jordan, he cried out to Seth his son, *saying*: Declare unto thy sons the patriarchs and the prophets all that thou didst hear from Michael the archangel, when I sent thee unto the gates of paradise that thou mightest entreat God to send thee his angel to give thee the oil of the tree of mercy to anoint my body when I was sick. Then Seth drew near unto the holy patriarchs and prophets, and said: When I, Seth, was praying at the gates of paradise, behold Michael the angel of the Lord appeared unto me, saying: I am sent unto thee from the Lord: it is I that am set over the body of man. And I say unto thee, Seth, vex not thyself with tears, praying and entreating

Greek.

to proclaim that the only begotten Son of God cometh hither, that whosoever believeth on him may be saved, and whoso believeth not on him may be condemned. Therefore say I unto you all, that when ye behold him ye shall worship him, for now only is the time of repentance for you, for that ye did worship idols in the vain world that is above, and for the sins which ye have committed: but at another time it is impossible that this should come to pass.

Latin B.

For if by his voice only all my might hath been thus overthrown, what, thinkest thou, will he do when his presence is come unto us?

2 Unto whom Satan the prince of death answered thus: Why keepest thou this crying? Fear not, my friend of old time, thou most evil one, for I stirred up the people of the Jews against him, and commanded him to be smitten with buffets, and did contrive against him betrayal by his disciple: and he is a man that feareth death greatly, for he said in his fear: My soul is sorrowful even unto death: yet unto death have I brought him, for now he hangeth lifted up upon a cross.

3 Then saith Hell unto him: If it be he that by the word of his command alone made Lazarus, which was four days dead, to fly out of my bosom like an eagle, then is he not a man in his manhood, but God in his majesty. I beseech thee, bring him not unto me. Satan saith to him: Notwithstanding, make thyself ready, fear not: for already he hangeth upon a cross, and I can do no other. Then Hell spake thus unto Satan: If, then, thou canst do no other, lo thy destruction draweth near, and I shall at last be cast down and remain without honour; but thou wilt be tormented under my dominion.

Latin A.

for the oil of the tree of mercy, that thou mayest anoint thy
father Adam for the pain of his body: for thou wilt not be able to
receive it save in the last days and times, save when five thousand
and five hundred (*al.* 5,952) years are accomplished: then shall
the most beloved Son of God come upon the earth to raise up
the body of Adam and the bodies of the dead, and he shall
come and be baptized in Jordan. And when he is come forth
of the water of Jordan, then shall he anoint with the oil of mercy
all that believe on him, and that oil of mercy shall be unto all
generations of them that shall be born of water and of the Holy
Ghost, unto life eternal. Then shall the most beloved Son of

Greek. III (XIX)

And as John was thus teaching them that were in hell, the
first-created Adam, the first father, also heard it, and said unto
Seth his son: My son, I would have thee to tell the forefathers
of the race of men, and the prophets; when I laid me down to
die, whither I did send thee. And Seth said: Ye prophets and
patriarchs, hearken: My father Adam, the first-created, laid him
down on a time to die, and sent me to make supplication unto
God hard by the gate of paradise, that he would lead me by his
angel unto the tree of mercy, and I should take the oil and anoint
my father, and he should arise from his sickness. Which also
I did; and after my prayer an angel of the Lord came and said
unto me: What askest thou, Seth? askest thou for the oil that
raiseth up the sick, or for the tree that floweth with that oil, for
the sickness of thy father? this cannot be found at this time.
Depart therefore and say unto thy father, that after there are
accomplished from the creation of the world five thousand five
hundred years, then shall the only-begotten Son of God become
man and come down upon the earth, and he shall anoint him
with that oil, and he shall arise: and with water and the Holy
Ghost shall he wash him and them that come of him. And then

Latin B. IV (XX)

1 Now the saints of God heard the contention between Satan
and Hell: but as yet they knew not each other among themselves:
nevertheless they were at the point to know. But our holy
father Adam made answer unto Satan thus: O prince of death,
wherefore fearest thou and tremblest? Behold the Lord cometh
which shall destroy all thy creatures, and thou shalt be taken
captive of him and be bound, world without end.
2 Then all the saints, when they heard the voice of our father
Adam, how valiantly he made answer unto Satan, were glad and
were comforted: and all of them ran together unto father Adam

Latin A.

God, even Christ Jesus, come down upon the earth and shall bring in our father Adam into paradise unto the tree of mercy.

And when they heard all these things of Seth, all the patriarchs and prophets rejoiced with a great rejoicing.

IV (XX)

1 And while all the saints were rejoicing, behold Satan the prince and chief of death said unto Hell: Make thyself ready to receive Jesus who boasteth himself that he is the Son of God, whereas

---

Greek.

shall he be healed of every disease: but now it is not possible that this should come to pass.

And when the patriarchs and prophets heard these things, they rejoiced greatly.

IV (XX)

1 And while all of them were thus joyful, Satan the inheritor of darkness cometh and saith unto Hades: O thou that devourest all and art insatiable, hearken to my words. There is one of the

---

Latin B.

and were gathered about him in that place. Then our father Adam, looking earnestly upon all that multitude, marvelled if they all were begotten of him into the world. And he embraced them that stood near round about him, and shed exceeding bitter tears, and spake unto Seth his son: Declare, my son Seth, unto the holy patriarchs and prophets that which the keeper of paradise said unto thee when I sent thee to bring me of the very oil of mercy that thou mightest anoint my body when I was sick.

3 Then he answered: I, when thou sentest me before the gates of paradise, prayed and besought the Lord with tears, and I called the keeper of paradise to give me thereof. Then Michael the archangel came forth and said unto me: Seth, wherefore mournest thou? know thou before, that thy father Adam shall not receive of this oil of mercy now, but after many generations of the world. For the most beloved Son of God shall come down from heaven into the world and shall be baptized of John in the river Jordan: and then shall thy father Adam receive of this oil of mercy, and all they that believe in him: and the kingdom of them which have believed in him shall endure, world without end.

V (XXI)

1 Then all the saints when they heard these things rejoiced again with *great* joy, and one of them that stood by, Isaias by name, proclaimed with a loud voice, saying: Father Adam and all ye

Latin A.

he is a man that feareth death, and sayeth: My soul is sorrowful
even unto death. And he hath been much mine enemy, doing
me great hurt, and many that I had made blind, lame, dumb,
leprous, and possessed he hath healed with a word: and some
whom I have brought unto thee dead, them hath he taken
away from thee.

2 Hell answered and said unto Satan the prince: Who is he
that is so mighty, if he be a man that feareth death? for all the
mighty ones of the earth are held in subjection by my power,
even they whom thou hast brought me subdued by thy power.
If, then, thou art mighty, what manner of man is this Jesus who,
though he fear death, resisteth thy power? If he be so mighty
in his manhood, verily I say unto thee he is almighty in his godhead, and no man can withstand his power. And when he saith
that he feareth death, he would ensnare thee, and woe shall be

---

Greek.

race of the Jews, Jesus, who calleth himself the Son of God; but
he is a man, and by our contrivance the Jews have crucified him.
And now that he hath died, be thou prepared that we may make
him fast here. For I know that he is a man, and I have heard
him saying: My soul is exceeding sorrowful, even unto death.
And he hath done me much hurt in the world that is above while
he walked among men. For wheresoever he found my servants
he did persecute them, and as many as I caused to be maimed, or
blind, or lame, or leprous, or any such thing, he healed them with
a word only: and whereas I made ready many to be buried, them
also he quickened again only with a word.

2 Hades saith: And is he indeed so mighty that he can do
such things with a word only? or, if he be such, art thou able to
withstand him? it seemeth to me, no man will be able to with-

---

Latin B.

that stand by hearken unto my sayings. While I was upon earth,
and the Holy Ghost taught me, I did sing in prophecy concerning
this light, saying: The people which sat in darkness have seen
a great light: unto them which dwell in the land of the shadow
of death hath the light shined. And at his word Father Adam
and they all turned unto him and asked him: Who art thou?
for that which thou sayest is true. And he answered and said:
I am named Isaias.

2 Then appeared there another beside him, as it were a dweller
in the wilderness, and they asked him and said: Who art thou
that bearest in thy body such signs? and he answered stoutly:
I am John the Baptist, the voice and the prophet of the Most
High. I went before the face of the same Lord to make the

870 K

Latin A.

unto thee for everlasting ages. But Satan the prince of Tartarus
said: Why doubtest thou and fearest to receive this Jesus,
which is thine adversary and mine? For I tempted him, and
I have stirred up mine ancient people of the Jews with envy and
wrath against him. I have sharpened a spear to thrust him
through, gall and vinegar have I mingled to give him to drink,
and I have prepared a cross to crucify him and nails to pierce
him: and his death is nigh at hand, that I may bring him unto
thee to be subject unto thee and me.

Greek.

stand him: but whereas thou sayest that thou hast heard him
fearing death, this he said to mock thee and in sport, willing to
seize on thee with a mighty hand: and woe, woe unto thee for
everlasting! Satan saith: O thou Hades that devourest all and
art insatiable, didst thou fear so much at that thou hast heard
concerning our common adversary? I feared him not, but I did
set on the Jews, and they crucified him and gave him also gall to
drink mingled with vinegar. Prepare thyself, therefore, that
when he cometh thou mayest hold him fast.

Latin B.

desert and rough ways into plain paths. I did show with my
finger unto them of Jerusalem the lamb of the Lord and the Son
of God, and glorified him. I baptized him in the river Jordan.
I heard the voice of the Father out of heaven thundering upon
him and proclaiming: This is my beloved Son in whom I am
well pleased. I have received an answer from him that he
would himself descend into hell.

Then Father Adam, when he heard that, cried with a loud voice,
and shouted again and again Alleluia, which is, being interpreted:
The Lord cometh.

VI (XXII)

1 After this another that stood by and was adorned as it were
with the marks of an emperor, by name David, cried out thus
and said: When I was upon earth I did reveal unto the people
concerning the mercy of God and his visitation, and prophesied
joyful things to come throughout all ages, saying: Let them
give thanks unto the Lord, even his mercies: and his wonders
unto the children of men.[1] For he hath broken the gates of brass
and smitten the bars of iron in sunder.

Then did the holy patriarchs and prophets begin to recognize
one another, and each one of them to speak words out of their
prophecies. Then holy Jeremias, looking upon his prophecies,
said to the patriarchs and prophets: When I was upon earth

[1] So the Latin Psalter has it.

Latin A.

3 Hell answered and said: Thou hast told me that it is he that hath taken away dead men from me. For there be many which while they lived on the earth have taken dead men from me, yet not by their own power but by prayer to God, and their almighty God hath taken them from me. Who is this Jesus which by his own word without prayer hath drawn dead men from me? Perchance it is he which by the word of his command did restore to life Lazarus which was four days dead and stank and was corrupt, whom I held here dead. Satan the prince of death answered and said: It is that same Jesus. When Hell heard that he said unto him: I adjure thee by thy strength and mine own that thou bring him not unto me. For at that time I, when I heard the command of his word, did quake and was overwhelmed with fear, and all my ministries with me were troubled. Neither could we keep Lazarus, but he like an eagle shaking himself leaped forth with all agility and swiftness, and departed from us, and the earth also which held the dead body of

Greek.

3 Hades answered: O inheritor of darkness, son of perdition devil, thou saidst but now unto me that many of them whom thou hadst made ready to be buried he did quicken again with a word only: now if he hath set free many from burial, how and by what strength shall he be held by us? I indeed of late swallowed up a certain dead man named Lazarus, and after a little, one of the living by force snatched him up out of mine entrails by a word only: and I think this is he of whom thou speakest. If, then, we receive him here, I fear lest we be imperilled for the rest also; for I have swallowed up all men from the beginning: behold, I perceive that they are unquiet, and my belly paineth me, and this Lazarus that before was caught away from me I take to be no good sign, for he flew away from me, not like to a dead man but to an eagle, so instantly did the earth cast him out. Wherefore also I adjure thee by thy gifts and by mine own, that

Latin B.

I prophesied of the Son of God, *saying* that he was seen upon earth and conversed among men.

2 Then all the saints rejoicing in the light of the Lord and at the sight of their father Adam, and at the answer of all the patriarchs and prophets, cried out, saying: Alleluia, blessed is he that cometh in the name of the Lord. So that at the cry of them Satan feared, and sought a way to flee by, and could not, for Hell and his ministers did hold him bound in hell and fenced in on every side. And they said unto him: Why fearest thou? we will in no wise suffer thee to go out hence; but thou must receive these things

Latin A.

Lazarus straightway gave him up alive. Wherefore now I know that that man which was able to do these things is a God strong in command and mighty in manhood, and that he is the saviour of mankind. And if thou bring him unto me he will set free all that are here shut up in the hard prison and bound in the chains of their sins that cannot be broken, and will bring them unto the life of his godhead for ever.

V (XXI)

1 And as Satan the prince, and Hell, spoke thus together, suddenly there came a voice as of thunder and a spiritual cry: Remove, O princes, your gates, and be ye lift up, ye everlasting doors, and the King of glory shall come in. When Hell heard that he said unto Satan the prince: Depart from me and go out of mine abode: if thou be a mighty man of war, fight thou against the King of glory. But what hast thou to do with him? And Hell cast Satan forth out of his dwelling. Then said Hell unto

---

Greek.

thou bring him not to this place, for I believe that he cometh hither to raise up all the dead. And this I say unto thee: by the outer darkness, if thou bring him hither, not one of all the dead will be left in me.

V (XXI)

1 And as Satan and Hades spake thus with one another, there came a great voice as of thunder, saying: Lift up, O princes, your gates, and be ye lift up, ye everlasting doors, and the King of glory shall come in. When Hades heard, he said unto Satan: Go forth, if thou art able, and withstand him. So Satan went forth. Then said Hades unto his devils: Make fast the gates of brass well and strongly, and the bars of iron, and keep my locks, and

---

Latin B.

as thou art worthy, at his hands whom thou didst fight against every day: and if not, know thou that thou shalt be bound by him and committed unto my keeping for ever.

VII (XXIII)

1 And again there came the voice of the Son of the most high Father, as the voice of a great thunder, saying: Lift up, O princes, your gates, and be ye lift up, ye everlasting doors, and the King of glory shall come in. Then Satan and Hell cried out, saying: Who is this King of glory? And it was answered them by the Lord's voice: The Lord strong and mighty, the Lord mighty in battle.

2 After that voice there came unto us a man whose appearance was as that of a robber, bearing a cross upon his shoulder, who cried without and said: Open unto me that I may enter in. And Satan opened the gate unto him a little way and brought him

Latin A.

his wicked ministers: Shut ye the hard gates of brass and put
on them the bars of iron and withstand stoutly, lest we that hold
captivity be taken captive.

2 But when all the multitude of the saints heard it, they
spake with a voice of rebuking unto Hell: Open thy gates, that
the King of glory may come in. And David cried out, saying:
Did I not when I was alive upon earth, foretell unto you: Let
them give thanks unto the Lord, even his mercies and his
wonders unto the children of men; who hath broken the gates
of brass and smitten the bars of iron in sunder? he hath taken
them out of the way of their iniquity. And thereafter in like
manner Esaias said: Did not I when I was alive upon earth
foretell unto you: The dead shall arise, and they that are in the
tombs shall rise again, and they that are in the earth shall
rejoice, for the dew which cometh of the Lord is their healing?
And again I said: O death, where is thy sting? O Hell, where
is thy victory?

Greek.

stand upright, and beware at all points, for if he come in hither,
woe will take hold on us.

2 When the forefathers heard that, they began all of them to
insult him, saying: Thou that devourest all and art insatiate,
open, that the King of glory may come in. David the prophet
said: Knowest thou not, blind one, that when I lived in the
world I did prophesy that word, Lift up, O princes, your gates.
Esaias said: This I foresaw by the Holy Ghost and wrote: The
dead shall arise, and they that are in the tombs shall awake, and
they that are in the earth shall rejoice: and again: O death,
where is thy sting? O Hell, where is thy victory?

Latin B.

within into the house, and shut the gate again after him. And
all the saints saw him that he shone brightly, and said unto him
straightway: Thine appearance is that of a robber: show us,
what is that which thou bearest on thy back? And he answered
humbly and said: Of a truth I was a robber altogether, and the
Jews hanged me upon a cross with my Lord Jesus Christ, the Son
of the most high Father. And at the last I have come hither
before him; but himself cometh after me immediately.

3 Then the holy David's anger was kindled against Satan, and
he cried aloud: Open, thou most foul one, thy gates, that the
King of glory may come in. Likewise also all the saints of God
rose up against Satan and would have laid hold on him and parted
him among them.

And again there was a cry without: Lift up, ye princes, your

Latin A.

3 When they heard that of Esaias, all the saints said unto Hell: Open thy gates: now shalt thou be overcome and weak and without strength. And there came a great voice as of thunder, saying: Remove, O princes, your gates, and be ye lift up ye doors of hell, and the King of glory shall come in. And when Hell saw that they so cried out twice, he said, as if he knew it not: Who is the King of glory? And David answered Hell and said: The words of this cry do I know, for by his spirit I prophesied the same; and now I say unto thee that which I said before: The Lord strong and mighty, the Lord mighty in battle, he is the King of glory. And: The Lord looked down from heaven that he might hear the groanings of them that are in fetters and deliver the children of them that have been slain. And now, O thou most foul and stinking Hell, open thy gates, that the King of glory may come in. And as David spake thus unto Hell, the Lord of majesty appeared in the form of a man and lightened the eternal darkness and brake the bonds that could not be loosed: and the succour of his everlasting might visited us that sat in the deep darkness of our transgressions and in the shadow of death of our sins.

Greek.

3 Then came there again a voice, saying: Lift up the gates. And when Hades heard the voice the second time, he answered as if he knew it not, and said: Who is this King of glory? The angels of the Lord said: The Lord strong and mighty, the Lord mighty in battle. And straightway at the word the gates of brass were broken in pieces and the bars of iron were ground to powder, and all the dead that were bound were loosed from their chains, and we with them, and the King of glory entered in, *in fashion* as a man, and all the dark places of Hell were enlightened.

Latin B.

gates, and be ye lift up, ye everlasting doors, and the King of glory shall come in. And again at that clear voice Hell and Satan inquired, saying: Who is this King of glory? and it was said unto them by that marvellous voice: The Lord of hosts, he is the King of glory.

VIII (XXIV)

And lo, suddenly Hell did quake, and the gates of death and the locks were broken small, and the bars of iron broken, and fell to the ground, and all things were laid open. And Satan remained in the midst and stood put to confusion and cast down,

Latin A. VI (XXII)

1 When Hell and death and their wicked ministers saw that, they were stricken with fear, they and their cruel officers, at the sight of the brightness of so great light in their own realm, seeing Christ of a sudden in their abode, and they cried out, saying: We are overcome by thee. Who art thou that art sent by the Lord for our confusion? Who art thou that without all damage of corruption, and with the signs (?) of thy majesty unblemished, dost in wrath condemn our power? Who art thou that art so great and so small, both humble and exalted, both soldier and commander, a marvellous warrior in the shape of a bondsman, and a King of glory dead and living, whom the cross bare slain upon it? Thou that didst lie dead in the sepulchre hast come down unto us living: and at thy death all creation quaked and all the stars were shaken: and thou hast become free among the dead and dost rout our legions. Who art thou that settest free the prisoners that are held bound by original sin and restorest them into their former liberty? Who art thou that sheddest thy divine and bright light upon them that were blinded with the darkness of their sins? After the same manner all the legions of devils were stricken with like fear and cried out all together in the terror of their confusion, saying: Whence art thou, Jesus, a man so mighty and bright in majesty, so excellent, without spot and clean from sin? For that world of earth which hath been alway subject unto us until now, and did pay tribute to our profit, hath never sent unto us a dead man like thee,

Greek. VI (XXII)

1 Hades cried out straightway: We are overcome, woe unto us. But who art thou that hast so great authority and power? and what manner of man art thou that art come hither without sin? thou that appearest small and canst do great things, that art humble and exalted, a bondsman and a master, a soldier and a commander, that exercisest authority over the dead and the living? thou wast nailed to the cross, and laid in the sepulchre, and now art thou become free and hast destroyed our whole power.

Art thou then that Jesus of whom the chief ruler Satan said unto us, that by thy cross and death thou shouldest inherit the whole world?

Latin B.

and bound with a fetter about his feet. And behold, the Lord Jesus Christ coming in the glory of the light of the height, in meekness, great and yet humble, bearing a chain in his hands bound therewith the neck of Satan, and also, binding his hands behind his back, cast him backward into Tartarus, and set his holy foot upon his throat and said: Throughout all ages hast thou done much

Latin A.

nor ever dispatched such a gift unto Hell. Who then art thou
that so fearlessly enterest our borders, and not only fearest not
our torments, but besides essayest to bear away all men out of our
bonds? Peradventure thou art that Jesus, of whom Satan our
prince said that by thy death of the cross thou shouldest receive
the dominion of the whole world.

2 Then did the King of glory in his majesty trample upon
death, and laid hold on Satan the prince and delivered him unto
the power of Hell, and drew Adam to him unto his own brightness.

VII (XXIII)

Then Hell, receiving Satan the prince, with sore reproach
said unto him: O prince of perdition and chief of destruction,
Beelzebub, the scorn of the angels and spitting of the righteous,
why wouldest thou do this? Thou wouldest crucify the King
of glory, and at his decease didst promise us great spoils of his
death: like a fool thou knewest not what thou didst. For behold,
now, this Jesus putteth to flight by the brightness of his majesty
all the darkness of death, and hath broken the strong depths of
the prisons, and let out the prisoners, and loosed them that were
bound. And all that were sighing in our torments do rejoice
against us, and at their prayers our dominions are vanquished

Greek.

2 Then the King of glory took hold upon the head of the chief
ruler Satan, and delivered him unto the angels and said: Bind
down with irons his hands and his feet and his neck and his
mouth. And then he delivered him unto Hades, saying: Take
him and keep him safely until my second coming.

VII (XXIII)

Then Hades, when he had taken Satan, said unto him: O Beelzebub, inheritor of fire and torment, adversary of the saints,
what need hadst thou to provide that the King of glory should be
crucified, so that he should come hither and strip us naked?
Turn thee and see that not one dead man is left in me, but all
whatsoever thou didst gain by the tree of knowledge thou hast
lost by the tree of the cross, and all thy joy is turned into sorrow,
and when thou wouldest slay the King of glory thou hast slain
thyself: for since I have received thee to keep thee safely, thou—

Latin B.

evil and hast never been quiet at any time. To-day do I deliver
thee unto eternal fire. And he called Hell quickly and gave him
commandment, saying: Take this most evil and wicked one and
hold him in thy keeping until that day when I shall command
thee. And he took him from beneath the Lord's feet, and he was
cast down together with him into the depth of the bottomless pit.

Latin A.

and our realms conquered, and now no nation of men feareth us any more. And beside this, the dead which were never wont to be proud triumph over us, and the captives which never could be joyful do threaten us. O prince Satan, father of all the wicked and ungodly and renegades, wherefore wouldest thou do this? They that from the beginning until now have despaired of life and salvation—now is none of their wonted roarings heard, neither doth any groan from them sound in our ears, nor is there any sign of tears upon the face of any of them. O prince Satan, holder of the keys of hell, those thy riches which thou hadst gained by the tree of transgression and the losing of paradise, thou hast lost by the tree of the cross, and all thy gladness hath perished. When thou didst hang up Christ Jesus the King of glory thou wroughtest against thyself and against me. Henceforth thou shalt know what eternal torments and infinite pains thou art to suffer in my keeping for ever. O prince Satan, author of death and head of all pride, thou oughtest first to have sought out matter of evil in this Jesus: Wherefore didst thou adventure without cause to crucify him unjustly against whom thou foundest no blame, and to bring into our realm the innocent and righteous one, and to lose the guilty and the ungodly and unrighteous of the whole world?

And when Hell had spoken thus unto Satan the prince, then said the King of glory unto Hell: Satan the prince shall be in thy power unto all ages in the stead of Adam and his children, even those that are my righteous ones.

VIII (XXIV)

1 And the Lord stretching forth his hand, said: Come unto me, all ye my saints which bear mine image and my likeness. Ye

---

Greek.

shalt learn by trial what evils I will practise upon thee. O thou head-devil, the beginning of death, and root of sin, and end of all evil, what ill didst thou find in Jesus that thou wentest about his destruction? how didst thou dare to do so great wickedness? how didst thou desire to bring down such an one into this darkness, whereby thou art bereaved of all them that have died since the beginning.

VIII (XXIV)

1 And as Hades talked thus with Satan, the King of glory spread forth his right hand and took hold on our forefather Adam

---

Latin B. IX (XXV)

1 Then the Lord Jesus, the Saviour of all men, pitiful and most gracious, greeted Adam with kindness, saying unto him: Peace

Latin A.

that by the tree and the devil and death were condemned, behold
now the devil and death condemned by the tree. And forthwith
all the saints were gathered in one under the hand of the Lord.
And the Lord holding the right hand of Adam, said unto him:
Peace be unto thee with all thy children that are my righteous
ones. But Adam, casting himself at the knees of the Lord,
entreated him with tears and beseechings, and said with a loud
voice: I will magnify thee, O Lord, for thou hast set me up
and not made my foes to triumph over me: O Lord my God,
I cried unto thee and thou hast healed me; Lord, thou hast
brought my soul out of hell, thou hast delivered me from them
that go down to the pit. Sing praises unto the Lord all ye saints
of his, and give thanks unto *him for the* remembrance of his
holiness. For there is wrath in his indignation and life is in his
good pleasure. In like manner all the saints of God kneeled
and cast themselves at the feet of the Lord, saying with one
accord: Thou art come, O redeemer of the world: that which
thou didst foretell by the law and by thy prophets, that hast
thou accomplished in deed. Thou hast redeemed the living by
thy cross, and by the death of the cross thou hast come down
unto us, that thou mightest save us out of hell and death through
thy majesty. O Lord, like as thou hast set the name of thy

Greek.

and raised him up; and then turned himself unto the rest and
said: Come with me all ye, as many as have suffered death
through the tree which this man touched. For lo, I do raise you
all up again through the tree of the cross. And with that he put
them all forth, and our forefather Adam was seen full of gladness
of soul and said: I give thanks to thy greatness, O Lord, for thou
hast brought me up out of the lowest hell. Likewise also all the
prophets and the saints said: We give thanks unto thee, O Christ,
Saviour of the world, for that thou hast brought up our life from
corruption.

Latin B.

be unto thee, Adam, and unto thy children unto everlasting ages.
Amen. Then Father Adam cast himself at the Lord's feet, and
rose up and kissed his hands, and shed abundant tears, saying:
Behold the hands which formed me: testifying unto all. And
he said to the Lord: Thou art come, O King of glory, to set men
free and gather them to thine everlasting kingdom. Then our
mother Eve also in like manner cast herself at the feet of the
Lord, and rose up and kissed his hands, and shed tears abundantly,
and said: Behold the hands which fashioned me: testifying
unto all.

Latin A.

glory in the heavens and set up thy cross for a token of redemption upon the earth, so, Lord, set thou up the sign of the victory of thy cross in hell, that death may have no more dominion.

2 And the Lord stretched forth his hand and made the sign of the cross over Adam and over all his saints, and he took the right hand of Adam and went up out of hell, and all the saints followed him. Then did holy David cry aloud and say: Sing unto the Lord a new song, for he hath done marvellous things. His right hand hath wrought salvation for him and his holy arm. The Lord hath made known his saving health, before the face of all nations hath he revealed his righteousness. And the whole multitude of the saints answered, saying: Such honour have all his saints. Amen, Alleluia.

Greek.

2 And when they had thus said, the Saviour blessed Adam upon his forehead with the sign of the cross, and so did he also unto all the patriarchs and prophets and martyrs and forefathers. And he took them and leaped up out of hell. And as he went the holy fathers sang praises, following him and saying: Blessed is he that cometh in the name of the Lord. Unto him be the glory of all the saints.

Latin B.

2 Then all the saints adoring him cried out, saying: Blessed is he that cometh in the name of the Lord: God the Lord hath showed us light. Amen throughout all ages. Alleluia, world without end: laud, honour, might, and glory, because thou hast come from on high to visit us. And they gathered them beneath the hands of the Lord, singing always Alleluia, and rejoicing together at the glory. Then the Saviour searched throughout and did bite hell (al. hell was in affliction), forasmuch as he cast down part into Tartarus, and part he brought again with him on high.

X (XXVI)

Then all the saints of God besought the Lord that he would leave the sign of victory—even of the holy cross—in hell, that the wicked ministers thereof might not prevail to keep back any that was accused, whom the Lord absolved. And so it was done, and the Lord set his cross in the midst of hell, which is the sign of victory; and it shall remain there for ever.

Then all we went out thence with the Lord, and left Satan and Hell in Tartarus.

Latin A.

3 And thereafter Habacuc the prophet cried out and said: Thou wentest forth for the salvation of thy people to set free thy chosen. And all the saints answered, saying: Blessed is he that cometh in the name of the Lord. God is the Lord and hath showed us light. Amen, Alleluia.

Likewise after that the prophet Micheas also cried, saying: What God is like thee, O Lord, taking away iniquity and removing sins? and now thou withholdest thy wrath for a testimony that thou art merciful of free will, and thou dost turn away and have mercy on us, thou forgivest all our iniquities and hast sunk all our sins in the depths of the sea, as thou swarest unto our fathers in the days of old. And all the saints answered, saying: This is our God for ever and ever, he shall be our guide, world without end. Amen, Alleluia. And so spake all the prophets, making mention of holy words out of their praises, and all the saints followed the Lord, crying Amen, Alleluia.

IX (XXV)

But the Lord holding the hand of Adam delivered him unto Michael the archangel, and all the saints followed Michael the archangel, and he brought them all into the glory and beauty (grace) of paradise. And there met with them two men, ancients of days, and when they were asked of the saints: Who are ye that have not yet been dead in hell with us and are set in paradise in the body? then one of them answering, said: I am Enoch which was translated hither by the word of the Lord, and this that is with me is Elias the Thesbite which was taken up in a chariot of fire: and up to this day we have not tasted death, but we are received unto the coming of Antichrist to fight against him with signs and wonders of God, and to be slain of him in Jerusalem, and after three days and a half to be taken up again alive on the clouds.

Greek.   IX (XXV)

He went therefore into paradise holding our forefather Adam by the hand, and delivered him, and all the righteous, unto Michael the archangel. And as they were entering in at the gate of paradise, there met them two aged men, unto whom said the holy fathers: Who are ye, which have not seen death nor come down into hell, but dwell in paradise with your bodies and souls? And one of them answered and said: I am Enoch that pleased God and was translated hither by him: and this is Elias the Thesbite: and we shall live unto the end of the world, but at that time we shall be sent by God to withstand Antichrist and to be slain of him, and after three days to rise and be caught up in the clouds to meet the Lord.

Latin A.   X (XXVI)

And as Enoch and Elias spake thus with the saints, behold there came another man of vile habit, bearing upon his shoulders the sign of the cross; whom when they beheld, all the saints said unto him: Who art thou? for thine appearance is as of a robber; and wherefore is it that thou bearest a sign upon thy shoulders? And he answered them and said: Ye have rightly said: for I was a robber, doing all manner of evil upon the earth. And the Jews crucified me with Jesus, and I beheld the wonders in the creation which came to pass through the cross of Jesus when he was crucified, and I believed that he was the maker of all creatures and the almighty king, and I besought him, saying: Remember me, Lord, when thou comest into thy kingdom. And forthwith he received my prayer, and said unto me: Verily I say unto thee, this day shalt thou be with me in paradise: and he gave me the sign of the cross, saying: Bear this and go unto paradise, and if the angel that keepeth paradise suffer thee not to enter in, show him the sign of the cross; and thou shalt say unto him: Jesus Christ the Son of God who now is crucified hath sent me. And when I had so done, I spake all these things unto the angel that keepeth paradise; and when he heard this of me, forthwith he opened the door and brought me in and set me at the right hand of paradise, saying: Lo now, tarry a little, and Adam the father of all mankind will enter in with all his children that are holy and righteous, after the triumph and glory of the ascending up of Christ the Lord that is crucified. When they heard all these words of the robber, all the holy patriarchs

---

Greek.   X (XXVI)

And as they thus spake there came another man, humble of aspect, and bearing also a cross upon his shoulder, unto whom the holy fathers said: Who art thou that hast the appearance of a robber, and what is that cross that thou bearest on thy shoulder? He answered: I as ye say was a robber and a thief in the world, and therefore the Jews took me and delivered me unto the death of the cross together with our Lord Jesus Christ. When, therefore, he hung upon the cross, I beheld the signs which came to pass, and I believed on him and besought him and said: Lord, when thou shalt reign, forget not me. And straightway he said to me: Verily, verily, to-day, I say unto thee, thou shalt be with me in paradise.

I came, therefore, bearing my cross, into paradise, and found Michael the archangel, and said unto him: Our Lord Jesus Christ that was crucified hath sent me hither; bring me therefore unto the gate of Eden. And when the flaming sword saw the sign of the cross, it opened unto me and I entered in. Then said the archangel unto me: Tarry a little, for Adam the forefather

Latin A.

and prophets said with one voice: Blessed be the Lord Almighty, the Father of eternal good things, the Father of mercies, thou that hast given such grace unto thy sinners and hast brought them again into the beauty of paradise and into thy good pastures: for this is the most holy life of the spirit. Amen, Amen.

XI (XXVII)

These are the divine and holy mysteries which we saw and heard, even I, Karinus, and Leucius: but we were not suffered to relate further the rest of the mysteries of God, according as Michael the archangel strictly charged us, saying: Ye shall go with your brethren unto Jerusalem and remain in prayer, crying out and glorifying the resurrection of the Lord Jesus Christ, who hath raised you from the dead together with him: and ye shall not be speaking with any man, but sit as dumb men, until the hour come when the Lord himself suffereth you to declare the mysteries of his godhead. But unto us Michael the archangel gave commandment that we should go over Jordan unto a place rich and fertile, where are many which rose again together with us for a testimony of the resurrection of Christ the Lord. For three days only were allowed unto us who rose from the dead, to keep the passover of the Lord in Jerusalem with our kindred (parents) that are living for a testimony of the resurrection of Christ the Lord: and we were baptized in the holy river of Jordan and received white robes, every one of us. And after the three days, when we had kept the passover of the Lord, all

Greek.

of mankind cometh with the righteous, that they also may enter in. And now, having seen you, I am come to meet you. And when the saints heard these things, they cried aloud with a great voice, saying: Great is our Lord, and great is his power.

XI (XXVII)

All these things did we see and hear, even we the two brethren which also were sent by Michael the archangel and appointed to proclaim the resurrection of the Lord, but first to go unto Jordan and be baptized; whither also we went and were baptized,

Latin B.

But unto us and many others was it commanded that we should rise again with our bodies, and bear witness in the world of the resurrection of our Lord Jesus Christ, and concerning those things that were done in hell.

These are the things, brethren beloved, which we have seen, and do testify being adjured of you, as he beareth witness who died for us and rose again. For like as it is written, so was it performed in every point.

Latin A.

they were caught up in the clouds which had risen again with us, and were taken over Jordan and were no more seen of any man. But unto us it was said that we should remain in the city of Arimathaea and continue in prayer.

These be all things which the Lord bade us declare unto you: give praise and thanksgiving (confession) unto him, and repent that he may have mercy upon you. Peace be unto you from the same Lord Jesus Christ which is the Saviour of us all. Amen.

And when they had finished writing all things in the several volumes of paper they arose; and Karinus gave that which he

Greek.

together with other dead that had risen again. Thereafter we went unto Jerusalem also and accomplished the passover of the resurrection: but now we depart, for we are not able to abide in this place. And the love of God and the Father, and the grace of our Lord Jesus Christ, and ⟨the fellowship⟩ of the Holy Ghost be with you all. Amen.

When they had thus written and had closed up the books, they gave the one half unto the high priests and the one half unto Joseph and Nicodemus: and they themselves vanished suddenly.

To the glory of our Lord Jesus Christ. Amen.

Latin B.   XI (XXVII)

But when the paper was wholly read through, all that heard it fell upon their faces weeping bitterly and smote hard upon their breasts, crying out and saying: Woe unto us: wherefore cometh this to pass unto us wretched men? Pilate did flee, Annas and Caiaphas did flee, the priests and Levites did flee, and all the people of the Jews beside, lamenting and saying: Woe unto us miserable men; we have shed innocent blood upon the earth.

Therefore for three days and three nights they tasted not at all either bread or water, neither did any of them return unto the synagogue. But on the third day the council gathered together again, and the other paper, to wit of Leucius, was read, and neither more nor less was found in it, even to one letter, than what was contained in the writing of Karinus.

Then was the synagogue troubled and they mourned all of them forty days and forty nights, looking for death at the hand of God and for the vengeance of God. But the Most High God, which is merciful and pitiful, destroyed them not immediately, but gave them freely a place of repentance: but they were not found worthy to be turned unto the Lord.

These be the testimonies, beloved brethren, of Karinus and Leucius, concerning Christ the Son of God and his holy acts in Hell: unto whom let us all give praise and glory unto ages without end. Amen.

Latin A.

had written into the hands of Annas and Caiaphas and Gamaliel; likewise Leucius gave that which he had written into the hands of Nicodemus and Joseph. And suddenly they were transfigured and *became* white exceedingly and were no more seen. But their writings were found to be the same (*lit.* equal), neither more nor less by one letter.

And when all the synagogue of the Jews heard all these marvellous sayings of Karinus and Leucius, they said one to another: Of a truth all these things were wrought by the Lord, and blessed be the Lord, world without end, Amen. And they went out all of them in great trouble of mind, smiting their breasts with fear and trembling, and departed every man unto his own home.

And all these things which were spoken by the Jews in their synagogue, did Joseph and Nicodemus forthwith declare unto the governor. And Pilate himself wrote all the things that were done and said concerning Jesus by the Jews, and laid up all the words in the public books of his judgement hall (*praetorium*).

XII (XXVIII)
This chapter is not found in the majority of copies.

After these things Pilate entered into the temple of the Jews and gathered together all the chief of the priests, and the teachers (*grammaticos*) and scribes and doctors of the law, and went in with them into the holy place of the temple and commanded all the doors to be shut, and said unto them: We have heard that ye have in this temple a certain great Bible; wherefore I ask you that it be presented before us. And when that great Bible adorned with gold and precious jewels was brought by four ministers, Pilate said to them all: I adjure you by the God of your fathers which commanded you to build this temple in the place of his sanctuary, that ye hide not the truth from me. Ye know all the things that are written in this Bible; but tell me now if ye have found in the scriptures that this Jesus whom ye have crucified is the Son of God which should come for the salvation of mankind, and in what year of the times he must come. Declare unto me whether ye crucified him in ignorance or knowingly.

And Annas and Caiaphas when they were thus adjured commanded all the rest that were with them to go out of the temple; and they themselves shut all the doors of the temple and of the sanctuary, and said unto Pilate: Thou hast adjured us, O excellent judge, by the building of this temple to make manifest unto thee the truth and reason (*or* a true account). After that we had crucified Jesus, knowing not that he was the Son of God, but supposing that by some chance he did his wondrous works, we made a great assembly (synagogue) in this temple; and as we conferred one with another concerning the signs of the mighty

Latin A.

works which Jesus had done, we found many witnesses of our own nation who said that they had seen Jesus alive after his passion, and that he was passed into the height of the heaven. Moreover, we saw two witnesses whom Jesus raised from the dead, who declared unto us many marvellous things which Jesus did among the dead, which things we have in writing in our hands. Now our custom is that every year before our assembly we open this holy Bible and inquire the testimony of God. And we have found in the first book of the Seventy how that Michael the angel spake unto the third son of Adam the first man concerning the five thousand and five hundred years, wherein should come the most beloved Son of God, even Christ: and furthermore we have thought that peradventure this same was the God of Israel which said unto Moses: Make thee an ark of the covenant in length two cubits and a half, and in breadth one cubit and a half, and in height one cubit and a half. For by those five cubits and a half we have understood and known the fashion of the ark of the old covenant, for that in five thousand and a half *thousand* years Jesus Christ should come in the ark of his body: and we have found that he is the God of Israel, even the Son of God. For after his passion, we the chief of the priests, because we marvelled at the signs which came to pass on his account, did open the Bible, and searched out all the generations unto the generation of Joseph, and Mary the mother of Christ, taking *her* to be the seed of David: and we found that *from the day* when God made the heaven and the earth and the first man, from that time unto the Flood are 2,212 years: and from the Flood unto the building of the tower 531 years: and from the building of the tower unto Abraham 606 years: and from Abraham unto the coming of the children of Israel out of Egypt 470 years: and from the going of the children of Israel out of Egypt unto the building of the temple 511 years: and from the building of the temple unto the destruction of the same temple 464 years: so far found we in the Bible of Esdras: and inquiring from the burning of the temple unto the coming of Christ and his birth we found it to be 636 years, which together were five thousand and five hundred years,[1] like as we found it written in the Bible that Michael the archangel declared before unto Seth the third son of Adam, that after five thousand and a half *thousand* years Christ the Son of God hath (? should) come. Hitherto have we told no man, lest there should be a schism in our synagogues; and now, O excellent judge, thou hast adjured us by this holy Bible of the testimonies of God, and we do declare it unto thee: and we also have adjured thee by thy life and health that thou declare not these words unto any man in Jerusalem.

[1] Really 5430 : no MS. gives a correct calculation.

Latin A.   XIII (XXIX)

And Pilate, when he heard these words of Annas and Caiaphas, laid them all up amongst the acts of the Lord and Saviour in the public books of his judgement hall, and wrote a letter unto Claudius the king of the city of Rome, saying:

[The following Epistle or Report of Pilate is inserted in Greek into the late Acts of Peter and Paul (§ 40) and the Pseudo-Marcellus Passion of Peter and Paul (§ 19). We thus have it in Greek and Latin, and the Greek is used here as the basis of the version.]

Pontius Pilate unto Claudius, greeting.

There befell of late a matter which I myself brought to light (*or* made trial of): for the Jews through envy have punished themselves and their posterity with fearful judgements of their own fault; for whereas their fathers had promises (*al.* had announced unto them) that their God would send them out of heaven his holy one who should of right be called their king, and did promise that he would send him upon earth by a virgin; he, then (*or* this God of the Hebrews, then), came when I was governor of Judaea, and they beheld him enlightening the blind, cleansing lepers, healing the palsied, driving devils out of men, raising the dead, rebuking the winds, walking upon the waves of the sea dry-shod, and doing many other wonders, and all the people of the Jews calling him the Son of God: the chief priests therefore, moved with envy against him, took him and delivered him unto me and brought against him one false accusation after another, saying that he was a sorcerer and did things contrary to their law.

But I, believing that these things were so, having scourged him, delivered him unto their will: and they crucified him, and when he was buried they set guards upon him. But while my soldiers watched him he rose again on the third day: yet so much was the malice of the Jews kindled that they gave money to the soldiers, saying: Say ye that his disciples stole away his body. But they, though they took the money, were not able to keep silence concerning that which had come to pass, for they also have testified that they saw him arisen and that they received money from the Jews. And these things have I reported ⟨unto thy mightiness⟩ for this cause, lest some other should lie *unto thee* (*Lat.* lest any lie otherwise) and thou shouldest deem right to believe the false tales of the Jews.

COPTIC NARRATIVES OF THE MINISTRY AND THE PASSION

There is a large mass of fragments in Coptic (Sahidic), some relating to the Ministry of our Lord and others to his Passion, which demand some notice here.

The largest collections of them (I pass over earlier publications such as those of Zoega and Dulaurier) are in Forbes Robinson's *Coptic Apocryphal Gospels*, E. Revillout's *Apocryphes Coptes*, I (Patrologia Orientalis II. 2), P. Lacau's *Fragments d'Apocryphes Coptes* (Mémoires de l'Institut Français d'Archéologie Orientale du Caire, 1904).

The fragments relating to the Life of Christ before the Passion are none of them attributed definitely to any author. They are mostly in homiletic form: the writer addresses his readers or congregation from time to time, directly, and not seldom he makes definite mention of the Gospels.

In one passage which Forbes Robinson humorously makes to serve as a motto to his volume, we read, 'But some one will say to me, Art thou then adding a supplement to the Gospels? Let that beloved one listen attentively and . . .', the fragment ends. Whatever his defence or explanation may have been, he certainly does add a great many supplements to the Gospels. It seems likely (judging from the analogy of other Coptic documents) that he personated, if not an apostle, a disciple of the apostles. The names of Evodius of Antioch and Gamaliel are found attached to similar writings. It would be quite in order for such a person to postulate the existence of the canonical Gospels, and to profess to offer information which was not contained in them.

It is conceivable that some of the narrative matter in these fragments may be taken from earlier books; but the fragments themselves cannot, I think, be earlier in date than the fifth century.

They will not be translated here in full: but a list, and a brief description of their contents, shall be given.

1. Robinson, p. 162. Birth and childhood of John Baptist. Birth of Christ. His star in the form of a wheel, its figure like a cross, letters on it: This is Jesus the Son of God. The wise men see it and come to Herod.

2. Robinson, p. 163. The Feast at Cana. The wine has failed; the parents of the bridegroom complain to Mary, who is their sister, and ask her to approach Christ. She does so. He orders that the water-pots be filled. *We* (the servants) hasted and filled them.

This, then, belongs to a narrative written by an eyewitness.

3. Revillout no. 1.
Herod accuses Philip to Tiberius.
Tiberius orders him to confiscate all Philip's goods.
Herod does so: Philip knows not the reason.

4. Revillout no. 2. Robinson, p. 168.

This is one of the longest of the fragments. It begins with
a passage addressed to the hearers, and quotes John the Evangelist on the feeding of the 5,000: the story is filled out with
dialogue, and tells how Judas was the last to receive the bread
and 'had no inheritance' in it. Thomas then says that he wishes
to see the power of Christ displayed in the raising of the dead
from their tombs, not only from the bier, as at Nain. Jesus
replies in a long and rhetorical address of many clauses, beginning,
'Come with me, Didymus, to the tomb of Lazarus'. Then the
raising of Lazarus is told, and the risen man says that when the
voice, 'Lazarus, come forth!' sounded in Amente (Hades), Adam
knew it and bore witness to it.

We then hear of one Carius, a Roman officer appointed to
look after the confiscated lands of Philip (see fragment 3).
He came to see Jesus and reported his mighty works to Herod,
saying that he ought to be made king. Herod threatened
any one who consented thereto with death. Annas and
Caiaphas went to Carius and accused Jesus—he is a magician,
was born of fornication, breaks the sabbath, has abolished
the synagogue of the Jews. Joseph and Nicodemus opposed
them.

(Robinson's text ends here: Revillout's (p. 145) continues
without break.)

Herod cast Joseph and Nicodemus into prison. Carius
threatened the Jews with destruction if any ill befell them. Then
Herod got a pound of gold from every one of the chiefs of the
Jews and bribed Carius with it not to tell Tiberius. And Carius
kept silence.

Joseph escaped to Arimathaea.

Carius sent the apostle John to Tiberius to tell him about
Jesus, and the emperor honoured him, and wrote that Jesus
should be made king: and as the Gospel (John vi. 15) says, Jesus
departed into a mountain alone.

After that he summoned the apostles; and now we have
a lengthy blessing of Peter on the mountain, at the end of which
Peter sees the seven heavens open, and the Trinity. All the
armies of heaven and the very stones of the mountain cry out the
trisagios to Peter.

5. Revillout no. 4, p. 151. Robinson, p. 176.

Jesus is comforting the apostles on the mountain. The
messengers of Theophilus come to fetch him to make him king.
'My kingdom is not of this world.'

The 'authorities' of Tiberius prevailed the second time concerning Jesus, with Pilate also, to commend Jesus to make him
king. Pilate advocated the plan strongly. Herod who was there
abused him: 'Thou art a Galilaean foreign Egyptian Pontus!'
There was enmity between Pilate and Herod, and Herod bribed
the Roman authorities and slandered Jesus.

Jesus' address to the apostles, ending 'let us go hence, for
Herod seeketh me to kill me '.

They came down from the mountain, and met the devil in the
form of a fisherman with attendant demons carrying nets and
hooks, &c.: and they cast their nets and hooks on the mount.[1]
The apostles questioned Jesus about this: John, Philip, and
Andrew, in particular. John was sent to speak to the devil and
ask him what he was catching. The devil said: 'It is not a wonder
to catch fish in the waters: the wonder is in this desert, to catch
fish there.' He cast his nets and caught all manner of fish (really
men), some by their eyes, others by their lips, &c.

(Here follows a fragment given only by Lacau, p. 108.) Jesus
told John to tell the devil to cast his nets again. He did so, and
a great smoke rose up, and the devil's power disappeared. John
threw a stone at him and he fled, cursing. Bartholomew then
asked to be permitted to see 'him whom thou didst create to
laugh at him' (Leviathan), and Jesus said that the sight was
almost too terrible for human eyes; but the request was granted.
A cloud—that of the Transfiguration—appeared in the heaven.

(Here the piece ends.)

And here Revillout would place a few lines which he calls
no. 4 *bis* (p. 189), which paraphrase John vii. 8–11, about Jesus
refusing at first to go to the feast, and subsequently going in
secret. The only detail worth noting is that (at Jerusalem)
Jesus sojourns in the house of Irmeël.

We next have a group of pieces relating to the Passion.

First we place two fragments relating to Judas and his wife.

6. Revillout no. 5, p. 156.

Some speaker tells how Judas used to take his ill-gotten gains
home to his wife: sometimes he cheated her of them, and then
she mocked him.

She counselled him to betray his Master.

He listened to her as Adam did to Eve, and went and covenanted
with the Jews. The prophecy (Zech.) was fulfilled.

He took the money to his wife: he said to her . . .

7. Lacau, p. 34. Revillout, Suppl. 1, p. 195.

Judas received the thirty pieces.

His wife was foster-mother to the child of Joseph of Arimathaea, which was seven months old. When the money was brought
into the house, the child (fell ill or would not stop crying).
Joseph was summoned: the child cried out, begging him to take
it away 'from this evil beast, for yesterday at the ninth hour
they received the price (of blood)'. Joseph took the child away.

Judas went to the priests. They arrested Jesus and took him
to Pilate. . . . He was crowned with thorns and crucified, and
said: Father forgive them.

[1] Compare with this the Gospel of Bartholomew, iv. 44.

8. Revillout no. 6, p. 157. Lacau, p. 33.

Jesus and the apostles at table. The table turned of itself after Jesus had partaken of a dish, to present it to each apostle.

Matthias set a dish on the table in which was a cock, and told Jesus how, when he was killing it, the Jews said: 'The blood of your master shall be shed like that of this cock.' Jesus smiled and answered that it was true ; and after some more words, bade the cock come to life and fly away and 'announce the day whereon they will deliver me up'. And it did so.

Here a reference will not be out of place to the Ethiopic 'Book of the Cock' which is read in the Abyssinian Church on Maundy Thursday. It has been translated by Marius Chaîne, in the *Revue Sémitique*, 1905, p. 276.

The contents are as follows :

After these things Akrosina, the wife of Simon the Pharisee, brought a cock cut up with a knife, put it in a magnificent dish, and set it on the table before our Lord. Jesus said, 'My time is at hand'. He blessed the bread and gave it to Judas. Satan entered into him and he went out—without receiving the blessing of Jesus.

Jesus touched the slain cock and it stood up whole. He bade it follow Judas and see what he did, and return and report it: he endowed it with human speech. It followed Judas home: his wife urged him to betray Jesus. He went to the temple. The dialogue with the Jews is reported, and Paul of Tarsus, 'son of Josue Almason, son of Cadafanâ', a rough man, says, 'Now, thou, deliver him into my hands without error'.

The cock returned to Bethany, and sat before Jesus and wept bitterly, and told all the story. The disciples wept. Jesus dismissed the cock to mount up into the sky for a thousand years.[1]

The fragments 7 and 8 most probably belong to the beginning of the Book of Bartholomew, which has to be noticed hereafter. Certainly this is the case with Revillout no. 12, p. 165 (Lacau 3, p. 34), which narrates the death of Ananias.

9. Revillout no. 10, p. 161. A dialogue between Christ and Pilate expanded from that in St. John.

[1] By way of a curiosity another Ethiopic narrative of the Passion may find mention here. It is noticed in Dillmann's catalogue of the Ethiopic MSS. in the British Museum (no. 40, Add. 16, 254) under the name of Liber Vivificans (Dirsan Mahyawi), and contains the story of the Passion written by the Evangelists and by three Virgins, Berzeda, Mathilda, and Elisabeth, to whom the Lord revealed his Passion. Another copy, apparently, is in the D'Abbadie MS. 29. The 'three Virgins' are evidently SS. Birgitta of Sweden (fourteenth century), Mechtildis (twelfth or thirteenth century), and Elisabeth of Schönau (twelfth century), all of whom had revelations about the Passion. How their writings made their way to Abyssinia it would be curious and interesting to ascertain.

10. Revillout no. 11, p. 163. A further piece of a like dialogue, including long speeches of our Lord, and ending with *Ecce homo*.

The place and order of the two next is uncertain.

11. Revillout no. 13, p. 168. An address of our Lord (to Thomas) reminding him of the signs at the crucifixion, and exhorting him to touch him.

12. Revillout no. 14, p. 169. Mary (the Virgin) at the sepulchre. Jesus appears to her and addresses her, forbidding her to touch him. The scene is assimilated to that of the appearance to Mary Magdalene (as elsewhere in Coptic writings): see above on the 'XXth Discourse of Cyril', pp. 87, 88.

13. Revillout no. 15, p. 170. Lacau, p. 19. Two leaves with a gap of two between them.

This fragment has a definite attribution, to Gamaliel.

It is a narrative connected with the resurrection.

We find Pilate examining four soldiers as to their statement that the body of Jesus was stolen. One (the second: the testimony of the first is gone) says the eleven apostles took the body; the third says, Joseph and Nicodemus; the fourth, 'we were asleep'. They are imprisoned, and Pilate goes with the centurion and the priests to the tomb and finds the grave-clothes. He says, 'If the body had been stolen, these would have been taken too'. They say, 'These grave-clothes belong to some one else'. Pilate remembers the words of Jesus, 'Great wonders must happen in my tomb', and goes in, and weeps over the shroud. Then he turns to the centurion, who had but one eye, having lost the other in battle.

Here is a gap, in which no doubt the centurion's eye is healed by touching the grave clothes, and he is converted. Also it is clear that Joseph and Nicodemus are sent for, and that the Jews point out to Pilate that in a well in the garden there is the body of a crucified man.

The other leaf begins with a dialogue between Pilate and the centurion. Then all go to the well. 'I, Gamaliel, followed them also among the band.' They see the body, and the Jews cry, 'Behold the sorcerer'. . . . Pilate asks Joseph and Nicodemus whether this is the body of Jesus. They answer, the grave-clothes are his, but the body is that of the thief who was crucified with him. The Jews are angry and wish to throw Joseph and Nicodemus into the well. . . . Pilate remembers the words of Jesus, 'The dead shall rise again in my tomb', and says to the Jews, 'You believe that this is truly the Nazarene'. They say, 'Yes'. 'Then', says Pilate, 'it is but right to lay his body in his own tomb.' . . .

Here the leaf ends; but we can see that when the body is laid in Jesus' tomb it will revive and declare the truth.

A detached sheet of an Ethiopic MS. which was in private

hands in 1892 (see *Newbery House Magazine*, 1892, p. 641), contains a like story in another form.

Here we have the Jews explaining to Pilate that the sweet odour of the sepulchre is due to the spices put on the body by Joseph, and to the flowers in the garden. Pilate rebukes them, and they retort that he has no business to come to the sepulchre. He addresses the centurion. After a gap is a prayer of Pilate's, in which he asks pardon for having put 'another body in the place where they put thy body'. At the end of the prayer a voice comes from the mouth of the dead bidding Pilate remove the stone that he (the dead) may come out.

An Arabic Life of Pilate, noticed by De Sacy, extant in manuscript at Paris (Arab. 160), seems likely to contain the whole story, of which we here have fragments. It purports to have been written by Gamaliel and Annas (or Ananias). Migne, *Dict. des Apocr.* I. 1101.

This, I believe, completes the list of the fragments of this character which have been published up to date. Nearly all of them are put together by Revillout under the title of the Gospel of the Twelve Apostles. But we have seen that at least one (13) is from a narrative under Gamaliel's name; and it is also pretty clear that not all the rest can belong to a single writing.

Nos. 1, 3, 4, 5 must go together: they are from the 'homiletic' book. 1 is the least certainly pertinent.

These pieces have an element which links them together in the *motif* of the intrigues to make Jesus a king. Their late date is apparent in the long rhetorical speeches, and in the tremendous exaltation of St. Peter.

No. 2 is by an eyewitness, assigned by Baumstark to *Gamaliel*.

No. 6 may belong to *Gamaliel*.

Nos. 7, 8 to *Bartholomew*.

Nos. 9, 10, with their interest in Pilate, are probably from *Gamaliel*.

Nos. 11, 12 uncertain. Baumstark refers them to *Gamaliel*.

No. 13, *Gamaliel*.

Baumstark's article referred to here is in the *Revue Biblique Internationale* for 1906, p. 245. He would refer nos. 2, 3, 4, 5 to *Gamaliel*, as well as the later ones.

Other Coptic documents will come up for notice when we deal with the Gospel of Bartholomew, the Death of the Virgin, and the Acts of the Apostles: and also with the Apocalypses. It may be as well, however, to register here the statement or warning that the Copts were tireless in producing embroideries upon the Biblical stories, and perhaps in rewriting older documents to suit their own taste. Only fresh discoveries of older texts can enable us to decide how much, if any, of the details which these later fragments supply, is really archaic.

OTHER APPENDIXES TO THE ACTS OF PILATE

Under this heading may be noticed the various forms of Reports of Pilate to the Emperor, and other Letters attributed to him: of his death, of the Vengeance of the Saviour, and also the Greek writing called the Story of Joseph of Arimathaea.

It is probable that some sort of Report of Pilate to Tiberius was concocted very early. Tertullian states it as a fact that Pilate reported all the events of the Passion to Tiberius, and that the Emperor tried, without success, to induce the Senate to declare Jesus a God.[1] What the source of this story was is unknown, but it is a very obvious one to invent. The texts of the apocryphal Reports which we have are all late, but in some of the Greek ones there are faint similarities to the Gospel of Peter.

Tischendorf prints a short

LETTER OF PILATE TO TIBERIUS,

which cannot be traced further back than the fifteenth century. It is written in rather elegant Latin, evidently, I think, by an Italian of the early Renaissance. The tenor of it is this :

'Jesus Christ of whom I recently wrote to you has been executed against my will. So pious and austere a man has never been seen, nor will be again. But there was a wonderful unanimity in the request of the Jews and their leader that he should be crucified, though their own prophets, and the Sibyls, testified against them, and signs appeared at his death which the philosophers said threatened the collapse of the whole world. His disciples who still live do not belie their master's teaching, but are active in good works. Had I not feared a general rising, the man might have been yet alive.' He ends, feebly excusing his conduct. Date, the 5th of the Kalends of April.

REPORT OF PILATE (ANAPHORA).

There are two Greek texts of this which do not differ in essentials. In some manuscripts one form is appended to the Acts of Pilate. It is a late document, and not of much interest in its present form: but, as has been said, it contains faint reminders of the Gospel of Peter, and may be based on a briefer document of early date. After the address it begins:

'I have received a communication, O most mighty, which oppresses me with fear and trembling.'

He goes on to say that in Jerusalem, a city of his province, the Jews delivered him a man named Jesus, charging him with much that they could not substantiate, and in particular with violating the sabbath. The miracles are then described with some rhetorical ornament, particularly in the case of Lazarus.

[1] A letter of Tiberius to Abgar of Edessa, quoted by Moses of Chorene (*History of Armenia*, II, ch. 33) gives exactly the same account of the proceedings in the Senate, and mentions the report of Pilate.

Jesus was delivered to him by Herod, Archelaus, Philip, Annas, Caiaphas, and all the people.

At his crucifixion the sun was darkened; the stars appeared, and in all the world people lighted lamps from the sixth hour till evening; the moon appeared like blood, and the stars and Orion lamented at the sin of the Jews. (The other recension says that Abraham, Isaac, Jacob, the twelve patriarchs, and Moses and Job, who were seen by the Jews, and many others 'whom I, too, saw', appeared in the body and thus lamented.)

On the first day of the week, at the third hour of night, there was a great light: the sun shone with unwonted brightness, men in shining garments appeared in the air and cried out to the souls in Hades to come up, and proclaimed the resurrection of Jesus.

The light continued all night. Many Jews disappeared in the chasms which the earthquake had caused: and all the synagogues except one fell down.

Under the stress of the consternation caused by all these portents Pilate writes to Caesar.

To this is appended in one recension the 'Delivering up, Paradosis, of Pilate'.

On receipt of the letter there was great astonishment at Rome, and Caesar in wrath ordered Pilate to be brought to him as a prisoner.

On hearing of his arrival Caesar took his seat 'in the temple of the gods before all the senate, and with all his army and all the multitude of his power', and said to Pilate: How didst thou dare, thou, most impious, to do such a thing, when thou hadst seen such signs concerning that man? by thy wicked daring thou hast destroyed the whole world.

Pilate threw the blame on the Jews, on Herod, Archelaus, Philip, Annas, and Caiaphas (see the Anaphora). *Caesar.* Why didst thou yield to them? *Pilate.* The nation is rebellious and disobedient. *Caesar.* Thou oughtest to have kept him safe and sent him to me, and not have yielded and crucified one who had done all those mighty works of which thou spakest in thy report. It is plain that he was the Christ, the king of the Jews.

When Caesar named Christ, all the images of the gods fell down and became as dust. There was great consternation: Caesar remanded Pilate to prison.

Next day he sat in the Capitol with all the senate, and a dialogue similar to the last took place. After it Caesar wrote to Licianus, the chief governor of the East, bidding him enslave all the nation of the Jews, and make them few in number for their wickedness. This Licianus did.

Caesar then commanded a ruler named Albius to behead Pilate. He was led forth to death, and prayed: Number me not among the wicked Hebrews. Remember not evil against me or against thy servant Procla which standeth here, whom thou didst make to prophesy that thou must be nailed to the cross. But pardon us and number us among thy righteous ones.

A voice from heaven came, saying: All the generations and the families of the Gentiles shall call thee blessed, because in thy days were fulfilled all these things which were spoken by the prophets concerning me; and thou also shalt appear as my witness (or martyr) at my second coming, when I shall judge the twelve tribes of Israel and them that have not confessed my name.

The prefect cut off Pilate's head, and an angel of the Lord received it: whom when Procla his wife saw, she was filled with joy, and straightway gave up the ghost and was buried with her husband.

This extraordinarily favourable view of Pilate is characteristic of the East. From the same workshop as the Report and the Paradosis come two letters—of Pilate to Herod, and Herod to Pilate—which exist in Greek and in Syriac (the latter in a manuscript of the sixth or seventh century). There is some divergence between the two versions.

THE LETTER OF PILATE TO HEROD

It was no good thing which I did at your persuasion when I crucified Jesus. I ascertained from the centurion and the soldiers that he rose again, and I sent to Galilee and learned that he was preaching there to above five hundred believers.

My wife Procla took Longinus, the believing centurion, and ten (or twelve) soldiers (who had kept the sepulchre), and went forth and found him 'sitting in a tilled field' teaching a multitude. He saw them, addressed them, and spoke of his victory over death and hell. Procla and the rest returned and told me. I was in great distress, and put on a mourning garment and went with her and fifty soldiers to Galilee. We found Jesus: and as we approached him there was a sound in heaven and thunder, and the earth trembled and gave forth a sweet odour. We fell on our faces and the Lord came and raised us up, and I saw on him the scars of the passion, and he laid his hands on my shoulders, saying: All generations and families shall call thee blessed (see above), because in thy days the Son of Man died and rose again.

THE LETTER OF HEROD TO PILATE

It is in no small sorrow—according to the divine Scriptures— (i. e. as I might have anticipated from the teaching of Scripture) that I write to you.

My dear daughter Herodias was playing upon the water (i. e. the ice) and fell in up to her neck. And her mother caught at her head to save her, and it was cut off, and the water swept her body away. My wife is sitting with the head on her knees, weeping, and all the house is full of sorrow.

I am in great distress of mind at the death of Jesus, and reflecting on my sins in killing John Baptist and massacring the Innocents. 'Since, then, you are able to see the man Jesus again, strive for me and intercede for me: for to you Gentiles the kingdom is given, according to the prophets and Christ.'

Lesbonax my son is in the last stages of a decline. I am afflicted with dropsy, and worms are coming out of my mouth. My wife's left eye is blinded through weeping. Righteous are the judgements of God, because we mocked at the eye of the righteous. Vengeance will come on the Jews and the priests, and the Gentiles will inherit the kingdom, and the children of light be cast out.

And, Pilate, since we are of one age, bury my family honourably: it is better for us to be buried by you than by the priests, who are doomed to speedy destruction. Farewell. I have sent you my wife's earrings and my own signet ring. I am already beginning to receive judgement in this world, but I fear the judgement hereafter much more. This is temporary, that is everlasting.

If the Eastern Christians—or at least those of Egypt and Syria—regarded Pilate as a saint and martyr, those of the West thought of him only as a criminal. The biography of him which is given in the *Golden Legend* (cap. 53, on the Passion) is of too late a date to be reproduced here; but the legends of his death are older. In summarizing them we will begin with one of the few Greek writings which takes the Western, the unfavourable, view of Pilate. It is assuredly not early in date: it has points of connexion with the B recension (Greek) of the Acts of Pilate. It is the

LETTER OF TIBERIUS TO PILATE

This was delivered to Pilate by means of the messenger Raab (cf. Rachaab in Recension B, p. 116), who was sent with 2,000 soldiers to bring him to Rome.

Since you have given a violent and iniquitous sentence of death against Jesus of Nazareth, showing no pity, and having received gifts to condemn him, and with your tongue have expressed sympathy (a reference to the Anaphora), but in your heart have delivered him up, you shall be brought home a prisoner to answer for yourself.

I have been exceedingly distressed at the reports that have reached me: a woman, a disciple of Jesus, has been here, called Mary Magdalene,[1] out of whom he is said to have cast seven devils, and has told of all his wonderful cures. How could you permit him to be crucified? If you did not receive him as a God, you

---

[1] Cf. Recension B of the Acts of Pilate.

might at least have honoured him as a physician.   Your own deceitful writing to me has condemned you.

As you unjustly sentenced him, I shall justly sentence you, and your accomplices as well.

Pilate, Archelaus, Philip, Annas, and Caiaphas were arrested.

Rachaab and the soldiers slew all the Jewish males, defiled the women, and brought the leaders to Rome.   On the way Caiaphas died in Crete: the earth would not receive his body, and he was covered with a cairn of stones.

It was the old law that if a condemned criminal saw the face of the emperor he was spared: so Tiberius would not see Pilate, but shut him up in a cave.

Annas was sewed into a fresh bull's-hide, which, contracting as it dried, squeezed him to death.   The other chiefs of the Jews were beheaded: Archelaus and Philip were crucified.

One day the emperor went out to hunt, and chased a hind to the door of Pilate's prison.   Pilate looked out, trying to see the emperor's face, but at that moment the emperor shot an arrow at the hind, which went in at the window and killed Pilate.

The same tale is told in a Greek life of Mary Magdalene, which I have transcribed from a manuscript at Holkham, and which is evidently under strong Western influence, since it tells the story of her mission to Marseilles and of a miracle wrought on a prince there, which is a very favourite subject with French mediaeval artists.

THE DEATH OF PILATE

The Latin legend of Pilate's death hardly ranks as an apocryphal book. It is printed by Tischendorf from a Milan manuscript of the fourteenth century—the illustrated manuscript mentioned above (p. 66) under the heading of Infancy Gospels, facsimiled under the title of *Canonical Histories and Apocryphal Legends*.   It is also found in the Golden Legend, cap. 53, as the conclusion of the fabulous life of Pilate, and is there said to be taken from 'a certain history, though an apocryphal one'.   This life is found separate—usually in company with a similar life of Judas Iscariot—in manuscripts of an earlier date than the Golden Legend; but the whole composition is thoroughly mediaeval and has nothing antique about it.

The story is this:

The Emperor Tiberius, being sorely diseased, heard that there was a wonderful physician in Jerusalem, named Jesus, who healed all sicknesses.   He sent an officer of his named Volusianus to Pilate to bid him send the physician to him.   Pilate was terrified, knowing that Jesus had been crucified (and begged for fourteen days delay, *Golden Legend*).   On the way back to his inn, Volusianus met a matron called Veronica and asked her about Jesus.   She told him the truth, to his great grief, and, to console him added that when our Lord was away teaching she had desired to have a picture of him always by her, and went to carry a linen cloth to a painter for that purpose. Jesus met her, and on hearing what she wished, took the cloth from her and imprinted the features of his face upon it. This cloth, she said, will cure your lord: I cannot sell it, but I will go with you to him.

Volusianus and Veronica returned to Rome, and Tiberius, when the likeness was to be brought to him, spread the path with silken cloths. He was instantly healed by looking at the likeness.

Pilate was arrested and brought before the emperor at Rome. Now he was wearing the seamless tunic of Jesus. When he came before the emperor, he, who had been raging against him before, became quite mild. He sent Pilate away and immediately his rage returned. This happened again. Then, either by divine inspiration or on the suggestion of some Christian, he had him stripped of the tunic, sent him back to prison, and shortly after sentenced him to die by the basest of deaths. On hearing this, Pilate killed himself with his own knife. Caesar had a millstone tied to his neck and threw him into the Tiber. The demons gathered in crowds, and storms disturbed the place so that all were in great fear. The corpse was taken out of the river and carried off to Vienne (via Gehennae) on the Rhone, with the same result. Thence it was taken to be buried in the territory of Lausanne; but disturbances continued there till the inhabitants dug it up and threw it into a well surrounded by mountains, where diabolical manifestations are still said to occur.

The last class of these legends is somewhat older. We have it in several forms in Latin and also in an old Anglo-Saxon version. It has something in common with the Death of Pilate, and it merges into the romances of the Destruction of Jerusalem which were very popular in the thirteenth and fourteenth centuries. The oldest form is that called the Healing of Tiberius (*Cura sanitatis Tiberii*), which goes back in manuscripts to the eighth century.

This runs as follows: Tiberius was sorely diseased. He heard from a Jew named Thomas of the miracles of Jesus, and sent a great officer, Volusianus, to bring him from Jerusalem. The voyage took a year and three months. Pilate and the Jews were much frightened. Pilate had to be persuaded by one of his soldiers that it was the crucified Jesus who was meant: the evidence for the resurrection was confirmed by Joseph of Arimathaea and others. Pilate, imprisoned meanwhile, was made to avow his guilt publicly.

A young man named Marcius now informed Volusian that a woman of Tyre, Veronica (who is also called Basilla, say some early copies), possessed the likeness of Jesus, who had cured her issue of blood three years before. Denying it at first, she at last produced it under compulsion. Volusian adored it, and threatened with punishment all who had taken part in Jesus' death. He then set off for Rome with Veronica and Pilate, and reached it in a short time. Tiberius inquired why Pilate had not been executed. Volusian said he did not wish to anticipate the emperor's judgement. Tiberius banished Pilate, without seeing him, to Ameria in Tuscany. Volusian then brought Veronica and the likeness to Tiberius, who adored it and was healed. He gave money to Veronica, and made a precious shrine for the likeness, was baptized, and died after some years in peace.[1]

The next development of the legend is thought to originate in Aquitaine. The manuscripts go back to the tenth century, and the Anglo-Saxon version is not later than the eleventh. The name of this is

THE VENGEANCE OR AVENGING OF THE SAVIOUR,

and a brief summary of it shall be given.

There was a king Titus (*or* Tyrus) under Tiberius, in Aquitaine, in a city of Libia called Burgidalla (Bordeaux). He had a cancer in his right nostril and his face was eaten away up to his eye.

There was also a Jew named Nathan, son of Naum, whom the Jews had sent to Tiberius to bear a treaty to him. Tiberius, too, was ill of fever and ulcers and had nine kinds of leprosy. Nathan's ship was driven ashore at Titus's city. Nathan was sent for and told his story. Titus asked if he knew any one who could cure him. Nathan said: If you had been in Jerusalem lately there was a prophet called Emanuel (the miracles are enumerated, and the Passion, descent into hell, and resurrection described). Titus said: Woe to you, Tiberius, in whose realm such things are done. I would have slain these Jews with my own hand for destroying my Lord. At this word the wound fell from his face and he was healed, and so were all the sick who were there. Titus cried out, confessing his belief in Christ, and made Nathan baptize him (and instead of Tyrus he was called Titus, which in our tongue means Pious, *Anglo-Saxon*).

Then he sent for Vespasian to come with all his forces, and he came with 5,000 men, and said: What do you want me for? 'To destroy the enemies of Jesus.' So they sailed off to Jerusalem. Archelaus in terror gave his kingdom to his son, and stabbed himself. The son allied himself with other kings and fortified Jerusalem, which was besieged seven years, till the inhabitants had to eat earth. At last they took counsel to surrender, and gave the keys to Titus and Vespasian. Some were slain, some crucified head downwards, or pierced

---

[1] An appendix or continuation tells how, in Nero's days, Simon Magus came to Rome and claimed to be the risen Son of God. How Pilate was sent for, and his letter to Claudius read; how Pilate returned into exile at Ameria, and soon died; and of Nero's evil end.

with lances, sold, cast lots upon, and divided into four parts, and the rest sold at thirty for a penny.

Then they made search for the likeness of Jesus and found Veronica, who had it. Pilate they delivered to four quaternions of soldiers. (Veronica was the woman healed of the issue of blood. She abode with Titus and Vespasian till the emperor's kinsman Velosian came.)

A message was sent by Titus to Tiberius to send Velosian. He told him to go to Jerusalem and bring some one to heal him, to whom he might promise half the kingdom.

Velosian arrived after a year and seven days, and first found Joseph and Nicodemus. Joseph told of the burial, of his imprisonment, and his deliverance by Jesus.

Then Veronica came and told of her healing. Velosian arraigned and imprisoned Pilate (put him in an iron cage, *Anglo-Saxon*). He then examined Veronica, who denied that she had the likeness. He threatened her with torture; at last she confessed that she had it in (*or* on) a linen cloth and adored it every day. She produced it. Velosian adored it, took it, put it in a gold cloth and locked it in a box, and embarked for Rome. Veronica left all she had and insisted on coming with him. They sailed up the Tiber to Rome, after a year's journey.

Tiberius heard of their arrival and summoned Velosian, who told him all the story at length, including the destruction of the Jews. Then Tiberius asked for the likeness. It was brought, and he adored it, and at his flesh was cleansed and he prayed. Then he asked if there were any there who had seen Christ and knew how to baptize. And Nathan was brought, and baptized him, and he blessed God, and was instructed in all the articles of the Christian faith.

Another form of the legend is given in the *Golden Legend*,[1] and incorporated, with pictures, in the Milan manuscript referred to before.

This begins by telling how Pilate sent a messenger, Albanus, to Caesar to excuse himself for the condemnation of Jesus. Albanus was driven ashore in Galicia and brought to Vespasian, who derived his name from the fact that from his childhood he had been troubled with a wasps' nest in his nose. Vespasian said to Albanus: You come from the land of the wise; you must cure me. Albanus said: I am not skilled in medicine. Vespasian: You must cure me or die. Albanus: There was a man who could have cured you with a word; he cast out devils, and raised the dead. He was Jesus of Nazareth, whom the Jews killed for envy. If you believed in him you would recover. Vespasian: I do firmly believe that he is the Son of God and that he can cure me. And immediately the wasps fell from his nose

---

[1] Cap. 67, of St. James the Less.

and he was healed. Vespasian then vowed to go to Tiberius and get forces wherewith to destroy the city and nation of the Jews. And after some years spent in gathering an army he besieged Jerusalem. The Christians, warned by the Holy Ghost, had fled to Pella.

Then there is a meeting between the historian Josephus and Vespasian; the latter's elevation to the empire is prophesied and takes place. Then we have the story of Titus falling ill from joy at his father's triumph, and being cured by having a slave whom he hated set next him at table. This was contrived by Josephus. Thereafter the famine in Jerusalem, and the incident of the woman Mary eating her child. Then the city is taken and the Jews are sold thirty for a penny.

Then the discovery of an old man built up in a very massive wall, who is Joseph of Arimathaea. Delivered by Jesus, as the Gospel of Nicodemus tells, he had been imprisoned again by the Jews because he continued to preach the gospel, and had been miraculously sustained ever since with light and food from heaven.

The very last of these late fictions which shall be noticed here is the

STORY OF JOSEPH OF ARIMATHAEA

which we have in Greek only. The earliest manuscript used by Tischendorf is said to be of the twelfth century.

I. 1 I, Joseph of Arimathaea, who begged the body of the Lord Jesus from Pilate, was imprisoned by the Jews on that account. These are the people who provoked their lawgiver Moses, and failing to recognize their God crucified his Son.

Seven days before the passion of Christ, two condemned robbers were sent from Jericho to Pilate, whose crimes were these.

2 The first, Gestas, used to strip and murder wayfarers, hang up women by the feet and cut off their breasts, drink the blood of babes: he knew not God nor obeyed any law, but was violent from the beginning.

The other, Demas, was a Galilaean who kept an inn; he despoiled the rich but did good to the poor, even burying them, like Tobit. He had committed robberies on the Jews, for he stole (plundered) the law itself at Jerusalem, and stripped the daughter of Caiaphas, who was a priestess of the sanctuary, and he took away even the mystic deposit of Solomon which had been deposited in the (holy) place.

3 Jesus also was taken at even on the third day before the passover. But Caiaphas and the multitude of the Jews had no passover but were in great grief because of the robbery of the sanctuary by the thief. And they sent for Judas Iscariot who was brother's son to Caiaphas, and had been persuaded by

the Jews to become a disciple of Jesus, not to follow his teachings,
but to betray him. They paid him a didrachm of gold daily;
and as one of Jesus' disciples, called John, says, he had been
two years with Jesus.

4 On the third day before Jesus was taken, Judas said to
the Jews: Let us assemble a council and say that it was not
the robber who took away the law, but Jesus. Nicodemus,
who had the keys of the sanctuary, said No: for he was a truthful
man. But Sarra, Caiaphas' daughter, cried out that Jesus said
in public, 'I can destroy the temple' (&c.). All the Jews said:
We believe you. For they held her as a prophetess. So Jesus
was taken.

II. 1 On the morrow, being Wednesday, at the ninth hour,
they brought him into Caiaphas' hall, and Annas and Caiaphas
asked him: Why didst thou take away the law? He was silent.
Why wouldst thou destroy the temple of Solomon? He was
silent.

2 In the evening the multitude sought the daughter of
Caiaphas, to burn her with fire, because the law was stolen
and they could not keep the passover. But she said: Wait
a little, my children, and let us destroy Jesus, and the law will
be found and the feast kept. Then Annas and Caiaphas privily
gave gold to Judas and said: Say as you said before, that it
was Jesus who stole the law. Judas agreed, but said: The people
must not know that you have told me this: and you must let
Jesus go, and I will persuade them. So they fraudulently let
Jesus go.

3 At dawn of the Thursday Judas went into the sanctuary
and said to all the people: What will ye give me if I deliver
to you the destroyer of the law and robber of the prophets?
They said: Thirty silver pieces of gold (!). But they did not
know that it was Jesus of whom he spoke, for many thought him
to be the Son of God. And Judas received the thirty pieces.

4 At the fourth and fifth hours he went out and found Jesus
walking in the street. Towards evening he obtained a guard
of soldiers. As they went, Judas said: Whomsoever I shall
kiss, take him: he it is that stole the law and the prophets.
He came to Jesus and kissed him, saying: Hail, Rabbi. They
took Jesus to Caiaphas and examined him. 'Why didst thou
do this?' but he answered nothing. Nicodemus and I left
the seat of the pestilent, and would not consent to perish in the
council of sinners.

III. 1 They did many evil things to Jesus that night, and on
the dawn of Friday delivered him to Pilate. He was condemned
and crucified with the two robbers, Gestas on the left, Demas
on the right.

2 He on the left cried out to Jesus: See what evils I have
wrought on the earth; and had I known thou wert the king,

I would have killed thee too. Why callest thou thyself Son of God and canst not help thyself in the hour of need? or how canst thou succour any other that prayeth? if thou be the Christ, come down from the cross that I may believe thee. But now I behold thee, not as a man but as a wild beast caught and perishing along with me. And much else he spake against Jesus, blaspheming and gnashing his teeth upon him: for he was caught in the snare of the devil.

3 But Demas, on the right, seeing the divine grace of Jesus, began to cry out thus: I know thee, Jesus Christ, that thou art the Son of God. I see thee, Christ, worshipped by ten thousand times ten thousand angels; forgive my sins that I have committed: make not the stars to enter into judgement with me, or the moon, when thou judgest all the world: for in the night did I work my evil plans: stir not up the sun that now is darkened for thy sake to tell the evil of my heart: for I can give thee no gift for remission of sins. Already death cometh on me for my sins, but pardon belongeth unto thee: save me, Lord of all things, from thy terrible judgement: give not power unto the enemy to swallow me up and be inheritor of my soul, as of his that hangeth on the left; for I see how the devil taketh his soul rejoicing, and his flesh vanisheth away. Neither command me to depart into the lot of the Jews, for I see Moses and the patriarchs weeping sore, and the devil exulting over them. Therefore before my spirit departeth, command O Lord that my sins be blotted out, and remember me the sinner in thy kingdom when thou sittest on the great throne of the Most High and shalt judge the twelve tribes of Israel: for thou hast prepared great punishment for thy world for thy sake.

4 And when the thief had so said, Jesus saith unto him: Verily, verily, I say unto thee, Demas, that to-day thou shalt be with me in paradise: but the sons of the kingdom, the children of Abraham, Isaac, and Jacob, and Moses shall be cast out into the outer darkness: there shall be weeping and gnashing of teeth. But thou only shalt dwell in paradise until my second coming, when I shall judge them that have not confessed my name. And he said to the thief: Go and say unto the cherubim and the powers that turn about the flaming sword, that keep the garden since Adam the first-created was in paradise and transgressed and kept not my commandments and I cast him out thence—but none of the former men shall see paradise until I come the second time to judge the quick and dead—And he wrote thus: Jesus Christ the Son of God that came down from the heights of heaven, that proceeded out of the bosom of the invisible Father without separation, and came down into the world to be incarnate and to be nailed to the cross, that I might save Adam whom I formed: unto my powers the archangels, that keep the doors of paradise, the servants of

my Father: I will and command that he that is crucified with
me [enter in,] receive remission of his sins for my sake, and
being clothed with an incorruptible body enter in to paradise,
and that he dwell there where no man *else* is ever able to dwell.

And when this was said, Jesus gave up the ghost on Friday
at the ninth hour. And there was darkness over all the land
and a great earthquake, so that the sanctuary fell, and the
pinnacle of the temple.

IV. 1 And I, Joseph, begged the body and laid it in my new
tomb. The body of Demas was not found: that of Gestas
was in appearance like that of a dragon.

The Jews imprisoned me on the evening of the sabbath.

2 When it was evening on the first day of the week, at the
fifth hour of the night, Jesus came to me with the thief on the
right hand. There was great light; the house was raised up
by the four corners and I went forth: and I perceived Jesus
first, and then the thief bringing a letter to him, and as we
journeyed to Galilee there was a very great light, and a sweet
fragrance came from the thief.

3 Jesus sat down in a certain place and read as follows: The
cherubim and the six-winged that are commanded by thy Godhead to keep the garden of paradise make known to thee this
by the hand of the robber that by thy dispensation was crucified
with thee. When we saw the mark of the nails on the robber
that was crucified with thee and the light of the letters of thy
Godhead, the fire was quenched, being unable to bear the light
of the mark, and we were in great fear and crouched down. For
we heard that the maker of heaven and earth and all creation
had come to dwell in the lower parts of the earth for the sake
of Adam the first-created. For we beheld the spotless cross,
with the robber flashing with light and shining with seven times
the light of the sun, and trembling came on us, when we heard
the crashing of them beneath the earth, and with a great voice
the ministers of Hades said with us: Holy, Holy, Holy, is he
that was in the highest in the beginning: and the powers sent
up a cry, *saying*, Lord, thou hast been manifested in heaven and
upon earth, giving joy unto the worlds (ages) and saving thine
own creation from death.

V. 1 And as I went with Jesus and the robber to Galilee, the
form of Jesus was changed and he became wholly light, and
angels ministered to him and he conversed with them. I stayed
with him three days, and none of the disciples were there.

2 In the midst of the days of unleavened bread his disciple
John came, and the robber disappeared. John asked who it
was, but Jesus did not answer. John said: Lord, I know that
thou hast loved me from the beginning: why dost thou not
reveal this man to me? Jesus said: Seekest thou to know
hidden things? art thou wholly without understanding? per-

ceivest thou not the fragrance of paradise filling the place? knowest thou not who it was? The thief that was on the cross is become heir of paradise: verily, verily, I say unto you, that it is his alone until the great day come. John said: Make me worthy to see him.

3 Then suddenly the thief appeared and John fell to the earth: for he was now like a king in great might, clad with the cross. And a voice of a multitude was heard: Thou art come into the place of paradise prepared for thee: we are appointed to serve thee by him that sent thee until the great day. After that both the thief and I, Joseph, vanished, and I was found in my own house, and I saw Jesus no more.

All this I saw and have written, that all might believe on Jesus and no longer serve Moses' law, but believe in the signs and wonders of Christ, and believing obtain eternal life and be found in the kingdom of heaven.

For His is glory, might, praise, and majesty, world without end. Amen.

There is a certain amount of inventiveness in this: none of the picturesque detail, however, can be called antique, and several phrases betray the influence of the same workshop that produced the Letters of Herod to Pilate. The ignorance of Jewish customs which it betrays is colossal.

GOSPEL OF BARTHOLOMEW

JEROME, in the prologue to his Commentary on Matthew, mentions a number of apocryphal Gospels—those according to the Egyptians, Thomas, Matthias, *Bartholomew*, the Twelve, Basilides, and Apelles: probably he depends upon Origen, for he himself disliked and avoided apocryphal books, with few exceptions; the Gospel according to the Hebrews, for instance, he hardly reckoned as apocryphal. Of this Gospel of Bartholomew we have no sort of description: we find it condemned in the Gelasian Decree, which may mean either that the compiler of the Decree knew a book of that name, or that he took it on trust from Jerome. In the pseudo-Dionysian writings two sentences are quoted from 'the divine Bartholomew', and a third has just been brought to light from the kindred 'book of Hierotheus'.[1] But one cannot be sure that these writers are quoting real books.

We have, however, a writing attributed to Bartholomew which attained some popularity; the manuscripts do not call it a Gospel, but the Questions of Bartholomew. It contains ancient elements, and I think that MM. Wilmart and Tisserant have made out their claim that it at least represents the old Gospel. I therefore give a translation of it here.

It exists in three languages, and not, apparently, in a very original form in any of them : Greek is the original language, of which we have two manuscripts, at Vienna and Jerusalem ; Latin 1, consisting of two leaves of extracts, of the ninth century ; Latin 2, complete : see below ; Slavonic (i–iv. 15). The Greek text may be as old as the fifth century ; the Latin 2 of the sixth or seventh.

In the *Revue Biblique* for 1913 the Latin fragments and a fresh Greek text were published by MM. Wilmart and Tisserant, with the variants of the other authorities, and in 1921-2 yet another text, a complete Latin one, appeared in the same periodical, edited by Professor Moricca from a manuscript in the Casanatensian library at Rome, in which the text is, in parts, tremendously expanded. This copy is of the eleventh century and came from the monastery of Monte Amiata. The Latin is exceedingly incorrect, and there are many corruptions, and interpolations which extend to whole pages of closely printed text. I cite it as Lat. 2.

I take the Greek and Slavonic, where they exist, as the basis of my version, and add some passages from the Latin. The main topics, common to two or more of the texts, are:

    i. The descent into Hell: the number of souls saved and lost.
    ii. The Virgin's account of the Annunciation.
    iii. The apostles see the bottomless pit.
    iv. The devil is summoned and gives an account of his doings.
    v. Questions about the deadly sins. Commission of the apostles to preach. Departure of Christ. (This reads like a late addition.)

[1] By the Rev. F. Marsh, *Journal of Theol. Studies*, 1922.

GOSPEL (QUESTIONS) OF ST. BARTHOLOMEW

I[1]

Greek. 1 After the resurrection from the dead of our Lord Jesus Christ, Bartholomew came unto the Lord and questioned him, saying: Lord, reveal unto me the mysteries of the heavens.

2 Jesus answered and said unto him: If I put ⟨not⟩ off the body of the flesh, I shall not be able to tell them unto thee.

3 *Om.*

Slavonic. 1 Before the resurrection of our Lord Jesus Christ from the dead, the apostles said: Let us question the Lord: Lord, reveal unto us the wonders.

2 And Jesus said unto them: If I put ⟨not⟩ off the body of the flesh, I cannot tell them unto you.

3 But when he was buried and risen again, they all durst not question him, because it was not ⟨possible⟩ to look upon him, but the fullness of his Godhead was seen.

4 But Bartholomew, &c.

Latin 2. 1 At that time, before the Lord Jesus Christ suffered, all the disciples were gathered together, questioning him and saying: Lord, show us the mystery in the heavens.

2 But Jesus answered and said unto them: If I put not off the body of flesh I cannot tell you.

3 But after that he had suffered and risen again, all the apostles, looking upon him, durst not question him, because his countenance was not as it had been aforetime, but showed forth the fullness of power.

Greek. 4 Bartholomew therefore drew near unto the Lord and said: I have a word *to speak* unto thee, Lord.

5 And Jesus said to him: I know what thou art about to say; say then what thou wilt, and I will answer thee.

6 And Bartholomew said: Lord, when thou wentest to be hanged upon the cross, I followed thee afar off and saw thee hung upon the cross, and the angels coming down from heaven and worshipping thee. And when there came darkness, 7 I beheld, and I saw thee that thou wast vanished away from the cross, and I heard only a voice in the parts under the earth, and great wailing and gnashing *of teeth* on a sudden. Tell me, Lord, whither wentest thou from the cross?

8 And Jesus answered and said: Blessed art thou, Bartholomew, my beloved, because thou sawest this mystery; and now will I tell thee all things whatsoever thou askest me. 9 For when I vanished away from the cross, then went I down into Hades that I might bring up Adam and all them that were with him, according to the supplication of Michael the archangel.

10 Then said Bartholomew: Lord, what was the voice which was heard?

---

[1] I give the opening verses in all three texts.

11 Jesus saith unto him: Hades said unto Beliar: As I perceive, *a* God cometh hither.

[*Slavonic and Latin 2 continue*: And the angels cried unto the powers, saying: Remove your gates, ye princes, remove the everlasting doors, for behold the King of glory cometh down. 12 Hades said: Who is the King of glory, that cometh down from heaven unto us?

13 And when I had descended five hundred steps, Hades was troubled, saying: I hear the breathing of the Most High, and I cannot endure it. (*Latin 2*. He cometh with great fragrance and I cannot bear it.) 14 But the devil answered and said: Submit not thyself, O Hades, but be strong: for God himself hath not descended upon the earth. 15 But when I had descended yet five hundred steps, the angels and the powers cried out: Take hold, remove the doors, for behold the King of glory cometh down. And Hades said: O, woe unto me, for I hear the breath of God.]

Greek. 16–17 And Beliar said unto Hades: Look carefully who it is that ⟨cometh⟩, for it is Elias, or Enoch, or one of the prophets that this man seemeth to me to be. But Hades answered Death and said: Not yet are six thousand years accomplished. And whence are these, O Beliar; *for* the sum of the number is in mine hands.

[*Slavonic.* 16 And the devil said unto Hades: Why affrightest thou me, Hades? it is a prophet, and he hath made himself like unto God: this prophet will we take and bring him hither unto those that think to ascend into heaven. 17 And Hades said: Which of the prophets is it? Show me: Is it Enoch the scribe of righteousness? But God hath not suffered him to come down upon the earth before the end of the six thousand years. Sayest thou that it is Elias, the avenger? But before ⟨the end⟩ he cometh not down. What shall I do, whereas the destruction is of God: for surely our end is at hand? For I have the number (of the years) in mine hands.]

Greek. 18 ⟨And Beliar said unto Hades⟩: Be not troubled, make safe thy gates and strengthen thy bars: consider, God cometh not down upon the earth.

19 Hades saith unto him: These be no good words that I hear from thee: my belly is rent, and mine inward parts are pained: it cannot be but that God cometh hither. Alas, whither shall I flee before the face of the power of the great king? Suffer me to enter into myself (thyself, *Latin*): for before (of, *Latin*) thee was I formed.

20 Then did I enter in and scourged him and bound him with chains that cannot be loosed, and brought forth thence all the patriarchs and came again unto the cross.

21 Bartholomew saith unto him: [*Latin 2*, I saw thee again, hanging upon the cross, and all the dead arising and worshipping thee, and going up again into their sepulchres.] Tell me, Lord,

who was he whom the angels bare up in their hands, even that
man that was very great of stature? [*Slav.*, *Lat.* 2, And what
spakest thou unto him that he sighed so sore?]
  22 Jesus answered and said unto him: It was Adam the first-
formed, for whose sake I came down from heaven upon earth.
And I said unto him: I was hung upon the cross for thee and for
thy children's sake. And he, when he heard it, groaned and said:
So was thy good pleasure, O Lord.
  23 Again Bartholomew said: Lord, I saw the angels ascending
before Adam and singing praises. 24 But one of the angels
which was very great, above the rest, would not ascend up with
them: and there was in his hand a sword of fire, and he was
looking steadfastly upon thee only.
  [*Slav.* 25 And all the angels besought him that he would
go up with them, but he would not. But when thou didst
command him to go up, I beheld a flame of fire issuing out of
his hands and going even unto the city of Jerusalem. 26 And
Jesus said unto him: Blessed art thou, Bartholomew my beloved,
because thou sawest these mysteries. This was one of the angels
of vengeance which stand before my Father's throne: and this
angel sent he unto me. 27 And for this cause he would not
ascend up, because he desired to destroy all the powers of the
world. But when I commanded him to ascend up, there went
a flame out of his hand and rent asunder the veil of the temple,
and parted it in two pieces for a witness unto the children of
Israel for my passion because they crucified me. (*Lat.* 1. But the
flame which thou sawest issuing out of his hands smote the
house of the synagogue of the Jews, for a testimony of me,
wherein they crucified me.)].
  Greek. 28 And when he had thus spoken, he said unto the
apostles: Tarry for me in this place, for to-day a sacrifice is
offered in paradise. 29 And Bartholomew answered and said
unto Jesus: Lord, what is the sacrifice which is offered in
paradise? And Jesus said: *There be* souls of the righteous
which to-day have departed out of the body and go unto
paradise, and unless I be present they cannot enter into paradise.
  30 And Bartholomew said: Lord, how many souls depart out
of the world daily? Jesus saith unto him: Thirty thousand.
  31 Bartholomew saith unto him: Lord, when thou wast with us
teaching the word, didst thou receive the sacrifices in paradise? [1]
Jesus answered and said unto him: Verily I say unto thee, my
beloved, that I both taught the word with you and continually
sat with my Father, and received the sacrifices in paradise every
day. 32 Bartholomew answered and said unto him: Lord, if
thirty thousand souls depart out of the world every day, how
many souls out of them are found righteous? Jesus saith unto
him: Hardly fifty [three] my beloved. 33 Again Bartholomew
  [1] In Lat. 2, 31 follows 29.

saith: And how do three only enter into paradise? Jesus saith
unto him: The [fifty] three enter into paradise or are laid up in
Abraham's bosom: but the others go into the place of the resurrection, for the three are not like unto the fifty.

34 Bartholomew saith unto him: Lord, how many souls above
the number are born into the world daily? Jesus saith unto him:
One soul only is born above the number of them that depart.
[30, &c., *Latin* 1. Bartholomew said: How many are the souls
which depart out of the body every day? Jesus said: Verily
I say unto thee, twelve (thousand) eight hundred, four score
and three souls depart out of the body every day.][1]

35 And when he had said this he gave them the peace, and
vanished away from them.

II

1 Now the apostles were in the place [Cherubim, Cheltoura,
Chritir] with Mary. 2 And Bartholomew came and said unto
Peter and Andrew and John: Let us ask her that is highly
favoured how she conceived the incomprehensible, or how she
bare him that cannot be carried, or how she brought forth so
much greatness. But they doubted to ask her. 3 Bartholomew
therefore said unto Peter: Thou that art the chief, and my
teacher, draw near and ask her. But Peter said to John: Thou
art a virgin and undefiled (and beloved) and thou must ask her.
4 And as they all doubted and disputed, Bartholomew came near
unto her with a cheerful countenance and said to her: Thou that
art highly favoured, the tabernacle of the Most High, unblemished,
·we, even all the apostles, ask thee (*or* All the apostles have sent
me to ask thee) to tell us how thou didst conceive the incomprehensible, or how thou didst bear him that cannot be carried, or
how thou didst bring forth so much greatness.

5 But Mary said unto them: Ask me not (*or* Do ye indeed
ask me) concerning this mystery. If I should begin to tell you,
fire will issue forth out of my mouth and consume all the world.
6 But they continued yet the more to ask her. And she, for she
could not refuse to hear the apostles, said: Let us stand up in
prayer. 7 And the apostles stood behind Mary: but she said
unto Peter: Peter, thou chief, thou great pillar, standest thou
behind us? Said not our Lord: the head of the man is Christ
⟨but the head of the woman is the man, *Slav.*, *Lat.* 2⟩? now
therefore stand ye before me and pray. 8 But they said unto
her: In thee did the Lord set his tabernacle, and it was his good
pleasure that thou shouldest contain him, and thou oughtest to be

[1] Lat. 2, 30–4 has: 6,074 souls depart out of the body every day.
Three go into paradise. 33 How three only? Fifty-three go into
paradise, but only three into Abraham's bosom. The rest are in the
place of repose, for they are not like the three. 34 One more soul
departs every day than is born.

the leader in the prayer (al. to go with us to). 9 But she said
unto them: Ye are shining stars, and as the prophet said, 'I did
lift up mine eyes unto the hills, from whence shall come mine
help'; ye, therefore, are the hills, and it behoveth you to pray.
10 The apostles say unto her: Thou oughtest to pray, thou
art the mother of the heavenly king. 11 Mary saith unto them:
In your likeness did God form the sparrows,[1] and sent them forth
into the four corners of the world. 12 But they say unto her:
He that is scarce contained by the seven heavens was pleased to
be contained in thee.

13 Then Mary stood up before them and spread out her hands
toward the heaven and began to speak thus: Elphuë Zarethra
Charboum Nemioth Melitho Thraboutha Mephnounos Chemiath
Aroura Maridōn Elisōn Marmiadōn Seption Hesaboutha Ennouna
Saktinos Athoōr Belelam Ōpheōth Abō Chrasar (this is the reading of one Greek copy: the others and the Slavonic have many
differences,[2] as in all such cases: but as the original words—assuming
them to have once had a meaning—are hopelessly corrupted, the
matter is not of importance), which is in the Greek tongue
(Hebrew, Slav.): O God the exceeding great and all-wise and
king of the worlds (ages), that art not to be described, the ineffable, that didst establish the greatness of the heavens and all
things by a word, that out of darkness (or the unknown) didst
constitute and fasten together the poles of heaven in harmony,
didst bring into shape the matter that was in confusion, didst
bring into order the things that were without order, didst part
the misty darkness from the light, didst establish in one place
the foundations of the waters, thou that makest the beings of the
air to tremble, and art the fear of them that are on (or under) the
earth, that didst settle the earth and not suffer it to perish, and
filledst it, which is the nourisher of all things, with showers of
blessing: (Son of) the Father, thou whom the seven heavens
hardly contained, but who wast well-pleased to be contained
without pain in me, thou that art thyself the full word of the
Father in whom all things came to be: give glory to thine
exceeding great name, and bid me to speak before thy holy
apostles.

14 And when she had ended the prayer she began to say unto
them: Let us sit down upon the ground; and come thou, Peter
the chief, and sit on my right hand and put thy left hand beneath
mine armpit; and thou, Andrew, do so on my left hand; and
thou, John, the virgin, hold together my bosom; and thou,
Bartholomew, set thy knees against my back and hold my

---

[1] See the Infancy Gospels.
[2] Lat. 2. Helfoith . Alaritha . arbar . Neniotho . Melitho . Tarasunt .
Chanebonos . Umia . Theirura . Marado . Seliso . Heliphomar . Mabon .
Saruth . Gefutha . Enunnas . Sacinos . Thatis . Etelelam . Tetheo .
abocia . Rusar.

shoulders, lest when I begin to speak my bones be loosed *one from another*.

15 And when they had so done she began to say: When I abode in the temple of God and received my food from an angel, on a certain day there appeared unto me one in the likeness of an angel, but his face was incomprehensible, and he had not in his hand bread or a cup, as did the angel which came to me aforetime. 16 And straightway the robe (veil) of the temple was rent and there was a very great earthquake, and I fell upon the earth, for I was not able to endure the sight of him. 17 But he put his hand beneath me and raised me up, and I looked up into heaven and there came a cloud of dew and sprinkled me from the head to the feet, and *he* wiped me with his robe. 18 And said unto me: Hail, thou that art highly favoured, the chosen vessel, grace inexhaustible. And he smote his garment upon the right hand and there came a very great loaf, and he set it upon the altar of the temple and did eat of it first himself, and gave unto me also. 19 And again he smote his garment upon the left hand and there came a very great cup full of wine: and he set it upon the altar of the temple and did drink of it first himself, and gave also unto me. And I beheld and saw the bread and the cup whole *as they were*.[1]

20 And he said unto me: Yet three years, and I will send my word unto thee and thou shalt conceive my (*or* a) son, and through him shall the whole creation be saved. Peace be unto thee, my beloved, and my peace shall be with thee continually. 21 And when he had so said he vanished away from mine eyes, and the temple was restored as it had been before.

22 And as she was saying this, fire issued out of her mouth; and the world was at the point to come to an end: but Jesus appeared quickly (*Lat.* 2, and laid his hand upon her mouth) and said unto Mary: Utter not this mystery, or this day my whole creation will come to an end (*Lat.* 2, and the flame from her mouth ceased). And the apostles were taken with fear lest haply the Lord should be wroth with them.

III

1 And he departed with them unto the mount Mauria (*Lat.* 2, Mambre), and sat in the midst of them. 2 But they doubted to question him, being afraid. 3 And Jesus answered and said unto them: Ask me what ye will that I should teach you, and I will show it you. For yet seven days, and I ascend unto my Father, and I shall no more be seen of you in this likeness. 4 But they, yet doubting, said unto him: Lord, show us the deep (abyss) according unto thy promise. 5 And Jesus said unto them: It is

[1] Compare the appearance of the angel to Aseneth in the *History of Aseneth*.

not good (*Lat.* 2, is good) for you to see the deep: notwithstanding, if ye desire it, according to my promise, come, follow me and behold. 6 And he led them away into a place that is called Cherubim (Cherukt *Slav.*, Chairoudec *Gr.*, *Lat.* 2 omits), that is the place of truth. 7 And he beckoned unto the angels of the West, and the earth was rolled up like a *volume of a* book and the deep was revealed unto them. 8 And when the apostles saw it, they fell on their faces upon the earth. 9 But Jesus raised them up, saying: Said I not unto you, 'It is not good for you to see the deep'. And again he beckoned unto the angels, and the deep was covered up.

IV

1 And he took them and brought them again unto the Mount of Olives.

2 And Peter said unto Mary: Thou that art highly favoured, entreat the Lord that he would reveal unto us the things that are in the heavens.

3 And Mary said unto Peter: O stone hewn out of the rock, did not the Lord build his church upon thee? Go thou therefore first and ask him.

4 Peter saith again: O tabernacle that art spread abroad ⟨it behoveth thee to ask⟩. 5 Mary saith: Thou art the image of Adam: was not he first formed and then Eve? Look upon the sun, that according to the likeness of Adam it is bright, and upon the moon, that because of the transgression of Eve it is full of clay. For God did place Adam in the east and Eve in the west, and appointed the lights that the sun should shine on the earth unto Adam in the east in *his* fiery chariots, and the moon in the west should give light unto Eve with a countenance like milk. And she defiled the commandment of the Lord. Therefore was the moon stained with clay (*Lat.* 2, is cloudy) and her light is not bright. Thou therefore, since thou art the likeness of Adam, oughtest to ask *him*: but in me was he contained that I might recover the strength of the female.

6 Now when they came up to the top of the mount, and the Master was withdrawn from them a little space, Peter saith unto Mary: Thou art she that hast brought to nought the transgression of Eve, changing it from shame into joy; it is lawful, therefore, for thee to ask.

7 When Jesus appeared again, Bartholomew saith unto him: Lord, show us the adversary of men that we may behold him, of what fashion he is, and what is his work, and whence he cometh forth, and what power he hath that he spared not even thee, but caused thee to be hanged upon the tree. 8 But Jesus looked upon him and said: Thou bold heart! thou askest for that which thou art not able to look upon. 9 But Bartholomew was troubled and fell at Jesus' feet and began to speak thus: O lamp that

cannot be quenched, Lord Jesu Christ, maker of the eternal light, that hast given unto them that love thee the grace that beautifieth all, and hast given us the eternal light by thy coming into the world, that hast† . . . † the heavenly essence by a word † . . . † hast accomplished the work of the Father, hast turned the shame-facedness of Adam into mirth, hast done away the sorrow of Eve with a cheerful countenance by thy birth from a virgin: re-member not evil against me but grant me the word of mine asking. (*Lat.* 2, who didst come down into the world, who hast confirmed the eternal word of the Father, who hast called the sadness of ⟨Adam⟩ joy, who hast made the shame of Eve glad, and restored her by vouchsafing to be contained in the womb.)

10 And as he thus spake, Jesus raised him up and said unto him: Bartholomew, wilt thou see the adversary of men? I tell thee that when thou beholdest him, not thou only but the rest of the apostles and Mary will fall on your faces and become as dead corpses.

11 But they all said unto him: Lord, let us behold him.

12 And he led them down from the Mount of Olives and looked wrathfully upon the angels that keep hell (Tartarus), and beckoned unto Michael to sound the trumpet in the height of the heavens. And Michael sounded, and the earth shook, and Beliar came up, being held by 660 (560 *Gk.*, 6,064 *Lat.* 1, 6,060 *Lat.* 2) angels and bound with fiery chains. 12 And the length of him was 1,600 cubits and his breadth 40 (*Lat.* 1, 300 ; *Slav.* 17) cubits (*Lat.* 2, his length 1,900 cubits, his breadth 700, one wing of him 80), and his face was like a lightning of fire and his eyes full of darkness (like sparks, *Slav.*). And out of his nostrils came a stinking smoke ; and his mouth was as the gulf of a precipice, and the one of his wings was four-score cubits. 14 And straight-way when the apostles saw him, they fell to the earth on their faces and became as dead. 15 But Jesus came near and raised the apostles and gave them a spirit of power, and he saith unto Bartholomew: Come near, Bartholomew, and trample *with* thy feet on his neck, and he will tell thee his work, what it is, and how he deceiveth men. 16 And Jesus stood afar off with the rest of the apostles. 17 And Bartholomew feared, and raised his voice and said: Blessed be the name of thine immortal kingdom from henceforth even for ever. And when he had spoken, Jesus permitted him, *saying*: Go and tread upon the neck of Beliar: and Bartholomew ran quickly upon him and trode upon his neck: and Beliar trembled. (For this verse the Vienna MS. has: And Bartholomew raised his voice and said thus: O womb more spacious than a city, wider than the spreading of the heavens, that contained him whom the seven heavens contain not, but thou without pain didst contain sanctified in thy bosom, &c.: evidently out of place.

Latin 1 has only: Then did Antichrist tremble and was filled with fury.)

18 And Bartholomew was afraid, and fled, and said unto Jesus: Lord, give me an hem of thy garments (*Lat.* 2, the kerchief (?) from thy shoulders) that I may have courage to draw near unto him. 19 But Jesus said unto him: Thou canst not take an hem of my garments, for these are not my garments which I wore before I was crucified. 20 And Bartholomew said: Lord, I fear lest, like as he spared not thine angels, he swallow me up also. 21 Jesus saith unto him: Were not all things made by my word, and by the will of my Father the spirits were made subject unto Solomon? thou, therefore, being commanded by my word, go in my name and ask him what thou wilt. (*Lat.* 2 omits 20.) 22[1] [And Bartholomew made the sign of the cross and prayed unto Jesus and went behind him. And Jesus said to him: Draw near. And as Bartholomew drew near, fire was kindled on every side, so that his garments appeared fiery. Jesus saith to Bartholomew: As I said unto thee, tread upon his neck and ask him what is his power.] And Bartholomew went and trode upon his neck, and pressed down his face into the earth as far as his ears. 23 And Bartholomew saith unto him: Tell me who thou art and what is thy name. And he said to him: Lighten me a little, and I will tell thee who I am and how I came hither, and what my work is and what my power is. 24 And he lightened him and saith to him: Say all that thou hast done and all that thou doest. 25 And Beliar answered and said: If thou wilt know my name, at the first I was called Satanael, which is interpreted a messenger of God, but when I rejected the image of God my name was called Satanas, that is, an angel that keepeth hell (Tartarus).[2] 26 And again Bartholomew saith unto him: Reveal unto me all things and hide nothing from me. 27 And he said unto him: I swear unto thee by the power of the glory of God that even if I would hide aught I cannot, for he is near that would convict me. For if I were able I would have destroyed you like one of them that were before you. 28 For, indeed, I was formed (*al.* called) the first angel: for when God made the heavens, he took a handful of fire and formed me first, Michael second [Vienna MS. here has these sentences: for he had his Son before the heavens and the earth and we were formed (for when he took thought to create all things, his Son spake a word), so that we also were created by the will of the Son and the consent of the Father. He formed, *I say*, first me, next Michael the chief captain of the hosts that are above], Gabriel third, Uriel fourth, Raphael fifth, Nathanael sixth, and other angels of whom I cannot tell the names. [*Jerusalem MS.*, Michael, Gabriel, Raphael, Uriel, Xathanael, and

[1] 22 [   ] is from Gk. (Jerusalem MS.) and Latin 1.
[2] 25. Lat. 2 adds about seven lines descriptive of Satan's character: not interesting.

other 6,000 angels. *Lat.* 1, Michael the† honour of power, third Raphael, fourth Gabriel, and other seven. *Lat.* 2, Raphael third, Gabriel fourth, Uriel fifth, Zathael sixth, and other six.] For they are the rod-bearers (lictors) of God, and they smite me with their rods and pursue me seven times in the night and seven times in the day, and leave me not at all and break in pieces all my power. These are the (twelve, *Lat.* 2) angels of vengeance which stand before the throne of God: these are the angels that were first formed. 30 And after them were formed all the angels. In the first heaven are an hundred myriads, and in the second an hundred myriads, and in the third an hundred myriads, and in the fourth an hundred myriads, and in the fifth an hundred myriads, and in the sixth an hundred myriads, and in the seventh (an hundred myriads, and outside the seven heavens, *Jerusalem MS.*) is the first firmament (flat surface) wherein are the powers which work upon men. 31 For there are four other angels set over the winds. The first angel is over the north, and he is called Chairoum (. . . broïl, *Jerusalem MS.*; *Lat.* 2, angel of the north,[1] Mauch), and hath in his hand a rod of fire, and restraineth the superfluity of moisture that the earth be not overmuch wet. 32 And the angel that is over the north [2] is called Oertha (*Lat.* 2, Alfatha): he hath a torch of fire and putteth it to his sides, and they warm the great coldness of him that he freeze not the world. 33 And the angel that is over the south is called Kerkoutha (*Lat.* 2, Cedar), and they break his fierceness that he shake not the earth. 34 And the angel that is over the south-west is called Naoutha, and he hath a rod of snow in his hand and putteth it into his mouth, and quencheth the fire that cometh out of his mouth. And if the angel quenched it not at his mouth it would set all the world on fire. 35 And there is another angel over the sea which maketh it rough with the waves thereof. 36 But the rest I will not tell thee, for he that standeth by suffereth me not.

37 Bartholomew saith unto him: How chastisest thou the souls of men? 38 Beliar saith unto him: Wilt thou that I declare unto thee the punishment of the hypocrites, of the backbiters, of the jesters, of the idolaters, and the covetous, and the adulterers, and the wizards, and the diviners, and of them that believe in us, and of all whom I †look upon† (deceive?)? (38 *Lat.* 2: When I *will* show any illusion by them. But they that do these things, and they that consent unto them or follow them, do perish with me. 39 Bartholomew said unto him: Declare quickly how thou persuadest men not to follow God, and thine evil arts, that are slippery and dark, that they should leave the straight and shining paths of the Lord.) 39 Bartholomew saith unto him: †I will that thou declare† it in few words. 40 And he smote his teeth together, gnashing them, and there came up out of the bottomless pit a wheel having a sword flash-

---

[1] Boreas.　　　　[2] Aparktios.

ing with fire, and in the sword were pipes. 41 And I (he) asked
him, saying: What is this sword? 42 And he said: This sword
is *the sword* of the gluttonous: for into this pipe are sent they
that through their gluttony devise all manner of sin; into the
second pipe are sent the backbiters which backbite their neighbour secretly; into the third pipe are sent the hypocrites and
the rest whom I overthrow by my contrivance. (*Lat.* 2: 40
And Antichrist said: I will tell thee. And a wheel came up
out of the abyss, having seven fiery knives. The first knife
hath twelve pipes (*canales*). . . . 42 Antichrist answered: The
pipe of fire in the first knife, in it are put the casters of lots
and diviners and enchanters, and they that believe in them
or have sought them, because in the iniquity of their heart they
have invented false divinations. In the second pipe of fire are
first the blasphemers . . . suicides . . . idolaters. . . . In the rest are
first perjurers . . . (long enumeration).) 43 And Bartholomew
said: Dost thou then do these things by thyself alone? 44 And
Satan said: If I were able to go forth by myself, I would have
destroyed the whole world in three days: but neither I nor
any of the six hundred go forth. For we have other swift
ministers whom we command, and we furnish them with an hook
of many points [1] and send them forth to hunt, and they catch
for us souls of men, enticing them with sweetness of divers
baits, that is by drunkenness and laughter, by backbiting,
hypocrisy, pleasures, fornication, and the rest of the †trifles†
that come out of their treasures. (*Lat.* 2 amplifies enormously.)

45 And I will tell thee also the rest of the names of the angels.
The angel of the hail is called Mermeōth, and he holdeth the
hail upon his head, and my ministers do adjure him and send
him whither they will. And other angels are there over the
snow, and other over the thunder, and other over the lightning,
and when any spirit of us would go forth either by land or by
sea, these angels send forth fiery stones and set our limbs on fire.
(*Lat.* 2 enumerates all the transgressions of Israel and all
possible sins in two whole pages.)

46 Bartholomew saith: Be still (be muzzled) thou dragon of
the pit. 47 And Beliar said: Many things will I tell thee of
the angels. They that run together throughout the heavenly
places and the earthly are these: Mermeōth, Onomatath, Douth,
Melioth, Charouth, Graphathas, Oethra, Nephonos, Chalkatoura.
With them †do fly† (are administered?) the things that are in
heaven and on earth and under the earth.

48 Bartholomew saith unto him: Be still (be muzzled) and
be faint, that I may entreat my Lord. 49 And Bartholomew
fell upon his face and cast earth upon his head and began to
say: O Lord Jesu Christ, the great and glorious name. All

---

[1] hook of many points, &c. This passage recalls the Coptic fragment
No. 5, above, p. 149.

the choirs of the angels praise thee, O Master, and I that am
unworthy with my lips † . . . † do praise thee, O Master. Hearken
unto me thy servant, and as thou didst choose me from the receipt
of custom and didst not suffer me to have my conversation
unto the end in my former deeds, O Lord Jesu Christ, hearken
unto me and have mercy upon the sinners. 50 And when he
had so said, the Lord saith unto him: Rise up, suffer him that
groaneth *to arise*: I will declare the rest unto thee. 51 And
Bartholomew raised up Satan and said unto him: Go unto
thy place, with thine angels; but the Lord hath mercy upon
all his world. (50, 51, again enormously amplified in *Lat.* 2.
Satan complains that he has been tricked into telling his secrets
before the time. The interpolation is to some extent dated
by this sentence: 'Simon Magus and Zaroës and Arfaxir and
Jannes and Mambres are my brothers.' Zaroës and Arfaxat
are wizards who figure in the Latin Acts of Matthew and of
Simon and Jude (see below). 49 follows 51 in this text.)

52 But the devil said: Suffer me, and I will tell thee how
I was cast down into this place and how the Lord did make
man. 53 I was going to and fro in the world, and God said unto
Michael: Bring me a clod from the four corners of the earth,
and water out of the four rivers of paradise. And when Michael
brought them *God* formed Adam in the regions of the east, and
shaped the clod which was shapeless, and stretched sinews and
veins *upon it* and established it with joints; and he worshipped
him, himself for his own sake first, because he was the image
of God, *therefore* he worshipped him. 54 And when I came from
the ends of the earth Michael said: Worship thou the image
of God, which he hath made according to his likeness. But
I said: I am fire of fire, I was the first angel formed, and shall
I worship clay and matter? 55 And Michael saith to me: Worship, lest God be wroth with thee. But I said to him: God
will not be wroth with me; but I will set my throne over against
his throne, and I will be as he is. Then was God wroth with me
and cast me down, having commanded the windows of heaven
to be opened. 56 And when I was cast down, he asked also
the six hundred that were under me, if they would worship:
but they said: Like as we have seen the first *angel do*, neither
will we worship him that is less than ourselves. Then were
the six hundred also cast down by him with me. 57 And when
we were cast down upon the earth we were senseless for forty
years; and when the sun shone forth seven times brighter
than fire, suddenly I awaked; and I looked about and saw the
six hundred that were under me senseless. 58 And I awaked my
son Salpsan and took him to counsel how I might deceive the
man on whose account I was cast out of the heavens. 59 And
thus did I contrive it. I took a vial in mine hand and scraped
the sweat from off my breast and the hair of mine armpits, and

washed myself (*Lat.* 2, I took fig-leaves in my hands and wiped the sweat from my bosom and below mine arms and cast it down beside the streams of waters. 59 is greatly prolonged in this text) in the springs of the waters whence the four rivers flow out, and Eve drank of it and desire came upon her: for if she had not drunk of that water I should not have been able to deceive her. 60 Then Bartholomew commanded him to go into hell.

61 And Bartholomew came and fell at Jesus' feet and began with tears to say thus: Abba, Father, that art past finding out by us, Word of the Father, whom the seven heavens hardly contained, but who wast pleased to be contained easily and without pain within the body of the Virgin: whom the Virgin knew not that she bare: thou by thy thought hast ordained all things to be: thou givest us †that which we need† before thou art entreated. 62 Thou that didst wear a crown of thorns that thou mightest prepare for us that repent the precious crown from heaven; that didst hang upon the tree, that (*a clause gone*): (*Lat.* 2, that thou mightest turn from us the tree of lust and concupiscence (etc., etc.). The verse is prolonged for over 40 lines) (*that didst drink wine mingled with gall*) that thou mightest give us to drink of the wine of compunction, and wast pierced in the side with a spear that thou mightest fill us with thy body and thy blood: 63 Thou that gavest names unto the four rivers: to the first Phison, because of the faith (*pistis*) which thou didst appear in the world to preach; to the second Geon, for that man was made of earth (*gē*); to the third Tigris, because by thee was revealed unto us the consubstantial Trinity in the heavens (*to make anything of this we must read Trigis*); to the fourth Euphrates, because by thy presence in the world thou madest every soul to rejoice (*euphrānai*) through the word of immortality. 64[1] My God and Father, the greatest, my King: save, Lord, the sinners. 65 When he had thus prayed Jesus said unto him: Bartholomew, my Father did name me Christ, that I might come down upon earth and anoint every man that cometh *unto me* with the oil of life: and he did call me Jesus that I might heal every sin of them that know not . . . and give unto men (*several corrupt words : the Latin has*) the truth of God.

66 And again Bartholomew saith unto him: Lord, is it lawful for me to reveal these mysteries unto every man? 67 Jesus saith unto him: Bartholomew, my beloved, as many as are faithful and are able to keep them unto themselves, to them mayest thou entrust these things. For some there are

[1] In Lat. 2, vv. 64–71 occupy 83 lines: verse 65 fills nearly 50 of these; Jesus dwells on the words, 'I am the way, the truth, and the life', and speaks at some length of his benefits to the Jewish nation and their blindness and ingratitude (recalling the Improperia and 2 Esdras 1): there are also many clauses from John xiii–xv.

that be worthy of them, but there are also other some unto
whom it is not fit to entrust them: for they are vain (swaggerers),
drunkards, proud, unmerciful, partakers in idolatry, authors
of fornication, slanderers, teachers of foolishness, and doing
all works that are of the devil, and therefore are they not worthy
that these should be entrusted to them. 68 And also they are
secret, because of those that cannot contain them; for as many
as can contain them shall have a part in them. Herein (Hitherto ?),
therefore, my beloved, have I spoken unto thee, for blessed art
thou and all thy kindred which of their choice have this word
entrusted unto them; for all they that can contain it shall receive
whatsoever they will in the ⟨day ?⟩ of my judgement.

69 Then I, Bartholomew, which wrote these things in mine
heart, took hold on the hand of the *Lord the* lover of men and
began to rejoice and to speak thus:
Glory be to thee, O Lord Jesus Christ, that givest unto all
thy grace which all we have perceived. Alleluia.
Glory be to thee, O Lord, the life of sinners.
Glory be to thee, O Lord, death is put to shame.
Glory be to thee, O Lord, the treasure of righteousness.
For unto God do we sing.

70 And as Bartholomew thus spake again, Jesus put off
his mantle and took a kerchief from the neck of Bartholomew
and began to rejoice and say (70 *Lat.* 2, Then Jesus took a
kerchief(?)[1] and said: I am good: mild and gracious and merciful,
strong and righteous, wonderful and holy): I am good. Alleluia.
I am meek and gentle. Alleluia. Glory be to thee, O Lord:
for I give gifts unto all them that desire me. Alleluia.
Glory be to thee, O Lord, world without end. Amen. Alleluia.

71 And when he had ceased, the apostles kissed him, and he
gave them the peace of love.

V

1 Bartholomew saith unto him:[2] Declare unto us, Lord,
what sin is heavier than all sins? 2 Jesus saith unto him:
Verily I say unto thee that hypocrisy and backbiting is heavier
than all sins: for because of them, the prophet said in the
psalm, that 'the ungodly shall not rise in the judgement, neither
sinners in the council of the righteous', neither the ungodly in
the judgement of my Father. Verily, verily, I say unto you,
that every sin shall be forgiven unto every man, but the sin
against the Holy Ghost shall not be forgiven. 3 And Bartholomew saith unto him: What is the sin against the Holy
Ghost? 4 Jesus saith unto him: Whosoever shall decree against
any man that hath served my holy Father hath blasphemed
against the Holy Ghost: For every man that serveth God

[1] *toracem.*   [2] In Lat. 2, vv. 1–6 occupy 58 lines.

worshipfully is worthy of the Holy Ghost, and he that speaketh
anything evil against him shall not be forgiven.[1]
5 Woe unto him that sweareth by the head of God, yea woe (?)
to him that sweareth falsely by him †truly†. For there are
twelve heads of God the most high: for he is the truth, and in
him is no lie, neither forswearing. 6 Ye, therefore, go ye and
preach unto all the world the word of truth, and thou, Bartholomew, preach this word unto every one that desireth it; and
as many as believe thereon shall have eternal life.
7 Bartholomew saith:[2] O Lord, and if any sin with sin of the
body, what is their reward? 8 And Jesus said: It is good if he
that is baptized present his baptism blameless: but the pleasure
of the flesh will †become a lover†. For a single marriage belongeth to sobriety: for verily I say unto thee, he that sinneth after
the third marriage (wife) is unworthy of God. (8 Lat. 2 is to
this effect: . . . But if the lust of the flesh come upon him,
he ought to be the husband of one wife. The married, if they
are good and pay tithes, will receive a hundredfold. A second
marriage is lawful, on condition of the diligent performance
of good works, and due payment of tithes: but a third marriage
is reprobated: and virginity is best.) 9 But ye, preach ye
unto every man that they keep themselves from such things:
for I depart not from you and I do supply you with the Holy
Ghost. (Lat. 2, At the end of 9, Jesus ascends in the clouds,
and two angels appear and say: 'Ye men of Galilee', and the
rest.) 10 And Bartholomew worshipped him with the apostles,
and glorified God earnestly, saying: Glory be to thee, Holy
Father, Sun unquenchable, incomprehensible, full of light.
Unto thee be glory, unto thee honour and adoration, world
without end. Amen. (Lat. 2, End of the questioning of the
most blessed Bartholomew and (or) the other apostles with
the Lord Jesus Christ.)

THE BOOK OF THE RESURRECTION OF CHRIST
BY BARTHOLOMEW THE APOSTLE

This exists in Coptic only. There are several recensions of it: the
most complete is in a manuscript recently acquired by the British
Museum (Or. 6804), and translated first by W. E. Crum (Rustafjaell's
Light of Egypt, 1910) and then edited and translated by Sir E. A. Wallis
Budge (*Coptic Apocrypha in the dialect of Upper Egypt*, 1913). Other
fragments are in the publications of Lacau and Revillout. No full
translation, but only an analysis, will be offered here.

---

[1] Lat. 2 enumerates seventeen other sins—chiefly forms of idolatry
and wrong belief.
[2] In Lat. 2, vv. 7–10 fill 69 lines.

Five leaves are wanting at the beginning of the British Museum MS. The contents of these can be partly filled up from Lacau and Revillout. But in the first place a passage (p. 193, Budge) may be quoted which shows something of the setting of the book : 'Do not let this book come into the hand of any man who is an unbeliever and a heretic. Behold, this is the seventh time that I have commanded thee, O my son Thaddaeus, concerning these mysteries. Reveal not thou them to any impure man, but keep them safely.' We see that the book was addressed by Bartholomew to his son Thaddaeus, and this would no doubt have been the subject of some of the opening lines of the text.

Next we may place the two fragments, one about the child of Joseph of Arimathaea, the other about the cock raised to life, which have been already described as nos. 7 and 8 of the Coptic narratives of the Passion (pp. 149, 150). The order is uncertain.

Then we have a piece which in Revillout is no. 12 (p. 165), in Lacau no. 3 (p. 34). Lacau gives it partly in two recensions.

Christ is on the cross, but his side has been pierced, and he is dead.

A man in the crowd named Ananias, of Bethlehem, rushes to the cross and embraces and salutes the body breast to breast, hand to hand, and denounces the Jews. A voice comes from the body of Jesus and blesses Ananias, promising him incorruption, and the name of 'the firstfruits of the immortal fruit'. The priests decide to stone Ananias: he utters words of exultation. The stoning produces no effect. They cast him into a furnace, where he remains till Jesus has risen. At last they pierce him with a spear.

The Saviour takes his soul to heaven, and blesses him.

There can be but little matter lost between this and the opening of the British Museum MS., in the first lines of which the taking of Ananias' soul to heaven is mentioned.

We now take up the British Museum MS. as our basis. Certain passages of it are preserved in Paris fragments which partly overlap each other, and so three different texts exist for some parts: but it will not be important for our purpose to note many of the variations.

Joseph of Arimathaea buried the body of Jesus. Death came into Amente (the underworld), asking who the new arrival was, for he detected a disturbance.

He came to the tomb of Jesus with his six sons in the form of serpents. Jesus lay there (it was the second day, i. e. the Saturday) with his face and head covered with napkins.

Death addressed his son the Pestilence, and described the commotion which had taken place in his domain. Then he spoke to the body of Jesus and asked, 'Who art thou?' Jesus removed the napkin that was on his face and looked in the face of Death and laughed at him. Death and his sons fled. Then they approached again, and the same thing happened. He addressed Jesus again at some length, suspecting, but not certain, who he was.

Then Jesus rose and mounted into the chariot of the Cherubim. He wrought havoc in Hell, breaking the doors, binding the demons Beliar and Melkir (cf. Melkira in the Ascension of Isaiah), and delivered Adam and the holy souls.

Then he turned to Judas Iscariot and uttered a long rebuke, and described the sufferings which he must endure. Thirty names of sins are given, which are the snakes which were sent to devour him.

Jesus rose from the dead, and Abbaton (Death) and Pestilence came back to Amente to protect it, but they found it wholly desolate, only three souls were left in it (those of Herod, Cain, and Judas, says the Paris MS.).

Meanwhile the angels were singing the hymn which the Seraphim sing at dawn on the Lord's day over his body and his blood.

Early in the morning of the Lord's day the women went to the tomb. They were Mary Magdalene, Mary the mother of James whom Jesus delivered out of the hand of Satan, Salome who tempted him, Mary who ministered to him and Martha her sister, Joanna (al. Susanna) the wife of Chuza who had renounced the marriage bed, Berenice who was healed of an issue of blood in Capernaum, Lia (Leah) the widow whose son he raised at Nain, and the woman to whom he said, 'Thy sins which are many are forgiven thee'.

These were all in the garden of Philogenes, whose son Simeon Jesus healed when he came down from the Mount of Olives with the apostles (probably the lunatic boy at the Mount of Transfiguration).

Mary said to Philogenes: If thou art indeed he, I know thee. Philogenes said: Thou art Mary the mother of Thalkamarimath, which means joy, blessing, and gladness. Mary said: If thou have borne him away, tell me where thou hast laid him and I will take him away: fear not. Philogenes told how the Jews sought a safe tomb for Jesus that the body might not be stolen, and he offered to place it in a tomb in his own garden and watch over it: and they sealed it and departed. At midnight he rose and went out and found all the orders of angels: Cherubim, Seraphim, Powers, and Virgins. Heaven opened, and the Father raised Jesus. Peter, too, was there and supported Philogenes, or he would have died.

The Saviour then appeared to them on the chariot of the Father and said to Mary: Mari Khar Mariath (Mary the mother of the Son of God). Mary answered: Rabbouni Kathiathari Miôth (The Son of God the Almighty, my Lord, and my Son). A long address to Mary from Jesus follows, in the course of which he bids her tell his brethren, 'I ascend unto my Father and your Father', &c. Mary says: If indeed I am not permitted to touch thee, at least bless my body in which thou didst deign to dwell.

Believe me, my brethren the holy apostles, I, Bartholomew, beheld the Son of God on the chariot of the Cherubim. All the heavenly hosts were about him. He blessed the body of Mary.

She went and gave the message to the apostles, and Peter blessed her, and they rejoiced.

Jesus and the redeemed souls ascended into Heaven, and the Father crowned him. The glory of this scene Bartholomew could not describe. It is here that he enjoins his son Thaddaeus not to let this book fall into the hands of the impure (quoted above).

Then follows a series of hymns sung in heaven, eight in all, which accompany the reception of Adam and the other holy souls into glory. Adam was eighty cubits high and Eve fifty. They were brought to the Father by Michael. Bartholomew had never seen anything to compare with the beauty and glory of Adam, save that of Jesus. Adam was forgiven, and all the angels and saints rejoiced and saluted him, and departed each to their place.

Adam was set at the gate of life to greet all the righteous as they enter, and Eve was set over all the women who had done the will of God, to greet them as they come into the city of Christ.

As for me, Bartholomew, I remained many days without food or drink, nourished by the glory of the vision.

The apostles thanked and blessed Bartholomew for what he had told them: he should be called the apostle of the mysteries of God. But he protested: I am the least of you all, a humble workman. Will not the people of the city say when they see me, 'Is not this Bartholomew the man of Italy, the gardener, the dealer in vegetables? Is not this the man that dwelleth in the garden of Hierocrates the governor of our city? How has he attained this greatness?'

The next words introduce a new section.

At the time when Jesus took us up into the Mount of Olives he spoke to us in an unknown tongue, which he revealed to us, saying: Anetharath (or Atharath Thaurath). The heavens were opened and we all went up into the seventh heaven (so the London MS.: in the Paris copy only Jesus went up, and the apostles gazed after him). He prayed the Father to bless us. The Father, with the Son and the Holy Ghost, laid His hand on the head of Peter (and made him archbishop of the whole world: Paris B). All that is bound or loosed by him on earth shall be so in heaven; none who is not ordained by him shall be accepted. Each of the apostles was separately blessed (there are omissions of single names in one or other of the three texts). Andrew, James, John, Philip (the cross will precede him wherever he goes), Thomas, Bartholomew (he will be the depositary of the mysteries of the Son), Matthew (his shadow will heal the sick), James son of Alphaeus, Simon Zelotes, Judas of James, Thaddeus, Matthias (who was rich and left all to follow Jesus). And now, my brethren the apostles, forgive me: I, Bartholomew, am not a man to be honoured.

The apostles kissed and blessed him. And then, with Mary, they offered the Eucharist.

The Father sent the Son down into Galilee to console the apostles and Mary: and he came and blessed them and showed them his wounds, and committed them to the care of Peter, and gave them their commission to preach. They kissed his side and sealed themselves with the blood that flowed thence. He went up to heaven.

Thomas was not with them, for he had departed to his city, hearing that his son Siophanes (Theophanes ?) was dead: it was the seventh day since the death when he arrived. He went to the tomb and raised him in the name of Jesus.

Siophanes told him of the taking of his soul by Michael: how it sprang from his body and lighted on the hand of Michael, who wrapped it in a fine linen cloth: how he crossed the river of fire and it seemed to him as water, and was washed thrice in the Acherusian lake: how in heaven he saw the twelve splendid thrones of the apostles, and was not permitted to sit on his father's throne.[1]

Thomas and he went into the city to the consternation of all who saw them. He, Siophanes, addressed the people and told his story: and Thomas baptized 12,000 of them, founded a church, and made Siophanes its bishop.

Then Thomas mounted on a cloud and it took him to the Mount of Olives and to the apostles, who told him of the visit of Jesus: and he would not believe. Bartholomew admonished him. Then Jesus appeared, and made Thomas touch his wounds: and departed into heaven.

This is the second time that he showed himself to his disciples after that he had risen from the dead.

This is the Book of the Resurrection of Jesus the Christ, our Lord, in joy and gladness. In peace. Amen.

Peter said to the apostles: Let us offer the offering before we separate. They prepared the bread, the cup, and incense.

Peter stood by the sacrifice and the others round the Table. They waited (break in the text: Budge and others suppose an appearance of Christ, but I do not think this is correct: 4½ lines are gone: then there are broken words):

table . . . their hearts rejoiced . . . worshipped the Son of God. He took his seat . . . his Father (probably, who sitteth at the right hand of the Father). His Body was on the Table about which

[1] This vision resembles one inserted in the end of the Coptic version of the Apocalypse of Paul.

they were assembled; and they divided it. They saw the blood of Jesus pouring out as living blood down into the cup. Peter said: God hath loved us more than all, in letting us see these great honours: and our Lord Jesus Christ hath allowed us to behold and hath revealed to us the glory of his body and his divine blood. They partook of the body and blood—and then they separated and preached the word. (What is clearly indicated is a change in the elements: there is not room for a description of an appearance of Jesus: he says no word, and his departure is not mentioned.)

This writing may be better described as a rhapsody than a narrative. It bristles with contradictions of itself: Joseph and Philogenes both bury Jesus; Thomas raises the dead and will not believe in Christ's resurrection: and so forth. That Mary the mother of Jesus is identified with Mary Magdalene is typical of the disregard of history, and we have seen it in other Coptic documents. The interest of the author is centred in the hymns, blessings, salutations, and prayers, which in this analysis have been wholly omitted, but which occupy a large part of the original text. The glorification of St. Bartholomew is another purpose of the writer: the special blessings given to him recall the attitude which he takes in the *Gospel* (i. 1, 8) as inquiring into the mysteries of heaven, and seeing things which are hidden from others. Both *Gospel* and *Book* are specially interested in the Descent into Hell, the Resurrection, and the redemption of Adam.

Bartholomew (Nathanael) was told (in St. John's Gospel) that he would see the angels ascending and descending upon the Son of Man. This promise is fulfilled in the *Gospel* (i. 6, 23) and very often in the *Book*: in St. John we also read of his being 'under the fig-tree', and this was probably enough to suggest to the Coptic author of the *Book* that he was a gardener.

A date is hard to suggest. The British Museum MS. is assigned to the twelfth century; the Paris fragments are older. That of the Coptic literature of this class is usually supposed to belong to the fifth and sixth centuries; and I think this, or at latest the seventh century, may be the period when the book was produced.

THERE is a fairly large class of books, early and late, which consists, like the Gospel of Bartholomew, of questions addressed to our Lord and his answers to them. Earliest of all are perhaps the Gnostic books preserved in Coptic in a Berlin MS. and not yet edited. One of these was used by Irenaeus. We hear of lost books of a similar kind: Questions of Mary, and a Gospel of Philip. We also possess, in Greek, late specimens of this class: e. g. Questions of John to Christ about the Last Things, which go by the name of the Apocryphal Apocalypse of John and have been printed by Tischendorf. Another like book is the Liber S. Joannis which was found in use in a Latin version among the Albigensian heretics in Southern France: it is printed by Thilo. Yet another is the Dispute of the Devil with Christ, printed in two texts, in Greek, by Vassiliev, and on the same general lines are Questions of St. James the brother of the Lord to St. John, also printed by Vassiliev. Various late Testaments or Dialogues of Jesus with the apostles remain unprinted.

BOOK OF JOHN THE EVANGELIST

Reprinted by Thilo from I. Benoist's *Histoire des Albigeois*, &c., Paris, 1691, T. 1, 283–96. Döllinger in his *Beiträge zur mittelalter-lichen Sektengeschichte*, vol. ii, printed another text from a fourteenth-century manuscript at Vienna. I have not given the variants. Thilo's reprint is followed. The Vienna MS. is rather imperfect at the end. Benoist derived his text from the Archives of the Inquisition at Carcassonne. The manuscript of it had this annotation in Latin:

'This is the secret *book* of the heretics of Concoréze, brought from Bulgaria by their bishop Nazarius; full of errors.'

This Nazarius was examined by Rainer (Contra Waldenses, vi : printed in *Bibl. Patr. max.* xxv. 271). He said that the Blessed Virgin was an angel, and that Christ did not take upon him a human nature but an angelic or heavenly one: and that he had this erroneous teaching from a bishop and elder son of the church of Bulgaria almost sixty years since.

The book is a Bogomile production, denying that the world was made by God, and attributing creation to the devil. Catholic Christians are disciples of John Baptist: baptism has no value, nor, probably, the Eucharist: but the statement about this has dropped out of the text. The law of sacrifices (promulgated by Enoch) and the Mosaic law are works of the devil.

The account of the Last Judgement, I agree with Thilo, seems too orthodox and conventional to square with the rest of the book: one suspects dilution from another source. In its Latin dress the book can hardly be older than the twelfth century. The original might be of the sixth or seventh.

I, John, your brother and partaker in tribulation, and that shall be also a partaker in the kingdom of heaven, when I lay upon the breast of our Lord Jesus Christ and said unto him: Lord, who is he that shall betray thee ? [and] he answered and said: He that dippeth his hand with me in the dish: then Satan entered unto him and he sought how he might betray me.

And I said: Lord, before Satan fell, in what glory abode he with thy Father? And he said unto me: In such glory was he that he commanded the powers of the heavens: but I sat with my Father; and he did order all the followers of the Father, and went down from heaven unto the deep and ascended up out of the deep unto the throne of the invisible Father. And he saw the glory of him that moveth the heavens, and he thought to set his seat above the clouds of heaven and desired to be like unto the Most High.

And when he had descended into the air, he said unto the angel of the air: Open unto me the gates of the air. And he opened them unto him. And he sought to go further downward and found the angel which held the waters, and said unto him: Open unto me the gates of the waters. And he opened to him. And he passed through and found all the face of the earth covered with waters. And he passed through beneath the earth and found two fishes lying upon the waters, and they were as oxen yoked for ploughing, holding the whole earth by the commandment of the invisible Father, from the west even unto the sunrising. And when he had gone down he found clouds hanging which held the waters of the sea. And he went down yet further and found hell, that is the gehenna of fire,[1] and thereafter he could go down no further because of the flame of the burning fire. And Satan returned back and filled up (passed over again) the paths and entered in unto the angel of the air and to him that was over the waters, and said unto them: All these things are mine: if ye will hearken unto me, I will set my seat in the clouds and be like the Most High, and I will take the waters from this upper firmament and gather together the other parts (places) of the sea, and thereafter there shall be no water upon the face of all the earth, and I will reign with you world without end.

And when he had said thus unto the angels, he went up unto the other angels, even unto the fifth heaven, and thus spake he unto each of them: How much owest thou unto thy lord? He said: An hundred measures (cors) of wheat. And he said unto him: Take pen and ink and write sixty. And unto others he said: And thou, how much owest thou unto thy lord? and he answered: An hundred jars of oil. And he said: Sit down and write fifty. And as he went up through all the heavens he said thus, even unto the fifth heaven, seducing the angels of the invisible Father. And there came forth a voice out of the throne of the Father, saying: What doest thou, O denier of the Father,

[1] Here (in Thilo's text only) occurs the word *ossop* which means nothing. A marginal note in Döllinger's Vienna MS. speaks of *oseph* and says that it is a place, apparently the *Vallis Josaphat*.

seducing the angels? doer of iniquity, that thou hast devised do quickly.

Then the Father commanded his angels, saying: Take away their garments. And the angels took away their garments and their thrones and their crowns from all the angels that hearkened unto him.

And I asked of the Lord: When Satan fell, in what place dwelt he? And he answered me: My Father changed his appearance because of his pride, and the light was taken from him, and his face became like unto heated iron, and his face became wholly like that of a man: and he drew with his tail the third part of the angels of God, and was cast out from the seat of God and from the stewardship of the heavens. And Satan came down into this firmament, and he could find (make) no rest for himself nor for them that were with him. And he asked the Father, saying: Have patience with me and I will pay thee all. And the Father had mercy on him and gave him rest and them that were with him, as much as they would even unto seven days.

And so sat he in the firmament and commanded the angel that was over the air and him that was over the waters, and they raised the earth up and it appeared dry: and he took the crown of the angel that was over the waters, and of the half thereof he made the light of the moon and of the half the light of the stars: and of the *precious* stones he made all the hosts of the stars.

And thereafter he made the angels his ministers according to the order of the form of the Most High, and by the commandment of the invisible Father *he made* thunder, rain, hail, and snow.

And he sent forth angels to be ministers over them. And he commanded the earth to bring forth every beast for food (fatling), and every creeping thing, and trees and herbs: and he commanded the sea to bring forth fishes, and the fowls of the heaven.

And he devised furthermore and made man in his likeness, and commanded the (*or* an) angel of the third heaven to enter into the body of clay. And he took thereof and made another body in the form of a woman, and commanded the (*or* an) angel of the second heaven to enter into the body of the woman. But the angels lamented when they beheld a mortal shape upon them and that they were unlike in shape. And he commanded them to do the deed of the flesh in the bodies of clay, and they knew not how to commit sin.

Then did the contriver of evil devise in his mind to make paradise, and he brought the man and woman into it. And he commanded to bring a reed, and the devil planted it in the midst of paradise, and so did the wicked devil hide his device that they knew not his deceit. And he came in and spake unto them, saying: Of every fruit which is in paradise eat ye, but of the fruit of the knowledge of good and evil eat not. Notwithstanding, the devil entered into a wicked serpent and seduced the angel that was in the form of the woman, and † . . . † and he wrought his lust with Eve in the †song† of the serpent. And therefore are they called sons of the devil and sons of the serpent that do the lust of the devil their father, even unto the end of this world. And again the devil poured out upon the angel that was in Adam the poison of his lust, and it begetteth the sons of the serpent and the sons of the devil even unto the end of this world.

And after that I, John, asked of the Lord, saying: How say men that Adam and Eve were created by God and set in paradise to keep the commandments of the Father, and were delivered unto death? And the Lord said to me: Hearken, John, beloved of my Father; foolish men say thus in their deceitfulness that my Father made bodies of clay: but by the Holy Ghost made he all the powers of the heavens, and holy ones were found having bodies of clay because of their transgression, and therefore were delivered unto death.

And again I, John, asked the Lord: How beginneth a man to be in the Spirit (to have a spirit) in a body of flesh? And the Lord said unto me: *Certain* of the angels which fell do enter unto the bodies of women, and receive flesh from the lust of the flesh, and so is a spirit born of spirit, and flesh of flesh, and so is the kingdom of Satan accomplished in this world and among all nations.

⟨And again I asked the Lord: How long shall be the reign of Satan?⟩ And he said to me: My Father hath suffered him to reign seven days, which are seven ages.

And I asked the Lord and said: What shall be in that time? And he said to me: From the time when the devil fell from the glory of the Father and (lost) his own glory, he sat upon the clouds, and sent his ministers, even angels flaming with fire, unto men from Adam even unto Henoch his servant. And he raised up Henoch upon the firmament and showed him his godhead, and commanded pen and ink to be given him: and he sat down and wrote threescore and seven books. And he commanded that he should take them to the earth and deliver them unto his sons. And Henoch let his books down upon the earth and delivered them unto his sons, and began to teach them to perform the custom of sacrifice, and unrighteous mysteries, and so did he hide the kingdom of heaven from men. And he said unto them: Behold that I am your god and beside me is none other god. And therefore did my Father send me into the world that I might make it known unto men, that they might know the evil device of the devil.

And then when he perceived that I had come down out of heaven into the world, he sent an angel and took of three sorts of wood and gave them unto Moses that I might be crucified, and now are they reserved for me. But then (now) did *the devil* proclaim unto him (Moses) his godhead, *and* unto his people, and commanded a law to be given unto the children of Israel, and brought them out through the midst of the sea which was dried up.

When my Father thought to send me into the world, he sent his angel before me, by name Mary, to receive me. And I when I came down entered in by the ear and came forth by the ear. And Satan the prince of this world perceived that I was come to seek and save them that were lost, and sent his angel, even Helias the prophet, baptizing with water: who is called John the Baptist. And Helias asked the prince of this world : How can I know him ? Then his lord said : On whomsoever thou shalt see the spirit descending like a dove and resting upon him, he it is that baptizeth with the Holy Ghost unto forgiveness of sins : thou wilt be able to destroy him and †to save†.

And again I, John, asked the Lord : Can a man be saved by the baptism of John without thy baptism ? And the Lord answered : Unless I have baptized *him* unto forgiveness of sins, by the baptism of water can no man see the kingdom of heaven : for I am the bread of life that came down from the seventh heaven, and they that eat my flesh and drink my blood, they shall be called the sons of God.

And I asked the Lord and said : What meaneth it, to eat my flesh and drink my blood ? (An answer and question seem to have fallen out.) And the Lord said unto me : Before the falling of the devil with all his host from the glory of the Father [in prayer], they did glorify the Father in their prayers thus, saying : Our Father, which art in heaven ; and so did all their songs come up before the throne of the Father. But when they had fallen, after that they are not able to glorify God with that prayer.

And I asked the Lord : How do all men receive the baptism of John, but thine not at all ? And the Lord answered : Because their deeds are evil and they come not unto the light.

The disciples of John marry and are given in marriage ; but my disciples neither marry nor are given in marriage, but are as the angels of God in heaven. But I said : If, then, it be sin to have to do with a woman, it is not good to marry. And the Lord said unto me : Not every one can receive this saying (&c., Matt. xix. 11, 12).

I asked the Lord concerning the day of judgement : What shall be the sign of thy coming ? And he answered and said unto me : When the numbers of the righteous shall be accomplished, that is, the number of the righteous that are crowned,† that have fallen,† then shall Satan be loosed out of his prison, having great wrath, and shall make war with the righteous, and they shall cry unto the Lord with a loud voice. And immediately the Lord shall command an angel to blow with the trumpet, and the voice of the archangel shall be heard in the trumpet from heaven even unto hell.

And then shall the sun be darkened and the moon shall not

give her light, and the stars shall fall, and the four winds shall be loosed from their foundations, and shall cause the earth and the sea and the mountains to quake together. And the heaven shall immediately shake and the sun shall be darkened, and it shall shine even to the fourth hour. Then shall appear the sign of the Son of man, and all the holy angels with him, and he shall set his seat upon the clouds, and sit on the throne of his majesty with the twelve apostles on the twelve seats of their glory. And the books shall be opened and he shall judge the whole world and the faith which he proclaimed. And then shall the Son of man send his angels, and they shall gather his elect from the four winds, from the heights of the heavens unto the boundaries of them, and shall bring them †to seek†.

Then shall the Son of God send the evil spirits, to bring all nations before him, and shall say unto them: Come, ye that did say: We have eaten and drunk and received the gain of this world. And after that they shall again be brought, and shall all stand before the judgement-seat, even all nations, in fear. And the books of life shall be opened and all nations shall show forth their ungodliness. And he shall glorify the righteous for their patience: and glory and honour and incorruption *shall be the reward of* their good works: but as for them that kept the commandments of the angels and obeyed unrighteously, indignation and trouble and anguish shall take hold on them.

And the Son of God shall bring forth the elect out of the midst of the sinners and say unto them: Come, ye blessed of my Father, inherit the kingdom prepared for you from the foundation of the world. Then shall he say unto the sinners: Depart from me, ye cursed, into everlasting fire, which was prepared for the devil and his angels. And the rest, beholding the last cutting off, shall cast the sinners into hell by the commandment of the invisible Father. Then shall the spirits of them that believe not go forth out of the prisons, and then shall my voice be heard, and there shall be one fold and one shepherd: and the darkness and obscurity shall come forth out of the lower parts of the earth— that is to say, the darkness of the gehenna of fire—and shall burn all things from below even to the air of the firmament. †And the Lord shall be in the firmament and† even to the lower parts of the earth. (*read* And the distance from the firmament unto the lower parts of the earth shall be) as if a man of thirty years old should take up a stone and cast it down, hardly in three years would it reach the bottom: so great is the depth of the pit and of the fire wherein the sinners shall dwell. And then shall Satan and all his host be bound and cast into the lake of fire. And the Son of God shall walk with his elect above the firmament and shall shut up the devil, binding him with strong chains that cannot be loosed. At that time the sinners, weeping and mourning, shall say: O earth, swallow us up and cover us in death. And then shall the righteous shine as the sun in the kingdom of their Father. And he shall bring them before the throne of the invisible Father, saying: Behold, I and my children whom God hath given me: O righteous one, the world hath not known thee, but I have known thee in truth, because thou hast sent me. And then shall the Father answer his Son and say: My beloved Son, sit thou on my right hand until I make thine enemies the footstool of thy feet, which have denied me and said: We are gods, and beside us there is none other god: which have slain thy prophets and persecuted thy righteous ones, and thou hast persecuted them even unto the outer darkness: there shall be weeping and gnashing of teeth.

And then shall the Son of God sit on the right hand of his Father, and the Father shall command his angels, and they shall minister unto them (i. e. the righteous) and set them among the choirs of the angels, to clothe them with incorruptible garments, and shall give them crowns that fade not and seats that cannot be moved. And God shall be in the midst of them ; and they shall not hunger nor thirst any more, neither shall the sun light on them nor any heat. And God shall wipe away every tear from their eyes. And he shall reign with his holy Father, and of his kingdom there shall be no end for ever and ever.

THE ASSUMPTION OF THE VIRGIN

As was the case with the Acts of Pilate, we must admit that we have as yet no critical edition of the very numerous forms of this legend.

We have texts in Greek, Latin, Syriac, Coptic, Arabic, not to mention derivatives in many vernacular mediaeval versions, all of which would have to be dealt with in a comprehensive survey. Clearly the present collection cannot attempt to do that. What it can do is to present a statement of the contents of the principal ancient versions.

My own belief is that the legend was first elaborated, if it did not originate, in Egypt: and therefore the Sahidic and Bohairic texts will receive special attention.

The standard *Greek* writing on the subject is one attributed to St. John, which is edited from five manuscripts (of eleventh–fourteenth centuries) by Tischendorf. This was exploited and inflated in sermon-form by John, archbishop of Thessalonica, in the seventh century. It will be translated here.

The standard *Latin* form is that attributed to Melito, bishop of Sardis: often printed, last by Tischendorf (Transitus Mariae B).

What Tischendorf calls the Latin A form is attributed to Joseph of Arimathaea. The text, which is very divergent in various copies, is printed by Tischendorf from three late manuscripts, all Italian.

Of the Syriac, of which there are many forms, we have editions by Wright, Budge, and Mrs. Lewis.

The Arabic, edited by Enger in 1854, is akin to the Syriac; it is not very important for our purpose, nor is the Ethiopic, edited by Chaîne in *Apocrypha de B. V. M.*

THE ASSUMPTION. COPTIC TEXTS

Of these we have two complete texts in Bohairic and one in Sahidic, with fragments of others.

The first Bohairic account is in a Homily attributed to Evodius (usually described as first bishop of Antioch, but here), archbishop of Rome, the successor and spiritual son of Peter; he insists that he was an eyewitness of all that he tells. (Ed. by Robinson, *Coptic Apocryphal Gospels*.)

The first four sections of the homily are panegyric. The narrative begins with V.

Evodius first tells of his calling by Jesus. He was with Peter and Andrew and Alexander and Rufus his kinsmen, and followed Jesus when Peter and Andrew did, and was of the seventy-two disciples.

They lived with Mary after the Passion, as did Salome and Joanna and the rest of the virgins who were with her, and Peter sanctified an altar in the house.

VI. On the twentieth of the month Tobi, they were all gathered

at the altar, and Jesus appeared and greeted them. He bade
Peter prepare the altar because 'I must needs take a great offering
from your midst on the morrow, before that each one of you goes
to the lot that hath fallen to him to preach therein'. He then
ordained Peter archbishop, and others, including Evodius, presbyters, and also deacons, readers, psalmists, and doorkeepers;
and departed to heaven. They remained, wondering what the
offering was to be.

VII. On the twenty-first of Tobi Jesus returned, on the
chariot of the cherubim, with thousands of angels, and David the
sweet singer. 'We' besought him to tell what the great offering
was to be, and he told them that it was his Mother whom he was
to take to himself. (Here, as elsewhere, I do not pretend to give
the long discourses which occur, but only the bare skeleton of
the story.) [1]

VIII. We all wept, and Peter asked if it was not possible that
Mary should never die, and then if she might not be left to them
for a few days. But the Lord said that her time was accomplished.

IX. The women, and also Mary, wept, but Jesus consoled her.
She said: I have heard that Death has many terrible faces. How
shall I bear to see them ? He said: How dost thou fear his divine
shape when the Life of all the world is with thee ? And he kissed
her, and blessed them all, and bade Peter look upon the altar for
heavenly garments which the Father had sent to shroud Mary in.

X.[2] Mary arose and was arrayed in the garments, and turned
to the east and uttered a prayer in the language of heaven, and
then lay down, still facing eastward.

Jesus made us stand for the prayer, and the virgins also who
used to minister in the temple and had come to wait on Mary
after the Passion. We asked them why they left it. They said:
When we saw the darkness at the crucifixion we fled into the holy
of holies and shut the door. We saw a strong angel come down
with a sword, and he rent the veil in twain : and we heard a great
voice (from the house of the altar *Sah.*), saying, Woe to thee,
Jerusalem, which killest the prophets. The angel of the altar
flew up into the canopy of the altar with the angel of the sword :
and we knew that God had left his people, and we fled to his
Mother.

XI. The virgins stood about Mary singing, and Jesus sat by
her. She besought him to save her from the many terrors of the
next world—the accusers of Amenti, the dragon of the abyss,
the river of fire that proves the righteous and the wicked. (All
this *Sah.* omits.)

[1] Parts of VII and VIII exist in Sahidic fragment I (Robinson,
p. 66).
[2] At this point begins Sahidic fragment II (Robinson, p. 70) and
continues into XVII: it has important differences.

XII. He comforted her and said to the apostles: Let us withdraw outside for a little while, for Death cannot approach while I am here. And they went out and he sat on a stone, and looked up to heaven and groaned and said: I have overcome thee, O Death, that dwellest in the storehouses of the south. Come, appear to my virgin mother: but not in a fearful shape. He appeared, and when she saw him, her soul leaped into the bosom of her son—white as snow, and he wrapped it in garments of fine linen and gave it to Michael.

All the women wept; Salome ran to Jesus and said: Behold, she whom thou lovest is dead. David the singer rejoiced and said: Right dear in the sight of the Lord is the death of his saints. (The Sahidic does not describe the moment of death, but says it took place at the ninth hour of the 21st of Tobi: and omits David.)

XIII. They re-entered the house and found her lying dead, and Jesus blessed her.

XIV. Jesus shrouded the body in the heavenly garments, and they were fastened thereto. He bade the apostles take up the body, Peter bearing the head and John the feet, and carry it to a new tomb in the field of Jehoshaphat, and watch it for three and a half days.

David rejoiced, saying: She shall be brought unto the King, &c. (Ps. xlv. 14), and: Arise, O Lord, into thy resting place (Ps. cxxxii. 8).

(*Sah.* omits details: the order is merely to carry the body to the tomb: David again omitted.)

XV. Jesus ascended with Mary's soul in the chariot of the Cherubim. (*Sah.* merely: he hid himself from us.) We took up the body, and when we came to the field of Jehoshaphat, the Jews heard the singing and came out intending to burn the body. But a wall of fire encompassed us, and they were blinded: and the body was laid in the tomb and watched for three and a half days.

(*Sah.* omits all after the blindness.)

XVI. The Jews were in terror and confessed their sin and asked pardon. Their eyes were opened and they sought and found not the body: and they were amazed and confessed themselves guilty.

(Here *Sah.* has a very confusing insertion. When the eyes of the Jews have been opened: 'there came a great choir of angels and caught away the body of the Virgin, and Peter and John and we looked on while she was carried to heaven, until we lost sight of it. And the Jews saw it also, and confessed themselves guilty.

XVII. At mid-day on the fourth day all were gathered at the tomb. A great voice came, saying: Go every one to his place till the seventh month: for I have hardened the heart of the Jews, and they will not be able to find the tomb or the body till I take it up to heaven. Return on the 16th of Mesore. We returned to the house.

In the seventh month after the death, i. e. on 15th of Mesore, we reassembled at the tomb and spent the night in watching and singing. (*Sah.* has only: We returned to the house.)

XVIII. At dawn on the 16th of Mesore, Jesus appeared. Peter said: We are grieved that we have not seen thy Mother since her death. Jesus said: She shall now come. The chariot of the Cherubim appeared with the Virgin seated in it. There were greetings. Jesus bade the apostles go and preach in all the world. He spent all that day with us and with his Mother, and gave us the salutation of peace and went up to heaven in glory.

XIX. Such was the death of the Virgin on the 21st of Tobi, and her assumption on 16th Mesore. I, Evodius, saw it all. The sermon ends with a blessing.

(*Sah.* has: XVIII. At dawn on the eighth day after her death Jesus appeared (as in *Boh.*), and the fragment ends at his promise that the apostles shall now see the Virgin.)

The other Sahidic account is in the 'Twentieth Discourse of Cyril of Jerusalem', edited by Budge (*Misc. Copt. texts*). We have seen what he says of the early part of the life of the Virgin. At p. 642 (Eng. trans.) he takes up the subject of her death. A considerable portion of this had been already edited by Robinson as Sahidic Fragment IV of the *Life of the Virgin*, pp. 24–40.

For ten (*Rob.* fifteen) years after the resurrection, according to Josephus and Irenaeus (!), John and Mary lived together at Jerusalem. One day the Virgin bade John summon Peter and James: and they sat down before her and she addressed them, reminding them of the life of Jesus (up to the Ascension and Pentecost). She went on to say that Jesus had come to her and warned her that her time was accomplished. ' I will hide thy body in the earth, no man shall find it until the day when I raise it incorruptible. A great church shall be built over it.' Now therefore summon the virgins.

It was done. Mary took the hand of one of them, Mary Magdalene, now very old, and committed the others to her charge.

She bade Peter fetch from the house of his disciple Birrus the linen clothes she had committed to him: James was to buy for a stater (shekel, *Rob.*) spices and perfumes.

John lighted the lamps. Mary spread the linen on the ground and poured the spices upon it and stood and prayed, facing east: she asked to be delivered from the terrors of the next world—the dragon and the river of fire. Then she lay down facing east.

Jesus appeared on the Cherubim and bade her not fear death. And said to Death: Come, O thou who art in the chambers of the south. When Mary saw him her soul leaped into the bosom of her Son, and he wrapped it in a garment of light.

She fell asleep on the night of the 20th day of Tobi (early on the 21st, *Rob.*).

The Lord bade the apostles take the body to the valley of Jehoshaphat and set down the bier, because of the Jews, and he would hide it.

In the morning they took it forth. The Jews heard the singing, and took counsel and set out with fire to burn it. The apostles saw them coming, and dropped the bier and fled. The Jews found nothing but the bier, and that they burnt. A sweet odour came from the place where the body was laid, and a voice said: Let no man give himself the trouble of seeking it till the great day of the appearing of Christ. The Jews were ashamed and fled, and told their neighbours, but bade them tell no one.

This is Cyril's account, which entirely shuts out a corporal assumption, but has frequent coincidences of language and matter with the Bohairic account of Evodius, and the Sahidic fragments of the same.

THE DISCOURSE OF THEODOSIUS

Archbishop of Alexandria (probably the Jacobite Patriarch of 536–68). It is in Bohairic, edited by Robinson (p. 90), who calls it the Second Bohairic account: he omits fifteen pages of homiletic matter at the beginning.

I. At the moment of the Ascension Jesus charged Peter, 'his bishop'. and John to remain with Mary till her death.

II. She was living in Jerusalem with a number of virgins. 'We also, the apostles Peter and John', were with her.

On the 20th of Tobi we came to her and found her amazed. She explained that that night, after she had finished the 'little office (synaxis)', she slumbered and saw a beautiful youth about thirty years of age, 'and you also standing at his right hand, with garments in your hands'. She perceived that it was Jesus, and he told her that the garments were her shroud; and he vanished.

Then Mary makes a long discourse on the horrors of death— the river of fire, the two powers of light and darkness, the avengers with diverse faces, the worm, the unquenchable fire which three tears will put out, the ruler of darkness.

On hearing this we wept.

III. There was a knocking at the door. It was the virgins who had come from the Mount of Olives, with censers and lamps. They had been warned by a voice in the night to come to Mary, who was to die next day.

Mary bade us withdraw a little, and uttered a (long) thanksgiving to her Son, and a prayer to be delivered from the terrors of the next world.

IV. There were thunderings and lightnings. Jesus came on a chariot of light with Moses, David, the prophets, and the righteous kings, and addressed Mary. (There is a refrain to the speech, 'O my beloved Mother, arise, let us go hence'.)

Mary spoke comfort to the apostles. Jesus spoke of the necessity of death. If she were translated, 'wicked men will think concerning thee that thou art a power which came down from heaven, and that the dispensation (the Incarnation) took place in appearance'.

V. He turned to the apostles—to me Peter and to John—and said that Mary should appear to them again. 'There are 206 days from her death unto her holy assumption. I will bring her unto you arrayed in this body.'

He bade them bring garments and perfumes from the altar, which were sent from heaven.

They spread them on the bed.

The Virgin arose and prayed him to receive her.

VI. She lay down on the garments, turned her face to him, and straightway commended her spirit into his hands.

He bade us prepare her for burial, and gave us three palms from paradise and three branches of the olive-tree which Noah's dove brought to Noah, and we laid them on her body. Peter was to bear the head, John the feet. The Jews would plot against her, but they should be blinded. The body was to be placed in the stone coffin and watched, and in 206 days he would bring the soul to it.

He went up to heaven and presented the soul to the Father and the Holy Ghost. And the voice of the Holy Trinity was heard welcoming the soul.

VII. We carried the body out to the field of Jehoshaphat. The Jews saw it and took counsel to come and burn it. The apostles set down the bier and fled.

Darkness came on the Jews, and they were blinded and smitten by their own fire. They cried out for mercy and were healed, and many were converted.

We returned to Jerusalem, and often came back to the tomb.

VIII. When the 206 days were over, on the evening of the 15th, that is the morning of the 16th of Mesore, we gathered at the tomb and watched all night.

At the tenth hour there were thunderings, and a choir of angels was heard, and David's harp. Jesus came on the chariots of the Cherubim with the soul of the Virgin seated in his bosom, and greeted us.

He called over the coffin and bade the body arise (a long address).

IX. The coffin, which had been shut like Noah's ark, opened. The body arose and 'embraced its own soul, even as two brothers who are come from a strange country, and they were united one with another'. David said, 'Mercy and truth are met together' (&c.).

Jesus went up to heaven, blessing us, and we heard the voice of the powers singing : Bring to the Lord the honour due unto his name. The virgins that be her fellows (her holy deeds) shall be her company (&c.).

Here we have the corporal assumption after 206 days.

Yet another Sahidic fragment is to be found in Revillout (*Patrol. Orient. Apocryphes Coptes*, I, fr. 16, p. 174). He attributes it quite without reason to the Gospel of the Twelve Apostles. It is told by an eyewitness, but he cannot be identified.

We here encounter the high priest whose hand is smitten off when he touches the bier: he appears in the other versions.

The high priest begs to be healed. Peter says, if he believes in Jesus Christ he can be healed.

The high priest acknowledges that he and his people crucified Jesus (knowing him to be the Son of God) because he drove the traders out of the temple.

Peter bids him, if he believes, to embrace the body of the Virgin and profess his belief.

He does so and takes his own cut-off hand and puts it to the stump, and it adheres.

Peter bids him take 'this palm branch' and go to the city and lay it on the eyes of those who are blind. He found many of them lamenting, and all who believed were healed.

Meanwhile the apostles laid the body in the tomb and remained there, to wait till the Lord should come and raise it up as he had said.

They bade the virgins go home in peace: but they wanted to stay there too. Peter and John reassured them. They asked to be blessed, and Peter blessed them.

At the third hour of the day the converted high priest came and told Peter that the Jews were still plotting to burn the body and the tomb.

Peter warned the disciples: but God sent forgetfulness upon the Jews. And the apostles took courage. And a voice from heaven came also, promising safety.

It came to pass after that we reached the 16th of Mesore, and were gathered with the apostles at the tomb. We saw lightnings and were afraid. There was a sweet odour and a sound of trumpets. The door of the tomb opened: there was a great light within. A chariot descended in fire: Jesus was in it; he greeted us.

He called into the tomb: Mary, my mother, arise! And we saw her in the body, as if she had never died. Jesus took her into the chariot. The angels went before them. A voice called, 'Peace be to you, my brethren'.

The miracle was even greater than that of the resurrection of Jesus, which no one saw except Mary and Mary Magdalene.

We, then, the apostles, are witnesses of these things, and have added or diminished nothing.

We went to the tomb and found the garments where the body had lain: we buried them.

Here the fragment ends. It forms a link between the Egyptian and the other forms of the story.

To sum up. All the narratives except the Discourse of Cyril tell of a corporal assumption, and all but one place it on the 16th of Mesore, the exception being the Sahidic fragment II, which puts it on the eighth day after the death.

The same fragment seems to indicate that the body was taken up at the burial: whether it was brought back and taken up a second time we cannot tell.

The other versions will mostly agree in assembling all the apostles at the death-bed. In the Coptic group the death takes place before the dispersion of the apostles, and we do not hear of any of them individually except Peter and John.

GREEK NARRATIVE

THE DISCOURSE OF ST. JOHN THE DIVINE CONCERNING THE FALLING ASLEEP OF THE HOLY MOTHER OF GOD

1 Whenas the all-holy glorious mother of God and ever-virgin Mary according to her custom went unto the holy sepulchre of our Lord to burn incense, and bowed her holy knees, she besought Christ our God that was born of her to come and abide with her (*rather*, that she might depart unto him).

2 And when the Jews saw her resorting unto the holy sepulchre they came to the chief priests, saying: Mary goeth every day unto the sepulchre. And the chief priests called the watchmen which were charged by them not to suffer any to pray at the holy sepulchre, and inquired of them if it were so in truth. But the watch answered and said that they saw no such thing; for God did not suffer them to see her venerable presence.

3 Now on one day, which was Friday, the holy Mary came as she was wont to the sepulchre, and as she prayed it came to pass that the heavens were opened and the archangel Gabriel came down unto her and said: Hail, thou that didst bear Christ our God: thy prayer hath passed through the heavens unto him that was born of thee and hath been accepted, and henceforth according to thy petition thou shalt leave the world and come unto the heavenly places unto thy Son, unto the true life that hath no successor.

4 And when she heard that from the holy archangel she returned unto Bethlehem the holy, having with her three virgins that ministered unto her. And when she had rested a little space she sat up and said to the virgins: Bring me a censer that I may pray. And they brought it as it was commanded them.

5 And she prayed, saying: My Lord Jesu Christ, who didst vouchsafe of thine excellent goodness to be born of me, hear my voice and send unto me thine apostle John, that seeing him I may have the firstfruits of joy: and send unto me also the rest of thine apostles, both them that have already come to dwell with thee and them that are in this present world, in whatever land they may be, by thy holy commandment, that I may behold them and bless thy name that is greatly extolled, for I have confidence that thou hearest thine handmaid in every thing.

6 And as she prayed I, John, came unto her, for the Holy Ghost caught me up by a cloud from Ephesus and set me in the place where the mother of my Lord lay. And I entered in unto her and gave glory to him that was born of her and said: Hail, thou mother of my Lord, that didst bear Christ our God: rejoice for that thou departest out of this life with great glory.

7 And the holy mother of God glorified God that I, John, was come to her, remembering the word of the Lord which he spake: Behold thy mother, and behold thy son. And the three virgins came and worshipped.

8 And the holy mother of God said unto me: Pray thou and put on incense. And I prayed thus: O Lord Jesu Christ that doest marvellous things, do now marvellous things before her that bare thee, and let thy mother depart out of this life, and let them that crucified thee and believed not in thee be troubled.

9 And after I had finished the prayer the holy Mary said unto me: Bring me the censer. And she cast in incense and said: Glory be to thee, my God and my Lord, because in me are fulfilled all things that thou didst promise me before thou didst ascend into the heavens, that whenever I should depart out of this world thou wouldest come unto me in glory, thou and the multitude of thine angels.

10 And I, John, said unto her: Our Lord and our God Jesus Christ cometh, and thou beholdest him according as he promised thee. And the holy mother of God answered and said to me: The Jews have sworn that when mine end cometh they will burn my body. And I answered and said unto her: Thy holy and precious body shall not see corruption. And she answered and said unto me: Bring a censer and put incense therein and pray. And there came a voice from heaven ànd said the Amen.

11 And I, John, listened unto that voice, and the Holy Ghost said unto me: John, heardest thou this voice which was uttered in heaven after the ending of the prayer? And I answered and said: Yea, I heard it. And the Holy Ghost said unto me: This voice which thou heardest signifieth the coming of thy brethren the apostles and of the holy powers which is to be: for to-day they are coming hither.

12 And thereupon I, John, fell to prayer. And the Holy Ghost said unto the apostles: All of you together mount up upon

clouds from the ends of the world and gather yourselves together
at Bethlehem the holy because of the mother of our Lord Jesus
Christ, in a moment of time: Peter from Rome, Paul from
Tiberia, Thomas out of the inmost Indies, James from Jerusalem:
13 Andrew the brother of Peter, and Philip, Luke and Simon the
Canaanite, and Thaddaeus, which were fallen asleep, were raised
up by the Holy Ghost out of their sepulchres; unto whom said
the Holy Ghost: Think not that the resurrection is now; but for
this cause are ye risen up out of your graves, that ye may go to
salute for an honour and a wonderful sign for the mother of your
Lord and Saviour Jesus Christ: for the day is come near of her
departure and going to abide in heaven. 14 And Mark, who was
yet alive, came also from Alexandria with the rest, as hath been
said, from their several countries.

15 But Peter when he was lifted up by the cloud stood between
the heaven and the earth, for the Holy Ghost sustained him, and
beheld[1] while the rest of the apostles also were caught up in the
clouds to be present with Peter. And so all came together by the
means of the Holy Ghost, as hath been said.

15*[2] And we entered in unto the mother of our Lord and God
and did her worship and said: Fear not, neither be grieved: the
Lord God that was born of thee shall bring thee out of this world
with glory. And she rejoicing in God her Saviour sat up in the
bed and said to the apostles: Now believe I that our teacher and
our God cometh from heaven, and I *shall* behold him, and so
depart out of this life, even as I have seen you come unto me.
And I would that you would tell me whence ye knew that I was
departing and came unto me, and from what lands and how far
ye are come hither, that ye have been so quick to visit me: for
neither hath he that was born of me, even our Lord Jesus Christ,
hidden *it* from me. For I have believed now also that he is the
Son of the Most High.

16 And Peter answered and said unto the apostles: Let each
one certify the mother of our Lord, in what *manner* the Holy
Ghost announced it unto us and charged us.

17 And I, John, answered and said: I, whenas I was entering
in unto the holy altar in Ephesus to minister, the Holy Ghost
said unto me: The time of the departure of the mother of thy
Lord is come near: go unto Bethlehem to salute her. And a cloud
of light caught me up and set me at the door *of the house* where
thou liest. 18 And Peter also answered: I also was in Rome,
and about the dawn I heard a voice by the Holy Ghost saying
unto me: The mother of thy Lord must depart, for the time is
come nigh: go thou unto Bethlehem to salute her: and lo,
a cloud of light caught me up, and I beheld the rest of the

---

[1] Greek, corruptly, συνοδα: probably συνορᾷ, for the Syriac has
'beheld the apostles', or the like.

[2] The number 15 is, by an error, repeated in Tischendorf.

apostles also coming unto me upon clouds, and a voice saying to me: Go all of you unto Bethlehem.   19 Paul also answered and said: I also was abiding in a city not very far off from Rome; and the place is called Tiberia.   And I heard the Holy Ghost saying unto me: The mother of thy Lord leaveth this world to go unto the heavenly places, and endeth (maketh) her course by departure: but go thou also unto Bethlehem to salute her.   And lo, a cloud of light caught me up and set me where it did set you also.   20 Thomas also answered and said: I also had passed through the land of the Indians, and my preaching was increased in strength by the grace of Christ, and the son of the king's sister, by name Labdanes, was about to be sealed (baptized) by me in the palace, and suddenly the Holy Ghost saith unto me: Thou also, Thomas, go unto Bethlehem to salute the mother of thy Lord, for she maketh her removal unto heaven.   And a cloud of light caught me up and set me with you.   21 And Mark also answered and said: As I also was finishing the service (canon) of the third hour in the city of Alexandria, while I prayed, the Holy Ghost caught me up and brought me unto you.

22 And James also answered and said: While I was in Jerusalem the Holy Ghost admonished (permitted) me, saying: Be thou present at Bethlehem, for the mother of thy Lord maketh her departure.   And lo, a cloud of light caught me up and brought me unto you.

23 And Matthew also answered and said: I glorified and do glorify God, for that as I was in a ship and it was tossed, for the sea was boisterous with waves, suddenly a cloud of light overshadowed *us*, and overcame (shook off) the billows of the tempest and made them calm, and me it caught up and brought me unto you.   24 Likewise they that had departed *this life* before told how they were come.   And Bartholomew said: I was preaching the word in the country of Thebes, and lo, the Holy Ghost said to me: The mother of thy Lord maketh her departure: go therefore to salute her at Bethlehem.   And lo, a cloud of light caught me up and brought me unto you.

25 All these things spake the apostles unto the holy mother of God, how and in what fashion they came.   And she spread forth her hands unto heaven and prayed, saying: I worship and praise and glorify thy name, which is greatly extolled, O Lord, because thou hast regarded the lowliness of thine handmaiden, and thou that art mighty hast magnified me, and behold all generations shall call me blessed.   26 And after the prayer she said unto the apostles: Cast on incense and pray.   And when they had prayed there came a thunder from heaven and a terrible sound as of chariots, and lo, a multitude of the host of angels and powers, and a voice as of the Son of man was heard, and the Seraphim *came* round about the house wherein the holy and spotless mother of God, the virgin, lay: so that all that were in

Bethlehem beheld all the marvellous sights, and went to Jerusalem and declared all the wonderful things that were come to pass.

27 And it came to pass after that sound that the sun and the moon appeared about the house, and an assembly of the first-begotten saints came unto the house where the mother of the Lord lay, for her honour and glory. And I saw also many signs come to pass, blind receiving sight, deaf hearing, lame walking, lepers cleansed, and them that were possessed of unclean spirits healed. And every one that was under any sickness or disease *came and* touched the wall where she lay, and cried: Holy Mary, thou that didst bear Christ our God, have mercy on us. And forthwith they were cured.

28 And many multitudes that were dwelling in Jerusalem out of every country because of a vow, when they heard the signs that were being done in Bethlehem by means of the Lord's mother, came unto the place seeking to be healed of divers diseases; and they obtained *health*. And there was joy unspeakable on that day of the multitude of them that were healed, with them also that beheld, glorifying Christ our God and his mother. And all Jerusalem *returned* from Bethlehem, keeping holiday with singing of psalms and spiritual songs.

29 But the priests of the Jews, together with their people, were amazed at that which was done, and were taken with bitter (heavy) envy, and again with vain thoughts they gathered a council and advised themselves to send *men* against the holy mother of God and the holy apostles which were there at Bethlehem. And when the multitude of the Jews were now set forward toward Bethlehem, as it were about a mile therefrom, it came to pass that they saw a terrible vision, and their feet were bound: and they departed thence to them of their nation, and declared all the fearful vision unto the chief priests. 30 But they being yet more inflamed in spirit went unto the governor, crying out and saying: The nation of the Jews is destroyed because of this woman: drive thou her away from Bethlehem and from the province of Jerusalem. But the governor was astonied at the wonders and said unto them: I will not drive her out from Bethlehem nor from any other place. But the Jews continued crying out and adjuring him by the safety of Tiberius Caesar that he should lead the apostles out of Bethlehem: and if thou doest it not we will report it unto Caesar. And being now compelled he sent a captain of a thousand against the apostles unto Bethlehem.

31 But the Holy Ghost said unto the apostles and the mother of the Lord: Behold, the governor hath sent a captain of a thousand against you, because the Jews have made a tumult. Go out therefore from Bethlehem, and fear not; for behold, I will bring you by a cloud unto Jerusalem; for the power of the Father and of the Son and of the Holy Ghost is with you.

32 The apostles therefore rose up straightway and went out of the house, bearing the bed of their lady the mother of God, and set forward toward Jerusalem: and immediately, according as the Holy Ghost said, they were lifted up by a cloud and were found at Jerusalem in the house of their lady. And we stood up and for five days we sung praise without ceasing.

33 But when the captain came unto Bethlehem and found not there the mother of the Lord, neither the apostles, he laid hold upon the Bethlehemites, saying unto them: Did ye not come and tell the governor and the priests all the signs and wonders which were come to pass, and how the apostles came out of every land? where then are they? come ye hither to Jerusalem unto the governor. For the captain knew not of the departure of the apostles and the mother of the Lord unto Jerusalem. So the captain took the Bethlehemites and went unto the governor, saying that he had found no man.

34 Now after five days it was made known to the governor and to the priests and to all the city that the mother of the Lord was in her own house in Jerusalem with the apostles, by means of the signs and wondrous things that came to pass there; and a multitude of men and women were assembled, crying out: O holy virgin that didst bear Christ our God, forget not the race of men. 35 And because of this the people of the Jews, moved yet more with envy, together with the priests, took wood and fire and came on, desiring to burn the house where the mother of the Lord lay, together with the apostles. But the governor stood beholding the sight afar off. And when the people of the Jews were come unto the door of the house, behold, suddenly a force of fire came from within it by means of an angel and burnt a great multitude of the Jews, and there was great fear throughout all the city and they glorified God which was born of her. 36 But when the governor saw what was done, he cried aloud before all the people, saying: Of a truth he is the Son of God, which was born of the virgin whom ye thought to drive out: for these signs are of a true God. And there was a division betwixt the Jews, and many believed on the name of our Lord Jesus Christ because of the signs which came to pass.

37 Now after all these wonders were come to pass because of Mary the mother of God and ever virgin, the mother of the Lord, as we the apostles were with her in Jerusalem, the Holy Ghost said unto us: Ye know that on the Lord's day the good tidings were told unto the Virgin Mary by the archangel Gabriel, and on the Lord's day the Saviour was born in Bethlehem, and on the Lord's day the children of Jerusalem went forth with palm-branches to meet him, saying: Hosanna in the highest: blessed is he that cometh in the name of the Lord. And on the Lord's day he rose from the dead, and on the Lord's day he shall come to judge the quick and the dead, and on the Lord's day he

shall come from heaven for the glory and honour of the departure
of the holy and glorious virgin which bare him. 38 And upon the
same Lord's day the mother of the Lord said unto the apostles:
Cast on incense, for Christ cometh with an host of angels: and
behold Christ cometh sitting upon the throne of the Cherubim.
And as we all prayed there appeared innumerable multitudes of
angels, and the Lord riding upon the Cherubim in great power.
And lo, an appearance of light going before him and lighting upon
the holy virgin because of the coming of her only-begotten Son:
and all the powers of the heavens fell down and worshipped him.
39 And the Lord called unto his mother and said: Mary. And
she answered and said: Behold, here am I, Lord. And the Lord
said unto her: Be not grieved, but let thine heart rejoice and be
glad; for thou hast found grace to behold the glory that was
given me of my Father. And the holy mother of God looked up
and saw in him glory which the mouth of man cannot utter nor
comprehend. And the Lord abode by her, saying: Behold,
henceforth shall thy precious body be translated unto paradise,
and thine holy soul shall be in the heavens in the treasuries of
my Father in surpassing brightness, where is peace and rejoicing
of the holy angels, and continuance *thereof*. 40 And the mother
of the Lord answered and said unto him: Lay thy right hand
upon me, Lord, and bless me. And the Lord spread out his
unstained right hand and blessed her: and she, holding his
unstained right hand, kissed it, saying: I worship this right hand
which made the heaven and the earth; and I beseech thy name
which is greatly extolled, O Christ, God, King of the ages, only-
begotten of the Father, receive thine handmaid, thou that didst
vouchsafe to be born of me the lowly one to save mankind by
thine unutterable dispensation. Every man that calleth upon
or entreateth or nameth the name of thine handmaid, grant him
thine help. 41 And as she thus spake, the apostles came near
unto her feet and worshipped the Lord and said: O mother of
the Lord, leave unto the world a blessing, for thou departest out
of it: for thou didst bless it and raise it up from destruction
when thou barest the light of the world. And the mother of the
Lord prayed, and thus spake she in her prayer: O God, who of
thy great goodness didst send thine only-begotten Son to dwell
in my lowly body, who didst vouchsafe to be born of me the
lowly one, have mercy upon the world and upon every soul that
calleth upon thy name.

42 And again she prayed and said: O Lord, King of the
heavens, Son of the living God, accept every man that calleth
upon thy name, that thy birth may be glorified. And again she
prayed and said: O Lord Jesu Christ, that hast all power in
heaven and on earth, I entreat thine holy name with this supplication: At every time and in every place where there is a
memorial of my name, sanctify thou that place, and glorify them

that glorify thee through my name, accepting every offering of such, and every supplication and every prayer. 43 And when she had thus prayed, the Lord said unto his own mother: Let thine heart be glad and rejoice; for every grace and every gift hath been given thee of my Father which is in heaven and of me and of the Holy Ghost. Every soul that calleth upon thy name shall not be put to shame, but shall find mercy and consolation and succour and confidence, both in this world and in that which is to come, before my Father which is in heaven. 44 And the Lord turned and said unto Peter: The time is come to begin the song of praise. And when Peter began the song of praise, all the powers of the heavens answered Alleluia. And then the countenance of the mother of the Lord did shine above the light. And she rose up and with her own hand blessed every one of the apostles, and all of them gave glory to God; and the Lord spread forth his unstained hands and received her holy and spotless soul. 45 And at the going forth of her spotless soul the place was filled with sweet odour and light unspeakable, and lo, a voice from heaven was heard, saying: Blessed art thou among women. And Peter ran, and I, John, and Paul and Thomas, and embraced her precious feet to receive sanctification: and the twelve apostles laid her honourable and holy body upon a bed and bare it forth.

46 And behold as they bare her, a certain Hebrew named Jephonias, mighty of body, ran forth and set upon the bed, as the apostles bare it, and lo, an angel of the Lord with invisible power smote his two hands from off his shoulders with a sword of fire and left them hanging in the air about the bed. 47 And when this miracle came to pass, all the people of the Jews that beheld it cried out: Verily he is the true God that was born of thee, Mary, mother of God, ever virgin. And Jephonias himself, being commanded by Peter, that the wonderful works of God might be showed, stood up behind the bed and cried: Holy Mary that didst bear Christ which is God, have mercy on me. And Peter turned and said unto him: In the name of him that was born of her thine hands which were taken from thee shall cleave to their place. And immediately at the word of Peter the hands that did hang beside the bed of our lady went back and clave unto Jephonias: and he also believed and glorified Christ, even God, that was born of her.

48 And after this miracle the apostles bare the bed and laid her precious and holy body in Gethsemane in a new tomb. And lo, an odour of sweet savour came out of the holy sepulchre of our lady the mother of God: and until three days were past the voices of invisible angels were heard glorifying Christ our God which was born of her. And when the third day was fulfilled the voices were no more heard, and thereafter we all perceived that her spotless and precious body was translated into paradise.

[Other MSS.: When the apostles went forth from the city of

Jerusalem bearing the bed, suddenly twelve clouds of light
caught them up, together with the body of our lady, and translated
them into paradise.]

49 Now after it was translated, lo, we beheld Elisabeth the
mother of the holy John the Baptist, and Anna the mother of
our lady, and Abraham and Isaac and Jacob, and David singing
Alleluia, and all the choirs of the saints worshipping the precious
body of the mother of the Lord, and *we saw* a place of light, than
which light nothing is brighter, and a great fragrance *came* from
that place whereto her precious and holy body was translated
in paradise, and a melody of them that praised him that was born
of her: and unto virgins only is it given to hear that sweet
melody wherewith no man can be sated.

50 We, therefore, the apostles, when we beheld thus suddenly
the translation of her holy body, glorified God who had shown
unto us his wonders at the departure of the mother of our Lord
Jesus Christ: by the prayer and intercession of whom may we
all be accounted worthy to come into her protection and succour
and guardianship, both in this world and in that which is to come:
at all times and in all places glorifying her only-begotten Son,
with the Father and the Holy Ghost, world without end. Amen.

[For 49 and 50 one manuscript has only: And we all glorified
God: unto whom be glory and power, world without end. Amen.]

The other Greek narrative of the Assumption is not yet fully
known. It is that which is embodied in a sermon of John, archbishop of Thessalonica.

Tischendorf gives only extracts, from several manuscripts,
which show that the story begins with the bringing of a palm to
the Virgin by the angel as a token of her approaching departure.

We have the same gathering of the apostles, who do not know
why they have been summoned. They tell of the manner in
which they were brought.

The Jews are blinded and burnt, and healed by the palm-
branch.

The apostles lay the body in the tomb and remain there
watching until it is translated. In one text Christ appears and
takes the body.

THE ASSUMPTION : LATIN NARRATIVE OF PSEUDO-MELITO

This is Tischendorf's B text, but though he places it second, it is
the leading Latin authority, the other being a late Italian fiction.

I. *Prologue.*

Melito, servant of God, bishop of the church of Sardis, unto
the brethren which are established in peace at Laodicea, reverend
in the Lord, greeting.

I remember that I have oft-times written concerning a certain Leucius, who, after that with us he had been a companion of the apostles, with alienated sense and rash mind departed from the way of righteousness and put into his books many things concerning the acts of the apostles, and spake many and diverse things of their mighty deeds, but concerning their teaching lied much, affirming that they taught otherwise, and establishing his own wicked position as if by their words. Nor did he account this sufficient, but also corrupted with so evil a pen the departure of the blessed Mary ever virgin, the mother of God, that it is unlawful not only to read but even to hear it in the church of God. We therefore at your petition have written simply those things which we heard from the apostle John, and have sent them unto your brotherhood: believing no alien doctrines which sprout out from heretics, but that the Father is in the Son, the Son in the Father, the triune person of godhead and undivided essence abiding: and that not two natures of man were created, a good and a bad, but that one good nature was created by a good God, which by the fraud of the serpent was corrupted through sin, and restored by the grace of Christ.

II. When therefore the Lord and Saviour Jesus Christ for the life of the whole world hung on the tree of the cross pierced with nails, he saw standing beside the cross his mother and John the evangelist, whom he more especially loved beyond the other apostles because he alone of them was a virgin in body. Unto him therefore he committed the charge of the holy Mary, saying to him: Behold thy mother; and to her: Behold thy son. From that hour the holy mother of God continued in the especial care of John so long as she endured the sojourn of this life. And when the apostles had taken the world by their lots for preaching, she abode in the house of his parents beside the Mount of Olivet.

III. In the second year after Christ having overcome death had ascended into heaven, upon a certain day, Mary fervent with desire of Christ betook herself alone into the refuge of her dwelling to weep. And lo, an angel shining in a garment of great brightness stood before her and came forth with words of greeting, saying: Hail thou blessed of the Lord, receive the greeting of him that granted salvation to Jacob by his prophets. Behold, said he, this palm-branch. I have brought it to thee from the paradise of the Lord, and thou shalt cause it to be carried before thy bier on the third day when thou shalt be taken up out of the body. For behold thy Son with the thrones and the angels and all the powers of heaven awaiteth thee. 2 Then Mary said to the angel: I ask that all the apostles of the Lord Jesus Christ be gathered together to me. And the angel said: Lo, this day by the power of my Lord Jesus Christ all the apostles shall come to thee. And Mary said to him: I ask that thou wouldest put thy blessing upon me, that no power of hell may meet me in that hour wherein my soul goeth out of the body, and that I may not see the prince of darkness. And the angel said: The power of hell shall not hurt thee; but an eternal blessing hath the Lord thy God given thee, of whom I am the servant and messenger: but think not that the power not to see the prince of darkness can be given by me, but by him whom thou didst bear in thy womb: for his is all power, world without end. And thus saying, the angel departed with great light. 3 Now the palm-branch shone with exceeding brightness. Then Mary put off her garments and clothed herself in her best raiment, and taking the palm which she had received of the angel's hand she went out into the Mount of Olivet and began to pray and to say: I was not worthy to receive thee, Lord, if thou hadst not had mercy on me; nevertheless I kept the treasure which thou didst commit to me. Therefore I pray thee, O king of glory, that no power of hell may hurt me. For if the heavens and the angels quake before thee every day, how much more a man created of the earth, in whom is no good save what he hath received of thy bounty. Thou, Lord, art God, blessed for ever, world without end. And having thus said, she returned to her dwelling.

IV. And behold, suddenly, while Saint John was preaching at Ephesus, on the Lord's day, at the third hour, there was a great earthquake, and a cloud raised him up and took him out of the sight of all and brought him before the door of the house where Mary was. And he knocked at the door and straightway went in. But when Mary saw him she rejoiced greatly and said: I pray thee, my son John, remember the words of my Lord Jesus Christ wherewith he commended me to thee. For behold on the third day, [when] I am to depart out of the body—*and* I have heard the counsels of the Jews who say: Let us wait until the day when she shall die who bore that deceiver, and let us burn her body with fire. 2 So she called Saint John and took him into the secret part of the house and showed him her grave-clothes and that palm of light which she had received from the angel, and charged him to cause it to be borne before her bed when she should go to the tomb.

V. And Saint John said to her: How shall I alone prepare thy burial unless my brethren and fellow apostles of my Lord Jesus Christ come to pay honour to thy body?

And lo, suddenly by the commandment of God all the apostles were lifted up on a cloud and caught away from the places where they were preaching and set down before the door of the house wherein Mary dwelt. And they greeted each other and marvelled, saying: What is the cause wherefore the Lord hath gathered us together here?

[*In another text is this addition.* And Paul came with them who was turned from the circumcision and taken with Barnabas to minister to the Gentiles. And when there arose among them a godly contention, which of them should first pray the Lord to show them the cause *of their coming*, and Peter exhorted Paul to pray first, Paul answered, saying: That is thine office, to begin first, since thou wast chosen of God to be a pillar of the church, and thou art before all in the apostleship: but me it befits not at all, for I am the least of all you, and Christ was seen of me as of one born out of due time, neither presume I to even myself with you; yet by the grace of God I am what I am.]

VI. Then all the apostles rejoicing with one mind finished their prayer: and when they had said Amen, lo, suddenly the blessed John came and showed them all these things. And the apostles entered the house and found Mary and saluted her, saying: Blessed be thou of the Lord which made heaven and earth. And she said to them: Peace be unto you my most beloved brethren. How came ye hither? And they told her how they had come, each one of them being lifted up on a cloud by the Spirit and set down in that place. And she said to them: God hath not deprived me of the sight of you. Behold I go the way of all the earth, and I doubt not that the Lord hath now brought you hither to give me comfort in the anguish that is to come upon me. Now therefore I beseech you that we all keep watch together without ceasing, until the hour when the Lord shall come and I shall depart out of the body.

VII. And as they sat about her comforting her, and for three days gave themselves to the praises of God, lo, on the third day, about the third hour of the day, sleep fell upon all that were in that house, and no man at all could keep waking save only the apostles and three virgins that were there. And behold, suddenly the Lord Jesus Christ came with a great multitude of angels, and a great light came down upon that place, and the angels were singing hymns and praising the Lord. Then the Saviour spake, saying: Come, thou most precious pearl, enter into the treasury (receptacle) of eternal life.

VIII. Then Mary fell on her face on the pavement, worshipping God, and said: Blessed be the name of thy glory, O Lord my God, who hast vouchsafed to choose me thy handmaid and to commit to me thy secret mystery. Remember me, therefore, O king of glory; for thou knowest that with all my heart I have loved thee and have kept the treasure committed unto me. Receive me therefore thy servant and deliver me from the power of darkness, and let not any assault of Satan meet me, neither let me see ugly spirits coming to meet me. 2 And the Saviour answered her: When I was sent by the Father and for the salvation of the world was hung on the cross, the prince of darkness came to me : but whereas he prevailed not to find in me any sign of his work, he departed vanquished and trodden down. Thou when thou seest him shalt see him indeed according to the law of mankind whereby the end, even death, is allotted thee: but he cannot hurt thee, for I am with thee to help thee. Come thou without fear, for the heavenly host awaiteth thee to bring thee into the joy of paradise. 3 And as the Lord thus spake, Mary arose from the pavement and laid herself on her bed, and giving thanks to God she gave up the ghost. But the apostles saw her soul, that it was of such whiteness that no tongue of mortal men can worthily express it; for it excelled all whiteness of snow and of all metal and silver that glistereth with great brightness of light.

IX. Then the Saviour spake, saying: Arise, Peter, and take the body of Mary and bear it unto the right-hand side of the city toward the east, and thou wilt find there a new sepulchre wherein ye shall place it, and wait till I come unto you.

2 And when the Lord had so said, he delivered the soul of the holy Mary to Michael which was set over paradise and *is* the prince of the people of the Jews: and Gabriel went with them. And immediately the Saviour was received up into heaven with the angels.

X. Now the three virgins that were there and watched took the body of the blessed Mary to wash it after the custom of burials. And when they had stripped it of its apparel, that holy body shone with such brightness that it could indeed be touched to do the service thereof, but the appearance could not be looked upon for the exceeding flashing of light: and a great splendour appeared in it, and nothing was perceived by the sense when the body was washed, but it was most pure and not stained with any manner of defilement. And the body of the blessed Mary was like the flowers of the lily, and a great sweetness of fragrance issued from it, so that nothing like that sweetness could elsewhere be found.

XI. Then therefore the apostles laid the holy body upon a bier and said one to another: Who shall bear the palm before her bier? Then John said to Peter: Thou who art before us in the apostleship oughtest to bear this palm before her bed. And Peter answered him: Thou only of us art a virgin chosen of the Lord, and hast found such favour that thou didst lie on his breast: and he when he hung for our salvation on the tree of the cross committed her unto thee with his own mouth. Thou therefore oughtest to carry this palm; and let us take up the body to bear it unto the place of the sepulchre. 2 Thereafter Peter lifted up the head of the body and began to sing, saying: Israel is come out of Egypt. Alleluia. And with him the other apostles bore the body of the blessed Mary, and John carried the palm of light before the bier. And the rest of the apostles sang with exceeding sweet voices.

XII. And behold a new miracle. There appeared a very great cloud over the bier like the great circle that useth to be seen about the splendour of the moon: and an host of angels was in the cloud sending forth a song of sweetness, and the earth resounded with the noise of that great melody. Then the people came out of the city, about fifteen thousand, and marvelled and said: What is this sound of such sweetness? 2 Then there stood one and told them: Mary is gone out of the body, and the disciples of Jesus are singing praises about her. And they looked and saw the bier crowned with great glory and the apostles singing with a loud voice. And behold, one of them who was a prince of the priests of the Jews in his degree was filled with fury and wrath and said to the rest: Behold the tabernacle of him that hath troubled us and all our nation, what glory it hath received. And he came near and would have overthrown the bier and cast the body on the earth. And forthwith his hands dried up from his elbows and clave to the bier. And when the apostles lifted the bier, part of him was hanging and part clave to the bier, and he was wrung with extreme torment as the apostles went on and sang. But the angels that were in the clouds smote the people with blindness.

XIII. Then that prince cried out, saying: I beseech thee, holy Peter, despise me not in this so great necessity, for I am sore tormented with great pains. Remember that when the damsel that kept the door knew thee in the judgement hall and told the rest, that they might challenge thee, then I spake good on thy behalf. Then Peter answered and said: It is not mine to give thee ought: but if thou believest with thy whole heart on the Lord Jesus Christ, whom this woman bare in her womb and continued a virgin after the birth, the mercy of the Lord, which by his great pity saveth the unworthy, shall give thee healing.

2 Whereunto he answered: Do we not believe? but what shall we do? The enemy of mankind hath blinded our hearts, and shame hath covered our faces that we should not confess the mighty works of God; especially when we did curse ourselves, crying out against Christ: His blood be on us and on our children. Then said Peter: See, that curse will hurt him that continueth unbelieving in him, but unto them that turn to God mercy is not denied. And he said: I believe all that thou sayest to me: only I beseech thee, have mercy on me lest I die.

XIV. Then Peter made the bier stand still and said to him: If thou believest with thy whole heart in Jesus Christ, thine hands shall be loosed from the bier. And when he had so said, straightway his hands were loosed from the bier and he began to stand on his feet: but his arms were yet withered, neither did the pain depart from him. 2 Then Peter said to him: Go near to the body and kiss the bed and say: I believe in God and in the Son of God whom this woman bare, even Jesus Christ, and I believe all things whatsoever Peter the apostle of God hath told me. And he came near and kissed the bed, and forthwith all pain left him and his hands were made whole. 3 Then began he to bless God greatly and to speak out of the books of Moses testimonies unto the praise of Christ, so that even the apostles themselves marvelled and wept for gladness, praising the name of the Lord.

XV. But Peter said to him: Take this palm at the hand of our brother John, and go into the city and thou wilt find much people blinded; and declare unto them the mighty works of God, and whosoever believeth on the Lord Jesus Christ, lay this palm upon their eyes and they shall see: but whoso believe not shall continue blind. 2 And when he had so done, he found much people blinded and lamenting thus: Woe unto us, for we are become like the men of Sodom that were stricken with blindness. Nothing remaineth for us now save to perish. But when they had heard the words that the prince spake which was healed, they believed on the Lord Jesus Christ, and when he laid the palm upon their eyes, they recovered sight; but whoso of them continued in hardness of heart died. And the prince of the priests went forth to the apostles and gave back the palm and declared all that had come to pass.

XVI. But the apostles carrying Mary came into the place of the valley of Josaphat which the Lord had showed them, and laid her in a new tomb and shut the sepulchre. But they sat down at the door of the tomb as the Lord had charged them: and lo, suddenly the Lord Jesus Christ came with a great multitude of angels, and light flashing with great brightness, and said to the apostles: Peace be with you. And they answered and said: Let thy mercy, O Lord, be upon us, like as we have hoped in thee.

2 Then the Saviour spake unto them, saying: Before I ascended up unto my Father I promised you, saying, that ye which have followed me, in the regeneration when the Son of man shall sit on the throne of his majesty, ye also shall sit on twelve thrones, judging the twelve tribes of Israel. Now this woman did I choose out of the tribes of Israel by the commandment of my Father, to dwell in her. What then will ye that I do with her? 3 Then said Peter and the other apostles: Lord, thou didst before choose this thine handmaid to become thine immaculate chamber, and us thy servants for thy ministry. All things didst thou foreknow before the worlds with thy Father, with whom to thee and the Holy Ghost there belongeth equal Godhead and infinite power. If therefore it might come to pass before the power of thy grace, it hath appeared right to us thy servants that, as thou having overcome death dost reign in glory, so thou shouldest raise up the body of thy mother and take her with thee rejoicing into heaven.

XVII. Then said the Saviour: Be it done according to your

will. And he commanded Michael the archangel to bring the soul of the holy Mary. And behold, Michael the archangel rolled away the stone from the door of the sepulchre, and the Lord said: Rise up, my love and my kinswoman: thou that didst not suffer corruption by union of the flesh, shalt not suffer dissolution of the body in the sepulchre. 2 And immediately Mary rose up from the grave and blessed the Lord, and fell at the Lord's feet and worshipped him, saying: I am not able to render thee worthy thanks, O Lord, for thine innumerable benefits which thou hast vouchsafed to grant unto me thy handmaid. Let thy name be blessed for ever, redeemer of the world, thou God of Israel.

XVIII. And the Lord kissed her and departed, and delivered her to the angels to bear her into paradise. And he said to the apostles: Come near unto me; and when they had come near, he kissed them and said: Peace be unto you; as I have been always with you, so will I be even unto the end of the world.

2 And immediately when the Lord had so said he was lifted up in a cloud and received into heaven, and the angels with him, bearing the blessed Mary into the paradise of God.

But the apostles were taken up upon clouds and returned every one unto the lot of his preaching, declaring the mighty works of God and praising the Lord Jesus Christ, who liveth and reigneth with the Father and the Holy Ghost in a perfect unity and in one substance of the Godhead, world without end. Amen.

THE ASSUMPTION : NARRATIVE BY JOSEPH OF ARIMATHAEA

This is Tischendorf's A text. It is of late complexion, and one of the three manuscripts used by Tischendorf (C) presents a very divergent text throughout. An analysis will suffice.

1 Before the Passion the Virgin asked Jesus to certify her of her death on the third day before it, and to receive her with his angels. 2, 3 He promised that this should be so (the speech is fairly long).

4 In the second year after the ascension she was constantly praying. On the third day before her death an angel (Gabriel, C) came and gave her a palm and told her of her departure.

5 She sent for Joseph of Arimathaea and other disciples, and told them, and then washed and arrayed herself as a queen. Three virgins were with her—Sepphora, Abigea, and Žael. The apostles were already dispersed about the world.

6 At the third hour, thunder, rain, earthquake. John was suddenly brought from Ephesus and entered the chamber and

greeted her. She said: Dearest son, why have you left me for so long?

7 All the disciples except Thomas now arrived on clouds, and greeted her.

8 They were John, James his brother, Peter, Paul, Andrew, Philip, Luke, Barnabas, Bartholomew, Matthew, Matthias surnamed Justus, Simon the Canaanite, Jude and his brother, Nicodemus, Maximianus (this must be the legendary Maximin of Aix en Provence who figures in the late legend of Mary Magdalene's mission to Marseilles).

9 Mary asked: why have you all come? Peter said: It is for us to ask thee. None of us know. I was at Antioch, and now I am here. And all told where they had been. 10 Mary told them the reason, that she was to depart on the morrow, and asked them to watch and pray with her. So they did, all night, with lights and psalmody.

11 On the Sunday at the third hour Christ came down with a host of angels and took the soul of his mother. Such was the light and fragrance that all fell on their faces (as at Mount Tabor) and none could rise for an hour and a half. 12 As the light receded, the soul of Mary was taken up with it, with singing: and as the cloud went up, the earth shook, and all in Jerusalem saw the death of Mary in one instant.

13 Then Satan entered into them and they took arms to burn the body and kill the apostles; but they were struck blind, and smote their heads against walls, and hit one another.

14 The apostles took up the body to bear it from Mount Sion to the valley of Josaphat. As they went, a Jew named Ruben tried to upset the bier, but his hands withered to the elbow and willy-nilly he had to go on into the valley weeping and crying, for his hands clave to the bier. 15 He began to ask the apostles to pray for him that he might be saved and become a Christian. They knelt and prayed, and his hands were loosed and he was healed. He was baptized at once, and began to proclaim Christ.

16 'Then the apostles laid the body in the tomb with great honour, weeping and singing for pure love and sweetness. And suddenly a light from heaven shone round about them, and as they fell to the earth, the holy body was taken up by angels into heaven' (the apostles not knowing it).

17 Thomas was suddenly brought to the Mount of Olives and saw the holy body being taken up, and cried out to Mary: 'make thy servant glad by thy mercy, for now thou goest to heaven'. And the girdle with which the apostles had girt the body was thrown down to him; he took it and went to the valley of Josaphat. 18 When he had greeted the apostles, Peter said: 'Thou wast always unbelieving, and so the Lord hath not suffered thee to be at his mother's burial.' He smote his breast and said: 'I know

it and I ask pardon of you all,' and they all prayed for him.
19 Then he said: 'Where have ye laid her body?' and they
pointed to the sepulchre. But he said: 'The holy body is not
there.' Peter said: 'Formerly you would not believe in the
resurrection of the Lord before you touched him: how should
you believe us?' Thomas went on saying: 'It is not here.'
Then in anger they went and took away the stone, and the body
was not there; and they knew not what to say, being vanquished
by Thomas's words. 20 Then Thomas told them how he had
been saying mass in India (and he still had on his priestly vest-
ments), how he had been brought to the Mount of Olives and
seen the ascension of Mary and she had given him her girdle:
and he showed it. 21 They all rejoiced and asked his pardon,
and he blessed them and said : Behold how good and pleasant
a thing it is, brethren, to dwell together in unity.

22 The same clouds which had brought them, now carried
them back, as we read in the Acts about Philip who baptized
the eunuch, and as Abacuc was brought to Daniel and taken
back.

23 Nor is it wonderful that Christ should do such things
(miracles are enumerated).

24 I am that Joseph who laid the body of the Lord in my
tomb and saw him rise again, and always watched over his
most holy temple, even the blessed Mary, ever virgin, before
the ascension of the Lord and after it: and upon this page
and in my heart have I written the things that came out of the
mouth of God, and how the aforesaid matters came to pass,
and I have made known to all the Jews and Gentiles what I saw
with my eyes and heard with my ears, and as long as I live
I shall not cease to proclaim them.

'Whose assumption is this day reverenced and honoured
throughout all the world: let us constantly pray her that she
remember us before her most merciful son in heaven: to whom
is praise and glory for infinite ages. Amen.'

(C has a statement that any Christian who has this writing in
his house will be safe from various afflictions—lunacy, deafness,
blindness, sudden death—and he will have the protection of the
Virgin at his end.)

The episode of Thomas and the girdle is peculiar to this writing.
The girdle is the great relic of Prato; and the prominence given to
this incident is another indication that we have here a mediaeval
Italian composition, not earlier, I imagine, than the thirteenth century.

THE SYRIAC NARRATIVES

The Syriac narratives of the Assumption of the Virgin form a very large mass of writing.
The principal texts are:
1. That edited by W. Wright in the *Journal of Sacred Literature* for 1865, and again by Mrs. Agnes Smith Lewis in *Studia Sinaitica*, XI. *Apocrypha Syriaca*, 1902. In the latter the translation fills pp. 12–69 in quarto.
2, 2 a. Edited by Wright in *Contributions to the Apocryphal Literature of the N. T.*, 1865, pp. 18–24 (2), and 24–41 (2 a). These are pieces of two distinct works, which he has put together under one heading. Both are fragmentary: the first is the simplest of the Syriac versions. The second (2 a) is akin to 1.
3. That in Sir E. A. Wallis Budge's *History of the B. V. M.*, Luzac's Semitic Text and Translation Series, vol. v, 1899, pp. 97–153.
4. The fragments in Wright's *Contributions* called Obsequies of the Holy Virgin (pp. 42–51 and Preface, 10–15).
Of these nos. 1, 2, 2 a, 3 have much in common; 4 is very peculiar. Some account of each shall be given.

No. 1 (Wright and Lewis) is a congeries of documents divided into six books (really five, but six are promised).
Book I, after a panegyrical introduction, tells how the narrative was found. It was attested in autograph by James, bishop of Jerusalem. Two apostles wrote each of the six books, and they were entrusted to John.
His copy was found at Ephesus, attested by the Twelve and the Seventy-two, and written in Hebrew, Greek, and Latin.
Book II. In the year 344 (of the era of the Greeks), on the third day of the latter Teshrin (September), being the third day of the week at the third hour, Mary went to the tomb.
The Jews immediately after the Passion had closed it with great stones, and forbidden resort to it on pain of death. They also hid the cross, spear, sponge, robe, crown of thorns, and nails.
The priests told the guardians of the tomb to stone Mary if she came there again. They said, 'Do it yourselves'. On the Friday Mary burnt incense there: Gabriel came down and told her of her approaching death. (There is no mention of a palm.)
The guards informed the priests that Mary had come again. The priests asked the governor to forbid her.
At this time Abgar of Edessa (converted by Addai) wished to destroy Jerusalem because of Christ's death, and came as far as Euphrates, but hesitated to cross it. He wrote to the procurator Sabinus, who sent the letter to Tiberius,[1] who was greatly moved

---

[1] A letter of Abgar to Tiberius on the subject, and the answer of Tiberius, are given by Moses of Chorene in his *History of Armenia* (ii. 33).

against the Jews. The Jews were alarmed. They said to the governor: Forbid Mary to go to the tomb. He said: Forbid her yourselves. A long abusive speech of the Jews to Mary follows.

She left Jerusalem and went to Bethlehem with her three virgins, Callĕtha, daughter of Nicodemus, Neshra, daughter of Gamaliel, Tabitha, daughter of Archelaus. (There is a description of the service which these did to Mary: Gabriel tells her to go to Bethlehem.)

On Friday Mary burnt incense and prayed that John might be sent to her. John was brought from Ephesus. His arrival and conversation with Mary.

The other apostles were brought. Here we are following the Greek text pretty closely.

John received the apostles. They each told Mary how they had come. The correspondence with the Greek is curiously exact. Mark was performing the service of the third hour. Matthew says: 'I have given and am giving glory to God,' and so on. The Greek, however, does not give the speeches of those who had been raised from the grave to come, but the Syriac does, for Philip, Simon, Luke, and Andrew. And after Andrew, Bartholomew (not already dead) follows, as in the Greek.

There was a great concourse of angels, and the Bethlehemites in fear went and told the governor and the priests.

Book III. All the great signs attracted people from many quarters. Before this many used to come to the Virgin to be healed. (Five instances are given of cures.)

There was now a festival at Jerusalem, and many sick went out to Bethlehem to be healed. 2,800 were cured. = Gk. 28, but more diffuse.

On the 21st of Teshrin II in the night, men rose up to attack the house. Angels of fire descended from heaven. = Gk. 29, but there the attackers are confounded and turned back. Syr. has nothing of this.

The priests insisted on Mary's banishment by the governor. He sent a chiliarch to Bethlehem with thirty men. The Spirit told the apostles to take Mary to Jerusalem. They did so and held a five days' service.

Meanwhile the chiliarch found nothing at Bethlehem, and the priests said this was due to magic. This last is not in Gk. 31–3, which is, otherwise, represented well.

After the five days, Mary's presence in Jerusalem was realized. The Jews wished the governor to burn the house: he told them to do so themselves, and watched from a distance. The attackers were scorched and burnt. The governor declared his belief in Christ. = Gk. 34–5. Here the Syriac has a very long digression not represented in the Greek, and belonging properly, it seems, to the story of the Cross (pp. 39–50).

Caleb the Sadducee, who was a secret believer, whispered to

the governor that he should adjure the Jews by the God of Israel to tell him their real opinion about Jesus.

So all Jerusalem was assembled: and there follows a long altercation between the believers and unbelievers before the governor. Eventually some of the latter are forced by scourging to tell how they had hidden the cross, &c. The governor (rather inconsequently) has the place obstructed with great stones.

He then goes to see Mary. He greets the apostles (and they tell him how they came there. This is only in 2). Mary at his request tells him the story of the Annunciation. The governor left Jerusalem and went to Rome and told the emperor, and the account of all this was written down by disciples at Rome, who also wrote to the apostles telling them of various miracles (seven are told) which Mary had wrought.

The text then leaps to § 45 of the Greek, omitting (in this place) all notice of the death of the Virgin.

The Spirit told the apostles to bear her to a place where were three caves, and to lay her on a bench there and await his bidding.

Jephonias, 'strong and tall, and handsome of figure', attacked them—was smitten and healed (but Mary is not dead yet, for she speaks to him). Peter gave a dry rod to Jephonias and sent him to the Jews. The rod blossomed. He healed a man born blind, and many others. = Gk. 45–7, and Lat. xii–xv. The Greek has not the healing of the Jews, and the Syriac has distorted it.

The apostles laid Mary in the eastern cave and held a service of three days and nights. Some Jews came to the cave: three ventured in, and were burnt and swallowed up. Many believed, but the priests threatened and bribed them.

This, which concludes Book III, is badly confused in the Syriac, which has made the great mistake of saying that the apostles bore the Virgin to the cave before she was dead.

Book IV. While the apostles were ministering about Mary in the cave the Spirit spoke to them, and told the story of the Annunciation. He spoke also of the date of her death, and then told how Sunday is the day of the Annunciation, the Nativity, the Entry, Resurrection, Ascension, and Judgement. = Gk. 36.

Eve, Anna, Elisabeth, Adam, and other patriarchs now came and greeted Mary, and then the procession of heavenly chariots, and then Christ. His words to her, and her answer. Her kissing of his hand, and prayers and blessing and death, are as in Gk. 38–44, but the blessing is far longer.

Then the body was prepared for burial. Twelve chariots took up the apostles and bore them all to Paradise (cf. the alternative text of Gk. 48): and they returned thence and ordained a commemoration of her three times a year. Cf. Gk. 49.

After this is a very long disquisition on the rules which the apostles made about the commemoration: it need not even be summarized here (pp. 59–62).

When they had come back to the cave they agreed to write a book in Hebrew, Greek, and Latin, and commit it to John: and, with more unimportant matter following on this, the book ends.

Book V, pp. 64–9. This is a diffuse account of the Virgin's visit to Paradise. One paragraph tells of her seeing Gehenna.

John and Peter were with her, and she revealed everything to John and told him to write it: it would be made public at the end of the world.

Christ then says he will tell her what is to happen at his second coming: but nothing is told. Mary answers with thanksgiving and prayer—and Book V ends. Book VI does not appear.

2. (Wright: *Contributions*, p. 18.)

A prefatory section declares the apostles to be the witnesses and authors of what follows.

The story then begins, and gives a shorter form of what we have had, in this order:

Mary goes to the tomb.

The Jews threaten to stone her.

She asks Jesus to take her out of the world.

The angel comes to tell her her prayer is heard.

The guards of the tomb report this.

The Jews ask Sabinus the governor to banish her.

He refers them to her. They come and abuse her.

She goes to Bethlehem with the three virgins (named as in 1).

She prays that John may be sent. He comes.

The other apostles arrive.

They begin to tell how they came. The first fragment ends in John's narrative. It was left unfinished by the scribe.

2 a. p. 24. This begins in the midst of the dispute between believers and unbelievers before the governor, and the story follows the course of 1 down to the point where the apostles lay Mary in the cave. Here the first fragment of 2 a ends.

p. 39. The second fragment of 2 a does not seem to have an exact textual equivalent in 1.

Chariots of light and saints arrive, and Mary is borne to paradise.

The apostles return to the Mount of Olives, and pray to be allowed to ordain a commemoration of Mary.

And so with rather a long doxology the book ends.

It is, so far as we have it, far more compact and coherent than 1 or 3.

3. (Budge.)

This is mainly identical in content with 1, but has points of its own.

Mary goes to the tomb.

The Jews plot to kill her, close the cave, set guards on it.

Gabriel comes.

The guards report it.

Mary goes to Bethlehem with the three virgins (as above).

The Jews hid the cross, &c., and asserted that 'here are buried the Book of Moses and the box of manna and the rod of Aaron and the mantle of Elijah', so that if miracles did happen there, they could be attributed to those relics.

Abgar's letter. Sabinus is angry with the Jews. Mary prayed that the apostles might be sent.

John came.

Then the others. The statement that they came and the circumstances of their doing so are put into one narrative, not repeated as in 1.

After the apostles had greeted Mary, Anne, Elisabeth, Adam, &c., came, and all the various orders of saints and angels: and Christ. This dialogue and her prayers are rather shortened, but essentially as in 1.

Mary died and her soul was taken up.

Then we have a bad dislocation.

The believers in the city went to the governor and told him the truth about Jesus and the Jews. He was angry with the chiefs, and smote them and told them not to harm the Christians. This is a condensation into a few lines of the dispute before the governor. Yet this dispute occurs later on. Here, however, we have the sequel.

The governor visited Mary with his sick son (who was healed). The apostles told him of their miraculous coming. The governor went to Rome and told the emperor, and the believers there wrote down the wonderful record. This is a shorter form of 1.

A paragraph on the age of Mary (52) follows.

The apostles said, 'Let us make a distinction between the burial of believers and non-believers, and make a beginning with Mary'. They prepared her body for burial, and set out in procession.

The Jews saw it and bribed the governor not to interfere with them. They also bribed a gigantic soldier of his, Yophana, to go with them and attack the bier.

Then we have the affliction and cure of Yophana, who goes back to the governor, and he laughs at the Jews.

The apostles laid the body in the cave.

Peter asked the multitude to set guards over it. He also spoke to the believers of the glory of Mary.

The Jews plotted and put a number of dead bodies in the cave, but in vain: and then tried to burn the body but were burnt themselves.

Then the apostles brought out the body and laid it on a bier.

Then came all the chariots of light, and the body was put in a chariot of light, and it and all the apostles went up to Paradise.

And the cloud took them back to Jerusalem. And they wrote down all the triumphs of the Virgin and sent the books everywhere, and ordained three yearly commemorations; and were taken back to the places whence they had come.

Then a homiletical paragraph. It introduces the revelation of John about the Virgin in Paradise. = No. 1, Book V.

The Jews thought the body was still in the cave, and they went in and found it not. Many believed.

The unbelievers (again?) put dead bodies in the cave.

The believers told the governor, and he sent Yophana, who confiscated all the goods of the offenders.

'Here I will write of the miracles which the Bethlehemites saw wrought in the upper chamber where Mary lay.'

Visions of angels, multitudes of sick healed: six miracles narrated, as in 1. The healing of 2,800 people.

Plot to attack the house. Descent of angels of fire. All this is in 1.

The priests insisted on the banishment of Mary. The chiliarch sent. The apostles bore Mary to Bethlehem (*read* Jerusalem). The five days' service. The house in Jerusalem attacked, the besiegers burnt, the governor's declaration of belief.

The dispute between believers and unbelievers before the governor. The hiding-place of the cross obstructed.

Then afterwards the disciples of the apostles wrote (to various places), and wrote an account of the departure of Mary, and took it with them to Byzantium.

And then a series of miracles is narrated, which are nearly all identical with those in 1.

4. Wright. (Obsequies of the Holy Virgin, *Contributions*, p. 42.)

The fragments printed and summarized by Wright in the Preface contain these incidents:

The appearance of the Lord to his mother: her last words and death. Her soul is delivered to Michael. Peter begins to speak to Christ.

The funeral procession. Jews are blinded, and he who tries to overset the bier has his arms fixed to it. They are restored. Peter gives him a staff with which he heals 5,000 blinded people.

p. 42. First long fragment. Paul is speaking, and telling a long story about Solomon, who had been told by a demon that a certain young man would die. A form of this story occurs in the Testament of Solomon.

The apostles ask Paul to go on speaking, 'for our Lord hath sent thee to gladden us during these three days'. Paul asks them what they will preach when they go forth: and is answered by Peter, John, and Andrew. He criticizes them as too severe, and recommends a gentler policy. They are angry.

And as they were all sitting disputing before the entrance to Mary's tomb, Jesus appeared and justified Paul's view, as against the others.

He summoned Michael and bade him bring forth the body of Mary into the clouds. They were all carried to Paradise.

The apostles then asked the Lord to show them the place of torment, reminding him of his promise that on the day of the departure of Mary they should see it.

They were all taken on a cloud to the west. The Lord spoke to the angels of the pit, and the earth sprang upwards and they saw the pit.[1]

The lost saw Michael and begged for respite. Mary and the apostles fell down and interceded for them. Michael spoke to them, telling them that at all the twelve hours of the day and of the night the angels intercede for creation. The angel of the waters intercedes for the waters. Here the fragment ends.

p. 48. The next fragment is a story told by Michael to Mary, of the concealing of the bones of Joseph in the Nile by Pharaoh and their discovery by Moses. It seems as if this must have been told in answer to some inquiry of Mary's about her own body, and therefore it should be placed earlier in order.

p. 50. The last fragment is a curious story about Jesus testing the apostles, evidently during his life on earth. It is so puzzling and uncommon as to be worth quoting in full:

'them according to their wish. And he sent by the hand of the apostles to them [2] (to ask) were these things not so?

And he said: These are the shepherds of the house of Israel, who are praying for the sheep, that they may be sanctified and made glorious before the sons of men: and themselves they are not able to sanctify, because they exalt themselves like the strong. Did I not give them many signs?

And the apostles said: Lord, lo they beseech and pray, and repent, and kneel upon their knees. Why dost thou not hear them? Our Lord says unto them: I too was willing to hear them, but there is deception in them (as) ye too know.

And when Jesus wished to show the apostles for what reason he did not hear them, he took them up into a mountain and let them become hungry. And when the apostles had gone, they asked of him, and say unto him: Lord we are hungry; what have we then to eat in this desert? And Jesus told them to go to the trees which were before them. And he said to them: Go to those trees which are over against us, whose branches are many and fair and beautiful at a distance, and from them ye shall get food. And when the apostles went, they did not find fruit on the trees.

And they returned to Jesus, and said: Good Teacher, thou

[1] I have pointed out, and the Rev. St. J. Seymour has elaborated the thesis, that this visit of the apostles to Hell was known in *Ireland* at an early date, and that the Irish form must be derived somehow from this Syriac text.

[2] Evidently the leaders of the Jews.

didst send us to those trees which are over against us, and we went and found on them no fruit, but only branches which were fair and beautiful, but there was no fruit on them.

And Jesus said to them: Ye have not seen them, because the trees grow straight upwards. Go therefore at once, because the trees are bending themselves, and ye shall find on them fruit, and get yourselves food. And when they went, they found the trees bending down, but they did not find fruit upon them.

And they returned again to Jesus in great distress, and say to him: What is this, Teacher, that we are mocked? For at first thou didst say to us, 'Ye shall find trees which are straight, and there is fruit on them,' and we found none. Why are we mocked? But it is fitting that thou shouldest teach us what this is that has happened; for we think that what thou didst wish to teach us is false; for by a visible power the trees were laid hold of and bent down. If this be a temptation, make known to us what it is.

And Jesus said to them: Go and sit under them, and ye shall see what it is that abides on them, but ye shall not be able to bend them again. And when the apostles went and sat under the trees, straightway the trees threw down stinking worms. And the apostles came again to Jesus and say to him: Teacher, dost thou wish to lead us astray or to turn us away from thee.' . . .

The trees of course represent the leaders or priests of the Jews whose prayers are ineffectual because of their moral defects. The story has no parallel that I know of, and to my mind has a rather ancient complexion.

This whole book of the Obsequies stands quite apart from the rest of the narratives: it had, we see, the framework, with the Jew attacking the bier and so forth ; but this framework was evidently used for the insertion of a number of quite extraneous discourses and stories, and what we have of these is so unusual that we must greatly regret the loss of the rest. The undoubted fact that this form of the story somehow penetrated to Ireland gives additional interest to the book.

Wright assigned the manuscript to the latter part of the fifth century.

Besides the forms we have reviewed there are versions in Arabic (ed. Enger, 1854), Aethiopic (Chaine, *Corpus script. christ. Orient.*, 1909), Armenian (Vetter, *Theol. Quartalschrift*, 1902). These agree in their main features with the Syriac books and do not demand a detailed analysis. The Armenian, as usual, has its own peculiar and 'unauthorized' additions.

Our survey of the narratives shows that there are two great groups, one of which is represented in Coptic only—but not uniformly by all the Coptic authorities. In this there is a long interval between the death of Mary and her corporal assumption—206 days, from 21 Tobi to 16 Mesore (one authority gives only seven days, and one excludes a corporal assumption). Also we hear nothing of the summoning of the apostles from their missionary work: Peter and John are the only two who are prominent. Further, only one fragment (Copt. 4) has the story of a Jew smitten for touching the bier, and healed.

Also in all Mary is warned of her death by her Son, not by an angel.

In the Greek, Latin, and Syriac (1, 2, 3) the death is announced by an angel; in Greek and Latin he brings a palm-branch (and so, too, in Copt. 4), but not in Syriac.

The apostles are summoned from all parts of the world and from their graves, and tell how they came.

The 'governor' figures largely in Syriac and appears in Greek. The controversy before him, which is only in the oriental versions, seems to have been borrowed from another writing: the real point of it is the hiding of the cross at the end.

The Jew who attacks the bier (usually Jephonias, but Ruben in the latest text, Lat. A) is a constant feature: he also figures in the Coptic fragment 4.

In Greek, Latin, and Copt. 4 he heals the blinded people with the palm-branch: in Syriac with Peter's staff.

The corporal assumption takes place very soon after the death. Less emphasis is laid upon it than in the Coptic texts.

ACTS

WE begin with the five books which were formed into a corpus by the Manichaeans and substituted by them for our canonical Acts.

They are of different dates.

Earliest are the *Acts of John*, not later than the middle of the second century.

Next the *Acts of Paul*, composed by a presbyter of Asia before Tertullian's time: *cir.* 160–170 ?

The *Acts of Peter*, usually assigned to about the year 200.

The *Acts of Andrew*, less well preserved than the rest, and probably to be dated well after 200; even after 250, perhaps.

The *Acts of Thomas*, composed in Syriac, according to the weight of authority, date from the third century.

Photius (890), who read all five and has written a criticism of them in his *Bibliotheca* or *Myriobiblon*, found them all attributed to one author, Leucius. But it is now agreed that Leucius (a supposed disciple of John) [1] was the ostensible author of the *Acts of John* only.

ACTS OF JOHN

The length of this book is given in the Stichometry of Nicephorus as 2,500 lines: the same number as for St. Matthew's Gospel. We have large portions of it in the original, and a Latin version (purged, it is important to note, of all traces of unorthodoxy) of some lost episodes, besides a few scattered fragments. These will be fitted together in what seems the most probable order.

The best edition of the Greek remains is in Bonnet, *Acta Apost. Apocr.* II. 1, 1898: the Latin is in Book V of the Historia Apostolica of Abdias (Fabricius, *Cod. Apocr. N. T.*: there is no modern edition).

The beginning of the book is lost. It probably related in some form a trial, and banishment of John to Patmos. A distinctly late Greek text printed by Bonnet (in two forms) as cc. 1–17 of his work tells how Domitian, on his accession, persecuted the Jews. They accused the Christians in a letter to him: he accordingly persecuted the Christians. He heard of John's teaching in Ephesus and sent for him: his ascetic habits on the voyage impressed his captors. He was brought before Domitian, and made to drink poison, which did not hurt him: the dregs of it killed a criminal on whom it was tried: and John revived him; he also raised a girl who was slain by an

---

[1] He is once mentioned, without reference to the Acts, as a disciple of John, viz. by Epiphanius, Heresy 51. 6. The early heretics Cerinthus, Ebion, &c., &c., often opposed the Lord's disciples, and 'they were often opposed by Saint John and his companions, Leucius and many others'.

unclean spirit. Domitian, who was much impressed, banished him to Patmos. Nerva recalled him. The second text tells how he escaped shipwreck on leaving Patmos, swimming on a cork; landed at Miletus, where a chapel was built in his honour, and went to Ephesus. All this is late: but an old story, known to Tertullian and to other Latin writers, *but to no Greek*, said that either Domitian at Rome or the Proconsul at Ephesus cast John into a caldron of boiling oil which did him no hurt. The scene of this was eventually fixed at the Latin Gate in Rome (hence the St. John Port Latin of our calendar, May 6th). We have no detailed account of this, but it is conjectured to have been told in the early part of the Leucian Acts. If so, it is odd that no Greek writer mentions it.

Leaving for the time certain small fragments which may perhaps have preceded the extant episodes, I proceed to the first long episode (Bonnet, c. 18).

[John is going from Miletus to Ephesus.]

18 Now John was hastening to Ephesus, moved thereto by a vision. Damonicus therefore, and Aristodemus his kinsman, and a certain very rich man Cleobius, and the wife of Marcellus, hardly prevailed to keep him for one day in Miletus, reposing themselves with him. And when very early in the morning they had set forth, and already about four miles of the journey were accomplished, a voice came from heaven in the hearing of all of us, saying: John, thou art about to give glory to thy Lord in Ephesus, whereof thou shalt know, thou and all the brethren that are with thee, and certain of them that are there, which shall believe by thy means. John therefore pondered, rejoicing in himself, what it should be that should befall (meet) him at Ephesus, and said: Lord, behold I go according to thy will: let that be done which thou desirest.

19 And as we drew near to the city, Lycomedes the praetor of the Ephesians, a man of large substance, met us, and falling at John's feet besought him, saying: Is thy name John? the God whom thou preachest hath sent thee to do good unto my wife, who hath been smitten with palsy now these seven days and lieth incurable. But glorify thou thy God by healing her, and have compassion on us. For as I was considering with myself what resolve to take in this matter, one stood by me and said: Lycomedes, cease from this thought which warreth against thee, for it is evil (hard): submit not thyself unto it. For I have compassion upon mine handmaid Cleopatra, and have sent from Miletus a man named John who shall raise her up and restore her to thee whole. Tarry not, therefore, thou servant of the God who hath manifested himself unto me, but hasten unto my wife who hath no more than breath. And straightway John went from the gate, with the brethren that were with

him and Lycomedes, unto his house. But Cleobius said to
his young men: Go ye to my kinsman Callippus and receive
of him comfortable entertainment—for I am come hither with
his son—that we may find all things decent.

20 Now when Lycomedes came with John into the house
wherein his wife lay, he caught hold again of his feet and said:
See, lord, the withering of the beauty, see the youth, see the
renowned flower of my poor wife, whereat all Ephesus was wont
to marvel: wretched me, I have suffered envy, I have been
humbled, the eye of mine enemies hath smitten me: I have
never wronged any, though I might have injured many, for
I looked before to this very thing, and took care, lest I should
see any evil or any such ill fortune as this. What profit, then,
hath Cleopatra from my anxiety? what have I gained by being
known for a pious man until this day? nay, I suffer more than
the impious, in that I see thee, Cleopatra, lying in such plight.
The sun in his course shall no more see me conversing with
thee: I will go before thee, Cleopatra, and rid myself of life:
I will not spare mine own safety though it be yet young. I will
defend myself before Justice, that I have rightly deserted, for
I may indict her as judging unrighteously. I will be avenged
on her when I come before her as a ghost ⟨bereft⟩ of life. I will
say to her: Thou didst force me to leave the light when thou
didst rob me of Cleopatra: thou didst cause me to become
a corpse when thou sentest me this *ill fortune*: thou didst compel
me to insult Providence, by cutting off my joy in life (my confidence).

21 And with yet more words Lycomedes addressing Cleopatra
came near to the bed and cried aloud and lamented: but John
pulled him away, and said: Cease from these lamentations
and from thine unfitting words: thou must not disobey him
that (?) appeared unto thee: for know that thou shalt receive
thy consort again. Stand, therefore, with us that have come
hither on her account and pray to the God whom thou sawest
manifesting himself unto thee in dreams. What, then, is it,
Lycomedes? Awake, thou also, and open thy soul. Cast off
the heavy sleep from thee: beseech the Lord, entreat him for
thy wife, and he will raise her up. But he fell upon the floor
and lamented, fainting.[1]

John therefore said with tears: Alas for the fresh (new)
betraying of my vision! for the new temptation that is prepared
for me! for the new device of him that contriveth against me!
the voice from heaven that was borne unto me in the way,
hath it devised this for me? was it this that it foreshowed me
should come to pass here, betraying me to this great multitude of the citizens because of Lycomedes? the man lieth with-

[1] It is evident from what follows that Lycomedes died: but the
text does not say so; some words may have fallen out.

out breath, and I know well that they will not suffer me to go out of the house alive. Why tarriest thou, Lord (*or*, what wilt thou do)? why hast thou shut off from us thy good promise? Do not, I beseech thee, Lord, do not give him cause to exult who rejoiceth in the suffering of others; give him not cause to dance who alway derideth us; but let thy holy name and thy mercy make haste. Raise up these two dead *whose death is* against me.

22 And even as John thus cried out, the city of the Ephesians ran together to the house of Lycomedes, *hearing* that he was dead. And John, beholding the great multitude that was come, said unto the Lord: Now is the time of refreshment and of confidence toward thee, O Christ; now is the time for us who are sick to have the help that is of thee, O physician who healest freely; keep thou mine entering in hither safe from derision. I beseech thee, Jesu, succour this great multitude that it may come to thee who art Lord of all things: behold the affliction, behold them that lie here. Do thou prepare, even from them that are assembled for that end, holy vessels for thy service, when they behold thy gift. For thyself hast said, O Christ, 'Ask, and it shall be given you'. We ask therefore of thee, O king, not gold, not silver, not substance, not possessions, nor aught of what is on earth and perisheth, but two souls, by whom thou shalt convert them that are here unto thy way, unto thy teaching, unto thy liberty (confidence), unto thy most excellent (*or* unfailing) promise: for when they perceive thy power in that those that have died are raised, they will be saved, some of them. Do thou thyself, therefore, give *them* hope in thee: and so go I unto Cleopatra and say: Arise in the name of Jesus Christ.

23 And he came to her and touched her face and said: Cleopatra, He saith, whom every ruler feareth, and every creature and *every* power, the abyss and all darkness, and unsmiling death, and the height of heaven, and the circles of hell [and the resurrection of the dead, and the sight of the blind], and the whole power of the prince of this world, and the pride of the ruler: Arise, and be not an occasion unto many that desire not to believe, or an affliction unto souls that are able to hope and to be saved. And Cleopatra straightway cried with a loud voice: I arise, master: save thou thine handmaid.

Now when she had arisen ⟨who had lain incurable for⟩ seven days, the city of the Ephesians was moved at the unlooked-for sight. And Cleopatra asked concerning her husband Lycomedes, but John said to her: Cleopatra, if thou keep thy soul unmoved and steadfast, thou shalt forthwith have Lycomedes thine husband standing here beside thee, if at least thou be not disturbed nor moved at that which hath befallen, having believed on my God, who by my means shall grant him *unto thee* alive.

Come therefore with me into thine other bedchamber, and thou shalt behold him, a dead corpse indeed, but raised again by the power of my God.

24 And Cleopatra going with John into her bedchamber, and seeing Lycomedes dead for her sake, had no power to speak (suffered in her voice), and ground her teeth and bit her tongue, and closed her eyes, raining down tears: and with calmness gave heed to the apostle. But John had compassion on Cleopatra when he saw that she neither raged nor was beside her-self, and called upon the perfect and condescending mercy, saying: Lord Jesus Christ, thou seest the pressure *of sorrow*, thou seest the need; thou seest Cleopatra shrieking her soul out in silence, for she constraineth within her the frenzy that cannot be borne; and I know that for Lycomedes' sake she also will die upon his body. And she said quietly to John: That have I in mind, master, and nought else.

And the apostle went to the couch whereon Lycomedes lay, and taking Cleopatra's hand he said: Cleopatra, because of the multitude that is present, and thy kinsfolk that have come in, with strong crying, say thou to thine husband: Arise and glorify the name of God, for he giveth back the dead to the dead. And she went to her husband and said to him according as she was taught, and forthwith raised him up. And he, when he arose, fell on the floor and kissed John's feet, but he raised him, saying: O man, kiss not my feet but the feet of God by whose power ye are both arisen.

25 But Lycomedes said to John: I entreat and adjure thee by the God in whose name thou hast raised us, to abide with us, together with all them that are with thee. Likewise Cleopatra also caught his feet and said the same. And John said to them: For to-morrow I will be with you. And they said to him again: We *shall* have no hope in thy God, but shall have been raised to no purpose, if thou abide not with us. And Cleobius with Aristodemus and Damonicus were touched in the soul and said to John: Let us abide with them, that they continue without offence towards the Lord. So he continued there with the brethren.

26 There came together therefore a gathering of a great multitude on John's account; and as he discoursed to them that were there, Lycomedes, who had a friend who was a skilful painter, went hastily to him and said to him: You see me in a great hurry to come to you: come quickly to my house and paint the man whom I show you without his knowing it. And the painter, giving some one the necessary implements and colours, said to Lycomedes: Show him to me, and for the rest have no anxiety. And Lycomedes pointed out John to the painter, and brought him near *him*, and shut him up in a room from which the apostle of Christ could be seen. And Lycomedes was with the blessed man, feasting on the faith and the know-

ledge of our God, and rejoiced yet more in the thought that he should possess him in a portrait.

27 The painter, then, on the first day made an outline of him and went away. And on the next he painted him in with his colours, and so delivered the portrait to Lycomedes to his great joy. And he took it and set it up in his own bedchamber and hung it with garlands: so that later John, when he perceived it, said to him: My beloved child, what is it that thou always doest when thou comest in from the bath into thy bedchamber alone? do not I pray with thee and the rest of the brethren? or is there something thou art hiding from us? And as he said this and talked jestingly with him, he went into the bedchamber, and saw the portrait of an old man crowned with garlands, and lamps and altars set before it. And he called him and said: Lycomedes, what meanest thou by this matter of the portrait? can it be one of thy gods that is painted here? for I see that thou art still living in heathen fashion. And Lycomedes answered him: My only God is he who raised me up from death with my wife: but if, next to that God, it be right that the men who have benefited us should be called gods—it is thou, father, whom I have had painted in that portrait, whom I crown and love and reverence as having become my good guide.

28 And John who had never at any time seen his own face said to him: Thou mockest me, child: am I like that in form, ⟨excelling⟩ thy Lord? how canst thou persuade me that the portrait is like me? And Lycomedes brought him a mirror. And when he had seen himself in the mirror and looked earnestly at the portrait, he said: As the Lord Jesus Christ liveth, the portrait is like me: yet not like me, child, but like my fleshly image; for if this painter, who hath imitated this my face, desireth to draw me in a portrait, he will be at a loss, ⟨needing more than⟩ the colours that are now given †to thee†, and boards and plaster (?) and glue (?), and the position of my shape, and old age and youth and all things that are seen with the eye.

29 But do thou become for me a good painter, Lycomedes. Thou hast colours which he giveth thee through me, who painteth all of us for himself, even Jesus, who knoweth the shapes and appearances and postures and dispositions and types of our souls. And the colours wherewith I bid thee paint are these: faith in God, knowledge, godly fear, friendship, communion, meekness, kindness, brotherly love, purity, simplicity, tranquillity, fearlessness, grieflessness, sobriety, and the whole band of colours that painteth the likeness of thy soul, and even now raiseth up thy members that were cast down, and levelleth them that were lifted up, and tendeth thy bruises, and healeth thy wounds, and ordereth thine hair that was disarranged, and washeth thy face, and chasteneth thine eyes, and purgeth thy bowels, and emptieth thy belly, and cutteth off that which is

beneath it; and in a word, when the whole company and mingling of such colours is come together, into thy soul, it shall present it to our Lord Jesus Christ undaunted, whole (unsmoothed), and firm of shape. But this that thou hast now done is childish and imperfect: thou hast drawn a dead likeness of the dead.

There need be no portion of text lost at this point: but possibly some few sentences have been omitted. The transition is abrupt and the new episode has not, as elsewhere, a title of its own.

30 And he commanded Verus (Berus), the brother that ministered to him, to gather the aged women that were in all Ephesus, and made ready, he and Cleopatra and Lycomedes, all things for the care of them. Verus, then, came to John, saying: Of the aged women that are here over threescore years old I have found four only sound in body, and of the rest some . . . (a word gone) and some palsied and others sick. And when he heard that, John kept silence for a long time, and rubbed his face and said: O the slackness (weakness) of them that dwell in Ephesus! O the state of dissolution, and the weakness toward God! O devil, that hast so long mocked the faithful in Ephesus! Jesus, who giveth me grace and the gift to have my confidence in him, saith to me in silence: Send after the old women that are sick and come (be) with them into the theatre, and through me heal them: for there are some of them that will come unto this spectacle whom by these healings I will convert and make them useful for some end.

31 Now when all the multitude was come together to Lycomedes, he dismissed them on John's behalf, saying: To-morrow come ye to the theatre, as many as desire to see the power of God. And the multitude, on the morrow, while it was yet night, came to the theatre: so that the proconsul also heard of it and hasted and took his seat with all the people. And a certain praetor, Andronicus, who was the first of the Ephesians at that time, put it about that John had promised things impossible and incredible: But if, said he, he is able to do any such thing as I hear, let him come into the public theatre, when it is open, naked, and holding nothing in his hands, neither let him name that magical name which I have heard him utter.

32 John therefore, having heard this and being moved by these words, commanded the aged women to be brought into the theatre: and when they were all brought into the midst, some of them upon beds and others lying in a deep sleep, and all the city had run together, and a great silence was made, John opened his mouth and began to say:

33 Ye men of Ephesus, learn first of all wherefore I am visiting in your city, or what is this great confidence which I have towards you, so that it may become manifest to this general assembly and to all of you (or, so that I manifest myself to). I have been sent, then, upon a mission which is not of man's ordering, and

not upon any vain journey; neither am I a merchant that
make bargains or exchanges; but Jesus Christ whom I preach,
being compassionate and kind, desireth by my means to convert
all of you who are held in unbelief and sold unto evil lusts,
and to deliver you from error; and by his power will I confound even the unbelief of your praetor, by raising up them
that lie before you, whom ye all behold, in what plight and
in what sicknesses they are. And to do this (to confound Andronicus) is not possible for me if they perish: therefore shall they
†be healed†.

34 But this first I have desired to sow in your ears, even that
ye should take care for your souls—on which account I am come
unto you—and not expect that this time will be for ever, for
it is but a moment, and not lay up treasures upon the earth
where all things do fade. Neither think that when ye have
gotten children ye can rest upon them (?), and try not for their
sakes to defraud and overreach. Neither, ye poor, be vexed
if ye have not wherewith to minister unto pleasures; for men
of substance when they are diseased call you happy. Neither,
ye rich, rejoice that ye have much money, for by possessing
these things ye provide for yourselves grief that ye cannot be
rid of when ye lose them; and besides, while it is with you, ye
are afraid lest some one attack you on account of it.

35 Thou also that art puffed up because of the shapeliness
of thy body, and art of an high look, shalt see the end of the
promise thereof in the grave; and thou that rejoicest in adultery,
know that both law and nature avenge it upon thee, and before
these, conscience; and thou, adulteress, that art an adversary
of the law, knowest not whither thou shalt come in the end.
And thou that sharest not with the needy, but hast monies
laid up, when thou departest out of this body and hast need of
some mercy when thou burnest in fire, shalt have none to pity
thee; and thou the wrathful and passionate, know that thy
conversation is like the brute beasts; and thou, drunkard and
quarreller, learn that thou losest thy senses by being enslaved
to a shameful and dirty desire.

36 Thou that rejoicest in gold and delightest thyself with
ivory and jewels, when night falleth, canst thou behold what
thou lovest? thou that art vanquished by soft raiment, and
then leavest life, will those things profit thee in the place whither
thou goest? And let the murderer know that the condign
punishment is laid up for him twofold after his departure hence.
Likewise also thou poisoner, sorcerer, robber, defrauder, sodo-
mite, thief, and as many as are of that band, ye shall come at
last, as your works do lead you, unto unquenchable fire, and
utter darkness, and the pit of punishment, and eternal threatenings. Wherefore, ye men of Ephesus, turn yourselves, knowing
this also, that kings, rulers, tyrants, boasters, and they that

have conquered in wars, stripped of all things when they depart hence, do suffer pain, lodged in eternal misery.

37 And having thus said, John by the power of God healed all the diseases.

This sentence must be an abridgement of a much longer narration. The manuscript indicates no break at this point: but we must suppose a not inconsiderable loss of text. For one thing, Andronicus, who is here an unbeliever, appears as a convert in the next few lines. Now he is, as we shall see later, the husband of an eminent believer, Drusiana; and his and her conversion will have been told at some length; and I do not doubt that among other things there was a discourse of John persuading them to live in continence.

37 *continued.* Now the brethren from Miletus said unto John: We have continued a long time at Ephesus; if it seem good to thee, let us go also to Smyrna; for we hear already that the mighty works of God have reached it also. And Andronicus said to them: Whensoever the teacher willeth, then let us go. But John said: Let us first go unto the temple of Artemis, for perchance there also, if we show ourselves, the servants of the Lord will be found.

38 After two days, then, was the birthday of the idol temple. John therefore, when all were clad in white, alone put on black raiment and went up into the temple. And they took him and essayed to kill him. But John said: Ye are mad to set upon me, a man that is the servant of the only God. And he gat him up upon an high pedestal and said unto them:

39 Ye run hazard, men of Ephesus, of being like in character to the sea: every river that floweth in and every spring that runneth down, and the rains, and waves that press upon each other, and torrents full of rocks are made salt together by the bitter †element† (*MS.* promise!) that is therein. So ye also remaining unchanged unto this day toward true godliness are become corrupted by your ancient rites of worship. How many wonders *and* healings of diseases have ye seen *wrought* through me? And yet are ye blinded in your hearts and cannot recover sight. What is it, then, O men of Ephesus? I have adventured now and come up even into this your idol temple. I will convict you of being most godless, and dead from the understanding of mankind. Behold, I stand here: ye all say that ye have a goddess, even Artemis: pray then unto her that I alone may die; or else I only, if ye are not able to do this, will call upon mine own god, and for your unbelief I will cause every one of you to die.

40 But they who had beforetime made trial of him and had seen dead men raised up, cried out: Slay us not so, we beseech thee, John. We know that thou canst do it. And John said to them: If then ye desire not to die, let that which ye worship be confounded, †and wherefore it is confounded,† that ye also may

depart from your ancient error. For now is it time that either
ye be converted by my God, or I myself die by your goddess;
for I will pray in your presence and entreat my God that mercy
be shown unto you.

41 And having so said he prayed thus: O God that art God
above all that are called gods, that until this day hast been set
at nought in the city of the Ephesians; that didst put into my
mind to come into this place, whereof I never thought; that
dost convict every manner of worship by turning *men* unto thee;
at whose name every idol fleeth and every evil spirit and every
unclean power; now also by the flight of the evil spirit here at
thy name, *even of him* that deceiveth this great multitude, show
thou thy mercy in this place, for they have been made to err.

42 And as John spake these things, immediately the altar of
Artemis was parted into many pieces, and all the things that
were dedicated in the temple fell, and †[*MS.* that which seemed
good to him]† was rent asunder, and likewise of the images *of the
gods* more than seven. And the half of the temple fell down, so
that the priest was slain at one blow by the falling of the (? roof,
? beam). The multitude of the Ephesians therefore cried out:
One is the God of John, one is the God that hath pity on us, for
thou only art God: now are we turned *to thee*, beholding thy
marvellous works! have mercy on us, O God, according to thy
will, and save us from our great error! And some of them, lying
on their faces, made supplication, and some kneeled and besought,
and some rent their clothes and wept, and others tried to escape.

43 But John spread forth his hands, and being uplifted in soul,
said unto the Lord: Glory be to thee, my Jesus, the only God
of truth, for that thou dost gain (receive) thy servants by divers
devices. And having so said, he said to the people: Rise up
from the floor, ye men of Ephesus, and pray to my God, and
recognize the invisible power that cometh to manifestation, and
the wonderful works which are wrought before your eyes.
Artemis ought to have succoured herself: her servant ought to
have been helped of her and not to have died. Where is the power
of the evil spirit? where are her sacrifices? where her birthdays?
where her festivals? where are the garlands? where is all that
sorcery and the poisoning (witchcraft) that is sister thereto?

44 But the people rising up from off the floor went hastily and
cast down the rest of the idol temple, crying: The God of John
only do we know, and him hereafter do we worship, since he hath
had mercy upon us! And as John came down from thence, much
people took hold of him, saying: Help us, O John! Assist us
that do perish in vain! Thou seest our purpose: thou seest the
multitude following thee and hanging upon thee in hope toward
thy God. We have seen the way wherein we went astray when
we lost him: we have seen our gods that were set up in vain:
we have seen the great and shameful derision that is come to

them: but suffer us, we pray thee, to come unto thine house and to be succoured without hindrance. Receive us that are in bewilderment.

45 And John said to them: Men (of Ephesus), believe that for your sakes I have continued in Ephesus, and have put off my journey unto Smyrna and to the rest of the cities, that there also the servants of Christ may turn to him. But since †I am not yet perfectly assured concerning you†, I have continued praying to my God and beseeching him that I should then depart from Ephesus when I have confirmed you *in the faith*: and whereas I see that this is come to pass and yet more is being fulfilled, I will not leave you until I have weaned you like children from the nurse's milk, and have set you upon a firm rock.

46 John therefore continued with them, receiving them in the house of Andronicus. And one of them that were gathered laid down the dead body of the priest of Artemis before the door [of the temple], for he was his kinsman, and came in quickly with the rest, saying nothing *of it*. John, therefore, after the discourse to the brethren, and the prayer and the thanksgiving (eucharist) and the laying of hands upon every one of the congregation, said by the spirit: There is one here who moved by faith in God hath laid down the priest of Artemis before the gate and is come in, and in the yearning of his soul, taking care first for himself, hath thought thus in himself: It is better for me to take thought for the living than for my kinsman that is dead: for I know that if I turn to the Lord and save mine own soul, John will not deny to raise up the dead also. And John arising from his place went to that into which that kinsman of the priest who had so thought was entered, and took him by the hand and said: Hadst thou this thought when thou camest unto me, my child? And he, taken with trembling and affright, said: Yes, lord, and cast himself at his feet. And John said: Our Lord is Jesus Christ, who will show his power in thy dead kinsman by raising him up.

47 And he made the young man rise, and took his hand and said: It is no great matter for a man that is master of great mysteries to continue wearying himself over small things: or what great thing is it to rid *men* of diseases of the body? And yet holding the young man by the hand he said: I say unto thee, child, go and raise the dead thyself, saying nothing but this only: John the servant of God saith to thee, Arise. And the young man went to his kinsman and said this only—and much people was with him—and entered in unto John, bringing him alive. And John, when he saw him that was raised, said: Now that thou art raised, thou dost not truly live, neither art partaker or heir of the true life: wilt thou belong unto him by whose name and power thou wast raised? And now believe, and thou shall live unto all ages. And he forthwith believed upon the Lord Jesus and thereafter clave unto John.

[Another manuscript (Q. Paris Gr. 1468, of the eleventh century) has another form of this story. John destroys the temple of Artemis, and then 'we' go to Smyrna and all the idols are broken: Bucolus, Polycarp, and Andronicus are left to preside over the district. There were there two priests of Artemis, brothers, and one died. The raising is told much as in the older text, but more shortly.

'We' remained four years in the region, which was wholly converted, and then returned to Ephesus.]

48 Now on the next day John, having seen in a dream that he must walk three miles outside the gates, neglected it not, but rose up early and set out upon the way, together with the brethren.

And a certain countryman who was admonished by his father not to take to himself the wife of a fellow labourer of his who threatened to kill him—this young man would not endure the admonition of his father, but kicked him and left him without speech (*sc.* dead). And John, seeing what had befallen, said unto the Lord: Lord, was it on this account that thou didst bid me come out hither to-day?

49 But the young man, beholding the violence (sharpness) of death, and looking to be taken, drew out the sickle that was in his girdle and started to run to his own abode; and John met him and said: Stand still, thou most shameless devil, and tell me whither thou runnest bearing a sickle that thirsteth for blood. And the young man was troubled and cast the iron on the ground, and said to him: I have done a wretched and barbarous deed and I know it, and so I determined to do an evil yet worse and more cruel, even to die myself at once. For because my father was alway curbing me to sobriety, that I should live without adultery, and chastely, I could not endure him to reprove me, and I kicked him and slew him, and when I saw what was done, I was hasting to the woman for whose sake I became my father's murderer, with intent to kill her and her husband, and myself last of all: for I could not bear to be seen of the husband of the woman, and undergo the judgement of death.

50 And John said to him: That I may not by going away and leaving you in danger give place to him that desireth to laugh and sport with thee, come thou with me and show me thy father, where he lieth. And if I raise him up for thee, wilt thou hereafter abstain from the woman that is become a snare to thee. And the young man said: If thou raisest up my father himself for me alive, and if I see him whole and †continuing† in life, I will hereafter abstain from her.

51 And while he was speaking, they came to the place where the old man lay dead, and many passers-by were standing near thereto. And John said to the youth: Thou wretched man, didst thou not spare even the old age of thy father? And he, weeping and tearing his hair, said that he repented thereof; and

John the servant of the Lord said: Thou didst show me I was to
set forth for this place, thou knewest that this would come to pass,
from whom nothing can be hid of things done in life, that givest
me power to work every cure and healing by thy will: now
also give me this old man alive, for thou seest that his murderer is become his own judge: and spare him, thou only Lord,
that spared not his father (because he) counselled him for the
best.

52 And with these words he came near to the old man and
said: My Lord will not be weak to spread out his kind pity and
his condescending mercy even unto thee: rise up therefore and
give glory to God for the work that is come to pass †at this
moment†. And the old man said: I arise, Lord. And he rose
and sat up and said: I was released from a terrible life and had
to bear the insults of my son, dreadful and many, and his want
of natural affection, and to what end hast thou called me back,
O man of the living God? (And John answered him: If) thou
art raised only for the same end, it were better for thee to die;
but raise thyself unto better things. And he took him and led
him into the city, preaching unto him the grace of God, so that
before he entered the gate the old man believed.

53 But the young man, when he beheld the unlooked-for
raising of his father, and the saving of himself, took a sickle and
mutilated himself, and ran to the house wherein he had his
adulteress, and *reproached her*, saying : For thy sake I became
the murderer of my father and of you two and of myself : there
thou hast that which is alike guilty of all. For on me God hath
had mercy, that I should know his power.

54 And he came back and told John in presence of the brethren
what he had done. But John said to him: He that put it into
thine heart, young man, to kill thy father and become the
adulterer of another man's wife, the same made thee *think it*
a right deed to take away also the unruly members. But thou
shouldest have done away, not with the place *of sin*, but the
thought which through those members showed itself harmful:
for it is not the instruments that are injurious, but the unseen
springs by which every shameful emotion is stirred and cometh
to light. Repent therefore, my child, of this fault, and having
learnt the wiles of Satan thou shalt have God to help thee in all
the necessities of thy soul. And the young man kept silence and
attended, having repented of his former sins, that he should
obtain pardon from the goodness of God: and he did not separate
from John.

55 When, then, these things had been done by him in the city
of the Ephesians, they of Smyrna sent unto him saying: We
hear that the God whom thou preachest is not envious, and hath
charged thee not to show partiality by abiding in one place.
Since, then, thou art a preacher of such a God, come unto Smyrna

and unto the other cities, that we may come to know thy God, and having known him may have our hope in him.

[Q has the above story also, and continues with an incident which is also quoted in a different form (and not as from these Acts) by John Cassian. Q has it thus:

Now one day as John was seated, a partridge flew by and came and played in the dust before him; and John looked on it and wondered. And a certain priest came, who was one of his hearers, and came to John and saw the partridge playing in the dust before him, and was offended in himself and said: Can such and so great a man take pleasure in a partridge playing in the dust? But John perceiving in the spirit the thought of him, said to him: It were better for thee also, my child, to look at a partridge playing in the dust and not to defile thyself with shameful and profane practices: for he who awaiteth the conversion and repentance of all men hath brought thee here on this account: for I have no need of a partridge playing in the dust. For the partridge is thine own soul.

Then the elder, hearing this and seeing that he was not hidden, but that the apostle of Christ had told him all that was in his heart, fell on his face on the earth and cried aloud, saying: Now know I that God dwelleth in thee, O blessed John! for he that tempteth thee tempteth him that cannot be tempted. And he entreated him to pray for him. And he instructed him and delivered him the rules (canons) and let him go to his house, glorifying God that is over all.

Cassian, Collation XXIV. 21, has it thus:

It is told that the most blessed Evangelist John, when he was gently stroking a partridge with his hands, suddenly saw one in the habit of a hunter coming to him. He wondered that a man of such repute and fame should demean himself to such small and humble amusements, and said: Art thou that John whose eminent and widespread fame hath enticed me also with great desire to know thee? Why then art thou taken up with such mean amusements? The blessed John said to him: What is that which thou carriest in thy hands? A bow, said he. And why, said he, dost thou not bear it about always stretched? He answered him: I must not, lest by constant bending the strength of its vigour be wrung and grow soft and perish, and when there is need that the arrows be shot with much strength at some beast, the strength being lost by excess of continual tension, a forcible blow cannot be dealt. Just so, said the blessed John, let not this little and brief relaxation of my mind offend thee, young man, for unless it doth sometimes ease and relax by some remission the force of its tension, it will grow slack through unbroken rigour and will not be able to obey the power of the spirit.

The only common point of the two stories is that St. John amuses

242   ACTS OF JOHN

himself with a partridge, and a spectator thinks it unworthy of him.
The two morals differ wholly. The amount of text lost here is of quite
uncertain length. It must have told of the doings at Smyrna, and
also, it appears, at Laodicea (see the title of the next section). One
of the episodes must have been the conversion of a woman of evil life
(see below, ' the harlot that was chaste ').]

Our best manuscript prefixes a title to the next section:

From Laodicea to Ephesus the second time.

58 Now when some long time had passed, and none of the
brethren had been at any time grieved by John, they were then
grieved because he had said: Brethren, it is now time for me to go
to Ephesus (for so have I agreed with them that dwell there) lest
they become slack, now for a long time having no man to confirm
them. But all of you must have your minds *steadfast* towards
God, who never forsaketh us.

But when they heard this from him, the brethren lamented
because they were to be parted from him. And John said: Even
if I be parted from you, yet Christ is alway with you: whom if
ye love purely ye will have his fellowship without reproach, for
if he be loved, he preventeth (anticipateth) them that love him.

59 And having so said, and bidden farewell to them, and left
much money with the brethren for distribution, he went forth
unto Ephesus, while all the brethren lamented and groaned.
And there accompanied him, of Ephesus, both Andronicus and
Drusiana and Lycomedes and Cleobius and their *families*. And
there followed him Aristobula also, who had heard that her
husband Tertullus had died on the way, and Aristippus with
Xenophon, and the harlot that was chaste, and many others,
whom he exhorted at all times *to cleave* to the Lord, and they
would no more be parted from him.

60 Now on the first day we arrived at a deserted inn, and when
we were at a loss for a bed for John, we saw a droll matter. There
was one bedstead lying somewhere there without coverings,
whereon we spread the cloaks which we were wearing, and we
prayed him to lie down upon it and rest, while the rest of us all
slept upon the floor. But he when he lay down was troubled by
the bugs, and as they continued to become yet more troublesome
to him, when it was now about the middle of the night, in the
hearing of us all he said to them: I say unto you, O bugs, be-
have yourselves, one and all, and leave your abode for this night
and remain quiet in one place, and keep your distance from the
servants of God. And as we laughed, and went on talking for
some time, John addressed himself to sleep; and we, talking low,
gave him no disturbance (*or*, thanks to him we were not disturbed).

61 But when the day was now dawning I arose first, and with
me Verus and Andronicus, and we saw at the door of the house
which we had taken a great number of bugs standing, and while
we wondered at the great sight of them, and all the brethren

were roused up because of them, John continued sleeping. And when he was awaked we declared to him what we had seen. And he sat up on the bed and looked at them and said: Since ye have well behaved yourselves in hearkening to my rebuke, come unto your place. And when he had said this, and risen from the bed, the bugs running from the door hasted to the bed and climbed up by the legs thereof and disappeared into the joints. And John said again: This creature hearkened unto the voice of a man, and abode by itself and was quiet and trespassed not; but we which hear the voice and commandments of God disobey and are light-minded: and for how long?

62 After these things we came to Ephesus: and the brethren there, who had for a long time known that John was coming, ran together to the house of Andronicus (where also he came to lodge), handling his feet and laying his hands upon their own faces and kissing them (and many rejoiced even to touch his vesture, and were healed by touching the clothes of the holy apostle. *So the Latin, which has this section; the Greek has:* so that they even touched his garments).

63 And whereas there was great love and joy unsurpassed among the brethren, a certain one, a messenger of Satan, became enamoured of Drusiana, though he saw and knew that she was the wife of Andronicus. To whom many said: It is not possible for thee to obtain that woman, seeing that for a long time she has even separated herself from her husband for godliness' sake. Art thou only ignorant that Andronicus, not being aforetime that which now he is, a God-fearing man, shut her up in a tomb, saying: Either I must have thee as the wife whom I had before, or thou shalt die. And she chose rather to die than to do that foulness. If, then, she would not consent, for godliness' sake, to cohabit with her lord and husband, but even persuaded him to be of the same mind as herself, will she consent to thee desiring to be her seducer? depart from this madness which hath no rest in thee: give up this deed which thou canst not bring to accomplishment.

64 But his familiar friends saying these things to him did not convince him, but with shamelessness he courted her with messages; and †when he learnt the insults and disgraces which she returned, he spent his life in melancholy† (*or better,* she, when she learnt of this disgrace and insult at his hand, spent her life in heaviness). And after two days Drusiana took to her bed from heaviness, and was in a fever and said: Would that I had not now come home to my native place, I that have become an offence to a man ignorant of godliness! for if it were one who was filled with the word of God, he would not have gone to such a pitch of madness. But now (therefore) Lord, since I am become the occasion of a blow unto a soul devoid of knowledge, set me free from this chain and remove me unto thee quickly. And in the presence of John, who knew nothing at all of such a matter,

Drusiana departed out of life not wholly happy, yea, even troubled because of the spiritual hurt of the man.

65 But Andronicus, grieved with a secret grief, mourned in his soul, and wept openly, so that John checked him often and said to him: Upon a better hope hath Drusiana removed out of this unrighteous life. And Andronicus answered him: Yea, I am persuaded of it, O John, and I doubt not at all in regard of trust in my God: but this very thing do I hold fast, that she departed out of life pure.

66 And when she was carried forth, John took hold on Andronicus, and now that he knew the cause, he mourned more than Andronicus. And he kept silence, considering the provocation of the adversary, and for a space sat still. Then, the brethren being gathered there to hear what word he would speak of her that was departed, he began to say:

67 When the pilot that voyageth, together with them that sail with him, and the ship herself, arriveth in a calm and stormless harbour, then let him say that he is safe. And the husbandman that hath committed the seed to the earth, and toiled much in the care and protection of it, let him then take rest from his labours, when he layeth up the seed with manifold increase in his barns. Let him that enterpriseth to run in the course, then exult when he beareth home the prize. Let him that inscribeth his name for the boxing, then boast himself when he receiveth the crowns: and so in succession is it with all contests and crafts, when they do not fail in the end, †but show themselves to be like that which they promised† (*corrupt*).

68 And thus also I think is it with the faith which each one of us practiseth, that it is then discerned whether it be indeed true, when it continueth like itself even until the end of life. For many obstacles fall into the way, and prepare disturbance for the minds of men: care, children, parents, glory, poverty, flattery, prime of life, beauty, conceit, lust, wealth, anger, uplifting, slackness, envy, jealousy, neglect, fear, insolence, love, deceit, money, pretence, and other such obstacles, as many as there are in this life: as also the pilot sailing a prosperous course is opposed by the onset of contrary winds and a great storm and mighty waves out of calm, and the husbandman by untimely winter and blight and creeping things rising out of the earth, and they that strive in the games 'just do not win', and they that exercise crafts are hindered by the *divers difficulties* of them.

69 But before all things it is needful that the believer should look before at his ending and understand it in what manner it will come upon him, whether it will be vigorous and sober and without any obstacle, or disturbed and clinging to the things that are here, and bound down by desires. So is it right that a body should be praised as comely when it is wholly stripped, and a general as great when he hath accomplished every promise of the

war, and a physician as excellent when he hath succeeded in every cure, and a soul as full of faith and worthy (*or* receptive) of God when it hath paid its promise in full: not that soul which began *well* and was dissolved into all the things of this life and fell away, nor that which is numb, having made an effort to attain to better things, and then is borne down to temporal things, nor that which hath longed after the things of time more than those of eternity, nor that which exchangeth ⟨enduring things for⟩ those that endure not, nor that which hath honoured the works of dishonour that deserve shame, nor that which taketh pledges of Satan, nor that which hath received the serpent into its own house, nor that which suffereth reproach for God's sake and then is [not] ashamed, nor that which with the mouth saith yea, but indeed approveth not itself: but that which hath prevailed not to be made weak by foul pleasure, not to be overcome by light-mindedness, not to be caught by the bait of love of money, not to be betrayed by vigour of body or wrath.

70 And as John was discoursing yet further unto the brethren that they should despise temporal things in respect of the eternal, he that was enamoured of Drusiana, being inflamed with an horrible lust and possession of the many-shaped Satan, bribed the steward of Andronicus who was a lover of money with a great sum: and he opened the tomb and gave him opportunity to wreak the forbidden thing upon the dead body. Not having succeeded with her when alive, he was still importunate after her death to her body, and said: If thou wouldst not have to do with me while thou livedst, I will outrage thy corpse now thou art dead. With this design, and having managed for himself the wicked act by means of the abominable steward, he rushed with him to the sepulchre; they opened the door and began to strip the grave-clothes from the corpse, saying: What art thou profited, poor Drusiana? couldest thou not have done this in life, which perchance would not have grieved thee, hadst thou done it willingly?

71 And as these men were speaking thus, and only the accustomed shift now remained on her body, a strange spectacle was seen, such as they deserve to suffer who do such deeds. A serpent appeared from some quarter and dealt the steward a single bite and slew him: but the young man it did not strike; but coiled about his feet, hissing terribly, and when he fell mounted on his body and sat upon him.

72 Now on the next day John came, accompanied by Andronicus and the brethren, to the sepulchre at dawn, it being now the third day from Drusiana's death, that we might break bread there. And first, when they set out, the keys were sought for and could not be found; but John said to Andronicus: It is quite right that they should be lost, for Drusiana is not in the sepulchre; nevertheless, let us go, that thou mayest not be

neglectful, and the doors shall be opened of themselves, even as the Lord hath done for us many such things.

73 And when we were at the place, at the commandment of the master, the doors were opened, and we saw by the tomb of Drusiana a beautiful youth, smiling : and John, when he saw him, cried out and said: Art thou come before us hither too, beautiful one? and for what cause? And we heard a voice saying to him: For Drusiana's sake, whom thou art to raise up—for I was within a little of finding her ⟨shamed⟩—and for his sake that lieth dead beside her tomb. And when the beautiful one had said this unto John he went up into the heavens in the sight of us all. And John, turning to the other side of the sepulchre, saw a young man—even Callimachus, one of the chief of the Ephesians—and a huge serpent sleeping upon him, and the steward of Andronicus, Fortunatus by name, *lying* dead. And at the sight of the two he stood perplexed, saying to the brethren: What meaneth such a sight? or wherefore hath not the Lord declared unto me what was done here, he who hath never neglected me?

74 And Andronicus seeing those corpses, leapt up and went to Drusiana's tomb, and seeing her lying in her shift only, said to John: I understand what has happened, thou blessed servant of God, John. This Callimachus was enamoured of my sister; and because he never won her, though he often assayed it, he hath bribed this mine accursed steward with a great sum, perchance designing, as now we may see, to fulfil by his means the tragedy of his conspiracy, for indeed Callimachus avowed this to many, saying: If she will not consent to me when living, she shall be outraged when dead. And it may be, master, that the beautiful one knew it and suffered not her body to be insulted, and therefore have these died who made that attempt. And can it be that the voice that said unto thee, 'Raise up Drusiana', foreshowed this? because she departed out of this life in sorrow of mind. But I believe him that said that this is one of the men that have gone astray; for thou wast bidden to raise him up: for as to the other, I know that he is unworthy of salvation. But this one thing I beg of thee: raise up Callimachus first, and he will confess to us what is come about.

75 And John, looking upon the body, said to the venomous beast: Get thee away from him that is to be a servant of Jesus Christ; and stood up and prayed over him thus: O God whose name is glorified by us, as of right: O God who subduest every injurious force: O God whose will is accomplished, who alway hearest us: now also let thy gift be accomplished in this young man; and if there be any dispensation to be wrought through him, manifest it unto us when he is raised up. And straightway the young man rose up, and for a whole hour kept silence.

76 But when he came to his right senses, John asked of him

about his entry into the sepulchre, what it meant, and learning
from him that which Andronicus had told him, namely, that
he was enamoured of Drusiana, John inquired of him again
if he had fulfilled his foul intent, to insult a body full of holiness.
And he answered him: How could I accomplish it when this
fearful beast struck down Fortunatus at a blow in my sight:
and rightly, since he encouraged my frenzy, when I was already
cured of that unreasonable and horrible madness: but me it
stopped with affright, and brought me to that plight in which ye
saw me before I arose. And another thing yet more wondrous
I will tell thee, which yet went nigh to slay and was within
a little of making me a corpse. When my soul was stirred up
with folly and the uncontrollable malady was troubling me,
and I had now torn away the grave-clothes in which she was
clad, and I had then come out of the grave and laid them as
thou seest, I went again to my unholy work: and I saw a beautiful
youth covering her with his mantle, and from his eyes sparks
of light came forth unto her eyes; and he uttered words to
me, saying: Callimachus, die that thou mayest live. Now
who he was I knew not, O servant of God; but that now thou
hast appeared here, I recognize that he was an angel of God,
that I know well; and this I know of a truth that it is a true
God that is proclaimed by thee, and of it I am persuaded. But
I beseech thee, be not slack to deliver me from this calamity
and this fearful crime, and to present me unto thy God as a
man deceived with a shameful and foul deceit. Beseeching
help therefore of thee, I take hold on thy feet. I would become
one of them that hope in Christ, that the voice may prove true
which said to me, 'Die that thou mayest live': and that voice
hath also fulfilled its effect, for he is dead, that faithless, disorderly, godless one, and I have been raised by thee, I who will
be faithful, God-fearing, knowing the truth, which I entreat
thee may be shown me by thee.

77 And John, filled with great gladness and perceiving the
whole spectacle of the salvation of man, said: What thy power
is, Lord Jesu Christ, I know not, bewildered as I am at thy
much compassion and boundless long-suffering. O what a
greatness that came down into bondage! O unspeakable liberty
brought into slavery by us! O incomprehensible glory *that
is come. unto* us! thou that hast kept the dead tabernacle safe
from insult; that hast redeemed the man that stained himself
with blood and chastened *the soul of him that would defile* the
corruptible body; Father that hast had pity and compassion
on the man that cared not for thee; We glorify thee, and praise
and bless and thank thy great goodness and long-suffering,
O holy Jesu, for thou only art God, and none else: whose is
the might that cannot be conspired against, now and world
without end. Amen.

78 And when he had said this John took Callimachus and saluted (kissed) him, saying: Glory be to our God, my child, who hath had mercy on thee, and made me worthy to glorify his power, and thee also by a good course to depart from that thine abominable madness and drunkenness, and hath called thee unto his own rest and unto renewing of life.

79 But Andronicus, beholding the dead Callimachus raised, besought John, with the brethren, to raise up Drusiana also, saying: O John, let Drusiana arise and spend happily that short space (of life) which she gave up through grief about Callimachus, when she thought she had become a stumbling-block to him: and when the Lord will, he shall take her again *to himself*. And John without delay went unto her tomb and took her hand and said: Upon thee that art the only God do I call, the more than great, the unutterable, the incomprehensible: unto whom every power of principalities is subjected: unto whom all authority boweth: before whom all pride falleth down and keepeth silence: whom devils hearing of tremble: whom all creation perceiving keepeth its bounds. Let thy name be glorified by us, and raise up Drusiana, that Callimachus may yet more be confirmed unto thee who dispensest that which unto men is without a way and impossible, but to thee only possible, even salvation and resurrection: and that Drusiana may now come forth in peace, having about her not any the least hindrance —now that the young man is turned unto thee—in her course toward thee.

80 And after these words John said unto Drusiana: Drusiana, arise. And she arose and came out of the tomb; and when she saw herself in her shift only, she was perplexed at the thing, and learned the whole accurately from Andronicus, the while John lay upon his face, and Callimachus with voice and tears glorified God, and she also rejoiced, glorifying him in like manner.

81 And when she had clothed herself, she turned and saw Fortunatus lying, and said unto John: Father, let this man also rise, even if he did assay to become my betrayer. But Callimachus, when he heard her say that, said: Do not, I beseech thee, Drusiana, for the voice which I heard took no thought of him, but declared concerning thee only, and I saw and believed: for if he had been good, perchance God would have had mercy on him also and would have raised him by means of the blessed John: †he knew† therefore that the man was come to a bad end [*Lat.* he judged him worthy to die whom he did not declare worthy to rise again]. And John said to him: We have not learned, my child, to render evil for evil: for God, though we have done much ill and no good toward him, hath not given retribution unto us, but repentance, and though we were ignorant of his name he did not neglect us but had mercy on us, and when we blasphemed him, he did not punish but pitied us,

and when we disbelieved him he bore us no grudge, and when we persecuted his brethren he did not recompense us evil but put into our minds repentance and abstinence from evil, and exhorted us to come unto him, as he hath thee also, my son Callimachus, and not remembering thy former evil hath made thee his servant, waiting upon his mercy. Wherefore if thou allowest not me to raise up Fortunatus, it is for Drusiana so to do.

82 And she, delaying not, went with rejoicing of spirit and soul unto the body of Fortunatus and said: Jesu Christ, God of the ages, God of truth, that hast granted me to see wonders and signs, and given to me to become partaker of thy name; that didst breathe thyself into me with thy many-shaped countenance, and hadst mercy on me in many ways; that didst protect me by thy great goodness when I was oppressed by Andronicus that was of old my husband; that didst give me thy servant Andronicus to be my brother; that hast kept me thine handmaid pure unto this day; that didst raise me up by thy servant John, and when I was raised didst show me him that was made to stumble free from stumbling; that hast given me perfect rest in thee, and lightened me of the secret madness; whom I have loved and affectioned: I pray thee, O Christ, refuse not thy Drusiana that asketh thee to raise up Fortunatus, even though he assayed to become my betrayer.

83 And taking the hand of the dead man she said: Rise up, Fortunatus, in the name of our Lord Jesus Christ. And Fortunatus arose, and when he saw John in the sepulchre, and Andronicus, and Drusiana raised from the dead, and Callimachus a believer, and the rest of the brethren glorifying God, he said: O, to what have the powers of these clever men attained! I did not want to be raised, but would rather die, so as not to see them. And with these words he fled and went out of the sepulchre.

84 And John, when he saw the unchanged mind (soul) of Fortunatus, said: O nature that is not changed for the better! O fountain of the soul that abideth in foulness! O essence of corruption full of darkness! O death exulting in them that are thine! O fruitless tree full of fire! O tree that bearest coals for fruit! O matter that dwellest with the madness of matter (al. O wood of trees full of unwholesome shoots) and neighbour of unbelief! Thou hast proved who thou art, and thou art always convicted, with thy children. And thou knowest not how to praise the better things: for thou hast *them* not. Therefore, such as is thy way (? fruit), such also is thy root and thy nature. Be thou destroyed from among them that trust in the Lord: from their thoughts, from their mind, from their souls, from their bodies, from their acts, their life, their conversation, from their †business†, their occupations, their counsel, from the resurrection unto (or rest in) God, from their sweet savour wherein thou wilt ⟨not⟩ share, from their faith, their prayers, from the

holy bath, from the eucharist, from the food of the flesh, from drink, from clothing, from love, from care, from abstinence, from righteousness: from all these, thou most unholy Satan, enemy of God, shall Jesus Christ our God and ⟨the judge⟩ of all that are like thee and have thy character, make thee to perish.

85 And having thus said, John prayed, and took bread and bare it into the sepulchre to break it; and said: We glorify thy name, which converteth us from error and ruthless deceit: we glorify thee who hast shown before our eyes that which we have seen: we bear witness to thy loving-kindness which appeareth in divers ways: we praise thy merciful name, O Lord (we thank thee), who hast convicted them that are convicted of thee: we give thanks to thee, O Lord Jesu Christ, that we are persuaded of thy ⟨grace⟩ which is unchanging: we give thanks to thee who hadst need of *our* nature that should be saved: we give thanks to thee that hast given us this sure ⟨faith⟩, for thou art ⟨God⟩ alone, both now and ever. We thy servants give thee thanks, O holy one, who are assembled with ⟨good⟩ intent and are gathered *out of the world* (or risen from death).

86 And having so prayed and given glory *to God*, he went out of the sepulchre after imparting unto all the brethren of the eucharist of the Lord. And when he was come unto Andronicus' house he said to the brethren: Brethren, a spirit within me hath divined that Fortunatus is about to die of blackness (poisoning of the blood) from the bite of the serpent; but let some one go quickly and learn if it is so indeed. And one of the young men ran and found him dead and the blackness spreading over him, and it had reached his heart: and came and told John that he had been dead three hours. And John said: Thou hast thy child, O devil.

'John therefore was with the brethren rejoicing in the Lord.' This sentence is in the best manuscript. In Bonnet's edition it introduces the last section of the Acts, which follows immediately in the manuscript. It may belong to either episode. The Latin has: And that day he spent joyfully with the brethren.

There cannot be much of a gap between this and the next section, which is perhaps the most interesting in the Acts.

The greater part of this episode is preserved only in one very corrupt fourteenth-century manuscript at Vienna. Two important passages (93-5 (part) and 97-8 (part)) were read at the Second Nicene Council and are preserved in the Acts thereof: a few lines of the Hymn are also cited in Latin by Augustine (Ep. 237 (253) to Ceretius): he found it current separately among the Priscillianists. The whole discourse is the best popular exposition we have of the Docetic view of our Lord's person.

87 Those that were present inquired the cause, and were especially perplexed, because Drusiana had said: The Lord

appeared unto me in the tomb in the likeness of John, and in
that of a youth. Forasmuch, therefore, as they were perplexed
and were, in a manner, not yet stablished in the faith, so as to
endure it steadfastly, John said (*or* John bearing it patiently, said):

88 Men and brethren, ye have suffered nothing strange or
incredible as concerning your perception of the ⟨Lord⟩, inasmuch
as we also, whom he chose for himself to be apostles, were tried
in many ways: I, indeed, am neither able to set forth unto you
nor to write the things which I both saw and heard: and now
is it needful that I should fit them for your hearing; and according as each of you is able to contain it I will impart unto you
those things whereof ye are able to become hearers, that ye
may see the glory that is about him, which was and is, both
now and for ever.

For when he had chosen Peter and Andrew, which were
brethren, he cometh unto me and James my brother, saying:
I have need of you, come unto me. And my brother *hearing*
that, said: John, what would this child have that is upon the
sea-shore and called us? And I said: What child? And he
said to me again: That which beckoneth to us. And I answered:
Because of our long watch we have kept at sea, thou seest not
aright, my brother James; but seest thou not the man that
standeth there, comely and fair and of a cheerful countenance?
But he said to me: Him I see not, brother; but let us go forth
and we shall see what he would have.

89 And so when we had brought the ship to land, we saw
him also helping along with us to settle the ship: and when
we departed from that place, being minded to follow him, again
he was seen of me as having ⟨a head⟩ rather bald, but the beard
thick and flowing, but of James as a youth whose beard was
newly come. We were therefore perplexed, both of us, as to
what that which we had seen should mean. And after that,
as we followed him, both of us were by little and little ⟨yet more⟩
perplexed as we considered the matter. Yet unto me there
then appeared this yet more wonderful thing: for I would try
to see him privily, and I never at any time saw his eyes closing
(winking), but only open. And oft-times he would appear to
me as a small man and uncomely, and †then again† as one
reaching unto heaven. Also there was in him another marvel:
when I sat at meat he would take me upon his own breast; and
sometimes his breast was felt of me to be smooth and tender,
and sometimes hard like unto stones, so that I was perplexed
in myself and said: Wherefore is this so unto me? And as
I considered this, he . . .

90 And at another time he taketh with him me and James
and Peter unto the mountain where he was wont to pray, and
we saw in him a light such as it is not possible for a man that
useth corruptible (mortal) speech to describe what it was like.

Again in like manner he bringeth us three up into the mountain, saying: Come ye with me. And we went again: and we saw him at a distance praying. I, therefore, because he loved me, drew nigh unto him softly, as though he could not see *me*, and stood looking upon his hinder parts: and I saw that he was not in any wise clad with garments, but was seen of us naked, and not in any wise as a man, and that his feet were whiter than any snow, so that the earth there was lighted up by his feet, and that his head touched the heaven: so that I was afraid and cried out, and he, turning about, appeared as a man of small stature, and caught hold on my beard and pulled it and said to me: John, be not faithless but believing, and not curious. And I said unto him: But what have I done, Lord? And I say unto you, brethren, I suffered so great pain in that place where he took hold on my beard for thirty days, that I said to him: Lord, if thy twitch when thou wast in sport hath given me so great pain, what were it if thou hadst given me a buffet? And he said unto me: Let it be thine henceforth not to tempt him that cannot be tempted.

91 But Peter and James were wroth because I spake with the Lord, and beckoned unto me that I should come unto them and leave the Lord alone. And I went, and they both said unto me: He (the old man) that was speaking with the Lord upon the top *of the mount*, who was he? for we heard both of them speaking. And I, having in mind his great grace, and his unity which hath many faces, and his wisdom which without ceasing looketh upon us, said: That shall ye learn if ye inquire of him.

92 Again, once when all we his disciples were at Gennesaret sleeping in one house, I alone having wrapped myself in my mantle, watched (*or* watched from beneath my mantle) what he should do: and first I heard him say: John, go thou to sleep. And I thereon feigning to sleep saw another like unto him [sleeping], whom also I heard say unto my Lord: Jesus, they whom thou hast chosen believe not yet on thee (*or* do they not yet, &c.?). And my Lord said unto him: Thou sayest well: for they are men.

93 Another glory also will I tell you, brethren: Sometimes when I would lay hold on him, I met with a material and solid body, and at other times, again, when I felt him, the substance was immaterial and as if it existed not at all. And if at any time he were bidden by some one of the Pharisees and went to the bidding, we went with him, and there was set before each one of us a loaf by them that had bidden us, and with us he also received one; and his own he would bless and part it among us: and of that little every one was filled, and our own loaves were saved whole, so that they which bade him were amazed. And oftentimes when I walked with him, I desired to see the print of his foot, whether it appeared on the earth; for I saw

him as it were lifting himself up from the earth: and I never
saw it. And these things I speak unto you, brethren, for the
encouragement of your faith toward him; for we must at the
present keep silence concerning his mighty and wonderful works,
inasmuch as they are unspeakable and, it may be, cannot *at all*
be either uttered or heard.

94 Now before he was taken by the lawless Jews, †who also
were governed by (had their law from) the lawless serpent,† he
gathered all of us together and said: Before I am delivered up
unto them let us sing an hymn to the Father, and so go forth
to that which lieth before us. He bade us therefore make as
it were a ring, holding one another's hands, and himself standing
in the midst he said: Answer Amen unto me. He began, then,
to sing an hymn and to say:

Glory be to thee, Father.

And we, going about in a ring, answered him: Amen.

Glory be to thee, Word: Glory be to thee, Grace. Amen.

Glory be to thee, Spirit: Glory be to thee, Holy One:

Glory be to thy glory. Amen.

We praise thee, O Father; we give thanks to thee, O Light,
   wherein darkness dwelleth not. Amen.

95 Now whereas (*or* wherefore) we give thanks, I say:

I would be saved, and I would save. Amen.

I would be loosed, and I would loose. Amen.

I would be wounded, and I would wound. Amen.

I would be born, and I would bear. Amen.

I would eat, and I would be eaten. Amen.

I would hear, and I would be heard. Amen.

I would be thought, being wholly thought. Amen.

I would be washed, and I would wash. Amen.

Grace danceth. I would pipe; dance ye all. Amen.

I would mourn: lament ye all. Amen.

The number Eight (*lit.* one ogdoad) singeth praise with
   us. Amen.

The number Twelve danceth on high. Amen.

†The Whole on high hath part in *our* dancing. Amen.

Whoso danceth not, knoweth not what cometh to pass.
   Amen.

I would flee, and I would stay. Amen.

I would adorn, and I would be adorned. Amen.

I would be united, and I would unite. Amen.

A house I have not, and I have houses. Amen.

A place I have not, and I have places. Amen.

A temple I have not, and I have temples. Amen.

A lamp am I to thee that beholdest me. Amen.

A mirror am I to thee that perceivest me. Amen.

A door am I to thee that knockest at me. Amen.

A way am I to thee a wayfarer. ⟨Amen⟩.

96 Now answer thou (*or* as thou respondest) unto my dancing.
Behold thyself in me who speak, and seeing what I do, keep
silence about my mysteries.

Thou that dancest, perceive what I do, for thine is this passion
of the manhood, which I am about to suffer. For thou couldest
not at all have understood what thou sufferest if I had not been
sent unto thee, as the word of the Father. Thou that sawest
what I suffer sawest me as suffering, and seeing it thou didst
not abide but wert wholly moved, †moved to make wise†.
Thou hast me as a bed, rest upon me. Who I am, thou shalt
know when I depart. What now I am seen to be, that I am not.
Thou shalt see when thou comest. If thou hadst known how
to suffer, thou wouldest have been able not to suffer. Learn
thou to suffer, and thou shalt be able not to suffer. What thou
knowest not, I myself will teach thee. Thy God am I, not the
God of the traitor. I would keep tune with holy souls. In
me know thou the word of wisdom. Again with me say thou:
Glory be to thee, Father; glory to thee, Word; glory to thee,
Holy Ghost. †And if thou wouldst know concerning me, what
I was, *know that*† with a word did I deceive all things and I was
no whit deceived. I have leaped: but do thou understand the
whole, and having understood it, say: Glory be to thee, Father.
Amen.

97 Thus, my beloved, having danced with us the Lord went
forth. And we as men gone astray or dazed with sleep fled
this way and that. I, then, when I saw him suffer, did not
even abide by his suffering, but fled unto the Mount of Olives,
weeping at that which had befallen. And when he was crucified
on the Friday, at the sixth hour of the day, darkness came upon
all the earth. And my Lord standing in the midst of the cave
and enlightening it, said: John, unto the multitude below in
Jerusalem I am being crucified and pierced with lances and
reeds, and gall and vinegar is given me to drink. But unto
thee I speak, and what I speak hear thou. I put it into thy
mind to come up into this mountain, that thou mightest hear
those things which it behoveth a disciple to learn from his teacher
and a man from his God.

98 And having thus spoken, he showed me a cross of light
fixed (set up), and about the cross a great multitude, †not having
one form: and in it (the cross) was one form and one likeness†
[*so the MS.; I would read*: and therein was one form and one
likeness: and in the cross another multitude, not having one
form]. And the Lord himself I beheld above the cross, not
having any shape, but only a voice: and a voice not such as
was familiar to us, but one sweet and kind and truly of God,
saying unto me: John, it is needful that one should hear these
things from me, for I have need of one that will hear. This
cross of light is sometimes called the (*or* a) word by me for your

sakes, sometimes mind, sometimes Jesus, sometimes Christ, sometimes door, sometimes a way, sometimes bread, sometimes seed, sometimes resurrection, sometimes Son, sometimes Father, sometimes Spirit, sometimes life, sometimes truth, sometimes faith, sometimes grace. And by these names *it is called* as toward men: but that which it is in truth, as conceived of in itself and as spoken of unto you (MS. us), it is the marking-off of all things, and the firm uplifting of things fixed out of things unstable, and the harmony of wisdom, and indeed wisdom in harmony [this last clause in the MS. is joined to the next: 'and being wisdom in harmony']. There are ⟨places⟩ of the right hand and the left, powers *also*, authorities, lordships and demons, workings, threatenings, wraths, devils, Satan, and the lower root whence the nature of the things that come into being proceeded.

99 This cross, then, is that which fixed all things apart (*al.* joined all things unto itself) by the (*or* a) word, and separate off the things that are from those that are below (*lit.* the things from birth and below it), and then also, being one, streamed forth into all things (*or*, made all flow forth. *I suggested*: compacted all into ⟨one⟩). But this is not the cross of wood which thou wilt see when thou goest down hence: neither am I he that is on the cross, whom now thou seest not, but only hearest his (*or* a) voice. I was reckoned to be that which I am not, not being what I was unto many others: but they will call me (say of me) something else which is vile and not worthy of me. As, then, the place of rest is neither seen nor spoken of, much more shall I, the Lord thereof, be neither seen ⟨nor spoken of⟩.

100 Now the multitude of one aspect (*al.* ⟨not⟩ of one aspect) that is about the cross is the lower nature: and they whom thou seest in the cross, if they have not one form, *it is because* not yet hath every member of him that came down been comprehended. But when the human nature (*or* the upper nature) is taken up, and the race which draweth near unto me and obeyeth my voice, he that now heareth me shall be united therewith, and shall no more be that which now he is, but above them, as I also now am. For so long as thou callest not thyself mine, I am not that which I am (*or* was): but if thou hear me, thou, hearing, shalt be as I am, and I shall be that which I was, when I ⟨have⟩ thee as I am with myself. For from me thou art that (which I am). Care not therefore for the many, and them that are outside the mystery despise; for know thou that I am wholly with the Father, and the Father with me.

101 Nothing, therefore, of the things which they will say of me have I suffered: nay, that suffering also which I showed unto thee and the rest in the dance, I will that it be called a mystery. For what thou art, thou seest, for I showed it thee; but what I am I alone know, and no man else. Suffer me then

to keep that which is mine, and that which is thine behold thou
through me, and behold me in truth, that I am, not what I said,
but what thou art able to know, because thou art akin *thereto*.
Thou hearest that I suffered, yet did I not suffer; that I suffered
not, yet did I suffer; that I was pierced, yet I was not smitten;
hanged, and I was not hanged; that blood flowed from me,
and it flowed not; and, in a word, what they say of me, that
befell me not, but what they say not, that did I suffer. Now
what those things are I signify unto thee, for I know that
thou wilt understand. Perceive thou therefore in me the
praising (*al.* slaying *al.* rest) of the (*or* a) Word (Logos), the piercing
of the Word, the blood of the Word, the wound of the Word,
the hanging up of the Word, the suffering of the Word, the nailing
(fixing) of the Word, the death of the Word. And so speak I,
separating off the manhood. Perceive thou therefore in the
first place of the Word; then shalt thou perceive the Lord, and
in the third place the man, and what he hath suffered.

102 When he had spoken unto me these things, and others
which I know not how to say as he would have me, he was taken
up, no one of the multitudes having beheld him. And when
I went down I laughed them all to scorn, inasmuch as he had
told me the things which they have said concerning him; holding fast this one thing in myself, that the Lord contrived all
things symbolically and by a dispensation toward men, for their
conversion and salvation.

103 Having therefore beheld, brethren, the grace of the Lord
and his kindly affection toward us, let us worship him as those
unto whom he hath shown mercy, not with our fingers, nor
our mouth, nor our tongue, nor with any part whatsoever
of our body, but with the disposition of our soul—even him who
became a man apart from this body: and let us watch because
(*or* we shall find that) now also he keepeth ward over prisons
for our sake, and over tombs, in bonds and dungeons, in reproaches and insults, by sea and on dry land, in scourgings,
condemnations, conspiracies, frauds, punishments, and in a word,
he is with all of us, and himself suffereth with us when we suffer,
brethren. When he is called upon by each one of us, he endureth
not to shut his ears to us, but as being everywhere he hearkeneth
to all of us; and now both to me and to Drusiana,—forasmuch as
he is the God of them that are shut up—bringing us help by
his own compassion.

104 Be ye also persuaded, therefore, beloved, that it is not a
man whom I preach unto you to worship, but God unchangeable,
God invincible, God higher than all authority and all power,
and elder and mightier than all angels and creatures that are
named, and all aeons. If then ye abide in him, and are builded
up in him, ye shall possess your soul indestructible.

105 And when he had delivered these things unto the brethren,

John departed, with Andronicus, to walk. And Drusiana also followed afar off with all *the brethren*, that they might behold the acts that were done by him, and hear his speech at all times in the Lord.

The remaining episode which is extant in the Greek is the conclusion of the book, the Death or Assumption of John. Before it must be placed the stories which we have only in the Latin (of ' Abdias ' and another text by 'Mellitus', i. e. Melito), and the two or three isolated fragments.

(Lat. XIV.) Now on the next (*or* another) day Craton, a philosopher, had proclaimed in the market-place that he would give an example of the contempt of riches: and the spectacle was after this manner. He had persuaded two young men, the richest of the city, who were brothers, to spend their whole inheritance and buy each of them a jewel, and these they brake in pieces publicly in the sight of the people. And while they were doing this, it happened by chance that the apostle passed by. And calling Craton the philosopher to him, he said: That is a foolish despising of the world which is praised by the mouths of men, but long ago condemned by the judgement of God. For as that is a vain medicine whereby the disease is not extirpated, so is it a vain teaching by which the faults of souls and of conduct are not cured. But indeed my master taught a youth who desired to attain to eternal life, in these words; saying that if he would be perfect, he should sell all his goods and give to the poor, and so doing he would gain treasure in heaven and find the life that has no ending. And Craton said to him: Here the fruit of covetousness is set forth in the midst of men, and hath been broken to pieces. But if God is indeed thy master and willeth this to be, that the sum of the price of these jewels should be given to the poor, cause thou the gems to be restored whole, that what I have done for the praise of men, thou mayest do for the glory of him whom thou callest thy master. Then the blessed John gathered together the fragments of the gems, and holding them in his hands, lifted up his eyes to heaven and said: Lord Jesu Christ, unto whom nothing is impossible: who when the world was broken by the tree of concupiscence, didst restore it again in thy faithfulness by the tree of the cross: who didst give to one born blind the eyes which nature had denied him, who didst recall Lazarus, dead and buried, after the fourth day unto the light; and has subjected all diseases and all sicknesses unto the word of thy power: so also now *do* with these precious stones which these, not knowing the fruits of almsgiving, have broken in pieces for the praise of men: recover thou them, Lord, now by the hands of thine angels, that by their value the work of mercy may be fulfilled, and make these men believe in thee the un-begotten Father through thine only-begotten Son Jesus Christ our Lord, with the Holy Ghost the illuminator and sanctifier of the whole Church, world without end. And when the faithful who were with the apostle had answered and said Amen, the fragments of the gems were forthwith so joined in one that no mark at all that they had been broken remained in them. And Craton the philosopher, with his disciples, seeing this, fell at the feet of the apostle and believed thenceforth (or immediately) and was baptized, with them all, and began himself publicly to preach the faith of our Lord Jesus Christ.

XV. Those two brothers, therefore, of whom we spake, sold the gems which they had bought by the sale of their inheritance, and gave *the price* to the poor; and thereafter a very great multitude of believers began to be joined to the apostle.

And when all this was done, it happened that after the same example, two honourable men of the city of the Ephesians[1] sold all their goods and distributed them to the needy, and followed the apostle as he went through the cities preaching the word of God. But it came to pass, when they entered the city of Pergamum, that they saw their servants walking abroad arrayed in silken raiment and shining with the glory of this world: whence it happened that they were pierced with the arrow of the devil and became sad, seeing themselves poor and clad with a single cloak while their own servants were powerful and prosperous. But the apostle of Christ, perceiving these wiles of the devil, said: I see that ye have changed your minds and your countenances on this account, that, obeying the teaching of my Lord Jesus Christ, ye have given all ye had to the poor. Now, if ye desire to recover that which ye formerly possessed of gold, silver, and precious stones, bring me some straight rods, each of you a bundle. And when they had done so, he called upon the name of the Lord Jesus Christ, and they were turned into gold. And the apostle said to them: Bring me small stones from the seashore. And when they had done this also, he called upon the majesty of the Lord, and all the pebbles were turned into gems. Then the blessed John turned to those men and said to them: Go about to the goldsmiths and jewellers for seven days, and when ye have proved that these are true gold and true jewels, tell me. And they went, both of them, and after seven days returned to the apostle, saying: Lord, we have gone about the shops of all the goldsmiths, and they have all said that they never saw such pure gold. Likewise the jewellers have said the same, that they never saw such excellent and precious gems.

XVI. Then the holy John said unto them: Go, and redeem to you the lands which ye have sold, for ye have lost the estates of heaven. Buy yourselves silken raiment, that for a time ye may shine like the rose which showeth its fragrance and redness and suddenly fadeth away. For ye sighed at beholding your *servants* and groaned that ye were become poor. Flourish, there-

[1] Rather, as Pseudo-Mellitus has it, the same two brothers.

fore, that ye may fade: be rich for the time, that ye may be beggars for ever. Is not the Lord's hand able to make riches overflowing and unsurpassably glorious? but he hath appointed a conflict for souls, that they may believe that they shall have eternal riches, who for his name's sake have refused temporal wealth. Indeed, our master told us concerning a certain rich man who feasted every day and shone with gold and purple, at whose door lay a beggar, Lazarus, who desired to receive even the crumbs that fell from his table, and no man gave unto him. And it came to pass that on one day they died, both of them, and that beggar was taken into the rest which is in Abraham's bosom, but the rich man was cast into flaming fire: out of which he lifted up his eyes and saw Lazarus, and prayed him to dip his finger in water and cool his mouth, for he was tormented in the flames. And Abraham answered him and said: Remember, son, that thou receivedst good things in thy life, but this Lazarus likewise evil things. Wherefore rightly is he now comforted, while thou art tormented, and besides all *this*, a great gulf is fixed between you and us, so that neither can they come thence hither, nor hither thence. But he answered: I have five brethren: I pray that some one may go to warn them, that they come not into this flame. And Abraham said to him: They have Moses and the prophets, let them hear them. To that he answered: Lord, unless one rise up again, they will not believe. Abraham said to him: If they believe not Moses and the prophets, neither will they believe, if one rise again. And these words our Lord and Master confirmed by examples of mighty works: for when they said to him: Who hath come hither from thence, that we may believe him? he answered: Bring hither the dead whom ye have. And when they had brought unto him a young man which was dead (Ps.-Mellitus: three dead corpses), he was waked up by him as one that sleepeth, and confirmed all his words.

But wherefore should I speak of my Lord, when at this present there are those whom in his name and in your presence and sight I have raised from the dead : in whose name ye have seen palsied men healed, lepers cleansed, blind men enlightened, and many delivered from evil spirits? But the riches of these mighty works they cannot have who have desired to have earthly wealth. Finally, when ye yourselves went unto the sick and called upon the name of Jesus Christ, they were healed: ye did drive out devils and restore light to the blind. Behold, this grace is taken from you, and ye are become wretched, who were mighty and great. And whereas there was such fear of you upon the devils that at your bidding they left the men whom they possessed, now ye will be in fear of the devils. For he that loveth money is the servant of Mammon: and Mammon is the name of a devil who is set over carnal gains, and is the master of them that love the world. But even the lovers of the world do not possess riches, but are possessed of them. For it is out of reason that for one belly there should be laid up so much food as would suffice a thousand, and for one body so many garments as would furnish clothing for a thousand men. In vain, therefore, is that stored up which cometh not into use, and for whom it is kept, no man knoweth, as the Holy Ghost saith by the prophet: In vain is every man troubled who heapeth up riches and knoweth not for whom he gathereth them. Naked did our birth from women bring us into this light, destitute of food and drink: naked will the earth receive us which brought us forth. We possess in common the riches of the heaven; the brightness of the sun is equal for the rich and the poor, and likewise the light of the moon and the stars, the softness of the air and the drops of rain, and the gate of the church and the fount of sanctification, and the forgiveness of sins, and the sharing in the altar, and the eating of the body and drinking of the blood of Christ, and the anointing of the chrism, and the grace of the giver, and the visitation of the Lord, and the pardon of sin: *in* all these the dispensing of the Creator is equal, without respect of persons. Neither doth the rich man use these gifts after one manner and the poor after another.

But wretched and unhappy is the man who would have something more than sufficeth him: for of this come heats of fevers, rigours of cold, divers pains in all the members of the body, and he can neither be fed with food nor sated with drink; that covetousness may learn that money will not profit it, which being laid up bringeth to the keepers thereof anxiety by day and night, and suffereth them not even for an hour to be quiet and secure. For while they guard their houses against thieves, till their estate, ply the plough, pay taxes, build storehouses, strive for gain, try to baffle the attacks of the strong, and to strip the weak, exercise their wrath on whom they can, and hardly bear it from others, shrink not from playing at tables and from public shows, fear not to defile or to be defiled, suddenly do they depart out of this world, naked, bearing only their own sins with them, for which they shall suffer eternal punishment.

XVII. While the apostle was thus speaking, behold there was brought to him by his mother, who was a widow, a young man who thirty days before had first married a wife. And the people which were waiting upon the burial came with the widowed mother and cast themselves at the apostle's feet all together with groans, weeping, and mourning, and besought him that in the name of his God, as he had done with Drusiana, so he would raise up this young man also. And there was so great weeping of them all that the apostle himself could hardly refrain from crying and tears. He cast himself down, therefore, in prayer, and wept a long time: and rising from prayer spread out his hands to heaven, and for a long space prayed within himself. And when he had so done thrice, he commanded the body which was swathed to be loosed, and said: Thou youth Stacteus, who for love of thy flesh hast quickly lost thy soul: thou youth which knewest not thy creator, nor perceivedst the Saviour of men, and wast ignorant of thy true friend, and therefore didst fall into the snare of the worst enemy: behold, I have poured out tears and prayers unto my Lord for thine ignorance, that thou mayest rise from the dead, the bands of death being loosed, and declare unto these two, to Atticus and Eugenius, how great glory they have lost, and how great punishment they have incurred. Then Stacteus arose and worshipped the apostle, and began to reproach his disciples, saying: I beheld your angels weeping, and the angels of Satan rejoicing at your overthrow. For now in a little time ye have lost the kingdom that was prepared for you, and the dwelling-places builded of shining stones, full of joy, of feasting and delights, full of everlasting life and eternal light : and have gotten yourselves places of darkness, full of dragons, of roaring flames, of torments, and punishments unsurpassable, of pains and anguish, fear and horrible trembling. Ye have lost the places full of unfading flowers, shining, full of the sounds of instruments of music (organs), and have gotten on the other hand places wherein roaring and howling and mourning ceaseth not day nor night. Nothing else remaineth for you save to ask the apostle of the Lord that like as he hath raised me to life, he would raise you also from death unto salvation and bring back your souls which now are blotted out of the book of life.

XVIII. Then both he that had been raised and all the people, together with Atticus and Eugenius, cast themselves at the apostle's feet and besought him to intercede for them with the Lord. Unto whom the holy apostle gave this answer: that for thirty days they should offer penitence to God, and in that space pray especially that the rods of gold might return to their nature and likewise the stones return to the meanness wherein they were made. And it came to pass that after thirty days were accomplished, and neither the rods were turned into wood nor the gems into pebbles, Atticus and Eugenius came and said to the apostle: Thou hast always taught mercy, and preached forgiveness, and bidden that one man should spare another. And if God willeth that a man should forgive a man, how much more shall he, as he is God, both forgive and spare men. We are confounded for our sin: and whereas we have cried with our eyes which lusted after the world, we do now repent with eyes that weep. We pray thee, Lord, we pray thee, apostle of God, show in deed that mercy which in word thou hast always promised. Then the holy John said unto them as they wept and repented, and all interceded for them likewise: Our Lord God used these words when he spake concerning sinners: I will not the death of a sinner, but I will rather that he be converted and live. For when the Lord Jesus Christ taught us concerning the penitent, he said: Verily I say unto you, there is great joy in heaven over one sinner that repenteth and turneth himself from his sins: and there is more joy over him than over ninety and nine which have not sinned. Wherefore I would have you know that the Lord accepteth the repentance of these men. And he turned unto Atticus and Eugenius and said: Go, carry back the rods unto the wood whence ye took them, for now are they returned to their own nature, and the stones unto the sea-shore, for they are become *common* stones as they were before. And when this was accomplished, they received again the grace which they had lost, so that again they cast out devils as before time and healed the sick and enlightened the blind, and daily the Lord did many mighty works by their means.

XIX tells shortly the destruction of the temple of Ephesus and the conversion of 12,000 people.

Then follows the episode of the poison-cup in a form which probably represents the story in the Leucian Acts. (We have seen that the late Greek texts place it at the beginning, in the presence of Domitian.)

XX. Now when Aristodemus, who was chief priest of all those idols, saw this, filled with a wicked spirit, he stirred up sedition among the people, so that one people prepared themselves to fight against the other. And John turned to him and said: Tell me, Aristodemus, what can I do to take away the anger from thy soul? And Aristodemus said: If thou wilt have me believe in thy God, I will give thee poison to drink, and if thou drink it, and die not, it will appear that thy God is true. The apostle answered: If thou give me poison to drink, when I call on the name of my Lord, it will not be able to harm me. Aristodemus said again: I will that thou first see others drink it and die straightway, that so thy heart may recoil from that cup. And the blessed John said: I have told thee already that I am prepared to drink it, that thou mayest believe on the Lord Jesus Christ when thou seest me whole after the cup of poison. Aristodemus therefore went to the proconsul and asked of him two men who were to undergo the sentence of death. And when he had set them in the midst of the market-place before all the people, in the sight of the apostle he made them drink the poison: and as soon as they had drunk it, they gave up the ghost. Then Aristodemus turned to John and said: Hearken to me and depart from thy teaching wherewith thou callest away the people from the worship of the gods; or take and drink this, that thou mayest show that thy God is almighty, if after thou hast drunk, thou canst remain whole. Then the blessed John, as they lay dead which had drunk the poison, like a fearless and brave man took the cup, and making the sign of the cross, spake thus: My God, and the Father of our Lord Jesus Christ, by whose word the heavens were established, unto whom all things are subject, whom all creation serveth, whom all power obeyeth, feareth, and trembleth, when we call on thee for succour: whose name the serpent hearing is still, the dragon fleeth, the viper is quiet, the toad (which is called a frog) is still and strengthless, the scorpion is quenched, the basilisk vanquished, and the phalangia (spider) doth no hurt; in a word, all venomous things, and the fiercest reptiles and noisome beasts, are pierced (*or* covered with darkness). [Ps.- Mellitus adds: and all roots hurtful to the health of men dry up.] Do thou, I say, quench the venom of this poison, put out the deadly workings thereof, and void it of the strength which it hath in it: and grant in thy sight unto all these whom thou hast created, eyes that they may see, and ears that they may hear, and a heart that they may understand thy greatness. And when he had thus said, he armed his mouth and all his body with the sign of the cross and drank all that was in the cup. And after he had drunk, he said: I ask that they for whose sake I have drunk, be turned unto thee, O Lord, and by thine enlightening receive the salvation which is in thee. And when for the space of three hours the people saw that John was of a cheerful countenance, and that there was no sign at all of paleness or fear in him, they began to cry out with a loud voice: He is the one true God whom John worshippeth.

XXI. But Aristodemus even so believed not, though the people reproached him: but turned unto John and said: This one thing I lack—if thou in the name of thy God raise up these that have died by this poison, my mind will be cleansed of all doubt. When he said that, the people rose against Aristodemus, saying: We will burn thee and thine house if thou goest on to trouble the apostle further with thy words. John, therefore, seeing that there was a fierce sedition, asked for silence, and said in the hearing of all: The first of the virtues of God which we ought to imitate is patience, by which we are able to bear with the foolishness of unbelievers. Wherefore if Aristodemus is still held by unbelief, let us loose the knots of his unbelief. He shall be compelled, even though late, to acknowledge his creator; for I will not cease from this work until a remedy shall bring help to his wounds, and like physicians which have in their hands a sick man needing medicine, so also, if Aristodemus be not yet cured by that which hath now been done, he shall be cured by that which I will now do. And he called Aristodemus to him, and gave him his coat, and he himself stood clad only in his mantle. And Aristodemus said to him: Wherefore hast thou given me thy coat? John said to him: That thou mayest even so be put to shame and depart from thine unbelief. And Aristodemus said: And how shall thy coat make me to depart from unbelief? The apostle answered: Go and cast it upon the bodies of the dead, and thou shalt say thus: The apostle of our Lord Jesus Christ hath sent me that in his name ye may rise again, that all may know that life and death are servants of my Lord Jesus Christ. Which when Aristodemus had done, and had seen them rise, he worshipped John, and ran quickly to the proconsul and began to say with a loud voice: Hear me, hear me, thou proconsul; I think thou rememberest that I have often stirred up thy wrath against John and devised many things against him daily, wherefore I fear lest I feel his wrath: for he is a god hidden in the form of a man, and hath drunk poison, and not only continueth whole, but them also which had died by the poison he hath recalled to life by my means, by the touch of his coat, and they have no mark of death upon them. Which when the proconsul heard he said: And what wilt thou have me to do? Aristodemus answered: Let us go and fall at his feet and ask pardon, and whatever he commandeth us let us do. Then they came together and cast themselves down and besought forgiveness: and he received them and offered prayer and thanksgiving to God, and he ordained them a fast of a week, and when it was fulfilled he baptized them in the name of the Lord Jesus Christ and his Almighty Father, and the Holy Ghost the illuminator. [And when they were baptized, with all their house and their servants and their kindred, they brake all their idols and built a church in the name of Saint John: wherein he himself was taken up, in manner following:]

This bracketed sentence, of late complexion, serves to introduce the last episode of the book.

Here we may insert a notice of three detached fragments of the Acts.

a. The upper portion of a papyrus leaf of the fourth century, *Oxyrhynchus papyri*, no. 850 (vol. vi, 1908). The order of the two pages is doubted by the editors, who suggest that the *recto* should follow the *verso*.

Recto

departure.

. . . . Andronicus and his wife . . . .

(this is the title of the following episode)

ll. 1, 2 And when a few days had passed, John went forth with many of the brethren to . . . .

3 . . . . to cross a bridge under which a *deep* river ran

4 (and as John) went to the brethren

5 (behold a man) came towards him clad in the manner of a soldier

6 and standing before him said: John, into

7 (my) hands thou shall shortly come. And John (in wrath)

8 (said): the Lord shall quench thy threatening and thy wrath and

9 (thy trans)gression. And lo he vanished away. (When therefore)

10 John was come to those to whom he went, and found

11 (them) gathered together, he said: Rise up my breth-
12 (ren) let us bow our knees unto the Lord and
12, 13 brought to nought the unseen working of the great
enemy
14 bowed his knees together with them ... said
15 . . . . God
Here is the appearance of a demon disguised as a soldier who
threatens John, perhaps predicting his arrest, and is routed. John is
about to pray with the brethren.

Verso

1 for him
2 groanings and
3 but John
4 to Zeuxis, having risen and taken up a (cup)
5 . . . . who didst compel me with
6, 7 thinking to strangle himself: that dost turn things
despaired of unto thee: 7, 8 that makest known . . . . the
things that
8 are known to no man: that weepest for the afflicted
9 that raisest up those that have been put to death
10 of the helpless: Jesu the comforter of the
11 we praise thee and worship and give thanks
12 for all thy gifts: and for thy present dispensation
13, 14 and ministry. And unto Zeuxis only *he gave* of the
eucharist. and afterward gave to them that would receive
15 looking on him durst not: but the proconsul
16 (? sending a) centurion in the midst of the assembly
(church ?) saith to John
17 : Servant of the unnameable (God
18 hath brought letters from Caesar
19 (? in which is contained: Domitianus Caesar) and the
sen(ate . . . .

Zeuxis has tried to hang himself. He has been delivered and a
service of thanksgiving is held. The proconsul is already there and
has seen the miracle: he brings letters from the emperor.

The editor questions whether there is room in the lower part of the
recto to finish John's prayer and introduce the episode of Zeuxis.
But the author, while often very prolix, can also get over much ground
in few lines. And it is equally difficult to see how the emperor's letter
should be dismissed and done with in half a page and a story about
Andronicus follow immediately.

The interest of the fragment for the general course of the story
lies in this, that it confirms our belief that John was represented as
coming under the notice of the emperor; and probably either exile
or the caldron of oil, or both, were the sequels of the transaction:
I doubt, however, whether the trial was laid at Rome.

b and *c* are quotations preserved in a barbarous Latin Apocryphon
called the Epistle of Titus, mainly a declamation about virginity, which

exists in one manuscript at Würzburg (eighth century). Dom Donatien de Bruyne printed them in the *Revue Bénédictine* for 1908 (pp. 149–60).

b. Or is that outside the law which we are taught, how the very devils [when they] confessed to Dyrus (*read* Verus) the deacon as to the coming of John: consider what they said: Many will come to us in the last times to turn us out of our vessels (i. e. the bodies possessed by them), saying that they are pure and clean from women and are not held by desire of them: whom (MS. while) if we desired, we (could) possess them also.

This should come from an early part of the book. I take it to precede John's first visit to Ephesus. My rendering indicates the obscurity of the original.

c is so confused (and wearisome) that it defies translation. It is a diatribe of John's against matrimony and begins thus:

Receive therefore in thy heart the admonition of the blessed John, who, when he was bidden to a marriage, came not save for the sake of chastity, and consider what he said: Little children, while yet your flesh is pure and ye have your body untouched and not destroyed, and are not defiled by Satan, the great enemy and shameless (foe) of chastity: know therefore more fully the mystery of the nuptial union: it is the experiment of the serpent, the ignorance of teaching, injury of the seed, the gift of death, . . . (thirty-one (!) clauses follow, many of which are quite corrupt; the last are) the impediment which separateth from the Lord, the beginning of disobedience, the end of life, and death. Hearing this, little children, join yourselves together in an inseparable marriage, holy and true, waiting for the one true incomparable bridegroom from heaven, even Christ, the ever-lasting bridegroom.

If, then, the apostle severed a marriage, lest it should be an occasion of sin . . . &c.

This is the most avowedly Encratite passage in the Acts: true, John persuaded Andronicus and others to dissolve their marriage in all but name: but there is nowhere else such a wealth of abuse of the institution of marriage as such. The speech belongs to an episode of which we know nothing; it cannot refer to Andronicus or Lycomedes, who were both married when first we hear of them.

A third quotation in the Epistle of Titus is taken from an extant part of the Acts, the last prayer of John.

The last episode of these Acts (as is the case with several others of the Apocryphal Acts) was preserved separately for reading in church on the Saint's day. We have it in at least nine Greek manuscripts, and in many versions: Latin, Syriac, Armenian, Coptic, Ethiopic, Slavonic.

106 John therefore continued with the brethren, rejoicing in the Lord. And on the morrow, being the Lord's day, and all the brethren being gathered together, he began to say unto them: Brethren and fellow-servants and coheirs and partakers with me in the kingdom of the Lord, ye know the Lord, how

many mighty works he hath granted you by my means, how many wonders, healings, signs, how great *spiritual* gifts, teachings, governings, refreshings, ministries, knowledges, glories, graces, gifts, beliefs, communions, all which ye have seen given you by him in your sight, *yet* not seen by these eyes nor heard by these ears. Be ye therefore stablished in him, remembering him in your every deed, knowing the mystery of the dispensation which hath come to pass towards men, for what cause the Lord hath accomplished it. He beseecheth you by me, brethren, and entreateth you, desiring to remain without grief, without insult, not conspired against, not chastened: for he knoweth even the insult that cometh of you, he knoweth even dishonour, he knoweth even conspiracy, he knoweth even chastisement, from them that hearken not to his commandments.

107 Let not then our good God be grieved, the compassionate, the merciful, the holy, the pure, the undefiled, the immaterial, the only, the one, the unchangeable, the simple, the guileless, the unwrathful, even our God Jesus Christ, who is above every name that we can utter or conceive, and more exalted. Let him rejoice with us because we walk aright, let him be glad because we live purely, let him be refreshed because our conversation is sober. Let him be without care because we live continently, let him be pleased because we communicate *one with another*, let him smile because we are chaste, let him be merry because we love him. These things I now speak unto you, brethren, because I am hasting unto the work set before me, and already being perfected by the Lord. For what else could I have to say unto you? Ye have the pledge of our God, ye have the earnest of his goodness, ye have his presence that cannot be shunned. If, then, ye sin no more, he forgiveth you that ye did in ignorance: but if after that ye have known him and he hath had mercy on you, ye walk again in the like *deeds*, both the former will be laid to your charge, and also ye will not have a part nor mercy before him.

108 And when he had spoken this unto them, he prayed thus: O Jesu who hast woven this crown with thy weaving, who hast joined together these many blossoms into the unfading flower of thy countenance, who hast sown in them these words: thou only tender of thy servants, and physician who healest freely: only doer of good and despiser of none, only merciful and lover of men, only saviour and righteous, only seer of all, who art in all and everywhere present and containing all things and filling all things: Christ Jesu, God, Lord, that with thy gifts and thy mercy shelterest them that trust in thee, that knowest clearly the wiles and the assaults of him that is everywhere our adversary, which he deviseth against us: do thou only, O Lord, succour thy servants by thy visitation. Even so, Lord.

109 And he asked for bread, and gave thanks thus: What praise or what offering or what thanksgiving shall we, breaking this bread, name save thee only, O Lord Jesu? We glorify thy name that was said by the Father: we glorify thy name that was said through the Son (*or* we glorify the name of Father that was said by thee . . . the name of Son that was said by thee): we glorify thine entering of the Door. We glorify the resurrection shown unto us by thee. We glorify thy way, we glorify of thee the seed, the word, the grace, the faith, the salt, the unspeakable (*al.* chosen) pearl, the treasure, the plough, the net, the greatness, the diadem, him that for us was called Son of man, that gave unto us truth, rest, knowledge, power, the commandment, the confidence, hope, love, liberty, refuge in thee. For thou, Lord, art alone the root of immortality, and the fount of incorruption, and the seat of the ages: called by all these *names* for us now, that calling on thee by them we may make known thy greatness which at the present is invisible unto us, but visible only unto the pure, being portrayed in thy manhood only.

110 And he brake the bread and gave unto all of us, praying over each of the brethren that he might be worthy of the grace of the Lord and of the most holy eucharist. And he partook also himself likewise, and said: Unto me also be there a part with you, and: Peace be with you, my beloved.

111 After that he said unto Verus: Take with thee some two men, with baskets and shovels, and follow me. And Verus without delay did as he was bidden by John the servant of God. The blessed John therefore went out of the house and walked forth of the gates, having told the more part to depart from him. And when he was come to the tomb of a *certain* brother of ours, he said to the young men: Dig, my children. And they dug: and he was instant with them yet more, saying: Let the trench be deeper. And as they dug he spoke unto them the word of God and exhorted them that were come with him out of the house, edifying and perfecting them unto the greatness of God, and praying over each one of us. And when the young men had finished the trench as he desired, we knowing nothing of it, he took off his garments wherein he was clad and laid them as it were for a pallet in the bottom of the trench: and standing in his shift only he stretched his hands upward and prayed thus:

112 O thou that didst choose us out for the apostleship of the Gentiles: O God that sentest us into the world: that didst reveal thyself by the law and the prophets: that didst never rest, but alway from the foundation of the world savedst them that were able to be saved: that madest thyself known through all nature: that proclaimedst thyself even among beasts: that didst make the desolate and savage soul tame and quiet; that gavest thyself to it when it was athirst for thy words: that didst appear to it in haste when it was dying: that didst show thyself

to it as a law when it was sinking into lawlessness: that didst manifest thyself to it when it had been vanquished by Satan: that didst overcome its adversary when it fled unto thee: that gavest it thine hand and didst raise it up from the things of Hades: that didst not leave it to walk after a bodily sort (in the body): that didst show to it its own enemy: that hast made for it a clear knowledge toward thee: O God, Jesu, the Father of them that are above the heavens, the Lord of them that are in the heavens, the law of them that are in the ether, the course of them that are in the air, the keeper of them that are on the earth, the fear of them that are under the earth, the grace of them that are thine own: receive also the soul of thy John, which it may be is accounted worthy by thee.

113 O thou who hast kept me until this hour for thyself and untouched by union with a woman: who when in my youth I desired to marry didst appear unto me and say to me: John, I have need of thee: who didst prepare for me also a sickness of the body: who when for the third time I would marry didst forthwith prevent me, and then at the third hour of the day saidst unto me on the sea: John, if thou hadst not been mine, I would have suffered thee to marry: who for two years didst blind me (or afflict mine eyes), and grant me to mourn and entreat thee: who in the third year didst open the eyes of my mind and also grant me my visible eyes: who when I saw clearly didst ordain that it should be grievous to me to look upon a woman: who didst save me from the temporal fantasy and lead me unto that which endureth always: who didst rid me of the foul madness that is in the flesh: who didst take me from the bitter death and establish me on thee alone: who didst muzzle the secret disease of my soul and cut off the open deed: who didst afflict and banish him that raised tumult in me: who didst make my love of thee spotless: who didst make my joining unto thee perfect and unbroken: who didst give me undoubting faith in thee, who didst order and make clear my inclination toward thee: thou who givest unto every man the due reward of his works, who didst put into my soul that I should have no possession save thee only: for what is more precious than thee? Now therefore Lord, whereas I have accomplished the dispensation wherewith I was entrusted, account thou me worthy of thy rest, and grant me that end in thee which is salvation unspeakable and unutterable.

114 And as I come unto thee, let the fire go backward, let the darkness be overcome, let the gulf be without strength, let the furnace die out, let Gehenna be quenched. Let angels follow, let devils fear, let rulers be broken, let powers fall; let the places of the right hand stand fast, let them of the left hand not remain. Let the devil be muzzled, let Satan be derided, let his wrath be burned out, let his madness be stilled, let his

vengeance be ashamed, let his assault be in pain, let his children be smitten and all his roots plucked up. And grant me to accomplish the journey unto thee without suffering insolence or provocation, and to receive that which thou hast promised unto them that live purely and have loved thee only.

115 And having sealed himself in every part, he stood and said: Thou art with me, O Lord Jesu Christ: and laid himself down in the trench where he had strown his garments: and having said unto us: Peace be with you, brethren, he gave up his spirit rejoicing.

The less good Greek manuscripts and some versions are not content with this simple ending. The Latin says that after the prayer a great light appeared over the apostle for the space of an hour, so bright that no one could look at it. (Then he laid himself down and gave up the ghost.) We who were there rejoiced, some of us, and some mourned. . . . And forthwith manna issuing from the tomb was seen of all, which manna that place produceth even unto this day, &c. But perhaps the best conclusion is that of one Greek manuscript:

We brought a linen cloth and spread it upon him, and went into the city. And on the day following we went forth and found not his body, for it was translated by the power of our Lord Jesus Christ, unto whom be glory, &c.

Another says: On the morrow we dug in the place, and him we found not, but only his sandals, and the earth moving (*lit.* springing up like a well), and after that we remembered that which was spoken by the Lord unto Peter, &c.

Augustine (*on John* xxi) reports the belief that in his time the earth over the grave was seen to move as if stirred by John's breathing.

ACTS OF PAUL (See Appendix II)

This book, Tertullian tells us, was composed shortly before his time in honour of Paul by a presbyter of Asia, who was convicted of the imposture and degraded from his office. The date of it may therefore be about A. D. 160. The author was an orthodox Christian.

Our authorities for it are:

1. The sadly mutilated Coptic MS. at Heidelberg, of the sixth century at latest.

2. The Acts of Paul and Thecla, a single episode which has been preserved complete in Greek and many versions: parts of it exist in the Coptic.

3. The correspondence with the Corinthians, partly preserved in the Coptic, and current separately in Armenian and Latin.

4. The Martyrdom, the concluding episode of the Acts, preserved separately (as in the case of John and others) in Greek and other versions.

5. Detached fragments or quotations.

The length of the whole book is given as 3,600 lines (Stichometry of Nicephorus), or 3,560 (Stichometry of the Codex Claromontanus): the Canonical Acts are given by the same two authorities respectively as 2,800 and 2,600. We have, perhaps, 1,800 lines of the Acts of Paul.

The text of the Coptic MS. is miserably defective, and the restoration of it, in the episodes which are preserved in it alone, is a most difficult process: Professor Carl Schmidt has done practically all that can be expected, with infinite labour and great acuteness. In treating the defective episodes I shall follow him closely, but shall not attempt to represent all the broken lines.

I

The first extant page of the Coptic MS. seems to be p. 9.

p. 9. Paul went into (the house) at the place where the (dead) was. But Phila the wife of Panchares (Anchares, MS., see below) was very wroth and said to her husband in (great anger): Husband, thou hast gone . . . . the wild beasts, thou hast not begotten . . . . thy son . . . . where is mine?

. . . .

p. 10. . . . . (he hath not) desired food . . . . to bury him. But (Panchares) stood in the sight of all and made his prayer at the ninth hour, until the people of the city came to bear the boy out. When he had prayed, Paul (came) and saw . . . . and of Jesus Christ . . . . the boy . . . . the prayer.

. . . .

p. 11 (a small piece only). . . . . multitude . . . . eight days . . . . they thought that he raised up the (boy). But when Paul had remained

p. 12. They asked? him? . . . . the men listened to him . . . . they sent for Panchares . . . and cried out, *saying*: We believe, Panchares, ... but save the city *from* . . . . many things, which they said. Panchares said unto them: Judge ye whether your good deeds (?)

p. 13. . . . . is not possible . . . . but to (testify) . . . . God who hath . . . . his Son according to . . . . salvation, and I also believe that, my brethren, there is no other God, save Jesus Christ the son of the Blessed, unto whom is glory *for ever*, Amen. But when they saw that he would not turn to them, they pursued Paul, and caught him, and brought him back into the city, ill-using (?) him, and cast stones at him and thrust him out of their city and out of their country. But Panchares would not return evil for evil: he shut the door *of his house* and went in with his wife . . . . fasting. . . . . But when it was evening *Paul came* to him and said:

p. 14. *God* hath . . . . Jesus Christ.

These are the last words of the episode. The situation is a little cleared by a sentence in the Greek Acts of Titus ascribed to Zenas (not earlier than the fifth century?): 'They arrived at Antioch and found Barnabas the son of Panchares, whom Paul raised up.' Barnabas may be a mistake, but Panchares is, I doubt not, right: for the Coptic definite article is *p* prefixed to the word, and the Coptic translator finding Panchares in his text has confused the initial of it with his own definite article, and cut it out.

We have, then, a husband Panchares and wife Phila at Antioch (in Pisidia perhaps: this is disputed), and their son (possibly named Barnabas) is dead. Phila reproaches Panchares with want of parental affection. I take it that he is a believer, and has not mourned over his son, perhaps knowing that Paul was at hand and hoping for his help. Panchares prays till his fellow-townsmen come to carry out the body for burial. Paul arrives: at some point he raises the dead: but the people are irritated and some catastrophe threatens them at Paul's hands.

Panchares makes a profession of faith, the result of which is Paul's ill-treatment and banishment. But Paul returns secretly and reassures Panchares.

II

The next episode is that of Paul and Thecla, in which the Greek text exists, and will be followed. In the Coptic it has a title:

After the flight from Antioch, when he would go to Iconium.

It is possible that in this episode the author of the Acts may have used a local legend, current in his time, of a real Christian martyr Thecla. It is otherwise difficult to account for the very great popularity of the cult of St. Thecla, which spread over East and West, and made her the most famous of virgin martyrs. Moreover, one historical personage is introduced into the story, namely, Queen Tryphaena, who was the widow, it seems, of Cotys, King of Thrace, and the mother of Polemo II, King of Pontus. She was a great-niece of the Emperor Claudius. Professor W. M. Ramsay has contended that there was a *written* story of Thecla which was adapted by the author of the Acts: but his view is not generally accepted.

1 When Paul went up unto Iconium after he fled from Antioch, there journeyed with him Demas and Hermogenes the coppersmith, which were full of hypocrisy, and flattered Paul as though they loved him. But Paul, looking only unto the goodness of Christ, did them no evil, but loved them well, so that he assayed to make sweet unto them all the oracles of the Lord, and of the teaching and the interpretation (of the Gospel) and of the birth and resurrection of the Beloved, and related unto them word by word all the great works of Christ, how they were revealed unto him (*Copt.* adds: how that Christ was born of Mary the virgin, and of the seed of David).

2 And a certain man named Onesiphorus, when he heard that Paul was come to Iconium, went out with his children Simmias and Zeno and his wife Lectra to meet him, that he might receive him *into his house*: for Titus [1] had told him what manner of man Paul was in appearance; for he had not seen him in the flesh, but only in the spirit.

[1] The Acts of Titus tell us that Paul sent Titus before him to announce his coming in every city which he was to visit.

3 And he went by the king's highway that leadeth unto Lystra and stood expecting him, and looked upon them that came, according to the description of Titus. And he saw Paul coming, a man little of stature, thin-haired upon the head, crooked in the legs, of good state of body, with eyebrows joining, and nose somewhat hooked, full of grace: for sometimes he appeared like a man, and sometimes he had the face of an angel.

4 And when Paul saw Onesiphorus he smiled, and Onesiphorus said: Hail, thou servant of the blessed God. And he said: Grace be with thee and with thine house. But Demas and Hermogenes were envious, and stirred up their hypocrisy yet more, so that Demas said: Are we not *servants* of the Blessed, that thou didst not salute us so? And Onesiphorus said: I see not in you any fruit of righteousness, but if ye be such, come ye also into my house and refresh yourselves.

5 And when Paul entered into the house of Onesiphorus, there was great joy, and bowing of knees and breaking of bread, and the word of God concerning abstinence (*or* continence) and the resurrection; for Paul said:

Blessed are the pure in heart, for they shall see God.

Blessed are they that keep the flesh chaste, for they shall become the temple of God.

Blessed are they that abstain (*or* the continent), for unto them shall God speak.

Blessed are they that have renounced this world, for they shall be well-pleasing unto God.

Blessed are they that possess their wives as though they had them not, for they shall inherit God.

Blessed are they that have the fear of God, for they shall become angels of God.

6 Blessed are they that tremble at the oracles of God, for they shall be comforted.

Blessed are they that receive *the* wisdom of Jesus Christ, for they shall be called sons of the Most High.

Blessed are they that have kept their baptism *pure*, for they shall rest with the Father and with the Son.

Blessed are they that have compassed the understanding of Jesus Christ, for they shall be in light.

Blessed are they that for love of God have departed from the fashion of this world, for they shall judge angels, and shall be blessed at the right hand of the Father.

Blessed are the merciful, for they shall obtain mercy and shall not see the bitter day of judgement.

Blessed are the bodies of the virgins, for they shall be well-pleasing unto God and shall not lose the reward of their continence (chastity), for the word of the Father shall be unto them a work of salvation in the day of his Son, and they shall have rest world without end.

7 And as Paul was saying these things in the midst of the assembly (church) in the house of Onesiphorus, a certain virgin, Thecla, whose mother was Theocleia, which was betrothed to an husband, Thamyris, sat at the window hard by, and hearkened night and day unto the word concerning chastity which was spoken by Paul: and she stirred not from the window, but was led onward (or pressed onward) by faith, rejoicing exceedingly: and further, when she saw many women and virgins entering in to Paul, she also desired earnestly to be accounted worthy to stand before Paul's face and to hear the word of Christ; for she had not yet seen the appearance of Paul, but only heard his speech.

8 Now as she removed not from the window, her mother sent unto Thamyris, and he came with great joy as if he were already to take her to wife. Thamyris therefore said to Theocleia: Where is my Thecla? And Theocleia said: I have a new tale to tell thee, Thamyris: for for three days and three nights Thecla ariseth not from the window, neither to eat nor to drink, but looking earnestly as it were upon a joyful spectacle, she so attendeth to a stranger who teacheth deceitful and various words, that I marvel how the great modesty of the maiden is so hardly beset.

9 O Thamyris, this man upsetteth the *whole* city of the Iconians, and thy Thecla also, for all the women and the young men go in to him and are taught by him. Ye must, saith he, fear one only God and live chastely. And my daughter, too, like a spider at the window, bound by his words, is held by a new desire and a fearful passion: for she hangeth upon the things that he speaketh, and the maiden is captured. But go thou to her and speak to her; for she is betrothed unto thee.

10 And Thamyris went to her, alike loving her and fearing because of her disturbance (ecstasy), and said: Thecla, my betrothed, why sittest thou thus? and what passion is it that holdeth thee in amaze; turn unto thy Thamyris and be ashamed. And her mother also said the same: Thecla, why sittest thou thus, looking downward, and answering nothing, but as one stricken? And they wept sore, Thamyris because he failed of a wife, and Theocleia of a child, and the maidservants of a mistress; there was, therefore, great confusion of mourning in the house. And while all this was so, Thecla turned not away, but paid heed to the speech of Paul.

11 But Thamyris leapt up and went forth into the street and watched them that went in to Paul and came out. And he saw two men striving bitterly with one another, and said to them: Ye men, tell me who ye are, and who is he that is within with you, that maketh the souls of young men and maidens to err, deceiving them that there may be no marriages but they should

live as they are. I promise therefore to give you much money if ye will tell me of him: for I am a chief *man* of the city.

12 And Demas and Hermogenes said unto him: Who this man is, we know not; but he defraudeth the young men of wives and the maidens of husbands, saying: Ye have no resurrection otherwise, except ye continue chaste, and defile not the flesh but keep it pure.

13 And Thamyris said to them: Come, ye men, into mine house and refresh yourselves with me. And they went to a costly banquet and much wine and great wealth and a brilliant table. And Thamyris made them drink, for he loved Thecla and desired to take her to wife: and at the dinner Thamyris said: Tell me, ye men, what is his teaching, that I also may know it: for I am not a little afflicted concerning Thecla because she so loveth the stranger, and I am defrauded of my marriage.

14 And Demas and Hermogenes said: Bring him before Castelius the governor as one that persuadeth the multitudes with the new doctrine of the Christians; and so will he destroy him and thou shalt have thy wife Thecla. And we will teach thee of that resurrection which he asserteth, that it is already come to pass in the children which we have, and we rise again when we have come to the knowledge of the true God.

15 But when Thamyris heard this of them, he was filled with envy and wrath, and rose up early and went to the house of Onesiphorus with the rulers and officers and a great crowd with staves, saying unto Paul: Thou hast destroyed the city of the Iconians and her that was espoused unto me, so that she will not have me: let us go unto Castelius the governor. And all the multitude said: Away with the wizard, for he hath corrupted all our wives. And the multitude rose up together against him.

16 And Thamyris, standing before the judgement seat, cried aloud and said: O proconsul, this is the man—we know not whence he is—who alloweth not maidens to marry: let him declare before thee wherefore he teacheth such things. And Demas and Hermogenes said to Thamyris: Say thou that he is a Christian, and so wilt thou destroy him. But the governor kept his mind steadfast and called Paul, saying unto him: Who art thou, and what teachest thou? for it is no light accusation that these bring against thee.

17 And Paul lifted up his voice and said: If I am this day examined what I teach, hearken, O proconsul. The living God, the God of vengeance, the jealous God, the God that hath need of nothing, but desireth the salvation of men, hath sent me, that I may sever them from corruption and uncleanness and all pleasure and death, that they may sin no more. Wherefore God hath sent his own Child, whom I preach and teach that men should have hope in him who alone hath had compassion upon the world that was in error; that men may no more be under

judgement but have faith and the fear of God and the knowledge of sobriety and the love of truth. If then I teach the things that have been revealed unto me of God, what wrong do I, O proconsul? And the governor having heard that, commanded Paul to be bound and taken away to prison until he should have leisure to hear him more carefully.

18 But Thecla at night took off her bracelets and gave them to the doorkeeper, and when the door was opened for her she went into the prison, and gave the jailer a mirror of silver and so went in to Paul and sat by his feet and heard the wonderful works of God. And Paul feared not at all, but walked in the confidence of God: and her faith also was increased as she kissed his chains.

19 Now when Thecla was sought by her own people and by Thamyris, she was looked for through the streets as one lost; and one of the fellow-servants of the doorkeeper told that she went out by night. And they examined the doorkeeper and he told them that she was gone to the stranger unto the prison; and they went as he told them and found her as it were bound with him, in affection. And they went forth thence and gathered the multitude to them and showed it to the governor.

20 And he commanded Paul to be brought to the judgement seat; but Thecla rolled herself upon the place where Paul taught when he sat in the prison. And the governor commanded her also to be brought to the judgement seat, and she went exulting with joy. And when Paul was brought the second time the people cried out more vehemently: He is a sorcerer, away with him! But the governor heard Paul gladly concerning the holy works of Christ: and he took counsel, and called Thecla and said: Why wilt thou not marry Thamyris, according to the law of the Iconians? but she stood looking earnestly upon Paul, and when she answered not, her mother Theocleia cried out, saying: Burn the lawless one, burn her that is no bride in the midst of the theatre, that all the women which have been taught by this man may be affrighted.

21 And the governor was greatly moved: and he scourged Paul and sent him out of the city, but Thecla he condemned to be burned. And straightway the governor arose and went to the theatre: and all the multitude went forth unto the dreadful spectacle. But Thecla, as the lamb in the wilderness looketh about for the shepherd, so sought for Paul: and she looked upon the multitude and saw the Lord sitting, like unto Paul, and said: As if I were not able to endure, Paul is come to look upon me. And she earnestly paid heed to him: but he departed into the heavens.

22 Now the boys and the maidens brought wood and hay to burn Thecla: and when she was brought in naked, the governor wept and marvelled at the power that was in her. And they laid the wood, and the executioner bade her mount upon the

pyre: and she, making the sign of the cross, went up upon the wood. And they lighted it, and though a great fire blazed forth, the fire took no hold on her; for God had compassion on her, and caused a sound under the earth, and a cloud overshadowed her above, full of rain and hail, and all the vessel *of it* was poured out so that many were in peril of death, and the fire was quenched, and Thecla was preserved.

23 Now Paul was fasting with Onesiphorus and his wife and their children in an open sepulchre on the way whereby they go from Iconium to Daphne. And when many days were past, as they fasted, the boys said unto Paul: We are anhungered. And they had not wherewith to buy bread, for Onesiphorus had left the goods of this world, and followed Paul with all his house. But Paul took off his upper garment and said: Go, child, buy several loaves and bring them. And as the boy was buying, he saw his neighbour Thecla, and was astonished, and said: Thecla, whither goest thou? And she said: I seek Paul, *for* I was preserved from the fire. And the boy said: Come, I will bring thee unto him, for he mourneth for thee and prayeth and fasteth now these six days.

24 And when she came to the sepulchre unto Paul, who had bowed his knees and was praying and saying: O Father of Christ, let not the fire take hold on Thecla, but spare her, for she is thine: she standing behind him cried out: O Father that madest heaven and earth, the Father of thy beloved child Jesus Christ, I bless thee for that thou hast preserved me from the fire, that I might see Paul. And Paul arose and saw her and said: O God the knower of hearts, the Father of our Lord Jesus Christ, I bless thee that thou hast speedily accomplished that which I asked of thee, and hast hearkened unto me.

25 And there was much love within the sepulchre, for Paul rejoiced, and Onesiphorus, and all of them. And they had five loaves, and herbs, and water (and salt), and they rejoiced for the holy works of Christ. And Thecla said unto Paul: I will cut my hair round about and follow thee whithersoever thou goest. But he said: The time is ill-favoured and thou art comely: *beware* lest another temptation take thee, worse than the first, and thou endure it not but play the coward. And Thecla said: Only give me the seal in Christ, and temptation shall not touch me. And Paul said: Have patience, Thecla, and thou shalt receive the water.

26 And Paul sent away Onesiphorus with all his house unto Iconium, and so took Thecla and entered into Antioch: and as they entered in, a certain Syriarch, Alexander by name, saw Thecla and was enamoured of her, and would have bribed (flattered) Paul with money and gifts. But Paul said: I know not the woman of whom thou speakest, neither is she mine. But as he was of great power, he himself embraced her in the highway; and she endured it not, but sought after Paul and cried out

bitterly, saying: Force not the stranger, force not the handmaid of God. I am of the first of the Iconians, and because I would not marry Thamyris, I am cast out of the city. And she caught at Alexander and rent his cloak and took the wreath [1] from his head and made him a mocking-stock.

27 But he alike loving her and being ashamed of what had befallen him, brought her before the governor; and when she confessed that she had done this, he condemned her to the beasts.[2] But the women were greatly amazed, and cried out at the judgement seat: An evil judgement, an impious judgement! And Thecla asked of the governor that she might remain a virgin until she should fight the beasts; and a certain rich queen, Tryphaena by name, whose daughter had died, took her into her keeping, and had her for a consolation.

28 Now when the beasts were led in procession, they bound her to a fierce lioness, and the queen Tryphaena followed after her: but the lioness, when Thecla was set upon her, licked her feet, and all the people marvelled. Now the writing (title) of her accusation was: Guilty of sacrilege. And the women with their children cried out from above: O God, an impious judgement cometh to pass in this city. And after the procession Tryphaena took her again. For her daughter Falconilla, which was dead, had said to her in a dream: Mother, thou shalt take in my stead Thecla the stranger that is desolate, that she may pray for me and I be translated into the place of the righteous.

29 When therefore Tryphaena received her after the procession, she alike bewailed her because she was to fight the beasts on the morrow, and also, loving her closely as her own daughter Falconilla; and said: Thecla, my second child, come, pray thou for my child that she may live for ever; for this have I seen in a dream. And she without delay lifted up her voice and said: O my God, Son of the Most High that art in heaven, grant unto her according to her desire, that her daughter Falconilla may live for ever. And after she had said this, Tryphaena bewailed her, considering that so great beauty was to be cast unto the beasts.

30 And when it was dawn, Alexander came to take her—for it was he that was giving the games—saying: The governor is set and the people troubleth us: give me her that is to fight the beasts, that I may take her away. But Tryphaena cried aloud so that he fled away, saying: A second mourning for my Falconilla cometh about in mine house, and there is none to help, neither child, for she is dead, nor kinsman, for I am a widow. O God of Thecla my child, help thou Thecla.

31 And the governor sent soldiers to fetch Thecla: and Tryphaena left her not, but herself took her hand and led her up, saying: I did bring my daughter Falconilla unto the sepulchre;

[1] With the figure of Caesar, *Syr.*

[2] *Syr. Lat. add*: for it was Alexander that gave the spectacle.

but thee, Thecla, do I bring to fight the beasts. And Thecla wept bitterly and groaned unto the Lord, saying: Lord God in whom I believe, with whom I have taken refuge, that savedst me from the fire, reward thou Tryphaena who hath had pity on thine handmaid, and hath kept me pure.

32 There was therefore a tumult, and a voice of the beasts, and shouting of the people, and of the women which sat together, some saying: Bring in the sacrilegious one! and the women saying: Away with the city for this unlawful deed! away with all us, thou proconsul! it is a bitter sight, an evil judgement!

33 But Thecla, being taken out of the hand of Tryphaena, was stripped and a girdle put upon her, and was cast into the stadium: and lions and bears were set against her. And a fierce lioness running to her lay down at her feet, and the press of women cried aloud. And a bear ran upon her; but the lioness ran and met him, and tore the bear in sunder. And again a lion, trained against men, which was Alexander's, ran upon her, and the lioness wrestled with him and was slain along with him. And the women bewailed yet more, seeing that the lioness also that succoured her was dead.

34 Then did they put in many beasts, while she stood and stretched out her hands and prayed. And when she had ended her prayer, she turned and saw a great tank full of water, and said: Now is it time that I should wash myself. And she cast herself in, saying: In the name of Jesus Christ do I baptize myself on the last day. And all the women seeing it and all the people wept, saying: Cast not thyself into the water: so that even the governor wept that so great beauty should be devoured by seals. So, then, she cast herself into the water in the name of Jesus Christ; and the seals, seeing the light of a flash of fire, floated dead on the top of the water. And there was about her a cloud of fire, so that neither did the beasts touch her, nor was she seen to be naked.

35 Now the women, when other more fearful beasts were put in, shrieked aloud, and some cast leaves, and others nard, others cassia, and some balsam, so that there was a multitude of odours; and all the beasts that were struck thereby were held as it were in sleep and touched her not; so that Alexander said to the governor: I have some bulls exceeding fearful, let us bind the criminal to them. And the governor frowning, allowed it, saying: Do that thou wilt. And they bound her by the feet between the bulls, and put hot irons under their bellies that they might be the more enraged and kill her. They then leaped forward; but the flame that burned about her, burned through the ropes, and she was as one not bound.

36 But Tryphaena, standing by the arena, fainted at the entry, so that her handmaids said: The queen Tryphaena is dead! And the governor stopped *the games* and all the city was

frightened, and Alexander falling at the governor's feet said:
Have mercy on me and on the city, and let the condemned go,
lest the city perish with her; for if Caesar hear this, perchance
he will destroy us and the city, because his kinswoman the queen
Tryphaena hath died at the entry.

37 And the governor called Thecla from among the beasts,
and said to her: Who art thou? and what hast thou about thee
that not one of the beasts hath touched thee? But she said:
I am the handmaid of the living God; and what I have about
me—it is that I have believed on that his Son in whom God is
well pleased; for whose sake not one of the beasts hath touched
me. For he alone is the goal (or way) of salvation and the
substance of life immortal; for unto them that are tossed about
he is a refuge, unto the oppressed relief, unto the despairing
shelter, and in a word, whosoever believeth not on him, shall not
live, but die everlastingly.

38 And when the governor heard this, he commanded garments
to be brought and said: Put on these garments. And she said:
He that clad me when I was naked among the beasts, the same
in the day of judgement will clothe me with salvation. And she
took the garments and put them on. And the governor forthwith
issued out an act, saying: I release unto you Thecla the godly,
the servant of God. And all the women cried out with a loud
voice and as with one mouth gave praise to God, saying: One
is the God who hath preserved Thecla: so that with their voice
all the city shook.

39 And Tryphaena, when she was told the good tidings, met
her with much people and embraced Thecla and said: Now do
I believe that the dead are raised up: now do I believe that my
child liveth: come within, and I will make thee heir of all my
substance. Thecla therefore went in with her and rested in her
house eight days, teaching her the word of God, so that the more
part of the maid-servants also believed, and there was great joy
in the house.

40 But Thecla yearned after Paul and sought him, sending
about in all places; and it was told her that he was at Myra.
And she took young men and maids, and girded herself, and
sewed her mantle into a cloak after the fashion of a man, and
departed into Myra, and found Paul speaking the word of God,
and went to him. But he when he saw her and the people that
were with her was amazed, thinking in himself: Hath some
other temptation come upon her? But she perceived it, and
said to him: I have received the washing, O Paul; for he that
hath worked together with thee in the Gospel hath worked with
me also unto my baptizing.

41 And Paul took her by the hand and brought her into the
house of Hermias, and heard all things from her; so that Paul
marvelled much, and they that heard were confirmed, and prayed

for Tryphaena. And Thecla arose and said to Paul: I go unto
Iconium. And Paul said: Go, and teach the word of God. Now
Tryphaena *had* sent her much apparel and gold, so that she left
of it with Paul for the ministry of the poor.

42 But she herself departed unto Iconium. And she entered
into the house of Onesiphorus, and fell down upon the floor
where Paul had sat and taught the oracles of God, and wept,
saying: O God of me and of this house, where the light shone
upon me, Jesu Christ the Son of God, my helper in prison, my
helper before the governors, my helper in the fire, my helper
among the beasts, thou art God, and unto thee be the glory for
ever. Amen.

43 And she found Thamyris dead, but her mother living. And
she saw her mother and said unto her: Theocleia my mother,
canst thou believe that the Lord liveth in the heavens? for
whether thou desirest money, the Lord will give it thee through
me: or thy child, lo, I am here before thee. And when she had
so testified, she departed unto Seleucia, and after she had enlightened many with the word of God, she slept a good sleep.

A good many manuscripts add that Theocleia was not converted,
but the Coptic does not support them: it ends the episode as above.

A long appendix is given by other Greek copies, telling how in
Thecla's old age (she was ninety) she was living on Mount Calamon or
Calameon, and some evil-disposed young men went up to ill-treat her:
and she prayed, and the rock opened and she entered it, and it closed
after her. Some add that she went underground to Rome: this, to
account for the presence of her body there.

Copt., p. 38 of the MS.   III

When he was departed from Antioch and taught in Myra (Myrrha).

When Paul was teaching the word of God in Myra, there was
there a man, Hermocrates by name, who had the dropsy, and he
put himself forward in the sight of all, and said to Paul: Nothing
is impossible with God, but especially with him whom thou
preachest; for when he came he healed many, even that God
whose servant thou art. Lo, I and my wife and my children, we
cast ourselves at thy feet: *have pity on me* that I also may believe
as thou hast believed on the living God.

Paul said unto him: I will restore thee (thine health) *not* for
reward, but through the name of Jesus Christ thou shalt become
whole in the presence of all these. (*And he touched his body*)
drawing his hand downwards: and his belly opened and much
water ran from him and . . . . he fell down like a dead man,
so that some said: It is better for him to die than to continue in
pain. But when Paul had quieted the people, he took his hand

and raised him up and asked him, saying: Hermocrates, *ask for* what thou desirest. And he said: I would eat. And he took a loaf and gave him to eat. And in that hour he was whole, and received the grace of the seal in the Lord, he and his wife.

But Hermippus his son was angry with Paul, and sought for a set time wherein to rise up with them of his own age and destroy him. For he wished that his father should not be healed but should die, that he might soon be master of his goods. But Dion, his younger son, heard Paul gladly.

Now all they that were with *Hermippus* took counsel to fight against Paul so that Hermippus . . . . and sought to kill him. . . . . Dion fell down and died: but Hermippus watered Dion with his tears.

But Hermocrates mourned sore, for he loved Dion more than his other son. (Yet) he sat at Paul's feet, and forgat that Dion was dead. But when Dion was dead, his mother Nympha rent her clothes and went unto Paul and set herself before the face of Hermocrates her husband and of Paul. And when Paul saw her, he was affrighted and said: Wherefore art thou thus, Nympha? But she said to him: Dion is dead; and the whole multitude wept when they beheld her. And Paul looked upon the people that mourned and sent young men, saying to them: Go and bring me him hither. And they went: but Hermippus *caught hold of* the body (of Dion) in the street and cried out

A leaf lost.[1]

. . . . the word in him (them?). But an angel of the Lord had said unto him in the night: Paul, thou hast to-day a great conflict against thy body, but God, the Father of his Son Jesus Christ, will *protect* thee.

When Paul had arisen, he went unto his brethren, and remained (*sorrowful?*) saying: What meaneth this vision? And while Paul thought upon this, he saw Hermippus coming, having a sword drawn in his hand, and with him many other young men with staves. And Paul said unto them: I am not a robber, neither a murderer. The God of all things, the Father of Christ, will turn your *hands* backward, and your sword into its sheath, and your strength into weakness: for I am a servant of God, *though I be* alone and a stranger, and small and of no reputation(?) among the Gentiles. But do thou, O God, look down upon their counsel and suffer me not to be brought to nought by them.

And when Hermippus ran upon Paul with his sword drawn, *straightway* he ceased to see, so that he cried out aloud, saying: My dear comrades, forget not your friend Hermippus. For I have sinned, O Paul, I have pursued after *innocent* blood. *Learn,* ye foolish and ye of understanding, that this world is nought, gold is nought, all money is nought: I that glutted

[1] In the lost text Dion is raised from the dead.

myself with all manner of goods am now a beggar and entreat of you all: Hearken to me all ye my companions, and every one that dwelleth in Myra. *I have* mocked at a man *who hath saved* my father: I have mocked *at a man who* hath raised up my brother *Dion* . . . . *I have mocked* at a man who . . . . *without* doing me any *evil.* But entreat ye of him: behold, he hath saved my father and raised up my brother; he is able therefore to save me also. But Paul stood there weeping alike before God, for that he heard him quickly, and before man, for that the proud was brought low. And he turned himself and went up . . . . But the young men *took the feet* and bore Hermippus and brought him to the place where Paul was *teaching* and laid him *down* before the *door* and went unto their house. *And when they* were gone a great multitude came to the house of Hermocrates, and another great *multitude entered in,* to see whether *Hermippus* were shut up there. And *Hermippus* besought every one that went in, *that they would entreat Paul,* with him. But they that went in *saw Hermocrates* and Nympha, how they rejoiced greatly at the raising up of Dion, and distributed victuals and money unto the widows for his recovery. And they beheld Hermippus their son in the state of *this second affliction,* and how he took hold on the feet of every one, and on the feet of his parents also, and prayed them, as one of the strangers, that he might be healed. And his parents were troubled, and lamented to every one that came in, so that some said: Wherefore do these weep? for Dion is arisen. But Hermocrates possessed goods . . . . and brought the value of the goods and took it and distributed it. And Hermocrates, troubled in mind and desiring that they might be satisfied, said: Brethren, let us leave the food . . . . and occupy ourselves . . . . Hermocrates. *And immediately* Nympha *cried out* in great affliction unto *Paul* . . . .
. . . . *they said:* Nympha, Hermocrates calleth upon God . . . . that *your son* Hermippus may see and cease to grieve, for he hath resisted Christ and his minister. But they and Paul *prayed* to God. And when Hermippus recovered his sight, he turned himself to his mother Nympha, and said to her: Paul came unto me and laid his hand upon me while I wept, and in that hour I saw all things clearly.[1] And she took his hand and led him unto the widows and Paul. But while Paul wept bitterly, Hermippus gave thanks, saying unto them: Every one that believeth, shall . . . .

A leaf gone.

. . . . concord and peace. . . . . Amen.
And when Paul had confirmed the brethren that were in Myra, he departed unto Sidon.

[1] It seems clear to me that it was Christ in the form of Paul who healed Hermippus while Paul himself was within the house engaged in worship with the widows.

IV

When he was departed from Myra ⟨and would go unto Sidon⟩.

Now *when Paul was departed from Myra and would* go *unto*
Sidon there was great sadness of the brethren that were in
Pisidia and Pamphylia, because they yearned after his word and
his holy appearance in Christ ; so that some from Perga followed
Paul, namely Thrasymachus and Cleon with their wives Aline (?)
and Chrysa, Cleon's wife. And on the way they nourished Paul:
and they were eating their bread under a tree (?). And as he was
about to say Amen, there came (five lines broken: the words 'the
brethren' and 'idol' occur) . . . . table of devils . . . .
he dieth therefor, but every one that believeth on Jesus Christ
who hath saved us from all defilement and all uncleanness and all
evil thoughts, he shall be manifest. And they drew near unto the
table (three lines broken. 'Idol' occurs) . . . . stood . . . .
a mighty idol. And an old man . . . . stood up among them,
saying unto them: Ye men, (wait a little and see) what befalleth
the priests which would draw near unto our gods: for verily
when our fellow-citizen Charinus hearkened and would . . . .
against the gods, there died he and his (father). And thereupon
died Xanthus also, Chrysa (?), and (*Hermocrates* ?) died, *sick of
the* dropsy, and his wife *Nympha.*

Two leaves at least gone.

(Paul is speaking)

after the manner of strange men. Wherefore presume ye to do
that which is not seemly (?) ? Or have ye not heard of that which
came to pass, which God brought upon Sodom and Gomorrha,
because they robbed . . . . after the manner of strangers
and of women ? God did not . . . . them but cast them
down into hell. Now therefore we are not men of this fashion
that ye say, nor *such as ye think*, but we are *preachers* of the living
God and his *Beloved.* But that ye may not marvel, understand
. . . . the miracles (?) which bear witness for *us.* But they
hearkened not unto him, but *took* the men and put them *into the
temple of* Apollo, to keep them until the *morrow*, whereon they
assembled the *whole* city. And many and costly were the victuals
which they gave them.

But Paul, who was fasting now the third day, testified all the
night long, being troubled, and smote his face and said: O God,
look down upon their threatenings and suffer us not to slide,
and let not our adversaries cast us down, but *save* us and bring
down quickly thy righteousness upon us. And as Paul cast himself
down, with the brethren, Thrasymachus and Cleon, then the
temple fell . . . . so that they that belonged to the temple
and the magistrates that were set over it . . . . others of
them in the . . . . for (the one part) fell down . . . .
fell down . . . . round about, in the midst of the two parts.

And they went in and *beheld* what had happened, and marvelled
that . . . . in their . . . . and that the . . . . *rejoiced
over the falling of the temple* (?). And they *cried out*, saying:
Verily *these are the works of* the men of a mighty God ! And
they departed and proclaimed in the city: Apollo the god of the
Sidonians is fallen, and the half of his temple. And all the
dwellers in the city ran to the temple and saw Paul and them that
were with him, how they wept at this temptation, that they were
made a spectacle for all men. But the multitude cried out:
Bring them into the theatre. And the magistrates came to fetch
them; and they groaned bitterly with one soul.

About two leaves gone.

(Paul speaking) through me. Consider . . . . (nine lines
much broken, 'the way of life (conversation) of Christ', 'not in the
faith', occur) . . . . Egyptians . . . . and they . . . .
But the multitude . . . . and followed after Paul, *crying*:
Praised be the God . . . . who hath sent Paul . . . .
that we should not . . . . of death. But Theudes . . . .
and prayed at Paul's feet and embraced his feet, *that he should
give him* the seal in the Lord. *But he* commanded *them* to go
to Tyre . . . . in health (*or* farewell), and they put Paul (in
a ship ?) and went with him.

The purpose of confining Paul and his companions in the temple
appears to have been connected with the sins of the cities of the plain
of which Paul speaks.

The Acts of Titus, quoted before, have a sentence referring to this
and the next episode: 'And Paul healed Aphphia the wife of Chrysippus
who was possessed with a devil: and fasting for seven days he over-
threw the idol of Apollo.' The Acts place this immediately after
the conversion and preaching at Damascus, and put the Panchares
episode later. They are not to be trusted, therefore, as a guide to the
order of our book.

V

When he was departed out of Sidon and would go unto Tyre.

Now when Paul was entered unto Tyre there came a multitude
of Jews . . . . in to him. These . . . . and they heard
the mighty works. . . . . They marvelled . . . . Amphion
(= Aphphia of the Acts of Titus) . . . . saying . . . . in
. . . . Chrysippus . . . . devil with him . . . . many
. . . . When Paul came . . . . he said: He . . . .
God and will not be an evil spirit (?) . . . . in (?) Amphion
. . . . through the evil spirit . . . . without any one's
having . . . . she said to him: Save me that I die not.
And while the multitude . . . . then arose the other (?) evil
spirit . . . . And forthwith the devils fled away. And when
the multitude saw this, by the power of God, they praised him
who had (given such power) unto Paul.

And there was there one by name ... rimus, who had a son born to him which was dumb.

On the next page is a proper name, Lix (or perhaps Kilix, a Cilician), and later the words, 'I preach the good tidings of the Saviour . . . . Son of God'.

On the next page. Lix perhaps occurs again, and 'Moses'.

The next begins: for that which we say cometh to pass forthwith. Behold we will bring him hither unto thee that he may . . . . thee, to hear *the truth of* thy . . . .

Next page. On God whose desire is come to pass in him, this is the wise man . . . .

. . . . the Father and he hath sent Jesus Christ.

Next page, turned toward the East. Moses

       . . . . in Syria
       . . . . in Cyrene

.   .   .   .

      Again I say unto you . . . .
I, that do the works . . . .

.   .   .   .

      that a man is not *justified by the Law*, but that he is justified *by the* works of righteousness, and he . . . .

Next page has the words 'liberty', 'and the yoke', 'all flesh'; *and*, 'and every one confess that Jesus Christ is the glory of the Father'.

Next page, lower part: is not water in him, but . . . . being water, I am not hungry but I am thirsty; I am not . . . . but not to . . . . to suffer *them*, to be (devoured) by wild beasts, not to be able . . . . from the earth, but not to suffer them to be burnt by the fire, are these things of the present age testified, he which was a persecutor . . . .

Next page, lower part, (Cle)anthes.

.   .   .   .

the law of God which is called . . . . who walketh here before them, hath he not followed us throughout all the cities. . . . . And when . . . . he turned himself toward the East after this (*after two lines*) such words, neither preacheth he as thou preachest them, O Paul, that thou mayest not . . . .

Next page begins: Thou art in the presence (sight, face) of Jerusalem, but I trust in the Lord that thou wilt . . . .

The name 'Saul' is almost certain some lines later.

Next page begins: whom they crucified.

And at the end: raised up our flesh.

Next page, 7th line, For since the day when . . . . persecuted the apostles which were (with me? *sc.* Peter) out of Jerusalem, I *hid* myself that I might have comfort, and we nourish *them which* stand, *through* the word according to the promise (?) of his grace. I have fallen into many troubles and have

subjected myself to the law, as *for* your *sakes*. But *I thought* by
night and by day in my *trouble* on *Jesus Christ*, waiting for him
as a lamb . . . . when they crucified him he did not
. . . . did not resist . . . . was not troubled.

The above may be a speech of Peter. We have seen some indication
that Paul is now at Jerusalem, and the conjecture is that a dialogue
between him and Peter occurred in this place.

The next page undoubtedly mentions Peter.
Line 1 has 'Paul', line 3, 'twelve (?) shepherds'.
Line 5, through Paul. But . . . . was troubled because
of the questioning (examination) that (was come) upon Peter
. . . . and he cried out, saying: *Verily*, God is one, and there
is no God beside him: one also *is Jesus* Christ his Son, whom we
. . . . this, whom thou preachest, did we crucify, whom
. . . . expect in great glory, but ye say that he is God and
Judge of the living and *the dead*, the King of the ages, for the
. . . . in the form of man.

. . . .

VI

Paul is condemned to the mines in an unknown place. Longinus
and Firmilla have a daughter, Frontina, who is to be thrown down
from a rock, and Paul with her. It is my distinct opinion that
Frontina is already dead: her body is to be thus contumeliously
treated because she has become a Christian.

The upper part of the page has Longinus twice in lines 1, 2;
'Paul' in l. 7. Then:

For since . . . . the mine, there hath not . . . . nothing
good hath befallen mine house. And he advised that the men
which were to throw Frontina down, should throw down Paul
also with her, alive. Now Paul knew these things, but he worked
fasting, in great cheerfulness, for two days with the prisoners.
They commanded that on the third day the men . . . . should
bring forth Frontina: and the whole city followed after her.
And Firmilla and Longinus lamented and the soldiers . . . .
But the prisoners carried the bed (bier). And when Paul saw the
great mourning with the daughter and eight . . . .

Next page, line 8. Paul alive with the daughter. But when
Paul had taken the daughter in his arms, he groaned unto the
Lord Jesus Christ because of the sorrow of Firmilla, and cast
himself on his knees in the mire . . . . praying for Frontina
with her in one (a) prayer. In that hour Frontina *rose up*. And
the whole multitude was afraid, and fled. Paul took the hand of
the daughter and led her through the city unto the house of
Longinus, and the whole multitude said with one voice: God
is one, who hath made heaven and earth, who hath granted

the life of the daughter in the presence of Paul. . . . . a loaf.
and he gave thanks to him.

Some lines later.

to Philippi (?).

VII

When he was departed from . . . . and would go ⟨to Philippi⟩.
Now when Paul was come to Philippi . . . . he entered into
the house of . . . . and there was great joy (among the brethren)
and to every one.

On the following page begins the episode of the correspondence with
the Corinthians, which was circulated separately in Syriac, Latin, and
Armenian, and found a place in the Syriac collection of Pauline
epistles (and is commented on with the rest by Ephraem the Syrian),
and in the Armenian Bible. We have it in (*a*) many Armenian MSS.,
(*b*) in Ephraem's commentary—only extant in Armenian, (*c*) in three
Latin MSS., at Milan, Laon, and Paris: as well as in the Coptic MS.,
which is here less fragmentary than in the preceding pages.

We begin with a short narrative, introducing the letter of the
Corinthians to Paul; then follows another short piece of narrative,
extant in Armenian only; then Paul's reply, commonly called the
'Third Epistle to the Corinthians'.

There are various phrases and whole sentences, especially in the
Armenian and the Milan MS. of the Latin, which are absent from the
Coptic and the Laon MS. and are regarded, rightly, as interpolations.
These will be distinguished by small capitals.

The page of the Coptic MS. on which the correspondence begins is
fragmentary at the beginning.

1. 1. the lawless one
1. 2. the reward. They . . . . in
1. 3. a prayer. . . . . every
1. 4. one, and every one (?)
1. 6. Paul . . . . again (*or* together).
1. 7. prayed that *a messenger be sent to Philippi.* For the
Corinthians were in great trouble concerning Paul, that he
would depart out of the world, before it was time. For
there were certain men come to Corinth, Simon and Cleobius,
saying: There is no resurrection of the flesh, but that of the
spirit *only*: and that the body of man is not the creation of God;
and also concerning the world, that God did not create it, and
that God knoweth not the world, and that Jesus Christ was not
crucified, but it was an *appearance* (i. e. but only in appearance),
and that he was not born of Mary, nor of the seed of David.
And in a word, there were many things which they had *taught*
in Corinth, deceiving many other men, (and deceiving also)
themselves. When therefore *the Corinthians* heard that *Paul
was at Philippi*, they sent a letter *unto Paul* to Macedonia *by*
Threptus and Eutychus the deacons. And the letter was after
this manner.

I. 1 Stephanus and the elders (presbyters) that are with him, *even* Daphnus and Eubulus and Theophilus and Zenon, unto Paul THEIR BROTHER ETERNAL greeting in the Lord.

2 There have come unto Corinth two men, Simon and Cleobius, which are overthrowing the faith of many with evil (CORRUPT) words, 3 which do thou prove AND EXAMINE: 4 for we have never heard such words from thee nor from the other apostles: 5 but all that we have received from thee or from them, that do we hold fast. 6 Since therefore the Lord hath had mercy on us, that while thou art still in the flesh we may hear these things again from thee, 7 if it be possible, either come unto us or write unto us. 8 For we believe, according as it hath been revealed unto Theonoë, that the Lord hath delivered thee out of the hand of the lawless one (enemy, *Laon*).

9 Now the things which these men say and teach are these: 10 They say that we must not use the prophets, 11 and that God is not Almighty, 12 and that there shall be no resurrection of the flesh, 13 and that man was not made by God, 14 and that Christ came not down (is not come, *Copt.*) in the flesh, neither was born of Mary, 15 and that the world is not of God, but of the angels.

16 Wherefore, brother, WE PRAY THEE use all diligence to come unto us, that the church of the Corinthians may remain without offence, and the madness of these *men* may be made plain. Farewell ALWAYS in the Lord.

II. 1 The deacons Threptus and Eutyches brought the letter unto Philippi, 2 so that Paul received it, being in bonds because of Stratonice the wife of Apollophanes, AND HE FORGAT HIS BONDS, and was sore afflicted, 3 and cried out, saying: It were better for me to die and to be with the Lord, than to continue in the flesh and to hear such things AND THE CALAMITIES OF FALSE DOCTRINE, so that trouble cometh upon trouble. 4 And over and above this so great affliction I am in bonds and behold these evils whereby the devices of Satan are accomplished. (4 Harnack: may not the priests (intrigues) of Satan anticipate *me* while (*or* after) I suffer (have suffered) fetters for the sake (?) of men.) 5 Paul therefore, in great affliction, wrote a letter, answering *thus*:

III. 1 Paul, a prisoner of Jesus Christ, unto the brethren which are in Corinth, greeting.

2 Being in the midst of many tribulations, I marvel not if the teachings of the evil one run abroad apace. 3 For my Lord Jesus Christ will hasten his coming, and will set at nought (no longer endure the insolence of) them that falsify his words. 4 For I delivered unto you in the beginning the things which I received of the HOLY apostles which were before me, who were at all times with Jesus Christ: 5 namely, that our Lord Jesus Christ was born of Mary WHICH IS of the seed of David ACCORDING TO THE FLESH, the Holy Ghost being sent forth from heaven from the Father unto her BY THE ANGEL GABRIEL, 6 that he

(Jesus) might come down into this world and redeem all flesh by his flesh, and raise us up from the dead in the flesh, like as he hath shown to us *in* himself for an ensample. 7 And because man was formed by his Father, 8 therefore was he sought when he was lost, that he might be quickened by adoption. 9 For to this end did God Almighty who made heaven and earth first send the prophets unto the Jews, that they might be drawn away from their sins. 10 For he designed to save the house of Israel: therefore he conferred a portion of the spirit of Christ upon the prophets and sent them unto the Jews first (*or* unto the first Jews), and they proclaimed the true worship of God for a long space of time. 11 But the prince of iniquity, desiring to be God, laid hands on them and slew them (banished them from God, *Laon MS.*), and bound all flesh by evil lusts (AND THE END OF THE WORLD BY JUDGEMENT DREW NEAR).

12 But God Almighty, who is righteous, would not cast away his own creation, BUT HAD COMPASSION ON THEM FROM HEAVEN, 13 and sent his spirit into Mary IN GALILEE, [14 *Milan MS. and Arm.*: WHO BELIEVED WITH ALL HER HEART AND RECEIVED THE HOLY GHOST IN HER WOMB, THAT JESUS MIGHT COME INTO THE WORLD,] 15 that by that flesh whereby that wicked one had brought in death (had triumphed), by the same he should be shown to be overcome. 16 For by his own body Jesus Christ saved all flesh [AND RESTORED IT UNTO LIFE], 17 that he might show forth the temple of righteousness in his body. 18 In whom (*or* whereby) we are saved (*Milan, Paris*: in whom if we believe we are set free).

19 They therefore (*Paris MS.*; *Arm. has*: Know therefore that. *Laon has*: They therefore who agree with them) are not children of righteousness but children of wrath who reject the wisdom (providence?) of God, saying that the heaven and the earth and all that are in them are not the work of God. 20 THEY THEREFORE ARE CHILDREN OF WRATH, for cursed are they, following the teaching of the serpent, 21 whom do ye drive out from you and flee from their doctrine. [*Arm., Milan, Paris*: 22 FOR YE ARE NOT CHILDREN OF DISOBEDIENCE, BUT OF THE WELL-BELOVED CHURCH. 23 THEREFORE IS THE TIME OF THE RESURRECTION PROCLAIMED UNTO ALL.]

24 And as for that which they say, that there is no resurrection of the flesh, they *indeed* shall have no resurrection UNTO LIFE, BUT UNTO JUDGEMENT, 25 because they believe not in him that is risen from the dead, NOT BELIEVING NOR UNDERSTANDING, 26 for they know not, O Corinthians, the seeds of wheat or of other seeds (grain), how they are cast bare into the earth and are corrupted and rise again by the will of God with bodies, and clothed.[1] 27 And not only that [body] which is cast in riseth again, but manifold more blessing itself [i. e. fertile and prosper-

---

[1] 26 sqq. The influence not only of 1 Cor. xv but of the Apocalypse of Peter is visible here.

ing]. 28 And if we must not take an example from seeds ONLY, BUT FROM MORE NOBLE BODIES, 29 ye know how Jonas the son of Amathi, when he would not preach to them of Nineve, BUT FLED, was swallowed by the sea-monster; 30 and after three days and three nights God heard the prayer of Jonas out of the lowest hell, and no part of him was consumed, not even an hair nor an eyelash. 31 How much more, O YE OF LITTLE FAITH, shall he raise up you that have believed in Christ Jesus, like as he himself arose. 32 Likewise also a dead man was cast upon the bones of the prophet Helisaeus by the children of Israel, and he arose, both body and soul and bones and spirit (*Laon*: arose in his body); how much more shall ye which have been cast upon the body and bones and spirit of the Lord [*Milan, Paris*: how much more, O ye of little faith, shall ye which have been cast *on him*] arise again in that day having your flesh whole, EVEN AS HE AROSE? [33 *Arm.*, *Milan, Paris* : LIKEWISE ALSO CONCERNING THE PROPHET HELIAS : HE RAISED UP THE WIDOW'S SON FROM DEATH : HOW MUCH MORE SHALL THE LORD JESUS RAISE YOU UP FROM DEATH AT THE SOUND OF THE TRUMPET, IN THE TWINKLING OF AN EYE ? FOR HE HATH SHOWED US AN ENSAMPLE IN HIS OWN BODY.]

34 If, then, ye receive any other *doctrine*, GOD SHALL BE WITNESS AGAINST YOU; AND let no man trouble me, 35 for I bear these bonds that I may win Christ, and I therefore bear his marks in my body that I may attain unto the resurrection of the dead. 36 And whoso receiveth (abideth in) the rule which he hath received by the blessed prophets and the holy gospel, shall receive a recompense from the Lord, AND WHEN HE RISETH FROM THE DEAD SHALL OBTAIN ETERNAL LIFE. 37 But whoso transgresseth these things, with him is the fire, and with them that walk in like manner (*Milan, Paris*: with them that go before in the same way, WHO ARE MEN WITHOUT GOD), 38 which are a generation of vipers, 39 whom do ye reject in the power of the Lord, 40 and peace, GRACE, AND LOVE shall be with you.

[*Laon adds*: This I found in an old book, entitled the third to the Corinthians, though it is not in the Canon.]

VIII
AT EPHESUS

This episode is not traceable in the Coptic MS. but it undoubtedly formed part of the Acts, though its place is uncertain. It is preserved in an allusion by Hippolytus (early third century) and in an abstract by Nicephorus Callisti (fourteenth century) in his *Ecclesiastical History* (ii. 25). There is also a sentence in the Acts of Titus:

'They departed from Crete and came to Asia: and at Ephesus twelve thousand believed at the teaching of the holy Paul: there also he fought with beasts, being thrown to a lion.'

HIPPOLYTUS in his *Commentary on Daniel*, iii. 29, says:

For if we believe that when Paul was condemned to the beasts the lion that was set upon him lay down at his feet and licked him, how shall we not believe that which happened in the case of Daniel?

NICEPHORUS:

Now they who drew up the travels of Paul have related that he did many other things, and among them this, *which befell when he was at Ephesus*. Hieronymus being governor, Paul used liberty of speech, and he (Hieronymus) said that he (Paul) was able to speak well, but that this was not the time for such words. But the people of the city, fiercely enraged, put Paul's feet into irons, and shut him up in the prison, till he should be exposed as a prey to the lions. But Eubula and Artemilla, wives of eminent men among the Ephesians, being his attached disciples, and visiting him by night, desired the grace of the divine washing. And by God's power, with angels to escort them and enlighten the gloom of night with the excess of the brightness that was in them, Paul, loosed from his iron fetters, went to the sea-shore and initiated them into holy baptism, and returning to his bonds without any of those in care of the prison perceiving it, was reserved as a prey for the lions.

A lion, then, of huge size and unmatched strength was let loose upon him, and it ran to him in the stadium and lay down at his feet. And when many other savage beasts, too, were let loose, it was permitted to none of them to touch the holy body, standing like a statue in prayer. At this juncture a violent and vast hailstorm poured down all at once with a great rush, and shattered the heads of many men and beasts as well, and shore off the ear of Hieronymus himself. And thereafter, with his followers, he came to the God of Paul and received the baptism of salvation. But the lion escaped to the mountains.

And thence Paul sailed to Macedonia and Greece, and thereafter through Macedonia came to Troas and to Miletus, and from there set out for Jerusalem.

Now it is not surprising that Luke has not narrated this fight with the beasts along with the other Acts: for it is not permitted to entertain doubt because (*or* seeing that) John alone of the evangelists has told of the raising of Lazarus: for we know that not every one writes, believes, or knows everything, but according as the Lord has imparted to each, as the spirit divides to each, so does he perceive and believe and write spiritually the things of the spirit.

Hippolytus is a voucher for the early date of the story, and Nicephorus for its source. It will be recognized, moreover, at once as being quite in the manner of our author. The anger of the Ephesians, it cannot be doubted, was roused by Paul's preaching of continence, to which Eubula and Artemilla had become converts. The episode is really little more than a repetition of *Thecla*, with Paul for the principal figure.

IX

FRAGMENTS: SCENES OF FAREWELL

(Paul speaking)   . . . . thanksgiving (?)
The grace of the Lord will walk with me until I have fulfilled all the dispensations which shall come upon me with patience. But they were sorrowful, and fasted. And Cleobius was in the Spirit and said unto them: Brethren, (the Lord) will suffer Paul to fulfil every dispensation and thereafter will suffer him to go up (to Jerusalem). But thereafter shall be . . . . in much instruction and knowledge and sowing of the word, so that men shall envy him, and so he shall depart out of this world. But when *Paul* and the brethren heard this, they lifted up their voices, saying:

Next page, first extant line, 'beheld'. *Second,* 'shall say'. *Third,* But the Spirit came upon Myrte *so that* she said unto them: Brethren . . . . and look upon this sign, that ye . . . . For Paul the servant of the Lord shall save many in Rome, so that of them shall be no number, and he will manifest himself more than all the faithful. Thereafter shall . . . . of the Lord Jesus Christ come . . . . a great grace is . . . . at Rome. And this is the manner wherein *the Spirit spake* unto Myrte. *And* every one took the bread, and they were in joy, according to the custom of the fast, through . . . . and the psalms of David and . . . . he rejoiced.

On the next page the only significant words are 'to Rome'; 'the brethren'; 'grieved'; 'took the *bread*'; 'praised the Lord'; 'were very sorrowful'.

The next has ends of lines: 'the Lord'; 'risen'; 'Jesus'; 'Paul *said* to him'. The last is 'he (or they) greeted'.

Two more pages have nothing of moment. The next is concerned with the Martyrdom.

X

THE MARTYRDOM

This, preserved separately to be read on the day of Commemoration, exists in two Greek copies, an incomplete Latin version, and versions in Syriac, Coptic, Ethiopic, Slavonic, besides fragments in our Coptic MS.

I. Now there were awaiting Paul at Rome Luke from Galatia (Gaul, *Gk.*) and Titus from Dalmatia: whom when Paul saw he was glad: and hired a grange outside Rome, wherein with the brethren he taught the word of truth, and he became noised abroad and many souls were added unto the Lord, so that there was a rumour throughout all Rome, and much people came unto him from the household of Caesar, believing, and there was great joy.

And a certain Patroclus, a cup-bearer of Caesar, came at even unto the grange, and not being able because of the press to enter in to Paul, he sat in a high window and listened to him teaching the word of God. But whereas the evil devil envied the love of the brethren, Patroclus fell down from the window and died, and forthwith it was told unto Nero.

But Paul perceiving it by the spirit said: Men and brethren, the evil one hath gained occasion to tempt you: go out of the house and ye shall find a lad fallen from the height and now ready to give up the ghost; take him up and bring him hither to me. And they went and brought him; and when the people saw it they were troubled. But Paul said: Now, brethren, let your faith appear; come all of you and let us weep unto our Lord Jesus Christ, that this lad may live and we continue in quietness. And when all had lamented, the lad received his spirit again, and they set him on a beast and sent him back alive, together with the rest that were of Caesar's household.

II. But Nero, when he heard of the death of Patroclus, was sore grieved, and when he came in from the bath he commanded another to be set over the wine. But his servants told him, saying: Caesar, Patroclus liveth and standeth at the table. And Caesar, hearing that Patroclus lived, was affrighted and would not go in. But when he went in, he saw Patroclus, and was beside himself, and said: Patroclus, livest thou? And he said: I live, Caesar. And he said: Who is he that made thee to live? And the lad, full of the mind of faith, said: Christ Jesus, the king of the ages. And Caesar was troubled and said: Shall he, then, be king of the ages and overthrow all kingdoms? Patroclus saith unto him: Yea, he overthroweth all kingdoms and he alone shall be for ever, and there shall be no kingdom that shall escape him. And he smote him on the face and said: Patroclus, art thou also a soldier of that king? And he said: Yea, Lord Caesar, for he raised me when I was dead. And Barsabas Justus of the broad feet, and Urion the Cappadocian, and Festus the Galatian, Caesar's chief men, said: We also are soldiers of the king of the ages. And he shut them up in prison, having grievously tormented them, whom he loved much, and commanded the soldiers of the great king to be sought out, and set forth a decree to this effect, that all that were found to be Christians and soldiers of Christ should be slain.

III. And among many others Paul also was brought, bound: unto whom all his fellow-prisoners gave heed; so that Caesar perceived that he was over the camp. And he said to him: Thou that art the great king's man, but my prisoner, how thoughtest thou well to come by stealth into the government of the Romans and levy soldiers out of my province? But Paul, filled with the Holy Ghost, said before them all: O Caesar, not only out of thy province do we levy soldiers, but out of the whole world. For so hath it been ordained unto us, that no man should be refused who wisheth to serve my king. And if it like thee also to serve him (*Lat.* thou wilt not repent thereof: but think not that the wealth, &c., *which seems better*), it is not wealth nor the splendour that is now in this life that shall save thee; but if thou submit and entreat him, thou shalt be saved; for in one day (*or* one day) he shall fight against the world with fire. And when Caesar heard that, he commanded all the prisoners to be burned with fire, but Paul to be beheaded after the law of the Romans.

But Paul kept not silence concerning the word, but communicated with Longus the prefect and Cestus the centurion.

Nero therefore went on (was) (*perhaps add* 'raging') in Rome, slaying many Christians without a hearing, by the working of the evil one; so that the Romans stood before the palace and cried: It sufficeth, Caesar! for the men are our own! thou destroyest the strength of the Romans! Then at that he was persuaded and ceased, and commanded that no man should touch any Christian, until he should learn throughly concerning them.

IV. Then was Paul brought unto him after the decree; and he abode by his word that he should be beheaded. And Paul said: Caesar, it is not for a little space that I live unto my king; and if thou behead me, this will I do: I will arise and show myself unto thee that I am not dead but live unto my Lord Jesus Christ, who cometh to judge the world.

But Longus and Cestus said unto Paul: Whence have ye this king, that ye believe in him and will not change your mind, even unto death? And Paul communicated unto them the word and said: Ye men that are in this ignorance and error, change your mind and be saved from the fire that cometh upon all the world: for we serve not, as ye suppose, a king that cometh from the earth, but from heaven, *even* the living God, who because of the iniquities that are done in this world, cometh as a judge; and blessed is that man who shall believe in him and shall live for ever when he cometh to burn the world and purge it throughly. Then they beseeching him said: We entreat thee, help us, and we will let thee go. But he answered and said: I am not a deserter of Christ, but a lawful soldier of the living God: if I had known that I should die, O Longus and Cestus, I would have done it, but seeing that I live unto God and love myself, I go unto the Lord, to come with him in the glory of his Father. They say unto him: How then shall we live when thou art beheaded?

V. And while they yet spake thus, Nero sent one Parthenius and Pheres to see if Paul were already beheaded; and they found him yet alive. And he called them to him and said: Believe on the living God, which raiseth me and all them that believe on him from the dead. And they said: We go now unto Nero; but when thou diest and risest again, then will we believe on thy God. And as Longus and Cestus entreated him yet more concerning salvation, he saith to them: Come quickly unto my grave in the morning and ye shall find two men praying, Titus and Luke. They shall give you the seal in the Lord.

Then Paul stood with his face to the east and lifted up his hands unto heaven and prayed a long time, and in his prayer he conversed in the Hebrew tongue with the fathers, and *then* stretched forth his neck without speaking. And when the executioner (*speculator*) struck off his head, milk spurted upon the cloak of the soldier. And the soldier and all that were there present when they saw it marvelled and glorified God which had given such glory unto Paul: and they went and told Caesar what was done.

VI. And when he heard it, while he marvelled long and was in perplexity, Paul came about the ninth hour, when many philosophers and the centurion were standing with Caesar, and stood before them all and said: Caesar, behold, I, Paul, the soldier of God, am not dead, but live in my God. But unto thee shall many evils befall and great punishment, thou wretched man, because thou hast shed unjustly the blood of the righteous, not many days hence. And having so said Paul departed from him. But Nero hearing it and being greatly troubled commanded the prisoners to be loosed, and Patroclus also and Barsabas and them that were with him.

VII. And as Paul charged them, Longus and Cestus the centurion went early in the morning and approached with fear unto the grave of Paul. And when they were come thither they saw two men praying, and Paul betwixt them, so that they beholding the wondrous marvel were amazed, but Titus and Luke being stricken with the fear of man when they saw Longus and Cestus coming toward them, turned to flight. But they pursued after them, saying: We pursue you not for death but for life, that ye may give it unto us, as Paul promised us, whom we saw just now standing betwixt you and praying. And when they heard that, Titus and Luke rejoiced and gave them the seal in the Lord, glorifying the God and Father of our Lord Jesus Christ (*Copt.* and glorified the Lord Jesus Christ and all the saints).

Unto whom be glory world without end. Amen.

The Coptic MS. has a colophon: The Acts of Paul according to the Apostle.

XI

UNPLACED AND UNCERTAIN FRAGMENTS

Among the very few ancient quotations of the Acts of Paul are two short phrases cited by Origen.

(*a*) *On First Principles*, i. 2, 3 : wherefore also that word seems to me to be truly said, which is written in the Acts of Paul: 'He is the word, a living creature.' But John in the beginning of his Gospel says more exaltedly and more excellently, &c.

(*b*) *On John*, xx. 12. But if any one likes to accept that which is recorded in the Acts of Paul as spoken by the Saviour: 'Again am I about to be crucified.'

Both phrases, but the second especially, have been thought by some to come from a context relating to the death of Peter. (*a*) is compared with Peter's speech at the cross; (*b*) appears in slightly different forms in all the Passions of Peter as Christ's answer to Peter when he is escaping from Rome. Whither goest thou Lord? (or, What doest thou here?) 'I come to be crucified again.' The inference is that an account of the martyrdom of Peter formed part of the Acts of Paul. But this I find very difficult to accept, though I acknowledge it to be possible, seeing that the author of these Acts evidently placed the martyrdom of Paul after that of Peter, and, to judge from the Acts of Peter, some little time (perhaps a whole year) after.

A probable fragment is a quotation made by Clement of Alexandria (*Strom.* vi. 5: ed. Stähelin, ii. 452).

He has been quoting the Preaching of Peter, and continues:

But *the proposition* that, just as God willed the Jews to be saved by giving them the prophets, so he raised up the most approved of the Greeks to be prophets suited to their language, according as they were capable of receiving the benefit from God, and distinguished them from the ruck of men—*this*, in addition to the Preaching of Peter, the apostle Paul will show when he says:

'Take also the Greek books, take knowledge of the Sibyl, how she declares one God, and things to come, take and read Hystaspes, and ye will find the Son of God described far more openly and plainly, and how many kings will make war against the Christ, hating him and those that bear his name, and his faithful ones: and his patience and his coming *again*.' And then in one word he asks of us: 'And the whole world and all that is in it, whose are they? are they not God's?' Therefore is it that Peter says (another quotation from the Preaching follows).

It has been usual to assume that these sentences are from a Preaching of Paul: but of such a book the very existence is doubtful. The passages supposed to establish it shall be given.

One is in Pseudo-Cyprian *de rebaptismate* (third century):

Now of this spurious, nay fatal, baptism an especial supporter is a book forged by these same heretics to favour this error, which is entitled 'the Preaching of Paul'. In which book, contrary to every scripture, you will find Christ, who alone never sinned at all, both confessing his own sin and being compelled almost against his will by his mother Mary to receive the baptism of John; and further, that when he was baptized, fire appeared upon the water, which is recorded in no gospel. And that after so long a time Peter and Paul (after their conference (comparison) on the gospel at Jerusalem, after their common counsels, their dispute, their settling of a course of action (?)) at last met in Rome as if then first known to each other: and some other things of the kind absurdly and disgracefully concocted, all of which you will find heaped together in that book.

The author, it may be noted, is wrong in his statement that the baptism story was not recorded in any Gospel: it was found, wholly or partly, in the Gospel according to the Hebrews and the Ebionite Gospel.

The other is in Lactantius' *Institutes,* iv. 21. 2 :

(Jesus) also revealed all things to come (to his disciples) which Peter and Paul preached at Rome, and that preaching continues in writing, for a memorial. Wherein, with many other wondrous things, they said that this too would come to pass, that after a little time God would send a king who would attack the Jews and lay their cities even with the ground and besiege them till they were exhausted with hunger and thirst: then would they feed on the bodies of their own kin, and devour one another: finally, that they would be taken and fall into the enemies' hands and see their wives maltreated before their faces, their maidens outraged and prostituted, their boys carried off, their infants dashed to the earth, all, in a word, wasted by fire and sword, and *themselves* captive and banished for ever from their land, because they rejoiced against the beloved and approved Son of God.

No other trace of a book called a Preaching of Paul remains, and, as I say, its existence is doubtful.

Commodian, the strange Christian poet, who according to some critics, was an African of the third century, and according to others lived in Gaul in the fifth, has in his Carmen Apologeticum (624 sqq.) allusions to the Acts of Peter and of Paul. Speaking of God's power, he says:

And whatever he willeth he can do: making dumb things to speak; he made Balaam's ass speak to him when he beat it; and a dog to say to Simon: 'Thou art called for by Peter!' For Paul when he preached, he caused dumb persons (*or perhaps* mules) to speak of him [1]: he made a lion speak to the people with God-given voice. Lastly, a thing which our nature does not permit—he made an infant five months old speak in public.

[1] The manuscript has *multi*, which may be for *muti* or *muli*. Or, keeping *multi* (as Zahn), we should translate, 'For Paul when he

ACTS OF PAUL 299

The incidents of the dog and of the child are from the Acts of Peter (only there the child is seven months old): but the lion and the dumb people (or mules) are not; and it seems that the lion is certainly from the Acts of Paul.[1] Perhaps it was the Ephesian lion. In the Ethiopic life of Paul we do find a talking lion.

Lastly, in John of Salisbury's *Policraticus* (finished in 1156) is this passage which, whatever its source, preserves a record of an apocryphal speech of Paul.

iv. 9. He has told the stories of the self-sacrifice of Codrus and Lycurgus, which he gets from the historian Justin. Then he continues:

I make use of these examples the more readily because I find that the apostle Paul when preaching to the Athenians made use of them also. That excellent preacher strove so to impress on their minds Jesus Christ and him crucified, that he might show by the example of heathens how the release of many came about through the shame of the cross. And this, he argued, could not happen save by the blood of the just, and of those who bore rule over the people. Further, no one could be found capable of freeing all, both Jews and Gentiles, save he unto whom the heathen are given for an inheritance, and the utmost parts of the earth assigned for his possession. And such a one he said could be no other than the Son of God Almighty, since no one but God has subjected to himself all nations and lands. As, then, he proclaimed the shame of the cross in such a way as gradually to purge away the foolishness of the heathen, little by little he raised the word of faith and the language of his preaching, up to the Word of God, the wisdom of God, and the very throne of the divine majesty: and, lest the power of the gospel should seem mean in the weakness of the flesh by dint of the slanders of Jews and the folly of heathens, he set forth the works of the crucified, which were confirmed by the witness of common report; since it was plain to all that none but God could do such things. But as report often falsifies, in both directions, report was assisted by the fact that *Christ's* disciples did even greater works, seeing that by the shadow of a disciple (Peter) the sick were healed of every kind of disease. What more? The ingenuities of an Aristotle, the subtleties of a Chrysippus, the gins of all the philosophers were defeated by the rising of one who had been dead. (This last sentence is borrowed from Jerome (Ep. (to Pammachius) 57 or 34.)

preached, in order that many might speak (*or* learn) of him, God made a lion ', &c. The miracle was done in order to attract the attention of ' many ' hearers.

[1] Jerome, quoting Tertullian, but adding some details to what he says (the source of them is doubtful), speaks of 'that whole fable about the baptized lion'. It reminds us of Commodian's words: but Jerome is a bad witness about apocryphal books, which he despises and reviles.

ACTS OF PETER

Written, probably by a resident in Asia Minor (he does not know much about Rome), not later than A. D. 200, in Greek. The author has read the Acts of John very carefully, and modelled his language upon them. However, he was not so unorthodox as Leucius, though his language about the Person of our Lord (ch. xx) has rather suspicious resemblances to that of the Acts of John.

The length of the book as given by the Stichometry of Nicephorus was 2,750 lines—fifty lines less than the canonical Acts. The portions we have may be about the length of St. Mark's Gospel; and about 1,000 lines may be wanting. Such is Zahn's estimate.

We have :

1. A short episode in Coptic.

2. A large portion in Latin preserved in a single manuscript of the seventh century at Vercelli : often called the Vercelli Acts. It includes the martyrdom.

3. The martyrdom, preserved separately, in two good Greek copies, in Latin, and in many versions—Coptic, Slavonic, Syriac, Armenian, Arabic, Ethiopic.

Also:

One or two important quotations from lost portions; a small fragment of the original in a papyrus; certain passages—speeches of Peter—transferred by an unscrupulous writer to the Life of St. Abercius of Hierapolis.[1]

A Latin paraphrase of the martyrdom, attributed to Linus, Peter's successor in the bishopric of Rome, was made from the Greek, and is occasionally useful.

I

THE COPTIC FRAGMENT

This is preserved separately, in an early papyrus manuscript (fourth–fifth century) now at Berlin; the other contents of it are Gnostic writings which have not yet been published. I follow C. Schmidt's rendering of it. It has a title at the end:

The Act of Peter

On the first day of the week, that is, on the Lord's day, a multitude gathered together, and they brought unto Peter many sick that he might heal them. And one of the multitude adventured to say unto Peter: Lo, Peter, in our presence thou hast made many blind to see and the deaf to hear and the lame to walk, and hast succoured the weak and given them strength: but wherefore hast thou not succoured thy daughter, the virgin, which grew up beautiful and hath believed in the name of God ? For behold, her one side is wholly palsied, and she lieth there

[1] chs. xxxviii, xxxix have also been extensively used in a prayer before the oblation in the Syrian (?) Testament of the Lord.

stretched out in the corner helpless. We see them that have
been healed by thee: thine own daughter thou hast neglected.
But Peter smiled and said unto him: My son, it is manifest
unto God alone wherefore her body is not whole. Know then
that God is not weak nor powerless to grant his gift unto my
daughter: but that thy soul may be convinced, and they that
are here present may the more believe—then he looked unto his
daughter and said to her: Raise thyself up from thy place,
without any helping thee save Jesus only, and walk whole before
all these, and come unto me. And she arose and came to him;
and the multitude rejoiced at that which was come to pass. Then
said Peter unto them: Behold, your heart is convinced that God
is not without strength concerning all things that we ask of him.
Then they rejoiced yet more and praised God. And Peter said to
his daughter: Go unto thy place, and lay thee down and be again
in thine infirmity, for this is expedient for me and for thee. And
the maiden went back and lay down in her place and was as
beforetime: and the whole multitude wept, and entreated Peter
to make her whole.

But Peter said unto them: As the Lord liveth, this is expedient
for her and for me. For on the day when she was born unto me
I saw a vision, and the Lord said unto me: Peter, this day is
a great temptation born unto thee, for this *daughter* will bring
hurt unto many souls if her body continue whole. But I thought
that the vision did mock me.

Now when the maiden was ten years old, a stumbling-block
was prepared for many by reason of her. And an exceeding rich
man, by name Ptolemaeus, when he had seen the maiden with
her mother bathing, sent unto her to take her to wife; *but* her
mother consented not. And he sent oft-times to her, and could
not wait.

[Here a leaf is lost: the sense, however, is not hard to supply.
Augustine speaks (quoting Apocryphal Acts) of a daughter of Peter
struck with palsy *at the prayer of her father.*
Ptolemaeus, unable to win the maiden by fair means, comes and
carries her off. Peter hears of it and prays God to protect her. His
prayer is heard. She is struck with palsy on one side of her body.
Then the text resumes.]

The servants of Ptolemaeus brought the maiden and laid her
down before the door of the house and departed.
But when I perceived it, I and her mother, we went down and
found the maiden, that one whole side of her body from her toes
even to her head was palsied and withered: *and* we bore her
away, praising the Lord which had preserved his handmaid from
defilement and shame and (corruption?). This is the cause of
the matter, why the maiden continueth so unto this day.
Now, then, it is fitting for you to know the end of Ptolemaeus.
He went home and sorrowed night and day over that which had

befallen him, and by reason of the many tears which he shed, he became blind. And when he had resolved to rise up and hang himself, lo, about the ninth hour of the day, he saw a great light which enlightened the whole house, and heard a voice saying unto him: Ptolemaeus, God hath not given thee the vessels for corruption and shame, and yet more doth it not become thee which hast believed in me to defile my virgin, whom thou shalt know as thy sister, even as if I were unto you both one spirit (*sic*). But rise up and go quickly unto the house of the apostle Peter, and thou shalt see my glory; he shall make known unto thee what thou must do.

But Ptolemaeus was not negligent, and bade his servants show him the way and bring him unto me. And when they were come to me, he told me all that had befallen him by the power of our Lord Jesus Christ. Then did he see with the eyes of his flesh, and with the eyes of his soul, and much people believed (hoped) in Christ: and he did them good and gave them the gift of God.

Thereafter Ptolemaeus died, departing out of this life, and went unto his Lord: and when he *made* his will he bequeathed a piece of land in the name of my daughter, because through her he had believed in God and was made whole. But I unto whom the disposition thereof fell, exercised it with great carefulness: I sold the land, and God alone knoweth neither I nor my daughter (received the price). I sold the land and kept nought back of the price, but gave all the money unto the poor.

Know therefore, thou servant of Jesus Christ, that God directeth (?) them that are his, and prepareth good for every one of them, although we think that God hath forgotten us. Therefore now, brethren, let us be sorrowful and watch and pray, and so shall the goodness of God look upon us, whereon we wait.

And yet further discourse did Peter hold before them all, and glorified the name of Christ the Lord and gave them all of the bread: and when he had distributed it, he rose up and went unto his house.

The scene of this episode is probably Jerusalem. The subject of it was often used by later writers, most notably, perhaps, by the author of the late Acts of SS. Nereus and Achilleus (fifth or sixth century), who gives the daughter a name, Petronilla, which has passed into Kalendars, and as Perronelle, Pernel, or Parnell has become familiar.

A few critics have questioned whether this piece really belongs to the Acts of Peter: but the weight of probability and of opinion is against them. Nothing can be plainer than that it is an extract from a larger book, and that it is ancient (the manuscript may be of the fourth century). Moreover, Augustine, in dealing with apocryphal Acts, alludes to the story contained in it. What other large book of ancient date dealing with Peter's doings can we imagine save the Acts?

II
THE GARDENER'S DAUGHTER

Augustine (*Against Adimantus*, xvii. 5), says to his Manichaean opponent : the story of Peter killing Ananias and Sapphira by a word is very stupidly blamed by those who in the apocryphal Acts read and admire both the incident I mentioned about the apostle Thomas (the death of the cup-bearer at the feast in his Acts) ' and that the daughter of Peter himself was stricken with palsy at the prayer of her father, and that the daughter of a gardener died at the prayer of Peter. Their answer is that it was expedient for them, that the one should be disabled by palsy and the other should die : but they do not deny that it happened at the prayer of the apostle '.

This allusion to the gardener's daughter remained a puzzle until lately. But a passage in the Epistle of Titus (already quoted) tells us the substance of the story.

A certain gardener had a daughter, a virgin, her father's only child: he begged Peter to pray for her. Upon his request, the apostle answered him that the Lord would give her that which was useful for her soul. Immediately the girl fell dead.

O worthy gain and suitable to God, to escape the insolence of the flesh and mortify the boastfulness of the blood ! But that old man, faithless, and not knowing the greatness of the heavenly favour, ignorant of the divine benefit, entreated Peter that his only daughter might be raised again. And when she was raised, not many days after, †as it might be to-day†, the slave of a believer who lodged in the house ran upon her and ruined the girl, and both of them disappeared.

This was evidently a contrast to the story of Peter's daughter, and probably followed immediately upon it in the Acts. There is another sentence appropriate to the situation, which Dom de Bruyne found in a Cambrai MS. of the thirteenth century—a collection of apophthegms—and printed with the extracts from the Epistle of Titus.

That the dead are not to be mourned overmuch, Peter, speaking to one who lamented without patience the loss of his daughter, said: So many assaults of the devil, so many warrings of the body, so many disasters of the world hath she escaped, and thou sheddest tears as if thou knewest not what thou sufferest in thyself (what *good* hath befallen thee).

This might very well be part of Peter's address to the bereaved gardener.

III

THE VERCELLI ACTS

I. At the time when Paul was sojourning in Rome and confirming many in the faith, it came also to pass that one by name Candida, the wife of Quartus that was over the prisons, heard Paul and paid heed to his words and believed. And when she had instructed her husband also and he believed, Quartus suffered Paul to go whither he would away from the city: to whom Paul said: If it be the will of God, he will reveal it unto me. And after Paul had fasted three days and asked of the Lord that which should be profitable for him, he saw a vision, even the Lord saying unto him: Arise, Paul, and become a physician in thy body (i. e. by going thither in person) to them that are in Spain.

He therefore, having related to the brethren what God had commanded, nothing doubting, prepared himself to set forth from the city. But when Paul was about to depart, there was great weeping throughout all the brotherhood, because they thought that they should see Paul no more, so that they even rent their clothes. For they had in mind also how that Paul had oftentimes contended with the doctors of the Jews and confuted them, *saying*: Christ, upon whom your fathers laid hands, abolished their sabbaths and fasts and holy-days and circumcision, and the doctrines of men and the rest of the traditions he did abolish. But the brethren lamented (and adjured) Paul by the coming of our Lord Jesus Christ, that he should not be absent above a year, saying: We know thy love for thy brethren; forget not us when thou art come thither, neither begin to forsake us, as little children without a mother. And when they besought him long with tears, there came a sound from heaven, and a great voice saying: Paul the servant of God is chosen to minister all the days of his life: by the hands of Nero the ungodly and wicked man shall he be perfected before your eyes. And a very great fear fell upon the brethren because of the voice which came from heaven : and they were confirmed yet more *in the faith*.

II. Now they brought unto Paul bread and water for the sacrifice, that he might make prayer and distribute it to every one. Among whom it befell that a woman named Rufina desired, she also, to receive the Eucharist at the hands of Paul: to whom Paul, filled with the spirit of God, said as she drew near: Rufina, thou comest not worthily unto the altar of God, arising from beside one that is not thine husband but an adulterer, and assayest to receive the Eucharist of God.[1] For behold Satan shall trouble thine heart and cast thee down in the sight of all

---

[1] This incident is quoted in the Epistle of Titus.

them that believe in the Lord, that they which see and believe may
know that they have believed in the living God, the searcher of
hearts. But if thou repent of thine act, he is faithful that is able
to blot out thy sin and set thee free from this sin: but if thou
repent not, while thou art yet in the body, devouring fire and
outer darkness shall receive thee for ever. And immediately
Rufina fell down, being stricken with palsy (?) from her head
unto the nails of her feet, and she had no power to speak (given
her) for her tongue was bound. And [1] when both they that
believed (in the faith) and the neophytes saw it, they beat their
breasts, remembering their old sins, and mourned and said: We
know not if God will forgive the former sins which we have
committed. Then Paul called for silence and said: Men and
brethren which now have begun to believe on Christ, if ye continue
not in your former works of the tradition of your fathers, and
keep yourselves from all guile and wrath and fierceness and
adultery and defilement, and from pride and envy and contempt
and enmity, Jesus the living God will forgive you that ye did in
ignorance. Wherefore, ye servants of God, arm yourselves every
one in your inner man with peace, patience, gentleness, faith,
charity, knowledge, wisdom, love of the brethren, hospitality,
mercy, abstinence, chastity, kindness, justice: then shall ye have
for your guide everlastingly the first-begotten of all creation, and
shall have strength in peace with our Lord. And when they had
heard these things of Paul, they besought him to pray for them.
And Paul lifted up his voice and said: O eternal God, God of
the heavens, God of unspeakable majesty (divinity), who hast
stablished all things by thy word, who hast bound upon all the
world the chain of thy grace, Father of thine holy Son Jesus
Christ, we together pray thee through thy Son Jesus Christ,
strengthen the souls which were before unbelieving but now are
faithful. Once I was a blasphemer, now I am blasphemed;
once I was a persecutor, now do I suffer persecution of others;
once I was the enemy of Christ, now I pray that I may be his
friend: for I trust in his promise and in his mercy; I account
myself faithful and that I have received forgiveness of my
former sins. Wherefore I exhort you also, brethren, to believe
in the Lord the Father Almighty, and to put all your trust
in our Lord Jesus Christ his Son, believing in him, and no man
shall be able to uproot you from his promise. Bow your
knees therefore together and commend me unto the Lord, who
am about to set forth unto another nation, that his grace may
go before me and dispose my journey aright, that he may receive
his vessels holy and believing, that *they*, giving thanks for my
preaching of the word of the Lord, may be well grounded *in the
faith.* But the brethren wept long and prayed unto the Lord
with Paul, saying: Be thou, Lord Jesus Christ, with Paul and

[1] This passage and Paul's speech are used in the Life of St. Abercius.

restore him unto us whole: for we know our weakness which is in us even to this day.

III. And a great multitude of women were kneeling and praying and beseeching Paul; and they kissed his feet and accompanied him unto the harbour. But Dionysius and Balbus, of Asia, knights of Rome, and illustrious men, and a senator by name Demetrius abode by Paul on his right hand and said: Paul, I would desire to leave the city if I were not a magistrate, that I might not depart from thee. Also from Caesar's house Cleobius and Iphitus and Lysimachus and Aristaeus and two matrons Berenice and Philostrate, with Narcissus the presbyter [after they had] accompanied him to the harbour: but whereas a storm of the sea came on, he (Narcissus ?) sent the brethren back to Rome, that if any ·would, he might come down and hear Paul until he set sail: and hearing that, the brethren went up unto the city. And when they told the brethren that had remained in the city, and the report was spread abroad, some on beasts, and some on foot, and others by way of the Tiber came down to the harbour, and were confirmed in the faith for three days, and on the fourth day until the fifth hour, praying together with Paul, and making the offering: and they put all that was needful on the ship and delivered him two young men, believers, to sail with him, and bade him farewell in the Lord and returned to Rome.

There has been great dispute about these three chapters, whether they are not an excerpt from the Acts of Paul, or whether they are an addition made by the writer of the Greek original of the Vercelli Acts.

If they are from the Acts of Paul, it means that in those Acts Paul was represented as visiting Rome twice, and going to Spain between the visits. Evidently, if this was so, he did not return straight from Spain to Rome: at least the Coptic gives no indication that the prophecies of Cleobius and Myrte were uttered in Spain.

The question is a difficult one. All allow that the writer of the Acts of Peter knew and used the Acts of Paul: but there is strong opposition to the idea that *Paul* related two visits to Rome.

The writer of *Paul* obviously knew the canonical Acts very well and obviously took great liberties with them. Did he go so far, one wonders, as to suppress and ignore the whole story of the trial before Felix and the shipwreck ? If he told of but one visit to Rome—the final one—it appears that he did: for the conditions described in the Martyrdom—Paul quite free and martyred very shortly after his arrival—are totally irreconcilable with Luke (Paul arriving in custody and living two years at least in the city).

IV. Now after a few days there was a great commotion in the midst of the church, for *some* said that they had seen wonderful *works done* by a certain man whose name was Simon, and that he was at Aricia, and they added further that he said he was a great power of God and without God he did nothing. Is not this the Christ? but we believe in him whom Paul preached

unto us; for by him have we seen the dead raised, and men
delivered from divers infirmities: †but this man seeketh contention, we know it† (or, but what this contention is, we know not)
for there is no small stir made among us. Perchance also he will
now enter into Rome ; for yesterday they besought him with
great acclamations, saying unto him: Thou art God in Italy,
thou art the saviour of the Romans: haste quickly unto Rome.
But he spake to the people with a shrill voice, saying: To-morrow
about the seventh hour ye shall see me fly over the gate of the
city in the form (habit) wherein ye now see me speaking unto you.
Therefore, brethren, if it seem good unto you, let us go and await
carefully the issue of the matter.

They all therefore ran together and came unto the gate.
And when it was the seventh hour, behold suddenly a dust was
seen in the sky afar off, like a smoke shining with rays stretching
far *from it*. And when he drew near to the gate, suddenly he
was not seen: and thereafter he appeared, standing in the midst
of the people; whom they all worshipped, and took knowledge
that he was the same that was seen of them the day before.

And the brethren were not a little offended among themselves,
seeing, moreover, that Paul was not at Rome, neither Timotheus
nor Barnabas, for they had been sent into Macedonia by Paul,
and that there was no man to comfort us, to speak nothing of
them that had but just become catechumens. And as Simon
exalted himself yet more by the works which he did, and many
of them daily called Paul a sorcerer, and others a deceiver, of
so great a multitude that had been stablished in the faith all
fell away save Narcissus the presbyter and two women in the
lodging of the Bithynians, and four that could no longer go out
of their house, but were shut up (day and night): *these* gave
themselves unto prayer (by day and night), beseeching the Lord
that Paul might return quickly, or some other that should visit
his servants, because the devil had made them fall by his
wickedness.

V. And as they prayed and fasted, God was already teaching
Peter at Jerusalem of that which should come to pass. *For*
whereas the twelve years which the Lord Christ had enjoined
upon him were fulfilled, he showed him a vision after this manner,
saying unto him: Peter, that Simon the sorcerer whom thou
didst cast out of Judaea, convicting him, hath again come before
thee (prevented thee) at Rome. And that shalt thou know
shortly (or, and that thou mayest know in few words): for all
that did believe in me hath Satan made to fall by his craft and
working: whose Power *Simon* approveth himself to be. But
delay thee not: set forth on the morrow, and there shalt thou
find a ship ready, setting sail for Italy, and within few days I will
show thee my grace which hath in it no grudging. Peter then,
admonished by the vision, related it unto the brethren without

delay, saying: It is necessary for me to go up unto Rome to fight with the enemy and adversary of the Lord and of our brethren.

And he went down to Caesarea and embarked quickly in the ship, whereof the ladder was already drawn up, not taking any provision with him. But the governor *of the ship* whose name was Theon looked on Peter and said: Whatsoever we have, all is thine. For what thank have we, if we take in a man like unto ourselves *who is* in uncertain case (difficulty) and share not all that we have with thee? but only let us have a prosperous voyage. But Peter, giving him thanks for that which he offered, himself fasted while he was in the ship, sorrowful in mind and again consoling himself because God accounted him worthy to be a minister in his service.

And after a few days the governor of the ship rose up at the hour of his dinner and asked Peter to eat with him, and said to him: O thou, whoever thou art, I know thee not, but as I reckon, I take thee for a servant of God. For as I was steering my ship at midnight I perceived the voice of a man from heaven saying to me: Theon, Theon! And twice it called me by my name and said to me: Among them that sail with thee let Peter be greatly honoured by thee, for by him shalt thou and the rest be preserved safe without any hurt after such a course as thou hopest not for. And Peter believed that God would vouchsafe to show his providence upon the sea unto them that were in the ship, and thenceforth began Peter to declare unto Theon the mighty works of God, and how the Lord had chosen him from among the apostles, and for what business he sailed unto Italy: and daily he communicated unto him the word of God. And considering him he perceived by his walk that he was of one mind in the faith and a worthy minister (deacon).

Now when there was a calm upon the ship in Hadria (the Adriatic), Theon showed it to Peter, saying unto him: If thou wilt account me worthy, whom thou mayest baptize with the seal of the Lord, thou hast an opportunity. For all that were in the ship had fallen asleep, being drunken. And Peter went down by a rope and baptized Theon in the name of the Father and the Son and the Holy Ghost: and he came up out of the water rejoicing with great joy, and Peter also was glad because God had accounted Theon worthy of his name. And it came to pass when Theon was baptized, there appeared in the same place a youth shining and beautiful, saying unto them: Peace be unto you. And immediately Peter and Theon went up and entered into the cabin; and Peter took bread and gave thanks unto the Lord which had accounted him worthy of his holy ministry, and for that the youth had appeared unto them, saying: Peace be unto you. *And he said*: Thou best and alone holy one, it is thou that hast appeared unto us, O God Jesu Christ, and in thy name hath *this man* now been washed and sealed with thy holy seal. Therefore in thy name do I impart unto him thine eucharist, that he may be thy perfect servant without blame for ever.

And as they feasted and rejoiced in the Lord, suddenly there came a wind, not vehement but moderate, at the ship's prow, and ceased not for six days and as many nights, until they came unto Puteoli.

VI. And when they had touched at Puteoli, Theon leapt out of the ship and went unto the inn where he was wont to lodge, to prepare to receive Peter. Now he with whom he lodged was one by name Ariston, which alway feared the Lord, and because of the Name Theon entrusted himself with him (had dealings with him). And when he was come to the inn and saw Ariston, Theon said unto him: God who hath accounted thee worthy to serve him hath communicated his grace unto me also by his holy servant Peter, who hath now sailed with me from Judaea, being commanded by our Lord to come unto Italy. And when he heard that, Ariston fell upon Theon's neck and embraced him and besought him to bring him to the ship and show him Peter. For Ariston said that since Paul set forth unto Spain there was no man of the brethren with whom he could refresh himself, and, moreover, a certain Jew had broken into the city, named Simon, and with his charms of sorcery and his wickedness hath he made all the brotherhood fall away this way and that, so that I also fled from Rome, expecting the coming of Peter: for Paul had told us of him, and I also have seen many things in a vision. Now, therefore, I believe in my Lord that he will build up again his ministry, for all *this* deceit shall be rooted out from among his servants. For our Lord Jesus Christ is faithful, who is able to restore our minds. And when Theon heard these things from Ariston, who wept, his spirit was raised (increased) yet more and he was the more strengthened, because he perceived that he had believed on the living God.

But when they came together unto the ship, Peter looked upon them and smiled, being filled with the Spirit; so that Ariston falling on his face at Peter's feet, said thus: Brother and lord, that hast part in the holy mysteries and showest the right way which is in the Lord Jesus Christ our God, who by thee hath shown unto us his coming: we have lost all them whom Paul had delivered unto us, by the working of Satan; but now I trust in the Lord who hath commanded thee to come unto us, sending thee as his messenger, that he hath accounted us worthy to see his great and wonderful works by thy means. I pray thee therefore, make haste unto the city: for I left the brethren which have stumbled, whom I saw fall into the temptation of the devil, and fled hither, saying unto them: Brethren, stand fast in the faith, for it is of necessity that within these two months the mercy of our Lord bring his servant unto you. For I had seen

a vision, even Paul, saying unto me: Ariston, flee thou out of
the city. And when I heard it, I believed without delay and
went forth in the Lord, although I had an infirmity in my flesh,
and came hither; and day by day I stood upon the sea-shore
asking the sailors: Hath Peter sailed with you? But now
through the abundance of the grace of God I entreat thee, let
us go up unto Rome without delay, lest the teaching of this
wicked man prevail yet further. And as Ariston said this with
tears, Peter gave him his hand and raised him up from the
earth, and Peter also groaning, said with tears: He hath prevented us which tempteth all the world by his angels; but he
that hath power to save his servants from all temptations shall
quench his deceits and put him beneath the feet of them that
have believed in Christ whom we preach.

And, as they entered in at the gate, Theon entreated Peter,
saying: Thou didst not refresh thyself on any day in so great
a voyage (sea): and now after (before) so hard a journey wilt
thou set out forthwith from the ship? tarry and refresh thyself,
and so shalt thou set forth: for from hence to Rome upon a pavement of flint I fear lest thou be hurt by the shaking. But Peter
answered and said to them: What if it come to pass that a
millstone were hung upon me, and likewise upon the enemy of
our Lord. even as my Lord said unto us of any that offended *one*
of the brethren, and I were drowned in the sea? but it might be
not only a millstone, but that which is far worse, †even that
I which am the enemy of this persecutor of his servants should
die afar off from them that have believed on the Lord Jesus
Christ† (so Ficker: the sentence is corrupt; the sense is that
Peter must at all costs be with his fellow-Christians, or he will
incur even worse punishment than that threatened by our Lord's
words). And by no exhortation could Theon prevail to persuade
him to tarry there even one day.

But Theon himself delivered all that was in the ship to be sold for
the price which he thought good, and followed Peter unto Rome;
whom Ariston brought unto the abode of Narcissus the presbyter.

VII. Now the report was noised through the city unto the
brethren that were dispersed, ⟨saying that Peter was come to
Rome [1]⟩ because of Simon, that he might show him to be a deceiver
and a persecutor of good men. All the multitude therefore
ran together to see the apostle of the Lord stay (himself, *or* the
brethren) on Christ. And on the first day of the week when the
multitude was assembled to see Peter, Peter began to say with
a loud voice: Ye men here present that trust in Christ, ye that
for a little space have suffered temptation, learn for what cause
God sent his Son into the world, and wherefore he made him to be
born of the Virgin Mary; *for would he so have done* if not to

[1] Professor Turner would read ' that Peter the disciple of the Lord
was come '.

procure *us* some grace or dispensation? even because he would *take away* all offence and all ignorance and all the contrivance of the devil, his attempts (beginnings) and his strength wherewith he prevailed aforetime, before our God shined forth in the world. And whereas men through ignorance fell into death by many and divers infirmities, Almighty God, moved with compassion, sent his Son into the world. With whom I was ; and he (*or* I) walked upon the water, whereof I myself remain a witness, *and do testify* that he then worked in the world by signs and wonders, all of which he did.

I do confess, dearly-beloved brethren, that I was with him : *yet* I denied him, even our Lord Jesus Christ, and that not once only, but thrice ; for there were evil dogs that were come about me as they did unto the Lord's prophets. And the Lord imputed it not unto me, but turned unto me and had compassion on the infirmity of my flesh, when (*or* so that) afterward I bitterly bewailed myself, and lamented the weakness of my faith, because I was befooled by the devil and kept not in mind the word of my Lord. And now I say unto you, O men and brethren, which are gathered together in the name of Jesus Christ: against you also hath the deceiver Satan aimed his arrows, that ye might depart out of the way. But faint not, brethren, neither let your spirit fall, but be strong and persevere and doubt not: for if Satan caused me to stumble, whom the Lord had in great honour, so that I denied the light of mine hope, and if he over-threw me and persuaded me to flee as if I had put my trust in a man, what think ye *will he do unto you* which are but young in the faith? Did ye suppose that he would not turn you away to make you enemies of the kingdom of God, and cast you down into perdition by a new (*or* the last) deceit? For whomsoever he casteth out from the hope of our Lord Jesus Christ, he is a son of perdition for ever. Turn yourselves, therefore, brethren, chosen of the Lord, and be strong in God Almighty, the Father of our Lord Jesus Christ, whom no man hath seen at any time, neither can see, save he who hath believed in him. And be ye aware whence this temptation hath come upon you. For it is not only by words that I would convince you that this is Christ whom I preach, but also by deeds and exceeding great works of power do I exhort you by the faith that is in Christ Jesus, that none of you look for any other save him that was despised and mocked of the Jews. even this Nazarene which was crucified and died and the third day rose again.

VIII. And the brethren repented and entreated Peter to fight against Simon: (who said that he was the power of God, and lodged in the house of Marcellus a senator, whom he had con-vinced by his charms) saying: Believe us, brother Peter: there was no man among men so wise as this Marcellus. All the widows that trusted in Christ had recourse unto him; all the fatherless were fed by him; and what more, brother? all the poor called Marcellus their patron, and his house was called the house of

the strangers and of the poor, and the emperor said unto him:
I will keep thee out of every office, lest thou despoil the provinces
to give gifts unto the Christians. And Marcellus answered:
All my goods are also thine. And Caesar said to him : Mine
they would be if thou keptest them for me; but now they are
not mine, for thou givest them to whom thou wilt, and I know
not to what vile persons. Having this, then, before our eyes,
brother Peter, we report it to thee, how the great mercy of this
man is turned unto blasphemy; for if he had not turned, neither
should we have departed from the holy faith of God our Lord.
And now doth this Marcellus in anger repent him of his good
deeds, saying: All this substance have I spent in all this time,
vainly believing that I gave it for the knowledge of God ! So that
if any stranger cometh to the door of his house, he smiteth him
with a staff and biddeth him be beaten, saying: Would God
I had not spent so much money upon these impostors: and yet
more doth he say, blaspheming. But if there abide in thee any
mercy of our Lord and aught of the goodness of his commandments, do thou succour the error of this man who hath done so
many alms-deeds unto the servants of God.

And Peter, when he perceived this, was smitten with sharp
affliction and said: O the divers arts and temptations of the
devil! O the contrivances and devices of the wicked! he that
nourisheth up for himself a mighty fire in the day of wrath, the
destruction of simple men, the ravening wolf, the devourer and
scatterer of eternal life! Thou didst enmesh the first man in
concupiscence and bind him with thine old iniquity and with
the chain of the flesh: thou art wholly the exceeding bitter fruit of
the tree of bitterness, who sendest divers lusts upon men. Thou
didst compel Judas my fellow-disciple and fellow-apostle to do
wickedly and deliver up our Lord Jesus Christ, who shall punish
thee therefor. Thou didst harden the heart of Herod and didst
inflame Pharaoh and compel him to fight against Moses the
holy servant of God; thou didst give boldness unto Caiaphas,
that he should deliver our Lord Jesus Christ unto the unrighteous
multitude; and even until now thou shootest at innocent souls
with thy poisonous arrows. Thou wicked one, enemy of all men,
be thou accursed from the Church of him the Son of the holy
God omnipotent, and as a brand cast out of the fire shalt thou
be quenched by the servants of our Lord Jesus Christ. Upon
thee let thy blackness be turned and upon thy children, an evil
seed ; upon thee be turned thy wickedness and thy threatenings ;
upon thee and thine angels be thy temptations, thou beginning
of malice and bottomless pit of darkness! Let thy darkness
that thou hast be with thee and with thy vessels which thou
ownest! Depart from them that shall believe in God, depart
from the servants of Christ and from them that desire to be his
soldiers. Keep thou to thyself thy garments of darkness! Without

cause knockest thou at other men's doors, which are not thine but of Christ Jesus that keepeth them. For thou, ravening wolf, wouldest carry off the sheep that are not thine but of Christ Jesus, who keepeth them with all care and diligence.

IX. As Peter spake thus with great sorrow of mind, many were added unto them that believed on the Lord. But the brethren besought Peter to join battle with Simon and not suffer him any longer to vex the people. And without delay Peter went quickly out of the synagogue (assembly) and went unto the house of Marcellus, where Simon lodged: and much people followed him. And when he came to the door, he called the porter and said to him: Go, say unto Simon: Peter because of whom thou fleddest out of Judaea waiteth for thee at the door. The porter answered and said to Peter: Sir, whether thou be Peter, I know not: but I have a command; for he had knowledge that yesterday thou didst enter into the city, and said unto me: Whether it be by day or by night, at whatsoever hour he cometh, say that I am not within. And Peter said to the young man: Thou hast well said in reporting that which he compelled thee to say. And Peter turned unto the people that followed him and said: Ye shall now see a great and marvellous wonder. And Peter seeing a great dog bound with a strong chain, went to him and loosed him, and when he was loosed the dog received a man's voice and said unto Peter: What dost thou bid me to do, thou servant of the unspeakable and living God? Peter said unto him: Go in and say unto Simon in the midst of his company: Peter saith unto thee, Come forth abroad, for for thy sake am I come to Rome, thou wicked one and deceiver of simple souls. And immediately the dog ran and entered in, and rushed into the midst of them that were with Simon, and lifted up his forefeet and in a loud voice said: Thou Simon, Peter the servant of Christ who standeth at the door saith unto thee: Come forth abroad, for for thy sake am I come to Rome, thou most wicked one and deceiver of simple souls. And when Simon heard it, and beheld the incredible sight, he lost the words wherewith he was deceiving them that stood by, and all of them were amazed.

X. But when Marcellus saw it he went out to the door and cast himself at Peter's feet and said: Peter, I embrace thy feet, thou holy servant of the holy God ; I have sinned greatly: but exact thou not my sins, if there be in thee the true faith of Christ, whom thou preachest, if thou remember his commandments, to hate no man, to be unkind to no man, as I learned from thy fellow apostle Paul ; keep not in mind my faults, but pray for me unto the Lord, the holy Son of God whom I have provoked to wrath—for I have persecuted his servants—that I be not delivered with the sins of Simon unto eternal fire ; who so persuaded me, that I set up a statue to him with this inscription :

'To Simon the new (young) God.' If I knew, O Peter, that thou couldest be won with money, I would give thee all my substance, *yea* I would give it and despise it, that I might gain my soul. If I had sons, I would account them as nothing, if only I might believe in the living God. But I confess that he would not have deceived me save that he said that he was the power of God; yet will I tell thee, O most gentle (sweet) Peter: I was not worthy to hear thee, thou servant of God, neither was I stablished in the faith of God which is in Christ; therefore was I made to stumble. I beseech thee, therefore, take not ill that which I am about to say, that Christ our Lord whom thou preachest in truth said unto thy fellow-apostles in thy presence: If ye have faith as a grain of mustard seed, ye shall say unto this mountain: Remove thyself: and straightway it shall remove itself. But this Simon said that thou, Peter, wast without faith when thou didst doubt, in the waters. And I have heard that Christ said this also: They that are with me have not understood me. If, then, ye upon whom he laid his hands, whom also he chose, did doubt, I, therefore, having this witness, repent me, and take refuge in thy prayers. Receive my soul who have fallen away from our Lord and from his promise. But I believe that he will have mercy upon me that repent. For the Almighty is faithful to forgive me my sins.

But Peter said with a loud voice: Unto thee, our Lord, be glory and splendour, O God Almighty, Father of our Lord Jesus Christ. Unto thee be praise and glory and honour, world without end. Amen. Because thou hast now fully strengthened and stablished us in thee in the sight of all, holy Lord, confirm thou Marcellus, and send thy peace upon him and upon his house this day: and whatsoever is lost or out of the way, thou alone canst turn them all again; we beseech thee, Lord, shepherd of the sheep that once were scattered, but now shall be gathered in one by thee. So also receive thou Marcellus as one of thy lambs and suffer him no longer to go astray (revel) in error or ignorance. Yea, Lord, receive him that with anguish and tears entreateth thee.

XI. And as Peter spake thus and embraced Marcellus, Peter turned himself unto the multitude that stood by him and saw there one that laughed (smiled), in whom was a very evil spirit. And Peter said unto him: Whosoever thou art that didst laugh, show thyself openly unto all that are present. And hearing this the young man ran into the court of the house and cried out with a loud voice and dashed himself against the wall and said: Peter, there is a great contention between Simon and the dog whom thou sentest; for Simon saith to the dog: Say that I am not here. Unto whom the dog saith more than thou didst charge him; and when he hath accomplished the mystery which thou didst command him, he shall die at thy feet. But Peter said:

And thou also, devil, whosoever thou art, in the name of our
Lord Jesus Christ, go out of that young man and hurt him not
at all: show thyself unto all that stand here. When the young
man heard it, he ran forth and caught hold on a great statue of
marble which was set in the court of the house, and brake it in
pieces with his feet. Now it was a statue of Caesar. Which
Marcellus beholding smote his forehead and said unto Peter:
A great crime hath been committed; for if this be made known
unto Caesar by some busybody, he will afflict us with sore
punishments. And Peter said to him: I see thee not the same
that thou wast a little while ago, for thou saidst that thou wast
ready to spend all thy substance to save thy soul. But if thou
indeed repentest, believing in Christ with thy whole heart, take
in thine hands of the water that runneth down, and pray to the
Lord, and in his name sprinkle it upon the broken pieces of the
statue and it shall be whole as it was before. And Marcellus,
nothing doubting, but believing with his whole heart, before he
took the water lifted up his hands and said: I believe in thee,
O Lord Jesu Christ: for I am *now* proved by thine apostle Peter,
whether I believe aright in thine holy name. Therefore I take
water in mine hands, and in thy name do I sprinkle these stones
that the statue may become whole as it was before. If, therefore,
Lord, it be thy will that I continue in the body and suffer nothing
at Caesar's hand, let this stone be whole as it was before. And
he sprinkled the water upon the stones, and the statue became
whole, whereat Peter exulted that Marcellus had not doubted
in asking of the Lord, and Marcellus was exalted in spirit for that
such a sign was first wrought by his hands; and he therefore
believed with his whole heart in the name of Jesus Christ the Son
of God, by whom all things impossible are *made* possible.

XII. But Simon within the house said thus to the dog: Tell
Peter that I am not within. Whom the dog answered in the
presence of Marcellus: Thou exceeding wicked and shameless
one, enemy of all that live and believe on Christ Jesus, here is
a dumb animal sent unto thee which hath received a human
voice to confound thee and show thee to be a deceiver and a
liar. Hast thou taken thought so long, to say *at last*: ' Tell
him that I am not within ' ? Art thou not ashamed to utter thy
feeble and useless words against Peter the minister and apostle
of Christ, as if thou couldst hide thee from him that hath commanded me to speak against *thee to* thy face: and that not for
thy sake but for theirs whom thou wast deceiving and sending
unto destruction ? Cursed therefore shalt thou be, thou enemy
and corrupter of the way of the truth of Christ, who shall prove
by fire that dieth not and in outer darkness, thine iniquities
that thou hast committed. And having thus said, the dog went
forth and the people followed him, leaving Simon alone. And
the dog came unto Peter as he sat with the multitude *that was*

come to see Peter's face, and the dog related what he had done unto Simon. And thus spake the dog unto the angel and apostle of the true God: Peter, thou wilt have a great contest with the enemy of Christ and his servants, and many that have been deceived by him shalt thou turn unto the faith; wherefore thou shalt receive from God the reward of thy work. And when the dog had said this he fell down at the apostle Peter's feet and gave up the ghost. And when the great multitude saw with amazement the dog speaking, they began then, some to throw themselves down at Peter's feet, and some said: Show us another sign, that we may believe in thee as the minister of the living God, *for* Simon also did many signs in our presence and therefore did we follow him.

XIII. And Peter turned and saw a herring (sardine) hung in a window, and took it and said to the people: If ye now see this swimming in the water like a fish, will ye be able to believe in him whom I preach? And they said with one voice: Verily we will believe thee. Then he said—now there was a bath for swimming at hand : In thy name, O Jesu Christ, forasmuch as hitherto it is not believed in, in the sight of all these live and swim like a fish. And he cast the herring into the bath, and it lived and began to swim. And all the people saw the fish swimming, and it did not so at that hour only, lest it should be said that it was a delusion (phantasm), but he made it to swim for a long time, so that they brought much people from all quarters and showed them the herring that was made a *living* fish, so that certain of the people even cast bread to it; and they saw that it was whole. And seeing this, many followed *Peter* and believed in the Lord.

And they assembled themselves day and night unto the house of Narcissus the presbyter. And Peter discoursed unto them of the scriptures of the prophets and of those things which our Lord Jesus Christ had wrought both in word and in deeds.

XIV. But Marcellus was confirmed daily by the signs which he saw wrought by Peter through the grace of Jesus Christ which he granted unto him. And Marcellus ran upon Simon as he sat in his house in the dining chamber, and cursed him and said unto him: Thou most adverse and pestilent of men, corrupter of my soul and my house, who wouldest have made me fall away from my Lord and Saviour Christ! and laying hands on him he commanded him to be thrust out of his house. And the servants having received such licence, covered him with reproaches; some buffeted his face, others *beat him* with sticks, others *cast* stones, others emptied out vessels full of filth upon his head, even those who on his account had fled from their master and been a long time fettered ; and other their fellow-servants of whom he had spoken evil to their master reproached him, saying to him: Now by the will of God who hath had mercy on us and on our master, do we recompense thee with a fit reward. And Simon, shrewdly beaten and cast out of the house, ran unto the house where Peter lodged, even the house of Narcissus, and standing at the gate cried out: Lo, here am I, Simon: come thou down, Peter, and I will convict thee that thou hast believed on a man which is a Jew and a carpenter's son.

XV. And when it was told Peter that Simon had said this, Peter sent unto him a woman which had a sucking child, saying to her: Go down quickly, and thou wilt find one that seeketh me. For thee there is no need that thou answer him at all, but keep silence and hear what the child whom thou holdest shall say unto him. The woman therefore went down. Now the child whom she suckled was seven months old; and it received a man's voice and said unto Simon: O thou abhorred of God and men, and destruction of truth, and evil seed of all corruption, O fruit by nature unprofitable! but only for a short and little season shalt thou be seen, and thereafter eternal punishment is laid up for thee. Thou son of a shameless father, that never puttest forth thy roots for good but for poison, faithless generation void of all hope! thou wast not confounded when a dog reproved thee; I a child am compelled of God to speak, and not even now art thou ashamed. But even against thy will, on the sabbath day that cometh, another shall bring thee into the forum of Julius that it may be shown what manner of man thou art. Depart therefore from the gate wherein walk the feet of the holy; for thou shalt no more corrupt the innocent souls whom thou didst turn out of the way and make sad; in Christ, therefore, shall be shown thine evil nature, and thy devices shall be cut in pieces. And now speak, I this last word unto thee: Jesus Christ saith to thee: Be thou stricken dumb in my name, and depart out of Rome until the sabbath that cometh. And forthwith he became dumb and *his speech* was bound; and he went out of Rome until the sabbath and abode in a stable. But the woman returned with the child unto Peter and told him and the rest of the brethren what the child had said unto Simon: and they magnified the Lord which had shown these things unto men.

XVI. Now when the night fell, Peter, while yet waking, beheld Jesus clad in a vesture of brightness, smiling and saying unto him: Already is much people of the brotherhood returned through me and through the signs which thou hast wrought in my name. But thou shalt have a contest of the faith upon the sabbath that cometh, and many more of the Gentiles and of the Jews shall be converted in my name unto me who was reproached and mocked and spat upon. For I will be present with thee when thou askest for signs and wonders, and thou shalt convert many: but thou shalt have Simon opposing thee by the works of his father; yet all his works shall be shown to be charms and contrivances of sorcery. But now slack thou not, and whomsoever I shall send unto thee thou shalt establish in my name. And when it was light, he told the brethren how the Lord had appeared unto him and what he had commanded him·

XVII. [This episode, inserted most abruptly, is believed by Vouaux to have been inserted here by the compiler of the Greek original of the Vercelli Acts: but it was not composed by him, but transferred with very slight additions from the earlier part of the Acts—now lost—of which the scene was laid in Judaea. I incline to favour this view.]

But believe ye me, men and brethren, I drove this Simon out of Judaea where he did many evils with his magical charms, lodging in Judaea with a certain woman Eubula, who was of honourable estate in this world, having store of gold and pearls of no small price. Here did Simon enter in by stealth with two others like unto himself, and none of the household saw them two, but Simon only, and by means of a spell they took away all the woman's gold, and disappeared. But Eubula, when she found what was done, began to torture her household, saying: Ye have taken occasion by this man of God and spoiled me, when ye saw him entering in to me to honour a mere woman; but his name is [1] *as* the name of the Lord.

As I fasted for three days and prayed that this matter should be made plain, I saw in a vision Italicus and Antulus (Antyllus?) whom I had instructed in the name of the Lord, and a boy naked and chained giving me a wheaten loaf and saying unto me: Peter, endure yet two days and thou shalt see the mighty works of God. As for all that is lost out of the house of Eubula, Simon hath used art magic and hath caused a delusion, and with two others hath stolen it away: whom thou shalt see on the third day at the ninth hour, at the gate which leadeth unto Neapolis, selling unto a goldsmith by name Agrippinus a young satyr of gold of two pound weight, having in it a precious stone. But for thee there is no need that thou touch it, lest thou be defiled; but let there be with thee some of the matron's servants, and thou shalt show them the shop of the goldsmith and depart from them. For by reason of this matter shall many believe on the name of the Lord, and all that which these men by their devices and wickedness have oft-times stolen shall be openly showed. When I heard that, I went unto Eubula and found her sitting with her clothes rent and her hair disordered, mourning; unto whom I said: Eubula, rise up from thy mourning and compose thy face and order thy hair and put on raiment befitting thee, and pray unto the Lord Jesus Christ that judgeth every soul: for he is the invisible Son of God, by whom thou must be saved, if only thou repent with thine whole heart of thy former sins:

[1] Here a leaf ends: there is no gap in the manuscript, but the sentence is abrupt, and Peter is very suddenly introduced into the story.

and receive thou power from him; for behold, by me the Lord saith to thee: Thou shalt find all whatsoever thou hast lost. And after thou hast received them, take thou care that he find thee, that thou mayest renounce this present world and seek for everlasting refreshment. Hearken therefore unto this: Let certain of thy people keep watch at the gate that leadeth to Neapolis on the day after to-morrow at about the ninth hour, and they shall see two young men *having* a young satyr of gold, of two pound weight, set with gems, as a vision hath shown me: which thing they will offer for sale to one Agrippinus of the household of godliness and of the faith which is in the Lord Jesus Christ: by whom it shall be showed thee that thou shouldest believe in the living God and not on Simon the magician, the unstable devil, who hath desired that thou shouldest remain in sorrow, and thine innocent household be tormented; who by fair words and speech only hath deceived thee, and with his mouth only spake of godliness, whereas he is wholly possessed of ungodliness. For when thou didst think to keep holy-day, and settedst up thine idol and didst veil it and set out all thine ornaments upon a table (round three-legged table), he brought in two young men whom no man of yours saw, by a magic charm, and they stole away thine ornaments and were no more seen. But his device hath had no success (place); for my God hath manifested it unto me, to the end thou shouldest not be deceived, neither perish in hell, for those sins which thou hast committed ungodly and contrary to God, who is full of all truth, and the righteous judge of quick and dead; and there is none other hope of life unto men save through him, by whom those things which thou hast lost are recovered unto thee: and now do thou gain thine own soul.

But she cast herself down before my feet, saying: O man, who thou art I know not; but him I received as a servant of God, and whatsoever he asked of me to give it unto the poor, I gave much by his hands, and beside that I did give much unto him. What hurt did I do him, that he should contrive all this against mine house? Unto whom Peter said:[1] There is no faith to be put in words, but in acts and deeds: but we must go on with that we have begun. So I left her and went with two stewards of Eubula and came to Agrippinus and said to him: See that thou take note of these men; for to-morrow two young men will come to thee, desiring to sell thee a young satyr of gold set with jewels, which belongeth to the mistress of these: and thou shalt take it as it were to look upon it, and praise the work of the craftsman, and then when these come in, God will bring the rest to the proof. And on the next day the stewards of the matron came about the ninth hour, and also those young men,

[1] Note the third person. It may be a mere slip, but, if not, it confirms the idea that the story has been transplanted from another place.

willing to sell unto Agrippinus the young satyr of gold. And they being forthwith taken, it was reported unto the matron, and she in distress of mind came to the deputy, and with a loud voice declared all that had befallen her. And when Pompeius the deputy beheld her in distress of mind, who never had come forth abroad, he forthwith rose up from the judgement seat and went unto the praetorium, and bade those men to be brought and tortured; and while they were being tormented they confessed that they did it in the service of Simon, which, *said they*, persuaded us thereto with money. And being tortured a long time, they confessed that all that Eubula had lost was laid up under the earth in a cave on the other side of the gate, and many other things besides. And when Pompeius heard this, he rose up to go unto the gate, *with* those two men, each of them bound with two chains. And lo, Simon came in at the gate, seeking them because they tarried long. And he seeth a great multitude coming, and those two bound with chains; and he understood and betook him to flight, and appeared no more in Judaea unto this day. But Eubula, when she had recovered all her goods, gave them for the service of the poor, and believed on the Lord Jesus Christ and was comforted; and despised and renounced this world, and gave unto the widows and fatherless, and clothed the poor. And after a long time she received her rest (sleep). Now these things, dearly beloved brethren, were done in Judaea, whereby he that is called the angel of Satan [1] was driven out thence.

XVIII. Brethren, dearest and most beloved, let us fast together and pray unto the Lord. For he that drove him out thence is able also to root him out of this place: and let him grant unto us power to withstand him and his magical charms, and to prove that he is the angel of Satan. For on the sabbath our Lord shall bring him, though he would not, unto the forum of Julius. Let us therefore bow our knees unto Christ, which heareth us, though we cry not; it is he that seeth us, though he be not seen with these eyes, yet is he in us: if we will, he will not forsake us. Let us therefore purify our souls of every evil temptation, and God will not depart from us. *Yea*, if we but wink with our eyes, he is present with us.

XIX. Now after these things were spoken by Peter, Marcellus also came in, and said: Peter, I have for thee cleansed mine whole house from the footsteps (traces) of Simon, and wholly done away even his wicked dust. For I took water and called upon the holy name of Jesus Christ, together with mine other servants which belong unto him, and sprinkled all my house and all the dining chambers and all the porticoes, even unto the outer gate, and said: I know that thou, Lord Jesu Christ, art pure and untouched of any uncleanness: so let mine enemy and adversary be driven

[1] *Or*, 'the angel of Satan which is called *Simon*'.

out from before thy face. And now, thou blessed one, have I bidden the widows and old *women* to assemble unto thee in my house which is purified (*MS*. common), that they may pray with us. And they shall receive every one a piece of gold in the name of the ministry (service), that they may be called indeed servants of Christ. And all else is now prepared for the service. I entreat thee, therefore, O blessed Peter, consent unto their request, so that thou also pay honour unto (ornament) their prayers in my stead; let us then go and take Narcissus also, and whosoever of the brethren are here. So then Peter consented unto his simplicity, to fulfil his desire, and went forth with him and the rest of the brethren.

XX. But Peter entered in, and beheld one of the aged *women*, a widow, that was blind, and her daughter giving her her hand and leading her into Marcellus' house; and Peter said unto her: Come hither, mother: from this day forward Jesus giveth thee his right hand, by whom we have light unapproachable which no darkness hideth; who saith unto thee by me: Open thine eyes and see, and walk by thyself. And forthwith the widow saw Peter laying his hand upon her.

And Peter entered into the dining-hall and saw that the Gospel was being read, and he rolled up *the book* and said: Ye men [1] that believe and hope in Christ, learn in what manner the holy Scripture of our Lord ought to be declared: whereof we by his grace wrote that which we could receive, though yet it appear unto you feeble, yet according to our power, even that which can be endured to be borne by (*or* instilled into) human flesh. We ought therefore first to know the will and the goodness of God, how that when error was everywhere spread abroad, and many thousands of men were being cast down into perdition, God was moved by his mercy to show himself in another form and in the likeness of man, concerning which neither the Jews nor we were able worthily to be enlightened. For every one of us according as he could contain the sight, saw, as he was able. Now will I expound unto you that which was newly read unto you. Our Lord, willing that I should behold his majesty in the holy mount— I, when I with the sons of Zebedee saw the brightness of his light, fell as one dead and shut mine eyes, and heard such a voice from him as I am not able to describe, and thought myself to be blinded by his brightness. And when I recovered (breathed again) a little I said within myself: Peradventure my Lord hath brought me hither that he might blind me. And I said: If this also be thy will, Lord, I resist not. And he gave me his hand and raised me up; and when I arose I saw him again in such a form as I was able to take in. As, therefore, the merciful God, dearly beloved brethren, carried our infirmities and bare our sins (as the prophet saith: He beareth our sins and suffereth for us;

---

[1] Parts of the speech are in Greek in the Life of St. Abercius.

but we did esteem him to be in affliction and smitten with plagues),
for he is in the Father and the Father in him—he also is himself
the fulness of all majesty, who hath shown unto us all his good
things: he did eat and drink for our sakes, himself being neither
an-hungered nor athirst; he carried and bare reproaches for our
sakes, he died and rose again because of us; who both defended
me when I sinned and comforted me by his greatness, and will
comfort you also that ye may love him: this *God* who is great and
small, fair and foul, young and old, seen in time and unto eternity
invisible; whom the hand of man hath not held, yet is he held
by his servants; whom no flesh hath seen, yet now seeth;
who is the word proclaimed by the prophets and now appearing
(*so Gk.*: *Lat.* not heard of but now known); not subject to suffering,
but having now made trial of suffering for our sake (*or* like unto
us); never chastised, yet now chastised; who was before the world
and hath been comprehended in time; the great beginning of all
principality, yet delivered over unto princes; beautiful, but among
us lowly; seen *of all* yet foreseeing *all* (*MS.* foul of view, yet
foreseeing). This Jesus ye have, brethren, the door, the light,
the way, the bread, the water, the life, the resurrection, the refreshment, the pearl, the treasure, the seed, the abundance (harvest),
the mustard seed, the vine, the plough, the grace, the faith, the
word: he is all things and there is none other greater than he.
Unto him be praise, world without end. Amen.

XXI. And when the ninth hour was fully come, they rose up
to make prayer. And behold certain widows, of the aged, unknown to Peter, which sat there, being blind and not believing [1],
cried out, saying unto Peter: We sit together here, O Peter,
hoping and believing in Christ Jesus: as therefore thou hast
made one of us to see, we entreat thee, lord Peter, grant unto us
also his mercy and pity. But Peter said to them: If there be in
you the faith that is in Christ, if it be firm in you, then perceive
in your mind that which ye see not with your eyes, and though
your ears are closed, yet let them be open in your mind within you.
These eyes shall again be shut, seeing nought but men and oxen
and dumb beasts and sticks and stones; but not every eye seeth
Jesus Christ. Yet now, Lord, let thy sweet and holy name succour
these *persons*; do thou touch their eyes; for thou art able—that
these may see with their eyes.

And when all had prayed, the hall wherein they were shone
as when it lighteneth, even with such *a light* as cometh in the
clouds, yet not such a light as that of the daytime, but unspeakable, invisible, such as no man can describe, even such that we
were beside ourselves with bewilderment, calling on the Lord
and saying: Have mercy, Lord, upon us thy servants: what we
are able to bear, that, Lord, give thou us; for this we can neither
see nor endure. And as we lay there, only those widows stood up

[1] *sic*: *qu.* not rising?

which were blind; and the bright light which appeared unto us entered into their eyes and made them to see. Unto whom Peter said: Tell us what ye saw. And they said: We saw an old man of such comeliness as we are not able to declare to thee; but others said: *We saw* a young man; and others: We saw a boy touching our eyes delicately, and so were our eyes opened. Peter therefore magnified the Lord, saying: Thou only art the Lord God, and of what lips have we need to give thee due praise? and how can we give thee thanks according to thy mercy? Therefore, brethren, as I told you but a little while since, God that is constant is greater than our thoughts, even as we have learned of these aged widows, how that they beheld the Lord in divers forms.

XXII. And having exhorted them all to think upon (understand) the Lord with their whole heart, he began together with Marcellus and the rest of the brethren to minister unto the virgins of the Lord, and to rest until the morning.

Unto whom Marcellus said: Ye holy and inviolate virgins of the Lord, hearken: Ye have a place to abide in, for these things that are called mine, whose are they save yours? depart not hence, but refresh yourselves: for upon the sabbath which cometh, *even* to-morrow, Simon hath a controversy with Peter the holy one of God: for as the Lord hath ever been with him, so will Christ the Lord now stand for him as his apostle. For Peter hath continued tasting nothing, but fasting yet a day, that he may overcome the wicked adversary and persecutor of the Lord's truth. For lo, my young men are come announcing that they have seen scaffolds being set up in the forum, and much people saying: To-morrow at daybreak two Jews are to contend here concerning the teaching (?) of God. Now therefore let us watch until the morning, praying and beseeching our Lord Jesus Christ to hear our prayers on behalf of Peter.

And Marcellus turned to sleep for a short space, and awoke and said unto Peter: O Peter, thou apostle of Christ, let us go boldly unto that which lieth before us. For just now when I turned myself to sleep for a little, I beheld thee sitting in a high place and before thee a great multitude, and a woman exceeding foul, in sight like an Ethiopian, not an Egyptian, but altogether black and filthy, clothed in rags, and with an iron collar about her neck and chains upon her hands and feet, dancing. And when thou sawest me thou saidst to me with a loud voice: Marcellus, the whole power of Simon and of his God is this *woman* that danceth; do thou behead her. And I said to thee: Brother Peter, I am a senator of a high race, and I have never defiled my hands, neither killed so much as a sparrow at any time. And thou hearing it didst begin to cry out yet more: Come thou, our true sword, Jesu Christ, and cut not off only the head of this devil, but hew all her limbs in pieces in the sight of all these whom I have approved in thy service. And immediately one like unto thee, O Peter, having a sword, hewed her in pieces: so that I looked earnestly upon you both, both on thee and on him that cut in pieces that devil, and marvelled greatly *to see* how alike ye were. And I awaked, and have told unto thee these signs of Christ. And when Peter heard it he was the more filled with courage, for that Marcellus had seen these things, *knowing* that the Lord alway careth for his own. And being joyful and refreshed by these words, he rose up to go unto the forum.

XXIII. Now the brethren were gathered together, and all that were in Rome, and took places every one for a piece of gold: there came together also the senators and the prefects and those in authority. And Peter came and stood in the midst, and all cried out: Show us, O Peter, who is thy God and what is his greatness which hath given thee confidence. Begrudge not the Romans; they are lovers of the gods. We have had proof of Simon, let us have it of thee; convince us, both of you, whom we ought truly to believe. And as they said these things, Simon also came in, and standing in trouble of mind at Peter's side, at first he looked at him.

And after long silence Peter said: Ye men of Rome, be ye true judges unto us, for I say that I have believed on the living and true God; and I promise to give you proofs of him, which are known unto me, as many among you also can bear witness. For ye see that this man is now rebuked and silent, *knowing* that I drove him out of Judaea because of the deceits which he practised upon Eubula, an honourable and simple woman, by his art magic; and being driven out from thence, he is come hither, thinking to escape notice among you; and lo, he standeth face to face with me. Say now, Simon, didst thou not at Jerusalem fall at my feet and Paul's, when thou sawest the healings that were wrought by our hands, and say: I pray you take of me a payment as much as ye will, that I may be able to lay hands *on men* and do such mighty works? And we when we heard it cursed thee, *saying*: Dost thou think to tempt us *as if* we desired to possess money? And now, fearest thou not at all? My name is Peter, because the Lord Christ vouchsafed to call me 'prepared for all things': for I trust in the living God by whom I shall put down thy sorceries. Now let him do in your presence the wonders which he did aforetime: and what I have now said of him, will ye not believe it?

But Simon said: Thou presumest to speak of Jesus of Nazareth, the son of a carpenter, and a carpenter himself, whose birth is recorded (*or* whose race dwelleth) in Judaea. Hear thou, Peter: the Romans have understanding: they are no fools. And he turned to the people and said: Ye men of Rome, is God born? is he crucified? he that hath a master is no God. And when he so spake, many said: Thou sayest well, Simon.

XXIV. But Peter said: Anathema upon thy words against (*or* in) Christ! Presumest thou to speak thus, whereas the

prophet saith of him: Who shall declare his generation? And
another prophet saith: And we saw him and he had no beauty
nor comeliness. And: In the last times shall a child be born of
the Holy Ghost: his mother knoweth not a man, neither doth
any man say that he is his father. And again he saith: *She
hath brought forth and not brought forth.*[1] And again: Is it
a small thing for you to weary men (*lit.* Is it a small thing that
ye make a contest for men)? Behold, a virgin shall conceive in
the womb. And another prophet saith, honouring the Father:
Neither did we hear her voice, neither did a midwife come in.[2]
Another prophet saith: Born not of the womb of a woman, but
from a heavenly place came he down. And: A stone was cut out
without hands, and smote all the kingdoms. And: The stone
which the builders rejected, the same is become the head of the
corner; and he calleth him a stone elect, precious. And again
a prophet saith concerning him: And behold, I saw one like the
Son of man coming upon a cloud. And what more? O ye men
of Rome, if ye knew the Scriptures of the prophets, I would
expound all unto you: by which Scriptures it was necessary *that
this should be spoken* in a mystery, and that the kingdom of God
should be perfected. But these things shall be opened unto you
hereafter. Now *turn I* unto thee, Simon: do thou some one thing
of those wherewith thou didst before deceive them, and I will
bring it to nought through my Lord Jesus Christ. And Simon
plucked up his boldness and said: If the prefect allow it (*prepare
yourselves* and delay not for my sake)[3].

XXV. But the prefect desired to show patience unto both,
that he might not appear to do aught unjustly. And the prefect
put forward one of his servants and said thus unto Simon:
Take this man and deliver him to death. And to Peter he said:
And do thou revive him. And unto the people the prefect said:
It is now for you to judge whether of these two is acceptable unto
God, he that killeth or he that maketh alive. And straightway
Simon spake in the ear of the lad and made him speechless, and
he died.

And as there began to be a murmuring among the people, one
of the widows who were nourished (refreshed) in Marcellus'
house, standing behind the multitude, cried out: O Peter, servant
of God, my son is dead, the only one that I had. And the people
made place for her and led her unto Peter: and she cast herself
down at his feet, saying: I had one only son, which with his
hands (shoulders) furnished me with nourishment: he raised me

[1] From the apocryphal *Ezekiel* (lost).
[2] From the *Ascension* of *Isaiah*, xi. 14.
[3] This appears to be the sense of the first line of the fragment in the
Oxyrhynchus Papyrus, no. 849 (of early fourth century), in which
parts of chs. xxv and xxvi are contained. The line is intrusive where
it occurs: I think it may have stood originally in this place.

up, he carried me: now that he is dead, who shall reach me
a hand? Unto whom Peter said: Go, with these for witness, and
bring hither thy son, that they may see and be able to believe
that by the power of God he is raised, †and that this man (Simon)
may behold it and fall† (or, and she when she saw him, fell down).
And Peter said to the young men: We have need of some young
men, and, moreover, of such as will believe. And forthwith thirty
young men arose, which were prepared to carry her or to bring
thither her son that was dead. And whereas the widow was
hardly returned to herself, the young men took her up; and she
was crying out and saying: Lo, my son, the servant of Christ
hath sent unto thee: tearing her hair and her face. Now the
young men which were come examined[1] (Gk. apparently, held)
the lad's nostrils to see whether he were indeed dead; and seeing
that he was dead of a truth, they had compassion on the old
woman and said: If thou so will, mother, and hast confidence in
the God of Peter, we will take him up and carry him thither that
he may raise him up and restore him unto thee.

XXVI. And as they said these things, the prefect (in the
forum, Lat.), looking earnestly upon Peter (said: What sayest
thou Peter?) Behold my lad is dead, who also is dear unto the
emperor, and I spared him not, though I had with me other
young men; but I desired rather to make trial (tempt) of thee
and of the God whom thou (preachest), whether ye be true, and
therefore I would have this lad die. And Peter said: God is not
tempted nor proved, O Agrippa, but if he be loved and entreated
he heareth them that are worthy. But since now [2] my God and
Lord Jesus Christ is tempted among you, who hath done so great
signs and wonders by my hands to turn you from your sins—now
also in the sight of all do thou, Lord, at my word, by thy power
raise up him whom Simon hath slain by touching him. And
Peter said unto the master of the lad: Go, take hold on his right
hand, and thou shalt have him alive and walking with thee.
And Agrippa the prefect ran and went to the lad and took his
hand and raised him up. And all the multitude seeing it cried:
One is the God, one is the God of Peter.

XXVII. In the meanwhile the widow's son also was brought
upon a bed by the young men, and the people made way for them
and brought them unto Peter. And Peter lifted up his eyes unto
heaven and stretched forth his hands and said: O holy Father
of thy Son Jesus Christ, who hast granted us thy power, that
we may through thee ask and obtain, and despise all that is in
the world, and follow thee only, who art seen of few and wouldest
be known of many: shine thou about us, Lord, enlighten us,

[1] Here begins the Greek fragment—a single vellum leaf—*Oxyrhynchus Papyri*, no. 849 (pl. VI): it is paged 167, 168. Each side
has 14 lines of 19–20 letters. I follow it here.
[2] End of the Greek fragment.

appear thou, raise up the son of this aged widow, which cannot
help herself without her son. And I, repeating the word of Christ
my Lord, say unto thee: Young man, arise and walk with thy
mother so long as thou canst do her good; and thereafter shalt
thou serve me after a higher sort, ministering in the lot of a deacon
of the bishop (or, and of a bishop). And immediately the dead
man rose up, and the multitudes saw it and marvelled, and the
people cried out: Thou art God the Saviour, thou, the God of
Peter, the invisible God, the Saviour. And they spake among
themselves, marvelling indeed at the power of a man that called
upon his Lord with a word; and they received it unto sanctification.

XXVIII. The fame of it therefore being spread throughout
the city, there came the mother of a certain senator, and cast
herself into the midst of the people, and fell at Peter's feet,
saying: I have learned from my people that thou art a servant
of the merciful God, and dost impart his grace unto all them that
desire this light. Impart therefore the light unto my son, for
I know that thou begrudgest none; turn not away from a matron
that entreateth thee. Unto whom Peter said: Wilt thou believe
on my God, by whom thy son shall be raised? And the mother
said with a loud voice, weeping: I believe, O Peter, I believe!
and all the people cried out: Grant the mother her son. But
Peter said: Let him be brought hither before all these. And
Peter turned himself to the people and said: Ye men of Rome,
I also am one of yourselves, and bear a man's body and am a sinner,
but have obtained mercy: look not therefore upon me as though
I did by mine own power that which I do, but by the power of
my Lord Jesus Christ, who is the judge of quick and dead. In
him do I believe and by him am I sent, and have confidence when
I call upon him to raise the dead. Go thou therefore also,
O woman, and cause thy son to be brought hither and to rise
again. And the woman passed through the midst of the people
and went into the street, running, with great joy, and believing
in her mind she came unto her house, and by means of her young
men she took him up and came unto the forum. Now she bade
the young men put caps [1] on their heads, and to walk before the
bier, and all that she had determined to burn upon the body of
her son to be borne before his bier; and when Peter saw it he had
compassion upon the dead body and upon her. And she came
unto the multitude, while all bewailed her; and a great crowd
of senators and matrons followed after, to behold the wonderful
works of God: for this Nicostratus which was dead was exceeding
noble and beloved of the senate. And they brought him and set
him down before Peter. And Peter called for silence, and with
a loud voice said: Ye men of Rome, let there now be a just
judgement betwixt me and Simon; and judge ye whether of us
two believeth in the living God, he or I. Let him raise up the

[1] *pilei*, a sign that they were now freed.

body that lieth here, and believe in him as the angel of God.
But if he be not able, and I call upon my God and restore the son
alive unto his mother, then believe ye that this man is a sorcerer
and a deceiver, which is entertained among you. And when all
they heard these things, they thought that it was right which
Peter had spoken, and they encouraged Simon, saying: Now,
if there be aught in thee, show it openly! either overcome, or
thou shall be overcome! (or, convince us, or thou shalt be convicted). Why standest thou still? Come, begin! But Simon,
when he saw them all instant with him, stood silent; and thereafter, when he saw the people silent and looking upon him, Simon
cried out, saying: Ye men of Rome, if ye behold the dead man
arise, will ye cast Peter out of the city? And all the people said:
We will not only cast him out, but on the very instant will we
burn him with fire.

Then Simon went to the head of the dead man and stooped
down and thrice raised himself up (or, and said thrice: Raise
thyself), and showed the people that he (the dead) lifted his
head and moved it, and opened his eyes and bowed himself
a little unto Simon. And straightway they began to ask for
wood and torches, wherewith to burn Peter. But Peter receiving
strength of Christ, lifted up his voice and said unto them that
cried out against him: Now see I, ye people of Rome, that ye
are—I must not say fools and vain, so long as your eyes and
your ears and your hearts are blinded. How long shall your
understanding be darkened? see ye not that ye are bewitched,
supposing that a dead man is raised, who hath not lifted himself
up? It would have sufficed me, ye men of Rome, to hold my
peace and die without speaking, and to leave you among the
deceits of this world; but I have the chastisement of fire unquenchable before mine eyes. If therefore it seem good unto
you, let the dead man speak, let him arise if he liveth, let him
loose his jaw that is bound, with his hands, let him call upon his
mother, let him say unto you that cry out: Wherefore cry ye?
let him beckon unto us with his hand. If now ye would see that
he is dead, and yourselves bewitched, let this man depart from
the bier, who hath persuaded you to depart from Christ, and ye
shall see that the *dead man* is such as ye saw him brought hither.

But Agrippa the prefect had no longer patience, but thrust
away Simon with his own hands, and again the dead man lay as
he was before. And the people were enraged, and turned away
from the sorcery of Simon and began to cry out: Hearken,
O Caesar! if now the dead riseth not, let Simon burn instead of
Peter, for verily he hath blinded us. But Peter stretched forth
his hand and said: O men of Rome, have patience! I say not
unto you that if the lad be raised Simon shall burn; for if I say
it, ye will do it. The people cried out: Against thy will, Peter,
we will do it. Unto whom Peter said: If ye continue in this mind.

the lad shall not arise: for we know not to render evil for evil, but we have learned to love our enemies and pray for our persecutors. For if even this man can repent, it were better; for God will not remember evil. Let him come, therefore, into the light of Christ; but if he cannot, let him possess the part of his father the devil, but let not your hands be defiled. And when he had thus spoken unto the people, he went unto the lad, and before he raised him, he said to his mother: These young men whom thou hast set free in the honour of thy son, can yet serve their God when he liveth, being free; for I know that the soul of some is hurt if they shall see thy son arise and *know* that these shall yet be in bondage: but let them all continue free and receive their sustenance as they did before, for thy son is about to rise again; and let them be with him. And Peter looked long upon her, to see her thoughts. And the mother of the lad said: What other can I do? therefore before the prefect I say: whatsoever I was minded to burn upon the body of my son, let them possess it. And Peter said: Let the residue be distributed unto the widows. Then Peter rejoiced in soul and said in the spirit: O Lord that art merciful, Jesu Christ, show thyself unto thy Peter that calleth upon thee like as thou hast always shown him mercy and loving-kindness: and in the presence of all these which have obtained freedom, that these may become *thy* servants, let Nicostratus now arise. And Peter touched the lad's side and said: Arise. And the lad arose and put off his *grave* clothes and sat up and loosed his jaw, and asked for other raiment; and he came down from the bier and said unto Peter: I pray thee, O man *of God*, let us go unto our Lord Christ whom I saw speaking with me; who also showed me unto thee and said to thee: Bring him hither unto me, for he is mine. And when Peter heard this of the lad, he was strengthened yet more in soul by the help of the Lord; and Peter said unto the people: Ye men of Rome, it is thus that the dead are raised up, thus do they converse, thus do they arise and walk, and live so long time as God willeth. Now therefore, ye that have come together unto the sight, if ye turn not from these your evil ways, and from all your gods that are made with hands, and from all uncleanness and concupiscence, ⟨ye shall perish for ever: Turn ye therefore and⟩ receive fellowship with Christ, believing, that ye may obtain everlasting life.

XXIX. And in the same hour they worshipped him as a God, falling down at his feet, and ⟨brought⟩ the sick whom they had at home, that he might heal them.

But the prefect seeing that so great a multitude waited upon Peter, signified to Peter that he should withdraw himself: and Peter told the people to come unto Marcellus' house. But the mother of the lad besought Peter to set foot in her house. But Peter had appointed to be with Marcellus on the Lord's day, to see the widows even as Marcellus had promised, to minister unto them with his own hands. The lad therefore that was risen again said: I depart not from Peter. And his mother, glad and rejoicing, went unto her own house. And on the next day after the sabbath she came to Marcellus' house bringing unto Peter two thousand pieces of gold, and saying unto Peter: Divide these among the virgins of Christ which serve him. But the lad that was risen from the dead, when he saw that he had given nothing to any man, went home and opened the press and himself offered four thousand pieces of gold, saying unto Peter: Lo, I also which was raised, offer a double offering, and myself also from this day forward as a speaking sacrifice unto God.

Here begins the original Greek text as preserved in one of our two manuscripts (that at Mt. Athos). The second (Patmos) manuscript begins, as do the versions, at ch. xxxiii. The Greek and not the Latin is followed in the translation.

XXX. Now on the Lord's day as Peter discoursed unto the brethren and exhorted them unto the faith of Christ, there being present many of the senate and many knights and rich women and matrons, and being confirmed in the faith, one woman that was there, exceeding rich, which was surnamed Chryse because every vessel of hers was of gold—for from her birth she never used a vessel of silver or glass, but golden ones only—said unto Peter: Peter, thou servant of God, he whom thou callest God appeared unto me in a dream and said: Chryse, carry thou unto Peter my minister ten thousand pieces of gold; for thou owest them to him. I have therefore brought them, fearing lest some harm should be done me by him that appeared unto me, which also departed unto heaven. And so saying, she laid down the money and departed. And Peter seeing it glorified the Lord, for that they that were in need should be refreshed. Certain, therefore, of them that were there said unto him: Peter, hast thou not done ill to receive the money of her? for she is ill spoken of throughout all Rome for fornication, and because she keepeth not to one husband, yea, she even hath to do with the young men of her house. Be not therefore a partner with the table of Chryse, but let that which came from her be returned unto her. But Peter hearing it laughed and said to the brethren: What this woman is in the rest of her way of life, I know not, but in that I have received this money, I did it not foolishly; for she did pay it as a debtor unto Christ, and giveth it unto the servants of Christ: for he himself hath provided for them.

XXXI. And they brought unto him also the sick on the sabbath, beseeching that they might recover of their diseases. And many were healed that were sick of the palsy, and the gout, and fevers tertian and quartan, and of every disease of the body were they healed, believing in the name of Jesus Christ, and very many were added every day unto the grace of the Lord.

But Simon the magician, after a few days were past, promised the multitude to convict Peter that he believed not in the true God but was deceived. And when he did many lying wonders, they that were firm in the faith derided him. For in dining-chambers he made certain spirits enter in, which were only an appearance, and not existing in truth. And what should I more say? though he had oft-times been convicted of sorcery, he made lame men seem whole for a little space, and blind likewise, and once he appeared to make many dead to live and move, as he did with Nicostratus (*Gk.* Stratonicus). But Peter followed him throughout and convicted him always unto the beholders: and when he now made a sorry figure and was derided by the people of Rome and disbelieved for that he never succeeded in the things which he promised to perform, being in such a plight at last he said to them: Men of Rome, ye think now that Peter hath prevailed over me, as more powerful, and ye pay more heed to him: ye are deceived. For to-morrow I shall forsake you, godless and impious that ye are, and fly up unto God whose Power I am, though I am become weak. Whereas, then, ye have fallen, I am He that standeth, and I shall go up to my Father and say unto him: Me also, even thy son that standeth, have they desired to pull down; but I consented not unto them, and am returned back unto myself.

XXXII. And already on the morrow a great multitude assembled at the Sacred Way to see him flying. And Peter came unto the place, having seen a vision (*or,* to see the sight), that he might convict him in this also; for when *Simon* entered into Rome, he amazed the multitudes by flying: but Peter that convicted him was *then* not yet living at Rome : which *city* he thus deceived by illusion, so that some were carried away by him (amazed at him).

So then this man standing on an high place beheld Peter and began to say: Peter, at this time when I am going up before all this people that behold me, I say unto thee : If thy God is able, whom the Jews put to death, and stoned you that were chosen of him, let him show that faith in him is *faith* in God, and let it appear at this time, if it be worthy of God. For I, ascending up, will show myself unto all this multitude, who I am. And behold when he was lifted up on high, and all beheld him raised up above all Rome and the temples thereof and the mountains, the faithful looked toward Peter. And Peter seeing the strangeness of the sight cried unto the Lord Jesus Christ: If thou suffer this man to accomplish that which he hath set about, now will all they that have believed on thee be offended, and the signs and wonders which thou hast given them through me will not be believed: hasten thy grace, O Lord, and let him fall from the height and be disabled; and let him not die but be brought to nought, and break his leg in three places. And he fell from the height and brake his leg in three places. Then every man cast stones at him and went away home, and thenceforth believed Peter.

But one of the friends of Simon came quickly out of the way (*or* arrived from a journey), Gemellus by name, of whom Simon had received much money, having a Greek woman to wife, and saw him that he had broken his leg, and said : O Simon, if the Power of God is broken to pieces, shall not that God whose Power thou art, himself be blinded ? Gemellus therefore also ran and followed Peter, saying unto him : I also would be of them that believe on Christ. And Peter said : Is there any that grudgeth it, my brother ? come thou and sit with us.

But Simon in his affliction found some to carry him by night on a bed from Rome unto Aricia; and he abode there a space, and was brought thence unto Terracina to one Castor that was banished from Rome upon an accusation of sorcery. And there he was sorely cut (*Lat.* by two physicians), and so Simon the angel of Satan came to his end.

[*Here the Martyrdom proper begins in the Patmos MS. and the versions.*]

XXXIII. Now Peter was in Rome rejoicing in the Lord with the brethren, and giving thanks night and day for the multitude which was brought daily unto the holy name by the grace of the Lord. And there were gathered also unto Peter the concubines of Agrippa the prefect, being four, Agrippina and Nicaria and Euphemia and Doris; and they, hearing the word concerning chastity and all the oracles of the Lord, were smitten in their souls, and agreeing together to remain pure from the bed of Agrippa they were vexed by him.

Now as Agrippa was perplexed and grieved concerning them—and he loved them greatly—he observed and sent men privily *to see* whither they went, and found that they went unto Peter. He said therefore unto them when they returned: That Christian hath taught you to have no dealings with me: know ye that I will both destroy you, and burn him alive. They, then, endured to suffer all manner of evil at Agrippa's hand, if only they might not suffer the passion of love, being strengthened by the might of Jesus.

XXXIV. And a certain woman which was exceeding beautiful, the wife of Albinus, Caesar's friend, by name Xanthippe, came, she also, unto Peter, with the rest of the matrons, and withdrew herself, she also, from Albinus. He therefore being mad, and loving Xanthippe, and marvelling that she would not sleep even upon the same bed with him, raged like a wild beast and would have dispatched Peter; for he knew that he was the cause

of her separating from his bed. Many other women also, loving
the word of chastity, separated themselves from their husbands,
because they desired them to worship God in sobriety and
cleanness. And whereas there was great trouble in Rome,
Albinus made known his state unto Agrippa, saying to him:
Either do thou avenge me of Peter that hath withdrawn my
wife, or I will avenge myself. And Agrippa said: I have suffered
the same at his hand, for he hath withdrawn my concubines.
And Albinus said unto him: Why then tarriest thou, Agrippa?
let us find him and put him to death for a dealer in curious arts,
that we may have our wives again, and avenge them also which
are not able to put him to death, whose wives also he hath parted
from them.

XXXV. And as they considered these things, Xanthippe took
knowledge of the counsel of her husband with Agrippa, and
sent and showed Peter, that he might depart from Rome. And
the rest of the brethren, together with Marcellus, besought him
to depart. But Peter said unto them: Shall we be runaways,
brethren? and they said to him: Nay, but that thou mayest yet
be able to serve the Lord. And he obeyed the brethren's voice
and went forth alone, saying: Let none of you come forth with
me, but I will go forth alone, having changed the fashion of
mine apparel. And as he went forth of the city, he saw the Lord
entering into Rome. And when he saw him, he said: Lord,
whither *goest thou* thus (*or* here)? And the Lord said unto
him: I go into Rome to be crucified. And Peter said unto
him: Lord, art thou (being) crucified again? He said unto him:
Yea, Peter, I am (being) crucified again. And Peter came to
himself: and having beheld the Lord ascending up into heaven,
he returned to Rome, rejoicing, and glorifying the Lord, for
that he said: I am being crucified: the which was about to
befall Peter.

XXXVI. He went up therefore again unto the brethren, and
told them that which had been seen by him: and they lamented
in soul, weeping and saying: We beseech thee, Peter, take
thought for us that are young. And Peter said unto them:
If it be the Lord's will, it cometh to pass, even if we will it not;
but for you, the Lord is able to stablish you in his faith, and
will found you therein and make you spread abroad, whom he
himself hath planted, that ye also may plant others through
him. But I, so long as the Lord will that I be in the flesh, resist
not; and again if he take me to him I rejoice and am glad.

And while Peter thus spake, and all the brethren wept, behold
four soldiers took him and led him unto Agrippa. And he in
his madness (disease) commanded him to be crucified on an
accusation of godlessness.

The whole multitude of the brethren therefore ran together,
both of rich and poor, orphans and widows, weak and strong,

desiring to see and to rescue Peter, while the people shouted
with one voice, and would not be silenced: What wrong hath
Peter done, O Agrippa? Wherein hath he hurt thee? tell the
Romans! And others said: We fear lest if this man die,
his Lord destroy us all.

And Peter when he came unto the place stilled the people
and said: Ye men that are soldiers of Christ! ye men that
hope in Christ! remember the signs and wonders which ye have
seen *wrought* through me, remember the compassion of God,
how many cures he hath wrought for you. Wait for him that
cometh and shall reward every man according to his doings.
And now be ye not bitter against Agrippa; for he is the minister
of his father's working. And this cometh to pass at all events,
for the Lord hath manifested unto me that which befalleth.
But why delay I and draw not near unto the cross?

XXXVII. And having approached and standing by the cross
he began to say: O name of the cross, *thou* hidden mystery!
O grace ineffable that is pronounced in the name of the cross!
O nature of man, that cannot be separated from God! O love
(friendship) unspeakable and inseparable, that cannot be shown
forth by unclean lips! I seize thee now, I that am at the end
of my delivery hence (*or*, of my coming hither). I will declare
thee, what thou art: I will not keep silence of the mystery
of the cross which of old was shut and hidden from my soul.
Let not the cross be unto you which hope in Christ, this which
appeareth: for it is another thing, different from that which
appeareth, *even* this passion which is according to that of Christ.
And now above all, because ye that can hear are able to hear
it *of me*, that am at the last and final hour of my life, hearken:
Separate your souls from every thing that is of the senses, from
every thing that appeareth, and does not exist in truth. Blind
these eyes of yours, close these ears of yours, put away your doings
that are seen; and ye shall perceive that which concerneth
Christ, and the whole mystery of your salvation: and let thus
much be said unto you that hear, as if it had not been spoken.
But now it is time for thee, Peter, to deliver up thy body unto
them that take it. Receive it then, ye unto whom it belongeth.
I beseech you the executioners, crucify me thus, with the head
downward and not otherwise: and the reason wherefore, I will
tell unto them that hear.

XXXVIII. And when they had hanged him up after the manner
he desired, he began again to say: Ye men unto whom it belongeth to hear, hearken to that which I shall declare unto you
at this especial time as I hang here. Learn ye the mystery of
all nature, and the beginning of all things, what it was. For
the first man, whose race I bear in mine appearance (*or*, of the
race of whom I bear the likeness), fell (was borne) head downwards, and showed forth a manner of birth such as was not

heretofore: for it was dead, having no motion. He, then, being pulled down—who also cast his first state down upon the earth—established this whole disposition of all things, being hanged up an image of the creation (*Gk.* vocation) wherein he made the things of the right hand into left hand and the left hand into right hand, and changed about all the marks of their nature, so that he thought those things that were not fair to be fair, and those that were in truth evil, to be good. Concerning which the Lord saith in a mystery: Unless ye make the things of the right hand as those of the left, and those of the left as those of the right, and those that are above as those below, and those that are behind as those that are before, ye shall not have knowledge of the kingdom.

This thought, therefore, have I declared unto you; and the figure wherein ye now see me hanging is the representation of that man that first came unto birth. Ye therefore, my beloved, and ye that hear me and that shall hear, ought to cease from your former error and return back again. For it is right to mount upon the cross of Christ, who is the word stretched out, the one and only, of whom the spirit saith: For what else is Christ, but the word, the sound of God? So that the word is the upright beam whereon I am crucified. And the sound is that which crosseth it, the nature of man. And the nail which holdeth the cross-tree unto the upright in the midst thereof is the conversion and repentance of man.

XXXIX. Now whereas thou hast made known and revealed these things unto me, O word of life, called now by me wood (*or*, word called now by me the tree of life), I give thee thanks, not with these lips that are nailed *unto the cross*, nor with *this* tongue by which truth and falsehood issue forth, nor with this word which cometh forth by means of art whose nature is material, but with that voice do I give thee thanks, O King, which is perceived (understood) in silence, which is not heard openly, which proceedeth not forth by organs of the body, which goeth not into ears of flesh, which is not heard of corruptible substance which existeth not in the world, neither is sent forth upon earth, nor written in books, which is owned by one and not by another: but with this, O Jesu Christ, do I give thee thanks, with the silence of a voice, wherewith the spirit that is in me loveth thee, speaketh unto thee, seeth thee, and beseecheth thee. Thou art perceived of the spirit only, thou art unto me father, thou my mother, thou my brother, thou my friend, thou my bondsman, thou my steward: thou art the All and the All is in thee: and thou Art, and there is nought else that IS save thee only.

Unto him therefore do ye also, brethren, flee, and if ye learn that in him alone ye exist, ye shall obtain those things whereof he saith unto you: 'which neither eye hath seen nor ear heard, neither have they entered into the heart of man.' We ask, therefore, for that which thou hast promised to give unto us, O thou undefiled Jesu. We praise thee, we give thee thanks, and confess to thee, glorifying thee, even we men that are yet without strength, for thou art God alone, and none other: to whom be glory now and unto all ages. Amen.

XL. And when the multitude that stood by pronounced the Amen with a great sound, together with the Amen Peter gave up his spirit unto the Lord.

And Marcellus not asking leave of any, for it was not possible, when he saw that Peter had given up the ghost, took him down from the cross with his own hands and washed him in milk and wine: and cut fine seven minae of mastic,[1] and of myrrh and aloes and *Indian* leaf other fifty, and perfumed (embalmed) his body and filled a coffin of marble of great price with Attic honey and laid it in his own tomb.

But Peter by night appeared unto Marcellus and said: Marcellus, hast thou heard that the Lord saith: Let the dead be buried of their own dead? And when Marcellus said: Yea, Peter said to him: That, then, which thou hast spent on the dead, thou hast lost: for thou being alive hast like a dead man cared for the dead. And Marcellus awoke and told the brethren of the appearing of Peter: and he was with them that had been stablished in the faith of Christ by Peter, himself also being stablished yet more until the coming of Paul unto Rome.[2]

XLI. [This last chapter, and the last sentence of XL, are thought by Vouaux to be an addition by the author of i–iii, in other words by the compiler of the Greek original of the Vercelli Acts.]

But Nero, learning thereafter that Peter was departed out of this life, blamed the prefect Agrippa, because he had been put to death without his knowledge; for he desired to punish him more sorely and with greater torment, because Peter had made disciples of certain of them that served him, and had caused them to depart from him: so that he was very wrathful and for a long season spake not unto Agrippa: for he sought to destroy all them that had been made disciples by Peter. And he beheld by night one that scourged him and said unto him: Nero, thou canst not now persecute nor destroy the servants of Christ: refrain therefore thine hands from them. And so Nero, being greatly affrighted by such a vision, abstained from *harming* the disciples at that time when Peter also departed this life.

And thenceforth the brethren were rejoicing with one mind and exulting in the Lord, glorifying the God and Saviour (Father?) of our Lord Jesus Christ with the Holy Ghost, unto whom be glory, world without end. Amen.

---

[1] *Gk.* Chian. The adjective was used by itself to signify mastic.

[2] The Latin omits this last sentence, but the other versions have it.

ACTS OF ANDREW

We have no ancient record of the length of this book, as we had in the cases of John, Paul, and Peter (but I suspect it was the most prolix of all the five), and we have fewer relics of the original text than for those. We have, however, a kind of abstract of the whole, written in Latin by Gregory of Tours: and there are Greek *Encomia* of the apostle which also help to the reconstruction of the story. The Martyrdom (as in other cases) exists separately, in many texts. Max Bonnet has established the relations of these to each other: and J. Flamion has made a most careful study of all the fragments.

The best specimen of the original text which we have is a fragment preserved in a Vatican MS., tenth–eleventh centuries, containing discourses of Andrew shortly before his passion. There are also a few ancient quotations.

These Acts may be the latest of the five leading apostolic romances. They belong to the third century: *c.* A. D. 260?

It was formerly thought that the Acts of Andrew and Matthias (Matthew) were an episode of the original romance: but this view has ceased to be held. That legend is akin to the later Egyptian romances about the apostles of which an immense number were produced in the fifth and later centuries. An abstract of them will be given in due course.

The epitome by Gregory of Tours is considered by Flamion to give on the whole the best idea of the contents of the original Acts. The latest edition of it is that by M. Bonnet in the *Monumenta Germaniae Historica* (Greg. Turon. II. 821–47). The greater part appears as Lib. III of the *Historia Apostolica* of (Pseudo-)Abdias, in a text much altered, it seems, in the sixteenth century by Wolfgang Lazius: reprinted in Fabricius' *Cod. Apocr. N. T.*

Gregory's prologue is as follows:

The famous triumphs of the apostles are, I believe, not unknown to any of the faithful, for some of them are taught us in the pages of the gospel, others are related in the Acts of the Apostles, and about some of them books exist in which the actions of each apostle are recorded; yet of the more part we have nothing but their Passions in writing.

Now I have come upon a book on the miracles (virtues, great deeds) of St. Andrew the apostle, which, because of its excessive verbosity, was called by some apocryphal. And of this I thought good to extract and set out the 'virtues' only, omitting all that bred weariness, and so include the wonderful miracles within the compass of one small volume, which might both please the reader and ward off the spite of the adverse critic: for it is not the multitude of words, but the soundness of reason and the purity of mind that produce unblemished faith.

1[1] After the Ascension the apostles dispersed to preach in various countries. Andrew began in the province of Achaia, but Matthew went to the city of Mermidona. (The rest of 1 and the whole of 2

[1] What follows is a full abstract, not a version, of Gregory's text.

give a short abstract of the Acts of Andrew and Matthew which
Gregory either found prefixed to his copy of the Acts of Andrew,
or thought himself obliged to notice, because of the popularity
of the story.)

2 Andrew left Mermidona and came back to his own allotted
district. Walking with his disciples he met a blind man who
said: 'Andrew, apostle of Christ, I know you can restore my
sight, but I do not wish for that: only bid those with you to
give me enough money to clothe and feed myself decently.'
Andrew said: 'This is the devil's voice, who will not allow the
man to recover his sight.' He touched his eyes and healed him.
Then, as he had but a vile rough garment, Andrew said: 'Take
the filthy garment off him and clothe him afresh.' All were
ready to strip themselves, and Andrew said: 'Let him have
what will suffice him.' He returned home thankful.

3 Demetrius of Amasea had an Egyptian boy of whom he
was very fond, who died of a fever. Demetrius hearing of
Andrew's miracles, came, fell at his feet, and besought help.
Andrew pitied him, came to the house, held a very long discourse,
turned to the bier, raised the boy, and restored him to his master.
All believed and were baptized.

4 A Christian lad named Sostratus came to Andrew privately
and told him: 'My mother cherishes a guilty passion for me:
I have repulsed her, and she has gone to the proconsul to throw
the guilt on me. I would rather die than expose her.' The
officers came to fetch the boy, and Andrew prayed and went
with him. The mother accused him. The proconsul bade him
defend himself. He was silent, and so continued, until the
proconsul retired to take counsel. The mother began to weep.
Andrew said: 'Unhappy woman, that dost not fear to cast
thine own guilt on thy son.' She said to the proconsul: 'Ever
since my son entertained his wicked wish he has been in constant
company with this man.' The proconsul was enraged, ordered
the lad to be sewn into the leather bag of parricides and drowned
in the river, and Andrew to be imprisoned till his punishment
should be devised. Andrew prayed, there was an earthquake,
the proconsul fell from his seat, every one was prostrated, and
the mother withered up and died. The proconsul fell at Andrew's
feet praying for mercy. The earthquake and thunder ceased,
and he healed those who had been hurt. The proconsul and his
house were baptized.

5 The son of Cratinus (Gratinus) of Sinope bathed in the
women's bath and was seized by a demon. Cratinus wrote
to Andrew for help: he himself had a fever and his wife dropsy.
Andrew went there in a vehicle. The boy tormented by the evil
spirit fell at his feet. He bade it depart and so it did, with
outcries. He then went to Cratinus' bed and told him he well
deserved to suffer because of his loose life, and bade him rise

and sin no more. He was healed. The wife was rebuked for her infidelity. 'If she is to return to her former sin, let her not now be healed: if she can keep from it, let her be healed.' The water broke out of her body and she was cured. The apostle brake bread and gave it her. She thanked God, believed with all her house, and relapsed no more into sin. Cratinus afterwards sent Andrew great gifts by his servants, and then, with his wife, asked him in person to accept them, but he refused saying: ' It is rather for you to give them to the needy.'

6 After this he went to Nicaea where were seven devils living among the tombs by the wayside, who at noon stoned passers-by and had killed many. And all the city came out to meet Andrew with olive branches, crying: 'Our salvation is in thee, O man of God.' When they had told him all, he said: 'If you believe in Christ you shall be freed.' They cried: 'We will.' He thanked God and commanded the demons to appear; they came in the form of dogs. Said he: 'These are your enemies: if you profess your belief that I can drive them out in Jesus' name, I will do so.' They cried out: 'We believe that Jesus Christ whom thou preachest is the Son of God.' Then he bade the demons go into dry and barren places and hurt no man till the last day. They roared and vanished. The apostle baptized the people and made Callistus bishop.

7 At the gate of Nicomedia he met a dead man borne on a bier, and his old father supported by slaves, hardly able to walk, and his old mother with hair torn, bewailing. 'How has it happened?' he asked. 'He was alone in his chamber and seven dogs rushed on him and killed him.' Andrew sighed and said: 'This is an ambush of the demons I banished from Nicaea. What will you do, father, if I restore your son?' 'I have nothing more precious than him, I will give him.' He prayed: 'Let the spirit of this lad return.' The faithful responded, 'Amen'. Andrew bade the lad rise, and he rose, and all cried: 'Great is the God of Andrew.' The parents offered great gifts which he refused, but took the lad to Macedonia, instructing him.

8 Embarking in a ship he sailed into the Hellespont, on the way to Byzantium. There was a great storm. Andrew prayed and there was calm. They reached Byzantium.

9 Thence proceeding through Thrace they met a troop of armed men who made as if to fall on them. Andrew made the sign of the cross against them, and prayed that they might be made powerless. A bright angel touched their swords and they all fell down, and Andrew and his company passed by while they worshipped him. And the angel departed in a great light.

10 At Perinthus he found a ship going to Macedonia, and an angel told him to go on board. As he preached the captain and the rest heard and were converted, and Andrew glorified God for making himself known on the sea.

11 At Philippi were two brothers, one of whom had two sons, the other two daughters. They were rich and noble, and said: 'There is no family as good as ours in the place: let us marry our sons to our daughters.' It was agreed and the earnest paid by the father of the sons. On the wedding-day a word from God came to them: 'Wait till my servant Andrew comes: he will tell you what you should do.' All preparations had been made, and guests bidden, but they waited. On the third day Andrew came: they went out to meet him with wreaths and told him how they had been charged to wait for him, and how things stood. His face was shining so that they marvelled at him. He said: 'Do not, my children, be deceived: rather repent, for you have sinned in thinking to join together those who are near of kin. We do not forbid or shun marriage [this cannot be the author's original sentiment: it is contradicted by all that we know of the Acts]. It is a divine institution: but we condemn incestuous unions.' The parents were troubled and prayed for pardon. The young people saw Andrew's face like that of an angel, and said: 'We are sure that your teaching is true.' The apostle blessed them and departed.

12 At Thessalonica was a rich noble youth, Exoös, who came without his parents' knowledge and asked to be shown the way of truth. He was taught, and believed, and followed Andrew, taking no care of his worldly estate. The parents heard that he was at Philippi and tried to bribe him with gifts to leave Andrew. He said: 'Would that you had not these riches, then would you know the true God, and escape his wrath.' Andrew, too, came down from the third storey and preached to them, but in vain: he retired and shut the doors of the house. They gathered a band and came to burn the house, saying: 'Death to the son who has forsaken his parents': and brought torches, reeds, and faggots, and set the house on fire. It blazed up. Exoös took a bottle of water and prayed: 'Lord Jesu Christ, in whose hand is the nature of all the elements, who moistenest the dry and driest the moist, coolest the hot and kindlest the quenched, put out this fire that thy servants may not grow evil, but be more enkindled unto faith.' He sprinkled the flames and they died. 'He is become a sorcerer,' said the parents, and got ladders, to climb up and kill them, but God blinded them. They remained obstinate, but one Lysimachus, a citizen, said: 'Why persevere? God is fighting for these. Desist, lest heavenly fire consume you.' They were touched, and said: 'This is the true God.' It was now night, but a light shone out, and they received sight. They went up and fell before Andrew and asked pardon, and their repentance made Lysimachus say: 'Truly Christ whom Andrew preaches is the Son of God,' All were converted except the youth's parents, who cursed him and went home again, leaving all their money to public uses. Fifty

days after they suddenly died, and the citizens, who loved the
youth, returned the property to him. He did not leave Andrew,
but spent his income on the poor.

13 The youth asked Andrew to go with him to Thessalonica.
All assembled in the theatre, glad to see their favourite. The
youth preached to them, Andrew remaining silent, and all
wondered at his wisdom. The people cried out: 'Save the son
of Carpianus who is ill, and we will believe.' Carpianus went
to his house and said to the boy: 'You shall be cured to-day,
Adimantus.' He said: 'Then my dream is come true: I saw
this man in a vision healing me.' He rose up, dressed, and ran
to the theatre, outstripping his father, and fell at Andrew's feet.
The people seeing him walk after twenty-three years, cried:
'There is none like the God of Andrew.'

14 A citizen had a son possessed by an unclean spirit and
asked for his cure. The demon, foreseeing that he would be
cast out, took the son aside into a chamber and made him hang
himself. The father said: 'Bring him to the theatre: I believe
this stranger is able to raise him.' He said the same to Andrew.
Andrew said to the people: 'What will it profit you if you see
this accomplished and do not believe?' They said: 'Fear not,
we will believe.' The lad was raised and they said: 'It is
enough, we do believe.' And they escorted Andrew to the
house with torches and lamps, for it was night, and he taught
them for three days.

15 Medias of Philippi came and prayed for his sick son.
Andrew wiped his cheeks and stroked his head, saying: 'Be
comforted, only believe,' and went with him to Philippi. As
they entered the city an old man met them and entreated
for his sons, whom for an unspeakable crime Medias had imprisoned, and they were putrefied with sores. Andrew said:
'How can you ask help for your son when you keep these men
bound? Loose their chains first, for your unkindness obstructs
my prayers.' Medias, penitent, said: 'I will loose these two and
seven others of whom you have not been told.' They were
brought, tended for three days, cured, and freed. Then the
apostle healed the son, Philomedes, who had been ill twenty-two
years. The people cried: 'Heal our sick as well.' Andrew told
Philomedes to visit them in their houses and bid them rise in
the name of Jesus Christ, by which he had himself been healed.
This was done, and all believed and offered gifts, which Andrew
did not accept.

16 A citizen, Nicolaus, offered a gilt chariot and four white
mules and four white horses as his most precious possession for
the cure of his daughter. Andrew smiled. 'I accept your gifts,
but not these visible ones: if you offer this for your daughter,
what will you for your soul? That is what I desire of you, that
the inner man may recognize the true God, reject earthly things

and desire eternal . . .' He persuaded all to forsake their idols,
and healed the girl. His fame went through all Macedonia.

17 Next day as he taught, a youth cried out: 'What hast thou
to do with us. Art thou come to turn us out of our own place?'
Andrew summoned him: 'What is your work?' 'I have dwelt
in this boy from his youth and thought never to leave him:
but three days since I heard his father say, "I shall go to
Andrew": and now I fear the torments thou bringest us and
I shall depart.' The spirit left the boy. And many came and
asked: 'In whose name dost thou cure our sick?'

Philosophers also came and disputed with him, and no one
could resist his teaching.

18 At this time, one who opposed him went to the proconsul
Virinus and said: 'A man is arisen in Thessalonica who says
the temples should be destroyed and ceremonies done away,
and all the ancient law abolished, and one God worshipped,
whose servant he says he is.' The proconsul sent soldiers and
knights to fetch Andrew. They found his dwelling: when they
entered, his face so shone that they fell down in fear. Andrew
told those present the proconsul's purpose. The people armed
themselves against the soldiers, but Andrew stopped them. The
proconsul arrived; not finding Andrew in the appointed place,
he raged like a lion and sent twenty more men. They, on arrival,
were confounded and said nothing. The proconsul sent a large
troop to bring him by force. Andrew said: 'Have you come
for me?' 'Yes, if you are the sorcerer who says the gods ought
not to be worshipped.' 'I am no sorcerer, but the apostle of
Jesus Christ whom I preach.' At this, one of the soldiers drew
his sword and cried: 'What have I to do with thee, Virinus, that
thou sendest me to one who can not only cast me out of this
vessel, but burn me by his power? Would that you would come
yourself! you would do him no harm.' And the devil went out
of the soldier and he fell dead. On this came the proconsul
and stood before Andrew but could not see him. 'I am he whom
thou seekest.' His eyes were opened, and he said in anger:
'What is this madness, that thou despisest us and our officers?
Thou art certainly a sorcerer. Now will I throw thee to the
beasts for contempt of our gods and us, and we shall see if the
crucified whom thou preachest will help thee.' *Andrew:* 'Thou
must believe, proconsul, in the true God and his Son whom he
hath sent, specially now that one of thy men is dead.' And
after long prayer he touched the soldier: 'Rise up: my God
Jesus Christ raiseth thee.' He arose and stood whole. The
people cried: 'Glory be to our God.' The proconsul: 'Believe
not, O people, believe not the sorcerer.' They said: 'This is no
sorcery but sound and true teaching.' The proconsul: 'I shall
throw this man to the beasts and write about you to Caesar,
that ye may perish for contemning his laws.' They would have

stoned him, and said: 'Write to Caesar that the Macedonians have received the word of God, and forsaking their idols, worship the true God.'

Then the proconsul in wrath retired to the praetorium, and in the morning brought beasts to the stadium and had the apostle dragged thither by the hair and beaten with clubs. First they sent in a fierce boar who went about him thrice and touched him not. The people praised God. A bull led by thirty soldiers and incited by two hunters, did not touch Andrew but tore the hunters to pieces, roared, and fell dead. 'Christ is the true God,' said the people. An angel was seen to descend and strengthen the apostle. The proconsul in rage sent in a fierce leopard, which left every one alone but seized and strangled the proconsul's son; but Virinus was so angry that he said nothing of it nor cared. Andrew said to the people: 'Recognize now that this is the true God, whose power subdues the beasts, though Virinus knows him not. But that ye may believe the more, I will raise the dead son, and confound the foolish father.' After long prayer, he raised him. The people would have slain Virinus, but Andrew restrained them, and Virinus went to the praetorium, confounded.

19 After this a youth who followed the apostle sent for his mother to meet Andrew. She came, and after being instructed, begged him to come to their house, which was devastated by a great serpent. As Andrew approached, it hissed loudly and with raised head came to meet him; it was fifty cubits long: every one fell down in fear. Andrew said: 'Hide thy head, foul one, which thou didst raise in the beginning for the hurt of mankind, and obey the servants of God, and die.' The serpent roared, and coiled about a great oak near by and vomited poison and blood and died.

Andrew went to the woman's farm, where a child killed by the serpent lay dead. He said to the parents: 'Our God who would have you saved hath sent me here that you may believe on him. Go and see the slayer slain.' They said: 'We care not so much for the child's death, if we be avenged.' They went, and Andrew said to the proconsul's wife (her conversion has been omitted by Gregory): 'Go and raise the boy.' She went, nothing doubting, and said: 'In the name of my God Jesus Christ, rise up whole.' The parents returned and found their child alive, and fell at Andrew's feet.

20 On the next night he saw a vision which he related. 'Hearken, beloved, to my vision. I beheld, and lo, a great mountain raised up on high, which had on it nothing earthly, but only shone with such light, that it seemed to enlighten all the world. And lo, there stood by me my beloved brethren the apostles Peter and John; and John reached his hand to Peter and raised him to the top of the mount, and turned to me and asked me to

go up after Peter, saying: "Andrew, thou art to drink Peter's cup." And he stretched out his hands and said: "Draw near to me and stretch out thy hands so as to join them unto mine, and put thy head by my head." When I did so I found myself shorter than John. After that he said to me: "Wouldst thou know the image of that which thou seest, and who it is that speaketh to thee?" and I said: "I desire to know it." And he said to me: "I am the word of the cross whereon thou shalt hang shortly, for his name's sake whom thou preachest." And many other things said he unto me, of which I must now say nothing, but they shall be declared when I come unto the sacrifice. But now let all assemble that have received the word of God, and let me commend them unto the Lord Jesus Christ, that he may vouchsafe to keep them unblemished in his teaching. For I am now being loosed from the body, and go unto that promise which he hath vouchsafed to promise me, who is the Lord of heaven and earth, the Son of God Almighty, very God with the Holy Ghost, continuing for everlasting ages.'

(I feel sure that John in the latter part of this vision has been substituted by Gregory for Jesus. The echoes of the Acts of John and of Peter are very evident here.)

All the brethren wept and smote their faces. When all were gathered, Andrew said: 'Know, beloved, that I am about to leave you, but I trust in Jesus whose word I preach, that he will keep you from evil, that this harvest which I have sown among you may not be plucked up by the enemy, that is, the knowledge and teaching of my Lord Jesus Christ. But do ye pray always and stand firm in the faith, that the Lord may root out all tares of offence and vouchsafe to gather you into his heavenly garner as pure wheat.' So for five days he taught and confirmed them: then he spread his hands and prayed: 'Keep, I beseech thee, O Lord, this flock which hath now known thy salvation, that the wicked one may not prevail against it, but that what by thy command and my means it hath received, it may be able to preserve inviolate for ever.' And all responded 'Amen'. He took bread, brake it with thanksgiving, gave it to all, saying: 'Receive the grace which Christ our Lord God giveth you by me his servant.' He kissed every one and commended them to the Lord, and departed to Thessalonica, and after teaching there two days, he left them.

21 Many faithful from Macedonia accompanied him in two ships. And all were desirous of being on Andrew's ship, to hear him. He said: 'I know your wish, but this ship is too small. Let the servants and baggage go in the larger ship, and you with me in this.' He gave them Anthimus to comfort them, and bade them go into another ship which he ordered to keep always near . . . that they might see him and hear the word of God. (This

is a little confused.) And as he slept a little, one fell overboard. Anthimus roused him, saying: 'Help us, good master; one of thy servants perisheth.' He rebuked the wind, there was a calm, and the man was borne by the waves to the ship. Anthimus helped him on board and all marvelled. On the twelfth day they reached Patrae in Achaia, disembarked, and went to an inn.

22 Many asked him to lodge with them, but he said he could only go where God bade him. That night he had no revelation, and the next night, being distressed at this, he heard a voice saying: 'Andrew, I am alway with thee and forsake thee not,' and was glad.

Lesbius the proconsul was told in a vision to take him in, and sent a messenger for him. He came, and entering the proconsul's chamber found him lying as dead with closed eyes; he struck him on the side and said: 'Rise and tell us what hath befallen thee.' Lesbius said: 'I abominated the way which you teach, and sent soldiers in ships to the proconsul of Macedonia to send you bound to me, but they were wrecked and could not reach their destination. As I continued in my purpose of destroying your Way, two black men (Ethiopes) appeared and scourged me, saying: " We can no longer prevail here, for the man is coming whom you mean to persecute. So to-night, while we still have the power, we will avenge ourselves on you." And they beat me sorely and left me. But now do you pray that I may be pardoned and healed.' Andrew preached the word and all believed, and the proconsul was healed and confirmed in the faith.

23 Now Trophima, once the proconsul's mistress, and now married to another, left her husband and clave to Andrew. Her husband came to her lady (Lesbius' wife) and said she was renewing her liaison with the proconsul. The wife, enraged, said: 'This is why my husband has left me these six months.' She called her steward (procurator) and had Trophima sentenced as a prostitute and sent to the brothel. Lesbius knew nothing, and was deceived by his wife, when he asked about her. Trophima in the brothel prayed continually, and had the Gospel on her bosom, and no one could approach her. One day one offered her violence, and the Gospel fell to the ground. She cried to God for help and an angel came, and the youth fell dead. After that, she raised him, and all the city ran to the sight.

Lesbius' wife went to the bath with the steward, and as they bathed an ugly demon came and killed them both. Andrew heard and said: 'It is the judgement of God for their usage of Trophima.' The lady's nurse, decrepit from age, was carried to the spot, and supplicated for her. Andrew said to Lesbius: 'Will you have her raised?' 'No, after all the ill she has done.' 'We ought not to be unmerciful.' Lesbius went to the praetorium; Andrew raised his wife, who remained shamefaced: he bade her go home and pray. 'First', she said, 'reconcile me to

Trophima whom I have injured.' 'She bears you no malice.'
He called her and they were reconciled. Callisto was the wife.
Lesbius, growing in faith, came one day to Andrew and confessed
all his sins. Andrew said: 'I thank God, my son, that thou
fearest the judgement to come. Be strong in the Lord in whom
thou believest.' And he took his hand and walked with him on
the shore.

24 They sat down, with others, on the sand, and he taught.
A corpse was thrown up by the sea near them. 'We must learn',
said Andrew, 'what the enemy has done to him.' So he raised
him, gave him a garment, and bade him tell his story. He said:
'I am the son of Sostratus, of Macedonia, lately come from Italy.
On returning home I heard of a new teaching, and set forth to
find out about it. On the way here we were wrecked and all
drowned.' And after some thought, he realized that Andrew
was the man he sought, and fell at his feet and said: 'I know
that thou art the servant of the true God. I beseech thee for
my companions, that they also may be raised and know him.'
Then Andrew instructed him, and thereafter prayed God to show
the bodies of the other drowned men: thirty-nine were washed
ashore, and all there prayed for them to be raised. Philopator,
the youth, said: 'My father sent me here with a great sum.
Now he is blaspheming God and his teaching. Let it not be so.'
Andrew ordered the bodies to be collected, and said: 'Whom
will you have raised first?' He said: 'Warus my foster-brother.'
So he was first raised and then the other thirty-eight. Andrew
prayed over each, and then told the brethren each to take the
hand of one and say: 'Jesus Christ the son of the living God
raiseth thee.'

Lesbius gave much money to Philopator to replace what he
had lost, and he abode with Andrew.

25 A woman, Calliopa, married to a murderer, had an illegitimate
child and suffered in travail. She told her sister to call on Diana
for help; when she did so the devil appeared to her at night and
said: 'Why do you trouble me with vain prayers? Go to Andrew
in Achaia.' She came, and he accompanied her to Corinth,
Lesbius with him. Andrew said to Calliopa: 'You deserve to
suffer for your evil life: but believe in Christ, and you will be
relieved, but the child will be born dead.' And so it was.

26 Andrew did many signs in Corinth. Sostratus the father
of Philopator, warned in a vision to visit Andrew, came first to
Achaia and then to Corinth. He met Andrew walking with
Lesbius, recognized him by his vision, and fell at his feet. Philopator said: 'This is my father, who seeks to know what he must
do.' *Andrew*: 'I know that he is come to learn the truth; we
thank God who reveals himself to believers.' Leontius the
servant of Sostratus, said to him: 'Seest thou, sir, how this
man's face shineth?' 'I see, my beloved,' said Sostratus; 'let

us never leave him, but live with him and hear the words of eternal life.' Next day they offered Andrew many gifts, but he said: 'It is not for me to take aught of you but your own selves. Had I desired money, Lesbius is richer.'

27 After some days he bade them prepare him a bath; and going there saw an old man with a devil, trembling exceedingly. As he wondered at him, another, a youth, came out of the bath and fell at his feet, saying: 'What have we to do with thee, Andrew? Hast thou come here to turn us out of our abodes?' Andrew said to the people: 'Fear not,' and drove out both the devils. Then, as he bathed, he told them: 'The enemy of mankind lies in wait everywhere, in baths and in rivers; therefore we ought always to invoke the Lord's name, that he may have no power over us.'

They brought their sick to him to be healed, and so they did from other cities.

28 An old man, Nicolaus, came with clothes rent and said: 'I am seventy-four years old and have always been a libertine. Three days ago I heard of your miracles and teaching. I thought I would turn over a new leaf, and then again that I would not. In this doubt, I took a Gospel and prayed God to make me forget my old devices. A few days after, I forgot the Gospel I had about me, and went to the brothel. The woman said: "Depart, old man, depart: thou art an angel of God, touch me not nor approach me, for I see in thee a great mystery." Then I remembered the Gospel, and am come to you for help and pardon.' Andrew discoursed long against incontinence, and prayed from the sixth to the ninth hour. He rose and washed his face and said: 'I will not eat till I know if God will have mercy on this man.' A second day he fasted, but had no revelation until the fifth day, when he wept vehemently and said: 'Lord, we obtain mercy for the dead, and now this man that desireth to know thy greatness, wherefore should he not return and thou heal him?' A voice from heaven said: 'Thou hast prevailed for the old man; but like as thou art worn with fasting, let him also fast, that he may be saved.' And he called him and preached abstinence. On the sixth day he asked the brethren all to pray for Nicolaus, and they did. Andrew then took food and permitted the rest to eat. Nicolaus went home, gave away all his goods, and lived for six months on dry bread and water. Then he died. Andrew was not there, but in the place where he was he heard a voice: 'Andrew, Nicolaus for whom thou didst intercede, is become mine.' And he told the brethren that Nicolaus was dead, and prayed that he might rest in peace.

29 And while he abode in that place (probably Lacedaemon) Antiphanes of Megara came and said: 'If there be in thee any kindness, according to the command of the Saviour whom thou preachest, show it now.' Asked what his story was, he told it.

'Returning from a journey, I heard the porter of my house crying out. They told me that he and his wife and son were tormented of a devil. I went upstairs and found other servants gnashing their teeth, running at me, and laughing madly. I went further up and found they had beaten my wife: she lay with her hair over her face unable to recognize me. Cure her, and I care nothing for the others.' Andrew said: 'There is no respect of persons with God. Let us go there.' They went from Lacedaemon to Megara, and when they entered the house, all the devils cried out: 'What dost thou here, Andrew? Go where thou art permitted: this house is ours.' He healed the wife and all the possessed persons, and Antiphanes and his wife became firm adherents.

30 He returned to Patrae where Egeas was now proconsul, and one Iphidamia, who had been converted by a disciple, Sosias, came and embraced his feet and said: 'My lady Maximilla who is in a fever has sent for you. The proconsul is standing by her bed with his sword drawn, meaning to kill himself when she expires.' He went to her, and said to Egeas: 'Do thyself no harm, but put up thy sword into his place. There will be a time when thou wilt draw it on me.' Egeas did not understand, but made way. Andrew took Maximilla's hand, she broke into a sweat, and was well: he bade them give her food. The proconsul sent him 100 pieces of silver, but he would not look at them.

31 [1] Going thence he saw a sick man lying in the dirt begging, and healed him.

32 [2] Elsewhere he saw a blind man with wife and son, and said: 'This is indeed the devil's work: he has blinded them in soul and body.' He opened their eyes and they believed.

33 [3] One who saw this said: 'I beg thee come to the harbour; there is a man, the son of a sailor, sick fifty years, cast out of the house, lying on the shore, incurable, full of ulcers and worms.' They went to him. The sick man said: 'Perhaps you are the disciple of that God who alone can save.' Andrew said: 'I am he who in the name of my God can restore thee to health,' and added: 'In the name of Jesus Christ, rise and follow me.' He left his filthy rags and followed, the pus and worms flowing from him. They went into the sea, and the apostle washed him in the name of the Trinity and he was whole, and ran naked through the city proclaiming the true God.

34 [4] At this time the proconsul's brother Stratocles arrived from Italy. One of his slaves, Alcman, whom he loved, was taken by a devil and lay foaming in the court. Stratocles hearing of it said: 'Would the sea had swallowed me before I saw this.'

[1] 31 This occurs in the Greek *Laudatio* 39.
[2] 32 In *Laudatio* 40.
[3] 33 In *Laudatio* 41, at considerable length.
[4] 34 In *Laudatio* 43, at considerable length.

Maximilla and Iphidamia said: 'Be comforted: there is here a man of God, let us send for him.' When he came he took the boy's hand and raised him whole. Stratocles believed and clave to Andrew.

35 Maximilla went daily to the praetorium and sent for Andrew to teach there. Egeas was away in Macedonia, angry because Maximilla had left him since her conversion. As they were all assembled one day, he returned, to their great terror. Andrew prayed that he might not be suffered to enter the place till all had dispersed. And Egeas was at once seized with indisposition, and in the interval the apostle signed them all and sent them away, himself last. But Maximilla on the first opportunity came to Andrew and received the word of God and went home. [At about this point we must place the episodes quoted by Evodius of Uzala : see below.]

36 After this Andrew was taken and imprisoned by Egeas, and all came to the prison to be taught. After a few days he was scourged and crucified; he hung for three days, preaching, and expired, as is fully set forth in his Passion. Maximilla embalmed and buried his body.

37 From the tomb comes manna like flour, and oil: the amount shows the barrenness or fertility of the coming season—as I have told in my first book of Miracles. I have not set out his Passion at length, because I find it well done by some one else.

38 This much have I presumed to write, unworthy, unlettered, &c. The author's prayer for himself ends the book. May Andrew, on whose death-day he was born, intercede to save him.

(The Passion to which Gregory alludes is that which begins 'Conversante et docente'.)

Of the detached fragments and quotations which precede the Passion there are three:

(a) One is in the Epistle of Titus (see p. 265).

When, finally, Andrew also [John has been cited shortly before] had come to a wedding, he too, to manifest the glory of God, disjoined certain who were intended to marry each other, men and women, and instructed them to continue holy in the single state.

No doubt this refers to the story in Gregory, ch. 11. Gregory, it may be noted, has altered the story (or has used an altered text), for the marriage of cousins was not forbidden till Theodosius' time (so Flamion). He or his source has imagined the relationship between the couples; in the original Acts none need have existed: the mere fact of the marriage was enough.

(b) The next are in a tract by Evodius, bishop of Uzala, against the Manichees:

Observe, in the Acts of Leucius which he wrote under the name of the apostles, what manner of things you accept about

Maximilla the wife of Egetes: who, refusing to pay her due to her husband (though the apostle has said: Let the husband pay the due to the wife and likewise the wife to the husband: 1 Cor. vii. 3), imposed her maid Euclia upon her husband, decking her out, as is there written, with wicked (*lit.* hostile) enticements and paintings, and substituted her as deputy for herself at night, so that he in ignorance used her as his wife.

There also is it written, that when this same Maximilla and Iphidamia were gone together to hear the apostle Andrew, a beautiful child, who, Leucius would have us understand, was either God or at least an angel, escorted them to the apostle Andrew and went to the praetorium of Egetes, and entering their chamber feigned a woman's voice, as of Maximilla, complaining of the sufferings of womankind, and of Iphidamia replying. When Egetes heard this dialogue, he went away. [These incidents must have intervened between cc. 35 and 36 of Gregory of Tours.]

(c) Evodius quotes another sentence, not certainly from the Acts of Andrew, but more in their manner than in that of *John* or *Peter*:

In the Acts written by Leucius, which *the Manichees* receive, it is thus written:

For the deceitful figments and pretended shows and collection (force, compelling) of visible things do not even proceed from their own nature, but from that man who of his own will has become worse through seduction.

It is obscure enough, in original and version: but is the kind of thing that would appeal to those who thought of material things and phenomena as evil.

We do not wonder that such narratives as that which Evodius quotes have been expunged, either by Gregory or his source, from the text.

The next passage is a fragment of some pages in length found by M. Bonnet in a Vatican MS. (Gr. 808) of tenth to eleventh century. There is no doubt that it is a piece of the original Acts. It is highly tedious in parts.

Andrew in prison discourses to the brethren.

1 . . . is there in you altogether slackness? are ye not yet convinced of yourselves that ye do not yet bear his goodness? let us be reverent, let us rejoice with ourselves in the bountiful (ungrudging) fellowship which cometh of him. Let us say unto ourselves: Blessed is our race! by whom hath it been loved? blessed is our state! of whom hath it obtained mercy? we are not cast on the ground, we that have been recognized by so great highness: we are not the offspring of time, afterward *to be* dissolved by time; we are not a contrivance (product) of motion, *made to be* again destroyed by itself, nor *things* of earthly birth, ending again therein. We belong, then, to a greatness, unto which we aspire, *of which* we are the property, and peradventure

to *a greatness* that hath mercy upon us. We belong to the better; therefore we flee from the worse: we belong to the beautiful, for whose sake we reject the foul; to the righteous, by whom we cast away the unrighteous; to the merciful, by whom we reject the unmerciful; to the Saviour, by whom we recognize the destroyer; to the light, by whom we have cast away the darkness; to the One, by whom we have turned away from the many; to the heavenly, by whom we have learned *to know* the earthly; to the abiding, by whom we have seen the transitory. If we desire to offer unto God that hath had mercy on us a worthy thanksgiving or confidence or hymn or boasting, *what better cause (theme) have we* than that we have been recognized by him?

2 And having discoursed thus to the brethren, he sent them away every one to his house, saying to them: Neither are ye ever forsaken of me, ye that are servants of Christ, because of the love that is in him: neither again shall I be forsaken of you, because of his intercession (mediation). And every one departed unto his house: and there was among them rejoicing after this sort for many days, while Aegeates took not thought to prosecute the accusation against the Apostle. Every one of them then was confirmed at that time in hope toward the Lord, and they assembled without fear in the prison, with Maximilla, Iphidamia, and the rest, continually†, being sheltered by the protection and grace of the Lord.

3 But one day Aegeates, as he was hearing causes, remembered the matter concerning Andrew: and as one seized with madness, he left the cause which he had in hand, and rose up from the judgement seat and ran quickly to the praetorium, inflamed with love of Maximilla and *desiring to persuade* her with flatteries. And Maximilla was beforehand with him, coming from the prison, and entering the house. And he went in and said to her:

4 Maximilla, thy parents counted me worthy of being thy consort, and gave me thine hand in marriage, not looking to wealth or descent or renown, but it may be to my good disposition of soul: and, that I may *pass over* much that I might utter in reproach of thee, both of that which I have enjoyed at thy parents' hands and thou from me during all our life, I am come, *leaving* the court, to learn of thee this one thing: *answer me then* reasonably; if thou wert as the wife of former days, living with me in the way we know, sleeping, conversing, bearing offspring with me, I would deal well with thee in all points; nay more, I would set free the stranger whom I hold in prison: but if thou wilt not—to thee I would do nothing harsh, for indeed I cannot; but him, whom thou affectionest more than me, I will afflict yet more. Consider, then, Maximilla, to whether of the two thou inclinest, and answer me to-morrow; for I am wholly armed for this *emergency*.

5 And with these words he went out; but Maximilla again at

the accustomed hour, with Iphidamia, went to Andrew: and putting his hands before her own eyes, and then putting them to her mouth, she began to declare to him the whole matter of the demand of Aegeates. And Andrew answered her:

I know, Maximilla my child, that thou thyself art moved to resist the whole attraction (promise) of nuptial union, desiring to be quit of a foul and polluted way of life: and this hath long been firmly held in thine (*MS.* mine) intention; but now thou wishest for the further testimony of mine opinion. I testify, O Maximilla: do it not; be not vanquished by the threat of Aegeates: be not overcome by his discourse: fear not his shameful counsels: fall not to his artful flatteries: consent not to surrender thyself to his impure spells; but endure all his torments, looking unto us for a little space, and thou shalt see him wholly numbed and withering away from thee and from all that are akin to thee. But (For) that which I most needed to say to thee—for I rest not till I fulfil the business which is seen, and which cometh to pass in thy person—hath escaped me: and rightly in thee do I behold Eve repenting, and in myself ,Adam returning; for that which she suffered in ignorance, thou now (for whose soul I strive) settest right by returning: and that which the spirit suffered which was overthrown with her and slipped away from itself, is set right in me, with thee who seest thyself being brought back. For her defect thou hast remedied by not suffering like her; and his imperfection I have perfected by taking refuge with God; that which she disobeyed thou hast obeyed: that whereto he consented I flee from: and that which they both transgressed we have been aware of; for it is ordained that every one should correct (and raise up again) his own fall.

6 I, then, having said this as I have said it, would go on to speak as followeth: Well done, O nature that art being saved, for †thou hast been strong† and hast not hidden thyself (*from God like Adam*)! Well done, O soul that criest out of what thou hast suffered, and returnest unto thyself! Well done, O man that understandest what is thine and dost press on to what is thine! Well done, thou that hearest what is spoken, for I see thee to be greater than things that are thought or spoken! I recognize thee as more powerful than the things which seemed to overpower thee; as more beautiful than those which cast thee down into foulness, which brought thee down into captivity. Perceiving then, O man, all this in thyself, that thou art immaterial, holy, light, akin to him that is unborn, that thou art intellectual, heavenly, translucent, pure, above the flesh, above the world, above rulers, above principalities, over whom thou art in truth, *then* comprehend thyself in thy condition and receive full *knowledge* and understand wherein thou excellest: and beholding thine own face in thine essence, break asunder all bonds—I say not *only* those that are of thy birth, but those that are above

birth, whereof we have set forth to thee the names which are exceeding great—desire earnestly to see him that is revealed unto thee, him who doth not come into being, whom perchance thou alone shalt recognize with confidence.

7 These things have I spoken of thee, Maximilla, for in their meaning the things I have spoken reach unto thee. Like as Adam died in Eve because he consented unto her †confession†, so do I now live in thee that keepest the Lord's commandment and stablishest thyself in the rank (dignity) of thy being. But the threats of Aegeates do thou trample down, Maximilla, knowing that we have God that hath mercy on us. And let not his noise move thee, but continue chaste; and let him punish me not only with such torments as bonds, but let him cast me to the beasts or burn me with fire, and throw me from a precipice. And what need I say? there is but this one body; let him abuse that as he will, for it is akin to himself.

8 And yet again unto thee is my speech, Maximilla: I say unto thee, give not thyself over unto Aegeates: withstand his ambushes; for indeed, Maximilla, I have seen my Lord saying unto me: Andrew, Aegeates' father the devil will loose thee from this prison. Thine, therefore, let it be henceforth to keep thyself chaste and pure, holy, unspotted, sincere, free from adultery, not reconciled to the discourses of our enemy, unbent, unbroken, tearless, unwounded, not storm-tossed, undivided, not stumbling, without fellow-feeling for the works of Cain. For if thou give not up thyself, Maximilla, to what is contrary to these, I also shall rest, though I be thus forced to leave this life for thy sake, that is, for mine own. But if I were thrust out hence, even I, who, it may be, might avail through thee to profit others that are akin to me, and if thou wert persuaded by the discourse of Aegeates and the flatteries of his father the serpent, so that thou didst turn unto thy former works, know thou that on thine account I should be tormented until thou thyself sawest that I had contemned life for the sake of a soul which was not worthy.

9 I entreat, therefore, the wise man that is in thee that thy mind continue †clear seeing†. I entreat thy mind that is not seen, that it be preserved *whole*: I beseech thee, love thy Jesus, and yield not unto the worse. Assist me, thou whom I entreat as a man, that I may become perfect: help me also, that thou mayest recognize thine own true nature: feel with me in my suffering, that thou mayest take knowledge of what I suffer, and escape suffering: see that which I see, and thou shalt be blind to what thou seest: see that which thou shouldst, and thou shalt not see that thou shouldst not: hearken to what I say, and cast away that which thou hast heard.

10 These things have I spoken unto thee and unto every one that heareth, if he will hear. But thou, O Stratocles, said he,

looking toward him, Why art thou so oppressed, with many tears and groanings to be heard afar off? what is the lowness of spirit that is on thee? why thy much pain and thy great anguish? dost thou take note of what is said, and wherefore I pray thee to be disposed in mind as my child? (or, my child, to be composed in mind): dost thou perceive unto whom my words are spoken? hath each of them taken hold on thine understanding? have they whetted (*MS*. touched) thine intellectual part? have I thee as one that hath hearkened to me? do I find myself in thee? is there in thee one that speaketh whom I see to be mine own? doth he love him that speaketh in me and desire to have fellowship with him? doth he wish to be made one with him? doth he hasten to become his friend? doth he yearn to be joined with him? doth he find in him any rest? hath he where to lay his head? doth nought oppose him there? nought that is wroth with him, resisteth him, hateth him, fleeth from him, is savage, avoideth, turneth away, starteth off, is burdened, maketh war, talketh with others, is flattered by others, agreeth with others? Doth nothing else disturb him? Is there one within that is strange to me? an adversary, a breaker of peace, an enemy, a cheat, a sorcerer, a crooked dealer, unsound, guileful, a hater of men, a hater of the word, one like a tyrant, boastful, puffed up, mad, akin to the serpent, a weapon of the devil, a friend of the fire, belonging to darkness? Is there in thee any one, Stratocles, that cannot endure my saying these things? Who is it? Answer: do I talk in vain? have I spoken in vain? Nay, saith the man in thee, Stratocles, who now again weepeth.

11 And Andrew took the hand of Stratocles and said: I have him whom I loved; I shall rest on him whom I look for; for thy yet groaning, and weeping without restraint, is a sign unto me that I have already found rest, that I have not spoken to thee these words which are akin to me, in vain.

12 And Stratocles answered him: Think not, most blessed Andrew, that there is aught else that afflicteth me but thee; for the words that come forth of thee are like arrows of fire shot against me, and every one of them reacheth me and verily burneth me up. That part of my soul which inclineth to what I hear is tormented, divining the affliction that is to follow, for thou thyself departest, and, I know, nobly: but hereafter when I seek thy care and affection, where shall I find it, or in whom? I have received the seeds of the words of salvation, and thou wast the sower: but that they should sprout up and grow needs none other but thee, most blessed Andrew. And what else have I say to thee but this? I need much mercy and help from thee, to become worthy of the seed I have from thee, which will not otherwise increase perpetually or grow up into the light except thou willest it, and prayest for them and for the whole of me.

13 And Andrew answered him: This, my child, was what
I beheld in thee myself. And I glorify my Lord that my thought
of thee walked not on the void, but knew what it said. But that
ye may know the truth, to-morrow doth Aegeates deliver me up
to be crucified: for Maximilla the servant of the Lord will enrage
the enemy that is in him, unto whom he belongeth, by not
consenting to that which is hateful to her; and by turning
against me he will think to console himself.

14 Now while the apostle spake these things, Maximilla was
not there, for she having heard throughout the words wherewith
he answered her, and being in part composed by them, and of
such a mind as the words pointed out, set forth not inadvisedly
nor without purpose and went to the praetorium. And she
bade farewell to all the life of the flesh, and when Aegeates
brought to her the same demand which he had told her to
consider, whether she would lie with him, she rejected it; and
thenceforth he bent himself to putting Andrew to death, and
thought to what death he should expose him. And when of all
deaths crucifixion alone prevailed with him, he went away with
his like and dined; and Maximilla, the Lord going before her in
the likeness of Andrew, with Iphidamia came back to the prison;
and there being therein a great gathering of the brethren, she
found *Andrew* discoursing thus:

15 I, brethren, was sent forth by the Lord as an apostle unto
these regions whereof my Lord thought me worthy, not to teach
any man, but to remind every man that is akin to such words,
that they live in evils which are temporal, delighting in their
injurious delusions: wherefrom I have always exhorted you also
to depart, and encouraged you to press toward things that
endure, and to take flight from all that is transitory (flowing);
for ye see that none of you standeth, but that all things, even to
the customs of men, are easily changeable. And this befalleth
because the soul is untrained and erreth toward nature and
holdeth pledges †of† its error. I therefore account them blessed
who have become obedient unto the word preached, and thereby
see the mysteries of their own nature; for whose sake all things
have been builded up.

16 I enjoin you therefore, beloved children, build yourselves
firmly upon the foundation that hath been laid for you, which
is unshaken, and against which no evil-willer can conspire. Be,
then, rooted upon this foundation: be established, remembering
what *ye have seen* (or *heard*) and all that hath come to pass while
I walked with you all. Ye have seen works wrought through me
which ye have no power to disbelieve, and such signs come to
pass as perchance even dumb nature will proclaim aloud; I have
delivered you words which I pray may so be received by you as
the words themselves would have it. Be established then,
beloved, upon all that ye have seen, and heard, and partaken of.

And God on whom ye have believed shall have mercy on you and present you unto himself, giving you rest unto all ages.

17 Now as for that which is to befall me, let it not really trouble you as some strange spectacle, that the servant of God, unto whom God himself hath granted much in deeds and words, should by an evil man be driven out of this temporal life: for not only unto me will this come to pass, but unto all them that have loved and believed on him and confess him. The devil that is wholly shameless will arm his own children against them, that they may consent unto him; and he will not have his desire.

And wherefore he essayeth this I will tell you. From the beginning of all things, and if I may so say, since he that hath no beginning came down to be under his rule, the enemy that is a foe to peace driveth away from (God) such a one as doth not belong indeed to him, but is some one of the weaker sort and not fully enlightened (?), nor yet able to recognize himself. And because he knoweth him not, therefore must he be fought against by him (the devil). For he, thinking that he possesseth him and is his master for ever, opposeth him so much, that he maketh their enmity to be a kind of friendship: for suggesting to him his own thoughts, he often portrayeth them as pleasurable and specious (*MS.* deceitful), by which he thinketh to prevail over him. He was not, then, openly shown to be an enemy, for he feigned a friendship that was worthy of him.

18 And this his work he carried on so long that† he (man) forgat to recognize it, but he (the devil) knew it himself: that is, he, because of his gifts ⟨was not seen to be an enemy⟩. But when the mystery of grace was lighted up, and the counsel of rest manifested, and the light of the word shown, and the race of them that were saved was proved, warring against many pleasures, ⟨he, seeing⟩ the enemy himself despised, and himself, through the goodness of him that had mercy on us, derided because of his own gifts, by which he had thought to triumph over man—he began to plot against us with hatred and enmity and assaults; and this hath he determined, not to cease from us till he thinketh to separate us (from God).

For before, our enemy was without care, and offered us a feigned friendship which was worthy of him, and was able not to fear that we, deceived by him, should depart from him. But when the *light of* dispensation was kindled, it made ⟨his enmity⟩, I say not stronger, ⟨but more plain⟩. For it exposed that part of his nature which was hidden and which thought to escape notice, and made it confess what it is.

Knowing therefore, brethren, that which shall be, let us be vigilant, not discontented, not making a proud figure, not carrying upon our souls marks of him which are not our own: but wholly lifted upward by the whole word, let us all gladly await the end, and take our flight away from him, that he may be henceforth shown as he is, who ⟨perverteth?⟩ our nature unto (*or* against) our . . .

THE MARTYRDOM

The original text of this, as Flamion shows, has to be picked out of several Greek and Latin authorities.

Bonnet prints the Martyrdom in several forms (*Act. Apost. Apocr.* ii. 1): on pp. 1–37 we have the *Passion* in three texts.

The uppermost is the Latin letter of the presbyters and deacons of Achaia. This, as Bonnet has proved, is the *original* of the two Greek versions printed below it. The first editors of this Letter thought it might be a genuine document. But it is really an artificial thing. The greater part of it consists of a dialogue between Andrew and Aegeates: the narrative of the actual Passion is rather brief.

Of the two Greek versions, the first, which begins ῎Α τοῖς ὀφθαλμοῖς is a faithful version of the Latin.

The other, which begins ῎Απερ τοῖς ὀφθαλμοῖς, has a number of insertions taken from the original Acts, ultimately, perhaps through the medium of a 'Passion', circulated separately, such as we have had in the cases of *John*, *Paul*, and *Peter*. This text is called by Flamion the *Épître grecque. Ep. gr.*

On pp. 38–45 follows the fragment of discourses which has just been translated. Very likely this is a relic of a separate Passion cut off from the end of the original Acts.

On pp. 46–57 is the 'Martyrium prius'. This tells (after speaking of the dispersion of the apostles) of the cure and conversion of Lesbius, destruction of temples, dismissal of Lesbius by Caesar, vision of Andrew that Aegeates is to put him to death, arrest of Andrew, and martyrdom. It contains many speeches. This is *Mart.* I.

On pp. 58–64 is the 'Martyrium alterum' in two texts, which begins at once with the arrest of the apostle by Aegeates—after he has spent the night in discoursing to the brethren.

Mart. II, A, B are the two texts of this.

Besides these Bonnet has published in the *Analecta Bollandiana* and separately (as *Supplementum Codicis Apocryphi*, ii, 1895) the following documents:

1. Acts of Andrew with Encomium: called for short *Laudatio*, which recounts the journeys at considerable length, and some of the miracles which we have seen in Gregory, and then the Passion (cc. 44–9) and the Translation to Constantinople.

2. A Greek Martyrdom, of which cc. 1–8 recount the journeys, and from 9 onwards the Passion, with a good deal of matter from the original Acts. This is called *Narratio*.

3. A Latin Passion—that known to Gregory, which begins *Conversante et docente*: it forms the end of Book III of Abdias' *Historia Apostolica*, and is there tacked on to Gregory's book of Miracles.

Using all these sources, Flamion has with great pains indicated which portions he assigns to the original Acts; and I shall follow him here. The resultant text is a kind of mosaic, of which the sources shall be indicated in the margin.

Narr. 22.
Mart. II,
A. 1.
And after he had thus discoursed throughout the night to the brethren, and prayed with them and committed them unto the Lord, early in the morning Aegeates the proconsul sent for the apostle Andrew out of the prison and said to him: The end of thy judgement is at hand, thou stranger, enemy of this present life and foe of all mine house. Wherefore hast thou thought good to intrude into places that are not thine, and to corrupt my wife who was of old obedient unto me? why hast thou done this against me and against all Achaia? Therefore shalt thou receive from me a gift in recompense of that thou hast wrought against me.

And he commanded him to be scourged by seven men and afterward to be crucified: and charged the executioners that his legs should be left unpierced, and so he should be hanged up: thinking by this means to torment him the more.

Now the report was noised throughout all Patrae that the stranger, the righteous man, the servant of Christ, whom Aegeates held prisoner, was being crucified, having done nothing amiss: and they ran together with one accord unto the sight, being wroth with the proconsul because of his impious judgement.

Ibid.
And as the executioners led him unto the place to fulfil that which was commanded them, Stratocles heard what was come to pass, and ran hastily and overtook them, and beheld the blessed Andrew violently haled by the executioners like a malefactor. And he spared them not, but beating every one of them soundly and tearing their coats from top to bottom, he caught Andrew away from them, saying: Ye may thank the blessed man who hath instructed me and taught me to refrain from extremity of wrath: for else I would have showed you what Stratocles is able to do, and what *is the power of* the foul Aegeates. For we have learnt to endure that which others inflict upon us. And he took the hand of the apostle and went with him to the place by the sea-shore where he was to be crucified.

Narr. 24
(Mart. II,
A. 3).
But the soldiers who had received him from the proconsul left him with Stratocles, and returned and told Aegeates, saying: As we went with Andrew, Stratocles prevented us, and rent our coats and pulled him away from us and took him with him, and lo, here we are as thou seest. And Aegeates answered them: Put on other raiment and go and fulfil that which I commanded you, upon the condemned man: but be not seen of Stratocles, neither answer him again if he ask aught of you; for I know the rashness of his soul,

ACTS OF ANDREW

what it is; and if he were provoked he would not even
spare me. And they did as Aegeates said unto them.

But as Stratocles went with the apostle unto the
place appointed, *Andrew* perceived that he was wroth
with Aegeates and was reviling him in a low voice, and
said unto him: My child Stratocles, I would have thee
henceforth possess thy soul unmoved, and remove from
thyself this temper, and neither be inwardly disposed
thus toward the things that seem hard to thee, nor be
inflamed outwardly: for it becometh the servant of
Jesus to be worthy of Jesus. And another thing will
I say unto thee and to the brethren that walk with me:
that the man that is against us, when he dareth aught
against us and findeth not one to consent unto him, is
smitten and beaten and wholly deadened because he
hath not accomplished that which he undertook; let
us therefore, little children, have him alway before our
eyes, lest if we fall asleep he slaughter us (you) like an
adversary.

And as he spake this and yet more unto Stratocles
and them that were with him, they came to the place
where he was to be crucified: and (seeing the cross set
up at the edge of the sand by the sea-shore) he left
them all and went to the cross and spake unto it (as
unto a living creature, with a loud voice):

Hail, O cross, yea be glad indeed ! Well know I that
thou shalt henceforth be at rest, thou that hast for a long
time been wearied, being set up and awaiting me. I come
unto thee whom I know to belong to me. I come unto
thee that hast yearned after me. I know thy mystery,
for the which thou art set up: for thou art planted in
the world to establish the things that are unstable:
and the one part of thee stretcheth up toward heaven
that thou mayest signify the heavenly word (*or*, the word
that is above) (the head of all things): and another part
of thee is spread out to the right hand and the left that
it may put to flight the envious and adverse power of
the evil one, and gather into one the things that are
scattered abroad (*or*, the world): And another part of
thee is planted in the earth, and securely set in the
depth, that thou mayest join the things that are in the
earth and that are under the earth unto the heavenly
things (*Laud.* that thou mayest draw up them that be
under the earth and them that are held in the places
beneath the earth, and join, &c.).

O cross, device (contrivance) of the salvation of the
Most High! O cross, trophy of the victory [of Christ]
over the enemies! O cross, planted upon the earth and

Mart. II, A.

Narr. 26 (Mart. II, A).

Laudatio 46, Mart I, 14 (Ep. Gr. 10).

Mart I.

having thy fruit in the heavens! O name of the cross, filled with all things (*lit.* a thing filled with all).

Well done, O cross, that hast bound down the mobility of the world (*or*, the circumference)! Well done, O shape of understanding that hast shaped the shapeless (earth?)! Well done, O unseen chastisement that sorely chastisest the substance of the knowledge that hath many gods, and drivest out from among mankind him that devised it! Well done, thou that didst clothe thyself with the Lord, and didst bear the thief as a fruit, and didst call the apostle to repentance, and didst not refuse to accept us!

Mart. I,
Laud.

But how long delay I, speaking thus, and embrace not the cross, that by the cross I may be made alive, and by the cross (win) the common death of all and depart out of life?

Come hither ye ministers of joy unto me, ye servants of Aegeates: accomplish the desire of us both, and bind the lamb unto the wood of suffering, the man unto the maker, the soul unto the Saviour.

Ep. Gr.,
Narr. 28.

And the blessed Andrew having thus spoken, standing upon the earth, looked earnestly upon the cross, and bade the brethren that the executioners should come and do that which was commanded them; for they stood afar off.

Laud.,
Mart. I,
Ep. Gr.,
Narr. 28.

And they came and bound his hands and his feet and nailed them not; for such a charge had they from Aegeates; for he wished to afflict him by hanging him up, and that in the night he might be devoured alive by dogs (*Laud.* that he might be wearied out and permit Maximilla to live with him). And they left him hanging and departed from him.

Narr.,
Ep. Gr.,
Mart. II.

And when the multitudes that stood by of them that had been made disciples in Christ by him saw that they had done unto him none of the things accustomed with them that are crucified, they hoped to hear something again from him. For as he hung, he moved his head and smiled. And Stratocles asked him, saying: Wherefore smilest thou, servant of God? thy laughter maketh us to mourn and weep because we are bereaved of thee. And the blessed Andrew answered him: Shall I not laugh, my son Stratocles, at the vain assault (ambush) of Aegeates, whereby he thinketh to punish us? we are strangers unto him and his conspiracies. He hath not ⟨ears⟩ to hear; for if he had, he would have heard that the man of Jesus cannot be punished, because he is henceforth known of him.

And thereafter he spake unto them all in common,

for the heathen also were come together, being wroth
at the unjust judgement of Aegeates.

Ye men that are here present, and women and Narr.,
children, old and young, bond and free, and all that Ep. Gr.
will hear, take ye no heed of the vain deceit of this
present life, but heed us rather who hang here for the
Lord's sake and are about to depart out of this body:
and renounce all the lusts of the world and contemn
(spit upon) the worship of the abominable idols, and
run unto the true worshipping of our God that lieth not,
and make yourselves a temple pure and ready to receive
the word. (*Narr.* then becomes obviously late: *Ep. Gr.*,
which is far shorter, ends : And hasten to overtake my
soul as it hasteneth toward heavenly things, and in
a word despise all temporal things, and establish your
minds as men believing in Christ.)

And the multitudes hearing the things which he Ep. Gr.,
spake departed not from the place; and Andrew con- Narr.,
tinued speaking yet more unto them, for a day and Mart. II,
a night. And on the day following, beholding his *Conver-*
endurance and constancy of soul and wisdom of spirit *sante.*
and strength of mind, they were wroth, and hastened
with one accord unto Aegeates, to the judgement-seat
where he sat, and cried out against him, saying: What
is this judgement of thine, O proconsul ? thou hast
ill judged! thou hast condemned unjustly: thy court
is against law! What evil hath this man done? wherein
hath he offended? The city is troubled: thou injurest
us all! destroy not Caesar's city! give us the righteous
man! restore us the holy man! slay not a man dear to
God! destroy not a man gentle and pious! lo, two days
is he hanged up and yet liveth, and hath tasted nothing,
and yet refresheth all us with his words, and lo, we
believe in the God whom he preacheth. Take down the
righteous man and we will all turn philosophers ; loose
the chaste man and all Patrae will be at peace ; set free
the wise man and all Achaia shall be set free by him!
(*or*, obtain mercy.)

But when at the first Aegeates would not hear them,
but beckoned with the hand to the people that they
should depart, they were filled with rage and were at
the point to do him violence, being in number about
two thousand (*Narr., Ep. Gr., Mart.* II : 20,000).

And when the proconsul saw them to be after a sort
mad, he feared lest there should be a rising against him,
and rose up from the judgement-seat and went with
them, promising to release Andrew. And some went
before and signified to the apostle and to the rest of

the people that were there, wherefore the proconsul was coming. And all the multitude of the disciples rejoiced, together with Maximilla and Iphidamia and Stratocles.

Narr.

But when Andrew heard it, he began to say: O the dullness and disobedience and simplicity of them whom I have taught! how much have I spoken, and even to this day I have not persuaded them to flee from the love of earthly things! but they are yet bound unto them and continue in them, and will not depart from them. What meaneth this affection and love and sympathy with the flesh? how long heed ye worldly and temporal things? how long understand ye not the things that be above us, and press not to overtake them? leave me henceforth to be put to death in the manner which ye behold, and let no man by any means loose me from these bonds; for so is it appointed unto me to depart out of the body and be present with the Lord, with whom also I am crucified. And this shall be accomplished.

Laud., Ep. Gr.

And he turned unto Aegeates and said with a loud voice: Wherefore art thou come, Aegeates, that art an alien unto me? what wilt thou dare afresh, what contrive, or what fetch? tell us that thou hast repented and art come to loose us? nay, not if thou repentest, indeed, Aegeates, will I now consent unto thee; not if thou promise me all thy substance will I depart from myself; not if thou say that thou art mine will I trust thee. And dost thou, proconsul, loose him that is ⟨not⟩ bound? him that hath been set free? that hath been recognized by his kinsman? that hath obtained mercy and is beloved of him? *dost thou loose* him that is alien to thee? the stranger? that only appeareth to thee? I have one with whom I shall be for ever, with whom I shall converse for unnumbered ages. Unto him do I go, unto him do I hasten, who made thee also known unto me, who said to me: Understand thou Aegeates and his gifts: let not that fearful one affright thee, nor think that he holdeth thee who art mine. He is thine enemy: he is pestilent, a deceiver, a corrupter, a madman, a sorcerer, a cheat, a murderer, wrathful, without compassion. Depart therefore from me, thou worker of all iniquity. (*Ep. Gr.* He is thine enemy. Therefore I know thee, through him that permitted me *to know.* I depart from thee. For I and they that are akin to me hasten toward that which is ours, and leave thee to be what thou wast, and what thou knowest not thyself to be.)

Ep. Gr., Narr., Conversante.

And the proconsul hearing this stood speechless, and as it were beside himself; but as all the city made an uproar that he should loose Andrew, he drew near to

ACTS OF ANDREW 363

the cross to loose him and take him down. But the blessed Andrew cried out with a loud voice: Suffer not, Lord, thine Andrew that hath been bound upon thy cross, to be loosed again; give not me that am upon thy mystery to the shameless devil; O Jesu Christ, let not thine adversary loose him that is hung upon thy grace; O Father, let not this mean (little) one humble any more him that hath known thy greatness. But do thou, Jesu Christ, whom I have seen, whom I hold, whom I love, in whom I am and shall be, receive me in peace into thine everlasting tabernacles, that by my going out there may be an entering in unto thee of many that are akin to me, and that they may rest in thy majesty. And having so said, and yet more glorified the Lord, he gave up the ghost, while we all wept and lamented at our parting from him.

And after the decease of the blessed Andrew, Maximilla together with Stratocles, caring nought for them that stood by, drew near and herself loosed his body: and when it was evening she paid it the accustomed care and buried it (hard by the sea-shore). And she continued separate from Aegeates because of his brutal soul and his wicked manner of life: and she led a reverend and quiet life, filled with the love of Christ, among the brethren. Whom Aegeates solicited much, and promised that she should have the rule over his affairs; but being unable to persuade her, he arose in the dead of night and unknown to them of his house cast himself down from a great height and perished.

But Stratocles, which was his brother after the flesh, would not touch aught of the things that were left of his substance; for the wretched man died without offspring: but said: Let thy goods go with thee, Aegeates.

For of these things we have no need, for they are polluted; but for me, let Christ be my friend and I his servant; and all my substance do I offer unto him in whom I have believed, and I pray that by worthy hearing of the blessed teaching of the apostle I may appear a partaker with him in the ageless and unending kingdom. And so the uproar of the people ceased, and all were glad at the amazing and untimely and sudden fall of the impious and lawless Aegeates.

[Not much of this last paragraph from *Narr.* can be original. All the texts end with a statement that the apostle suffered on the 30th of November.]

ACTS OF THOMAS

This is the only one of the five primary romances which we possess in its entirety. It is of great length and considerable interest. The Stichometry (see p. 24) gives it only 1,600 lines: this is far too little: it may probably apply only to a portion of the Acts, single episodes of which, in addition to the Martyrdom, may have been current separately. We do, in fact, find some separate miracles in some of the oriental versions.

There is a consensus of opinion among Syriac scholars that our Greek text of these Acts is a version from Syriac. The Syriac original was edited and translated by Wright in his Apocryphal Acts, and older fragments have since been published by Mrs. Lewis (*Horae Semiticae* IV, 1904. *Mythological Acts of the Apostles*).

Certain hymns occur in the Syriac which were undoubtedly composed in that language: most notable is the Hymn of the Soul (edited separately by A. A. Bevan, and others) which is not relevant to the context. It has been ascribed to Bardaisan the famous Syrian heretic. Only one Greek MS. of the Acts (the Vallicellian, at Rome, Bonnet's MS. U, of the eleventh century) contains it; it is paraphrased by Nicetas of Thessalonica in his Greek *réchauffé* of the Acts.

There is, in fact, no room to doubt that the whole text of the Acts, as preserved complete in MS. U and partially in other manuscripts, is a translation from the Syriac. But in the Martyrdom four manuscripts (including a very important Paris copy—Gr. 1510, of eleventh century, and another of ninth century) present a quite different, and superior, text, indubitably superior in one striking point: that whereas *Syr.* places the great prayer of Thomas in the twelfth Act, some little time before the Martyrdom (ch. 144 sqq.), the four manuscripts place it immediately before, after ch. 167, and this is certainly the proper place for it.

It is, I believe, still arguable (though denied by the Syriacists) that here is a relic of the original Greek text: in other words, the Acts *were* composed in Greek, and early rendered into Syriac. Becoming scarce or being wholly lost in Greek they were retranslated out of Syriac into Greek. But meanwhile the original Greek of the Martyrdom had survived separately, and we have it here. This was M. Bonnet's view, and it is one which I should like to adopt.

At the very least, we have a better text of the Martyrdom preserved in these four manuscripts than in U and its congeners.

As to other versions. The Latin Passions—one probably by Gregory of Tours—have been much adulterated. We have also Ethiopic versions of some episodes, and there is also an Armenian one of which little use has been made. However, versions are of little account in this case, where we have such comparatively good authorities as the Greek and Syriac for the whole book.

My version is made from the Greek text, (Bonnet, 1903) with an eye on the Syriac as rendered by Wright and by Mrs. Lewis and Bevan.

ACTS OF THE HOLY APOSTLE THOMAS

The First Act, when he went into India with Abbanes the merchant.

At that season all we the apostles were at Jerusalem, Simon which is called Peter and Andrew his brother, James the son of Zebedee and John his brother, Philip and Bartholomew, Thomas and Matthew the publican, James *the son* of Alphaeus and Simon the Canaanite, and Judas *the brother* of James: and we divided the regions of the world, that every one of us should go unto the region that fell to him and unto the nation whereunto the Lord sent him.

According to the lot, therefore, India fell unto Judas Thomas, which is also the twin: but he would not go, saying that by reason of the weakness of the flesh he could not travel, and 'I am an Hebrew man; how can I go amongst the Indians and preach the truth?' And as he thus reasoned and spake, the Saviour appeared unto him by night and saith to him: Fear not, Thomas, go thou unto India and preach the word there, for my grace is with thee. But he would not obey, saying: Whither thou wouldest send me, send me, but elsewhere, for unto the Indians I will not go.

2 And while he thus spake and thought, it chanced that there was there a certain merchant come from India whose name was Abbanes, sent from the King Gundaphorus,[1] and having commandment from him to buy a carpenter and bring him unto him.

Now the Lord seeing him walking in the market-place at noon said unto him: Wouldest thou buy a carpenter? And he said to him: Yea. And the Lord said to him: I have a slave that is a carpenter and I desire to sell him. And so saying he showed him Thomas afar off, and agreed with him for three litrae of silver unstamped, and wrote a deed of sale, saying: I, Jesus, the son of Joseph the carpenter, acknowledge that I have sold my slave, Judas by name, unto thee Abbanes, a merchant of Gundaphorus, king of the Indians. And when the deed was finished, the Saviour took Judas Thomas and led him away to Abbanes the merchant; and when Abbanes saw him he said unto him: Is this thy master? And the apostle said: Yea, he is my Lord. And he said: I have bought thee of him. And the apostle held his peace.

3 And on the day following the apostle arose early, and having prayed and besought the Lord he said: I will go whither thou wilt, Lord Jesus: thy will be done. And he departed unto Abbanes the merchant, taking with him nothing at all save only his price. For the Lord had given it unto him, saying: Let

[1] Gundaphorus is an historical personage who reigned over a part of India in the first century after Christ. His coins bear his name in Greek, as 'Hyndopherēs'.

thy price also be with thee, together with my grace, wheresoever thou goest.

And the apostle found Abbanes carrying his baggage on board the ship; so he also began to carry it aboard with him. And when they were embarked in the ship and were set down, Abbanes questioned the apostle, saying: What craftsmanship knowest thou? And he said: In wood *I can make* ploughs and yokes and augers (ox-goads, *Syr.*), and boats and oars for boats and masts and pulleys; and in stone, pillars and temples and court-houses for kings. And Abbanes the merchant said to him: Yea, it is of such a workman that we have need. They began then to sail homeward; and they had a favourable wind, and sailed prosperously till they reached Andrapolis, a royal city.

4 And they left the ship and entered into the city, and lo, there were noises of flutes and water-organs, and trumpets sounded about them; and the apostle inquired, saying: What is this festival that is in this city? And they that were there said to him: Thee also have the gods brought to make merry in this city. For the king hath an only daughter, and now he giveth her in marriage unto an husband: this rejoicing, therefore, and assembly of the wedding to-day is the festival which thou hast seen. And the king hath sent heralds to proclaim everywhere that all should come to the marriage, rich and poor, bond and free, strangers and citizens: and if any refuse and come not to the marriage he shall answer for it unto the king. And Abbanes hearing that, said to the apostle: Let us also go, lest we offend the king, especially seeing we are strangers. And he said: Let us go.

And after they had put up in the inn and rested a little space they went to the marriage; and the apostle seeing them all set down (reclining), laid himself, he also, in the midst, and all looked upon him, as upon a stranger and one come from a foreign land: but Abbanes the merchant, being his master, laid himself in another place.

5 And as they dined and drank, the apostle tasted nothing; so they that were about him said unto him: Wherefore art thou come here, neither eating nor drinking? but he answered them, saying: I am come here for somewhat greater than the food or the drink, and that I may fulfil the king's will. For the heralds proclaim the king's message, and whoso hearkeneth not to the heralds shall be subject to the king's judgement.

So when they had dined and drunken, and garlands and unguents were brought to them, every man took of the unguent, and one anointed his face and another his beard and another other parts of his body; but the apostle anointed the top of his head and smeared a little upon his nostrils, and dropped it into his ears and touched his teeth with it, and carefully anointed the parts about his heart: and the wreath that was brought to him, woven of myrtle and other flowers, he took, and set it on his head, and took a branch of calamus and held it in his hand.

Now the flute-girl, holding her flute in her hand, went about to them all and played, but when she came to the place where the apostle was, she stood over him and played at his head for a long space: now this flute-girl was by race an Hebrew.

6 And as the apostle continued looking on the ground, one of the cup-bearers stretched forth his hand and gave him a buffet; and the apostle lifted up his eyes and looked upon him that smote him and said: My God will forgive thee in the life to come this iniquity, but in this world thou shalt show forth his wonders, and *even* now shall I behold this hand that hath smitten me dragged by dogs. And having so said, he began to sing and to say this song :

The damsel *is* the daughter of light, in whom consisteth and dwelleth the proud brightness of kings, and the sight of her is delightful, she shineth with beauty and cheer. Her garments are like the flowers of spring, and from them a waft of fragrance is borne; and in the crown of her head the king is established, which with his immortal food (ambrosia) nourisheth them that are founded upon him ; and in her head is set truth, and with her feet she showeth forth joy. And her mouth is opened, and it becometh her well: thirty and two are they that sing praises to her. Her tongue is like the curtain of the door, which waveth to and fro for them that enter in: her neck is set in the fashion of steps which the first maker hath wrought, and her two hands signify and show, proclaiming the dance of the happy ages, and her fingers point out the gates of the city. Her chamber is bright with light, and breatheth forth the odour of balsam and all spices, and giveth out a sweet smell of myrrh and *Indian* leaf, and within are myrtles strown on the floor, and ⟨garlands⟩ of all manner of odorous flowers, and the †door-posts(?)† are adorned with †reeds†. 7 And surrounding her her groomsmen keep her, the number of whom is seven, whom she herself hath chosen. And her bridesmaids are seven, and they dance before her. And twelve in number are they that serve before her and are subject unto her, which have their aim and their look toward the bridegroom, that by the sight of him they may be enlightened; and for ever shall they be with her in that eternal joy, and shall be at that marriage whereto the princes are gathered together, and shall attend at that banquet whereof the eternal ones are accounted worthy, and shall put on royal raiment and be clad in bright robes; and in joy and exultation shall they both be, and shall glorify the Father of all, whose proud light they have received, and are enlightened by the sight of their lord; whose immortal food they have received, that hath no failing (excrementum, *Syr.*), and have drunk of the wine that giveth them neither thirst nor desire. And they have glorified and praised, with the living spirit, the Father of truth and the mother of wisdom.

8 And when he had sung and ended this song, all that were there present gazed upon him; and he kept silence; and they saw that his likeness was changed, but that which was spoken by him they understood not, forasmuch as he was an Hebrew and that which he spake was said in the Hebrew tongue. But the flute-girl alone heard all of it, for she was by race an Hebrew; and she went away from him and played to the rest, but for the most part she gazed and looked upon him, for she loved him well, as a man of her own nation; moreover he was comely to look upon beyond all that were there. And when the flute-girl had played to them all and ended, she sat down over against him, gazing and looking earnestly upon him. But he looked upon no man at all, neither took heed of any, but only kept his eyes looking toward the ground, waiting the time when he might depart thence.

But the cup-bearer that had buffeted him went down to the well to draw water; and there chanced to be a lion there, and it slew him and left him lying in that place, having torn his limbs in pieces, and forthwith dogs seized his members, and among them one black dog holding his right hand in his mouth bare it into the place of the banquet.

9 And all when they saw it were amazed and inquired which of them it was that was missing. And when it became manifest that it was the hand of the cup-bearer which had smitten the apostle, the flute-girl brake her flute and cast it away and went and sat down at the apostle's feet, saying: This is either a god or an apostle of God, for I heard him say in the Hebrew tongue: 'I shall now see the hand that hath smitten me dragged by dogs', which thing ye also have now beheld; for as he said, so hath it come about. And some believed her, and some not.

But when the king heard of it, he came and said to the apostle: Rise up and come with me, and pray for my daughter: for she is mine only-begotten, and to-day I give her in marriage. But the apostle was not willing to go with him, for the Lord was not yet revealed unto him in that place. But the king led him away against his will unto the bride-chamber that he might pray for them.

10 And the apostle stood, and began to pray and to speak thus: My Lord and my God, that travellest with thy servants, that guidest and correctest them that believe in thee, the refuge and rest of the oppressed, the hope of the poor and ransomer of captives, the physician of the souls that lie sick and saviour of all creation, that givest life unto the world and strengthenest souls; thou knowest things to come, and by our means accomplishest them: thou Lord art he that revealeth hidden mysteries

and maketh manifest words that are secret: thou Lord art the
planter of the good tree, and of thine hands are all good works
engendered: thou Lord art he that art in all things and passest
through all, and art set in all thy works and manifested in the
working of them all.   Jesus Christ, Son of compassion and
perfect saviour, Christ, Son of the living God, the undaunted
power that hast overthrown the enemy, and the voice that was
heard of the rulers, and made all their powers to quake, the
ambassador that wast sent from the height and camest down
even unto hell, who didst open the doors and bring up thence
them that for many ages were shut up in the treasury of darkness, and showedst them the way that leadeth up unto the
height: I beseech thee, Lord Jesu, and offer unto thee supplication for these young persons, that thou wouldest do for them the
things that shall help them and be expedient and profitable for
them.   And he laid his hands on them and said: The Lord shall
be with you, and left them in that place and departed.

11 And the king desired the groomsmen to depart out of the
bride-chamber; and when all were gone out and the doors were
shut, the bridegroom lifted up the curtain of the bride-chamber
to fetch the bride unto him. And he saw the Lord Jesus bearing
the likeness of Judas Thomas and speaking with the bride—
even of him that but now had blessed them and gone out from
them, the apostle; and he saith unto him: Wentest thou not
out in the sight of all? how then art thou found here? But the
Lord said to him: I am not Judas which is also called Thomas,
but I am his brother. And the Lord sat down upon the bed
and bade them also sit upon chairs, and began to say unto
them:

12 Remember, my children, what my brother spake unto you
and what he delivered before you: and know this, that if ye
abstain from this foul intercourse, ye become holy temples,
pure, being quit of impulses and pains, seen and unseen, and
ye will acquire no cares of life or of children, whose end is destruction: and if indeed ye get many children, for their sakes ye
become grasping and covetous, stripping orphans and over-
reaching widows, and by so doing subject yourselves to grievous
punishments.   For the more part of children become useless,
oppressed of devils, some openly and some invisibly, for they
become either lunatic or half withered or blind or deaf or dumb
or paralytic or foolish; and if they be sound, again they will be
vain, doing useless or abominable acts; for they will be caught
either in adultery or murder or theft or fornication, and by all
these will ye be afflicted.

But if ye be persuaded and keep your souls chaste before God,
there will come unto you living children whom these blemishes
touch not, and ye shall be without care, leading a tranquil life
without grief or anxiety, looking to receive that incorruptible

and true marriage, and ye shall be therein groomsmen entering into that bride-chamber which is full of immortality and light.

13 And when the young people heard these things, they believed the Lord and gave themselves up unto him, and abstained from foul desire and continued so, passing the night in that place. And the Lord departed from before them, saying thus: The grace of the Lord shall be with you.

And when the morning was come the king came to meet them, and furnished a table and brought it in before the bridegroom and the bride. And he found them sitting over against each other, and the face of the bride he found unveiled, and the bridegroom was right joyful.

And the mother came unto the bride and said: Why sittest thou so, child, and art not ashamed, but art as if thou hadst lived with thine husband a long season? And her father said: Because of thy great love toward thine husband dost thou not even veil thyself?

14 And the bride answered and said: Verily, father, I am in great love, and I pray my Lord that the love which I have perceived this night may abide with me, and I will ask for that husband of whom I have learned to-day: and therefore I will no more veil myself, because the mirror (veil) of shame is removed from me; and *therefore* am I no more ashamed or abashed, because the deed of shame and confusion is departed far from me; and that I am not confounded, it is because my astonishment hath not continued with me; and that I am in cheerfulness and joy, it is because the day of *my* joy hath not been troubled; and that I have set at nought this husband and this marriage that passeth away from before mine eyes, it is because I am joined in another marriage; and that I have had no intercourse with a husband that is temporal, whereof the end is with lasciviousness and bitterness of soul, it is because I am yoked unto a true husband.

15 And while the bride was saying yet more than this, the bridegroom answered and said: I give thee thanks, O Lord, that hast been proclaimed by the stranger, and found in us; who hast removed me far from corruption and sown life in me; who hast rid me of this disease that is hard to be healed and cured and abideth for ever, and hast implanted sober health in me; who hast shown me thyself and revealed unto me all my state wherein I am; who hast redeemed me from falling and led me to that which is better, and set me free from temporal things and made me worthy of those that are immortal and everlasting; that hast made thyself lowly even down to me and my littleness, that thou mayest present me unto thy greatness and unite me unto thyself; who hast not withheld thine own bowels from me that was ready to perish, but hast shown me how to seek myself and know who I was, and who and in what

manner I now am, that I may again become that which I was:
whom I knew not, but thyself didst seek me out: of whom I was
not aware, but thyself hast taken me to thee: whom I have
perceived, and now am not able to be unmindful of him: whose
love burneth within me, and I cannot speak it as is fit, but that
which I am able to say of it is little and scanty, and not fitly
proportioned unto his glory: yet he blameth me not that presume
to say unto him even that which I know not: for it is because of
his love that I say even this much.

16 Now when the king heard these things from the bridegroom
and the bride, he rent his clothes and said unto them that stood
by him: Go forth quickly and go about the whole city, and take
and bring me that man that is a sorcerer who by ill fortune
came unto this city; for with mine own hands I brought him
into this house, and I told him to pray over this mine ill-starred
daughter; and whoso findeth and bringeth him to me, I will
give him whatsoever he asketh of me. They went, therefore,
and went about seeking him, and found him not; for he had
set sail. They went also unto the inn where he had lodged and
found there the flute-girl weeping and afflicted because he had
not taken her with him. And when they told her the matter
that had befallen with the young people she was exceeding glad
at hearing it, and put away her grief and said: Now have I also
found rest here. And she rose up and went unto them, and was
with them a long time, until they had instructed the king also.
And many of the brethren also gathered there until they heard
the report of the apostle, that he was come unto the cities of
India and was teaching there: and they departed and joined
themselves unto him.

The Second Act : concerning his coming unto the king Gundaphorus.

17 Now when the apostle was come into the cities of India
with Abbanes the merchant, Abbanes went to salute the king
Gundaphorus, and reported to him of the carpenter whom he had
brought with him. And the king was glad, and commanded him
to come in to him. So when he was come in the king said unto
him: What craft understandest thou? The apostle said unto
him: The craft of carpentering and of building. The king saith
unto him: What craftsmanship, then, knowest thou in wood, and
what in stone? The apostle saith: In wood: ploughs, yokes,
goads, pulleys, and boats and oars and masts; and in stone:
pillars, temples, and court-houses for kings. And the king said:
Canst thou build me a palace? And he answered: Yea, I can
both build and furnish it; for to this end am I come, to build
and to do the work of a carpenter.

18 And the king took him and went out of the city gates and
began to speak with him on the way concerning the building of
the court-house, and of the foundations, how they should be

laid, until they came to the place wherein he desired that the building should be; and he said: Here will I that the building should be. And the apostle said: Yea, for this place is suitable for the building. But the place was woody and there was much water there. So the king said: Begin to build. But he said: I cannot begin to build now at this season. And the king said: When canst thou begin? And he said: I will begin in *the month* Dius and finish in Xanthicus. But the king marvelled and said: Every building is builded in summer, and canst thou in this very winter build and make ready a palace? And the apostle said: Thus it must be, and no otherwise is it possible. And the king said: If, then, this seem good to thee, draw me a plan, how the work shall be, because I shall return hither after some long time. And the apostle took a reed and drew, measuring the place; and the doors he set toward the sunrising to look toward the light, and the windows toward the west to the breezes, and the bakehouse he appointed to be toward the south, and the aqueduct for the service toward the north. And the king saw it and said to the apostle: Verily thou art a craftsman, and it befitteth thee to be a servant of kings. And he left much money with him and departed from him.

19 And from time to time he sent money and provision, and victual for him and the rest of the workmen. But *Thomas* receiving it all dispensed it, going about the cities and the villages round about, distributing and giving alms to the poor and afflicted, and relieving them, saying: The king knoweth how to obtain recompense fit for kings, but at this time it is needful that the poor should have refreshment.

After these things the king sent an ambassador unto the apostle, and wrote thus: Signify unto me what thou hast done, or what I shall send thee, or of what thou hast need. And the apostle sent unto him, saying: The palace (praetorium) is builded and only the roof remaineth. And the king hearing it sent him again gold and silver (*lit.* unstamped), and wrote unto him: Let the palace be roofed, if it is done. And the apostle said unto the Lord: I thank thee O Lord in all things, that thou didst die for a little space that I might live for ever in thee, and that thou hast sold me that by me thou mightest set free many. And he ceased not to teach and to refresh the afflicted, saying: This hath the Lord dispensed unto you, and he giveth unto every man his food: for he is the nourisher of orphans and steward of the widows, and unto all that are afflicted he is relief and rest.

20 Now when the king came to the city he inquired of his friends concerning the palace which Judas that is called Thomas was building for him. And they told him: Neither hath he built a palace nor done aught else of that he promised to perform, but he goeth about the cities and countries, and whatsoever he hath he giveth unto the poor, and teacheth of a new God, and

healeth the sick, and driveth out devils, and doeth many other wonderful things; and we think him to be a sorcerer. Yet his compassions and his cures which are done of him freely, and moreover the simplicity and kindness of him and his faith, do declare that he is a righteous man or an apostle of the new God whom he preacheth; for he fasteth continually and prayeth, and eateth bread only, with salt, and his drink is water, and he weareth but one garment alike in fair weather and in winter, and receiveth nought of any man, and that he hath he giveth unto others. And when the king heard that, he rubbed his face with his hands, and shook his head for a long space.

21 And he sent for the merchant which had brought him, and for the apostle, and said unto him: Hast thou built me the palace? And he said: Yea. And the king said: When, then, shall we go and see it? but he answered him and said: Thou canst not see it now, but when thou departest this life, *then* thou shalt see it. And the king was exceeding wroth, and commanded both the merchant and Judas which is called Thomas to be put in bonds and cast into prison until he should inquire and learn unto whom the king's money had been given, and so destroy both him and the merchant.

And the apostle went unto the prison rejoicing, and said to the merchant: Fear thou nothing, only believe in the God that is preached by me, and thou shalt indeed be set free from this world, but from the world to come thou shalt receive life. And the king took thought with what death he should destroy them. And when he had determined to flay them alive and burn them with fire, in the same night Gad the king's brother fell sick, and by reason of his vexation and the deceit which the king had suffered he was greatly oppressed; and sent for the king and said unto him: O king my brother, I commit unto thee mine house and my children; for I am vexed by reason of the provocation that hath befallen thee, and lo, I die; and if thou visit not with vengeance upon the head of that sorcerer, thou wilt give my soul no rest in hell. And the king said to his brother: All this night have I considered how I should put him to death, and this hath seemed good to me, to flay him and burn him with fire, both him and the merchant which brought him (*Syr.* Then the brother of the king said to him: And if there be anything else that is worse than this, do *it* to him; and I give thee charge of my house and my children).

22 And as they talked together, the soul of his brother Gad departed. And the king mourned sore for Gad, for he loved him much, and commanded that he should be buried in royal and precious apparel (*Syr.* sepulchre). Now after this angels took the soul of Gad the king's brother and bore it up into heaven, showing unto him the places and dwellings that were there, and inquired of him: In which place wouldest thou dwell? And

when they drew near unto the building of Thomas the apostle which he had built for the king, Gad saw it and said unto the angels: I beseech you, my lords, suffer me to dwell in one of the lowest rooms of these. And they said to him: Thou canst not dwell in this building. And he said: Wherefore? And they say unto him: This is that palace which that Christian builded for thy brother. And he said: I beseech you, my lords, suffer me to go to my brother, that I may buy this palace of him; for my brother knoweth not of what sort it is, and he will sell it unto me.

23 Then the angels let the soul of Gad go. And as they were putting his grave clothes upon him, his soul entered into him, and he said to them that stood about him: Call my brother unto me, that I may ask one petition of him. Straightway therefore they told the king, saying: Thy brother is revived. And the king ran forth with a great company and came unto his brother, and entered in and stood by his bed as one amazed, not being able to speak to him. And his brother said: I know and am persuaded, my brother, that if any man had asked of thee the half of thy kingdom, thou wouldest have given it him for my sake; therefore I beg of thee to grant me one favour which I ask of thee, that thou wouldest sell me that which I ask of thee. And the king answered and said: And what is it which thou askest me to sell thee? And he said: Convince me by an oath that thou wilt grant it me. And the king sware unto him: One of my possessions, whatsoever thou shalt ask, I will give thee. And he saith to him: Sell me that palace which thou hast in the heavens? And the king said: Whence should I have a palace in the heavens? And he said: Even that which that Christian built for thee which is now in the prison, whom the merchant brought unto thee, having purchased him of one Jesus: I mean that Hebrew slave whom thou desiredst to punish as having suffered deceit at his hand: whereat I was grieved and died, and am now revived.

24 Then the king considering the matter, understood it of those eternal benefits which should come to him and which concerned him, and said: That palace I cannot sell thee, but I pray to enter into it and dwell therein and to be accounted worthy of the inhabiters of it; but if thou indeed desirest to buy such a palace, lo, the man liveth and shall build thee one better than it. And forthwith he sent and brought out of prison the apostle and the merchant that was shut up with him, saying: I entreat thee, as a man that entreateth the minister of God, that thou wouldest pray for me and beseech him whose minister thou art to forgive me and overlook that which I have done unto thee or thought to do, and that I may become a worthy inhabiter of that dwelling for the which I took no pains, but thou hast builded it for me, labouring alone, the grace of thy God working with thee, and that I also may become a servant and serve this God whom

thou preachest. And his brother also fell down before the apostle and said: I entreat and supplicate thee before thy God that I may become worthy of his ministry and service, and that it may fall to me to be worthy of the things that were shown unto me by his angels.

25 And the apostle, filled with joy, said: I praise thee, O Lord Jesu, that thou hast revealed thy truth in these men; for thou only art the God of truth, and none other, and thou art he that knoweth all things that are unknown to the most; thou, Lord, art he that in all things showest compassion and sparest men. For men by reason of the error that is in them have overlooked thee, but thou hast not overlooked them. And now at my supplication and request do thou receive the king and his brother and join them unto thy fold, cleansing them with thy washing and anointing them with thine oil from the error that encompasseth them: and keep them also from the wolves, bearing them into thy meadows. And give them drink out of thine immortal fountain which is neither fouled nor drieth up; for they entreat and supplicate thee and desire to become thy servants and ministers, and for this they are content even to be persecuted of thine enemies, and for thy sake to be hated of them and to be mocked and to die, like as thou for our sake didst suffer all these things, that thou mightest preserve us, thou that art Lord and verily the good shepherd. And do thou grant them to have confidence in thee alone, and the succour that cometh of thee, and the hope of their salvation which they look for from thee alone; and that they may be grounded in thy mysteries and receive the perfect good of thy graces and gifts, and flourish in thy ministry and come to perfection in thy Father.

26 Being therefore wholly set upon the apostle, both the king Gundaphorus and Gad his brother followed him and departed not from him at all, and they also relieved them that had need, giving unto all and refreshing all. And they besought him that they also might henceforth receive the seal of the word, saying unto him: Seeing that our souls are at leisure and eager toward God, give thou us the seal; for we have heard thee say that the God whom thou preachest knoweth his own sheep by his seal. And the apostle said unto them: I also rejoice and entreat you to receive this seal, and to partake with me in this eucharist and blessing of the Lord, and to be made perfect therein. For this is the Lord and God of all, even Jesus Christ whom I preach, and he is the father of truth, in whom I have taught you to believe. And he commanded them to bring oil, that they might receive the seal by the oil. They brought the oil therefore, and lighted many lamps; for it was night (*Syr.* whom I preach: and the king gave orders that the bath should be closed for seven days, and that no man should bathe in it: and when the seven days were done, on the eighth day they three entered into the bath by

night that Judas might baptize them. And many lamps were lighted in the bath).

27 And the apostle arose and sealed them. And the Lord was revealed unto them by a voice, saying: Peace be unto you, brethren. And they heard his voice only, but his likeness they saw not, for they had not yet received the added sealing of the seal (*Syr.* had not been baptized). And the apostle took the oil and poured it upon their heads and anointed and chrismed them, and began to say (*Syr.* And Judas went up and stood upon the edge of the cistern and poured oil upon their heads and said):

Come, thou holy name of the Christ that is above every name.

Come, thou power of the Most High, and the compassion that is perfect.

Come, gift (charism) of the Most High.

Come, compassionate mother.

Come, communion of the male.

Come, she that revealeth the hidden mysteries.

Come, mother of the seven houses, that thy rest may be in the eighth house.

Come, elder of the five members, mind, thought, reflection, consideration, reason ; communicate with these young men.[1]

Come, holy spirit, and cleanse their reins and their heart, and give them the added seal, in the name of the Father and Son and Holy Ghost.

And when they were sealed, there appeared unto them a youth holding a lighted torch, so that their lamps became dim at the approach of the light thereof. And he went forth and was no more seen of them. And the apostle said unto the Lord: Thy light, O Lord, is not to be contained by us, and we are not able to bear it, for it is too great for our sight.

And when the dawn came and it was morning, he brake bread and made them partakers of the eucharist of the Christ. And they were glad and rejoiced.

And many others also, believing, were added to them, and came into the refuge of the Saviour.

28 And the apostle ceased not to preach and to say unto them: Ye men and women, boys and girls, young men and maidens, strong men and aged, whether bond or free, abstain from fornication and covetousness and the service of the belly: for under these three heads all iniquity cometh about. For fornication blindeth the mind and darkeneth the eyes of the soul, and is an impediment to the life (conversation) of the body, turning the whole man unto weakness and casting the whole body into sickness. And greed putteth the soul into fear and shame; being within the body it seizeth upon the goods of others, and is under fear lest if it restore other men's goods to their owners

---

[1] See Professor Burkitt's note at the end of this Act.

it be put to shame. And the service of the belly casteth the soul into thoughts and cares and vexations, taking thought lest it come to be in want, and have need of those things that are far from it. If, then, ye be rid of these ye become free of care and grief and fear, and that abideth with you which was said by the Saviour: Take no thought for the morrow, for the morrow shall take thought for the things of itself. Remember also that word of him of whom I spake: Look at the ravens and see the fowls of the heaven, that they neither sow nor reap nor gather into barns, and God dispenseth unto them; how much more unto you, O ye of little faith? But look ye for his coming and have your hope in him and believe on his name. For he is the judge of quick and dead, and he giveth to every one according to their deeds, and at his coming and his latter appearing no man hath any word of excuse when he is to be judged by him, as though he had not heard. For his heralds do proclaim in the four quarters (climates) of the world. Repent ye, therefore, and believe the promise and receive the yoke of meekness and the light burden, that ye may live and not die. These things get, these keep. Come forth of the darkness that the light may receive you! Come unto him that is indeed good, that ye may receive grace of him and implant his sign in your souls.

29 And when he had thus spoken, some of them that stood by said: It is time for the creditor to receive the debt. And he said unto them: He that is lord of the debt desireth alway to receive more; but let us give him that which is due. And he blessed them, and took bread and oil and herbs and salt and blessed and gave unto them; but he himself continued his fast, for the Lord's day was coming on (*Syr.* And he himself ate, because the Sunday was dawning).

And when night fell and he slept, the Lord came and stood at his head, saying: Thomas, rise early, and having blessed them all, after the prayer and the ministry go by the eastern road two miles and there will I show thee my glory: for by thy going shall many take refuge with me, and thou shalt bring to light the nature and power of the enemy. And he rose up from sleep and said unto the brethren that were with him: Children, the Lord would accomplish somewhat by me to-day, but let us pray, and entreat of him that we may have no impediment toward him, but that as at all times, so now also it may be done according to his desire and will by us. And having so said, he laid his hands on them and blessed them, and brake the bread of the eucharist and gave it them, saying: This eucharist shall be unto you for compassion and mercy, and not unto judgement and retribution. And they said Amen.

Note by Professor F. C. Burkitt, D.D.

In the *Acts of Thomas*, 27, the apostle, being about to baptize Gundaphorus the King of India with his brother Gad, invokes the holy name of the Christ, and among other invocations says (according to the best Greek text):

'Come, O elder of the five members, mind, idea, thoughtfulness, consideration, reasoning, communicate with these youths.'

What is the essential distinction of these five words for 'mind', and what is meant by the 'elder' (πρεσβύτερος)? We turn to the Syriac, as the original language in which our tale was composed, though our present text, which rests here on two manuscripts, has now and then been bowdlerized in the direction of more conventional phraseology, a process that the Greek has often escaped. Here in the Syriac we find (*Wright*, p. 193, l. 13; E. Tr., p. 166, last line but one):

'Come, Messenger of reconciliation, and communicate with the minds of these youths.'

The word for 'Come' is fem., while 'Messenger' (*Izgaddā*) is masc. This is because the whole prayer is an invocation of the Holy Spirit, which in old Syriac is invariably treated as feminine. The word for Messenger is that used in the Manichaean cosmogony for a heavenly Spirit sent from the Divine Light: this Spirit appeared as androgynous, so that the use of the word here with the feminine verb is not inappropriate.[1] It further leads us to look out for other indications of Manichaean phraseology in the passage. But first it suggests to us that πρεσβύτερος in our passage is a corruption of, or is used for, πρεσβευτής, 'an ambassador'.

As for the five words for 'mind', they are clearly the equivalents of *haunā, mad'ā, re'yānā, mahshĕbhāthā, tar'īthā,* named by Theodore bar Khōnī as the Five Shekhinas, or Dwellings, or Manifestations, of the Father of Greatness, the title by which the Manichaeans spoke of the ultimate Source of Light. There is a good discussion of these five words by M. A. Kugener in F. Cumont's *Recherches sur le Manichéisme* i, p. 10, note 3. In English we may say:

haunā	means	'sanity',
mad'ā	„	'reason',
re'yānā	„	'mind',
mahshabhĕthā	„	'imagination',
tar'īthā	„	'intention'.

The Greek terms, used here and also in *Acta Archelai*, § 9,[k] are in my opinion merely equivalents for the Syriac terms.

Act the Third : concerning the serpent

30 And the apostle went forth to go where the Lord had bidden him; and when he was near to the second mile (stone) and had turned a little out of the way, he saw the body of a comely youth lying, and said: Lord, is it for *this that* thou hast brought me forth, to come hither that I might see this

---

[1] So also it is used of 'holiness' in *Wright*, p. 255, l. 6, another fem.
[k] The Greek is preserved by Epiphanius, *Panar.* 645.

(*trial*) temptation? thy will therefore be done as thou desirest. And he began to pray and to say: O Lord, the judge of quick and dead, of the quick that stand by and the dead that lie *here*, and master and father of all things; and father not *only* of the souls that are in bodies but of them that have gone forth *of them*; for of the souls *also* that are in pollutions (*al.* bodies) thou art lord and judge; come thou at this hour wherein I call upon thee and show forth thy glory upon him that lieth here. And he turned himself unto them that followed him and said: This thing is not come to pass without cause, but the enemy hath effected it and brought it about that he may assault (?) *us* thereby; and see ye that he hath not made use of another sort, nor wrought through any other creature save that which is his subject.

31 And when he had so said, a great (*Syr.* black) serpent (dragon) came out of a hole, beating with his head and shaking his tail upon the ground, and with (using) a loud voice said unto the apostle: I will tell before thee the cause wherefor I slew this man, since thou art come hither for that end, to reprove my works. And the apostle said: Yea, say on. And the serpent: There is a certain beautiful woman in this village over against us; and as she passed by me (*or* my place) I saw her and was enamoured of her, and I followed her and kept watch upon her; and I found this youth kissing her, and he had intercourse with her and did other shameful acts with her: and for me it was easy to declare them before thee, for I know that thou art the twin brother of the Christ and alway abolishest our nature (*Syr.* easy for me to say, but to thee I do not dare to utter them because I know that the ocean-flood of the Messiah will destroy our nature): but because I would not affright her, I slew him not at that time, but waited for him till he passed by in the evening and smote and slew him, and especially because he adventured to do this upon the Lord's day.

And the apostle inquired of him, saying: Tell me of what seed and of what race thou art. 32 And he said unto him: I am a reptile of the reptile nature and noxious *son* of the noxious *father*: of him that hurt and smote the four brethren which stood upright (*om. Syr.*: the elements or four cardinal points may be meant): I am son to him that sitteth on a throne over all the earth, that receiveth back his own from them that borrow: I am son to him that girdeth about the sphere: and I am kin to him that is outside the ocean, whose tail is set in his own mouth: I am he that entered through the barrier (fence) into paradise and spake with Eve the things which my father bade me speak unto her: I am he that kindled and inflamed Cain to kill his own brother, and on mine account did thorns and thistles grow up in the earth: I am he that cast down the angels from above and bound them in lusts after women, that children born of earth might come of them and I might work my will in them: I am he that hardened Pharaoh's heart that he should slay the children of Israel and enslave them with the yoke of cruelty: I am he that caused the multitude to err in the wilderness when they made the calf: I am he that inflamed Herod and enkindled Caiaphas unto false accusation of a lie before Pilate; for this was fitting to me: I am he that stirred up Judas and bribed him to deliver up the Christ: I am he that inhabiteth and holdeth the deep of hell (Tartarus); but the Son of God hath wronged me, against my will, and taken (chosen) them that were his own from me: I am kin to him that is to come from the east, unto whom also power is given to do what he will upon the earth.

33 And when that serpent had spoken these things in the hearing of all the people, the apostle lifted up his voice on high and said: Cease thou henceforth, O most shameless one, and be put to confusion and die wholly, for the end of thy destruction is come; and dare not to tell of what thou hast done by them that have become subject unto thee. And I charge thee in the name of that Jesus who until now contendeth with you for the men that are his own, that thou suck out thy venom which thou hast put into this man, and draw it forth and take it from him. But the serpent said: Not yet is the end of our time come as thou hast said. Wherefore compellest thou me to take *back* that which I have put into this man, and to die before my time? for mine own father, when he shall draw forth and suck out that which he hath cast into the creation, then shall his end come. And the apostle said unto him: Show, *then*, now the nature of thy father. And the serpent came near and set his mouth upon the wound of the young man and sucked forth the gall out of it. And by little and little the colour of the young man which was as purple, became white, but the serpent swelled up. And when the serpent had drawn up all the gall into himself, the young man leapt up and stood, and ran and fell at the apostle's feet: but the serpent being swelled up, burst and died, and his venom and gall were shed forth; and in the place where his venom was shed there came a great gulf, and that serpent was swallowed up *therein*. And the apostle said unto the king and his brother: Take workmen and fill up that place, and lay foundations and build houses upon them, that it may be a dwelling-place for strangers.

34 But the youth said unto the apostle with many tears: Wherein have I sinned against thee? for thou art a man that hast two forms, and wheresoever thou wilt, *there* thou art found, and art restrained of no man, as I behold. For I saw that man that stood by thee and said unto thee: I have many wonders to show forth by thy means and I have great works to accomplish by thee, for which thou shalt receive *a reward*; and thou

shalt make many to live, and they shall be in rest in light eternal as children of God. Do thou then, saith he, speaking unto thee of me, quicken this youth that hath been stricken of the enemy, and be at all times his overseer. Well, therefore, art thou come hither, and well shalt thou depart again unto him, and yet he never shall leave thee at any time. But I am become without care or reproach: and he hath enlightened me from the care of the night and I am at rest from the toil of the day: and I am set free from him that provoked me to do thus, sinning against him that taught me to do contrary thereto: and I have lost him that is the kinsman of the night that compelled me to sin by his own deeds, and have found him that is of the light, and is my kinsman. I have lost him that darkeneth and blindeth his own subjects that they may not know what they do and, being ashamed at their own works, may depart from him, and their works come to an end; and have found him whose works are light and his deeds truth, which if a man doeth he repenteth not of them. And I have left him with whom lying abideth, and before whom darkness goeth as a veil, and behind him followeth shame, shameless in indolence; and I have found him that showeth me fair things that I may take hold on them, even the son of the truth, that is akin unto concord, who scattereth away the mist and enlighteneth his own creation, and healeth the wounds thereof and overthroweth the enemies thereof. But I beseech thee, O man of God, cause me to behold him again, and to see him that is now become hidden from me, that I may also hear his voice whereof I am not able to express the wonder, for it belongeth not to the nature of this bodily organ.

[Before this speech *Syr.* (Wright) inserts one of equal length, chiefly about man's free will and fall. But the fifth-century palimpsest edited by Mrs. Lewis agrees with the Greek.]

35 And the apostle answered him, saying: If thou depart from these things whereof thou hast received knowledge, as thou hast said, and if thou know who it is that hath wrought this in thee, and learn and become a hearer of him whom now in thy fervent love thou seekest; thou shalt both see him and be with him for ever, and in his rest shalt thou rest, and shalt be in his joy. But if thou be slackly disposed toward him and turn again unto thy former deeds, and leave that beauty and that bright countenance which now was showed thee, and forget the shining of his light which now thou desirest, not only wilt thou be bereaved of this life but also of that which is to come, and thou wilt depart unto him whom thou saidst thou hadst lost, and will no more behold him whom thou saidst thou hadst found.

36 And when the apostle had said this, he went into the city holding the hand of that youth, and saying unto him: These

things which thou hast seen, my child, are but a few of the many which God hath; for he doth not give us good tidings concerning these things that are seen, but greater things than these doth he promise us; but so long as we are in the body we are not able to speak and show forth those which he shall give unto our souls. If we say that he giveth us light, it is this which is seen, and we have it: and if *we say it of* wealth, which is and appeareth in the world, we name it (we speak of something which is in the world, *Syr.*), and we need it not, for it hath been said: Hardly shall a rich man enter into the kingdom of heaven: and if we speak of apparel of raiment wherewith they that are luxurious in this life are clad, it is named (we mention something that nobles wear, *Syr.*), and it hath been said: They that wear soft raiment are in the houses of kings. And if of costly banquets, concerning these we have received a commandment to beware of them, not to be weighed down with revelling and drunkenness and cares of this life—speaking of things that are—and it hath been said: Take no thought for your life (soul), what ye shall eat or what ye shall drink; neither for your body, what ye shall put on, for the soul is more than the meat and the body than the raiment. And of rest, if we speak of this temporal rest, a judgement is appointed for this also. But we speak of the world which is above, of God and angels, of watchers and holy ones, of the immortal (ambrosial) food and the drink of the true vine, of raiment that endureth and groweth not old, of things which eye hath not seen nor ear heard, neither have they entered into the heart of sinful men, the things which God hath prepared for them that love him. Of these things do we converse and of these do we bring good tidings. Do thou therefore also believe on him that thou mayest live, and put thy trust in him, and thou shalt not die. For he is not persuaded with gifts, that thou shouldest offer them to him, neither is he in need of sacrifices, that thou shouldest sacrifice unto him. But look thou unto him, and he will not overlook thee; and turn unto him, and he will not forsake thee. For his comeliness and his beauty will make thee wholly desirous to love him: and indeed he per-mitteth thee not to turn thyself away.

37 And when the apostle had said these things unto that youth, a great multitude joined themselves *unto them.* And the apostle looked and saw them raising themselves on high that they might see him, and they were going up into high places; and the apostle said unto them: Ye men that are come unto the assembly of Chiist, and would believe on Jesus, take exampie hereby, and see that if ye be not lifted up, ye cannot see me who am little, and are not able to spy me out who am like unto you. If, then, ye cannot see me who am like you unless ye lift yourselves up a little from the earth, how can ye see him that dwelleth in the height and now is found in the depth, unless

ye first lift yourselves up out of your former conversation, and your unprofitable deeds, and your desires that abide not, and the wealth that is left here, and the possession of earth that groweth old, and the raiment that corrupteth, and the beauty that waxeth old and vanisheth away, and yet more out of the whole body wherein all these things are stored up, and which groweth old and becometh dust, returning unto its own nature? For it is the body which maintaineth all these things. But rather believe on our Lord Jesus Christ, whom we preach, that your hope may be in him and in him ye may have life world without end, that he may become your fellow traveller in this land of error, and may be to you an harbour in this troublous sea. And he shall be to you a fountain springing up in this thirsty land and a chamber full of food in this place of them that hunger, and a rest unto your souls, yea, and a physician for your bodies.

38 Then the multitude of them that were gathered together hearing these things wept, and said unto the apostle: O man of God, the God whom thou preachest, we dare not say that we are his, for the works which we have done are alien unto him and not pleasing to him; but if he will have compassion on us and pity us and save us, overlooking our former deeds, and will set us free from the evils which we committed being in error, and not impute them unto us nor make remembrance of our former sins, we will become his servants and will accomplish his will unto the end. And the apostle answered them and said: He reckoneth not against you, neither taketh account of the sins which ye committed being in error, but overlooketh your transgressions which ye have done in ignorance.[1]

The Fourth Act: concerning the colt

39 And while the apostle yet stood in the highway and spake with the multitude, a she ass's colt came and stood before him (*Syr. adds*, And Judas said: It is not without the direction of God that this colt has come hither. But to thee I say, O colt, that by the grace of our Lord there shall be given to thee speech before these multitudes who are standing here; and do thou say whatsoever thou wilt, that they may believe in the God of truth whom we preach. And the mouth of the colt was opened, and it spake by the power of our Lord and said to him) and opened its mouth and said: Thou twin of Christ, apostle of the Most High and initiate in the hidden word of Christ, who receivest his secret oracles, fellow worker with the Son of God, who being free hast become a bondman, and being sold hast brought many into liberty. Thou kinsman of the great race that hath condemned the enemy and redeemed his own, that hast become an occasion of life unto many in the

---

[1] Cf. *Peter*, ch. III.

land of the Indians ; for thou hast come (against thy will, *Syr.*) unto men that were in error, and by thy appearing and thy divine words they are now turning unto the God of truth which sent thee : mount and sit upon me and repose thyself until thou enter into the city. And the apostle answered and said : O Jesu Christ (Son) that understandest the perfect mercy ! O tranquillity and quiet that now art spoken of (speakest, *Syr.*) by (among) brute beasts ! O hidden rest, that art manifested by thy working, Saviour of us and nourisher, keeping us and resting in alien bodies ! O Saviour of our souls ! spring that is sweet and unfailing ; fountain secure and clear and never polluted ; defender and helper in the fight of thine own servants, turning away and scaring the enemy from us, that fightest in many battles for us and makest us conquerors in all ; our true and undefeated champion (athlete) ; our holy and victorious captain : glorious, and giving unto thine own a joy that never passeth away, and a relief wherein is none affliction ; good shepherd that givest thyself for thine own sheep, and hast vanquished the wolf and redeemed thine own lambs and led them into a good pasture : we glorify and praise thee and thine invisible Father and thine holy Spirit [and] the mother of all creation.

40 And when the apostle had said these things, all the multitude that were there looked upon him, expecting to hear what he would answer to the colt. And the apostle stood a long time as it were astonied, and looked up into heaven and said to the colt: Of whom art thou and to whom belongest thou? for marvellous are the things that are shown forth by thy mouth, and amazing and such as are hidden from the many. And the colt answered and said: I am of that stock that served Balaam, and thy lord also and teacher sat upon one that appertained unto me by race. And I also have now been sent to give thee rest by thy sitting upon me: and (that) I may receive (*Syr.* these may be confirmed in) faith, and unto me may be added that portion which now I shall receive by thy service wherewith I serve thee; and when I have ministered unto thee, it shall be taken from me. And the apostle said unto him: He is able who granted thee this gift, to cause it to be fulfilled unto the end in thee and in them that belong unto thee by race: for as to this mystery I am weak and powerless. And he would not sit upon him. But the colt besought and entreated him that he might be blessed of him by ministering unto him. Then the apostle mounted him and sat upon him; and they followed him, some going before and some following after, and all of them ran, desiring to see the end, and how he would dismiss the colt.

41 But when he came near to the city gates he dismounted from him, saying: Depart, and be thou kept safe where thou wert. And straightway the colt fell to the ground at the apostle's feet and died. And all they that were present were sorry and

said to the apostle: Bring him to life and raise him up. But he answered and said unto them: I indeed am able to raise him by the name of Jesus Christ: but this is by all means expedient (*or*, this is ⟨not⟩ by any means expedient). For he that gave him speech that he might talk was able to cause that he should not die; and I raise him not, not as being unable, but because this is that which is expedient and profitable for him. And he bade them that were present to dig a trench and bury his body, and they did as they were commanded.

The Fifth Act : concerning the devil that took up his abode in the woman

42 And the apostle entered into the city and all the multitude followed him. And he thought to go unto the parents of the young man whom he had made alive when he was slain by the serpent; for they earnestly besought him to come unto them and enter into their house. But a very beautiful woman on a sudden uttered an exceeding loud cry, saying: O Apostle of the new God that art come into India, and servant of that holy and only good God; for by thee is he preached, the Saviour of the souls that come unto him, and by thee are healed the bodies of them that are tormented by the enemy, and thou art he that is become an occasion of life unto all that turn unto him: command me to be brought before thee that I may tell thee what hath befallen me, and peradventure of thee I may have hope, and these that stand by thee may be more confident in the God whom thou preachest. For I am not a little tormented by the adversary now this five years' space [*one Greek MS.* And the apostle bade her come unto him, and the woman stood before him and said: I, O servant of him that is indeed God, am a woman: *the rest have*, As a woman] I was sitting at the first in quiet, and peace encompassed me on every side and I had no care for anything, for I took no thought for any other. 43 And it fell out one day that as I came out from the bath there met me a man troubled and disturbed, and his voice and speech seemed to me exceeding faint and dim; and he stood before me and said: I and thou will be in one love, and we will have intercourse together as a man with his wife. And I answered and said to him: I never had to do with my betrothed, for I refused to marry, and how shall I yield myself to thee that wouldest have intercourse with me in adulterous wise? And having so said, I passed on, and I said to my handmaid that was with me: Sawest thou that youth and his shamelessness, how boldly he spake with me, and had no shame? but she said to me: I saw an old man speaking to thee. And when I was in mine house and had dined my soul suggested unto me some suspicion, and especially because he was seen of me in two forms; and having this in my mind I fell asleep. He came, therefore,

in that night and was joined unto me in his foul intercourse.
And when it was day I saw him and fled from him, and on the
night following that [1] he came and abused me; and now as thou
seest me I have spent five years being troubled by him, and
he hath not departed from me. But I know and am persuaded
that both devils and spirits and destroyers are subject unto
thee and are filled with trembling at thy prayers: pray thou
therefore for me and drive away from me the devil that ever
troubleth me, that I also may be set free and be gathered unto
the nature that is mine from the beginning, and receive the
grace that hath been given unto my kindred.

44 And the apostle said: O evil that cannot be restrained!
O shamelessness of the enemy! O envious one that art never
at rest! O hideous one that subduest the comely! O thou of
many forms! As he will he appeareth, but his essence cannot
be changed. O the crafty and faithless one! O the bitter tree,
whose fruits are like unto him! O the devil that overcometh
them that are alien to him! O the deceit that useth impudence!
O the wickedness that creepeth like a serpent, and that is of
his kindred! (*Syr.* wrongly adds a clause bidding the devil
show himself.) And when the apostle said this, the malicious one
came and stood before him, no man seeing him save the woman
and the apostle, and with an exceeding loud voice said in the
hearing of all: 45 What have we to do with thee, thou apostle
of the Most High! What have we to do with thee, thou servant
of Jesus Christ? What have we to do with thee, thou counsellor
of the holy Son of God? Wherefore wilt thou destroy us, whereas
our time is not yet come? Wherefore wilt thou take away our
power? for unto this hour we had hope and time remaining to
us. What have we to do with thee? Thou hast power over
thine own, and we over ours. Wherefore wilt thou act tyrannously
against us, when thou thyself teachest others not to act tyrannously? Wherefore dost thou crave other men's goods and
not suffice thyself with thine own? Wherefore art thou made
like unto the Son of God which hath done us wrong? for thou
resemblest him altogether as if thou wert born of him. For
we thought to have brought him under the yoke like as we
have the rest, but he turned and made us subject unto him:
for we knew him not; but he deceived us with his form of all
uncomeliness and his poverty and his neediness: for seeing him
to be such, we thought that he was a man wearing flesh, and
knew not that it is he that giveth life unto men. And he gave
us power over our own, and that we should not in this present
time leave them but have our walk in them: but thou wouldest
get more than thy due and that which was given thee, and
afflict us altogether.

[1] *or* on the night akin to him. *Syr. Lewis,* he used to come in the
shape of his race. *Syr. Wright,* he used to come in a terrible form.

46 And having said this the devil wept, saying: I leave thee, my fairest consort, whom long since I found and rested in thee; I forsake thee, my sure sister, my beloved in whom I was well pleased. What I shall do I know not, or on whom I shall call that he may hear me and help me. I know what I will do: I will depart unto some place where the report of this man hath not been heard, and peradventure I shall call thee, my beloved, by another name (*Syr.* for thee my beloved I shall find a substitute). And he lifted up his voice and said: Abide in peace, for thou hast taken refuge with one greater than I, but I will depart and seek for one like thee, and if I find her not, I will return unto thee again: for I know that whilst thou art near unto this man thou hast a refuge in him, but when he departeth thou wilt be such as thou wast before he appeared, and him thou wilt forget, and I shall have opportunity and confidence: but now I fear the name of him that hath saved thee. And having so said the devil vanished out of sight : only when he departed fire and smoke were seen there : and all that stood there were astonied.

47 And the apostle seeing it, said unto them: This devil hath shown nought that is alien or strange to him, but his own nature, wherein also he shall be consumed, for verily the fire shall destroy him utterly and the smoke of it shall be scattered abroad. And he began to say:

Jesu, the hidden mystery that hath been revealed unto us, thou art he that hast shown unto us many mysteries; thou that didst call me apart from all my fellows and spakest unto me three (one, *Syr.*) words wherewith I am inflamed, and am not able to speak them unto others. Jesu, man that wast slain, dead, buried! Jesu, God of God, Saviour that quickenest the dead, and healest the sick! Jesu, that wert in need like ⟨a poor man⟩ and savest as one that hath no need, that didst catch the fish for the breakfast and the dinner and madest all satisfied with a little bread. Jesu, that didst rest from the weariness of wayfaring like a man, and walkedst on the waves like a God. 48 Jesu most high, voice arising from perfect mercy, Saviour of all, the right hand of the light, overthrowing the evil one in his own nature, and gathering all his nature into one place; thou of many forms, that art only begotten, first-born of many brethren, God of the Most High God, man despised until now (*Syr.* and humble). Jesu Christ that neglectest us not when we call upon thee, that art become an occasion of life unto all mankind, that for us wast judged and shut up in prison, and loosest all that are in bonds, that wast called a deceiver and redeemest thine own from error: I beseech thee for these that stand here and believe on thee, for they entreat to obtain thy gifts, having good hope in thy help, and having their refuge in thy greatness; they hold their hearing ready to listen unto the words that are spoken by us. Let thy peace come and tabernacle in them and renew them from their former deeds, and let them put off the old man with his deeds, and put on the new that now is proclaimed unto them by me.

49 And he laid his hands on them and blessed them, saying: The grace of our Lord Jesus Christ shall be upon you for ever. And they said, Amen. And the woman besought him, saying: O apostle of the Most High, give me the seal, that that enemy return not again unto me. Then he caused her to come near unto him (*Syr.* went to a river which was close by there), and laid his hands upon her and sealed her in the name of the Father and the Son and the Holy Ghost; and many others also were sealed with her. And the apostle bade his minister (deacon) to set forth a table; and he set forth a stool which they found there, and spread a linen cloth upon it and set on the bread of blessing; and the apostle stood by it and said: Jesu, that hast accounted us worthy to partake of the eucharist of thine holy body and blood, lo, we are bold to draw near unto thine eucharist and to call upon thine holy name: come thou and communicate unto us (*Syr.* adds more).

50 And he began to say: Come, O perfect compassion, Come, O communion of the male, Come, she that knoweth the mysteries of him that is chosen, Come, she that hath part in all the combats of the noble champion (athlete), Come, the silence that revealeth the great things of the whole greatness, Come, she that manifesteth the hidden things and maketh the unspeakable things plain, the holy dove that beareth the twin young, Come, the hidden mother, Come, she that is manifest in her deeds and giveth joy and rest unto them that are joined unto her: Come and communicate with us in this eucharist which we celebrate in thy name and in the love-feast wherein we are gathered together at thy calling. (*Syr.* has other clauses and not few variants.) And having so said he marked out the cross upon the bread, and brake it, and began to distribute it. And first he gave unto the woman, saying: This shall be unto thee for remission of sins and eternal transgressions (*Syr.* and for the everlasting resurrection). And after her he gave unto all the others also which had received the seal (*Syr.* and said to them : Let this eucharist be unto you for life and rest, and not for judgement and vengeance. And they said, Amen. Cf. 29 fin.).

The Sixth Act: of the youth that murdered the woman.

51 Now there was a certain youth who had wrought an abominable deed, and he came near and received of the eucharist with his mouth: but his two hands withered up, so that he could no more put them unto his own mouth. And they that were there saw him and told the apostle what had befallen; and the apostle called him and said unto him : Tell me, my child, and be not ashamed, what was it that thou didst and camest

hither? for the eucharist of the Lord hath convicted thee. For this gift which passeth among many doth rather heal them that with faith and love draw near thereto, but thee it hath withered away; and that which is come to pass hath not befallen without some effectual cause. And the youth, being convicted by the eucharist of the Lord, came and fell at the apostle's feet and besought him, saying: I have done an evil deed, yet I thought to do somewhat good. I was enamoured of a woman that dwelleth at an inn without the city, and she also loved me; and when I heard of thee and believed, that thou proclaimest a living God, I came and received of thee the seal with the rest; for thou saidst: Whosoever shall partake in the polluted union, and especially in adultery, he shall not have life with the God whom I preach. Whereas therefore I loved her much, I entreated her and would have persuaded her to become my consort in chastity and pure conversation, which thou also teachest: but she would not. When, therefore, she consented not, I took a sword and slew her: for I could not endure to see her commit adultery with another man.

52 When the apostle heard this he said: O insane union, how runnest thou unto shamelessness! O unrestrained lust, how hast thou stirred up this man to do this! O work of the serpent, how art thou enraged against thine own! And the apostle bade water to be brought to him in a bason; and when the water was brought, he said: Come, ye waters from the living waters, that were sent unto us, the true from the true, the rest that was sent unto us from the rest, the power of salvation that cometh from that power which conquereth all things and subdueth them unto its own will: come and dwell in these waters, that the gift of the Holy Ghost may be perfectly consummated in them. And he said unto the youth: Go, wash thy hands in these waters. And when he had washed they were restored; and the apostle said unto him: Believest thou in our Lord Jesus Christ that he is able to do all things? And he said: Though I be the least, yet I believe. But I committed this deed, thinking that I was doing somewhat good: for I besought her, as I told thee, but she would not obey me, to keep herself chaste.

53 And the apostle said to him: Come, let us go unto the inn where thou didst commit this deed. And the youth went before the apostle in the way; and when they came to the inn they found her lying *dead*. And the apostle when he saw her was sorry; for she was a comely girl. And he commanded her to be brought into the midst of the inn: and they laid her on a bed and brought her forth and set her down in the midst of the court of the inn. And the apostle laid his hand upon her and began to say: Jesu, who alway showest thyself unto us— for this is thy will, that we should at all times seek thee, and thyself hast given us this power, to ask and to receive, and hast

not only permitted this, but hast taught us to pray: who art not seen of our bodily eyes, but art never hidden from the eyes of our soul, and in thine aspect art concealed, but in thy works art manifested unto us: and in thy many acts we have known thee so far as we are able, and thyself hast given us thy gifts without measure, saying: Ask and it shall be given unto you, seek and ye shall find, knock and it shall be opened unto you: we beseech thee, therefore, having the fear (suspicion) of our sins; and we ask of thee, not riches, not gold, not silver, not possessions, not aught else of the things which come of the earth and return again unto the earth; but this we ask of thee and entreat, that in thine holy name thou wouldest raise up the woman that lieth here, by thy power, to the glory and faith of them that stand by.

54 And he said unto the youth (*Syr.* 'Stretch thy mind towards our Lord,' and he signed him with the cross), having signed (sealed) him: Go and take hold on her hand and say unto her: I with my hands slew thee with iron, and with my hands in the faith of Jesus I raise thee up. So the youth went to her and stood by her, saying: I have believed in thee, Christ Jesu. And he looked unto Judas Thomas the apostle and said to him: Pray for me that my Lord may come to my help, whom I also call upon. And he laid his hand upon her hand and said: Come, Lord Jesu Christ: unto her grant thou life and unto me the earnest of faith in thee. And straightway as he drew her hand she sprang up and sat up, looking upon the great company that stood by. And she saw the apostle also standing over against her, and leaving the bed she leapt forth and fell at his feet and caught hold on his raiment, saying: I beseech thee, my lord, where is that other that was with thee, who left me not to remain in that fearful and cruel place, but delivered me unto thee, saying: Take thou this woman, that she may be made perfect, and hereafter be gathered into her place?

55 And the apostle said unto her: Relate unto us where thou hast been. And she answered: Dost thou who wast with me and unto whom I was delivered desire to hear? And she began to say:[1] A man took me who was hateful to look upon, altogether black, and his raiment exceedingly foul, and took me away to a place wherein were many pits (chasms), and a great stench and hateful odour issued thence. And he caused me to look into every pit, and I saw in the (first) pit flaming fire, and wheels of fire ran round there, and souls were hanged upon those wheels, and were dashed (broken) against each other; and very great crying and howling was there, and there was none to deliver. And that man said to me: These souls are of thy tribe, and when the number of their days is accomplished (*lit.*

[1] This description of hell-torments is largely derived from the Apocalypse of Peter, which see.

in the days of the number) they are (were) delivered unto torment and affliction, and then are others brought in in their stead, and likewise these into another *place*. These are they that have reversed the intercourse of male and female. And I looked and saw infants heaped one upon another and struggling with each other as they lay on them. And he answered and said to me : These are the children of those *others*, and therefore are they set here for a testimony against them. (*Syr.* omits this clause of the children, and lengthens and dilutes the preceding speech.)

56 And he took me unto another pit, and I stooped and looked and saw mire and worms welling up, and souls wallowing there, and a great gnashing of teeth was heard thence from them. And that man said unto me: These are the souls of women which forsook their husbands and committed adultery with others, and are brought into this torment. Another pit he showed me, whereinto I stooped and looked and saw souls hanging, some by the tongue, some by the hair, some by the hands, and some head downward by the feet, and tormented (smoked) with smoke and brimstone; concerning whom that man that was with me answered me: The souls which are hanged by the tongue are slanderers, that uttered lying and shameful words, and were not ashamed; and they that are hanged by the hair are unblushing ones which had no modesty and went about in the world bareheaded; and they that are hanged by the hands, these are they that took away and stole other men's goods, and never gave aught to the needy nor helped the afflicted, but did so, desiring to take all, and had no thought at all of justice or of the law; and they that hang upside down by the feet, these are they that lightly and readily ran in evil ways and disorderly paths, not visiting the sick nor escorting them that depart this life, and therefore each and every soul receiveth that which was done by it. (*Syr.* omits almost the whole section.)

57 Again he took me and showed me a cave exceeding dark, breathing out a great stench, and many souls were looking out desiring to get somewhat of the air, but their keepers suffered them not to look forth. And he that was with me said: This is the prison of those souls which thou sawest: for when they have fulfilled their torments for that which each did, thereafter do others succeed them: and there be some that are wholly consumed and (some, *Syr.*) that are delivered over unto other torments. And they that kept the souls which were in the dark cave said unto the man that had taken me: Give her unto us that we may bring her in unto the rest until the time cometh for her to be delivered unto torment. But he answered them: I give her not unto you, for I fear him that delivered her to me: for I was not charged to leave her here, but I take her back with me until I shall receive order concerning her. And he

took me and brought me unto another place wherein were men being sharply tormented (*Syr.* where men were). And he that was like unto thee took me and delivered me to thee, saying thus to thee: Take her, for she is one of the sheep that have gone astray. And I was taken by thee, and now am I before thee. I beseech thee, therefore, and supplicate that I may not depart unto those places of punishment which I have seen.

58 And the apostle said: Ye have heard what this woman hath related: and there are not these torments only, but others also, worse than these; and ye, if ye turn not unto this God whom I preach, and abstain from your former works and the deeds which ye committed without knowledge, shall have your end in those torments. Believe therefore on Christ Jesus, and he will forgive you the sins ye have committed hitherto, and will cleanse you from all your bodily lusts that abide on the earth, and will heal you of all your trespasses which follow you and depart with you and are found upon (before) you. Put off therefore every one of you the old man, and put on the new, and forsake your former walk and conversation; and let them that stole steal no more, but live by labouring and working; and let the adulterous no more fornicate, lest they deliver themselves unto eternal torment; for adultery is before God exceeding evil beyond other sins. And put away from you covetousness and lying and drunkenness and slandering, and render not evil for evil: for all these things are strange and alien unto the God who is preached by me: but rather walk ye in faith and meekness and holiness and hope, wherein God delighteth, that ye may become his own, expecting of him the gifts which some few only do receive.

59 All the people therefore believed and gave their souls obediently unto the living God and Christ Jesus, rejoicing in the blessed works of the Most High and in his holy service. And they brought much money for the service of the widows: for *the apostle* had them gathered together in the cities, and unto all of them he sent provision by his own ministers (deacons), both clothes and nourishment. And he himself ceased not preaching and speaking to them and showing that this is Jesus Christ whom the scriptures proclaimed, who is come and was crucified, and raised the third day from the dead. And next he showed them plainly, beginning from the prophets, the things concerning the Christ, that it was necessary that he should come, and that in him should be accomplished all things that were foretold of him. And the fame of him went forth into all the cities and countries, and all that had sick or them that were oppressed by unclean spirits brought them, and some they laid in the way whereby he should pass, and he healed them all by the power of the Lord. Then all that were healed by him said with one accord: Glory be to thee, Jesu, who hast granted us all alike

healing through thy servant and apostle Thomas. And *now* being whole and rejoicing, we beseech thee that we may be of thy flock, and be numbered among thy sheep; receive us therefore, Lord, and impute not unto us our transgressions and our former faults which we committed being in ignorance.

60 And the apostle said: Glory be to the only-begotten of the Father! Glory be to the first-born of many brethren! Glory be to thee, the defender and helper of them that come unto thy refuge! that sleepest not, and awakest them that are asleep, that livest and givest life to them that lie in death! O God, Jesu Christ, Son of the living God, redeemer and helper, refuge and rest of all that are weary (labour) in thy work, giver of healing to them that for thy name's sake bear the burden and heat of the day: we give thanks for (to) the gifts that are given us of thee and granted us by thy help and thy dispensation that cometh unto us from thee.

61 Perfect thou therefore these things in us unto the end, that we may have the boldness that is in thee: look upon us, for for thy sake have we forsaken our homes and our parents, and for thy sake have we gladly and willingly become strangers: look upon us, Lord, for we have forsaken our own possessions for thy sake, that we might gain thee, the possession that cannot be taken away: look upon us, Lord, for we have forsaken them that belong unto us by race, that we might be joined unto thy kinship: look upon us, Lord, that have forsaken our fathers and mothers and fosters, that we might behold thy Father, and be satisfied with his divine food: look upon us, Lord, for for thy sake have we forsaken our bodily consorts and our earthly fruits, that we might be partakers in that enduring and true fellowship, and bring forth true fruits, whose nature is from above, which no man can take from us, with whom we *shall* abide and who *shall* abide with us.

The Seventh Act: of the Captain.

62 Now while the apostle Thomas was proclaiming throughout all India the word of God, a certain captain of the king Misdaeus (Mazdai, *Syr.*) came to him and said unto him: I have heard of thee that thou takest no reward of any man, but even that thou hast thou givest to them that need. For if thou didst receive rewards, I would have sent thee a great sum, and would not have come myself, for the king doeth nought without me: for I have much substance and am rich, even one of the rich men of India. And I have never done wrong to any; but the contrary hath befallen me. I have a wife, and of her I had a daughter, and I am well affectioned toward her, as also nature requireth, and have never made trial of another wife. Now it chanced that there was a wedding in our city, and they that made the marriage feast were well beloved of me: they came in therefore and bade

me to it, bidding also *my wife* and her daughter. Forasmuch then as they were my good friends I could not refuse: I sent her therefore, though she desired not to go, and with them I sent also many servants: so they departed, both she and her daughter, decked with many ornaments.

63 And when it was evening and the time was come to depart from the wedding I sent lamps and torches to meet them: and I stood in the street to espy when she should come and I should see her with my daughter. And as I stood I heard a sound of lamentation. Woe for her! was heard out of every mouth. And my servants with their clothes rent came to me and told me what was done. We saw, said they, a man and a boy with him. And the man laid his hand upon thy wife, and the boy upon thy daughter: and they fled from them: and we smote (wounded) them with our swords, but our swords fell to the ground. And the same hour *the women* fell down, gnashing their teeth and beating their heads upon the earth; and seeing this we came to tell it thee. And when I heard this of my servants I rent my clothes and smote my face with my hands, and becoming like one mad I ran along the street, and came and found them cast in the market-place; and I took them and brought them to my house, and after a long space they awaked and stood up, and sat down.

64 I began therefore to inquire of my wife: What is it that hath befallen thee? And she said to me: Knowest thou not what thou hast done unto me? for I prayed thee that I might not go to the wedding, because I was not of even health in my body; and as I went on the way and came near to the aqueduct wherein the water floweth, I saw a black man standing over against me nodding at me with his head, and a boy like unto him standing by him; and I said to my daughter: Look at those two hideous men, whose teeth are like milk and their lips like soot. And we left them and went towards the aqueduct; and when it was sunset and we departed from the wedding, as we passed by with the young men and drew near the aqueduct, my daughter saw them first, and was affrighted and fled towards me; and after her I also beheld them coming against us: and the servants that were with us fled from them (*Syr.*) and they struck us, and cast down both me and my daughter. And when she had told me these things, the devils came upon them again and threw them down: and from that hour they are not able to come forth, but are shut up in one room or a second (*Syr.* in a room within another): and on their account I suffer much, and am distressed: for *the devils* throw them down wheresoever they find them, and strip them naked. I beseech and supplicate thee before God, help me and have pity on me, for it is now three years that a table hath not been set in my house, and my wife and my daughter have not sat at a table: and especially

for mine unhappy daughter, which hath not seen any good at all in this world.

65 And the apostle, hearing these things from the captain, was greatly grieved for him, and said unto him: Believest thou that Jesus will heal them? And the captain said: Yea. And the apostle said : Commit thyself then unto Jesus, and he will heal them and procure them succour. And the captain said : Show me him, that I may entreat him and believe in him. And the apostle said: He appeareth not unto these bodily eyes, but is found by the eyes of the mind. The captain therefore lifted up his voice and said: I believe thee, Jesu, and entreat and supplicate thee, help my little faith which I have in thee. And the apostle commanded Xenophon (*Syr.* Xanthippus) the deacon to assemble all *the brethren*; and when the whole multitude was gathered, the apostle stood in the midst and said:

66 Children and brethren that have believed on the Lord, abide in this faith, preaching Jesus who was proclaimed unto you by me, to bring you hope in him; and forsake not (be not forsaken of) him, and he will not forsake you. While ye sleep in this slumber that weigheth down the sleepers, he, sleeping not, keepeth watch over you: and when ye sail and are in peril and none can help, he walking upon the waters supporteth and aideth. For I am now departing from you, and it appeareth not if I shall again see you according to the flesh. Be ye not therefore like unto the people of Israel, who losing sight of their pastors for an hour, stumbled. But I leave unto you Xenophon the deacon in my stead; for he also like myself proclaimeth Jesus: for neither am I aught, nor he, but Jesus only; for I also am a man clothed with a body, a son of man like one of you; for neither have I riches as it is found with some, which also convict them that possess them, being wholly useless, and left behind upon the earth, whence also they came, and they bear away with them the transgressions and blemishes of sins which befall men by their means. And scantly are rich men found in almsgiving: but the merciful and lowly in heart, these shall inherit the kingdom of God: for it is not beauty that endureth with men, for they that trust in it, when age cometh upon them, shall suddenly be put to shame: all things therefore have their time ; in their season are they loved and hated. Let your hope then be in Jesus Christ the Son of God, which is always loved, and always desired: and be mindful of us, as we of you: for we too, if we fulfil not the burden of the commandments, are not worthy to be preachers of this name, and hereafter shall we pay the price (punishment) of our own head.

67 And he prayed with them and continued with them a long time in prayer and supplication, and committing them unto the Lord, he said: O Lord that rulest over every soul that is in the body; Lord, Father of the souls that have their hope in thee

and expect thy mercies: that redeemest from error the men that are thine own and settest free from bondage and corruption thy subjects that come unto thy refuge: be thou in the flock of Xenophon and anoint it with holy oil, and heal it of sores, and preserve it from the ravening wolves. And he laid his hand on them and said: The peace of the Lord shall be upon you and shall journey with us.

The Eighth Act : of the wild asses.[1]

68 The apostle therefore went forth to depart on the way: and they all escorted him, weeping and adjuring him to make remembrance of them in his prayers and not to forget them. He went up then and sat upon the chariot, leaving all the brethren, *and* the captain came and awaked the driver, saying: I entreat and pray that I may become worthy to sit beneath his feet, and I will be his driver upon this way, that he also may become my guide in that way whereby few go.

69 And when they had journeyed about two miles, the apostle begged of the captain and made him arise and caused him to sit by him, suffering the driver to sit in his own place. And as they went along the road, it came to pass that the beasts were wearied with the great heat and could not be stirred at all. And the captain was greatly vexed and wholly cast down, and thought to run on his own feet and bring other beasts for the use of the chariot; but the apostle said: Let not thine heart be troubled nor affrighted, but believe on Jesus Christ whom I have proclaimed unto thee, and thou shalt see great wonders. And he looked and saw a herd of wild asses feeding by the wayside, and said to the captain: If thou hast believed on Christ Jesus, go unto that herd of wild asses and say: Judas Thomas the apostle of Christ the new God saith unto you: Let four of you come, of whom we have need (*or*, of whom we may have use).

70 And the captain went in fear, for they were many; and as he went, they came to meet him; and when they were near, he said unto them : Judas Thomas the apostle of the new God commandeth you: Let four of you come, of whom I have need. And when the wild asses heard it, they ran with one accord and came to him, and when they came they did *him reverence*. [*Syr.* has a long prayer: And Judas Thomas the apostle of our Lord lifted up his voice in praise and said: Glorious art thou, God of truth and Lord of all natures, for thou didst will with thy will, and make all thy works and finish all thy creatures, and bring them to the rule of their nature, and lay upon them all thy fear that they might be subject to thy command. And thy will trod the path from thy secrecy to manifestation, and was caring for every soul that thou didst make, and was spoken of by the mouth of all the prophets, in all visions and sounds and voices; but Israel did not

[1] *Syr.* has no division here.

obey because of their evil inclination. And thou, because thou art Lord of all, hast a care for the creatures, so that thou spreadest over us thy mercy in him who came by thy will and put on the body, thy creature, which thou didst will and form according to thy glorious wisdom. He whom thou didst appoint in thy secrecy and establish in thy manifestation, to him thou hast given the name of Son, he who was thy will, the power of thy thought; so that ye are by various names, the Father and the Son and the Spirit, for the sake of the government of thy creatures, for the nourishing of all natures, and ye are one in glory and power and will; and ye are divided without being separated, and are one though divided; and all subsists in thee and is subject to thee, because all is thine. And I rely upon thee, Lord, and by thy command have subjected these dumb beasts, that thou mightest show thy ministering power upon us and upon them, because it is needful, and that thy name might be glorified in us and in the beasts that cannot speak.] And the apostle said unto them : Peace be unto you. Yoke ye four *of you* in the stead of these beasts that have come to a stand. And every one of them came and pressed to be yoked : there were then four stronger *than the rest*, which also were yoked. And the rest, some went before and some followed. And when they had journeyed a little way he dismissed the colts, saying: I say unto you the inhabiters of the desert, depart unto your pastures, for if I had had need of all, ye would all have gone with me; but now go unto your place wherein ye dwell. And they departed quietly until they were no more seen.

71 Now as the apostle and the captain and the driver went on, the wild asses drew the chariot quietly and evenly, lest they should disturb the apostle of God. And when they came near to the city gate they turned aside and stood still before the doors of the captain's house. And the captain said: It is not possible for me to relate what hath happened, but when I see the end I will tell it. The whole city therefore came to see the wild asses under the yoke; and they had heard also the report of the apostle that he was to come and visit them. And the apostle asked the captain: Where is thy dwelling, and whither dost thou bring us? And he said to him: Thou thyself knowest that we stand before the doors, and these which by thy commandment are come with thee know it better than I.

72 And having so said he came down from the chariot. The apostle therefore began to say: Jesu Christ, that art blasphemed by the ignorance of thee in this country; Jesu, the report of whom is strange in this city ; Jesu, that receivest all (*Syr.* sendest on before) the apostles in every country and in every city, and all thine that are worthy are glorified in thee; Jesu, that didst take a form and become as a man, and wert seen of all us that thou mightest not separate us from thine own love: thou, Lord,

art he that gavest thyself for us, and with thy blood hast purchased us and gained us as a possession of great price: and what have we to give thee, Lord, in exchange for thy life which thou gavest for us? for that which we would *give*, thou gavest us: and this is, that we should entreat of thee and live.

73 And when he had so said, many assembled from every quarter to see the apostle of the new God. And again the apostle said: Why stand we idle? Jesu, Lord, the hour is come: what wilt thou have done? command therefore that that be fulfilled which needeth to be done. Now the captain's wife and her daughter were sore borne down by the devils, so that they of the house thought they would rise up no more: for they suffered them not to partake of aught, but cast them down upon their beds, recognizing no man until that day when the apostle came thither. And the apostle said unto one of the wild asses that were yoked on the right hand: Enter thou within the gate, and stand there and call the devils and say to them: Judas Thomas the apostle and disciple of Jesus Christ saith unto you: Come forth hither : for on your account am I sent and unto them that pertain to you by race, to destroy you and chase you unto your place, until the time of the end come and ye go down into your own deep of darkness.

74 And that wild ass went in, a great multitude being with him, and said: Unto you I speak, the enemies of Jesus that is called Christ: unto you I speak that shut your eyes lest ye see the light: unto you I speak, children of Gehenna and of destruction, of him that ceaseth not from evil until now, that alway reneweth his workings and the things that befit his being: unto you I speak, most shameless, that *shall* perish by your own hands. And what I shall say of your destruction and end, and what I shall tell, I know not. For there are many things and innumerable to the hearing : and greater are your doings than the torment that is reserved for you (*Syr.* however great your bodies, they are too small for your retributions). But unto thee I speak, devil, and to thy son that followeth with thee: for now am I sent against you. And wherefore should I make many words concerning your nature and root, which yourselves know and are not ashamed? but Judas Thomas the apostle of Christ Jesus saith unto you, he that by much love and affection is sent hither: Before all this multitude that standeth here, come forth and tell me of what race ye are.

75 And straightway the woman came forth with her daughter, both like dead persons and dishonoured in aspect: and the apostle beholding them was grieved, especially for the girl, and saith unto the devils: God forbid that for you there should be sparing or propitiation, for ye know not to spare nor to have pity: but in the name of Jesus, depart from them and stand by their side.

And when the apostle had so said, the women fell down and became as dead; for they neither had breath nor uttered speech: but the devil answered with a loud voice and said : Art thou come hither again, thou that deridest our nature and race? art thou come again, that blottest out our devices? and as I take it, thou wouldest not suffer us to be upon the earth at all: but this at this time thou canst not accomplish. And the apostle guessed that this devil was he that had been driven out from that *other* woman.

76 And the devil said: I beseech thee, give me leave to depart even whither thou wilt, and dwell there and take commandment from thee, and I will not fear the ruler that hath authority over me. For like as thou art come to preach good tidings, so I also am come to destroy; and like as, if thou fulfil not the will of him that sent thee, he will bring punishment upon thy head, so I also, if I do not the will of him that sent me, before the season and time appointed, shall be sent unto mine own nature; and like as thy Christ helpeth thee in that thou doest, so also my father helpeth me in that I do ; and like as for thee he prepareth vessels worthy of thine inhabiting, so also for me he seeketh out vessels whereby I may accomplish his deeds ; and like as he nourisheth and provideth for his subjects, so also for me he prepareth chastisements and torments, with them that become my dwelling-places (*Syr.* those in whom I dwell) ; and like as for a recompense of thy working he giveth thee eternal life, so also unto me he giveth for a reward of my works eternal destruction ; and like as thou art refreshed by thy prayer and thy good works and spiritual thanksgivings, so I also am refreshed by murders and adulteries and sacrifices made with wine upon altars (*Syr.* sacrifices and libations of wine) ; and like as thou convertest men unto eternal life, so I also pervert them that obey me unto eternal destruction and torment: and thou receivest thine own and I mine.

77 And when the devil had said these things and yet more, the apostle said: Jesus commandeth thee and thy son by me to enter no more into the habitation of man: but go ye forth and depart and dwell wholly apart from the habitation of men. And the devils said unto him: Thou hast laid on us a harsh commandment: but what wilt thou do unto them that now are concealed from thee? for they that have wrought all the images rejoice in them more than thee: and many of them do the more part worship, and perform their will, sacrificing to them and bringing them food, by libations and by wine and water and offering with oblations. And the apostle said: They also shall now be abolished, with their works. And suddenly the devils vanished away: but the women lay cast upon the earth as it were dead, and without speech.

78 And the wild asses stood together and parted not one from

another; but he to whom speech was given by the power of the Lord—while all men kept silence, and looked to see what they would do—the wild ass said unto the apostle: Why standest thou idle, O apostle of Christ the Most High, who looketh that thou shouldest ask of him the best of learning? Wherefore then tarriest thou? (*Syr.* that thou shouldest ask him, and he would give thee? Why delayest thou, good disciple?) for lo, thy teacher desireth to show by thy hands his mighty works. Why standest thou still, O herald of the hidden one? for thy (Lord) willeth to manifest through thee his unspeakable things, which he reserveth for them that are worthy of him, to hear them. Why restest thou, O doer of mighty works in the name of the Lord? for thy Lord encourageth thee and engendereth boldness in thee. Fear not, therefore; for he will not forsake the soul that belongeth unto thee by birth. Begin therefore to call upon him and he will readily hearken to thee. Why standest thou marvelling at all his acts and his workings? for these are small things which he hath shown by thy means. And what wilt thou tell concerning his great gifts? for thou wilt not be sufficient to declare them. And why marvellest thou at his cures of the body which he worketh? (*Syr.* which come to an end) especially when thou knowest that healing of his which is secure and lasting, which he bringeth forth by his own nature? And why lookest thou unto this temporal life, and hast no thought of that which is eternal (*Syr.* when thou canst every day think on that which is eternal)?

79 But unto you the multitudes that stand by and look to see these that are cast down raised up, I say, believe in the apostle of Jesus Christ: believe the teacher of truth, believe him that showeth you the truth, believe Jesus, believe on the Christ that was born, that the born may live by his life: who also was raised up through infancy, that perfection might appear by his manhood (man). He did teach his own disciples: for he is the teacher of the truth and maketh wise men wise (*Syr.* who went to school that through him perfect wisdom might be known: he taught his teacher because he was the teacher of verity and the master of the wise). Who also offered the gift in the temple that he might show that all the (every) offering was sanctified. This is his apostle, the shewer-forth of truth: this is he that performeth the will of him that sent him. But there shall come false apostles and prophets of lawlessness, whose end shall be according to their deeds; preaching indeed and ordaining to flee from ungodliness, but themselves at all times detected in sins; clad indeed with sheep's clothing, but within, ravening wolves. Who suffice not themselves with one wife but corrupt many women; who, saying that they despise children, destroy many children (boys), for whom they will pay the penalty; that content not themselves with their own possessions, but desire that all useless things

should minister unto them only; professing to be his disciples; and with their mouth they utter one thing, but in their heart they think another; charging other men to beware of evil, but they themselves perform nought that is good; who are accounted temperate, and charge other men to abstain from fornication, theft, and covetousness, but in all these things do they *themselves* walk secretly, teaching other men not to do them.

80 And when the wild ass had declared all these things, all men gazed upon him. And when he ceased the apostle said: What I shall think concerning thy beauty, O Jesu, and what I shall tell of thee, I know not, or rather I am not able, for I have no power to declare it, O Christ that art in rest, and only wise, that only knowest the inward of the heart and understandest the thought. Glory be to thee, merciful and tranquil. Glory to thee, wise word. Glory to thy compassion that was born unto us. Glory to thy mercy that was spread out over us. Glory to thy greatness that was made small for us. Glory to thy most high kingship that was humbled for us. Glory to thy might which was enfeebled for us. Glory to thy Godhead that for us was seen in likeness of men. Glory to thy manhood that died for us that it might make us live. Glory to thy resurrection from the dead; for thereby rising and rest cometh unto our souls. Glory and praise (good report) to thine ascending into the heavens; for thereby thou hast shewed us the path of the height, and promised that we shall sit with thee on thy right hand and with thee judge the twelve tribes of Israel. Thou art the heavenly word of the Father: thou art the hidden light of the understanding, shewer of the way of truth, driver away of darkness, and blotter-out of error.

81 Having thus spoken, the apostle stood over the women, saying: My Lord and my God, I am not divided from thee (*or* doubt not concerning thee), nor as one unbelieving do I call upon thee, who art always our helper and succourer and raiser-up; who breathest thine own power into us and encouragest us and givest confidence in love unto thine own servants. I beseech thee, let these souls be healed and rise up and become such as they were before they were smitten of the devils. And when he thus spake the women turned and sat up. And the apostle bade the captain that his servants should take them and bring them within (*Syr.* and give them food, for they had not eaten for many days). And when they were gone in, the apostle said unto the wild asses, Follow me. And they went after him until he had brought them without the gate. And when they had gone out, he said to them: Depart in peace unto your pastures. The wild asses therefore went away willingly; and the apostle stood and took heed to them lest they should be hurt of any, until they had gone afar off and were no more seen. And the apostle returned with the multitude into the house of the captain.

The Ninth Act: of the wife of Charisius.

82 Now it chanced that a certain woman, the wife of Charisius, that was next unto the king, whose name was Mygdonia, came to see and behold the new name and the new God who was being proclaimed, and the new apostle who had come to visit their country: and she was carried by her own servants; and because of the great crowd and the narrow way they were not able to bring her near unto him. And she sent unto her husband to send her more to minister to her; and they came and approached her, pressing upon the people and beating them. And the apostle saw it and said to them: Wherefore overthrow ye them that come to hear the word, and are eager for it? and ye desire to be near me but are far off; as it was said of the multitude that came unto the Lord: Having eyes ye see not, and having ears ye hear not ; and he said to the multitudes : He that hath ears to hear, let him hear; and: Come unto me, all ye that labour and are heavy laden, and I will give you rest.

83 And looking upon them that carried her, he said unto them: This blessing and this admonition [Here and elsewhere there is a marked divergence between the texts of U and P, the Roman and Paris MSS.: Bonnet prints them separately. P is on the whole much shorter. *Syr.* differs from both. I follow U, but it is very corrupt.] which was promised unto them is for you that are heavily burdened now. Ye are they that carry burdens grievous to be borne, and are borne about by her command. And though ye are men, they lay on you loads as on brute beasts, for they that have authority over you think that ye are not men such as themselves, whether bond or free. For neither shall possessions profit the rich, nor poverty save the poor from judgement ; nor have we received a commandment which we are not able to perform ; nor hath he laid on us burdens grievous to be borne which we are not able to carry ; nor building which men build ; nor to hew stones and prepare houses, as your craftsmen do by their own knowledge. But this commandment have we received of the Lord, that that which pleaseth not us when it is done by another, this we should not do to any other man.

84 Abstain therefore first from adultery, for this is the beginning of all evils; and next from theft, which enticed Judas Iscariot, and brought him unto hanging ; (and from covetousness,) for as many as yield unto covetousness see not that which they do ; and from vainglory and from all foul deeds, especially them of the body, whereby cometh eternal condemnation. For this is the chief city of all evils; and likewise it bringeth them that hold their heads (necks) high unto tyranny, and draweth them down unto the deep, and subdueth them under its hands that they see not what they do; wherefore the things done of them are hidden from them.

85 But do ye become well-pleasing unto God in all good things, in meekness and quietness: for these doth God spare, and granteth eternal life and setteth death at nought. And in gentleness *which* followeth on all good things, and overcometh all enemies and alone receiveth the crown of victory: with gentleness (*Syr.*), and stretching out of the hand to the poor, and supplying the want of the needy, and distributing to them that are in necessity, especially them that walk in holiness. For this is chosen before God and leadeth unto eternal life: for this is before God the chief city of all good: for they that strive not in the course (stadium) of Christ shall not obtain holiness. And holiness did appear from God, doing away fornication, overthrowing the enemy, well-pleasing unto God: for she is an invincible champion (athlete), having honour from God, glorified of many: she is an ambassador of peace, announcing peace: if any gain her he abideth without care, pleasing the Lord, expecting the time of redemption: for she doeth nothing amiss, but giveth life and rest and joy unto all that gain her. [P has nothing of this, and *Syr.* makes better sense, but is not very interesting.]

86 But meekness hath overcome death and brought him under authority, meekness hath enslaved the enemy (U and P and *Syr.* now present the same text), meekness is the good yoke : meekness feareth not and opposeth not the many: meekness is peace and joy and exaltation of rest. Abide ye therefore in holiness and receive freedom from me, and be near unto meekness, for in these three heads is portrayed the Christ whom I proclaim unto you. Holiness is the temple of Christ, and he that dwelleth in her getteth her for an habitation ⟨*Syr.* and temperance is the rest of God⟩, because for forty days and forty nights he fasted, tasting nothing: and he that keepeth her shall dwell in her as on a mountain. And meekness is his boast: for he said unto Peter our fellow apostle : Turn back thy sword and put it again into the sheath thereof: for if I had willed so to do, could I not have brought more than twelve legions of angels from my Father ?

87 And when the apostle had said these things in the hearing of all the multitude, they trode and pressed upon one another: and the wife of Charisius the king's kinsman leapt out of her chair and cast herself on the earth before the apostle, and caught his feet and besought and said: O disciple of the living God, thou art come into a desert country, for we live in the desert, being like to brute beasts in our conversation; but now shall we be saved by thy hands; I beseech thee, therefore, take thought of me, and pray for me, that the compassion of the God whom thou preachest may come upon me, and I may become his dwelling-place and be joined in prayer and hope and faith in him, and I also may receive the seal and become an holy temple and he may dwell in me.

88 And the apostle said: I do pray and entreat for you all,

brethren, that believe on the Lord, and for you, sisters, that hope in Christ, that in all of you the word of God may tabernacle [and have his tabernacle therein]: for we have no power over them (*Syr.* because ye are given power over your own souls). And he began to say unto the woman Mygdonia: Rise up from the earth and compose thyself (take off thine ornaments, P; be mindful of thyself, *Syr.*). For this attire that is put on shall not profit thee, nor the beauty of thy body, nor thine apparel, neither yet the fame of thy rank, nor the authority of this world, nor the polluted intercourse with thine husband shall avail thee if thou be bereaved of the true fellowship: for the appearance (fantasy) of ornamenting cometh to nought, and the body waxeth old and changeth, and raiment weareth out, and authority and lordship pass away (U corrupt; P abridges; *Syr.* has: passeth away *accompanied* with punishment, according as each person hath conducted himself in it), and the fellowship of procreation also passeth away, and is as it were condemnation. Jesus only abideth ever, and they that hope in him. Thus he spake, and said unto the woman: Depart in peace, and the Lord shall make thee worthy of his own mysteries. But she said: I fear to go away, lest thou forsake me and depart unto another nation. But the apostle said to her: Even if I go, I shall not leave thee alone, but Jesus of his compassion will be with thee. And she fell down and did him reverence and departed unto her house.

89 Now Charisius, the kinsman of Misdaeus the king, bathed himself and returned and laid him down to dine. And he inquired concerning his wife, where she was; for she had not come out of her own chamber to meet him as she was wont. And her handmaids said to him: She is not well. And he entered quickly into the chamber and found her lying on the bed and veiled: and he unveiled her and kissed her, saying: Wherefore art thou sorrowful to-day? And she said: I am not well. And he said unto her: Wherefore then didst thou not keep the guise of thy freedom (*Syr.* pay proper respect to thy position as a free woman) and remain in thy house, but didst go and listen unto vain speeches and look upon works of sorcery? but rise up and dine with me, for I cannot dine without thee. But she said to him: To-day I decline it, for I am greatly afeared.

90 And when Charisius heard this of Mygdonia, he would not go forth to dinner, but bade his servants bring her to dine with him (*Syr.* bring food to him that he might sup in her presence): when then they brought it in, he desired her to dine with him, but she excused herself; since then she would not, he dined alone, saying unto her: On thine account I refused to dine with Misdaeus the king, and thou, wast thou not willing to dine with me? but she said: It is because I am not well. Charisius therefore rose up as he was wont and would sleep with her, but she said: Did I not tell thee that for to-day I refused it?

91 When he heard that he went to another bed and slept; and awaking out of sleep he said: My lady Mygdonia, hearken to the dream which I have seen. I saw myself lie at meat near to Misdaeus the king, and a dish of all sorts was set before us: and I saw an eagle come down from heaven and carry off from before me and the king two partridges, which he set against his heart; and again he came over us and flew about above us; and the king bade a bow to be brought to him; and the eagle again caught away from before us a pigeon and a dove, and the king shot an arrow at him, and it passed through him from one side to the other and hurt him not; and he being unscathed rose up into his own nest. And I awoke, and I am full of fear and sore vexed, because I had tasted of the partridge, and he suffered me not to put it to my mouth again. And Mygdonia said unto him: Thy dream is good: for thou every day eatest partridges, but this eagle had not tasted of a partridge until now.

92 And when it was morning Charisius went and dressed himself and shod his right foot with his left shoe ; and he stopped, and said to Mygdonia: What then is this matter? for look, the dream and this action *of mine*! But Mygdonia said to him: And this also is not evil, but seemeth to me very good; for from an unlucky act there will be a change unto the better. And he washed his hands and went to salute Misdaeus the king.

93 And likewise Mygdonia rose up early and went to salute Judas Thomas the apostle, and she found him discoursing with the captain and all the multitude, and he was advising them and speaking of the woman which had received the Lord in her soul, whose wife she was ; and the captain said : She is the wife of Charisius the kinsman of Misdaeus the king. And: Her husband is a hard man, and in every thing that he saith to the king he obeyeth him: and he will not suffer her to continue in this mind which she hath promised; for often-times hath he praised her before the king, saying that there is none other like her in love: all things therefore that thou speakest unto her are strange unto her. And the apostle said: If verily and surely the Lord hath risen upon her soul and she hath received the seed that was cast on her, she will have no care of this temporal life, nor fear death, neither will Charisius be able to harm her at all: for greater is he whom she hath received into her soul, if she have received him indeed.

94 And Mygdonia hearing this said unto the apostle: In truth, my lord, I have received the seed of thy words, and I will bear fruit like unto such seed. The apostle saith: *Our* souls give praise and thanks unto thee, O Lord, for they are thine: our bodies give thanks unto thee, which thou hast accounted worthy to become the dwelling-place of thy heavenly gift. And he said also to them that stood by: Blessed are the holy, whose souls have never condemned them, for they have gained them and are

not divided against themselves: blessed are the spirits of the pure, and they that have received the heavenly crown whole from the world (age) which hath been appointed them: blessed are the bodies of the holy, for they have been made worthy to become temples of God, that Christ may dwell in them: blessed are ye, for ye have power to forgive sins: blessed are ye if ye lose not that which is committed unto you, but rejoicing and departing bear it away with you: blessed are ye the holy, for unto you it is given to ask and receive: blessed are ye meek, for you hath God counted worthy to become heirs of the heavenly kingdom. Blessed are ye meek, for ye are they that have overcome the enemy: blessed are ye meek, for ye shall see the face of the Lord. Blessed are ye that hunger for the Lord's sake, for for you is rest laid up, and your souls rejoice from henceforth. Blessed are ye that are quiet, (for ye have been counted worthy) to be set free from sin [and from the exchange of clean and unclean beasts]. And when the apostle had said these things in the hearing of all the multitude, Mygdonia was the more confirmed in the faith and glory and greatness of Christ.

95 But Charisius the kinsman and friend of Misdaeus the king came to his breakfast and found not his wife in the house; and he inquired of all that were in his house: Whither is your mistress gone? And one of them answered and said: She is gone unto that stranger. And when he heard this of his servant, he was wroth with the other servants because they had not straightway told him what was done: and he sat down and waited for her. And when it was evening and she was come into the house he said to her: Where wast thou? And she answered and said: With the physician. And he said: Is that stranger a physician? And she said: Yea, he is a physician of souls: for most physicians do heal bodies that are dissolved, but he souls that are not destroyed. Charisius, hearing this, was very angry in his mind with Mygdonia because of the apostle, but he answered her nothing, for he was afraid; for she was above him both in wealth and birth: but he departed to dinner, and she went into her chamber. And he said to the servants: Call her to dinner. But she would not come.

96 And when he heard that she would not come out of her chamber, he went in and said unto her: Wherefore wilt thou not dine with me and perchance not sleep with me as the wont is? yea, concerning this I have the greater suspicion, for I have heard that that sorcerer and deceiver teacheth that a man should not live with his wife, and that which nature requireth and the godhead hath ordained he overthroweth. When Charisius said these things, Mygdonia kept silence. He saith to her again: My lady and consort Mygdonia, be not led astray by deceitful and vain words, nor by the works of sorcery which I have heard that this man performeth in the name of Father, Son, and Holy

Ghost; for it was never yet heard in the world that any raised the dead, and, as I hear, it is reported of this man that he raiseth dead men. And for that he neither eateth nor drinketh, think not that for righteousness' sake he neither eateth nor drinketh, but this he doth because he possesseth nought; for what should he do which hath not even his daily bread? And he hath one garment because he is poor; and as for his not receiving aught of any (he doth so, to be sure, because he knoweth in himself that he doth not verily heal any man, *Syr.*).

97 And when Charisius so said, Mygdonia was silent as any stone; but she prayed, *asking* when it should be day, that she might go to the apostle of Christ. And he withdrew from her and went to dinner heavy in mind, for he thought to sleep with her according to the wont. And when he was gone out, she bowed her knees and prayed, saying: Lord God and Master, merciful Father, Saviour Christ, do thou give me strength to overcome the shamelessness of Charisius, and grant me to keep the holiness wherein thou delightest, that I also may by it find eternal life. And when she had so prayed she laid herself on her bed and veiled herself.

98 But Charisius having dined came upon her, and she cried out, saying: Thou hast no more any room by me: for my Lord Jesus is greater than thou, who is with me and resteth in me. And he laughed and said: Well dost thou mock, saying this of that sorcerer, and well dost thou deride him, who saith : Ye have no life with God unless ye purify yourselves. And when he had so said he essayed to sleep with her, but she endured it not and cried out bitterly and said: I call upon thee, Lord Jesu, forsake me not! for with thee have I made my refuge; for when I learned that thou art he that seekest out them that are veiled in ignorance, and savest them that are held in error—— And now I entreat thee whose report I have heard and believed, come thou to my help, and save me from the shamelessness of Charisius, that his foulness may not get the upper hand of me. And she smote her hands together (tied his hands, *Syr.*) and fled from him naked, and as she went forth she pulled down the curtain of the bed-chamber and wrapped it about her ; and went to her nurse, and slept there with her.

99 But Charisius was in heaviness all night, and smote his face with his hands, and he was minded to go that very hour and tell the king concerning the violence that was done him, but he considered with himself, saying: If the great heaviness which is upon me compelleth me to go now unto the king, who will bring me in to him? for I know that my abuse hath overthrown me from my high looks and my vainglory and majesty, and hath cast me down into this vileness and separated my sister Mygdonia from me. Yea, if the king himself stood before the doors at this hour, I could not have gone out and answered

him. But I will wait until dawn; and I know that whatsoever I ask of the king, he granteth it me: and I will tell him of the madness of this stranger, how that it tyrannously casteth down the great and illustrious into the depth. For it is not this that grieveth me, that I am deprived of her companying, but for her am I grieved, because her greatness of soul is humbled: being an honourable lady in whom none of her house ever found fault (condemned), she hath fled away naked, running out of her own bedchamber; and I know not whither she is gone; and it may be that she is gone mad by the means of that sorcerer, and in her madness hath gone forth into the market-place to seek him; for there is nothing that appeareth unto her lovable except him and the things that are spoken by him.

100 And so saying he began to lament and say: Woe to me, O my consort, and to thee besides! for I am too quickly bereaved of thee. Woe is me, my most dear one, for thou excellest all my race : neither son nor daughter have I had of thee that I might find rest in them; neither hast thou yet dwelt with me a full year, and an evil eye hath caught thee from me. Would that the violence of death had taken thee, and I should *yet* have reckoned myself among kings and nobles : but that I should suffer this at the hands of a stranger, and belike he is a slave that hath run away, to mine ill fortune and *the sorrow* of mine unhappy soul ! Let there be no impediment for me until I destroy him and avenge this night; and may I not be well-pleasing before Misdaeus the king if he avenge me not with the head of this stranger; (and I will also tell him) of Siphor the captain who hath been the occasion *of this*. For by his means did *the stranger* appear here, and lodgeth at his house: and many there be that go in and come out, whom he teacheth a new doctrine ; saying that none can live if he quit not all his substance and become a renouncer like himself : and he striveth to make many partakers with him.

101 And as Charisius thought on these things, the day dawned; and after the night (?) he put on a mean habit, and shod himself, and went downcast and in heaviness to salute the king. And when the king saw him he said: Wherefore art thou sorrowful, and comest in such garb? and I see that thy countenance is changed. And Charisius said unto the king: I have a new thing to tell thee and a new desolation which Siphor hath brought into India, even a certain Hebrew, a sorcerer, whom he hath sitting in his house and who departeth not from him: and many are there that go in to him: whom also he teacheth of a new God, and layeth on them new laws such as never yet were heard, saying: It is impossible for you to enter into that eternal life which I proclaim unto you, unless ye rid you of your wives, and likewise the wives of their husbands. And it chanced that mine unlucky wife also went to him and became a hearer of his words, and she

believed them, and in the night she forsook me and ran unto the stranger. But send thou for both Siphor and that sorcerer that is hid with (in) him, and visit it (?) on their head, lest all that are of our nation perish.

102 And when Misdaeus his friend heard this he saith to him: Be not grieved nor heavy, for I will send for him and avenge thee, and thou shalt have thy wife again, and the others that cannot I will avenge. And the king went forth and sat on the judgement seat, and when he was set he commanded Siphor the captain to be called. They went therefore unto his house and found him sitting on the right hand of the apostle and Mygdonia at his feet, hearkening to him with all the multitude. And they that were sent from the king said unto Siphor: Sittest thou here listening to vain words, and Misdaeus the king in his wrath thinketh to destroy thee because of this sorcerer and deceiver whom thou hast brought into thine house? And Siphor hearing it was cast down, not because of the king's threat against him, but for the apostle, because the king was disposed contrary to him. And he said to the apostle: I am grieved concerning thee: for I told thee at the first that that woman is the wife of Charisius the king's friend and kinsman, and he will not suffer her to perform that she hath promised, and all that he asketh of the king he granteth him. But the apostle said unto Siphor: Fear nothing, but believe in Jesus that pleadeth for us all, for unto his refuge are we gathered together. And Siphor, hearing that, put his garment about him and went unto Misdaeus the king,

103 And the apostle inquired of Mygdonia : What was the cause that thy husband was wroth with thee and devised this against us? And she said: Because I gave not myself up unto his corruption (destruction): for he desired last night to subdue me and subject me unto that passion which he serveth: and he to whom I have committed my soul delivered me out of his hands; and I fled away from him naked, and slept with my nurse: but that which befell him I know not, wherefore he hath contrived this. The apostle saith: These things will not hurt us; but believe thou on Jesus, and he shall overthrow the wrath of Charisius and his madness and his impulse; and he shall be a companion unto thee in the fearful way, and he shall guide thee into his kingdom, and shall bring thee unto eternal life, giving thee that confidence which passeth not away nor changeth.

104 Now Siphor stood before the king, and he inquired of him: Who is that sorcerer and whence, and what teacheth he, whom thou hast lurking in thine house? And Siphor answered the king: Thou art not ignorant, O king, what trouble and grief I, with my friends, had concerning my wife, whom thou knowest and many others remember, and concerning my daughter, whom I value more than all my possessions, what a time and trial I suffered; for I became a laughing-stock and

a curse in all our country. And I heard the report of this man, and went to him and entreated him, and took him and brought him hither. And as I came by the way I saw wonderful and amazing things : and here also many did hear the wild ass, and concerning that devil whom he drove out, and healed my wife and daughter, and now are they whole; and he asked no reward but requireth faith and holiness, that men should become partakers with him in that which he doeth: and this he teacheth, to worship and fear one God, the ruler of all things, and Jesus Christ his Son, that they may have eternal life. And that which he eateth is bread and salt, and his drink is water from evening unto evening, and he maketh many prayers; and whatsoever he asketh of his God, he giveth him. And he teacheth that this God is holy and mighty, and that Christ is living and maketh alive, wherefore also he chargeth them that are there present to come unto him in holiness and purity and love and faith.

105 And when Misdaeus the king heard these things of Siphor, he sent many soldiers unto the house of Siphor the captain, to bring Thomas the apostle and all that were found there. And they that were sent entered in and found him teaching much people; and Mygdonia sat at his feet. And when they beheld the great multitude that were about him, they feared, and departed to their king and said: We durst not say aught unto him, for there was a great multitude about him, and Mygdonia sitting at his feet was listening to the things that were spoken by him. And when Misdaeus the king and Charisius heard these things, Charisius leaped out from before the king and drew much people with him and said: I will bring him, O king, and Mygdonia whose understanding he hath taken away. And he came to the house of Siphor the captain, greatly disturbed, and found him (Thomas) teaching: but Mygdonia he found not, for she had withdrawn herself unto her house, having learnt that it had been told her husband that she was there.

106 And Charisius said unto the apostle: Up, thou wicked one and destroyer and enemy of mine house: for me thy sorcery harmeth not, for I will visit thy sorcery on thine head. And when he so said, the apostle looked upon him and said unto him: Thy threatenings shall return upon thee, for me thou wilt not harm any whit: for greater than thee and thy king and all your army is the Lord Jesus Christ in whom I have my trust. And Charisius took a kerchief (turban, *Syr.*) of one of his slaves and cast it about the neck of the apostle, saying: Hale him and bring him away; let me see if his God is able to deliver him out of my hands. And they haled him and led him away to Misdaeus the king. And the apostle stood before the king, and the king said to him: Tell me who thou art and by what power thou doest these things. But the apostle kept silence. And the king commanded his officers (subjects) that he should be scourged

with an hundred and twenty-eight (hundred and fifty, *Syr.*)
blows, and bound, and be cast into the prison; and they bound
him and led him away.   And the king and Charisius considered
how they should put him to death, *for* the multitude worshipped
him as God. And they had it in mind to say: The stranger hath
reviled the king and is a deceiver.

107 But the apostle went unto the prison rejoicing and
exulting, and said: I praise thee, Jesu, for that thou hast not
only made me worthy of faith in thee, but also to endure much
for thy sake.   I give thee thanks therefore, Lord, that thou hast
taken thought for me and given me patience: I thank thee,
Lord, that for thy sake I am called a sorcerer and a wizard.
Receive thou me therefore with the blessing (*Syr.* let me receive of
the blessing) of the poor, and of the rest of the weary, and of the
blessings of them whom men hate and persecute and revile, and
speak evil words of them. For lo, for thy sake I am hated: lo,
for thy sake I am cut off from the many, and for thy sake they
call me such an one as I am not.

108 And as he prayed, all the prisoners looked on him, and
besought him to pray for them: and when he had prayed and
was set down, he began to utter a psalm in this wise:

[Here follows the Hymn of the Soul: a most remarkable
composition, originally Syriac, and certainly older than the
Acts, with which it has no real connexion. We have it in Greek
in one manuscript, the Vallicellian, and in a paraphrase by Nicetas
of Thessalonica, found and edited by Bonnet.]

1 When I was an infant child
   in the palace of my Father,
2 and resting in the wealth and luxury of my nurturers,
3 out of the East, our native country, my parents provisioned
   me and sent me.
4 And of the wealth of those their treasures they put together
   a load,
5 both great and light, that I might carry it alone.
6 Gold is the load, of them that are above (*or* of the land of the
   Ellaeans *or* Gilaeans),
   and silver of the great treasures (*or* of Gazzak the great), ,
7 and stones, chalcedonies from the Indians,
   and pearls from ⟨the land of⟩ the Kosani (Kushan).
8 And they armed me with adamant ⟨which breaketh iron⟩,
9 and they took off from me (*Gr.* put on me) the garment set
   with gems, spangled with gold, which they had made for
   me because they loved me,
10 and the robe that was yellow in hue, *made* for my stature.
11 And they made a covenant with me, and inscribed it on mine
   understanding, that I should ⟨not⟩ forget it, and said:
12 If thou go down into Egypt, and bring back thence the one pearl

13 which is there ⟨in the midst of the sea⟩ girt about by the
    devouring serpent,
14 thou shalt put on ⟨again⟩ the garment set with gems, and
    that robe whereupon it resteth (*or* which is thereon),
15 and become with thy brother that is next unto us (*Gr.* of the
    well-remembered) an heir (*Gr.* herald) in our kingdom.
109. 16 And I came out of the East by a road difficult and
    fearful, with two guides,
17 and I was untried in travelling by it.
18 And I passed by the borders of the Mosani (Maishan) where
    is the resort of the merchants of the East,
19 and reached the land of the Babylonians ⟨and came unto the
    walls of Sarbug⟩.
20 But when I entered into Egypt, the guides left me which
    had journeyed with me.
21 And I set forth by the quickest way to the serpent, and by
    his hole I abode,
22 watching for him to slumber and sleep, that I might take
    my pearl from him.
23 And forasmuch as I was alone I made mine aspect strange,
    and appeared as an alien to my people.
24 And there I saw my kinsman from the East, the free-born
25 a lad of grace and beauty, a son of princes (*or* an anointed
    one).
26 He came unto me and dwelt with me,
27 and I had him for a companion, and made him my friend and
    partaker in my journey (*or* merchandise).
28 And I charged him to beware of the Egyptians, and of par-
    taking of those unclean things (*or* consorting with those
    unclean men).
29 And I put on their raiment, lest I should seem strange, as one
    that had come from without
30 to recover the pearl; and lest the Egyptians should awake
    the serpent against me.
31 But, I know not by what occasion, they learned that I was
    not of their country.
32 And with guile they mingled for me a deceit, and I tasted of
    their food.
33 And I knew no *more* that I was a king's son, and I became
    a servant unto their king.
34 And I forgat also the pearl for which my fathers had sent me,
35 and by means of the heaviness of their food I fell into a deep
    sleep.
110. 36 But when this befell me, my fathers also were ware of
    it, and grieved for me,
37 and a proclamation was published in our kingdom, that all
    should meet at our doors.
38 And then the kings of Parthia and they that bare office and
    the great ones of the East

39 made a resolve concerning me, that I should not be left in Egypt,

40 and the princes wrote unto me signifying thus (and every noble signed his name to it, *Syr.*) :

41 From the (thy) Father the King of kings, and thy mother that ruleth the East,

42 and thy brother that is second unto us; unto our son that is in Egypt, peace.

43 Rise up and awake out of sleep, and hearken unto the words of the letter,

44 and remember that thou art a son of kings; lo, thou hast come under the yoke of bondage.

45 Remember the pearl for the which thou wast sent into Egypt (*Gr.* puts this after 46).

46 Remember thy garment spangled with gold,

47 ⟨and the glorious mantle which thou shouldest wear and wherewith thou shouldest deck thyself.⟩ Thy name is named *in* the book of life,

48 and with thy brother †whom thou hast received† ⟨thou shalt be⟩ in our kingdom.

111. 49 ⟨And my letter was a letter⟩ and the King [as ambassador] sealed it ⟨with his right hand⟩

50 because of the evil ones, even the children of the Babylonians and the tyrannous demons of Labyrinthus (Sarbug, *Syr.*).

51 ⟨It flew like the eagle, the king of all fowls.

52 It flew and lighted down by me, and became all speech.⟩

53 And I at the voice of it and the feeling of it started up out of sleep,

54 and I took it up and kissed it ⟨and brake the seal⟩ and read it.

55 And it was written concerning that which was recorded in mine heart.

56 And I remembered forthwith that I was a son of kings, and my freedom yearned (sought) after its kind.

57 I remembered also the pearl for the which I was sent down into Egypt,

58 and I began (*or* came) with charms against the terrible serpent,

59 and I overcame him (*or* put him to sleep) by naming the name of my Father upon him,

60 ⟨and the name of our second in rank, and of my mother the queen of the East⟩.

61 And I caught away the pearl and turned back to bear it unto my fathers.

62 And I stripped off the filthy garment and left it in their land,

63 and directed my way forthwith to the light of my fatherland in the East.

64 And on the way I found my letter that had awakened me,

65 and it, like as it had taken a voice and raised me when I slept, so also guided me with the light that came from it.

66 For at times the royal garment of silk ⟨shone⟩ before mine eyes,
67 ⟨and with its voice and its guidance it also encouraged me to speed,⟩
68 and with love leading me and drawing me onward,
69 I passed by Labyrinthus (Sarbug), and I left Babylon upon my left hand,
70 and I came unto Meson (Mesēnē; Maishan) the great, 71 that lieth on the shore of the sea,
72 ⟨and my bright robe which I had taken off, and the mantle wherewith I had been clad,
73 from the heights of Warkan (Hyrcania ?) had my parents sent thither
74 by the hand of their treasurers, unto whom they committed it because of their faithfulness⟩.
112. 75 But I remembered not the brightness of it; for I was yet a child and very young when I had left it in the palace of my Father,
76 but suddenly, [when] I saw the garment made like unto me as it had been in a mirror.
77 And I beheld upon it all myself (or saw it wholly in myself), and I knew and saw myself through it,
78 that we were divided asunder, being of one; and again were one in one shape.
79 Yea, the treasurers also which brought me the garment
80 I beheld, that they were two, yet one shape was upon both, one royal sign was set upon both of them.
81 The money and the wealth had they in their hands, and paid me the due price,
82 and the lovely garment, which was variegated with bright colours,
83 with gold and precious stones and pearls of comely hue
84 they were fastened above (or in the height),
85 ⟨and with stones of adamant were all its seams fastened⟩.
86 And the likeness of the King of kings was all in all of it.
87 Sapphire stones were fitly set in it above (or, like the sapphire stone also were its manifold hues).
113. 88 And again I saw that throughout it motions of knowledge were being sent forth,
89 and it was ready to utter speech.
90 And I heard it speak ⟨with them that had brought it⟩:
91 I am of him that is more valiant than all men, for whose sake I was reared up with the Father himself.
92 And I also perceived his stature (so Gr.; Syr. I perceived in myself that my stature grew in accordance with his working).
93 †And all its royal motions rested upon me as it grew toward the impulse of it† (And with its kingly motions it was spreading itself toward me).

94 And it hastened, reaching out from the hand of ⟨him that brought it⟩ unto him that would receive it,

95 and me also did yearning arouse to start forth and meet it and receive it.

96 And I stretched forth and received it, and adorned myself with the beauty of the colours thereof (mostly *Syr.*; *Gr.* corrupt),

97 and in my royal robe excelling in beauty I arrayed myself wholly.

98 And when I had put it on, I was lifted up unto the place of peace (salutation) and homage,

99 and I bowed my head and worshipped the brightness of the Father which had sent it unto me,

100 for I had performed his commandments, and he likewise that which he had promised,

101 and at the doors of his palace which was from the beginning I mingled among ⟨his nobles⟩,

102 and he rejoiced over me and received me with him into his palace,

103 and all his servants do praise him with sweet voices.

104 And he promised me that with him I shall be sent unto the gates of the king,

105 that with my gifts and my pearl we may appear together before the king.

[Immediately on this, in the Syriac, follows a Song of Praise of Thomas the apostle consisting of forty-two ascriptions of praise and four final clauses (Wright, pp. 245–51). It has no bearing on the Acts, and is not in itself so remarkable as to need to be inserted here.]

114 And Charisius went home glad, thinking that his wife would be with him, and that she had become such as she was before, even before she heard the divine word and believed on Jesus. And he went, and found her with her hair dishevelled and her clothes rent, and when he saw it he said unto her: My lady Mygdonia, why doth this cruel disease keep hold on thee? and wherefore hast thou done this? I am thine husband from thy virginity, and both the gods and the law grant me to have rule over thee; what is this great madness of thine, that thou art become a derision in all our nation? but put thou away the care that cometh of that sorcerer; and I will remove his face from among us, that thou mayest see him no more.

115 But Mygdonia when she heard that gave herself up unto grief, groaning and lamenting: and Charisius said again: Have I then so much wronged the gods that they have afflicted me with such a disease? what is my great offence that they have cast me into such humiliation? I beseech thee, Mygdonia, strangle my soul no more with the pitiful sight of thee and thy

mean appearance, and afflict not mine heart with care for thee. I am Charisius thine husband, whom all the nation honoureth and feareth. What must I do? I know not whither to turn. What am I to think? shall I keep silence and endure? yet who can be patient when men take his treasure? and who can endure *to lose* thy sweet ways? and what is there for me? (*Syr.* thy beauties which are ever before me) the fragrance of thee is in my nostrils, and thy bright face is fixed in mine eyes. They are taking away my soul, and the fair body which I rejoiced to see they are destroying, and that sharpest of eyes they are blinding, and cutting off my right hand: my joy is turning to grief and my life to death, and the light of it is being dyed (?) with darkness. Let no man of you my kindred henceforth look on me—from you no help hath come to me, nor will I hereafter worship the gods of the east that have enwrapped me in such calamities, nor pray to them any more nor sacrifice to them, for I am bereaved of my spouse. And what else should I ask of them? for all my glory is taken away, yet am I a prince and next unto the king in power; but Mygdonia hath set me at nought, and taken away all these things. (Would that some one would blind one of my eyes, and that thine eyes would look upon me as they were wont, *Syr.*, which has more clauses, to the same effect.)

116 And while Charisius spake thus with tears, Mygdonia sat silent and looking upon the ground; and again he came unto her and said: My lady Mygdonia, most desired of me, remember that out of all the women that are in India I chose and took thee as the most beautiful, though I might have joined to myself in marriage many more beautiful: but yet I lie, Mygdonia, for by the gods it would not have been possible to find another like thee in the land of India; but woe is me alway, for thou wilt not even answer me a word: but if thou wilt, revile me, so that I may only be vouchsafed a word from thee. Look at me, for I am more comely than that sorcerer: but thou art my wealth and honour: and all men know that there is none like me: and thou art my race and kindred—and lo, he taketh thee away from me.

117 And when Charisius had so said, Mygdonia saith unto him: He whom I love is better than thee and thy substance: for thy substance is of earth and returneth unto the earth; but he whom I love is of heaven and will take me with him unto heaven. Thy wealth shall pass away, and thy beauty shall vanish, and thy robes, and thy many works: and thou shalt be alone, naked, with thy transgressions. Call not to my remembrance thy deeds (unto me), for I pray the Lord that I may forget thee, so as to remember no more those former pleasures and the custom of the body; which shall pass away as a shadow, but Jesus only endureth for ever, and the souls which hope in him. Jesus himself shall quit me of the shameful deeds which I did with thee. And when Charisius heard this, he turned him

to sleep, vexed (dissolved) in soul, saying to her: Consider it by thyself all this night: and if thou wilt be with me such as thou wast before, and not see that sorcerer, I will do all according to thy mind, and if thou wilt remove thine affection from him, I will take him out of the prison and let him go and remove into another country, and I will not vex thee, for I know that thou makest much of the stranger. And not with thee first did this matter come about, for many other women also hath he deceived with thee; and they have awaked sober and returned to themselves: do not thou then make nought of my words and cause me to be a reproach among the Indians.

118 And Charisius having thus spoken went to sleep: but she took ten denarii (20 zūzē, *Syr.*), and went secretly to give them to the gaolers that she might enter in to the apostle. But on the way Judas Thomas came and met her, and she saw him and was afraid, for she thought that he was one of the rulers: for a great light went before him. And she said to herself as she fled: I have lost thee, O my unhappy soul! for thou wilt not again see Judas the apostle of ⟨Jesus⟩ the living ⟨God⟩, and not yet hast thou received the holy seal. And she fled and ran into a narrow place, and there hid herself, saying: I would rather choose to be killed (taken) by the poorer, whom it is possible to persuade, than to fall into the hand of this mighty ruler, who will despise gifts.

The Tenth Act: wherein Mygdonia receiveth baptism.

119 And while Mygdonia thought thus with herself, Judas came and stood over her, and she saw him and was afraid, and fell down and became lifeless with terror. But he stood by her and took her by the hand and said unto her: Fear not, Mygdonia: Jesus will not leave thee, neither will the Lord unto whom thou hast committed thy soul overlook thee. His compassionate rest will not forsake thee: he that is kind will not forsake thee, for his kindness' sake, nor he that is good for his goodness' sake. Rise up then from the earth, thou that art become wholly above it: look on the light, for the Lord leaveth not them that love him to walk in darkness: behold him that travelleth with his servants, that he is unto them a defender in perils. And Mygdonia arose and looked on him and said: Whither wentest thou, my lord? and who is he that brought thee out of prison to behold the sun? Judas Thomas saith unto her: My Lord Jesus is mightier than all powers and all kings and rulers.

120 And Mygdonia said: Give me the seal of Jesus Christ and I shall (let me) receive the gift at thy hands before thou departest out of life. And she took him with her and entered into the court and awaked her nurse, saying unto her: Narcia (*Gr.* Marcia), my mother and nurse, all thy service and refreshment thou hast done for me from my childhood until my present age are vain,

and for them I owe thee thanks which are temporal; do for me
now also a favour, that thou mayest for ever receive a recompense
from him that giveth great gifts. And Narcia in answer saith:
What wilt thou, my daughter Mygdonia, and what is to be done
for thy pleasure? for the honours which thou didst promise me
before, the stranger hath not suffered thee to accomplish, and
thou hast made me a reproach among all the nation. And now
what is this new thing that thou commandest me? And Mygdonia
saith: Become thou partaker with me in eternal life, that I may
receive of thee perfect nurture: take bread and bring it me, and
wine mingled with water, and spare my freedom (take pity on
me a free-born woman, *Syr.*). And the nurse said: I will bring
thee many loaves, and for water flagons of wine, and fulfil
thy desire. But she saith to the nurse: Flagons I desire not, nor
the many loaves: but this only, bring wine mingled with water,
and one loaf, and oil ⟨even if it be in a lamp, *Syr.*⟩.

121 And when Narcia had brought these things, Mygdonia
stood before the apostle with her head bare; and he took the oil
and poured it on her head, saying: Thou holy oil given unto us
for sanctification, secret mystery whereby the cross was shown
unto us, thou art the straightener of the crooked limbs, thou art
the humbler (softener) of hard things (works), thou art it that
showeth the hidden treasures, thou art the sprout of goodness;
let thy power come, let it be established upon thy servant
Mygdonia; and heal thou her by this freedom. And when the
oil was poured upon her he bade her nurse unclothe her and gird
a linen cloth about her; and there was there a fountain of water
upon which the apostle went up, and baptized Mygdonia in the
name of the Father and the Son and the Holy Ghost. And when
she was baptized and clad, he brake bread and took a cup of
water and made her a partaker in the body of Christ and the cup
of the Son of God, and said: Thou hast received thy seal, get for
thyself eternal life. And immediately there was heard from above
a voice saying: Yea, amen. And when Narcia heard that voice,
she was amazed, and besought the apostle that she also might
receive the seal; and the apostle gave it her and said: Let the
care of the Lord be about thee as about the rest.

122 And having done these things the apostle returned unto
the prison, and found the doors open and the guards still sleeping.
And Thomas said: Who is like thee, O God? who withholdest
not thy loving affection and care from any who is like thee, the
merciful, who hast delivered thy creatures out of evil. Life that
hath subdued death, rest that hath ended toil. Glory be to the
only-begotten of the Father. Glory to the compassionate that
was sent forth of his heart. And when he had said thus, the
guards waked and beheld all the doors open, and the prisoners
⟨+ asleep, *Syr.*⟩, and said in themselves: Did not we fasten the
doors? and how are they now open, and the prisoners within?

123 But at the dawn Charisius went unto Mygdonia ⟨and her nurse, *Syr.*⟩, and found them praying and saying: O new God that by the stranger hast come hither unto us, hidden God of the dwellers in India (*Syr.* who art hidden from); God that hast shown thy glory by thine apostle Thomas, God whose report we have heard and believed on thee; God, unto whom we are come to be saved; God, who for love of man and for pity didst come down unto our littleness; God who didst seek us out when we knew him (thee) not; God that dwellest in the heights and from whom the depths are not hid: turn thou away from us the madness of Charisius. And Charisius hearing that said to Mygdonia: Rightly callest thou me evil and mad and foul! for if I had not borne with thy disobedience, and given thee liberty, thou wouldest not have called *on God* against me and made mention of my name before God. But believe me, Mygdonia, that in that sorcerer there is no profit, and what he promiseth to perform he cannot: but I *will* perform before thy sight all that I promise, that thou mayest believe, and bear with my words, and be to me as thou wast beforetime.

124 And he came near and besought her again, saying: If thou wilt be persuaded of me, I shall henceforth have no grief; remember that day when thou didst meet me first; tell the truth: was I more beautiful unto thee at that time, or Jesus at this? And Mygdonia said: That time required its own, and this time also; that was the time of the beginning, but this of the end; that was the time of temporal life, this of eternal; that, of pleasure that passeth away, but this of pleasure that abideth for ever; that, of day and night, this of day without night. Thou sawest that marriage; that was passing, and here, and single, but this marriage continueth for ever; that was a partnership of corruption, but this of eternal life; those groomsmen (and maids) were men and women of time, but these abide unto the end. †That marriage upon earth† setteth up †dropping dew of the love of men† (*Syr.* That union was founded upon the earth where there is an unceasing press: this is founded upon the bridge of fire upon which is sprinkled grace: *both corrupt*); that bride-chamber is taken down again, but this remaineth always; that bed was strown with coverlets (that grow old), but this with love and faith. Thou art a bridegroom that passest away and art dissolved (changed), but Jesus is a true bridegroom, enduring for ever immortal; that dowry was of money and robes that grow old, but this is of living words which never pass away.

125 And when Charisius heard these things he went unto the king and told him all: and the king commanded Judas to be brought, that he might judge him and destroy him. But Charisius said: Have patience a little, O king, and first persuade the man, making him afraid, that he may persuade Mygdonia to be unto me as formerly. And Misdaeus sent and fetched the apostle of

Christ, and all the prisoners were grieved because the apostle departed from them, for they yearned after him, saying: Even the comfort which we had have they taken away from us.

126 And Misdaeus said unto Judas: Wherefore teachest thou this new doctrine, which both gods and men hate, and which hath nought of profit? And Judas said: What evil do I teach? And Misdaeus said: Thou teachest, saying that men ⟨cannot live well except they live chastely⟩ with the God whom thou preachest. Judas saith: Thou sayest true, O king: thus do I teach. For tell me, art thou not wroth with thy soldiers if they wait on thee in filthy garments? if then thou, being a king of earth and returning unto earth, requirest thy subjects to be reverend in their doings, are ye wroth and said ye that I teach ill when I say that they who serve my king must be reverend and pure and free from all grief and care, of children and unprofitable riches and vain trouble? For indeed thou wouldest have thy subjects follow thy conversation and thy manners, and thou punishest them if they despise thy commandments: how much more must they that believe on him serve my God with much reverence and cleanness and security, and be quit of all pleasures of the body, adultery and prodigality and theft and drunkenness and belly-service and foul deeds?

127 And Misdaeus hearing these things said: Lo, I let thee go: go then and persuade Mygdonia, the wife of Charisius, not to desire to depart from him. Judas saith unto him: Delay not if thou hast aught to do: for her, if she hath rightly received what she hath learned, neither iron nor fire nor aught else stronger than these will avail to hurt or to root out him that is held in her soul. Misdaeus saith unto Judas: Some poisons do dissolve other poisons, and a theriac cureth the bites of the viper; and thou if thou wilt canst give a solvent of those diseases, and make peace and concord betwixt this couple: for by so doing thou wilt spare thyself, for not yet art thou sated with life; and know thou that if thou do not persuade her, I will catch thee away out of this life which is desirable unto all men. And Judas said: This life hath been given as a loan, and this time is one that changeth; but that life whereof I teach is incorruptible; and beauty and youth that are seen shall in a little cease to be. The king saith to him: I have counselled thee for the best, but thou knowest thine own affairs.

128 And as the apostle went forth from before the king, Charisius came to him and entreated him and said: I beseech thee, O man: I have not sinned against thee or any other at any time, nor against the gods; wherefore hast thou stirred up this great calamity against me? and for what cause hast thou brought such disturbance upon mine house? and what profit hast thou of it? but if thou thinkest to gain somewhat, tell me the gain, what it is, and I will procure it for thee without labour. To what

end dost thou make me mad, and cast thyself into destruction? for if thou persuade her not, I will both dispatch thee and finally take myself out of life. But if, as thou sayest, after our departing hence there is there life and death, and also condemnation and victory and a place of judgement, then will I also go in thither to be judged with thee: and if that God whom thou preachest is just and awardeth punishment justly, I know that I shall gain my cause against thee; for thou hast injured me, having suffered no wrong at my hands: for indeed even here I am able to avenge myself on thee and bring upon thee all that thou hast done unto me. Therefore be thou persuaded, and come home with me and persuade Mygdonia to be with me as she was at first, before she beheld thee. And Judas saith to him: Believe me, my child, that if men loved God as much as they love one another, they would ask of him all things and receive them, and none would do them violence (there would be nothing which would not obey them, *Syr.*).

129 And as Thomas said this, they came unto the house of Charisius and found Mygdonia sitting and Narcia standing by her, and her hand supporting her cheek; and she was saying: Let the remainder of the days of my life, O mother, be cut off from me, and all the hours become as one hour, and let me depart out of life that I may go the sooner and behold that beautiful one, whose report I have heard, even that living one and giver of life unto them that believe on him, where is not day and night, nor light and darkness, nor good and evil, nor poor and rich, nor male and female, nor free and bond, nor proud that subjecteth the humble. And as she spake the apostle stood by her, and forthwith she rose up and did him reverence. Then Charisius said unto him: Seest thou how she feareth and honoureth thee, and all that thou shalt bid her she will do willingly?

130 And as he so spake, Judas saith unto Mygdonia: My daughter Mygdonia, obey that which *thy* brother Charisius saith. And Mygdonia saith: If thou wast not able ⟨to name⟩ the deed in word, wilt thou compel me to endure the act? for I have heard of thee that this life is of no profit, and this relief is for a time, and these possessions are transitory. And again thou saidst that whoso renounceth this life shall receive the life eternal, and whoso hateth the light of day and night shall behold a light that is not overtaken, that whoso despiseth this money shall find other and eternal money. But now ⟨thou sayest these things⟩ because thou art in fear. Who that hath done somewhat and is praised for the work changeth it? ⟨who buildeth a tower and⟩ straightway overthroweth it from the foundation? who diggeth a spring of water in a thirsty land and straightway filleth it in? who findeth a treasure and useth it not? And Charisius heard it and said: I will not imitate you, neither will I hasten to destroy you; nor though I may so do, will I put bonds about thee (but

thee I will bind, *Syr.*); and I will not suffer thee to speak with
this sorcerer; and if thou obey me, *well, but if not,* I know what
I must do.

131 And Judas went out of Charisius' house and departed
unto the house of Siphor and lodged there with him. And Siphor
said: I will prepare for Judas a hall (triclinium) wherein he may
teach (*Syr.* Siphor said to Judas: Prepare thyself an apartment,
&c.). And he did so; and Siphor said: I and my wife and
daughter will dwell henceforth in holiness, and in chastity, and
in one affection. I beseech thee that we may receive of thee
the seal, and become worshippers of the true God and numbered
among his sheep and lambs. And Judas said: I am afraid to
speak that which I think: yet I know somewhat, and what I know
it is not possible for me to utter.

132 And he began to say concerning baptism: This baptism
is remission of sins (the Greek MSS. U and P have divergent
texts, both obscure): this bringeth forth again light that is shed
about *us*: this bringeth to new birth the new man (this is the
restorer of understandings, *Syr.*): this mingleth the spirit (with
the body), raiseth up in threefoldwise a new man and ⟨maketh
him⟩ partaker of the remission of sins. Glory be to thee, hidden
one, that art communicated in baptism. Glory to thee the unseen
power that is in baptism. Glory to thee, renewal, whereby are
renewed they that are baptized and with affection take hold
upon thee.

And having thus said, he poured oil over their heads and said:
Glory be to thee the love of compassion (bowels). Glory to thee,
name of Christ. Glory to thee, power established in Christ.
And he commanded a vessel to be brought, and baptized them
in the name of the Father and the Son and the Holy Ghost.

133 And when they were baptized and clad, he set bread on
the table and blessed it, and said: Bread of life, the which who
eat abide incorruptible: Bread that filleth the hungry souls with
the blessing thereof: thou art he that vouchsafest to receive
a gift, that thou mayest become unto us remission of sins, and
that they who eat thee may become immortal: we invoke upon
thee the name of the mother, of the unspeakable mystery of the
hidden powers and authorities (? we name the name of the
unspeakable mystery, that is hidden from all, &c.): we invoke
upon thee the name of [thy ?] Jesus. And he said: Let the powers
of blessing come, and be established in this bread, that all the
souls which partake of it may be washed from their sins. And he
brake and gave unto Siphor and his wife and daughter.

The Eleventh Act: concerning the wife of Misdaeus.

134 Now Misdaeus the king, when he had let Judas go, dined
and went home, and told his wife what had befallen Charisius
their kinsman, saying: See what hath come to pass to that

unhappy man; and thou thyself knowest, my sister Tertia, that
a man hath nought better than his own wife on whom he resteth;
but it chanced that his wife went unto that sorcerer of whom
thou hast heard that he is come to the land of the Indians, and
fell into his charms and is parted from her own husband; and
he knoweth not what he should do. And when I would have
destroyed the malefactor, he would not have it. But do thou go
and counsel her to incline unto her husband, and forsake the
vain words of the sorcerer.

135 And as soon as she arose Tertia went to the house of
Charisius her husband's ⟨kinsman⟩, and found Mygdonia lying
upon the earth in humiliation; and ashes and sackcloth were
spread under her, and she was praying that the Lord would forgive
her her former sins and she might soon depart out of life. And
Tertia said unto her: Mygdonia, my dear sister and companion,
what is this †hand† (Syr. this folly)? what is the disease that hath
overtaken thee? and why doest thou the deeds of madmen? Know
thyself and come back unto thine own way, come near unto thy
many kinsfolk, and spare thy true husband Charisius, and do
not things unbefitting a free-woman. Mygdonia saith unto her:
O Tertia, thou hast not yet heard the preacher of life: not yet
hath he touched thine ears, not yet hast thou tasted the medicine
of life nor art freed from corruptible mourning. Thou standest
in the life of time, and the everlasting life and salvation thou
knowest not, and perceivest not the incorruptible fellowship.
Thou standest clad in robes that grow old and desirest not those
that are eternal; and art proud of this beauty which vanisheth,
and hast no thought of the ugliness of thy soul; and art rich in
a multitude of servants, (and hast not freed thine own soul from
servitude, Syr.) and pridest thyself in the glory that cometh
of many, but redeemest not thyself from the condemnation of
death.

136 And when Tertia heard this of Mygdonia she said: I pray
thee, sister, bring me unto that stranger that teacheth these
great things, that I also may go and hear him, and be taught
to worship the God whom he preacheth, and become partaker of
his prayers, and a sharer in all that thou hast told me of. And
Mygdonia saith to her: He is in the house of Siphor the captain;
for he is become the occasion of life unto all them that are being
saved in India. And hearing that, Tertia went quickly to Siphor's
house, that she might see the new apostle that was come thither.
And when she entered in, Judas said unto her: What art thou
come to see? a man that is a stranger and poor and contemptible
and needy, having neither riches nor substance; yet one thing
I possess which neither kings nor rulers can take away, that
neither perisheth nor ceaseth, which is Jesus the Saviour of all
mankind, the Son of the living God, who hath given life unto all
that believe on him and take refuge with him and are known to

be of the number of his servants (sheep, *Syr*.). Unto whom saith
Tertia: May I become a partaker of this life which thou promisest
that all they shall receive who come together unto the assembly
of God. And the apostle said: The treasury of the holy king is
opened wide, and they which worthily partake of the good things
that are therein do rest, and resting do reign: but first, no man
cometh unto him that is unclean and vile: for he knoweth our
inmost hearts and the depths of our thought, and it is not
possible for any to escape him. Thou, then, if verily thou believest
in him, shalt be made worthy of his mysteries; and he will
magnify thee and enrich thee, and make thee to be an heir of his
kingdom.

137 And Tertia having heard this returned home rejoicing,
and found her husband awaiting her, not having dined; and
when Misdaeus saw her he said: Whence is it that thine entering
in to-day is more beautiful? and wherefore art thou come
walking, which beseemeth not free-born women like thee? And
Tertia saith unto him: I owe thee the greatest of thanks for that
thou didst send me unto Mygdonia; for I went and heard of
a new life, and I saw the apostle of the God that giveth
life unto them that believe on him and fulfil his commandments;
I ought therefore myself to recompense thee for this favour and
admonition with good advice; for thou shalt be a great king in
heaven if thou obey me and fear the God that is preached by the
stranger, and keep thyself holy unto the living God. For this
kingdom passeth away, and thy comfort will be turned into
affliction: but go thou to that man, and believe him, and thou
shalt live unto the end. And when Misdaeus heard these things
of his wife, he smote his face with his hands and rent his clothes
and said: May the soul of Charisius find no rest, for he hath hurt
me to the soul; and may he have no hope, for he hath taken away
my hope. And he went out greatly vexed.

138 And he found Charisius his friend in the market-place,
and said unto him: Why hast thou cast me into hell to be another
companion to thyself? why hast thou emptied and defrauded
me to gain nought? why hast thou hurt me and profited thyself
not at all? why hast thou slain me and thyself not lived? why
hast thou wronged me and thyself not got justice? why didst
thou not suffer me to destroy that sorcerer before he corrupted
my house with his wickedness? And he kept hold upon (was up-
braiding, *Syr*.) Charisius. And Charisius saith: Why, what hath
befallen thee? Misdaeus said: He hath bewitched Tertia. And
they went both of them unto the house of Siphor the captain,
and found Judas sitting and teaching. And all they that were
there rose up before the king, but he arose not. And Misdaeus
perceived that it was he, and took hold of the seat and overset it,
and took up the seat with both his hands and smote his head so
that he wounded it, and delivered him to his soldiers, saying:

Take him away, and hale him with violence and not gently, that his shame may be manifest unto all men. And they haled him and took him to the place where Misdaeus judged, and he stood there, held of the soldiers of Misdaeus.

The Twelfth Act: concerning Ouazanes (Iuzanes) the son of Misdaeus.

139 And Ouazanes (Iuzanes, P ; Vizān, *Syr.*) the son of Misdaeus came unto the soldiers and said: Give me him that I may speak with him until the king cometh. And they gave him *up*, and he brought him in where the king gave judgement. And Iuzanes saith: Knowest thou not that I am the son of Misdaeus the king, and I have power to say unto the king what I will, and he will suffer thee to live? tell me then, who is thy God, and what power dost thou claim and glory in it? for if it be some power or art of magic, tell it me and teach me, and I will let thee go. Judas saith unto him: Thou art the son of Misdaeus the king who is king for a time, but I am the servant of Jesus Christ the eternal king; and thou hast power to say to thy father to save whom thou wilt in the temporal life wherein men continue not, which thou and thy father grant, but I beseech my Lord and intercede for men, and he giveth them a new life which is altogether enduring. And thou boastest thyself of possessions and servants and robes and luxury and unclean chamberings, but I boast myself of poverty and philosophy and humility and fasting and prayer and the fellowship of the Holy Ghost and of my brethren that are worthy of God: and I boast myself of eternal life. And thou reliest on (hast taken refuge with) a man like unto thyself, and not able to save his own soul from judgement and death, but I rely upon the living God, upon the saviour of kings and princes, who is the judge of all men. And ye indeed to-day perchance are, and to-morrow are no more, but I have taken refuge with him that abideth for ever and knoweth all our seasons and times. And if thou wilt become the servant of this God, thou shalt soon do so; but show that thou wilt be a servant worthy of him hereby: first by holiness (purity), which is the head of all good things, and then by fellowship with this God whom I preach, and philosophy and simplicity and love and faith and ⟨good hope⟩ in him, and unity of pure food (simplicity of pure life, *Syr.*).

140 And the young man was persuaded by the Lord and sought occasion how he might let Judas escape: but while he thought thereon, the king came; and the soldiers took Judas and led him forth. And Iuzanes went forth with him and stood beside him. And when the king was set he bade Judas be brought in, with his hands bound behind him; and he was brought into the midst and stood there. And the king saith: Tell me who thou art and by what power thou doest these things. And Judas

saith to him: I am a man like thee, *and* by the power of Jesus Christ I do these things. And Misdaeus saith: Tell me the truth before I destroy thee. And Judas saith: Thou hast no power against me, as thou supposest, and thou wilt not hurt me at all. And the king was wroth at his words, and commanded to heat *iron* plates and set him upon them barefoot; and as the soldiers took off his shoes he said: The wisdom of God is better than the wisdom of men. †Thou Lord and King† (do thou take counsel against them, *Syr.*) and let thy goodness resist his wrath. And they brought the plates which were like fire, and set the apostle upon them, and straightway water sprang up abundantly from the earth, so that the plates were swallowed up *in it*, and they that held him let him go and withdrew themselves.

141 And the king seeing the abundance of water said to Judas: Ask thy God that he deliver me from this death, that I perish not in the flood. And the apostle prayed and said: Thou that didst bind this element (nature) and gather it into one place and send it forth into divers lands; that didst bring disorder into order; that grantest mighty works and great wonders by the hands of Judas thy servant; that hast mercy on my soul, that I may alway receive thy brightness; that givest wages unto them that have laboured; thou saviour of my soul, restoring it unto its own nature that it may have no fellowship with hurtful things; that hast alway been the occasion of life: do thou restrain this element that it lift not up itself to destroy; for there are some of them that stand here who shall believe on thee and live. And when he had prayed, the water was swallowed up by little and little, and the place became dry. And when Misdaeus saw it he commanded him to be taken to the prison: Until I shall consider how he must be used.

142 And as Judas was led away to the prison they all followed him, and Iuzanes the king's son walked at his right hand, and Siphor at the left. And he entered into the prison and sat down, and Iuzanes and Siphor, and he persuaded his wife and his daughter to sit down, for they also were come in to hear the word of life. For they knew that Misdaeus would slay him because of the excess of his anger. And Judas began to say: O liberator of my soul from the bondage of the many, because I gave myself to be sold ⟨unto one, *Syr.*⟩; behold, I rejoice and exult, knowing that the times are fulfilled for me to enter in and receive ⟨thee my giver of rest, *Syr.*⟩. Lo, I am to be set free from the cares that are on the earth; lo, I fulfil mine hope and receive truth; lo, I am set free from sorrow and put on joy alone; lo, I become careless and griefless and dwell in rest; lo, I am set free from bondage and am called unto liberty; lo, I have served times and seasons, and I am lifted up above times and seasons; lo, I receive *my wages* from my recompenser, who giveth without reckoning (number) because his wealth sufficeth for the gift; ⟨lo, I put off

and on my raiment,⟩ and I shall not put it off again ; lo, I sleep and awake, and I shall no more go to sleep ; lo, I die and live again, and I shall no more taste of death ; lo, they rejoice and expect me, that I may come and be with their kindred and be set as a flower in their crown ; lo, I reign in the kingdom whereon I set my hope, *even* from hence ; lo, the rebellious fall before me, for I have escaped them ; lo, (unto me) the peace hath come, whereunto all are gathered.

143 And as the apostle spake thus, all that were there hearkened, supposing that in that hour he would depart out of life. And again he said: Believe on the physician of all ⟨diseases⟩, both seen and unseen, and on the saviour of the souls that need help from him. This is the free-born ⟨son⟩ of kings, this the physician of his creatures; this is he that was reproached of his own slaves ; this is the Father of the height and the Lord of nature and the Judge (? Father of nature and Lord of the height and supreme Judge, *Syr.*): he came of the greatest, the only-begotten son of the deep ; and he was called the son of (became visible through, *Syr.*) Mary the virgin, and was termed the son of Joseph the carpenter : he whose littleness (we beheld) with the eyes of our body, but his greatness we received by faith, and saw it in his works ; whose human body we felt also with our hands, and his aspect we saw transfigured (changed) with our eyes, but his heavenly semblance on the mount we were not able to see : he that made the rulers stumble and did violence unto death : he, the truth that lieth not, that at the last paid the tribute for himself and his disciples : whom the prince beholding feared and the powers that were with him were troubled ; and the prince bare witness (asked him, *Syr.*) who he was and from whence, and knew not the truth, because he is alien from truth : he that having authority over the world, and the pleasures therein, and the possessions and the comfort, ⟨rejected⟩ all these things, and turneth away his subjects, that they should not use them.

144 And having fulfilled these sayings, he arose and prayed thus: Our Father, which art in heaven: hallowed be thy name : Thy kingdom come : Thy will be done, as in heaven so upon earth : ⟨Give us the constant bread of the day, *Syr.*⟩ and forgive us our debts as we also have forgiven our debtors. And lead us not into temptation ; but deliver us from the evil *one*.

My Lord and God, hope and confidence and teacher, thou hast taught me to pray thus ; behold, I pray this prayer and fulfil thy commandment: be thou with me unto the end ; thou art he that from childhood hast sown life in me and kept me from corruption ; thou art he that hast brought me unto the poverty of this world, and exhorted me unto the true riches ; thou art he that hast made me known unto myself and showed me that I am thine; and I have kept myself pure from woman, that that which thou requirest be not found in defilement.

[At the words 'My Lord and God' begins the double text, represented on the one hand by the MS. U and on the other by the Paris MS. P, and three (partly four) others. These insert the prayer after ch. 167. Their text, I believe, may be the original Greek. I follow it here, repeating the first paragraph.]

(144) My Lord and God, my hope and my confidence and my teacher, that hast implanted courage in me, thou didst teach me to pray thus; behold, I pray thy prayer and bring thy will to fulfilment: be thou with me unto the end. Thou art he that from my youth up didst give me patience in temptation and ⟨sow in⟩ me life and preserve me from corruption; thou art he that didst bring me into the poverty of this world and fill me with the true riches; thou art he that didst show me that I was thine: wherefore I was never joined unto a wife, that the temple worthy of thee might not be found in pollution.

145 My mouth sufficeth not to praise thee, neither am I able to conceive the care and providence (carefulness) which hath been about me from thee (which thou hast had for me). For I desired to gain riches; but thou by a vision didst show me that they are full of loss and injury to them that gain them; and I believed thy showing, and continued in the poverty of the world until thou, the true riches, wert revealed unto me, who didst fill both me and the rest that were worthy of thee with thine own riches and set free thine own from care and anxiety. I have therefore fulfilled thy commandments, O Lord, and accomplished thy will, and become poor and needy and a stranger and a bondman and set at nought and a prisoner and hungry and thirsty and naked and unshod, and I have toiled for thy sake, that my confidence might not perish and my hope that is in thee might not be confounded, and my much labour might not be in vain and my weariness not be counted for nought: let not my prayers and my continual fastings perish, and my great zeal toward thee; let not my seed of wheat be changed *for tares* out of thy land ; let not the enemy carry it away and mingle his own tares therewith ; for thy land verily receiveth not his tares, neither indeed can they be laid up in thine houses.

146 I have planted thy vine in the earth; it hath sent down its roots into the depth and its growth is spread out in the height, and the fruits of it are stretched forth upon the earth, and they that are worthy of thee are made glad by them, whom also thou hast gained. The money which thou hast from me I laid down upon the table (bank); this, when thou requirest it, restore unto me with usury, as thou hast promised. With thy one mina have I traded and have made ten ; thou hast added *more* to me beside that I had, as thou didst covenant. I have forgiven my debtor the mina, require thou it not at my hands. I was bidden to the supper and I came: and I refused the land and the yoke of oxen and the wife, that I might not for their sake be rejected.

I was bidden to the wedding, and I put on white raiment, that I might be worthy of it and not be bound hand and foot and cast into the outer darkness. My lamp with its bright light expecteth the master coming from the marriage, that it may receive him, and I may not (? he may not) see it dimmed because the oil is spent. Mine eyes, O Christ, look upon thee, and mine heart exulteth with joy because I have fulfilled thy will and perfected thy commandments; that I may be likened unto that watchful and careful servant who in his eagerness neglecteth not to keep vigil (*other MSS.*: I have not slumbered idly in keeping thy commandments: in the first sleep and at midnight and at cockcrow, that mine eyes may behold thee, &c.). All the night have I laboured to keep mine house from robbers, lest it be broken through.

147 My loins have I girt close with truth and bound my shoes on my feet, that I may never see them gaping: mine hands have I put unto the yoked plough and have not turned away backward, lest my furrows go crooked. The plough-land is become white and the harvest is come, that I may receive my wages. My garment that groweth old I have worn out, and the labour that hath brought me unto rest have I accomplished. I have kept the first watch and the second and the third, that I may behold thy face and adore thine holy brightness. I have rooted out the worst (pulled down my barns, *Syr.*) and left them desolate upon earth, that I may be filled full from thy treasures (*Gr. MSS. add:* all my substance have I sold, that I may gain thee the pearl). The moist spring that was in me have I dried up, that I may live and rest *beside* thine inexhaustible spring (*al.* and *Syr.*: rest beside thy living spring). The captive whom thou didst commit to me I have slain, that he which is set free in me may not fall from his confidence. Him that was inward have I made outward and the outward ⟨inward⟩, and all thy fullness hath been fulfilled in me. I have not returned unto the things that are behind, but have gone forward unto the things that are before, that I become not a reproach. The dead man have I quickened, and the living one have I overcome, and that which was lacking have I filled up (*Syr. Wright*, not the older one, inserts negatives, '*not* quickened', &c.), that I may receive the crown of victory, and the power of Christ may be accomplished in me. I have received reproach upon earth, but give thou me the return and the recompense in the heavens. (U omits practically all this chapter.)

148 Let not the powers and the officers perceive me, and let them not have any thought concerning me; let not the publicans and exactors ply their calling upon me; let not the weak and the evil cry out against me *that am* valiant and humble; and when I am borne upward let them not rise up to stand before me, by thy power, O Jesu, which surroundeth me as a crown: for they

do flee and hide themselves, they cannot look on thee: but (for) suddenly do they fall upon them that are subject to them, and the portion of the sons of the evil *one* doth itself cry out and convict them; and it is not hid from them, for their nature is made known: the children of the evil one are separated off. Do thou then grant me, Lord, that I may pass by in quietness and joy and peace, and pass over and stand before the judge; and let not the devil (*or* slanderer) look upon me; let his eyes be blinded by thy light which thou hast made to dwell in me; close thou up (muzzle) his mouth: for he hath found nought against me.

[We revert to U.]

149 And he said again unto them that were about him: ⟨Believe, my children, in the God whom I proclaim; believe in Jesus Christ whom I preach; believe in the giver of life and helper of his servants, *Syr.*⟩ believe in the Saviour of them that have laboured in his service: for my soul already flourisheth, because my time is near to receive him; for he being beautiful draweth me on always to speak concerning his beauty, what it is, though I be not able and suffice not to speak it worthily: thou that art the light (feeder, *Syr.*) of my poverty and the supplier of my defects and nurturer of my need: be thou with me until I come and receive thee for evermore.

The Thirteenth Act: wherein Iuzanes receiveth baptism with the rest.

150 And Iuzanes the youth besought the apostle, saying: I pray thee, O man, apostle of God, suffer me to go, and I will persuade the gaoler to permit thee to come home with me, that by thee I may receive the seal, and become thy minister and a keeper of the commandments of the God whom thou preachest. For indeed, formerly I walked in those things which thou teachest, until my father compelled me and joined me unto a wife by name Mnesara; for I am in my one-and-twentieth year, and have now been seven years married, and before I was joined in marriage I knew no other woman ; wherefore also I was accounted useless of my father, nor have I ever had son or daughter of this wife, and also my wife herself hath lived with me in chastity all this time, and to-day, if she had been in health, and had listened to thee, I know well that both I should have been at rest and she would have received eternal life; but she is in peril and afflicted with much illness; I will therefore persuade the keeper that he promise to come with me; for I live by myself: and thou shalt also heal that unhappy one. And Judas the apostle of the Most High, hearing this, said to Iuzanes: If thou believest, thou shalt see the marvels of God, and how he saveth his servants.

151 And as they spake thus together, Tertia and Mygdonia and Narcia stood at the door of the prison, and they gave the gaoler 363 staters of silver and entered in to Judas; and found

ACTS OF THOMAS   431

Iuzanes and Siphor and his wife and daughter, and all the
prisoners sitting and hearing the word. And when they stood
by him he said to them: Who hath suffered you to come unto us?
and who opened unto you the sealed door that ye came forth? Tertia
saith unto him: Didst not thou open the door for us and tell us
to come into the prison that we might take our brethren that
were there, and then should the Lord show forth his glory in us?
And when we came near the door, I know not how, thou wast
parted from us and hid thyself and camest hither before us,
where also we heard the noise of the door, when thou didst shut
us out. We gave money therefore to the keepers and came in;
and lo, we are here praying thee that we may persuade thee and
let thee escape until the king's wrath against thee shall cease.
Unto whom Judas said: Tell us first of all how ye were shut up.

152 And she saith to him: Thou wast with us, and didst never
leave us for one hour, and askest thou how we were shut up?
but if thou desirest to hear, hear. The king Misdaeus sent for
me and said unto me: Not yet hath that sorcerer prevailed over
thee, for, as I hear, he bewitcheth men with oil and water and
bread, and hath not yet bewitched thee; but obey thou me, for
if not, I will imprison thee and wear thee out, and him I will
destroy; for I know that if he hath not yet given thee oil and
water and bread, he hath not prevailed to get power over thee.
And I said unto him: Over my body thou hast authority, and
do thou all that thou wilt; but my soul I will not let perish with
thee. And hearing that he shut me up in a chamber (beneath his
dining-hall, Syr.): and Charisius brought Mygdonia and shut her
up with me: and thou broughtest us out and didst bring us even
hither; but give thou us the seal quickly, that the hope of
Misdaeus who counselleth thus may be cut off.

153 And when the apostle heard this, he said: Glory be to thee,
O Jesu of many forms, glory to thee that appearest in the guise
of our poor manhood: glory to thee that encouragest us and
makest us strong and givest grace and consolest and standest by
us in all perils, and strengthenest our weakness. And as he thus
spake, the gaoler came and said: Put out the lamps, lest any
accuse you unto the king. And then they extinguished the
lamps, and turned to sleep; but the apostle spake unto the
Lord: It is the time now, O Jesu, for thee to make haste; for, lo,
the children of darkness sit (make us to sit, Syr.) in their own
darkness; do thou therefore enlighten us with the light of thy
nature. And on a sudden the whole prison was light as the day:
and while all they that were in the prison slept a deep sleep, they
only that had believed in the Lord continued waking.

154 Judas therefore saith to Iuzanes: Go thou before and
make ready the things for our need. Iuzanes therefore saith:
And who will open me the doors of the prison? for the gaolers
shut them and are gone to sleep. And Judas saith: Believe in

Jesus, and thou shalt find the doors open. And when he went forth and departed from them, all the rest followed after him. And as Iuzanes was gone on before, Mnesara his wife met him, coming unto the prison. And she knew him and said: My brother Iuzanes, is it thou? and he saith, Yea; and art thou Mnesara? and she saith, Yea. Iuzanes said unto her: Whither walkest thou, especially at so untimely an hour? and how wast thou able to rise up? And she said: This youth laid his hand on me and raised me up, and in a dream I saw that I should go where the stranger sitteth, and become perfectly whole. Iuzanes saith to her: What youth is with thee? And she said: Seest thou not him that is on my right hand, leading me by the hand?

155 And while they spake together thus, Judas, with Siphor and his wife and daughter and Tertia and Mygdonia and Narcia, came unto Iuzanes' house. And Mnesara the wife of Iuzanes, seeing him did reverence and said: Art thou come that savedst us from the sore disease? thou art he whom I saw in the night delivering unto me this youth to bring me to the prison. But thy goodness suffered me not to grow weary, but thou thyself art come unto me. And so saying she turned about and saw the youth no more; and finding him not, she saith to the apostle: I am not able to walk alone: for the youth whom thou gavest me is not here. And Judas said: Jesus will henceforth lead thee. *And* thereafter she came running unto him. And when they entered into the house of Iuzanes the son of Misdaeus the king, though it was yet night, a great light shined and was shed about them.

156 And then Judas began to pray and to speak thus: O companion and defender (ally) and hope of the weak and confidence of the poor: refuge and lodging of the weary: voice that came forth of the height (sleep, *Gr.*): comforter dwelling in the midst: port and harbour of them that pass through the regions of the rulers: physician that healest without payment: who among men wast crucified for many: who didst go down into hell with great might: the sight of whom the princes of death endured not; and thou camest up with great glory, and gathering all them that fled unto thee didst prepare a way, and in thy footsteps all they journeyed whom thou didst redeem; and thou broughtest them into thine own fold and didst join them with thy sheep: son of mercy, the son that for love of man wast sent unto us from the perfect country (fatherland) that is above; the Lord of all possessions (undefiled possessions, *Syr.*): that servest thy servants that they may live: that fillest creation with thine own riches: the poor, that wast in need and didst hunger forty days: that satisfiest thirsty souls with thine own good things; be thou with Iuzanes the son of Misdaeus and with Tertia and Mnesara; and gather them into thy fold and mingle them with thy number. Be unto them a guide in the land of error: be unto them a physi-

cian in the land of sickness: be unto them a rest in the land of
the weary: sanctify them in a polluted land: be their physician
both of bodies and souls: make them holy temples of thee, and
let thine holy spirit dwell in them.

157 Having thus prayed over them, the apostle said unto
Mygdonia: Unclothe thy sisters. And she took off their clothes
and girded them with girdles and brought them: but Iuzanes
had first gone before, and they came after him; and the apostle
took oil in a cup of silver and spake thus over it: Fruit more
beautiful than *all* other fruits, unto which none other whatsoever
may be compared: altogether merciful: fervent with the force of
the word: power of the tree which men putting upon them overcome their adversaries: crowner of the conquerors: help (symbol)
and joy of the sick: that didst announce unto men their salvation,
that showest light to them that are in darkness; whose leaf is
bitter, but in thy most sweet fruit thou art fair; that art rough
to the sight but soft to the taste; seeming to be weak, but in the
greatness of thy strength able to bear the power that beholdeth
all things. Having thus said [*a corrupt word follows*]: Jesu:
let his victorious might come and be established in this oil, like
as it was established in the tree (wood) that was its kin, even his
might at that time, whereof they that crucified thee could not
endure the word: let the gift also come whereby breathing upon
his (thine) enemies thou didst cause them to go backward and
fall headlong, and let it rest on this oil, whereupon we invoke
thine holy name. And having thus said, he poured it first upon
the head of Iuzanes and then upon the women's heads, saying:
In thy name, O Jesu Christ, let it be unto these souls for remission
of sins and for turning back of the adversary and for salvation
of their souls. And he commanded Mygdonia to anoint them,
but he himself anointed Iuzanes. And having anointed them he
led them down into the water in the name of the Father and the
Son and the Holy Ghost.

158 And when they were come up, he took bread and a cup,
and blessed it and said: Thine holy body which was crucified
for us do we eat, and thy blood that was shed for us unto salvation
do we drink; let therefore thy body be unto us salvation and
thy blood for remission of sins. And for the gall which thou
didst drink for our sakes let the gall of the devil be removed from
us: and for the vinegar which thou hast drunk for us, let our
weakness be made strong: and for the spitting which thou didst
receive for us, let us receive the dew of thy goodness: and by
(*or* for) the reed wherewith they smote thee for us, let us receive
the perfect house: and whereas thou receivedst a crown of thorns
for our sake, let us that have loved thee put on a crown that
fadeth not away; and for the linen cloth wherein thou wast
wrapped, let us also be girt about with thy power that is not
vanquished: and for the new tomb and the burial let us receive

renewing of soul and body: and for that thou didst rise up and revive, let us revive and live and stand before thee in righteous judgement. And he brake and gave the eucharist unto Iuzanes and Tertia and Mnesara and the wife and daughter of Siphor, and said: Let this eucharist be unto you for salvation and joy and health of your souls. And they said: Amen. And a voice was heard, saying: Amen: fear ye not, but only believe.

[THE MARTYRDOM]

Here we revert to the text of P and its companions.

159 And after these things Judas departed to be imprisoned.

And Tertia with Mygdonia and Narcia also went to be imprisoned. And the apostle Thomas said unto them—the multitude of them that had believed being present: Daughters and sisters and fellow-servants which have believed in my Lord and God, ministers of my Jesus, hearken to me this day: for I do deliver my word unto you, and I shall no more speak with you in this flesh nor in this world; for I go up unto my Lord and God Jesus Christ, unto him that sold me, unto that Lord that humbled himself even unto me the little, and brought me up unto eternal greatness, that vouchsafed to me to become his servant in truth and steadfastness: unto him do I depart, knowing that the time is fulfilled, and the day appointed hath drawn near for me to go and receive my recompense from my Lord and God: for my recompenser is righteous, who knoweth me, how I ought to receive my reward; for he is not grudging nor envious, but is rich in his gifts; he is not a lover of craft (*or* sparing) in that he giveth, for he hath confidence in his possessions which cannot fail.

160 I am not Jesus, but I am his servant: I am not Christ, but I am his minister: I am not the Son of God, but I pray to become worthy of God. Continue ye in the faith of Christ: continue in the hope of the Son of God: faint not at affliction, neither be divided in mind if ye see me mocked or that I am shut up in prison ⟨or die, *Syr.*⟩; for I do accomplish his will. For if I had willed not to die, I know in Christ that I am able *thereto*: but this which is called death, is not death, but a setting free from the body; wherefore I receive gladly this setting free from the body, that I may depart and see him that is beautiful and full of mercy, him that is to be loved: for I have endured much toil in his service, and have laboured for his grace that is come upon me, which departeth not from me. Let not Satan, then, enter you by stealth and catch away your thoughts: let there be in you no place for him: for he is mighty whom ye have received. Look for the coming of Christ, for he shall come and receive you, and this is he whom ye shall see when he cometh.

161 When the apostle had ended these sayings, they went into

the house; and the apostle Thomas said: Saviour that didst suffer many things for us, let these doors be as they were and let seals be set on them. And he left them and went to be imprisoned: and they wept and were in heaviness, for they knew that Misdaeus would slay him (not knowing that, M. would release him, P.).

162 And the apostle found the keepers wrangling and saying: Wherein have we sinned against this wizard? for by his art magic he hath opened the doors and would have had all the prisoners escape: but let us go and report it unto the king, and tell him concerning his wife and his son. And as they disputed thus, Thomas held his peace. They rose up early, therefore, and went unto the king and said unto him: Our lord and king, do thou take away that sorcerer and cause him to be shut up elsewhere, for we are not able to keep him; for except thy good fortune had kept the prison, all the condemned persons would have escaped, for now this second time have we found the doors open: and also thy wife, O king, and thy son and the rest depart not from him. And the king, hearing that, went, and found the seals that were set *on the doors* whole; and he took note of the doors also, and said to the keepers: Wherefore lie ye? for the seals are whole. How said ye that Tertia and Mygdonia come unto him into the prison? And the keepers said: We have told thee the truth.

163 And Misdaeus went to the prison and took his seat, and sent for the apostle Thomas and stripped him (and girded him with a girdle) and set him before him and saith unto him: Art thou bond or free? Thomas said: I am the bondsman of one only, over whom thou hast no authority. And Misdaeus saith to him: How didst thou run away and come into this country? And Thomas said: I was sold hither by my master, that I might save many, and by thy hands depart out of this world. And Misdaeus said: Who is thy lord? and what is his name? and of what country is he? And Thomas said: My Lord is thy master, and he is Lord of heaven and earth. And Misdaeus saith: What is his name? Thomas saith: Thou canst not hear his true name at this time: but the name that was given unto him is Jesus Christ. And Misdaeus saith unto him: I have not made haste to destroy thee, but have had long patience with thee: but thou hast added unto thine evil deeds, and thy sorceries are dispersed abroad and heard of throughout all the country: but this I do that thy sorceries may depart with thee, and our land be cleansed from them. Thomas saith unto him: These sorceries depart ⟨not, *Syr.*⟩ with me when I set forth hence, and know thou this, that I ⟨they, *Syr.*⟩ shall never forsake them that are here.

164 When the apostle had said these things, Misdaeus considered how he should put him to death; for he was afraid because of the much people that were subject unto him, for many also of the nobles and of them that were in authority believed on him. He took him therefore and went forth out of the city; and armed

soldiers also went with him. And the people supposed that the
king desired to learn somewhat of him, and they stood still and
gave heed. And when they had walked one mile, he delivered
him unto four soldiers and an officer, and commanded them to
take him into the mountain and there pierce him with spears
and put an end to him, and return again to the city. And saying
thus unto the soldiers, he himself also returned unto the city.

165 But the men ran after Thomas, desiring to deliver him
from death. And two *soldiers* went at the right hand of the
apostle and two on his left, holding spears, and the officer held
his hand and supported him. And the apostle Thomas said:
O the hidden mysteries which even until our departure are
accomplished in us! O riches of his glory, who will not suffer us
to be swallowed up in this passion of the body! Four are they
that cast me down, for of four am I made; and one is he that
draweth me, for of one I am, and unto him I go. And this I now
understand, that my Lord and God Jesus Christ, being of one,
was pierced by one, but I, which am of four, am pierced by four.

166 And being come up into the mountain unto the place
where he was to be slain, he said unto them that held him, and
to the rest: Brethren, hearken unto me now at the last; for
I am come to my departure out of the body. Let not then the
eyes of your heart be blinded, nor your ears be made deaf.
Believe on the God whom I preach, and be not guides unto
yourselves in the hardness of your heart, but walk in all your
liberty, and in the glory that is toward men, and the life that is
toward God.

167 And he said unto Iuzanes: Thou son (to the son, P) of
the (earthly) king Misdaeus and minister (to the minister) of our
Lord Jesus Christ: give unto the servants of Misdaeus their
price that they may suffer me to go and pray. And Iuzanes
persuaded the soldiers to let him pray. And the blessed Thomas
went to pray, and kneeled down, and rose up and stretched forth
his hands unto heaven, and spake thus:

[Here P and the rest give—rightly—the prayer of cc. 144–8.
U and its companions give the following: He turned to his
prayer; and it was this: My Lord and my God, and hope and
redeemer and leader and guide in all countries, be thou with all
them that serve thee, and guide me this day as I come unto thee.
Let not any take my soul which I have committed unto thee:
let not the publicans see me, and let not the exactors accuse me
falsely (play the sycophant with me). Let not the serpent see
me, and let not the children of the dragon hiss at me. Behold,
Lord, I have accomplished thy work and perfected thy commandment. I have become a bondman; therefore to-day do I receive
freedom. Do thou therefore give me this and perfect me: and
this I say, not for that I doubt, but that they may hear for whom
it is needful to hear.]

168 And when he had thus prayed he said unto the soldiers: Come hither and accomplish the commandments of him that sent you. And the four came and pierced him with their spears, and he fell down and died.

And all the brethren wept; and they brought beautiful robes and much and fair linen, and buried him in a royal sepulchre wherein the former (first) kings were laid.

169 But Siphor and Iuzanes would not go down to the city, but continued sitting by him all the day. And the apostle Thomas appeared unto them and said: Why sit ye here and keep watch over me? I am not here, but I have gone up and received all that I was promised. But rise up and go down hence; for after a little time ye also shall be gathered unto me.

But Misdaeus and Charisius took away Mygdonia and Tertia and afflicted them sorely: howbeit they consented not unto their will. And the apostle appeared unto them and said: Be not deceived: Jesus the holy, the living one, shall quickly send help unto you. And Misdaeus and Charisius, when they perceived that Mygdonia and Tertia obeyed them not, suffered them to live according to their own desire.

And the brethren gathered together and rejoiced in the grace of the Holy Ghost: now the apostle Thomas when he departed out of the world made Siphor a presbyter and Iuzanes a deacon, when he went up into the mountain to die. And the Lord wrought with them, and many were added unto the faith.

170 Now it came to pass after a long time that one of the children of Misdaeus the king was smitten by a devil, and no man could cure him, for the devil was exceeding fierce. And Misdaeus the king took thought and said: I will go and open the sepulchre, and take a bone of the apostle of God and hang it upon my son, and he shall be healed. But while Misdaeus thought upon this, the apostle Thomas appeared to him and said unto him: Thou believedst not on a living man, and wilt thou believe on the dead? yet fear not, for my Lord Jesus Christ hath compassion on thee and pitieth thee of his goodness.

And he went and opened *the sepulchre*, but found not the apostle there, for one of the brethren had stolen him away and taken him unto Mesopotamia; but from that place where the bones of the apostle had lain Misdaeus took dust and put it about his son's *neck*, saying: I believe on thee, Jesu Christ, now that he hath left me which troubleth men and opposeth them lest they should see thee. And when he had hung it upon his son, the lad became whole.

Misdaeus the king therefore was also gathered among the brethren, and bowed his head under the hands of Siphor the priest; and Siphor said unto the brethren: Pray ye for Misdaeus the king, that he may obtain mercy of Jesus Christ, and that he may no more remember evil against him. They all therefore, with one accord rejoicing, made prayer for him; and the Lord that loveth men, the King of kings and Lord of lords, granted Misdaeus also to have hope in him; and he was gathered with the multitude of them that had believed in Christ, glorifying the Father and the Son and the Holy Ghost; whose is power and adoration, now and for ever and world without end. Amen.

[U (and *Syr.*) ends: The acts of Judas Thomas the apostle are completed, which he did in India, fulfilling the commandment of him that sent him. Unto whom be glory, world without end. Amen.]

THE SECONDARY ACTS

The five principal apostolic romances which have been here translated had naturally many successors: it was not to be expected that the destinies of the other apostles would be left in obscurity when the possibilities of edifying fiction on this subject had been demonstrated to so great an extent. But a change is noticeable in the complexion of the later romances. The earlier ones had all a great interest in doctrine: the prayers and exhortations of the apostle are very evidently the centre of interest to the author. It is not so in the later Acts. In them it is the narrative and the accumulation of miracles which are the *raison d'être*. Religiously, then, these books are not very important: as storehouses of legend and folk-lore, and in their influence on later literature and art, they have considerable interest.

It is not easy to devise a scientific classification of the later Acts. They are multitudinous, fragmentary, imperfectly known: new recensions and new texts still emerge not unfrequently. But perhaps a line may be drawn between those which exist in Greek or Latin and those which we only have in Oriental languages—Coptic, Ethiopic, and Syriac. It may be said at once that Egypt was a prolific factory of the later Acts: in her monasteries it seems likely that in and after the fifth century a whole cycle of apostolic romances was produced. These we have partly in Coptic, which was very likely their original language, and more completely in Ethiopic and Arabic versions. There are two or three Greek texts also which attach themselves by their contents to this Egyptian cycle.

Outside it, and to be dealt with first here, are a few romances which exist in Greek and Latin. The Greek are separately current: the Latin, in their most accessible form, are embodied in the *Apostolic History*, put together—perhaps in France—perhaps in the sixth, at least not later than the seventh century, and associated with the name of Abdias, Bishop of Babylon: though properly he has no right to figure as its author at all.[1]

---

[1] In Book VI (Acts of SS. Simon and Jude) it is said that these apostles ordained Abdias, a disciple of Jesus, Bishop of Babylon: and that Craton their disciple wrote their Acts in ten books which were translated into Latin by (Julius) Africanus. But a preface to the whole work, purporting to be by Julius Africanus, says that he, Africanus, has taken his material from the books written about all

ACTS OF PHILIP

Now the first of the separate romances, which is most obviously an imitation of the Five, and is pretty certainly somewhat older than the others which we shall encounter, is the

ACTS OF PHILIP

No such suspicion of unorthodoxy as—rightly or wrongly—attaches to four out of the Five Acts, affects the Acts of Philip. If grotesque, it is yet a Catholic novel. In form it follows *Thomas*, for it is divided into separate Acts, of which the manuscripts mention fifteen: we have Acts i–ix and from xv to the end, including the Martyrdom, which last, as usual, was current separately and exists in many recensions.

One Act—the second—and the Martyrdom were first edited by Tischendorf. Batiffol printed the remainder in 1890, and Bonnet, using more manuscripts, gives the final edition in his *Acta Apost. Apocr.* ii. 1. Besides the Greek text, there is a single Act extant only in Syriac, edited by Wright, which, so far as its general character goes, might well have formed part of the Greek Acts: but it is difficult to fit it into the framework.

An analysis, with translations of the more interesting passages, will suffice for these Acts, and for the rest of their class.

I. *When he came out of Galilee and raised the dead man.*

1 When he was come out of Galilee, a widow was carrying out her only son to burial. Philip asked her about her grief: I have spent in vain much money on the gods, Ares, Apollo, Hermes, Artemis, Zeus, Athena, the Sun and Moon, and I think they are asleep as far as I am concerned. And I consulted a diviner to no purpose.

2 The apostle said: Thou hast suffered nothing strange, mother, for thus doth the devil deceive men. Assuage thy grief and I will raise thy son in the name of Jesus.

3 She said: It seems it were better for me not to marry, and to eat nothing but bread and water. Philip: You are right. Chastity is especially dear to God.

4 She said: I believe in Jesus whom thou preachest. He raised her son, who sat up and said: Whence is this light? and how comes it that an angel came and opened the prison of judgement where I was shut up? where I saw such torments as the tongue of man cannot describe.

5 So all were baptized. And the youth followed the apostle.

II. *When he went unto Greece of Athens* (!)

6 When he entered into the city of Athens which is called Hellas, 300 philosophers gathered and said: Let us go and see what his wisdom is, for they say of the wise men of Asia that

the apostles by Abdias the disciple of Simon and Jude. Abdias wrote in Hebrew: Eutropius his disciple translated him into Greek: Africanus put him into Latin, in ten books.

their wisdom is great. For they supposed Philip to be a philosopher: he travelled only in a cloak and an undergarment. So they assembled and looked into their books, lest he should get the better of them.

7 They said: If you have anything new to tell us, let us hear it, for we need nothing else but only to hear some new thing.

8 Philip: Then you must cast away the old man. The Lord said: Ye cannot put new wine into old bottles. I am glad to hear that you desire something new, for my Lord's teaching is new.

9 The philosophers: Who is thy Lord? Philip: Jesus Christ.

10 They: This is a new name to us. Give us three days to look into it.

11 They consulted, and said: Perhaps it will be best to send for the high priest of the Jews to discuss it with him.

12 So they wrote: The philosophers of Greece to Ananias the great high priest of the Jews at Jerusalem—and stated the case.

13 On reading the letter Ananias rent his clothes and said: Is that deceiver in Athens also? And Mansēmat, that is, Satan, entered into him. (This is another form of Mastema, the name of Satan in *Jubilees* and elsewhere.) And he consulted with the lawyers and Pharisees, and they said: Arm thyself and take 500 men and go and at all costs destroy Philip.

14 So he came in the high-priestly garments with great pomp, and he and the philosophers went to Philip's lodging, and he came out, and Ananias said: Thou sorcerer and wizard, I know thee, that thy master the deceiver at Jerusalem called thee son of thunder; did not Judaea suffice you, but must you come here to deceive? Philip said: May the veil of unbelief be taken from thee, and thou learn who is the deceiver, thou or I.

15 Ananias' address: how Jesus destroyed the law and allowed all meats—was crucified, the disciples stole his body, and did many wonders, and were cast out of Jerusalem, and now go all about the world deceiving every one, like this Philip. But I will take him to Jerusalem, for the king Archelaus seeketh him to kill him.

16 The people were not moved. Philip said: I will appeal to my God.

17 Ananias ran at him to smite him; his hand withered and he was blinded, and so were his 500 men: they cursed him, and prayed Philip for help.

18 Philip's prayer: O weak nature . . . O bitter sea. Come, Jesu, the holy light—thou overlookest us not when we cry to thee. . . .

19 Ananias to Philip: Thinkest thou to turn us from the traditions of our fathers, and the God of the manna in the wilderness, and Moses, to follow the Nazarene, Jesus? Philip: I will ask my God to manifest himself to thee and to these—perchance

thou wilt believe: but if not, a wonder shall befall thee. And he prayed God to send his Son.

20 The heavens opened and Jesus appeared in glory, his face seven times brighter than the sun, and his raiment whiter than snow. All the idols of Athens fell, and the devils in them fled, crying out. Philip said: Hearest thou not the devils, and believest thou not him that is here? Ananias: I have no God save him that gave the manna in the wilderness.

21 Jesus went up into heaven, and there was a great earthquake, and the people fled to the apostle, crying for mercy.

22 Philip: There is no envy in us, and the grace of Christ shall restore your sight, but first let the high priest see. A voice from heaven: Philip, once son of thunder but now of meekness, whatsoever thou askest my Father he will do for thee. The people were afraid at the voice. In the name of Christ, Philip made Ananias see. He said: How great is the art magic of Jesus! this Philip in a moment (or for a little) hath blinded me and in a moment restored my sight! I cannot be convinced by witchcraft. The 500 asked Philip to give back their sight that they might slay the unbelieving Ananias.

23 Philip: Render not evil for evil. To Ananias: There shall be a great sign shown in thee. Ananias: I know that thou art a sorcerer and disciple of Jesus; thou canst not bewitch me. Philip, to Jesus: Zabarthan, sabathabat, bramanouch, come quickly! The earth opened and swallowed Ananias to the knees. He cried: This is real magic, that the earth clave when Philip threatened it in Hebrew—and there are hooks below pulling at my legs to make me believe, but I will not, for I know his witchcraft from Jerusalem.

24 Philip, to the earth: Take him to the middle. And he sank further and said: One foot is frozen and the other hot—but I will not believe. The people wanted to stone him, but Philip checked them: This is for your salvation; if he repent, I will bring him up, but if not, he shall be swallowed into the deep.

25 He spread out his hand in the air over the 500, and their eyes were opened and they praised God. Philip, to Ananias: Confess now with a pure heart that Jesus is Lord, that thou mayest be saved like these. But he laughed at him.

26 Seeing him obstinate, Philip said to the earth: Open and swallow him to the neck. 27 And one of the first men of the city came and said: A devil has attacked my son, saying: As thou hast let a stranger come to the city, who destroys our idols, what can I do but kill thine only son? and he has suffocated him. Help me, for I also believe.

28 Bring me thy son. And he ran, calling to his son, and bade the servants bring him: he was 23 years old. Philip seeing him, grieved, and said to Ananias: This is through your folly: if I raise him will you believe? Ananias: I know you will raise

him by your magic, but I will not believe. Philip was wroth and
said: Catathema (cursed thing), go down into the abyss in the
sight of all. And he was swallowed up: but the high-priestly
robe flew away from him, and therefore no man knows where it is
from that day.

Philip raised the lad and drove away the devil.

29 The people cried out, believing in God, and the 500 were
baptized. And Philip stayed two years at Athens, and founded
a church and ordained a bishop and a presbyter, and departed
to Parthia to preach.

III. *Done in Parthia by Philip.*

30 When Philip came to Parthia he found in a city the apostle
Peter with disciples, and said: I pray you strengthen me, that
I may go and preach like you. 31 And they prayed for him.

32 And John was there also, and said to Philip: Andrew
is gone to Achaia and Thrace, and Thomas to India and the
wicked flesh-eaters, and Matthew to the savage troglodytes. And
do thou not be slack, for Jesus is with thee. And they let him
depart.

33 And he came to the sea in the borders of the Candaçi and
found a ship going to Azotus, and agreed with the sailors for
four staters, and sailed. A great wind came, and they began to
cast out the tackle and say farewell to each other and lament.

34 Philip consoled them: Not even the ship shall be lost. He
went up on the prow and said: Sea, sea, Jesus Christ by me his
servant bids thee still thy wrath. There was calm, and the
sailors thanked him and asked to become servants of Jesus.
35 And he instructed them to forsake the cares of this life.
36 And they believed, and Philip landed and baptized them all.

IV. *Of the daughter of Nicocleides, whom he healed at Azotus.*

37 There was great commotion in Azotus because of Philip's
miracles, and many came and were healed, and devils were cast
out and cried out against him. And people said divers things of
him, some that he was good, and others that he was a wizard,
and separated husbands and wives and preached chastity.

38 Evening came on and all dispersed. Philip sought a lodging,
and went to the warehouses of one Nicocleides, a recorder
(registrar), friend of the king, where many strangers lodged.

39 He stood in a corner and prayed for blessing and healing on
the house.

40 Charitine, daughter of Nicocleides, heard him and wept all
night. She had a sore disease in her eye. In the morning she
went to her father and said: I can no longer bear the taunts of
my companions about my eye. He said: What can I do? have
I not called in Leucius the king's physician and Elides the queen's

eunuch and Solgia her attendant. *She*: I know it; but there is a strange physician come here last night: call him.

41 He went to the warehouses and found Philip: Art thou the physician lately come? *Philip*: Jesus is my physician. I will come with thee. They found the daughter weeping. 42 After reassuring words she fell at his feet: I sprinkle my chamber with pure water and lay my linen garments under thy feet; help me, for I know thou canst. To her father: Let us bring him in, and let him see my disease.

43 Philip comforted and instructed them, and bade her rise and put her right hand on her face and say: In the name of Jesus Christ let my eye be healed. And it was. 44 And both believed and were baptized, and a number of servants. And Charitine put on male attire and followed Philip.

V. *Done in the city Nicatera; and of Ireus.*

45 Philip had in mind to go to Nicatera, a city of Greece, and many disciples accompanied him, and he taught continually. 46 And when he arrived there was great stir: What shall we do, for his teaching will prevail ... he separates husbands and wives. Let us cast him out before he begins to preach and our wives are deceived.

47 There were Jews, too, who spoke against him; but a chief of them, Ireus, said: Do not use force; let us test his teaching.

48 Ireus was wealthy. He was a just man and desired quietly to foil their counsel. He went to Philip and greeted him. And Philip saw there was no guile in him, and promised him salvation, for having stood up for him.

49 Ireus was surprised at his knowing this. Philip exhorted him to faith and constancy. 50 *Ircus*: Lodge at my house. *Philip*: First cleanse it. *Ireus*: How? *Philip*: Do no wrong, and leave thy wife. And he went home.

51 His wife said: I hear you foiled the counsel of the Jews about a strange sorcerer. *Ireus*: Would that we might be worthy to have him lodge here. *She*: I will not have him here, for he separates husbands and wives. I will go home to my parents and take my dowry and servants; four years I have been your wife and never contradicted you.

52 *Ireus* mildly: Have patience, and you also will believe. *She*: Rise, eat, drink and be merry, for you cannot deceive me. *Ireus*: How can I eat while the man of God is hungry? Put away this folly: he is a man of God, of mildness and grace. 53 *She*: Is his God like those of this city, of gold, fixed in the temple? *Ireus*: No, but in heaven, almighty: the gods of this city are made by ungodly men. *She*: Bring him, that I may see the god in him. 54 He went to meet Philip, who told him what had passed, and Ireus was amazed at his knowledge, but asked him not to publish the reproach of his wife. 55 Philip's

companions urged him to accept the refuge provided: and Ireus was glad. Philip consented to come, and followed Ireus. 56 The rulers and people saw it and determined not to allow it. Ireus arriving at his gate cried to the porter to open. Philip entered, saying: Peace be to this house. Ireus found that his wife was in her chamber and went and asked her to come, and put off her gay robes. But she was angry and said: No one of the house has ever seen my face, and shall I show it to a stranger?

57 So he went out and set fine gilt chairs for Philip and the rest. But he said: Take them away. *Ireus*: Do not grieve me. *Philip*: I grieve no one, but I have no use for gold, which passes away, &c. 58 *Ireus*: Can I be saved? for my former sins trouble me. *Philip*: Yes, Jesus is able to save you. And what of your wife who just now said to you: Depart from me, &c.? Ireus, surprised, went to his wife and said: Come and see a man who has told me what passed between you and me. She was scornful, and said: What is to become of our children if we have to give up all our worldly wealth? 59 Artemēla his daughter was listening, and said: If my father and mother are to enter a new life, may I not share it? She was very beautiful. Her mother Nerkela told her to rise and put off her gold-woven dress. Ireus said to Nerkela: Let us go out and see Philip [it seems Nerkela was converted, but the text does not show this clearly]. 60 The women changed their attire for a sober one, and they all went out. And when they saw Philip, he shone with a great light, so that they were afraid. 61 But he saw it, and returned to his former likeness: and Nerkela asked pardon of him and made him welcome. 62, 63 And they professed belief and were instructed and baptized.

VI. *In Nicatera, a city of Greece.*

64 The Jews and heathens were displeased at Ireus' conversion, 65 and sent seven men to his house. A handmaid told him of them; he came out smiling and asked their errand. 'The whole city wishes to see you.' He followed them. 66 And the assembly were surprised at his modest garb. One Onesimus asked him to explain about the sorcerer Philip. 67 *Ireus*: Why am I examined thus? do not trouble Philip. 68 But they said: Away with him. And Ireus went home and met Philip, who said: Are you afraid? No, he said. 69 The people now came with staves, crying out: Give us the deceiver. 70 Philip came forth and they took him to the assembly to scourge him, and said: Bind him hand and foot. 71 Ireus ran up the steps and cried: You shall not. But they would not hear, and Ireus pulled Philip away from them. 72 Philip said: If I choose, I can blind you. Aristarchus, son of Plegenes, a chief of the Jews, said: Do not be in a hurry to blind us: I know you can; but let us discuss, I am powerful, and if I let the people, they will stone you.

73 And he caught Philip by the beard; he was rather angry, because of the people, and said: Your hand and your ears and your right eye shall suffer for threatening me and insulting God. 74 His eye became hollow as if absent, his ears pained him, his right hand dangled useless. He cried out for mercy. 75 They all said: Heal our chief. 76 Philip told Ireus to go sign him with the cross and heal him in Jesus' name, which was done, and he asked pardon and indulgence and leave to discuss the matter. And the people said: We will judge of it. 77 Philip smiled and bade him speak first. He said: Do you receive the prophets or no? *Philip*: Because of your unbelief there is need of the prophets. *Aristarchus*: It is written: Who shall declare thy might, O God? and, No man can know thy glory; and, Thy glory hath filled the earth; and, The Lord is judge of quick and dead; and, God is a consuming fire and shall burn up his enemies on every side; and, One God hath made all these things. How then say you that Mary bore Jesus? . . . But you will say that he is the power and wisdom of God who was with him when he made the world. I do not deny that the first Scripture says: Let us make man. 78 Philip smiled and said: Hearken all: Isaiah said, Behold my servant (child) whom I have chosen. . . . And of the cross: He was led as a sheep to the slaughter. . . . And again: I gave my back to the scourger. . . . And another: I spread out my hands to a disobedient people. And: I was found of them that sought me not. . . . And David saith: Thou art my son. . . . And of his resurrection and Judas: Lord, why are they increased that trouble me. . . . And again David: I foresaw the Lord alway before me. . . . But David is dead. Take also of the twelve prophets: Say unto the daughter of Sion. . . . And: Out of Egypt have I called my son.

79 Aristarchus said: This Jesus is called Christ. Isaiah: Thus saith the Lord unto Christ my lord. . . . The Jews said: You are arguing for Christ. The people and rulers acclaimed Philip and said he should be received.

80 A bier was brought with a dead man, only son of a rich man: and with it ten slaves who were to be burnt with the corpse. The people said: Here is a great contest for the Christians. If theirs be God he will raise him and we will believe, and burn our idols. 81 Philip said to the parents: What will you do if I raise him? 'What you will.' The slaves made signs to him to remember them. There was this evil law of burning slaves, and sometimes even men's wives. 82 Philip said: Give me these slaves. 'Yes, and any more that you will.' He said to Aristarchus: Come, O Jew, raise him. And he touched his face and spat much on him and pulled his hand: in vain, and retired in confusion. 83 Nereus the father said: Raise my son and I will fight the Jews. *Philip*: If you will not promise not to hurt them, I will not raise him. *N.* As you will. 84 Philip went to the bier and

prayed, and breath entered into the lad Theophilus, and he opened his eyes and looked on Philip. A second time Philip said: Young man, in the name of Jesus Christ who was crucified under Pontius Pilate, arise. And he leapt from the bier. All cried: One is the God of Philip . . . and the slaves were made free. All believed. 86 Philip taught, baptized, destroyed idols, ordained, gave canons and rules.

VII. *Of Nerkela (and) Ireus at Nicatera.*

87 Nerkela and Artemela were blessed by Philip. 88 Ireus and Nereus consulted about building a church, and agreed to build it on Nereus' land. 89 Only the Jews were discontented, and decided to withdraw. 90 Philip came to the new building and addressed the people, 91 and made Ireus bishop and prayed over him, and announced that he was going away. 92 All wept, but he consoled them. 93 They loaded camels with provisions and accompanied him 20 stadia. He dismissed them and would only take five loaves: They all saluted him thrice, and fell on their faces and prayed for his blessing, and watched him out of sight, and returned to the city.

VIII. *Wherein the kid and the leopard in the wilderness believed.*

94 It came to pass when the Saviour divided the apostles and each went forth according to his lot, that it fell to Philip to go to the country of the Greeks: and he thought it hard, and wept. And Mariamne his sister (it was she that made ready the bread and salt at the breaking of bread, but Martha was she that ministered to the multitudes and laboured much) seeing it, went to Jesus and said: Lord, seest thou not how my brother is vexed? 95 And he said: I know, thou chosen among women; but go with him and encourage him, for I know that he is a wrathful and rash man, and if we let him go alone he will bring many retributions on men. But lo, I will send Bartholomew and John to suffer hardships in the same city, because of the much wickedness of them that dwell there; for they worship the viper, the mother of snakes. And do thou change thy woman's aspect and go with Philip. And to Philip he said: Why art thou fearful? for I am always with thee.

96 So they all set out for the land of the Ophiani; and when they came to the wilderness of dragons, lo, a great leopard came out of a wood on the hill, and ran and cast himself at their feet and spoke with human voice: I worship you, servants of the divine greatness and apostles of the only-begotten Son of God; command me to speak perfectly. 97 And Philip said: In the name of Jesus Christ, speak. And the leopard took perfect speech and said: Hear me Philip, groomsman of the divine word. Last night I passed through the flocks of goats over against the mount of the she-dragon, the mother of snakes,

and seized a kid; and when I went into the wood to eat, after I had wounded it, it took a human voice and wept like a little child, saying to me: O leopard, put off thy fierce heart and the beastlike part of thy nature, and put on mildness, for the apostles of the divine greatness are about to pass through this desert, to accomplish perfectly the promise of the glory of the only-begotten Son of God. At these words of the kid I was perplexed, and gradually my heart was changed, and my fierceness turned to mildness, and I did not eat it. And as I listened to its words, I lifted up my eyes and saw you coming, and knew that ye were the servants of the good God. So I left the kid and came to worship you. And now I beseech thee to give me liberty to go with thee everywhere and put off my beastlike nature.

98 And Philip said: Where is the kid? And he said: It is cast down under the oak opposite. Philip said to Bartholomew: Let us go and see him that was smitten, healed, and healing the smiter. And at Philip's bidding the leopard guided them to where the kid lay. 99 Philip and Bartholomew said: Now know we of a truth that there is none that surpasseth thy compassion, O Jesu, lover of man; for thou preventest us and dost convince us by these creatures to believe more and earnestly fulfil our trust. Now therefore, Lord Jesu Christ, come and grant life and breath and secure footing (existence?) to these creatures, that they may forsake their nature of beast and cattle and come unto tameness, and no longer eat flesh, nor the kid the food of cattle; but that men's hearts may be given them, and they may follow us wherever we go, and eat what we eat, to thy glory, and speak after the manner of men, glorifying thy name.

100 And in that hour the leopard and kid rose up and lifted up their forefeet and said: We glorify and bless thee that hast visited and remembered us in this desert, and changed our beastlike and wild nature into tameness, and granted us the divine word, and put in us a tongue and sense to speak and praise thy name, for great is thy glory. 101 And they fell and worshipped Philip and Bartholomew and Mariamne; and all set out together, praising God.

IX. *Of the dragon that was slain.*

102 They journeyed five days, and one morning after the midnight prayers a sudden wind arose, great and dark (misty), and out of it ran a great smoky (misty) dragon, with a black back, and a belly like coals of brass in sparkles of fire, and a body over 100 cubits long, and a multitude of snakes and their young followed it, and the desert quaked for a long distance. 103 And Philip said: Now is the time to remember the Lord's words: Fear nothing, neither persecution, nor the serpents of that land, nor the dark dragon. Let us stand fast and his power will fail; and pray and sprinkle the air from the cup and the smoke will

scatter. 104 So they took the cup and prayed: Thou that
sheddest dew on all pyres and bridlest darkness, putting a bit
into the dragon's mouth, bringing to nought his anger, turning
back the wickedness of the enemy and plunging him into his own
fire, shutting his doors and stopping the exits and buffeting his
pride: come and be with us in this desert, for we run by thy will
and at thy bidding. 105 And he said: Now stand and raise
your hands, with the cup you hold, and sprinkle the air in the
form of the cross. 106 And there was as a flash of lightning
which blinded the dragon and its brood; and they were withered
up; and the rays of the sun entered the holes and broke the eggs.
But the apostles closed their eyes, unable to face the lightning,
and remained unhurt.

It does not seem as if much could have intervened between this
Act and the Martyrdom, except perhaps the conversion of some people
in the snake-city. However, the manuscripts give a title thus:

*Out of the Travels of Philip the Apostle : from the fifteenth Act to
the end, wherein is the Martyrdom.*

107 (Introductory.) In the days of Trajan, after the Martyrdom
of Simon, son of Clopas, bishop of Jerusalem, successor to James,
Philip the apostle was preaching through all the cities of Lydia
and Asia. 108 And he came to the city Ophioryme (Snake-
street), which is called Hierapolis of Asia, and was received by
Stachys,[1] a believer. And with him were Bartholomew, one of
the Seventy, and his sister Mariamne, and their disciples. And
they assembled at Stachys' house. 109 And Mariamne sat and
listened to Philip discoursing. 110–112 He spoke of the snares of
the dragon, who has ' no shape' in creation, and is recognized and
shunned by beasts and birds. 113 For the men of the place
worshipped the snake and had images of it; and called Hierapolis
Ophioryme. And many were converted. 114 And Nicanora
the proconsul's wife believed; she was diseased, especially in
her eyes, and had been healed. She now came in a silver litter.
115 And Mariamne said in Hebrew: Alikaman, ikasame, marmari,
iachaman, mastranan, achaman, which means: O daughter of
the father, my lady, who wast given as a pledge to the serpent,
Christ is come to thee (and much more). 116 And Nicanora said:
I am a Hebrew, speak to me in my fathers' tongue. I heard of
your preaching and was healed. 117 And they prayed for her.
118 But her tyrant husband came and said: How is this? who
has healed you? 119 And she said: Depart from me, and lead
a chaste and sober life. 120 And he dragged her by the hair and
threatened to kill her. And the apostles were arrested, 121 and
scourged and dragged to the temple, 122 and shut up in it

[1] One manuscript tells that he had been cured of blindness that
lasted forty years.

(with the leopard and the kid. These are omitted in the principal text, but constantly occur in another recension: rightly, of course). 123 The people and priests came and demanded vengeance on the sorcerers. 124 The proconsul was afraid of his wife, for he had been almost blinded by a wonderful light when he looked through the window at her when praying. 125 They stripped and searched the apostles for charms, and pierced Philip's ankles and thighs and hung him head downward, and Bartholomew they hung naked by the hair. 126 And they smiled on each other, as not being tormented. But Mariamne on being stripped became like an ark of glass full of light and fire, and every one ran away. 127 And Philip and Bartholomew talked in Hebrew, and Philip said: Shall we call down fire from heaven? 128 And now John arrived, and asked what was happening, and the people told him. 129 And he was taken to the place. Philip said to Bartholomew in Hebrew: Here is John the son of Barĕga (or, he that is in Barek), that is (or, where is) the living water. And John said: The mystery of him that hanged between the heaven and the earth be with you.

130 Then John addressed the people, warning them against the serpent. *Inter alia*: When all matter was wrought and spread out throughout the system of heaven, the works of God entreated God that they might see his glory: and when they saw it, their desire became gall and bitterness, and the earth became the storehouse of that which went astray, and the result and the superfluity of the creation was gathered together and became like an egg: and the serpent was born.

131 The people said : We took you for a fellow citizen, but you are in league with these men. The priests are going to wring out your blood and mix it with wine and give it to the Viper. When they came to take John their hands were paralysed. John said to Philip: Let us not render evil for evil. Philip said: I shall endure it no longer. 132 The three others dissuaded him ; but he said: Abalo, arimouni, douthael, tharseleën, nachaoth, aeidounaph, teleteloein, which is (after many invocations descriptive of God): let the deep open and swallow these men: yea, Sabaoth. 133 It opened and the whole place was swallowed, about 7,000 men, save where the apostles were. And their voices came up, crying for mercy and saying: Lo, the cross enlighteneth us. And a voice was heard: I will have mercy on you in my cross of light. 134 But Stachys and his house, and Nicanora, and 50 others, and 100 virgins remained safe. 135 Jesus appeared and rebuked Philip. 136 But he defended himself. 137 And the Lord said: Since you have been unforgiving and wrathful, you shall indeed die in glory and be taken by angels to paradise, but shall remain outside it forty days, in fear of the flaming sword, and then I will send Michael and he shall let you in. And Bartholomew shall go to Lycaonia and be crucified there, and

Mariamne's body shall be laid up in the river Jordan. And I shall bring back those who have been swallowed up. 138 And he drew a cross in the air, reaching down into the abyss, and it was filled with light, and the cross was like a ladder. And Jesus called the people, and they all came up, save the proconsul and the Viper. And seeing the apostles they mourned and repented. 139 And Philip, still hanging, spoke to them and told them of his offence. 140 And some ran to take him down: but he refused and spoke to them. . . . " Be not grieved that I hang thus, for I bear the form (type) of the first man, who was brought upon earth head downwards, and again by the tree of the cross made alive from the death of his transgression. And now do I fulfil the precept. For the Lord said to me: Unless ye make that which is beneath to be above, and the left to be right (and the right left), ye shall not enter into my kingdom. Be like me in this: for all the world is turned the wrong way, and every soul that is in it." 141 Further he spoke to them of the incarnation, 142 and bade them loose Bartholomew, and told him and Mariamne of their destiny. Build a church in the place where I die, and let the leopard and kid be there, and let Nicanora look after them till they die, and then bury them at the church gate: and let your peace be in the house of Stachys: and he exhorted them to purity. " Therefore our brother Peter fled from every place where a woman was: and further, he had offence given by reason of his own daughter. And he prayed the Lord, and she had a palsy of the side that she might not be led astray." 143 Bury me not in linen like the Lord, but in papyrus, and pray for me forty days. Where my blood is dropping a vine will grow, and ye shall use the wine of it for the cup: and partake of it on the third day. 144 And he prayed the Lord to receive him, and protect him against all enemies. "Let not their dark air cover me, that I may pass the waters of fire and all the abyss. Clothe me in thy glorious robe and thy seal of light that ever shineth, until I have passed by all the rulers of the world and the evil dragon that opposeth us." 145 And he died. 146 And they buried him as he directed. And a heavenly voice said he had received the crown.

147 After three days the vine grew up. And they made the offering daily for forty days, and built the church and made Stachys bishop. And all the city believed. 148 And at the end of forty days the Saviour appeared in the form of Philip and told Bartholomew and Mariamne that he had entered paradise, and bade them go their ways. And Bartholomew went to Lycaonia and Mariamne to Jordan, and Stachys and the brethren abode where they were.

The narrative of the Act preserved in Syriac is this.

Philip, at Jerusalem, had a vision of Jesus, who commanded him to go to the city of Carthage, ' which is in Azotus ', and drive out the ruler of Satan, and preach the kingdom. He said:

I know not Latin or Greek, and the people there do not know Aramaic. Jesus said: Did I not create Adam and give him speech? Go, and I will be with thee.

He went to Samaria, thence to Caesarea, and to the harbour, and found a ship waiting for a wind. Asked to take Philip to Carthage, the captain said: Do not annoy me; we have waited twenty days: fetch your baggage and perhaps we shall get a wind, for you look like a servant of God. Philip: I have none; tell the passengers to come on board. . . . Let us pray for a fair wind. Turning to the west he commanded the angel of peace who has charge of fair winds to send a wind to take him to Carthage in a single day.

On board was a Jew, Ananias, who blasphemed (*sotto voce*, it seems) and said: May Adonai recompense thee, and the Christ on whom thou callest, who is become dust and lies in Jerusalem, while thou livest and leadest ignorant men astray by his name.

A wind came and filled the sail. The Jew rose to help to hoist the sail, and an angel bound him by the great toes and hung him head down on the top of the sail. The ship flew onward and the Jew cried out. Philip said: You shall not come down till you confess. He confessed his secret blasphemy. Philip: Dost thou now believe? Ananias confessed belief in a speech in which he enumerated Christ's (God's) mighty acts from creation to the deliverance of Susanna. Philip asked that he might be pardoned, and the angel brought him down. And the 495 men on the ship feared.

They looked up and saw the pharos of Carthage, and said : Can this be true ? O fools, said Ananias, did ye not see what befell me for unbelief ? If he commands that city in Christ's name, it will take all its inhabitants and go and stop in Egypt. The ship came into harbour. Philip dismissed the passengers, and stayed on board to confirm the captain.

On the Sunday he went up to the city to drive out Satan, and as he entered the gates, signed himself with the cross. He saw a black man on a throne with two serpents about his loins, and eyes like coals of fire, and flame coming from his mouth; there was a smell of smoke, and black men in troops were on his right and left. When Philip crossed himself the ruler fell backward, and all his troops. Philip said: Fall, and rise not. . . . The ruler said: Why curse me ? I do not abide here, but my troops wander over the earth and come to me at the third hour of the day, but they do not touch a disciple of Jesus. Woe is me! whither can I go ? In all the four quarters of the world his gospel is preached. I am completely overthrown.

The whole city heard him, but saw him not. Philip bade him go, and he took his throne and his troops and flew away bewailing till they came to Babel, and he settled there. The whole city was in fear, and Philip bade them leave their idols and turn to God. They praised God, and Philip went back to the ship.

On the Sabbath the Jews assembled in their synagogue and summoned Ananias, and asked if his adventures were true. He signed himself with the cross and said: It is true, and God forbid I should renounce Jesus the Christ. He then addressed them in a long and very abusive speech (modelled more or less on that of Stephen), enumerating all their wicked acts. 'Then arose Joshua, the son of Nun, and ye sought to kill him with deadly poison. . . . Isaiah the prophet, and ye sawed him with a saw of boxwood. . . . Ezekiel, and ye dragged him by his feet until his brains were dashed out. . . . Habakkuk, and through your sins he went astray from his prophetic office.' His face was like an angel. A priest arose and kicked him, and he died, and they buried him in the synagogue.

Next day Philip in the ship prayed and asked that Ananias might be delivered from the Jews. God commanded the earth and it gave a passage like a water-pipe, and conveyed Ananias to the bottom of the sea, and a dolphin bore up the body. Philip saw it, and after reassuring the people, bade it take the body back till he should go and convict the murderers.

Next day Philip went to the governor and got him to assemble all the Jews, and sit in judgement. Philip, to the Jews: Where is Ananias? They: Are we his keeper? Philip: Well are you called children of Cain, for, &c. Tell me where he is, and I will ask pardon for you. Jews: We have said we do not know. Philip: Do not lie. Jews: If the spirit were in you, you would know that we do not lie. Philip: If he is found with you, what do you deserve? Jews: Death from God and Caesar. Philip: Swear to me. They swore they knew nothing.

He looked and saw a man leading a sick ox to sell. He said to it: I command thee, go to the synagogue and call Ananias to rise and come and put these men to shame. The ox dragged his owner along and ran and called Ananias. He rose and laid hold of the ox with his right hand, and they came to Philip and prostrated themselves. Philip said: Whence comest thou? Ananias said: From the synagogue of these Jews, who murdered me for confessing Jesus: do me justice. Philip: The Lord has commanded us not to render evil for evil. The ox said: Order me and I will kill these men with my horns. Philip: Hurt no man, but go and serve thy master, and the Lord will heal thee. They went home in peace.

The governor said: These Jews deserve death. Philip: I am not come to kill but to give life. The Jews' mouths were closed.

Ananias spoke to the Jews and Philip also: but they did not ask pardon; so they were cast out. Three thousand Gentiles and fifteen hundred Jews believed; the unbelievers left the city, and before sunset an angel slew forty of the Jewish priests for shedding innocent blood: and all who saw it confessed and worshipped.

It is not clear, in the present state of our texts, where this episode could be fitted in to the Greek Acts. The Third Act, which has a voyage to Azotus, seems a possible place. But a glance at the Greek Acts shows that in spite of the appearance of method imparted by a division into Acts, there is no coherence at all in them, until we get to the city of the snake.

The first Act cannot have begun so abruptly as it now does. The second is equally abrupt in its introduction. The third is linked to it by the mention of Parthia, but there is great inconsequence in it, for it presupposes that Philip has done nothing as yet. The fourth is linked to the third by the scene, Azotus. The fifth, sixth, and seventh, at Nicatera, are wholly detached from what has gone before, and with the ninth we make a fresh start.

The next, and most famous of the secondary romances, is the

ACTS OF ANDREW AND MATTHIAS (MATTHEW)

which we have in Greek and Syriac and in part in Latin. The Anglo-Saxon poem, *Andreas*, by Cynewulf (?), preserved in the Vercelli MS., has given an unwonted celebrity to the story.

It was long thought that this must be an episode from the old Acts of Andrew: but Flamion's study of that book has finally made it clear that there is no place for the tale in those Acts: and that our story is an early member of that which we call the Egyptian cycle: it is a tale of wonder with no doctrinal purpose.

1 At that time all the apostles were gathered together and divided the countries among themselves, casting lots. And it fell to Matthias to go to the land of the anthropophagi. Now the men of that city ate no bread nor drank wine, but ate the flesh and drank the blood of men; and every stranger who landed there they took, and put out his eyes, and gave him a magic drink which took away his understanding. 2 So when Matthias arrived he was so treated; but the drink had no effect on him, and he remained praying for help in the prison. 3 And a light came and a voice: Matthias, my beloved, receive sight. And he saw. And the voice continued: I will not forsake thee: abide twenty-seven days, and I will send Andrew to deliver thee and all the rest. And the Saviour went up into heaven. Matthias remained singing praises; when the executioners came to take victims, he kept his eyes closed. They came and looked at the ticket on his hand and said: Three days more and we will slay him. For every victim had a ticket tied on his hand to show the date when his thirty days would be fulfilled.

4 When twenty-seven days had elapsed, the Lord appeared to Andrew in the country where he was teaching and said: In three days Matthias is to be slain by the man-eaters; go and deliver him. 'How is it possible for me to get there in time?' 'Early to-morrow, go to the shore and you will find a ship.' And he left him.

5 They went, Andrew and his disciples, and found a little boat and three men. The pilot was the Lord, and the other two were angels. Andrew asked whither they were going. 'To the land of the man-eaters.' 'I would go there too.' 'Every man avoids that place; why will you go?' 'I have an errand to do; and if you can, take us.' He said: 'Come on board.' 6 Andrew said: 'I must tell you we have neither money nor victuals.' 'How then do you travel?' 'Our master forbade us to take money and provisions. If you will do us this kindness, tell us: if not, we will look for another ship.' 'If these are your orders, come on board and welcome; I desire truly to have disciples of Jesus on my ship.' So they embarked. 7 Jesus ordered three loaves to be brought, and Andrew summoned his disciples to partake; but they could not answer him, for they were disturbed with the sea. So Andrew explained to the pilot, and he offered to set them ashore: but they refused to leave Andrew. 8 Jesus said: Tell your disciples some of the wonders your master did, to encourage them, for we are going to set sail: so they did, and Jesus steered. And Andrew told the disciples about the stilling of the storm, and prayed in himself that they might sleep: and they fell asleep. 9 Andrew said to Jesus: Tell me your art; sixteen years did I sail the sea, and this is the seventeenth, and I never saw such steering: the ship is as if on land. Jesus said: I, too, have often sailed the sea and been in danger; but because you are a disciple of Jesus, the sea knows you and is still. Andrew praised God that he had met such a man. 10 Jesus said: Tell me why the Jews did not believe on your master. Andrew enumerated the miracles: yet, he said, the Jews did not believe. 'Perhaps he did not do these signs before the high priests?' 11 'Yes, he did, both openly and privately, and they would not believe.' 'What were the signs he did in secret?' 'O man with the spirit of questioning, why do you tempt me thus?' 'I do not tempt you, but my soul rejoices to hear his wonderful works.' 'I will tell you, then. 12 Once when we the twelve went with our Lord to a heathen temple that he might show us the ignorance of the devil, the high priests saw us and said: Why do you follow this man who says he is the Son of God? has God a son? Is not this Joseph and Mary's son, and his brothers are James and Simon? and our hearts were weakened. And Jesus perceived it, and took us apart into the wilderness and did mighty signs [1] and strengthened our faith. And we said to the priests: Come and see; for he has convinced us.

13 'And the priests came to the heathen temple, and Jesus showed us the form of the heavens, "that we might learn whether it were true or no". Thirty men of the people and four priests were with us. On the right and left of the temple Jesus saw two

[1] Have we in the Syriac *Obsequies of the Virgin* a fragment of the story of these signs?

sphinxes carved, and turned to us and said: Behold the form of the heaven: these are like the cherubim and seraphim in heaven. And he said to the sphinx on the right: You semblance of that which is in heaven, made by craftsmen, come down and convince these priests whether I be God or man. 14 It came down and spoke and said: O foolish sons of Israel. This is God who made man. . . . Tell me not that I am a stone image: better are the temples than your synagogue. Our priests purify themselves seven days from women, and approach not the temple: but you come straight from defilement. The temples will abolish your synagogues, and become churches of the only-begotten Son of God. 15 The priests said: It speaks by magic; ye heard it say that this man spake with Abraham. How is that possible? . . . Jesus said to the sphinx: Go to the cave of Mambre and call Abraham; bid him rise with Isaac and Jacob and come to the temples of the Jebusaeans to convict the priests. It went and called, and the twelve patriarchs rose and came out. "To which of us wast thou sent?" "Not to you, but to the three patriarchs: go back and rest." They went back, and the three patriarchs came and convicted the priests. Jesus bade them return, and sent the sphinx back to its place. But the priests did not believe. And many other wonders he did.'

16 Jesus seeing that they were near land, leaned his head on one of the angels and ceased speaking to Andrew: and Andrew went to sleep. Then Jesus bade the angels take the men and lay them outside the city of the man-eaters and return: and then all departed to heaven.

17 Andrew awoke and looked about him and realized what had happened, and roused his disciples. They told him their dream: eagles came and bore them into paradise, and they saw the Lord on his throne, and angels, and the three patriarchs, and David singing, "and you the twelve apostles and twelve angels by you, whom the Lord bade to obey you in everything."

18 Andrew rejoiced and prayed the Lord to show himself: and Jesus appeared in the form of a beautiful young child. Andrew asked pardon for his boldness on the ship. Jesus reassured him and told him what trials awaited him in the city, and encouraged him to endure them, and departed. 19 They entered the city, unseen, and went to the prison. The seven guards fell dead at his prayer: at the sign of the cross the doors opened. He found Matthias and they greeted each other. 20 Andrew looked at the victims, who were naked and eating grass, and smote his breast and reproached the devil: How long warrest thou with men? thou didst cause Adam to be cast out of paradise: thou didst cause his bread that was on the table to be turned to stones.[1] Again, thou didst enter into the mind of the angels

---

[1] An allusion to something in the Penitence of Adam: we have not the complete story.

and cause them to be defiled with women and madest their savage sons the giants to devour men on the earth, so that God sent the flood. . . . 21 Then they both prayed, and they laid their hands on the prisoners and restored first their sight and then their sense, and Andrew bade them go out of the city and remain under a fig-tree and await him: there were 270 men and 49 women. And Andrew commanded a cloud, and it took Matthias and the disciples and brethren to the mount where Peter was teaching, and there they remained.

22 Andrew went out and walked in the city, and sat down by a brazen pillar with a statue on it, to see what would happen. The executioners came and found the prison empty and the guards dead, and reported to the rulers. They said: Go and fetch the seven dead men for us to eat to-day, and assemble, to-morrow, the old men, and we will cast lots for seven a day and eat them, till we can fit out ships and send and collect people to eat. So they fetched the seven corpses; there was a furnace in the midst of the city and a great vat for the blood: they put the men on the vat. A voice came: Andrew, look at this. Andrew prayed, and the men's swords fell and their hands turned to stone. The rulers cried: There are wizards in the city: go and gather the old men, for we are hungry. 23 They found 215, and lots were cast for 7. One of these said: Take my young son and kill him instead of me. They asked leave of the rulers, and it was granted, and the old man said: I have a daughter, take her too, and spare me. So the children were brought to the vat begging for their lives, but there was no pity. Andrew prayed, and again the swords fell from the men's hands; and there was much alarm. 24 Then came the devil in the guise of an old man, and said: Woe to you, you will all die of hunger ; but search now and look for a stranger named Andrew: he is the cause of your trouble. Andrew was looking at the devil, but the devil could not see him. And Andrew said: O Beliar, my lord will humble thee to the abyss. The devil said: I hear your voice and know it; but where you stand I see not. Andrew said: Art thou not called Amaël because thou art blind ? The devil said: Look for the man who spake to me, for it is he. And they shut the gates and looked everywhere, but could not find him. The Lord appeared and said to Andrew: Show thyself to them. 25 He rose and said: I am Andrew whom ye seek. And they ran and took him, and debated how to kill him: If we cut off his head, it will not pain him enough. Let us put a rope round his neck and drag him through the streets every day till he dies, and divide his body and eat it. They did so, and his flesh was torn and his blood flowed, and they cast him into prison with his hands bound behind him. 26 And so they did next day, and he wept and cried to the Lord: and the devil told the people to smite his mouth that he might not

speak; and they bound his hands behind him and left him in
the prison. The devil took seven other devils, whom Andrew
had driven out from places in the neighbourhood (this seems like
a reference to the older Acts), and they came to Andrew, and the
devil said: Now we will kill you like your master whom Herod
slew. 27 And he said: Now my children, kill him. But they
saw the seal on his forehead and were afraid, and said: Do you
kill him, for we cannot. And one of them said: If we cannot kill
him, let us mock him; and they stood before him and taunted
him with his helplessness, and he wept. And a voice—the devil's
voice disguised—said: Why weep? Andrew said: Because of our
Lord's word: Have patience with them; otherwise I would have
shown you! . . . But if the Lord grant me a visitation in this
city, I will chastise you as you deserve. And they fled. 28 Next
day the people dragged him again, and he cried out to the Lord:
Where are thy words: A hair of your heads shall not perish?
lo, my flesh is torn from me. And a voice said in Hebrew: My
words shall not pass away: look behind thee. And he saw great
fruit-bearing trees growing up where his flesh and blood had
fallen. And they took him back to prison, and said: Perhaps he
will die to-morrow. 29 And the Lord came and took his hand
and he rose up whole. And in the prison was a pillar, and on it
a statue. Andrew went to it and spread out his hands seven
times and said: Fear thou the sign of the cross, and let this
statue pour forth water as a flood. And say not, I am but a stone,
for God made us of earth, but ye are clean, and therefore God
gave his people the law on tables of stone. And the statue
poured water out of its mouth as from a canal, and it was bitter
and corroded men's flesh. 30 In the morning all the people
began to flee. The water killed their cattle and their children.
Andrew said: Let Michael wall the city about with fire. A cloud
of fire came and surrounded it, and they could not escape.
The water came up to their necks and consumed their flesh.
They cried and lamented till he saw their spirit was crushed,
and told the alabaster statue to cease. And Andrew went out
of the prison, the water parting before him, and the people
prayed for mercy. 31 The old man who had given up his children
came and besought. But Andrew said: I wonder at you; you
and the fourteen executioners shall be swallowed up and see
the places of torment and of peace. And he went as far as the
great vat, and prayed, and the earth opened and swallowed the
water and the old man and the executioners. And all feared
greatly, but he consoled them. 32 Then he bade them bring
all who had been killed by the water, but there were too many,
so he prayed and revived them. Then he drew out the plan of
a church, and baptized them and gave them the Lord's precepts.
And they begged him to stay with them a little; but he refused,
saying: I must first go to my disciples; and he set forth, and

they lamented grievously. 33 And Jesus appeared in the form
of a beautiful child and reproved him for leaving them, and told
him to stay seven days; and then he should go with his disciples
to the country of the barbarians, and then return and bring the
men out of the abyss. And he returned and they all rejoiced
greatly.

Whether originally intended to be so or not, there is a sequel to this
tale in the

ACTS OF PETER AND ANDREW

which we have in Greek and Slavonic and—told of Thaddaeus instead
of Andrew—in Ethiopic, where it forms part of the Egyptian cycle.

1 When Andrew left the city of the man-eaters, a cloud of
light took him up and carried him to the mountain where Peter
and Matthias and Alexander and Rufus were sitting. And Peter
said: Have you prospered? Yes, he said, but they did me much
hurt. Come then, said Peter, and rest awhile from your labours.
2 And Jesus appeared in the form of a little child and greeted
them, and told them to go to the city of the barbarians, and
promised to be with them, and left them.

3 So the four set out. And when they were near the city Andrew
asked Peter: Do many troubles await us here? ' I do not know,
but here is an old man sowing. Let us ask him for bread; if he
gives it us, we shall know that we are not to be troubled, but if
he says, I have none, troubles await us.' They greeted him and
asked accordingly. He said: If you will look after my plough
and oxen I will fetch you bread. . . . 'Are they your oxen?' 'No,
I have hired them.' And he went off. 4 Peter took off his
cloak and garment, and said: It is no time for us to be idle,
especially as the old man is working for us; and he took the
plough and began to sow. Andrew protested and took it from
him and sowed, and blessed the seed as he sowed. And Rufus and
Alexander and Matthias, going on the right, said: Let the sweet
dew and the fair wind come and rest on this field. And the
seed sprang up and the corn ripened. 5 When the farmer
returned with the bread and saw the ripe corn he worshipped
them as gods. But they told him who they were, and Peter gave
him the Commandments. . . . He said: I will leave all and
follow you. 'Not so, but go to the city, return your oxen to the
owner, and tell your wife and children and prepare us a lodging.'
6 He took a sheaf, hung it on his staff, and went off. The people
asked where he got the corn, for it was the time of sowing, but
he hastened home. 7 The chief men of the city heard of it and
sent for him and made him tell his story. 8 And the devil
entered them and they said: Alas! these are of the twelve
Galilaeans who go about separating men from their wives,

What are we to do? 9 One of them said: I can keep them out
of the city? 'How?' 'They hate all women, and specially unchaste
ones: let us put a naked wanton in the gate, and they will see
her and flee.' So they did. 10 The apostles perceived the snare
by the spirit, and Andrew said: Bid me, and I will chastise her.
Peter said: Do as you will. Andrew prayed, and Michael was
sent to catch her up by the hair and suspend her till they had
passed. 11 And she cried out, cursing the men of the city and
praying for pardon. 12 And many believed at her word and
worshipped the apostles, and they did many cures, and all
praised God.

13 There was a rich man named Onesiphorus who said: If
I believe, shall I be able to do wonders? Andrew said: Yes, if
you forsake your wife and all your possessions. He was angry
and put his garment about Andrew's neck and began to beat
him, saying: You are a wizard, why should I do so? 14 Peter
saw it and told him to leave off. He said: I see you are wiser
than he. What do *you* say? Peter said: I tell you this: it is
easier for a camel to go through a needle's eye than for a rich
man to enter the kingdom of God. Onesiphorus was yet more
angry, and took his garment off Andrew's neck and cast it on
Peter's and haled him along, saying: You are worse than the
other. If you show me this sign, I and the whole city will believe,
but if not you shall be punished. 15 Peter was troubled and
stood and prayed: Lord, help us at this hour, for thou hast
entrapped us by thy words. 16 The Saviour appeared in the
form of a boy of twelve years, wearing a linen garment 'smooth
within and without', and said: Fear not: let the needle and the
camel be brought. There was a huckster in the town who had
been converted by Philip; and he heard of it, and looked for a
needle with a large eye, but Peter said: Nothing is impossible
with God; rather bring a needle with a small eye. 17 When it
was brought, Peter saw a camel coming and stuck the needle in
the ground and cried: In the name of Jesus Christ crucified
under Pontius Pilate I command thee, camel, to go through the
eye of the needle. The eye opened like a gate and the camel
passed through; and yet again, at Peter's bidding. 18 Onesiphorus
said: You are a great sorcerer: but I shall not believe unless
I may send for a needle and a camel. And he said secretly to
a servant: Bring a camel and a needle, and find a defiled woman
and some swine's flesh and bring them too. And Peter heard
it in the spirit and said: O slow to believe, bring your camel and
woman and needle and flesh. 19 When they were brought,
Peter stuck the needle in the ground, with the flesh; the woman
was on the camel. He commanded it as before, and the camel
went through, and back again. 20 Onesiphorus cried out, convinced, and said: Listen. I have lands and vineyards, and
27 litrae of gold and 50 of silver, and many slaves: I will give

my goods to the poor and free my slaves if I may do a wonder like you. Peter said: If you believe, you shall. 21 Yet he was afraid he might not be able, because he was not baptized ; but a voice came: Let him do what he will. So Onesiphorus stood before the needle and camel and commanded it to go through, and it went as far as the neck and stopped. And he asked why. 'Because you are not yet baptized.' He was content, and the apostles went to his house, and 1,000 souls were baptized that night. 22 Next day the woman that was hung in the air said: Alas that I am not worthy to believe like the rest! I will give all my goods to the poor and my house for a monastery of virgins. Peter heard it and went out to her, and at his word she was let down unhurt, and gave him for the poor 4 litrae of gold and much raiment and her house for a monastery of virgins. 23 And the apostles consecrated a church and ordained clergy and committed the people to God.

THE MARTYRDOM OF MATTHEW

will be treated more shortly. It is evidently pretty late, and it starts with a perversion of the Acts of Andrew and Matthias, for it assumes that Matthew and not Matthias was Andrew's colleague among the man-eaters; and it would seem that very little had been done in the way of converting them.

The beginning also seems to imply a previous story, a vision of the Innocents in Paradise.

1 The holy Matthew remained alone on the Mount praying, in the apostolic robe, barefoot, and Jesus appeared to him in the form of one of the children that were singing in Paradise. 2 A dialogue. 3 Matthew said: That I saw thee in paradise singing with the other children that were slain at Bethlehem I know; but how thou camest hither so quickly, I marvel. But tell me, where is that ungodly Herod ? ' He dwelleth in hell, and there is prepared for him fire unquenchable, unending gehenna, boiling mire, the worm that sleepeth not, because he killed 3,000 children. 4 Now take my staff and go to Myrna the city of the man-eaters, and plant it at the gate of the church which you and Andrew founded. It will become a tree, and a spring will rise at its foot, and the man-eaters will eat of the tree and wash in the spring, and their bodies will be changed and they will be ashamed of their nakedness, and use fire to cook their food, and learn to know me.' 5 At the city gate he was met by Phulbana the king's wife, Phulbanos his son and Erba his wife, all possessed by devils—and the devils cried out and threatened Matthew that they would rouse the king against him. He cast them out. 6 The bishop Plato heard and came out to meet him with the clergy. And Matthew preached to the people, 7 and planted the staff. And the people became

humanized. 8 He baptized the queen and the rest. 9 At dawn the staff was become a tree. 10 Phulbanus the king was pleased with all this at first, but when they refused to quit Matthew he resolved to burn him. 11 Matthew had a consoling vision, and warned the people of his death. 12 The devil whom he had cast out disguised himself as a soldier and went to the king, and advised him to seize Matthew. 13 He sent four soldiers, who could only hear two men talking (Matthew and Plato), and then ten, who were routed by seeing a child with a torch. 14 The devil described to the king the difficulty of seizing Matthew, and all that he could do. The king said : Take him yourself. I cannot, for he has destroyed all our race. 15 Who, then, are you ? said the king. I am the demon Asmodaeus who was in your wife. The king adjured him to depart without harming any one, and he vanished as smoke. 16 That day the king remained quiet, but next day took two soldiers and went to the church and sent for Matthew. 17 He came out with Plato, but the king could not see him. Matthew opened his eyes. 18 The king treacherously led him to the palace. They pinned him hand and foot to the earth and covered him with papyrus soaked in dolphin oil, and poured brimstone, asphalt, and pitch on him, and heaped up tow and wood. 19 And the fire turned to dew, and all the people praised God. 20 Much charcoal from the royal baths was brought, and the twelve gods of gold and silver were set round the fire. 21 Matthew looking up to heaven, cried: Adonai Eloï Sabaoth marmari marmounth. The fire blazed up, and the king said: Where is now your magic ? But all the fire flew out about the idols and melted them—whose weight was 1,000 talents of gold. And the king lamented that gods of stone and clay were superior. 22 The fire burnt up many soldiers, and then took the form of a dragon and chased the king to the palace, and curled round so that he could not go in and made him come back to Matthew, crying for help. Matthew rebuked the fire and prayed, and gave up the ghost.

23 The king had him borne in state to the palace. The body and robes were intact, and sometimes he was seen on the bier, sometimes following or preceding it, and laying his hand on Plato's head. And many sick were healed.

24 When they reached the palace Matthew was seen to rise from the bier and ascend to heaven, led by a beautiful child, and twelve men in crowns, and we saw the child crown him. The king had a coffin made of iron and sealed it with lead, and privately put it on a ship at midnight and sank it in the sea.

25 All night the brethren watched at the palace gate, and at dawn a voice came: Plato, take the gospel and the psalter and go to the east of the palace and sing Alleluia, and read the gospel, and offer of the bread and the vine, pressing three clusters into the cup. and communicate with me, as the Lord Jesus showed

us the offering that is above, on the third day after he rose. So it was done, and the chanter went up on a great stone and sang : Precious in the sight of the Lord. . . . I slept and rose up again. . . . And they answered: Shall not the sleeper awake ? . . . Now will I arise, saith the Lord. Alleluia. They read the gospel and made the offering.

26 It was about the sixth hour, and Plato looked out to sea seven stadia away, and lo, Matthew standing on the sea between two men in bright apparel, and the beautiful child before them. And they said Amen, Alleluia. And the sea was to look upon like a crystal stone, and before the Child a cross came up out of the deep, and at the lower end of it the coffin of Matthew: and in a moment it was set on the land where they were.

27 The king beheld all from a window, and came down and fell at their feet and confessed his sin and his belief. He would give them the palace for a sanctuary, and the coffin should be laid on his golden couch in the great hall. Plato baptized and communicated him. 28 The apostle appeared and said: Thy name shall no more be Bulphamnus but Matthew ; thy son not Bulphandrus but also Matthew ; thy wife Ziphagia, Sophia ; and his wife Orba, Synesis. He ordained the king a priest, being 37. his son a deacon, being 17: his wife a priestess (presbytis) and his son's wife a deaconess, being 17. [29 (in one recension only) : The king destroyed his idols, and issued a decree establishing the new faith.] 30 Matthew bade them offer the offering daily for forty-nine days and repeat it yearly, and told Plato he should join him in three years, and be succeeded by the king, and he by his son. Then with two angels he departed to heaven. 31 And a voice came, promising peace and safety to the city.

His day is the 14th of Gorpiaeus (*al.* 16 November; *Lat.* 11 October).

The most effective part of these Acts is the vision after Matthew's death: the interest in liturgy is quite prominent here.

We will now take a review of the Latin Acts as contained in the

APOSTOLIC HISTORY OF ABDIAS

of which something has already been said.

It is in ten books. Book I treats of St. Peter. Chapters i–v are drawn from the Gospels and Acts; vi–xiv extracted from the Clementine literature; xv, the ordination of Clement; xvi, Paul arrives, and from this to the end (xx) is the contest with Simon and the Martyrdom from the Pseudo-Hegesippus *de excidio Hierosolymae*, lib. iii.

Book II, of Paul: i–vi from the canonical Acts; vii, viii from the Martyrdom.

Book III, of Andrew, is Gregory's book of miracles, and the Passion.

Book IV, of James the Great, gives us new matter, only found here, though doubtless there was a Greek original.

i. Describes James's preaching. ii. In the course of it he was opposed by Hermogenes and Philetus. Philetus was converted by James, and told Hermogenes he should leave him. Hermogenes in anger bound him by magical incantations and said: We will see if James can free you. Philetus found means to send a servant to James, who sent back his kerchief, and by it Philetus was freed and came to James.

iii. Hermogenes in anger sent devils to fetch both James and Philetus to him: but when they got there they began to howl in the air and complain that an angel had bound them with fiery chains. James sent them to bring Hermogenes bound. They tied his arms with ropes and brought him, mocking him. You are a foolish man, said James, but they shall not hurt you. The devils clamoured for leave to avenge themselves on him. Why do you not seize Philetus? said James. We dare not touch so much as an ant in your chamber, they said. James bade Philetus loose Hermogenes, and he stood confounded. Go free, said James, for we do not render evil for evil. I fear the demons, he said. And James gave him his staff to protect him.

iv. Armed with this, he went home and filled baskets with magical books and began to burn them. Not so, said James, lest the smoke vex the unwary ; cast them into the sea. He did so, and returned and begged for pardon. James sent him to undo his former work on those he had deceived, and spend in charity what he had gained by his art. He obeyed, and so grew in faith that he even performed miracles.

v. The Jews bribed two centurions, Lysias and Theocritus, to seize James. And while he was being taken away, there was a dispute between him and the Pharisees. He spoke to them first of Abraham, (vi.) and went on to cite prophecies. Isaiah : Behold a virgin . . . Jeremiah : Behold, thy redeemer shall come, O Jerusalem, and this shall be the sign of him : he shall open the eyes of the blind, restore hearing to the deaf, and raise the dead with his voice. Ezekiel : Thy king shall come, O Zion, he shall come humbly, and restore thee. Daniel : As the son of man, so shall he come and receive princedoms and powers. David : The Lord said unto my Lord . . . Again : He shall call me, thou art my Father . . . I will make him my first-born. Of the fruit of thy body . . . Isaiah again : Like a sheep to the slaughter. David : They pierced my hands . . . They gave me gall . . . My flesh shall rest . . . I will arise and be with thee . . . For the comfortless trouble's sake . . . He is gone up on high . . . God is gone up. He rode on the cherubim . . . The Lord shall come, and shall not keep silence, . . . vii. Isaiah : The dead shall rise. David : God spake once . . . They rewarded me evil for good . . . He that did eat my bread . . . The earth opened and swallowed up Dathan. viii. The people cried out : We have sinned. Abiathar the high priest stirred up a tumult, and a scribe cast a rope about James's neck and dragged him before Herod, who sentenced him to be beheaded. On the way he healed a paralytic.

ix. The scribe, named Josias, was convinced, and prayed for pardon. And Abiathar procured that he should be beheaded with James. Water was brought, James baptized him, they exchanged the kiss of peace, and were beheaded. (The tale of James forgiving his accuser is as old as Clement of Alexandria, who quotes it.)

Book V, of St. John. i. From the Gospels and Acts. ii. The caldron of oil at Ephesus, exile to Patmos, and recall. iii. The story of the robber (Clement of Alexandria the *ultimate* source). iv–xiii. Drusiana. xiv–xviii. Atticus and Eugenius (see above). xix. Destruction of temple of Artemis. xx, xxi. The poison (see above). Assumption of John.

Book VI, of St. James the Less. i–vi. from the Gospels and Acts and from Hegesippus as quoted by Eusebius (Rufinus).

vii sqq. SS. Simon and Jude, going to Persia, found there two magicians, Zaroës and Arfaxat, whom Matthew had driven out of Ethiopia (see the next book). Their doctrines were that the God of the Old Testament was the god of darkness, Moses and the Prophets deceivers, the soul the work of the good God, the body the work of the god of darkness, so that soul and body are contrary to each other: that the sun and moon are gods, and also water: that the incarnation of Christ was in appearance only (in fact, Manichaean doctrine).

viii. On entering the country they met Varardach, the general of King Xerxes, with an army preparing to repel an invasion of India. He had many priests and diviners with him: their gods explained that they could give no answers because of the presence of Simon and Jude. Varardach sent for them and they offered to expound their teaching: he said he would hear them after the campaign. Jude urged him to hear now. He asked them to foretell his success or failure.

ix. Simon said: We will allow your gods to answer your diviners. So they prayed, and the prophets said: There will be a great battle, and many will fall on either side. The apostles laughed, though Varardach was impressed; and they said: The truth is that to-morrow the Indians will send and offer you peace and become tributaries to Persia. After some dispute with the priests it was agreed (x.) that both parties should be kept in custody till the morrow; (xi.) when the apostles' prediction was fulfilled. But they interceded for the priests, whom Varardach would have killed. At least, said he, you will receive their goods. Their pay was reckoned up: 120 talents in all, besides the chief priest's, who had 4 pounds of gold a month: and much raiment, &c. (The apostles' refusal to take this has dropped out, it seems.) xii. On his return, Varardach reported all this to the king; but Zaroës and Arfaxat made light of it, and proposed a test before the apostles came. The lawyers of the land were to be summoned to dispute with them. And first they made them unable to speak, then restored their speech but took away their power of motion, and then made them unable to see. The lawyers retired in confusion. xiv. Varardach told the apostles, and they asked him to send for the lawyers, and proposed a second trial. If the lawyers would believe on their God, they would sign them with the cross and enable them to overcome the wizards. The lawyers were at first inclined to despise them for their mean appearance ; but, convinced by Simon's words, believed. xv. The apostles prayed over them: O God of Israel, who didst do away with the magic illusions of Jannes and Mambres and give them over to confusion and sores and cause them to perish: let thine hand be also on these magicians Zaroës and Arfaxat, &c. The contest took place and the magicians were powerless. One of the lawyers, Zebeus, explained to the king how they were the instruments of the evil angel ; and defied them to do as they had done the day before. xvi. They were enraged and called in a host of snakes. The apostles were hastily summoned, and made the snakes all turn on the magicians and bite them: they howled like wolves. Kill them outright, said the king ; but the apostles refused, and instead made the serpents suck out all their venom, which hurt still more. xvii. And for three days, in the hospital, the wizards continued screaming. When they were on the point of death, the apostles healed them, saying : Our God does not ask for forced service ; if you will not believe, you may go free. They wandered about Persia, slandering the apostles and telling the people to kill them when they came.

xviii. The apostles stayed in Babylon, healing the sick, and ordaining clergy. A deacon was accused of incontinence by the daughter of a satrap who had been seduced by another. The parents clamoured against the deacon Euphrosinus. The apostles sent for the infant who had been born that day, and on their bidding it spoke and cleared Euphrosinus: but the apostles refused to question it about the guilty man.

xix. Two fierce tigers had escaped from their cages and were devouring everybody they met. The apostles, appealed to, made the beasts follow them home, where they stayed three days. Then the apostles called the people together, and announced that they were going to leave them to visit the rest of Persia. On the urgent prayer of the people they stayed fifteen months longer, baptized 60,000 people, (xx) ordained Abdias bishop, and set out, accompanied by many disciples. For thirteen years they travelled, and Craton their disciple recorded their acts in ten books, which Africanus the historian translated into Latin, and from which we have here made extracts.

Zaroës and Arfaxat always went before the apostles and warned people against them, but were as regularly confuted.

At Suanir there were seventy priests who received a pound of gold apiece from the king at each of the feasts of the sun (at the beginning of each of the four seasons). The magicians warned these men that two Hebrews were coming, who would deprive them of all their gains: they should be compelled to sacrifice immediately on their arrival.

xxi. After travelling through all the twelve provinces, the apostles came to Suanir and lodged with a chief citizen, Sennes. The priests and mob flocked thither, crying out: Bring out the enemies of our gods. So they were taken to the temple of the sun ; and as they entered the devils began to cry out that they were being burned. In the east, in the temple, was a four-horse chariot of the sun in silver, and on the other side a four-oxed chariot of the moon, also silver. xxii. The priests would now compel the apostles to sacrifice. Jude said to Simon: I see the Lord calling us. Simon: I see him also among the angels; moreover, an angel has said to me: Go out hence and the temple shall fall, but I said: No, for some here may be converted. As they spoke (in Hebrew) an angel came and said: Choose either the death of all here or the palm of martyrdom. They chose the palm. As the priests pressed on them, they demanded silence. After a few words Simon commanded the devil to leave the chariot of the sun and break it, and Jude spoke likewise of the moon. Two hideous black men appeared and fled howling. The priests and people attacked the apostles and slew them. xxiii. This was on the first of July. Sennes suffered with them. Lightning struck the temple and split it into three pieces and burnt Zaroës and Arfaxat to coal. After three months Xerxes sent and confiscated the priests' goods and translated the bodies to his city, and built a marble basilica, octagonal, and 8 times 80 feet in circumference and 120 feet high, plated with gold inside, and the sarcophagus of silver in the middle. It took three years to build.

Book VII, of St. Matthew. i. He came to Naddaver in Ethiopia, where King Aeglippus reigned. There were two magicians, Zaroës and Arfaxat, who could make men immovable, blind, or deaf as they pleased, and also charmed serpents, like the Marsi. ii. Matthew counteracted all these acts, sent the snakes to sleep, and cured their bites with the cross. A eunuch named Candacis, whom Philip had baptized, took the apostle in, and he did many cures. iii. Candacis asked him how he, a Hebrew, could speak other tongues. Matthew told him the story of Babel and of Pentecost. iv. One came and announced that the magicians were coming with two crested dragons breathing fire and brimstone. Matthew crossed himself and rose to meet them. 'Speak from the window,' said Candacis. 'You can be at the window; I will go out.' When the dragons approached, both fell asleep at Matthew's feet, and he challenged the magicians to rouse them. They could not. Then he adjured them to go quietly and hurt no man, and so they did. v. The apostle then spoke, describing Paradise at length, and (vi) the Fall (the description of Paradise is rather interesting). vii. It was now announced that Euphranor the king's son was dead. The magicians, who could not raise him, said he had been taken up among the gods, and an image and temple ought to be built. Candacis said: Keep these men till Matthew comes. He came: the queen Euphenissa fell at his feet. He consoled her and raised Euphranor. viii. The people came to sacrifice to him as a god. He persuaded them to build a church: 11,000 men did it in thirty days: it was called the Resurrection. Matthew presided there twenty-three years, ordained clergy and founded churches; baptized the king, queen, prince, and princess Ephigenia, who vowed chastity. Zaroës and Arfaxat fled the country. It would be long to tell of all Matthew's cures and miracles: I will proceed to his martyrdom. ix. Aeglippus was succeeded by his brother Hyrtacus, who wished to marry Ephigenia, now presiding over more than 200 sacred virgins. He offered Matthew half his kingdom to persuade her. Matthew said: Assemble all the virgins to-morrow, and you shall hear what good things I will speak of marriage. x. His address on the divine institution and merits of matrimony. xi. Loudly applauded by Hyrtacus and his followers; he then pointed out that it would be sacrilege to marry Ephigenia. Hyrtacus went away in a rage. xii. But Matthew exhorted them not to fear man. xiii. Ephigenia prayed him to consecrate her and the other virgins. And he veiled them (with a long prayer). xiv. And as he stood at the altar praying, a soldier sent by Hyrtacus pierced him in the back and he died. The people threatened to burn the palace, but the clergy restrained them. xv. Ephigenia gave all her wealth to the church. Hyrtacus sent the nobles' wives to her, then tried to send demons to carry her off, then surrounded her house with fire. But an angel, and Matthew, appeared and encouraged her. And a great wind rose and drove all the fire on the palace, and only Hyrtacus and his son escaped. The son was seized by a devil, and rushed to Matthew's tomb and confessed his father's crimes. Hyrtacus was attacked with elephantiasis, and stabbed himself. Beor, the brother of Ephigenia, a Christian, succeeded and reigned twenty-five years, dying at 88, and appointing successors in his lifetime, and he had peace with the Romans and Persians, and all Ethiopia was filled with churches, unto this day.

This and the last book are linked together by the figures of Zaroës and Arfaxat, and strictly *Matthew* should, we see, precede *Simon and Jude*. The discourses in *Matthew* are much longer than in the other; and a certain consciousness of the existence of the Abyssinian church is shown.

Book VIII, of St. Bartholomew. This, as Bonnet has shown, is the original of the Greek Passion, edited by Tischendorf, of which there is but one manuscript, dated 1279. The Latin MSS. go back to the eighth or ninth century.

India is divided into three parts: Bartholomew came thither to a temple of Astaroth, who ceased to answer his worshippers. So they went to another city; and inquired of Beireth (Berith), who said Bartholomew was the cause. What is he like? they asked. 'He has black curly hair, white skin, large eyes, straight nose, his hair covers his ears, his beard long and grizzled, middle height: he wears a white *colobium* with a purple stripe, and a white cloak with four purple 'gems' at the corners: for twenty-six years he has worn these and they never grow old: his shoes have lasted twenty-six years: he prays 100 times a day and 100 times a night: his voice is like a trumpet: angels wait on him: he is always cheerful and knows all languages.' For two days they could not find him, but then he cast a devil out of a man. King Polymius heard of it and sent for him to heal his lunatic daughter who bit every one. She was loosed—the apostle having reassured her keepers—and cured. The king sent camels laden with riches, but the apostle could not be found. Next day, however, he came to the king and expounded the Christian faith, and offered to show him the devil who inhabited his idol. There was a dialogue, in which the demon explained his doings. Bartholomew made the people try to pull the statue down, but they could not. The ropes were removed and he bade the demon leave the statue, which was instantly broken. After a prayer of the apostle, an angel appeared and signed the four corners of the temple with the cross; and then showed them the devil : black, sharp-faced, with long beard, hair to the feet, fiery eyes, breathing flame, spiky wings like a hedgehog, bound with fiery chains; and then the angel sent him away howling. The king and the rest were baptized. But the heathen priests went and complained to his brother Astriges (Astyages), who had Bartholomew brought bound, and questioned him. It was told him that his idol Vualdath had fallen and was broken to pieces, and in anger he had Bartholomew beaten with clubs and beheaded (the Greek puts in 'flayed ', in accordance with the late tradition). And the people buried him honourably, and built a basilica over him. After twenty days Astriges was seized by a devil, and he and all the priests died. And there was great fear, and all believed: the king (Polymius) became bishop and presided twenty years.

Book IX, of Thomas. i. . . . I remember to have read a book in which his journey to India and acts there are set forth; but as it is by many not received because of its wordiness, I will omit what is superfluous and record what is plainly true, agreeable to the reader, and can edify the church. ii–iv. The sale to Abbanes and the marriage feast. v, vi. The palace. vii. Cure of possessed woman. The youth who killed the woman. viii, ix. Siphor's wife and daughter. ix–xi. Mygdonia and Charisius. xii. Tertia

(Treptia) and Zuzanes (who goes with his mother to Mygdonia and is converted with her). xiii. Thomas before Misdaeus. xiv. The iron plates. Thomas is put into the bath-furnace for a night: it cannot be heated: he is brought to the temple of the sun, with its gold four-horsed chariot. xv. Virgins enter, singing and playing. Thomas speaks with the demon in the image. The image is melted. Thomas and the rest are imprisoned. (These chapters are an interpolation.) xvi–xxv, epitomize the old Acts. The great prayer of Thomas immediately precedes his death.

Book X of St. Philip, is quite short. i. He goes to Scythia twenty years after the Ascension. ii. Before a statue of Mars: a great dragon comes out from beneath the statue and kills the priest's son and two tribunes, and makes many ill with its venomous breath. Philip banishes the dragon and raises and heals the dead and sick. iii. He teaches them for a year: they break the image, and many thousands are baptized. After ordaining bishop and clergy he returns to Asia, to Hierapolis, where he extinguishes the malignant heresy of the Ebionites, who said that the Son of God was not born as a man, but took his humanity from the Virgin. iv. And he had two daughters who converted many. Seven days before his death he calls the clergy together, exhorts them, and dies, aged 87, and is buried at Hierapolis, and his two daughters after a few years are laid at his right and left. Where many miracles are done by his intercession.

This is wholly divergent from the Greek accounts. Yet some Western texts, notably those current in Ireland, are aware of the story of his crucifixion at Hierapolis, and blend it awkwardly with the Latin legend.

NOTICES OF MINOR ACTS

Besides the Acts we have dealt with, there are others which demand a brief notice.

The Acts of John by Prochorus the deacon is a Greek romance of considerable length: it has been edited in full by Zahn (*Acta Joannis*). By far the greater part of it is taken up with miracles wrought by John on Patmos. It is not supposed to be earlier than the fifth century at most. Some of the manuscripts have been found to contain large excerpts from the Leucian Acts: the great episodes of Lycomedes, the temple of Artemis, and Drusiana—in fact almost all that we have of the Acts, except the discourse on our Lord's life and passion, and the death of John—have been thus preserved. Prochorus's own stories are not very interesting.

Wright has edited a Syriac history of John, attributed to Eusebius, 'who found it in a Greek book'. The scene is mainly at Ephesus. John takes service at a bath (as he does also in Prochorus), and there is a tale of the death and raising of a young man, Menelaus, which has attracted the attention of a recent anonymous writer on the resurrection—I do not quite know why. There is also a general baptism and a destruction of idols, in consequence of which Nero banishes John, and under stress of a rising recalls him. Finally, at the request of Peter and Paul, John writes his Gospel in one hour. He died at the age of 120. This text exists also in Arabic.

There are also Greek Acts of Barnabas, edited last by Bonnet, of which the interest is strictly local; they describe his travels and death in Cyprus—where they were doubtless written (not earlier than the 3fth century). With them must be classed the lives of other Cypriote saints of the apostolic age, Heraclides of Tamasus and Auxibius of Soli.

Acts of James the Great in Greek (ed. Ebersolt, Paris, 1902) are without interest.

Acts of Thomas in Greek, edited by me from a British Museum MS. (in *Apocr. Anecd.* ii), are a version (probably) of the Acts in the Egyptian cycle, which we have in Ethiopic.

More important, because more widely diffused, are the various late Acts and Passions of Peter and Paul. These occupy a large space in Lipsius's edition, where the following texts are printed :

1. The Passion of Peter, attributed to Linus, Peter's successor in the see of Rome, addressed to the churches of East and West: in Latin. It follows the course of the original Martyrdom, adding some details, e. g. the names of Processus and Martinian, Peter's gaolers, and a vision, when Peter is crucified, of 'angels standing with crowns of the flowers of roses and lilies, and upon the top of the upright cross Peter standing and receiving a book from Christ, and reading from it the words which he was speaking'.

2. The Passion of Paul, by Linus, in Latin. This, again, is the original Martyrdom with a few additions. On the way to execution Paul meets Plautilla, a noble matron, and borrows the kerchief from her head to bind his eyes: she is to wait for him and he will give it back. Returning, the soldiers met Plautilla rejoicing; and when they taunted her, she told them that Paul, with a celestial company, had come to her, and returned the blood-stained kerchief, which she showed them. There is a passage about Seneca, too: see below, p. 480.

In both, the speeches are variously altered and amplified.

The remaining texts all represent Peter and Paul as joining in the contest with Simon, and being martyred at the same time: the older legends making a year intervene between their deaths. We have first:

3. The Passion of Peter and Paul under the name of Marcellus. The Latin text is the better known: there is one manuscript of a Greek form of it. The opening words are *Cum venisset Paulus Romam.*

As in all these texts, there is a good deal about Simon's magic arts. When confronted with the apostles before Nero, he makes large dogs appear and attack the apostles: but Peter has foreseen this, and has some barley bread, which he has blessed, concealed in his sleeve, and, producing it, makes the dogs vanish.

Pilate's letter to Claudius (see p. 146) is produced and read before Nero.

When Simon flies in the air, Peter adjures the demons who are carrying him to let him fall; and his body is broken into four pieces. The death of Nero is mentioned, and an attempt of some devout men from the East to carry off the bodies of the apostles.

4. The Greek Acts of Peter and Paul. This text begins with Paul's

journey from the island of Gaudomelete to Rome. Dioscorus the shipmaster, who was bald like Paul, was arrested in mistake for him at Puteoli and beheaded, and his head sent to Caesar (for the Jews had induced the emperor to forbid Paul's landing in Italy). There are other local legends in this portion of the book. But after the arrival at Rome the story takes the same course as Pseudo-Marcellus.

5. A Latin Passion of Peter and Paul, largely borrowed from Pseudo-Hegesippus, has this peculiarity, that the apostles lodge in Rome with a believer who is a relation of Pontius Pilate. This person is called in by Nero to testify whether Simon is, as he asserts, Christ: and denies it, and further suggests that Peter and Paul should be called in to give their witness also. The dispute follows. The apostles are sentenced to death by Clement, not Agrippa, prefect of the city. Hardly anything is said of the Martyrdom.

The Greek Acts of Thaddaeus centre round the Edessene legend of the mission of King Abgarus to Christ, the miraculous portrait of him procured by Ananias, Abgarus's messenger, and the preaching of Thaddaeus at Edessa. The Syriac doctrine of Addai tells the same story. These are strictly local legends.

Acts and Passions of disciples of the apostles are sometimes interesting: such are those of Nereus and Achilleus which tell the story of Petronilla, Peter's daughter; and of Xanthippe and Polyxena which borrow matter and language from the Acts of Paul, Peter, Andrew, and Thomas. Those of Zenais and Philonilla—disciples of St. Paul—may prove to be interesting, and those of Hermione. The Acts of Titus by Zenas have already been shown to throw light on the Acts of Paul. The Acts of Mark, Luke, Timothy, Longinus, Cornelius, Aquila, Ananias are not of much interest, either as history or legend.

The Oriental Acts—mainly Coptic, Arabic, and Ethiopic—form a large mass of matter which it is not practicable to analyse. They may be read conveniently in the English versions of S. C. Malan, *Conflicts of the Holy Apostles*; Budge, *Contendings of the Apostles*; A. S. Lewis, *Mythological Acts of the Apostles*. The two first are from Ethiopic, the third from Arabic. They usually consist, in the case of each apostle, of his Preaching and his Martyrdom, related in separate chapters. Of the Martyrdoms, some (Peter, Paul, John, Thomas, James the Less) are the familiar stories: James ultimately from Hegesippus, the rest versions of the old Acts. The Ethiopic has a version of the first six episodes of the Acts of Thomas, and (in Budge) a long life of St. Paul which does not seem to have many points of contact with the old Acts : besides some stories which are loose and fabulous versions of the Clementine romance. The Acts of John are partly from Prochorus. The tales of the Preachings of the apostles vary greatly in interest. Those which make some impression are Andrew and Philemon in Scythia, where a dove is sent as a messenger by Philemon to Andrew; Andrew and Bartholomew, where a whale transports the party in their sleep, a ship with our Lord as captain (cf. Andrew and Matthias) conveys them, and a dog-headed man of hideous aspect is made to become their ally; Bartholomew in the Oasis practising vine-dressing; Matthew telling of his visit to the Land of Promise where the Lost Tribes dwell; Thaddaeus, identical with *Peter and Andrew*, but shorter. Andrew and Matthias figure here also.

One Arabic text is a wild story of Peter and Paul and an emperor of Rome called Bar'amus, which does not attach itself to any other legend of those apostles. It is as grotesque as the Slavonic Acts of Peter, of which a word has yet to be said. There is also a Preaching of Peter in which he heals a leprous girl.

Both Ethiopic and Arabic collections may be regarded as versions made from Coptic; but the Coptic texts themselves are for the most part very fragmentary. We have some of the older martyrdoms fairly complete, and some representative pieces of the other stories. But we have also pieces of stories which are not, so far, known to exist save in Coptic: for example, part of a Martyrdom of Simon Zelotes, and two tales about Andrew which are so curious as to deserve description.

THE ACTS OF ANDREW AND PAUL

is the name commonly given to the first. The beginning is gone. We find the captain of a ship which has brought Andrew and Paul to some city. Andrew has gone towards the city; Paul has plunged into the sea to visit the underworld, and leaves a message for Andrew to bring him up again. The shipman's mother—dim of sight—comes to meet her son, and he, having Paul's cloak to bring to Andrew, accidentally touches her eyes with it, and she sees clearly. Andrew takes the cloak and goes to the city with the multitude: a man meets him and begs him to visit and cure his only son, twelve years old, who is dying. But the Jews oppose his entrance ; he tells the father to return home: his boy will die, but he must not bury him till the morrow. The father goes home and finds him dead.

Andrew returns to the ship and makes the shipman point out the place where Paul dived into the sea. He takes a cup of fresh water, prays, and pours it into the sea, bidding the salt water retreat and the dry land appear. The abyss cleaves, and Paul leaps up, bearing a fragment of wood in his hand.

He has visited Amente and seen Judas and heard his story. Judas had repented and given back the money, and seen Jesus and pleaded for forgiveness. Jesus sent him to the desert to repent, bidding him fear no one but God. The prince of destruction came to him and threatened to swallow him up, and Judas was afraid and worshipped him. Then in despair he thought to go and ask Jesus again for pardon: but he had been taken away to the praetorium. So he resolved to hang himself and meet Jesus in Amente. Jesus came and took all the souls but his. The powers of Amente came and wept before Satan, who said: After all, we are stronger than Jesus ; he has had to leave a soul with us. Jesus ordered Michael to take away Judas's soul also, that Satan's boast might be proved vain, and told Judas how he had destroyed his own hopes by worshipping Satan and killing himself. Judas was sent back till the day of judgement. Paul tells also how he saw the streets of Amente desolate, and brought away a fragment of the broken gates in his hand. There were still some souls in punishment—the murderers, sorcerers, and those who cast little children into the water.

The apostles land, and with Apollonius the shipman go up to the city. The Jews refuse to let them in. They see 'a bird which is called True' digging in a wall. This is really a scarabaeus, δίκαιρον in Greek, which word has been mistaken for δίκαιον. Andrew says, 'Thou bird δίκαιος, go into the city to where the dead boy is, and tell them that we are at the gate and cannot enter; let them open to us.' The scarab gives the message and the people threaten to stone the Jews. At this point the governor comes out; the matter is explained to him by the people and by the Jews, who add, 'if they are the disciples of the living God, why does he not open the gate for them?' The governor is impressed by this and calls on the apostles to open for themselves. They consult, and Paul, suddenly inspired, strikes the gates with the fragment of wood from Amente, and they are swallowed up in the earth.

Here two leaves are lost. We gather that the Jews had practised some fraud about a dead, or supposedly dead, man, and had tied up his face with grave clothes, ' so that he could not breathe '. One guesses that the apostles bade the dead rise, but he was so tightly bound that nothing happened.

We find a dispute going on : the apostles say that the only thing is to order the dead to be loosed. The Jews seek to flee, but they are held by the soldiers till the grave clothes are loosed. The apostles pray : the dead rises and falls at the apostles' feet, saying, ' Forgive me for my folly,' and tells ' everything that had happened '. Andrew says to the Jews, ' Who is now the deceiver of the people ? We or you ? ' It appears from this that the dead man in question has been an accomplice of the Jews in their trick, and is not the dead child whom the apostles were to raise, and doubtless did raise when they first entered the city. This is confirmed by the next words of the Jews (fragmentary) : they fall at the apostles' feet and say . . . ' (we) killed him in folly, thinking that he would not rise '. They ask for baptism. And the act concludes with a general conversion—apparently of 27,000 Jews.

The other story, yet more fragmentary, tells of a woman who bore a child in the desert, killed it, cut it in pieces, and gave it to a dog to eat, to conceal her crime. At this moment Andrew and his companions came up. The woman fled, and the dog came to Andrew and spoke, and called him to come and see what had been done. Andrew consulted with Philemon (who figures as his companion in the Ethiopic Acts) and prayed. In his prayer he alludes to a miracle wrought by Christ on Mount Gebal, ' when, a great multitude being gathered, thou didst command that all the scattered stones and grains of sand should be gathered together, and we marvelled '. Evidently upon this the *disiecta membra* of the child are joined together, and, from words of Andrew which follow, it seems that it was made to weep and laugh. But we have no more of the story.

So much for the Oriental Acts of the fabulous cycle. With them I class a text which has only survived in Slavonic—certain Acts of Peter translated by Franko (*Zeitschr. f. Ntl. Wiss.*, 1902). It is imperfect at the beginning.

A Child (Jesus) comes to Peter and bids him go to the sea where a ship waits to take him to Rome. The captain of the ship (Michael) feigns reluctance to take Peter on board, because he is a disciple of the crucified. There is a storm which Peter stills; he then baptizes Michael, and Michael sells him the Child. When they arrived at Rome, Peter told the Child to catch some fish. 'Make me some hooks,' he said. And in an hour he caught 12,000 fish, which followed him about on dry land.

A Roman noble, Aravistus, bought the Child from Peter for 50 pieces of gold; and took him to a teacher, whom he speedily put to silence (a motif from the Infancy Gospels). In the night the house was wakened by angels singing the thrice-holy hymn over the Child. All in the house were baptized by him.

Nero arrested Peter, and the Child went and rebuked him ; his counsellor Cato smote the Child behind the ear, and was withered up (Infancy Gospel again). The city shook, and the dead rose, but the Child bade them go back till Michael should raise them.

Peter was crucified, head downwards. The Child was with him, and at the last revealed himself: the nails fell from Peter's head, breast, hands, and knees, and after praying for forgiveness for his murderers, he gave up the ghost.

Such are the main points of a rhapsody which serves to show how little the late story-teller cared about not merely history but older legend.

Not even now have all the texts been enumerated which could be classed as Apocryphal Acts: but the reader has before him a general view of the extent and character of the literature which I hope may be reckoned adequate. Put very broadly, the development is from rather dim historical reminiscences used as a framework for doctrinal teaching, to thaumaturgy plus doctrine, to pure thaumaturgy without any doctrine of significance.

John embodies some traditional memories of the residence of John at Ephesus. *Paul*, perhaps, in the Thecla-story uses an existing tale, true or fabulous. *Peter* has the crucifixion at Rome, the memory of Simon Magus, and little else. *Andrew* is a succession of miracles, and so is *Thomas* : but in all these the discourses of the apostles are the real *raison d'être* of the books. Not so with *Philip, Andrew and Matthias*, and the oriental cycle. In these the teaching is of a conventional kind, and becomes more and more perfunctory as we go on, while the miracles grow more and more sensational, until we perhaps reach the climax in the conversion and baptizing of an archangel.

The extent to which these Acts have been influenced by the sophistic romances of the pagan world has been much discussed, and probably exaggerated. The Canonical Acts at first served as the model of the *genre*: of that there can be no doubt. It is with *Andrew* that I begin to perceive the possibility that the author writes with an eye on his pagan colleagues in the art of fiction, just as Flamion has shown that he has also an eye on the philosophy that was popular in his day. *Xanthippe and Polyxena* seem to me more nearly related to the novels than any of the apostolic romances proper; the Clementine romance is another example of the borrowing of motifs from secular fiction. But on the whole it seems safer to say that these fables were intended rather to rival than to imitate the pagan novels—to supply Christians with a substitute and an antidote.

EPISTLES

THIS form did not find much favour with the makers of apocrypha. True, without going into the more destructive theories which would deny St. Paul all but four of the Epistles—or, all the Epistles which go under his name—many critics regard the Pastoral Epistles as, in their present form, not genuine writings of his, and a yet larger consensus is against the authenticity of 2 *Peter*. But, apart from possibilities of this kind, it does appear that the Epistle was on the whole too serious an effort for the forger, more liable to detection, perhaps, as a fraud, and not so likely to gain the desired popularity as a narrative or an Apocalypse. Certain it is that our apocryphal Epistles are few and not impressive. By far the most considerable is that Epistle of the Apostles which has only become known in recent years ; and the greater part of this is not an Epistle but a dialogue.

One famous apocryphal Epistle will not be produced here, viz. the Letter of Christ concerning Sunday, extant in almost every European language and in many Oriental versions. It was fabled to have fallen on the altar at Jerusalem, Rome, Constantinople—where not ?—and is a long, very dull denunciation of what we call Sabbath-breaking, with threats of disaster to the transgressors.

Another, not famous, must also be omitted, viz. the Epistle of Titus, of which something has been said apropos of the fragments of the Acts of John, Peter, and Andrew which it contains. Apart from these quotations and others of the same kind, it is incredibly dull. I believe it to be a Manichaean writing, or possibly Paulician. It has not yet been printed in full.

LETTERS OF CHRIST AND ABGARUS

Our earliest Greek text of these—which are found in many forms—is that given by Eusebius in his *Ecclesiastical History* (i. 13), extracted, as he says, by him from the archives of Edessa relating to Abgarus, and translated from Syriac word for word :

A copy of a letter written by Abgarus the toparch to Jesus, and sent to him by means of Ananias the runner, to Jerusalem.

Abgarus Uchama the toparch to Jesus the good Saviour that hath appeared in the parts (place) of Jerusalem, greeting. I have heard concerning thee and thy cures, that they are done of thee without drugs or herbs: for, as the report goes, thou makest blind men to see again, lame to walk, and cleansest lepers, and castest out unclean spirits and devils, and those that are afflicted with long sickness thou healest, and raisest the dead. And having heard all this of thee, I had determined one of two things, either that thou art God come down from heaven, and so doest these things, or art a Son of God that doest these things. Therefore now have I written and entreated thee to trouble thyself *to come* to me and heal the affliction which I have. For indeed I have heard that the Jews even murmur against thee and wish to do thee hurt. And I have a very little city but (and) comely (reverend), which is sufficient for us both.

The answer, written by Jesus, *sent* by Ananias the runner to Abgarus the toparch.

Blessed art thou that hast believed in me, not having seen me. For it is written concerning me that they that have seen me shall not believe in me, and that they that have not seen me shall believe and live. But concerning that which thou hast written to me, to come unto thee; it must needs be that I fulfil all things for the which I was sent here, and after fulfilling them should then be taken up unto him that sent me. And when I am taken up, I will send thee one of my disciples, to heal thine affliction and give life to thee and them that are with thee.

Later texts add a promise that where this letter is, no enemy shall prevail; and so we find the letter copied and used as an amulet. It was regarded naturally as the palladium of Edessa, but was also thought to act as a protection to individuals.

The letters form an integral part of the story of the mission of Thaddaeus and conversion of Edessa, and part of that legend is that Jesus gave the messenger of Abgarus a handkerchief miraculously imprinted with the picture of his face. Into all this we cannot enter.

LETTER OF LENTULUS

(E. von Dobschütz, *Christus-bilder* 318**)

This can hardly be earlier than the thirteenth century: probably it was written in Italy. The texts differ a good deal, especially in the introductory lines. The oldest does not present the document as a letter at all; but begins:

It is read in the annal-books of the Romans that our Lord Jesus Christ, who was called by the Gentiles the prophet of truth, was of stature . . .

Others, however, make a letter of it, with a prefatory note to this effect:

A certain Lentulus, a Roman, being an official for the Romans in the province of Judaea in the time of Tiberius Caesar, upon seeing Christ, and noting his wonderful works, his preaching, his endless miracles, and other amazing things about him, wrote thus to the Roman senate:

There hath appeared in these times, and still is, a man of great power named Jesus Christ, who is called by the Gentiles (peoples) the prophet of truth, whom his disciples call the Son of God: raising the dead and healing diseases, a man in stature middling tall, and comely, having a reverend countenance, which they that look upon may love and fear; having hair of the hue of an unripe hazel-nut and smooth almost down to his ears, but from the ears in curling locks somewhat darker and more shining, waving over (from) his shoulders; having a parting at the middle of the head according to the fashion of the Nazareans; a brow smooth and very calm, with a face without wrinkle or any blemish, which a moderate colour (red) makes beautiful; with the nose and mouth no fault at all can be found; having a full beard of the colour of his hair, not long, but a little forked at the chin; having an expression simple and mature, the eyes grey, glancing (?) (various) and clear; in rebuke terrible, in admonition kind and lovable, cheerful yet keeping gravity; sometimes he hath wept, but never laughed; in stature of body tall and straight, with hands and arms fair to look upon; in talk grave, reserved and modest [so that he was rightly called by the prophet] fairer than the children of men.

This follows the traditional portraits closely, and was no doubt written in presence of one. The Greeks, it may be added, had similar minute descriptions of the apostles and the Virgin—just as they had of the heroes of Troy.

I shall excuse myself from transcribing the letters of the Virgin to Ignatius and to the people of Messina and proceed to the forged Pauline Epistles. The most important of these we have already seen, viz. the 'Third Epistle to the Corinthians', in the Acts of Paul.

The Muratorian fragment mentions two of these: 'There is current also one to the Laodiceans, and another to the Alexandrians forged (plural) in favour of Marcion's heresy.' The statement is obscure, and has given rise to all sorts of guesses. We have an Epistle to the Laodiceans, but it is entirely colourless in doctrine. That to the Alexandrians is gone. We also know that Marcion cited the Epistle to the Ephesians as 'to the Laodiceans', but this does not help; the Muratorian writer knows *Ephesians*. Very possibly the word *forged* applies only to the second letter, and should be in the singular number. If so, the fragment may refer to our Epistle to the Laodiceans, which is quite old.

EPISTLE TO THE LAODICEANS

It exists only in Latin: the oldest copy is in the Fulda MS. written for Victor of Capua in 546. It is mentioned by various writers from the fourth century onwards, notably by Gregory the Great, to whose influence may ultimately be due the frequent occurrence of it in Bibles written in England; for it is commoner in English MSS. than in others. As will be seen, it is wholly uninteresting, and was merely written to justify or explain St. Paul's mention of the letter from Laodicea in Col. iv. 16.

1 Paul, an apostle not of men nor by man, but by Jesus Christ, unto the brethren that are at Laodicea.

2 Grace be unto you and peace from God the Father and the Lord Jesus Christ.

3 I give thanks unto Christ in all my prayers, that ye continue in him and persevere in his works, looking for the promise at the day of judgement.

4 Neither do the vain talkings of some overset you, which creep in, that they may turn you away from the truth of the Gospel which is preached by me.

5 And now shall God cause that they that are of me shall *continue* ministering unto the increase of the truth of the Gospel, and accomplishing goodness, and the work of salvation, *even* eternal life.

6 And now are my bonds seen of all men, which I suffer in Christ, wherein I rejoice and am glad.

7 And unto me this is for everlasting salvation; which also is brought about by your prayers, and the ministry of the Holy Ghost, whether by life or by death.

8 For verily to me life is in Christ, and to die is joy.

9 And unto him (*or* And also) shall he work his mercy in you, that ye may have the same love, and be of one mind.

10 Therefore, dearly beloved, as ye have heard in my presence, so hold fast and work in the fear of God, and it shall be unto you for life eternal.

11 For it is God that worketh in you.

12 And do ye without afterthought whatsoever ye do.

13 And for the rest, dearly beloved, rejoice in Christ, and beware of them that are filthy in lucre.

14 Let all your petitions be made openly before God, and be ye steadfast in the mind of Christ.

15 And what things are sound and true and sober and just and to be loved, do ye.

16 And what ye have heard and received, keep fast in your heart.

17 And peace shall be unto you.

18 The saints salute you.

19 The grace of the Lord Jesus be with your spirit.

20 And cause this *epistle* to be read unto them of Colossae, and *the epistle* of the Colossians *to be read* unto you.

It is not easy to imagine a more feebly constructed cento of Pauline phrases.

Zahn believed himself to have found a fragment of the Epistle to the Alexandrians in the shape of a lesson—a liturgical Epistle—in the (eighth century) Sacramentary and Lectionary of Bobbio (Paris Bib. Nat., Lat. 13246). It is headed 'Epistle of Paul the Apostle to the Colossians', but it is not from that letter or any other.

Brethren, we that are under the power of the Lord ought to keep the commandment of God. They that keep the Lord's precepts have eternal life, and they that deny his commandments get to themselves ruin and thereto the second death. Now the precept of the Lord is this: Thou shalt not swear falsely, thou shalt not steal, thou shalt not commit adultery, thou shalt not bear false witness, thou shalt not take gifts against the truth, neither for power. Whoso hath power and denieth the truth, shall be denied the kingdom of God and be trodden down into hell, whence he cometh not forth again. How are we frail and deceitful, workers of sin! We do not repent daily, but daily do we commit sin upon sin. That ye may know this, dearly beloved brethren, that our works ⟨are judged, hearken to that which⟩ is written in this book: 'it shall be for a memorial against us in the day of judgement.' There shall be neither witnesses nor companions; neither shall judgement be given by gifts; for there is nothing better than faith, truth, chastity, fasting, and almsgiving which putteth out all sins. And that which thou wouldest not have done to thyself, do not unto another. Agree thou for the kingdom of God and thou shalt receive the crown which is in Christ Jesus our Lord.

This, again, is a very incoherent little piece; it is rather like some curious fragmentary homilies printed by Dom de Bruyne from Carlsruhe (Reichenau) MSS. which I am sure are of Irish composition. I do not think it can be called an apocryphon at all; there are other pieces scattered about in manuscripts called 'preachings' of Paul, or the like, which are just centos of texts and precepts.

THE CORRESPONDENCE OF PAUL AND SENECA

existed in the fourth century, for Jerome mentions it, says it was 'read by many', and is led by it to insert Seneca in his catalogue of Christian authors; Augustine also, quoting the genuine Seneca, says, 'of whom some letters to the apostle Paul are current (read)'. The Pseudo-Linus inserts a paragraph in his *Passion of Paul* (see p. 470) telling how Seneca frequently conversed and corresponded with Paul, admired him much, and read some of his writings to Nero.

Manuscripts as old as the ninth century exist, and of the twelfth-fifteenth centuries there are many. The composition is of the poorest kind: only its celebrity induces me to translate it once again.

1. SENECA TO PAUL, greeting

I believe, Paul, that you have been informed of the talk which I had yesterday with my Lucilius about the apocrypha (*or possibly* the secret mysteries) and other things; for certain sharers in your teaching were with me. For we had retired to the gardens of Sallust, where, because of us, those whom I speak of, going in another direction, saw and joined us. Certainly we wished for your presence, and I would have you know it.

We were much refreshed by the reading of your book, by which I mean some of the many letters which you have addressed to some city or capital of a province, and which inculcate the moral life with admirable precepts. These thoughts, I take it, are not uttered by you but through you, *but* surely sometimes both by you and through you: for such is the greatness of them and they are instinct (warm) with such nobility, that I think *whole* generations (ages) of men could hardly suffice for the instilling and perfecting of them. I desire your good health, brother.

2. PAUL TO SENECA, greeting

I received your letter yesterday with delight, and should have been able to answer it at once, had I had by me the youth I meant to send to you. For you know when, and by whom, and at what moment, and to whom things ought to be given and entrusted. I beg, therefore, that you will not think *yourself* neglected, when I am respecting the dignity of your person. Now in that you somewhere write that you are pleased with my letter (*or*, write that you are pleased with part of my letter) I think myself happy in the good opinion of such a man: for you would not say it, you, a critic, a sophist, the teacher of a great prince, and indeed of all—unless you spoke truth. I trust you may long be in health.

3. SENECA TO PAUL, greeting

I have arranged some writings in a volume, and given them their proper divisions: I am also resolved to read them to Caesar, if only fortune be kind, that he may bring a new (an interested) ear *to the hearing*. Perhaps you, too, will be there. If not, I will at another time fix you a day, that we may look over the work together: indeed, I could not produce this writing to him, without first conferring with you, if only that could be done without risk: that you may know that you are not being neglected. Farewell, dearest Paul.

4. PAUL TO ANNAEUS SENECA, greeting

Whenever I hear your letters read, I think of you as present, and imagine nothing else but that you are always with us. As soon, then, as you begin to come, we shall see each other at close quarters. I desire your good health.

5. SENECA TO PAUL, greeting

We are much pained by your retirement. What is it? what causes keep you away? If it be the anger of the lady (Poppaea) because you have left the old rite and sect, and have converted others, there will be a possibility of pleading with her, that she may consider it as done on *due* reflection and not lightly.

6. PAUL TO SENECA AND LUCILIUS, greeting

Of the subject on which you have written I must not speak
with pen and ink, of which the former marks out and draws
somewhat, and the latter shows it clearly, especially as I know
that among you—that is, in your homes and in you—there are
those who understand me. Honour is to be paid to all, and
so much the more because men catch at opportunities of being
offended. If we are patient with them, we shall certainly overcome them at every point, provided they be men who can be
sorry for their actions. Farewell.

7. ANNAEUS SENECA TO PAUL AND THEOPHILUS, greeting

I profess myself well content with the reading of your letters
which you sent to the Galatians, Corinthians, and Achaeans;
and may we so live together as you show yourself to be *inspired*
with the divine frenzy (horror). For *it is* the holy spirit which
is in you and high above you which expresses these exalted and
adorable thoughts. I would therefore have you careful of other
points, that the polish of the style may not be wanting to the
majesty of the thought. And, brother, not to conceal anything
from you, and have it on my conscience, I confess to you that the
Augustus was moved by your views. When I read to him the
beginning of the power (virtue) that is in you (*perhaps he means*
your exordium about virtue) his words were these: that he
could wonder that a man not regularly educated could think
thus. I replied that the gods often speak by the mouths of
the simple (innocent), not of those who try deceitfully to show
what they can do by their learning. And when I cited him the
example of Vatienus the rustic, to whom two men appeared in
the territory of Reate, who afterwards were recognized as Castor
and Pollux, he appeared fully convinced. Farewell.

8. PAUL TO SENECA, greeting

Though I am aware that Caesar, even if he sometimes lapses,
is a lover of our wonders, you will suffer yourself to be, not
wounded but admonished. For I think that you took a very
serious step in bringing to his notice a matter alien to his religion
and training. For since he is a worshipper of the gods of the
nations, I do not see why you thought you would wish him to
know this matter, unless I am to think that you did it out of
excessive attachment to me. I beg you not to do so in future.
For you must be careful not to offend the empress in your
love for me: yet her anger will not hurt us if it lasts, nor do
good if it does not [*this is nonsense*]. As a queen, she will not
be angry: as a woman, she will be offended. Farewell.

9. SENECA TO PAUL, greeting

I know that you are not so much disturbed on your own account by my letter to you on the showing of your letters to Caesar, as by the nature of things, which so calls away the minds of men from all right learning and conduct—so that I am not surprised, for I have learnt this for certain by many examples. Let us then act differently, and if in the past anything has been done carelessly, you will pardon it. I have sent you a book on elegance of expression (store of words). Farewell, dearest Paul.

10. TO SENECA, PAUL, greeting

Whenever I write to you and do not place my name after yours (*see the heading*) I do a serious thing and one unbefitting my persuasion (sect). For I ought, as I have often declared, to be all things to all men, and to observe in your person that which the Roman law has granted to the honour of the senate, and choose the last place in writing (*text*, reading) a letter, not striving to do as I please in a confused and disgraceful way. Farewell, most devoted of masters. Given on the 5th of the kalends of July; Nero the fourth time, and Messala, consuls (A. D. 58).

11. SENECA TO PAUL, greeting

Hail, my dearest Paul. If you, so great a man, so beloved in all ways, be—I say not joined—but intimately associated with me and my name, it will indeed be well with your Seneca. Since, then, you are the summit and topmost peak of all people, would you not have me glad that I am so near you as to be counted a second self of yours? Do not, then, think that you are unworthy to be named first on the heading of letters, lest you make me think you are testing me rather than playing with me—especially as you know yourself to be a Roman citizen. For the rank that is mine, I would it were yours, and yours I would were mine. Farewell, dearest Paul. Given on the 10th of the kalends of April; Apronianus and Capito consuls (59).

12. SENECA TO PAUL, greeting

Hail, my dearest Paul. Think you that I am not in sadness and grief, that your innocent *people* are so often condemned to suffer? And next, that the whole people thinks you so callous and so prone to crime, that you are supposed to be the authors of every misfortune in the city? Yet let us bear it patiently and content ourselves with what fortune brings, until supreme happiness puts an end to our troubles. Former ages had to bear the Macedonian, Philip's son, and, after Darius, Dionysius, and our own times endured Gaius Caesar: to all of whom their will was law. The source of the many fires which Rome suffers is plain. But if humble men could speak out what the reason is, and if it were possible to speak without risk in this dark time, all would be plain to all. Christians and Jews are commonly executed as contrivers of the fire. Whoever the criminal is, whose pleasure is that of a butcher, and who veils himself with a lie, he is reserved for his due season: and as the best of men is sacrificed, the one for the many, so he, vowed to death for all, will be burned with fire. A hundred and thirty-two houses and four blocks have been burnt in six days; the seventh brought a pause. I pray you may be well, brother. Given the 5th of the kalends of April; Frugi and Bassus consuls (64).

13. SENECA TO PAUL, greeting

Much in every part of your works is enclosed in allegory and enigma, and therefore the great force that is given you of matter and talent (?) should be beautified, I do not say with elegance of words, but with a certain care. Nor should you fear what I remember you have often said; that many who affect such things vitiate the thought and emasculate the strength of the matter. But I wish you would yield to me and humour the genius of Latin, and give beauty to your noble words, that the great gift that has been granted you may be worthily treated by you. Farewell.

Given on the day before the nones of June; Leo and Sabinus consuls (non-existent).

14. PAUL TO SENECA, greeting

To your meditations have been revealed those things which the Godhead has granted to few. With confidence, therefore, I sow in a field already fertile a most prolific seed, not such matter as is liable to corruption, but the abiding word, an emanation from God who grows and abides for ever. This your wisdom has attained and you will see that it is unfailing—so as to judge that the laws of heathens and Israelites are to be shunned. You may become a new author, by showing forth with the graces of rhetoric the unblameable wisdom of Jesus Christ, which you, having wellnigh attained it, will instil into the temporal monarch, his servants, and his intimate friends; yet the persuading of them will be a rough and difficult task, for many of them will hardly incline to your admonitions. Yet the word of God, if it be instilled into them, will be a vital gain, producing a new man, incorrupt, and an everlasting soul that shall hasten from hence to God. Farewell, Seneca, most dear to me.

Given on the kalends of August; Leo and Sabinus consuls.

EPISTLE OF THE APOSTLES

The authorities for the text are : (a) a Coptic MS. of the fourth or fifth century at Cairo, mutilated; (b) a complete version in Ethiopic; (c) a leaf of a fifth-century MS. in Latin, palimpsest, at Vienna. The only edition which makes use of all the authorities is C. Schmidt's, 1919. The Ethiopic was previously edited by Guerrier in *Patrologia orientalis* under the title of *Testament of our Lord in Galilee*. A notice of this text by Guerrier in the *Revue de l'Orient Chrétien* (1907) enabled me to identify it with the Coptic text, of which Schmidt had given a preliminary account to the Berlin Academy. As to the date and character of the book, Schmidt's verdict is that it was written in Asia Minor about A. D. 160 by an orthodox Catholic. The orthodoxy has been questioned (see a review by G. Bardy in *Revue Biblique*, 1921). No ancient writer mentions it, and very few traces of its use can be found: the (third?)-century poet Commodian seems to use it in one place (see § 11).

There has so far been no English rendering of the text ; my version depends on Schmidt and Guerrier.

In the Ethiopic version another writing, a prophecy of our Lord concerning the signs of the end, is prefixed to the Epistle. Parts of this recur in the Syriac *Testament of the Lord* and part is repeated in the Epistle itself. It is noteworthy that this prophecy ends with a passage which is identical with one quoted by Clement of Alexandria from a source he does not name—only calling it 'the Scripture'.

Testament 11 in Guerrier.	Clem. Alex. *Protrept.* ciii.
And the righteous, that have walked in the way of righteousness, shall inherit the glory of God; and the power shall be given to them which no eye hath seen and no ear heard; and they shall rejoice in my kingdom	But the saints of the Lord shall inherit the glory of God, and his power. *Tell me what glory, O blessed one.* That which eye hath not seen nor ear heard, neither hath it come up upon the heart of man ; and they shall rejoice at the kingdom of their Lord for ever. Amen.

A similar passage is in the *Apostolic Constitutions,* vii. 22. On the possible derivation from the Apocalypse of Elias see my *Lost Apocrypha of O. T.*, p. 54.

The first four leaves of the Coptic MS. are lost, so we depend on the Ethiopic for the opening of the text.

1 The book which Jesus Christ revealed unto his disciples: and how that Jesus Christ revealed the book for the company (college) of the apostles, the disciples of Jesus Christ, even the book *which is* for all men. Simon and Cerinthus, the false apostles, concerning whom it is written that no man shall cleave unto them, for there is in them deceit wherewith they bring men to destruction. (The book hath been written) that ye may be steadfast and not flinch nor be troubled, and depart not from the word of the Gospel which ye have heard. Like as we heard

it, we keep it in remembrance and have written it for the whole world. We commend you our sons and our daughters in joy ⟨to the grace of God(?)⟩ in the name of God the Father the Lord of the world, and of Jesus Christ. Let grace be multiplied upon you.

2 *We*, John, Thomas, Peter, Andrew, James, Philip, Bartholomew, Matthew, Nathanael, Judas Zelotes, and Cephas, write unto the churches of the east and the west, of the north and the south, declaring and imparting unto you that which concerneth our Lord Jesus Christ: we do write according as we have seen and heard and touched him, after that he was risen from the dead: and how that he revealed unto us things mighty and wonderful and true.

3 This know we: that our Lord and Redeemer Jesus Christ is God the Son of God, who was sent of God [1] the Lord of the whole world, the maker and creator *of it*, who is named by all names, and high above all powers, Lord of lords, King of kings, Ruler of rulers, the heavenly one, that sitteth above the cherubim and seraphim at the right hand of the throne of the Father: who by his word *made* the heavens, and formed the earth and that which is in it, and set bounds to the sea that it should not pass: the deeps also and fountains, that they should spring forth and flow over the earth: the day and the night, the sun and the moon, did he establish, and the stars in the heaven: that did separate the light from the darkness: that called forth hell, and in the twinkling of an eye ordained the rain of the winter, the snow (cloud), the hail, and the ice, and the days in their several seasons: that maketh the earth to quake and again establisheth it: that created man in his own image, after his likeness, and by the fathers of old and the prophets is it declared (*or*, and spake in parables with the fathers of old and the prophets in verity), of whom the apostles preached, and whom the disciples did touch. In God, the Lord, the Son of God, do we believe, that he is the word become flesh: that of Mary the holy virgin he took a body, begotten of the Holy Ghost, not of the will (lust) of the flesh, but by the will of God: that he was wrapped in swaddling clothes in Bethlehem and made manifest, and grew up and came to ripe age, when *also* we beheld *it*.

4 This did our Lord Jesus Christ, who was sent by Joseph and Mary his mother to be taught. [And] when he that taught him said unto him: Say Alpha: then answered he and said: Tell thou me first what is Beta (*probably*: Tell thou me first what is ⟨Alpha and then will I tell thee what is⟩ Beta. Cf. the Marcosian story quoted by Irenaeus (see above, Gospel of Thomas, p. 15). The story is in our texts of the Gospel of Thomas, and runs through all the Infancy Gospels). This thing which then came to pass is true and of verity.

---

[1] Of the clauses that follow, some it seems should refer to the Father, others certainly to the Son: there is confusion in the text.

5 Thereafter was there a marriage in Cana of Galilee; and they bade him with his mother and his brethren, and he changed water into wine. He raised the dead, he caused the lame to walk: him whose hand was withered he caused to stretch it out, and the woman which had suffered an issue of blood twelve years touched the hem of his garment and was healed in the same hour. And when we marvelled at the miracle which was done, he said: Who touched me? Then said we: Lord, the press of men hath touched thee. But he answered and said unto us: I perceive that a virtue is gone out of me. Straightway that woman came before him, and answered and said unto him: Lord, I touched thee. And he answered and said unto her: Go, thy faith hath made thee whole. Thereafter he made the deaf to hear and the blind to see; out of them *that were possessed* he cast out the unclean spirits, and cleansed the lepers. The spirit which dwelt in a man, *whereof the name was* Legion, cried out against Jesus, saying: Before the time of our destruction is come, thou art come to drive us out. But the Lord Jesus rebuked him, saying: Go out of this man and do him no hurt. And he entered into the swine and drowned them in the water and they were choked.

Thereafter he did walk upon the sea, and the winds blew, and he cried out against them (rebuked them), and the waves of the sea were made calm. And when we his disciples had no money, we asked him: What shall we do because of the tax-gatherer? And he answered and told us: Let one of you cast an hook into the deep, and take out a fish, and he shall find therein a penny: that give unto the tax-gather for me and you. And thereafter when we had no bread, but only five loaves and two fishes, he commanded the people to sit them down, and the number of them was five thousand, besides children and women. We did set pieces of bread before them, and they ate and were filled, and there remained over, and we filled twelve baskets full of the fragments, asking one another and saying: What *mean* these five loaves? They are the symbol of our faith in the Lord of the Christians (in the great christendom), *even* in the Father, the Lord Almighty, and in Jesus Christ our redeemer, in the Holy Ghost the comforter, in the holy church, and in the remission of sins.

6 These things did our Lord and Saviour reveal unto us and teach us. And we do even as he, that ye may become partakers in the grace of our Lord and in our ministry and our giving of thanks (glory), and think upon life eternal. Be ye steadfast and waver not in the knowledge and confidence of our Lord Jesus Christ, and he will have mercy on you and save you everlastingly, world without end.

Here begins the Coptic text.

7 Cerinthus and Simon are come to go to and fro in the world, but they are enemies of our Lord Jesus Christ, for they do pervert

the word and the true thing, even (faith in) Jesus Christ. Keep yourselves therefore far from them, for death is in them, and great pollution and corruption, even in these on whom shall come judgement and the end and everlasting destruction.

8 Therefore have we not shrunk from writing unto you concerning the testimony of Christ our Saviour, of what he did, when we followed with him, how he enlightened our understanding . . .

9 Concerning whom we testify that the Lord is he who was crucified by Pontius Pilate and Archelaus between the two thieves (and with them he was taken down from the tree of the cross, *Eth.*), and was buried in a place which is called the place of a skull (*Kranion*). And thither went three women, Mary, she that was kin to Martha, and Mary Magdalene (Sarrha, Martha, and Mary, *Eth.*), and took ointments to pour upon the body, weeping and mourning over that which was come to pass. And when they drew near to the sepulchre, they looked in and found not the body (*Eth.* they found the stone rolled away and opened the entrance).

10 And as they mourned and wept, the Lord showed himself unto them and said to them: For whom weep ye? weep no more, I am he whom ye seek. But let one of you go to your brethren and say: Come ye, the Master is risen from the dead. Martha (Mary, *Eth.*) came and told us. We said unto her: What have we to do with thee, woman? He that is dead and buried, is it possible that he should live? And we believed her not that the Saviour was risen from the dead. Then she returned unto the Lord and said unto him: None of them hath believed me, that thou livest. He said: Let another of you go unto them and tell them again. Mary (Sarrha, *Eth.*) came and told us again, and we believed her not; and she returned unto the Lord and she also told him.

11 Then said the Lord unto Mary and her sisters: Let us go unto them. And he came and found us within (sitting veiled *or* fishing, *Eth.*), and called us out; but we thought that it was a phantom and believed not that it was the Lord. Then said he unto us: Come, fear ye not. I am your master, even he, O Peter, whom thou didst deny thrice; and dost thou now deny again? And we came unto him, doubting in our hearts whether it were he. Then said he unto us: Wherefore doubt ye still, and are unbelieving? I am he that spake unto you of my flesh and my death and my resurrection. But that ye may know that I am he, do thou, Peter, put thy finger into the print of the nails in mine hands, and thou also, Thomas, put thy finger into the wound of the spear in my side; but thou, Andrew, look on my feet and see whether they press the earth; for it is written in the prophet:[1] A phantom of a devil maketh no footprint on the earth.

[1] Not identified. The Christian poet Commodian appears to quote this passage : *Vestigium umbra non facit.*

12 And we touched him, that we might learn [1] of a truth whether he were risen in the flesh; and we fell on our faces (and worshipped him) confessing our sin, that we had been unbelieving. Then said our Lord and Saviour unto us: Rise up, and I will reveal unto you that which is above the heaven and in the heaven, and your rest which is in the kingdom of heaven. For my Father hath given me power (sent me, *Eth.*) to take you up thither, and them *also* that believe on me.

13 Now that which he revealed unto us is this, which he spake: It came to pass when I was about (minded) to come hither from the Father of all things, and passed through the heavens, then did I put on the wisdom of the Father, and I put on the power of his might. I was in heaven, and I passed by the archangels and the angels in their likeness, like as if I were one of them, among the princedoms and powers. I passed through them because I possessed the wisdom of him that had sent me. Now the chief captain of the angels, [is] Michael, and Gabriel and Uriel and Raphael followed me unto the fifth firmament (heaven), for they thought in their heart that I was one of them; such power was given me of my Father. And on that day did I adorn the archangels with a wonderful voice (so *Copt.: Eth., Lat.*, I made them quake—amazed them), so that they should go unto the altar of the Father and serve and fulfil the ministry until I should return unto him. And so wrought I the likeness by my wisdom; for I became all things in all, that I might praise the dispensation of the Father and fulfil the glory of him that sent me (*the verbs might well be transposed*) and return unto him. (*Here the Latin omits a considerable portion of text without notice, to near the beginning of c.* 17.)

14 For ye know that the angel Gabriel brought the message unto Mary. And we answered: Yea, Lord. He answered and said unto us: Remember ye not, then, that I said unto you a little while ago: I became an angel among the angels, and I became all things in all? We said unto him: Yea, Lord. Then answered he and said unto us: On that day whereon I took the form of the angel Gabriel, I appeared unto Mary and spake with her. Her heart accepted me, and she believed (She believed and laughed, *Eth.*), and I formed myself and entered into her body. I became flesh, for I alone was a minister unto myself in that which concerned Mary (I was mine own messenger, *Eth.*) in the appearance of the shape of an angel. *For* so must I needs (*or*, was I wont to) do. Thereafter did I return to my Father (*Copt.* After my return to the Father, *and run on*).

15 But do ye commemorate my death. Now when the Passover (Easter, pascha) cometh, one of you shall be cast into prison for my name's sake; and he will be in grief and sorrow, because ye keep the Easter while he is in prison and separated from you, for

[1] Here begins the Latin fragment.

he will be sorrowful because he keepeth not Easter with you. And I will send my power in the form of mine angel Gabriel, and the doors of the prison shall open. And he shall come forth and come unto you and keep the night-watch with you until the cock crow. And when ye have accomplished the memorial which is made of me, and the Agape (love-feast), he shall again be cast into prison for a testimony, until he shall come out thence and preach that which I have delivered unto you.

And we said unto him: Lord, is it then needful that we should again take the cup and drink? (Lord, didst not thou thyself fulfil the drinking of the Passover? is it then needful that we should accomplish it again? *Eth.*) He said unto us: Yea, it is needful, until the day when I come again, with them that have been put to death for my sake (come with my wounds, *Eth.*).

16 Then said we to him: Lord, that which thou hast revealed unto us (revealest, *Eth.*) is great. Wilt thou come in the power of any creature or in an appearance of any kind? (In what power or form wilt thou come? *Eth.*) He answered and said unto us: Verily I say unto you, I shall come like the sun when it is risen, and my brightness will be seven times the brightness thereof![1] The wings of the clouds shall bear me in brightness, and the sign of the cross shall go before me, and I shall come upon earth to judge the quick and the dead.

17 We said unto him: Lord, after how many years shall this come to pass? He said unto us:[2] When the hundredth part and the twentieth part is fulfilled, between the Pentecost and the feast of unleavened bread, then shall the coming of my Father be (*so Copt.*: When an hundred and fifty years are past, in the days of the feast of Passover and Pentecost, &c., *Eth.*: . . . (*imperfect word*) year is fulfilled, between the unleavened bread and Pentecost shall be the coming of my Father, *Lat.*).[3]

We said unto him: Now sayest thou unto us: I will come; and how sayest thou: He that sent me is he that shall come? Then said he to us: I am wholly in the Father and my Father is in me.[4] Then said we to him: Wilt thou indeed forsake us until thy coming? Where can we[5] find a master? But he answered and said unto us: Know ye not, then, that like as until now I have been here, so also was I there, with him that sent me? And we said to him: Lord, is it then possible that thou shouldest be both here and there? But he answered us: I am wholly in

---

[1] Probably from the Apocalypse of Peter.
[2] Here the *Latin* fragment resumes.
[3] Before the word 'year' in *Lat.* are the letters *inta* which may be the end of a numeral such as *quinquaginta* (fifty). It seems likely that in the archetype of the Latin one or more leaves were wanting.
[4] Here *Coptic* omits several clauses by homoeoteleuton. *Ethiopic* and *Latin* are followed.
[5] Here *Latin* ends.

the Father and the Father in me,[1] because of (in regard of) the likeness of the form and the power and the fullness and the light and the full measure and the voice. I am the word, I am become unto him a thing, that is to say (*word gone*) of the thought, fulfilled in the type (likeness); I have come into the Ogdoad (eighth number), which is the Lord's day.[2] (*In place of these sentences Eth. has*: I am of his resemblance and form, of his power and completeness, and of his light. I am his complete (fulfilled, entire) Word.

18 But it came to pass after he was crucified, and dead and arisen again, *when* the work *was fulfilled* which was accomplished in the flesh, and he was crucified and the ascension come to pass at the end of the days, then said he thus, &c. *It is an interpolation, in place of words which the translator did not understand, or found heretical.*) But the whole fulfilment of the fulfilment shall ye see after the redemption which hath come to pass by me, and ye shall see me, how I go up unto my Father which is in heaven. But behold, now, I give unto you a new commandment: Love one another and [*a leaf lost in Copt.*] obey one another, that peace may rule alway among you. Love your enemies, and what ye would not that man do unto you, that do unto no man.

19 And this preach ye also and teach them that believe on me, and preach the kingdom of heaven of my Father, and how my Father hath given me the power, that ye may bring near the children of my heavenly Father. Preach ye, and they shall obtain faith, that ye may be they for whom it is ordained that they shall bring his children unto heaven.

And we said unto him: Lord, unto thee it is possible to accomplish that whereof thou tellest us; but how shall we be able to do it? He said to us: Verily I say unto you, preach and proclaim as I *command you, for* I will be with you, for it is my good pleasure to be with you, that ye may be heirs with me in the kingdom of heaven, *even the kingdom* of him that sent me. Verily I say unto you, ye shall be my brethren and my friends, for my Father hath found pleasure in you: and so also shall they be that believe on me by your means. Verily I say unto you, such and so great joy hath my Father prepared for you that the angels and the powers desired and do desire to see it and look upon it; but it is not given unto them to behold the glory of my Father. We said unto him: Lord, what is this whereof thou speakest to us?

Copt. begins again : words are missing.

He answered us: Ye shall behold a light, more excellent than that which shineth ... (shineth more brightly than the light, and is more perfect than perfection. And the Son shall become perfect

[1] *Coptic* resumes.
[2] The Lord's day considered as the eighth day of the week.

through the Father who is Light, for the Father is perfect which bringeth to pass death and resurrection, and *ye shall see* a perfection more perfect than the perfect. And I am wholly at the right hand of the Father, even in him that maketh perfect. *So Eth.: Copt. has gaps*).

And we said unto him: Lord, in all things art thou become salvation and life unto us, for that thou makest known such a hope unto us. And he said to us: Be of good courage and rest in me. Verily I say unto you, your rest shall be above (?), in the place where is neither eating nor drinking, nor care (*Copt.* joy) nor sorrow, nor passing away of them that are therein : for ye *shall* have no part in (the things of earth, *Eth.*) but ye shall be received in the everlastingness of my Father. Like as I am in him, so shall ye also be in me.

Again we said unto him: In what form? in the fashion of angels, or in flesh? And he answered and said unto us: Lo, I have put on your flesh, wherein I was born and crucified, and am risen again through my Father which is in heaven, that the prophecy of David the prophet might be fulfilled, in regard of that which was declared concerning me and my death and resurrection, saying:

Lord, they are increased that fight with me, and many are they that are risen up against me.

Many there be that say to my soul: There is no help for him in his God.

But thou, O Lord, art my defender: thou art my worship, and the lifter up of my head.

I did call upon the Lord with my voice and he heard me (out of the high place of his temple, *Eth.*).

I laid me down and slept, and rose up again : for thou, O Lord, art my defender.

I will not be afraid for ten thousands of the people, that have set themselves against me round about.

Up, Lord, and help me, O my God : for thou hast smitten down all them that without cause are mine enemies: thou hast broken the teeth of the ungodly.

Salvation belongeth unto the Lord, and his good pleasure is upon his people (Ps. iii. 1-8).

If, therefore, all the words which were spoken by the prophets have been fulfilled in me (for I myself was in them), how much more shall that which I say unto you come to pass indeed, that he which sent me may be glorified by you and by them that believe on me?

20 And when he had said this unto us, we said to him: In all things hast thou had mercy on us and saved us, and hast revealed all things unto us ; but yet would we ask of thee somewhat if thou give us leave. And he said unto us: I know that ye pay heed, and that your heart is well-pleased when ye hear me: now concerning that which ye desire, I will speak good words unto you.

21 For verily I say unto you: Like as my Father hath raised me

from the dead, so shall ye also rise (in the flesh, *Eth.*) and be taken up into the highest heaven, unto the place whereof I have told you from the beginning, unto the place which he who sent me hath prepared for you. And so will I accomplish all dispensations (all grace, *Eth.*), even I who am unbegotten and yet begotten of mankind, who am without flesh and yet have borne flesh ⟨and have grown up like unto you that were born in flesh, *Eth.*⟩: for to that end am I come, that (*gap in Copt.: Eth. continues*) ye might rise from the dead in your flesh, in the second birth, *even* a vesture that shall not decay, together with all them that hope and believe in him that sent me: for so is the will of my Father, that I should give unto you, and unto them whom it pleaseth me, the hope of the kingdom.

Then said we unto him: Great is that which thou sufferest us to hope, and tellest us. And he answered and said: Believe ye that everything that I tell you shall come to pass? We answered and said: Yea, Lord. (*Copt. resumes for a few lines : then another gap. I follow Eth.*) He said unto us: Verily I say unto you, that I have obtained the whole power of my Father, that I may bring back into light them that dwell in darkness, them that are in corruption into incorruption, them that are in death into life, and that I may loose them that are in fetters. For that which is impossible with men, is possible with the Father. I am the hope of them that despair, the helper of them that have no saviour, the wealth of the poor, the health of the sick, and the resurrection of the dead.

22 When he had thus said, we said unto him: Lord, is it true that the flesh shall be judged together with the soul and the spirit, and that the one part shall rest in heaven and the other part be punished everlastingly yet living? And he said unto us: (*Copt. resumes*) How long will ye inquire and doubt?

23 Again we said unto him: Lord, there is necessity upon us to inquire of thee—because thou hast commanded us to preach— that we ourselves may learn assuredly of thee and be profitable preachers, and that they which are instructed by us may believe in thee. Therefore must we needs inquire of thee.

24 He answered us and said: Verily I say unto you, the resurrection of the flesh shall come to pass with the soul therein and the spirit. And we said unto him: Lord, is it then possible that that which is dissolved and brought to nought should become whole? and we ask thee not as unbelieving, neither as if it were impossible unto thee; but verily we believe that that which thou sayest shall come to pass. And he was wroth with us and said: O ye of little faith, how long will ye ask questions? But what ye will, tell it me, and I myself will tell you without grudging: only keep ye my commandments and do that which I bid you, and turn not away your face from any man, that I turn not my face away from you, but without shrinking and fear and

without respect of persons, minister ye in the way that is direct
and narrow and strait. So shall my Father himself rejoice
over you.

25 Again we said unto him: Lord, already are we ashamed
that we question thee oft-times and burden thee. And he answered and said unto us: I know that in faith and with your
whole heart ye do question me; therefore do I rejoice over you,
for verily I say unto you: I rejoice, and my Father that is in me,
because ye question me; and your importunity (shamelessness)
is unto me rejoicing and unto you it giveth life. And when he
had so said unto us, we were glad that we had questioned him,
and we said to him: Lord, in all things thou makest us alive and
hast mercy on us. Wilt thou now declare unto us that which we
shall ask thee? Then said he unto us: Is it the flesh that passeth
away, or is it the spirit? We said unto him: The flesh is it that
passeth away. Then said he unto us: That which hath fallen
shall rise again, and that which was lost shall be found, and that
which was weak shall recover, that in these things that are so
created the glory of my Father may be revealed. As he hath
done unto me, so will I do unto all that believe in me.

26 Verily I say unto you: the flesh shall arise, and the soul,
alive, that their defence may come to pass on that day in regard
of that that they have done, whether it be good or evil: that there
may be a choosing-out of the faithful who have kept the commandments of my Father that sent me; and so shall the judgement be accomplished with strictness. For my Father said unto
me: My Son, in the day of judgement thou shalt have no respect
for the rich, neither pity for the poor, but according to the sins
of every man shalt thou deliver him unto everlasting torment.
But unto my beloved that have done the commandments of my
Father that sent me will I give the rest of life in the kingdom of
my Father which is in heaven, and they shall behold that which
he hath given me. And he hath given me authority to do that
which I will, and to give that which I have promised and determined to give and grant unto them.

27 For to that end went I down unto the place of Lazarus,
and preached unto the righteous and the prophets, that they
might come out of the rest which is below and come up into that
which is above; and I poured out upon them with my right hand
the water (?) (baptism, *Eth.*) of life and forgiveness and salvation
from all evil, as I have done unto you and unto them that believe
on me. But if any man believe on me and do not my commandments, although he have confessed my name, he hath no profit
therefrom but runneth a vain race: for such will find themselves
in perdition and destruction, because they have despised my
commandments.

28 But so much the more have I redeemed you, the children
of light, from all evil and from the authority of the rulers (archons),

and every one that believeth on me by your means. For that which I have promised unto you will I give unto them also, that they may come out of the prison-house and the fetters of the rulers. We answered and said: Lord, thou hast given unto us the rest of life and hast given us ⟨joy ?⟩ by wonders, unto the confirmation of faith: wilt thou now preach the same unto us, seeing that thou hast preached it unto the ⟨righteous⟩ and the prophets ? Then said he unto us: Verily I say unto you, all that have believed on me and that believe in him that sent me will I take up into the heaven, unto the place which my Father hath prepared for the elect, and I will give you the kingdom, the chosen *kingdom*, in rest, and everlasting life.

29 But all they that have offended against my commandments and have taught other doctrine, (perverting) the Scripture and adding thereto, striving after their own glory, and that teach with other words them that believe on me in uprightness, if they make them fall thereby, shall receive everlasting punishment. We said unto him : Lord, shall there then be teaching by others, diverse from that which thou hast spoken unto us ? He said unto us : It must needs be, that the evil and the good may be made manifest ; and the judgement shall be manifest upon them that do these things, and according to their works shall they be judged and shall be delivered unto death..

Again we said unto him: Lord, blessed are we in that we see thee and hear thee declaring such things, for our eyes have beheld these great wonders that thou hast done. He answered and said unto us: Yea, rather blessed are they that have not seen and yet have believed, for they shall be called children of the kingdom, and they shall be perfect among the perfect, and I will be unto them life in the kingdom of my Father.

Again we said unto him: Lord, how shall men be able to believe that thou wilt depart and leave us ; for thou sayest unto us: There shall come a day and an hour when I shall ascend unto my Father ?

30 But he said unto us: Go ye and preach unto the twelve tribes, and preach also unto the heathen, and to all the land of Israel from the east to the west and from the south unto the north, and many shall believe on ⟨me⟩ the Son of God. But we said unto him: Lord, who will believe us, or hearken unto us, or (how shall we be able, *Eth.*) to teach the powers and signs and wonders which thou hast done? Then answered he and said to us: Go ye and preach the mercifulness of my Father, and that which he hath done through me will I myself do through you, for I am in you, and I will give you my peace, and I will give you a power of my spirit, that ye may prophesy to them unto life eternal. And unto the others also will I give my power, that they may teach the residue of the peoples.

(Six leaves lost in Copt.: Eth. continues.)

31 And behold a man shall meet you, whose name is Saul, which being interpreted is Paul: he is a Jew, circumcised according to the law, and he shall receive my voice from heaven with fear and terror and trembling. And his eyes shall be blinded, and by your hands by the sign of the cross shall they be protected (healed: *other Eth. MSS.* with spittle by your hands shall his eyes, &c.). Do ye unto him all that I have done unto you. Deliver it (? the word of God) unto the other. And at the same time that man shall open his eyes and praise the Lord, even my Father which is in heaven. He shall obtain power among the people and shall preach and instruct; and many that hear him shall obtain glory and be redeemed. But thereafter shall men be wroth with him and deliver him into the hands of his enemies, and he shall bear witness before kings that are mortal, and his end shall be that he shall turn unto me, whereas he persecuted me *at the first*. He shall preach and teach and abide with the elect, as a chosen vessel and a wall that shall not be overthrown, *yea*, the last of the last shall become a preacher unto the Gentiles, made perfect by the will of my Father. Like as ye have learned from the Scripture that your fathers the prophets spake of me, and in me it is indeed fulfilled.

And he said unto us: Be ye also therefore guides unto them; and all things that I said unto you, and that ye write concerning me (tell ye them), that I am the word of the Father and that the Father is in me. Such also shall ye be unto that man, as becometh you. Instruct him and bring to his mind that which is spoken of me in the Scripture and is fulfilled, and thereafter shall he become the salvation of the Gentiles.

32 And we asked him: Lord, is there for us and for them the self-same expectation of the inheritance? He answered and said unto us: Are then the fingers of the hand like unto each other, or the ears of corn in the field, or do *all* fruit-trees bear the same fruit? Doth not every one bear fruit according to its nature? And we said unto him: Lord, wilt thou again speak unto us in parables? Then said he unto us: Lament not. Verily I say unto you, ye are my brethren, and my companions in the kingdom of heaven unto my Father, for so is his good pleasure. Verily I say unto you, unto them also whom ye teach and who believe on me will I give that expectation.

33 And we asked him again: When shall we meet with that man, and when wilt thou depart unto thy Father and our God and Lord? He answered and said unto us: That man will come out of the land of Cilicia unto Damascus of Syria, to root up the church which ye must found there. It is I that speak through you; and he shall come quickly: and he shall become strong in the faith, that the word of the prophet may be fulfilled, which saith: Behold, out of Syria will I begin to call together a new Jerusalem, and Sion will I subdue unto me, and it shall be taken,

and the place which is childless shall be called the son and
daughter of my Father, and my bride. For so hath it pleased
him that sent me. But that man will I turn back, that he
accomplish not his evil desire, and the praise of my Father shall
be perfected in him, and after that I am gone home and abide
with my Father, I will speak unto him from heaven, and all
things shall be accomplished which I have told you before concerning him.

34 And we said unto him again: Lord, so many great things
hast thou told us and revealed unto us as never yet were spoken,
and in all hast thou given us rest and been gracious unto us.
After thy resurrection thou didst reveal unto us all things that
we might be saved indeed; but thou saidst unto us only: There
shall be wonders and strange appearances in heaven and on earth
before the end of the world come. Tell us now, how shall we
perceive it? And he answered us: I will teach it you; and not
that which shall befall you only, but them also whom ye shall
teach and who shall believe, as well as them who shall hear that
man and believe on me. In those years and days shall it come
to pass.

And we said again unto him: Lord, what shall come to pass?
And he said unto us:[1] Then shall they that believe and they
that believe not hear (see, *Eth.*) a trumpet in the heaven, a vision
of great stars which shall be seen in the day, wonderful sights in
heaven reaching down to the earth; stars which fall upon the
earth like fire, and a great and mighty hail of fire (a star shining
from the east unto this place, like unto fire, *Eth.* 2). The sun and
the moon fighting one with the other, a continual rolling and
noise of thunders and lightnings, thunder and earthquake; cities
falling and men perishing in their overthrow, a continual dearth
for lack of rain, a terrible pestilence and great mortality, mighty
and untimely, so that they that die lack burial: and the bearing
forth of brethren and sisters and kinsfolk shall be upon one bier.
The kinsman shall show no favour to his kinsman, nor any man
to his neighbour. And they that were overthrown shall rise up
and behold them that overthrew them, that they lack burial, for
the pestilence shall be full of hatred and pain and envy: and men
shall take from one and give to another. And thereafter shall it
wax yet worse than before. (Bewail ye them that have not
hearkened unto my commandments, *Eth.* 2.)

35 Then shall my Father be wroth at the wickedness of men,
for many are their transgressions, and the abomination of their
uncleanness weigheth heavy upon them in the corruption of
their life.

And we asked him: What of them that trust in thee? He
answered and said unto us: Ye are yet slow of heart; and how
long? Verily I say unto you, as the prophet David spake of me

[1] Here begins the parallel text in the prophecy (*Testament in Galilee*)
which is prefixed, in the Ethiopic version, to the Epistle: see above.

and of my people, so shall it be (?) for them also that believe on me. But they that are deceivers in the world and enemies of righteousness, upon them shall come the fulfilment of the prophecy of David, who said : Their feet are swift to shed blood, their tongue uttereth slander, adders' poison is under their lips. I behold thee companying with thieves, and partaking with adulterers, thou continuest speaking against thy brother and puttest stumbling-blocks before thine own mother's son. What thinkest thou, that I shall be like unto thee? Behold now how the prophet of God hath spoken of all, that all things may be fulfilled which he said aforetime.

36 And again we said unto him: Lord, will not then the nations say: Where is their God? And he answered and said unto us: Thereby shall the elect be known, that they, being plagued with such afflictions, come forth. We said: Will then their departure out of the world be by a pestilence which giveth them pain? He answered us: Nay, but if they suffer such affliction, it will be a proving of them, whether they have faith and remember these my sayings, and fulfil my commandments. These shall arise, and short will be their expectation, that he may be glorified that sent me, and I with him. For he hath sent me unto you to tell you these things; and that ye may impart them unto Israel and the Gentiles and they may hear, and they also be redeemed and believe on me and escape the woe of the destruction. But whoso escapeth from the destruction of death, him will they take and hold him fast in the prison-house in torments like the torments of a thief.

And we said unto him: Lord, will they *that believe* be *treated* like the unbelievers, and wilt thou punish them that have escaped from the pestilence? And he said unto us: If they that believe in my name deal like the sinners, then have they done as though they had not believed. And we said again to him: Lord, have they on whom this lot hath fallen no life? He answered and said unto us: Whoso hath accomplished the praise of my Father, he *shall abide in* the resting-place of my Father.

37 Then said we unto him: Lord, teach us what shall come to pass thereafter? And he answered us: In those years and days shall war be kindled upon war ;[1] the four ends of the earth shall be in commotion and fight against each other. Thereafter shall be quakings of clouds (*or*, clouds of locusts), darkness, and dearth, and persecutions of them that believe on me and against the elect. Thereupon shall come doubt and strife and transgressions against one another. And there shall be many that believe on my name and yet follow after evil and spread vain doctrine. And men shall follow after them and their riches, and be subject unto their pride, and lust for drink, and bribery, and there shall be respect of persons among them.

[1] Fragments of a leaf in Coptic exist for this passage.

38 But they that desire to behold the face of God and respect not the persons of the rich sinners, and are not ashamed before the people that lead them astray, but rebuke (?) them, they shall be crowned by the Father. And they also shall be saved that rebuke their neighbours, for they are sons of wisdom and of faith. But if they become not children of wisdom, whoso hateth his brother and persecuteth him and showeth him no favour, him will God despise and reject.

(Copt. resumes.)

But they that walk in truth and in the knowledge of the faith, and have love towards me—for they have endured insult—they shall be praised for that they walk in poverty and endure them that hate them and put them to shame. Men have stripped them naked, for they despised them because they continued in hunger and thirst, but after they have endured patiently, *they shall* have the blessedness of heaven, and they shall be with me for ever. But woe unto them that walk in pride and boasting, for their end is perdition.

39 And we said unto him: Lord, is this thy *purpose*, that thou leavest us, to come upon them? (Will all this come to pass, *Eth.*) He answered and said unto us: After what manner shall the judgement be? whether righteous or unrighteous? (In *Copt.* and *Eth.* the general sense is the same: but the answer of Jesus in the form of a question is odd, and there is probably a corruption.)

We said unto him: Lord, in that day they will say unto thee: Thou hast not distinguished between (*probably*: will they not say unto thee: Thou hast distinguished between) righteousness and unrighteousness, between the light and the darkness, and evil and good? Then said he: I will answer them and say: Unto Adam was power given to choose one of the two: he chose the light and laid his hand thereon, but the darkness he left behind him and cast away from him. Therefore have all men power to believe in the light which is life, and which is the Father that hath sent me. And every one that believeth and doeth the works of the light shall live in them; but if there be any that confesseth that he belongeth unto the light, and doeth the works of darkness, such an one hath no defence to utter, neither can he lift up his face to look upon the Son of God, which *Son* am I. For I will say unto him: As thou soughtest, so hast thou found, and as thou askedst, so hast thou received. Wherefore condemnest thou me, O man? Wherefore hast thou departed from me and denied me? And wherefore hast thou confessed me and yet denied me? hath not every man power to live and to die? Whoso then hath kept my commandments shall be a son of the light, that is, of the Father that is in me. But because of them that corrupt my words am I come down from heaven. I am the word: I became flesh, and I wearied myself (*or*, suffered) and taught, *saying*: The heavy laden shall be saved, and they that are gone astray shall go astray for ever. They shall be chastised and tormented in their flesh and in their soul.

40 And we said unto him: O Lord, verily we are sorrowful for their sake. And he said unto us: Ye do rightly, for the righteous are sorry for the sinners, and pray for them, making prayer unto my Father. Again we said unto him: Lord, is there none that maketh intercession unto thee (*so Eth.*)? And he said unto us: Yea, and I will hearken unto the prayer of the righteous which they make for them.

When he had so said unto us, we said to him: Lord, in all things hast thou taught us and had mercy on us and saved us, that we might preach unto them that are worthy to be saved, and that we might obtain a recompense with thee. (Shall we be partakers of a recompense from thee? *Eth.*) 41 He answered and said unto us: Go and preach, and ye shall be labourers, and fathers, and ministers. We said unto him: Thou art he (*or*, Art thou he) that shalt preach by us. (Lord, thou art our father. *Eth.*) Then answered he us, saying: Be not (*or*, Are not ye) all fathers or all masters. (Are then all fathers, or all servants, or all masters? *Eth.*) We said unto him: Lord, thou art he that saidst unto us: Call no man your father upon earth, for one is your Father, which is in heaven, and your master. Wherefore sayest thou now unto us: Ye shall be fathers of many children, and servants and masters? He answered and said unto us: According as ye have said (Ye have rightly said, *Eth.*). For verily I say unto you: whosoever shall hear you and believe on me, shall receive of you the light of the seal through me, and baptism through me: ye shall be fathers and servants and masters.

42 But we said unto him: Lord, how may it be that every one of us should be these three? He said unto us: Verily I say unto you: Ye shall be called fathers, because with praiseworthy heart and in love ye have revealed unto them the things of the kingdom of heaven. And ye shall be called servants, because they shall receive the baptism of life and the remission of their sins at my hand through you. And ye shall be called masters, because ye have given them the word without grudging, and have admonished them, and when ye admonished them, they turned themselves (were converted). Ye were not afraid of their riches, nor *ashamed* before their face, but ye kept the command-ments of my Father and fulfilled them. And ye shall have a great reward with my Father which is in heaven, and they shall have forgiveness of sins and everlasting life, and be partakers in the kingdom of heaven.

And we said unto him: Lord, even if every one of us had ten thousand tongues to speak withal, we could not thank thee, for that thou promisest such things unto us. Then answered he us, saying: Only do ye that which I say unto you, even as I myself also have done it. 43 And ye shall be like the wise virgins which watched and slept not, but went forth unto the lord into the bridechamber : but the foolish *virgins* were not able to watch, but slumbered. And we said unto him: Lord, who are the wise and who are the foolish? He said unto us: Five wise and five foolish; for these are they of whom the prophet hath spoken: Sons of God are they. Hear now their names.

But we wept and were troubled for them that slumbered. He said unto us: The five wise are Faith and Love and Grace and Peace and Hope. Now they of the faithful which possess this (these) shall be guides unto them that have believed on me and on him that sent me. For I am the Lord and I am the bridegroom whom they have received, and they have entered in to the house of the *bridegroom* and are laid down with me in the bridal chamber rejoicing. But the five foolish, when they had slept and had awaked, came unto the door of the bridal chamber and knocked, for *the doors* were shut. Then did they weep and lament that no man opened unto them.

We said unto him: Lord, and their wise sisters that were within in the bridegroom's house, did they continue without opening unto them, and did they not sorrow for their sakes nor entreat the bridegroom to open unto them? He answered us, saying: They were not yet able to obtain favour for them. We said unto him: Lord, on what day shall they enter in for their sisters' sake? Then said he unto us: He that is shut out, is shut out. And we said unto him: Lord, is this word (determined?). Who then are the foolish? He said unto us: Hear their names. They are Knowledge, Understanding (Perception), Obedience, Patience, and Compassion. These are they that slumbered in them that have believed and confessed me but have not fulfilled my commandments. 44 On account of them that have slumbered, they shall remain outside the kingdom and the fold of the shepherd and his sheep. But whoso shall abide outside the sheepfold, him will the wolves devour, and he shall be (condemned?) and die in much affliction: in him shall be no rest nor endurance, and (*Eth.*) although he be hardly punished, and rent in pieces and devoured in long and evil torment, yet shall he not be able to obtain death quickly.

45 And we said unto him: Lord, well hast thou revealed all this unto us. Then answered he us, saying: Understand ye not (*or*, Ye understand not) these words? We said unto him: Yea, Lord. By five shall men enter into thy kingdom ⟨and by five shall men remain without⟩: notwithstanding, they that watched were with thee the Lord and bridegroom, even though they rejoiced not because of them that slumbered (yet will they have no pleasure, because of, *Eth.*). He said unto us: They will

indeed rejoice that they have entered in with the bridegroom, the Lord; and they are sorrowful because of them that slumbered, for they are their sisters. For all ten are daughters of God, even the Father. Then said we unto him: Lord, is it then for thee to show them favour on account of their sisters? (It becometh thy majesty to show them favour, *Eth.*) He said unto us: ⟨It is not mine,⟩ but his that sent me, and I am consenting with him (It is not yours, &c., *Eth.*).

46 But be ye upright and preach rightly and teach, and be not abashed by any man and fear not any man, and especially the rich, for they do not my commandments, but boast themselves (swell) in their riches. And we said unto him: Lord, tell us if it be the rich only. He answered, saying unto us: If any man who is not rich and possesseth a small livelihood giveth unto the poor and needy, men will call him a benefactor.

47 But if any man fall under the load ⟨because⟩ of sin that he hath committed, then shall his neighbour correct him because of the good that he hath done unto his neighbour. And if his neighbour correct him and he return, he shall be saved, and he that corrected him shall receive a reward and live for ever. For a needy man, if he see him that hath done him good sin, and correct him not, shall be judged with severe judgement. Now if a blind man lead a blind, they both fall into a ditch: and whoso respecteth persons for their sake, shall be as the two ⟨blind⟩, as the prophet hath said: Woe unto them that respect persons and justify the ungodly for reward, even they whose God is their belly. Behold that judgement shall be their portion. For verily I say unto you: On that day will I neither have respect unto the rich nor pity for the poor.

48 If thou behold a sinner, admonish him betwixt him and thee: (if he hear thee, thou hast gained thy brother, *Eth.*) and if he hear thee not, then take to thee another, as many as three, and instruct thy brother: again, if he hear thee not, let him be unto thee

(Copt. defective from this point.)

as an heathen man or a publican.

49 If thou hear aught against thy brother, give it no credence; slander not, and delight not in hearing slander. For thus it is written: Suffer not thine ear to receive aught against thy brother: but if thou seest aught, correct him, rebuke him, and convert him. And we said unto him: Lord, thou hast in all things taught us and warned us. But, Lord, concerning the believers, even them to whom it belongeth to believe in the preaching of thy name: is it determined that among them also there shall be doubt and division, jealousy, confusion, hatred, and envy? For thou sayest: They shall find fault with one another and respect the person of them that sin, and hate them that rebuke them. And he answered and said unto us: How then shall the judgement

come about, that the corn should be gathered into the garner and the chaff thereof cast into the fire?

50 They that hate such things, and love me and rebuke them that fulfil not my commandments, shall be hated and persecuted and despised and mocked. Men will of purpose speak of them that which is not true, and will band themselves together against them that love me. But these will rebuke them, that they may be saved. But them that will rebuke and chasten and warn them, them will they (the others) hate, and thrust them aside, and despise them, and hold themselves far from them that wish them good. But they that endure such things shall be like unto the martyrs with the Father, because they have striven for righteousness, and have not striven for corruption.

And we asked him: Lord, shall such things be among us? And he answered us: Fear not; it shall not be in many, but in a few. We said unto him: Yet tell us, in what manner it shall come to pass. And he said unto us: There shall come forth another doctrine, and a confusion, and because they shall strive after their own advancement, they shall bring forth an unprofitable doctrine. And therein shall be a deadly corruption (of uncleanness), and they shall teach it, and shall turn away them that believe on me from my commandments and cut them off from eternal life. But woe unto them that falsify this my word and commandment, and draw away them that hearken to them from the life of the doctrine and separate themselves from the commandment of life: *for* together with them they shall come into everlasting judgement.

51 And when he had said this, and had finished his discourse with us, he said unto us again: Behold, on the third day and at the third hour shall he come which hath sent me, that I may depart with him. And as he so spake, there was thunder and lightning and an earthquake, and the heavens parted asunder, and there appeared a light (bright) cloud which bore him up. And *there came* voices of many angels, rejoicing and singing praises and saying: Gather us, O Priest, unto the light of the majesty. And when they drew nigh unto the firmament, we heard his voice *saying unto us*: Depart hence in peace.

APOCALYPSES

Of these it is my intention to include in this collection only such as bear the names of New Testament personages. There are several important books which are fathered upon patriarchs and prophets of the Old Testament, and some of these were composed by Christians, while others have received touches and insertions to adapt them for use by Christians. Most of these I have named in the Introduction.

Of Apocalypses attributed to New Testament personages there are not a very great many. That of *Peter* (early second century) leads the van in date and importance: that of *Paul* (fourth century) perhaps comes next in influence. That of *Thomas* has only come to light in recent years. A later stratum is represented by the Apocalypses of *John* (printed by Tischendorf) and the *Virgin*. The former is a series of questions and answers—the Byzantines were fond of this form of writing—about the end of the world, which contain nothing very interesting. A description of antichrist is perhaps the most notable feature: on this I have put together some matter in my *Lost Apocrypha of the O. T.*, to which I may refer the reader. That of the *Virgin* follows *Paul* closely.

The *Revelation of Stephen*, condemned in the Gelasian Decree along with *Paul* and *Thomas*, is something of a puzzle. A short section shall be devoted to it.

We hear of an *Apocalypse of James* the brother of the Lord, and one quotation from it occurs.[1]

The Syriac text printed by Rendel Harris, *The Gospel of the Twelve Apostles, with the Revelation of each one of them*, is in its present form late. It does not come up to its imposing title, for it only contains the utterances of Peter, John, and James.

Egypt has its contribution to offer. In Dr. Budge's volumes of Coptic texts will be found:

A Revelation of James the Less, telling how the Lord revealed the glory of John Baptist in the other world, where he figures as the ferryman of the blessed souls (*Coptic Apocrypha*, 1913, p. 343).

A book of 'Mysteries of St. John', questions of John the Evangelist addressed to the Cherubim: he is told about all manner of natural

---

[1] Von Dobschütz in *Byzantinische Zeitschrift*, 1903, p. 556, cites it from Coislin MS. 296 (Paris). It is to the effect that at the prayer of the apostles, the Lord 'added two sixtieths' to the time of his coming. The date indicated for the Second Coming is A. M. 6500. It is symbolized by the attitude of the priest's fingers when he blesses. The form of the citation is 'as James the brother of the Lord said in his Apocalypse'. The passage is not found in the Revelation of James contained in the late *Gospel of the Twelve Apostles* edited by Rendel Harris.

things, the rise of the Nile, the dew, &c., and also somewhat about Hezekiah and Solomon (*l. c.*, p. 241).

A revelation made by our Lord to the apostles about Abbaton the angel of death (*Coptic Martyrdoms*).

There is also a sort of Apocalypse of Philip extant only in Irish, which is apparently derived from a Latin original. It is called the *Evernew Tongue*. The tongue of the apostle Philip—which had been cut out seven times by his persecutors, ineffectually—discourses to an assembly of kings and prelates at Jerusalem, and tells them wonderful secrets of nature. See the *Journal of Theol. Studies*, 1918 (xx. 9), where I give an account of it.

In the same article I write on an apocalypse of which we do not know the name. Portions of it exist in Latin and in Irish—the latter embodied in the Vision of Adamnan. The Rev. St. J. Seymour also dealt with it more recently (*l. c.*, xxii. 16).

It tells of the sufferings of souls in the several heavens, and of their presentation to the Lord and acceptance or rejection. A distinctive mark of it is that the names of the heavens, and of the angelic guardian of each, are given.

Of the three Christian Apocalypses which will be presented here, two, *Peter* and *Paul*, are visions of the next world, the other, *Thomas*, is a prophecy of the end of this.

APOCALYPSE OF PETER

We have not a pure and complete text of this book, which ranked next in popularity and probably also in date to the Canonical Apocalypse of St. John.

We have, first, certain quotations made by writers of the first four centuries.

Next, a fragment in Greek, called the Akhmim fragment, found with the Passion-fragment of the Gospel of Peter in a manuscript known as the Gizeh MS. (discovered in a tomb) now at Cairo. This is undoubtedly drawn from the Apocalypse of Peter: but my present belief is that, like the Passion-fragment (see p. 90), it is part of the Gospel of Peter, which was a slightly later book than the Apocalypse and quoted it almost *in extenso*. There is also in the Bodleian Library a mutilated leaf of a very tiny Greek MS. of the fifth century which supplies a few lines of what I take to be the original Greek text.

Thirdly, an Ethiopic version contained in one of the numerous forms of the *Books of Clement*, a writing current in Arabic and Ethiopic, purporting to contain revelations—of the history of the world from the Creation, of the last times, and of guidance for the churches—dictated by Peter to Clement. The version of the Apocalypse contained in this has some extraneous matter at the beginning and end; but, as I have tried to show in a series of articles in the *Journal of Theological Studies* (1910–11) and the *Church Quarterly Review* (1915), it affords the best general idea of the contents of the whole book which we have. The second book of the Sibylline Oracles contains (in Greek hexameters) a paraphrase of a great part of the Apocalypse: and its influence can be traced in many early writings—the Acts of Thomas (55–57), the Martyrdom of Perpetua, the so-called Second Epistle of Clement, and, as I think, the Shepherd of Hermas: as well as in the Apocalypse of Paul, and many later visions.

The length of the book is given in the Stichometry of Nicephorus as 300 lines and in that of the Codex Claromontanus (D of the Epistles) as 270 : the latter is a Latin list of the Biblical books ; already cited for the Acts of Paul.

There is no mention of it in the Gelasian Decree, which is curious. At one time it was popular in Rome, for the Muratorian Canon mentions it (late in the second century?) along with the Apocalypse of John, though it adds, that ' some will not have it read in the church '. The fifth-century church historian Sozomen (vii. 19) says that to his knowledge it was still read annually in some churches in Palestine on Good Friday.

A translation of the ancient quotations shall be given first.

A

1. From Clement of Alexandria's so-called *Prophetical Extracts*, a series of detached sentences excerpted from some larger work, generally supposed to be his *Hypotyposes* or *Outlines* :

a. (41. 1) The Scripture saith that the children which have been exposed (by their parents) are delivered to a care-taking angel by whom they are educated, and *made to* grow up; and they shall be, it saith, as the faithful of an hundred years old are here (in this life). *b.* (41. 2) Wherefore also Peter in the Apocalypse saith: And a flash (lightning) of fire leaping from those children and smiting the eyes of the women.

2. *Ibid.* (48. 1) The providence of God doth not light upon them only that are in the flesh. For example, Peter in the Apocalypse saith that the children born out of due time (abortively) that would have been of the better part (i. e. would have been saved if they had lived)—these are delivered to a care-taking angel, that they may partake of knowledge and obtain the better abode, having suffered what they would have suffered had they been in the body. But the others (i. e. those who would not have been saved, had they lived) shall only obtain salvation, as *beings* that have been injured and had mercy shown to them, and shall continue without torment, receiving that as a reward.

But the milk of the mothers, flowing from their breasts and congealing, saith Peter in the Apocalypse, shall engender small beasts (snakes) devouring the flesh, and these running upon them devour them: teaching that the torments come to pass because of the sins (correspond to the sins).

3. From the *Symposium* (ii. 6) of Methodius of Olympus (third century). He does not name his source : Whence also we have received in inspired writings that children born untimely —even if they be the offspring of adultery—are delivered to care-taking angels. For if they had come into being contrary to the will and ordinance of that blessed nature of God, how could they have been delivered to angels to be nourished up in all repose and tranquillity? And how could they have confidently summoned their parents before the judgement seat of Christ to accuse them? saying : Thou, O Lord, didst not begrudge us this light that is common to all, but these exposed us to death, contemning thy commandment.

The word rendered *care-taking* in these passages is a very rare one—τημελοῦχος, *tēmelouchos*: so rare that it was mistaken by later readers for the proper name of an angel, and we find an angel Temeluchus in *Paul, John,* and elsewhere. A similar case is that of the word ταρταροῦχος, Tartaruchus, keeper of hell, which is applied to angels in our Apocalypse, and is also taken in the Ethiopic version, in *Paul,* and in other writings, to be a proper name.

4. From the *Apocritica* of Macarius Magnes (fourth century) of whom we know little. His book consists of extracts from a heathen opponent's attack on Christianity (Porphyry and Hierocles are named as possible authors of it) and his own answers. The heathen writer says (iv. 6, 7):

And by way of superfluity let this also be cited which is said in the Apocalypse of Peter. He introduces the heaven, to be judged along with the earth, thus: The earth, he says, shall present all men to God to be judged in the day of judgement, being itself also to be judged along with the heaven that encompasseth it.

5. *Ibid.* And this again he says, which is a statement full of impiety: And every power of heaven shall be melted, and the heaven shall be rolled up like a book, and all the stars shall fall like leaves from the vine, and as the leaves from the fig-tree.

This very nearly coincides with Isa. xxxiv. 4, and does not occur in our other texts of the Apocalypse.

6. In an old Latin homily on the Ten Virgins found and published by Dom Wilmart (*Bulletin d'anc. litt. et d'archéol. chrét.*) is this sentence:

The *closed door* is the river of fire by which the ungodly shall be kept out of the kingdom of God, as is written in Daniel and in Peter, in his Apocalypse. . . . That company of the foolish also shall arise and find the door shut, that is, the fiery river set against them.

The equivalent of all the above quotations is found in the Ethiopic text, with one exception, no. 5. The Akhmim text only contains something like no. 1 *b*: one indication out of many that it is a shortened and, I would say, secondary text.

B

THE AKHMIM FRAGMENT

which I should prefer to call Fragment II of the Gospel of Peter. It begins abruptly in a discourse of our Lord.

1 Many of them shall be false prophets, and shall teach ways

and diverse doctrines of perdition. 2 And they shall become
sons of of perdition. 8 And then shall God come unto my faithful ones that hunger and thirst and are afflicted and prove their
souls in this life, and shall judge the sons of iniquity.

4 And the Lord added and said: Let us go unto the mountain
(and) pray. 5 And going with him, we the twelve disciples
besought him that he would show us one of our righteous
brethren that had departed out of the world, that we might
see what manner of men they are in their form, and take courage,
and encourage also the men that *should* hear us.

6 And as we prayed, suddenly there appeared two men standing before the Lord (*perhaps add*, to the east) upon whom we
were not able to look. 7 For there issued from their countenance
a ray as of the sun, and their raiment was shining so as the eye
of man never saw the like: for no mouth is able to declare nor
heart to conceive the glory wherewith they were clad and the
beauty of their countenance. 8 Whom when we saw we were
astonied, for their bodies were whiter than any snow and redder
than any rose. 9 And the redness of them was mingled with
the whiteness, and, in a word, I am not able to declare their
beauty. 10 For their hair was curling and flourishing (flowery),
and fell comely about their countenance and their shoulders
like a garland woven of nard and various flowers, or like a rainbow in the air: such was their comeliness.

11 We, then, seeing the beauty of them were astonied at them,
for they appeared suddenly. 12 And I drew near to the Lord
and said: Who are these? 18 He saith to me: These are your
(our) righteous brethren whose appearance ye did desire to see.
14 And I said unto him: And where are all the righteous?
or of what sort is the world wherein they are, and possess this
glory? 15 And the Lord showed me a very great region outside
this world exceeding bright with light, and the air of that place
illuminated with the beams of the sun, and the earth of itself
flowering with blossoms that fade not, and full of spices and
plants, fair-flowering and incorruptible, and bearing blessed fruit.
16 And so great was the blossom that the odour thereof was
borne thence even unto us.

17 And the dwellers in that place were clad with the raiment
of shining angels, and their raiment was like unto their land.

18 And angels ran round about them there. 19 And the glory
of them that dwelt there was all equal, and with one voice they
praised the Lord God, rejoicing in that place.

20 The Lord saith unto us: This is the place of your leaders
(*or*, high priests), the righteous men.

21 And I saw also another place over against that one, very
squalid; and it was a place of punishment, and they that were
punished and the angels that punished them had their raiment
dark, according to the air of the place.

22 And some there were there hanging by their tongues; and these were they that blasphemed the way of righteousness, and under them was laid fire flaming and tormenting them.

23 And there was a great lake full of flaming mire, wherein were certain men that turned away from righteousness; and angels, tormentors, were set over them.

24 And there were also others, women, hanged by their hair above that mire which boiled up; and these were they that adorned themselves for adultery. And the men that were joined with them in the defilement of adultery were hanging by their feet, and had their heads hidden in the mire, and said: We believed not that we should come unto this place.

25 And I saw the murderers and them that were consenting to them cast into a strait place full of evil, creeping things, and smitten by those beasts, and so turning themselves about in that torment. And upon them were set worms like clouds of darkness. And the souls of them that were murdered stood and looked upon the torment of those murderers and said: O God, righteous is thy judgement.

26 And hard by that place I saw another strait place wherein the discharge and the stench of them that were in torment ran down, and there was as it were a lake there. And there sat women up to their necks in that liquor, and over against them many children which were born out of due time sat crying: and from them went forth rays of fire and smote the women in the eyes : and these were they that conceived out of wedlock (?) and caused abortion.

27 And other men and women were being burned up to their middle and cast down in a dark place and scourged by evil spirits, and having their entrails devoured by worms that rested not. And these were they that had persecuted the righteous and delivered them up.

28 And near to them again were women and men gnawing their lips and in torment, and having iron heated in the fire *set* against their eyes. And these were they that did blaspheme and speak evil of the way of righteousness.

29 And over against these were yet others, men and women, gnawing their tongues and having flaming fire in their mouths. And these were the false witnesses.

30 And in another place were gravel-stones sharper than swords or any spit, heated with fire, and men and women clad in filthy rags rolled upon them in torment.[1] And these were they that were rich and trusted in their riches, and had no pity upon orphans and widows but neglected the commandments of God.

---

[1] This is suggested by the LXX of two passages in Job: xli. 30, his bed is of sharp spits; viii. 17, on an heap of stones doth he rest, and shall live in the midst of gravel-stones.

31 And in another great lake full of foul matter (pus) and blood and boiling mire stood men and women up to their knees. And these were they that lent money and demanded usury upon usury.

32 *And* other men and women being cast down from a great rock (precipice) fell (came) to the bottom, and again were driven by them that were set over them, to go up upon the rock, and thence were cast down to the bottom and had no rest from this torment. And these were they that did defile their bodies, behaving as women: and the women that were with them were they that lay with one another as a man with a woman.

33 And beside that rock was a place full of much fire, and there stood men which with their own hands had made images for themselves instead of God, [And beside them other men and women][1] having rods of fire and smiting one another and never resting from this manner of torment. . . .

34 And yet others near unto them, men and women, burning and turning themselves about and roasted as in a pan. And these were they that forsook the way of God.

C

THE BODLEIAN LEAF

It measures but 2¾ by 2 inches and has 13 lines of 8 to 10 letters on each side (Madan's *Summary Catalogue*, No. 31810). The *verso* (second page) is difficult to read.

Recto = Gr. 33, 34 : women holding chains and scourging themselves before those idols of deceit. And they shall unceasingly have this torment. And near

Verso : them shall be other men and women burning in the burning of them that were mad after idols. And these are they which forsook the way of God wholly (?) and . . .

D

THE ETHIOPIC TEXT

First published by the Abbé Sylvain Grébaut in *Revue de l'Orient Chrétien*, 1910 : a fresh translation from his Ethiopic text by H. Duensing appeared in *Zeitschr. f. ntl. Wiss.*, 1913.

The Second Coming of Christ and Resurrection of the Dead (which *Christ* revealed unto Peter) who died because of their sins, for that they kept not the commandment of God their creator.

And he (Peter) pondered thereon, that he might perceive the mystery of the Son of God, the merciful and lover of mercy.

And when *the Lord* was seated upon the Mount of Olives, his *disciples* came unto him.

---

[1] The bracketed words are intrusive.

And we besought and entreated him severally and prayed him, saying unto him: Declare unto us what are the signs of thy coming and of the end of the world, that we may perceive and mark the time of thy coming and instruct them that come after us, unto whom we preach the word of thy gospel, and whom we set over (in) thy church, that they when they hear it may take heed to themselves and mark the time of thy coming.

And our Lord answered us, saying: Take heed that no man deceive you, and that ye be not doubters and serve other gods. Many shall come in my name, saying: I am the Christ. Believe them not, neither draw near unto them. For the coming of the Son of God shall not be plain (i. e. foreseen) ; but as the lightning that shineth from the east unto the west, so will I come upon the clouds of heaven with a great host in my majesty; with my cross going before my face will I come in my majesty; shining sevenfold more than the sun will I come in my majesty with all my saints, mine angels (mine holy angels). And my Father shall set a crown upon mine head, that I may judge the quick and the dead and recompense every man according to his works.

And ye, take ye the likeness thereof (learn a parable) from the fig-tree: so soon as the shoot thereof is come forth and the twigs grown, the end of the world shall come.

And I, Peter, answered and said unto him: Interpret unto me concerning the fig-tree, whereby we shall perceive it ; for throughout all its days doth the fig-tree send forth shoots, and every year it bringeth forth its fruit for its master. What *then* meaneth the parable of the fig-tree? We know it not.

And the Master (Lord) answered and said unto me: Understandest thou not that the fig-tree is the house of Israel? Even as a man *that* planted a fig-tree in his garden, and it brought forth no fruit. And he sought the fruit thereof many years, and when he found it not, he said to the keeper of his garden: Root up this fig-tree that it make not our ground to be unfruitful. And the gardener said unto God: (Suffer us) to rid it of weeds and dig the ground round about it and water it. If then it bear not fruit, we will straightway remove its roots out of the garden and plant another in place of it. Hast thou not understood that the fig-tree is the house of Israel? Verily I say unto thee, when the twigs thereof have sprouted forth in the last days, then shall feigned Christs come and awake expectation, *saying*: I am the Christ, that am now come into the world. And when they (Israel) shall perceive the wickedness of their deeds they shall turn away after them and deny him [whom our fathers did praise], even the first Christ whom they crucified and therein sinned a great sin. But this deceiver is not the Christ. [Something is wrong here: the sense required is that Israel perceives the wickedness of antichrist and does *not* follow him.] And when they reject him he shall slay with the sword, and there

shall be many martyrs. Then shall the twigs of the fig-tree, that
is, the house of Israel, shoot forth : many shall become martyrs
at his hand. Enoch and Elias shall be sent to teach them that this
is the deceiver which must come into the world and do signs and
wonders to deceive. And therefore shall they that die by his hand
be martyrs, and shall be reckoned among the good and righteous
martyrs who have pleased God in their life.[1]

And he showed me in his right hand the souls of all men.
And on the palm of his right hand the image of that which
shall be accomplished at the last day: and how the righteous
and the sinners shall be separated, and how they †do† that are
upright in heart, and how the evil-doers shall be rooted out unto
all eternity. We beheld how the sinners wept (weep) in great
affliction and sorrow, until all that saw it with their eyes wept,
whether righteous or angels, and he himself also.

And I asked him and said unto him: Lord, suffer me to speak
thy word concerning the sinners: It were better for them if they
had not been created. And the Saviour answered and said unto
me: Peter, wherefore speakest thou thus, *that* not to have been
created were better for them? Thou resistest God. Thou
wouldest not have more compassion than he for his image:
for he hath created them and brought them forth out of not
being. Now because thou hast seen the lamentation which
shall come upon the sinners in the last days, therefore is thine
heart troubled; but I will show thee their works, whereby they
have sinned against the Most High.

Behold now what shall come upon them in the last days,
when the day of God and the day of the decision of the judgement
of God cometh. From the east unto the west shall all the
children of men be gathered together before my Father that
liveth for ever. And he shall command hell to open its bars of
adamant and give up all that is therein.

And the wild beasts and the fowls shall he command to restore
all the flesh that they have devoured, because he willeth that
men should appear ; for nothing perisheth before God, and
nothing is impossible with him, because all things are his.

For all things *come to pass* on the day of decision, on the day
of judgement, at the word of God: and as all things were done
when he created the world and commanded all that is therein
and it was done—even so *shall it be* in the last days ; for all things
are possible with God. And therefore saith he in the scripture:[2]
Son of man, prophesy upon the several bones and say unto the
bones: bone unto bone in joints, sinew, nerves, flesh and skin
and hair thereon [and soul and spirit].

And soul and spirit shall the great Uriel give them at the

[1] Hermas, *Vision*, III. i. 9, speaks of 'those that have already been
well-pleasing unto God and have suffered for the Name's sake'.
[2] Ezek. xxxvii.

commandment of God; for him hath God set over the rising again of the dead at the day of judgement.

Behold and consider the corns of wheat that are sown in the earth. As things dry and without soul do men sow them in the earth: and they live again and bear fruit, and the earth restoreth them as a pledge entrusted unto it.

[And this that dieth, that is sown as seed in the earth, and shall become alive and be restored unto life, is man. *Probably a gloss.*]

How much more shall God raise up on the day of decision them that believe in him and are chosen of him, for whose sake he made [1] *the world*? And all things shall the earth restore on the day of decision, for it also shall be judged with them, and the heaven with it.[2]

And *this* shall come at the day of judgement upon them that have fallen away from faith in God and that have committed sin: Floods (cataracts) of fire shall be let loose; and darkness and obscurity shall come up and clothe and veil the whole world; and the waters shall be changed and turned into coals of fire, and all that is in them shall burn, and the sea shall become fire. Under the heaven *shall be* a sharp fire that cannot be quenched, and floweth *to fulfil* the judgement of wrath. And the stars shall fly in pieces by flames of fire, as if they had not been created, and the powers (firmaments) of the heaven shall pass away for lack of water and shall be as though they had not been. †And the lightnings of heaven shall be no more, and by their enchantment they shall affright the world† (*probably*: The heaven shall turn to lightning and the lightnings thereof shall affright the world). The spirits also of the dead bodies shall be like unto them (the lightnings?) and shall become fire at the commandment of God.

And so soon as the whole creation dissolveth, the men that are in the east shall flee unto the west, ⟨and they that are in the west⟩ unto the east; they that are in the south shall flee to the north, and they that are in ⟨the north unto⟩ the south. And in all places shall the wrath of a fearful fire overtake them; and an unquenchable flame driving them shall bring them unto the judgement of wrath, unto the stream of unquenchable fire that floweth, flaming with fire, and when the waves thereof part themselves one from another, burning, there shall be a great gnashing of teeth among the children of men.

Then shall they all behold me coming upon an eternal cloud of brightness: and the angels of God that are with me shall sit (*prob.* And I shall sit) upon the throne of my glory at the right hand of my heavenly Father; and he shall set a crown upon

[1] See the Third Epistle to the Corinthians (pp. 290–1) for a disquisition on the theme, most probably based on our passage.
[2] Quoted by the heathen writer in Macarius Magnes: see above among the fragments (p. 507).

mine head. And when the nations behold it, they shall weep, every nation apart.

Then shall he command them to enter into the river of fire while the works of every one of them shall stand before them (*something is wanting*) to every man according to his deeds. As for the elect that have done good, they shall come unto me and not see death by the devouring fire. But the unrighteous, the sinners, and the hypocrites shall stand in the depths of darkness that shall not pass away, and their chastisement is the fire, and angels bring forward their sins and prepare for them a place wherein they shall be punished for ever (every one according to his transgression).

Uriel (Urael) the angel of God shall bring forth the souls of those sinners (every one according to his transgression : *perhaps this clause should end the preceding paragraph : so Grébaut takes it*) who perished in the flood, and of all that dwelt in all idols, in every molten image, in every (object of) love, and in pictures, and of those that dwelt on all hills and in stones and by the wayside, whom men called gods: they shall burn them with them (the objects in which they dwelt, *or* their worshippers?) in everlasting fire ; and after that all of them with their dwelling-places are destroyed, they shall be punished eternally.

(Here begins the description of torments which we have, in another text, in the Akhmim fragment.)

Gr. 22.   Then shall men and women come unto the place prepared for them. By their tongues wherewith they have blasphemed the way of righteousness shall they be hanged up. There is spread *under* them unquenchable fire, that they escape it not.

Gr. 23.   Behold, another place: therein is a pit, great and full (of . .) In it are they that have denied righteousness: and angels of punishment chastise them and there do they kindle upon them the fire of their torment.

Gr. 24.   And again *behold* [two: *corrupt*] women: they hang them up by their neck and by their hair; they shall cast them into the pit. These are they which plaited their hair, not for good (*or*, not to make them beautiful) but to turn them to fornication, that they might ensnare the souls of men unto perdition. And the men that lay with them in fornication shall be hung by their loins in that place of fire ; and they shall say one to another: We knew not that we should come into everlasting punishment.

Gr. 25.   And the murderers and them that have made common cause with them shall they cast into the fire, in a place full of venomous beasts, and they shall be tormented without rest, feeling their pains ; and their worms shall be as many in number as a dark cloud. And the angel Ezraël shall bring forth the souls of them that have been slain, and they shall behold the torment of them that slew them, and say one to another: Righteousness and justice is the judgement of God. For we heard, but we believed not, that we should come into this place of eternal judgement.

And near by this flame shall be a pit, great and Gr. 26. very deep, and into it floweth from above all manner of †torment,† foulness, and issue. And women are swallowed up therein up to their necks and tormented with great pain. These are they that have caused their children to be born untimely, and have corrupted the work of God that created them. Over against them shall be another place where sit their children [both] alive, and they cry unto God. And flashes (lightnings) Clem. go forth from those children and pierce the eyes of them Alex. that for fornication's sake have caused their destruction.

Other men and women shall stand above them, Metho-naked; and their children stand over against them in dius. a place of delight, and sigh and cry unto God because of their parents, *saying*: These are they that have despised and cursed and transgressed thy commandments and delivered us unto death: they have cursed the angel that formed us, and have hanged us up, and withheld from us (*or*, begrudged us) the light which thou hast given unto all creatures. And the milk of Clem. their mothers flowing from their breasts shall congeal, Alex. and from it shall come beasts devouring flesh, which shall come forth and turn and torment them for ever with their husbands, because they forsook the commandments of God and slew their children. As for their children, they shall be delivered unto the angel Temlākos (i. e. a care-taking angel: *see above, in the Fragments*). And they that slew them shall be tormented eternally, for God willeth it so.

Ezraël the angel of wrath shall bring men and women, Gr. 27. the half of their bodies burning, and cast them into a place of darkness, even the hell of men; and a spirit of wrath shall chastise them with all manner of torment, and a worm that sleepeth not shall devour their entrails: and these are the persecutors and betrayers of my righteous ones.

And beside them that are there, *shall be* other men Gr. 28. and women, gnawing their tongues; and they shall torment them with red-hot iron and burn their eyes. These are they that slander and doubt of my righteousness.

Gr. 29.   Other men and women whose works *were done* in deceitfulness shall have their lips cut off; and fire entereth into their mouth and their entrails. These are the false witnesses (*al.* these are they that caused the martyrs to die by their lying).

Gr. 30.   And beside them, in a place near at hand, †upon the stone shall be a pillar of fire,† and the pillar is sharper than swords. *And there shall be* men and women clad in rags and filthy garments, and they shall be cast thereon, to suffer the *judgement* of a torment that ceaseth not: these are they that trusted in their riches, and despised the widows and the woman *with* fatherless children . . . before God.

Gr. 31.   And into another place hard by, full of filth, do they cast men and women up to the knees. These are they that lent money and took usury.

Gr. 32.   And other men and women cast themselves down from an high place and return again and run, and devils drive them. [These are the worshippers of idols] †and they put them to the end of their wits† (drive them up to the top of the height) and they cast themselves down. And thus do they continually, and are tormented for ever. These are they which have †cut† their flesh as [†apostles†] of a man: and the women that were with them . . . and these are the men that defiled themselves together as women. (*This is very corrupt : but the sense is clear in the Greek.*)

Gr. 33.   And beside them (shall be a brazier ?) . . . and beneath them shall the angel Ezraël prepare a place of much fire: and all the idols of gold and silver, all idols, the work of men's hands, and the semblances of images of cats and lions, of creeping things and wild beasts, and the men and women that have prepared the images thereof, *shall be* in chains of fire and shall be chastised because of their error before the *idols*, and this is their judgement for ever. (*In the Greek they beat each other with rods of fire : and this is better.*)

Gr. 34.   And beside them *shall be* other men and women, burning in the fire of the judgement, and their torment is ever-lasting. These are they that have forsaken the command-ment of God and followed the (persuasions ?) of devils.

(*Parts of these two sections are in the Bodleian fragment. At this point the Akhmim fragment ends. The Ethiopic continues :*)

And there shall be another place, very high (*corrupt sentences follow. Duensing omits them : Grébaut renders doubtfully :* There shall be a furnace and a brazier wherein shall burn fire. The fire that shall burn *shall come* from one end of the brazier). The men and women whose feet slip, shall go rolling down into a place where is fear. And again while the *fire* that is prepared floweth, they mount up and fall down again and continue to roll down. (*This suggests a narrow bridge over a stream of fire which they keep trying to cross.*) Thus shall they be tormented for ever. These are they that honoured not their father and mother and of their own accord withheld (withdrew) themselves from them. Therefore shall they be chastised eternally.

Furthermore the angel Ezraël shall bring children and maidens, to show them those that are tormented. They shall be chastised with pains, with hanging up (?) and with a multitude of wounds which flesh-devouring birds shall inflict upon them. These are they that boast themselves (trust) in their sins, and obey not their parents and follow not the instruction of their fathers, and honour not them that are more aged than they.

Beside them *shall be* girls clad in darkness for a garment, and they shall be sore chastised and their flesh shall be torn in pieces. These are they that kept not their virginity until they were given in marriage, and with these torments shall they be punished, and shall feel them.

And again, other men and women, gnawing their tongues without ceasing, and being tormented with everlasting fire. These are the servants (slaves) which were not obedient unto their masters; and this then is their judgement for ever.

And hard by this place of torment shall be men and women dumb and blind, whose raiment is white. They shall crowd one upon another, and fall upon coals of unquenchable fire. These are they that give alms and say: We are righteous before God: whereas they have not sought after righteousness.

Ezraël the angel of God †shall bring them forth out of this fire and establish a judgement of decision†. This then is their judgement. A river of fire shall flow and all †judgement† (they that are judged) shall be drawn down into the middle of the river. And Uriel shall set them there.

And there are wheels of fire, and men and women hung thereon by the strength of the whirling *thereof*. †And they that are in the pit shall burn†: now these are the sorcerers and sorceresses. †Those wheels shall be in all decision (judgement, punishment) by fire without number†.

Thereafter shall the angels bring mine elect and righteous which are perfect in all uprightness, and bear them in their hands, and clothe them with the raiment of the life that is above. They shall see their desire on them that hated them, when he punisheth them, *and* the torment of every one shall be for ever according to his works.

And all they that are in torment shall say with one voice: Have mercy upon us, for now know we the judgement of God, which he declared unto us aforetime, and we believed not. And the angel Tatîrōkos (Tartaruchus, *keeper of hell : a word corresponding in formation to* Temeluchus) shall come and chastise them with yet greater torment, and say unto them: Now do ye repent, when it is no longer the time for repentance, and nought of life remaineth. And they shall say: Righteous is the judgement of God, for we have heard and perceived that his judgement is good; for we are recompensed according to our deeds.

Then will I give unto mine elect and righteous the washing (baptism) and the salvation for which they have besought me, in the field of Akrosja (Acherousia, *a lake in other writings, e. g. Apocalypse of Moses—where the soul of Adam is washed in it: see also Paul* 22, 23) which is called Anēslaslejā (Elysium). They shall adorn with flowers the portion of the righteous, and I shall go . . . I shall rejoice with them. I will cause the peoples to enter in to mine everlasting kingdom, and show them that eternal *thing* (life?) whereon I have made them to set their hope, even I and my Father which is in heaven.

I have spoken this unto thee, Peter, and declared it unto thee. Go forth therefore and go unto the land (*or* city) of the west. (*Duensing omits the next sentences as unintelligible ; Grébaut and N. McLean render thus :* and enter into the vineyard which I shall tell thee of, in order that by the sickness (sufferings) of the Son who is without sin the deeds of corruption may be sanctified. As for thee, thou art chosen according to the promise which I have given thee. Spread thou therefore my gospel throughout all the world in peace. Verily men shall rejoice: my words shall be the source of hope and of life, and suddenly shall the world be ravished.)

(*We now have the section descriptive of paradise, which in the Akhmim text precedes that about hell.*)

Gr. 4. And my Lord Jesus Christ our king said unto me: Let us go unto the holy mountain. And his disciples
Gr. 6. went with him, praying. And behold there were two
Gr. 7. men there, and we could not look upon their faces, for a light came from them, shining more than the sun, and their raiment also was shining, and cannot be described, and nothing is sufficient to be compared unto them in this world. And the sweetness of them . . . that no mouth is able to utter the beauty of their appearance (*or*, the mouth hath not sweetness to express, &c.), for their aspect was astonishing and wonderful. †And the other, great, I say† (*probably*: and, in a word, I cannot describe it), shineth in his (*sic*) aspect above
Gr. 8, 9. crystal. *Like* the flower of roses is the appearance of the colour of his aspect and of his body . . . his head (*al.*
Gr. 10. their head was a marvel). And upon his (their) shoulders (*evidently something about their hair has dropped out*)

and on their foreheads was a crown of nard woven of
fair flowers. As the rainbow in the water,[1] so was
their hair. And such was the comeliness of their countenance, adorned with all manner of ornament. And when Gr. 11.
we saw them on a sudden, we marvelled. And I drew Gr. 12.
near unto the Lord (God) Jesus Christ and said unto
him: O my Lord, who are these? And he said unto Gr. 13.
me: They are Moses and Elias. And I said unto him: Gr. 14.
⟨Where then are⟩ Abraham and Isaac and Jacob and
the rest of the righteous fathers? And he showed us Gr. 15.
a great garden, open, full of fair trees and blessed fruits,
and of the odour of perfumes. The fragrance thereof Gr. 16.
was pleasant and came even unto us. And thereof
(al. of that tree) . . . saw I much fruit. And my Lord (Gr. 20).
and God Jesus Christ said unto me: Hast thou seen
the companies of the fathers?

As is their rest,[2] such also is the honour and the glory of them
that are persecuted for my righteousness' sake. And I rejoiced
and believed [and believed] and understood that which is written
in the book of my Lord Jesus Christ. And I said unto him:
O my Lord, wilt thou that I make here three tabernacles, one
for thee, and one for Moses, and one for Elias? And he said
unto me in wrath: Satan maketh war against thee, and hath
veiled thine understanding; and the good things of this world
prevail against thee. Thine eyes therefore must be opened and
thine ears unstopped that ⟨thou mayest see ?⟩ [3] a tabernacle,
not made with men's hands, which my heavenly Father hath
made for me and for the elect. And we beheld *it and were* full
of gladness.

And behold, suddenly there came a voice from heaven, saying:
This is my beloved Son in whom I am well pleased: ⟨he hath
kept⟩ my commandments. And then came a great and exceeding
white cloud over our heads and bare away our Lord and Moses
and Elias. And I trembled and was afraid: and we looked up;
and the heaven opened and we beheld men in the flesh, and they
came and greeted our Lord and Moses and Elias and went into
another heaven. And the word of the scripture was fulfilled:
This is the generation that seeketh him and seeketh the face of the
God of Jacob. And great fear and commotion was there in heaven,
and the angels pressed one upon another that the word of the
scripture might be fulfilled which saith: Open the gates, ye princes.
Thereafter was the heaven shut, that had been open.

And we prayed and went down from the mountain, glorifying
God, which hath written the names of the righteous in heaven
in the book of life.

[1] Probably: in the time of rain. From the LXX of Ezek. i. 28.
[2] Here Eth. inserts the clause, 'And I rejoiced', &c., rightly removed
to the next sentence by Duensing. [3] *Or*, There is but one tabernacle.

There is a great deal more of the Ethiopic text, but it is very evidently of later date; the next words are:

'Peter opened his mouth and said to me: Hearken, my son Clement; God created all things for his glory,' and this proposition is dwelt upon. The glory of those who duly praise God is described in terms borrowed from the Apocalypse: 'The Son at his coming will raise the dead . . . and will make my righteous ones shine *seven times more than the sun*, and will make their crowns shine *like crystal* and like the *rainbow in the time of rain*, (crowns) which are perfumed with *nard* and *cannot be contemplated*, (adorned) with rubies, with the colour of emeralds shining brightly, with topazes, gems, and yellow pearls that shine like the stars of heaven, and like the rays of the sun, sparkling, which cannot be gazed upon.' Again, of the angels: 'Their faces *shine more than the sun*; their crowns are as *the rainbow in the time of rain*. (They are perfumed) *with nard*. Their eyes shine like the morning star. *The beauty of their appearance cannot be expressed*. . . . Their raiment is not woven, but white as that of the fuller, according as I saw on the mountain where Moses and Elias were. Our Lord showed at the transfiguration the apparel of the last days, of the day of resurrection, unto Peter, James and John the sons of Zebedee, and a bright cloud overshadowed *us*, and we heard the voice of the Father saying unto us: This is my Son whom I love and in whom I am well pleased: hear him. And being afraid we forgat all the things of this life and of the flesh, and knew not what we said because of the greatness of the wonder of that day, and of the mountain whereon he showed us the second coming in the kingdom that passeth not away.'

Next: 'The Father hath committed all judgement unto the Son.' The destiny of sinners—their eternal doom—is more than Peter can endure: he appeals to Christ to have pity on them.

And my Lord answered me and said to me: 'Hast thou understood that which I said unto thee before? It is permitted unto thee to know that concerning which thou askest: but thou must not tell that which thou hearest unto the sinners lest they transgress the more, and sin.' Peter weeps many hours, and is at last consoled by an answer which, though exceedingly diffuse and vague, does seem to promise ultimate pardon for all: 'My Father will give unto them all the life, the glory, and the kingdom that passeth not away,' . . . 'It is because of them that have believed in me that I am come. It is also because of them that have believed in me, that, at their word, I shall have pity *on men*.' The doctrine that sinners will be saved at last by the prayers of the righteous is, rather obscurely, enunciated in the Second Book of the Sibylline Oracles (a paraphrase, in this part, of the Apocalypse), and in the (Coptic) Apocalypse of Elias (see *post*).

Ultimately Peter orders Clement to hide this revelation in a box, that foolish men may not see it.

The passage in the Second Book of the Sibylline Oracles which seems to point to the ultimate salvation of all sinners will be found in the last lines of the translation given below.

The passage in the Coptic Apocalypse of Elias is guarded and obscure in expression, but significant. It begins with a sentence which has a parallel in *Peter*.

The righteous will behold the sinners in their punishment, and those who have persecuted them and delivered them up. Then will the sinners on their part behold the place of the righteous and be partakers of grace. In that day will that for which the (righteous) shall often pray, be granted to them.

That is, as I take it, the salvation of sinners will be granted at the prayer of the righteous.

Compare also the Epistle of the Apostles, 40: 'the righteous are sorry for the sinners, and pray for them. . . . And I will hearken unto the prayer of the righteous which they make for them.'

I would add that the author of the Acts of Paul, who (in the Third Epistle to the Corinthians and elsewhere) betrays a knowledge of the Apocalypse of Peter, makes Falconilla, the deceased daughter of Tryphaena, speak of Thecla's praying for her that she may be translated into the place of the righteous (Thecla episode, 28).

My impression is that the maker of the Ethiopic version (or of its Arabic parent, or of another ancestor) has designedly omitted or slurred over some clauses in the passage beginning: 'Then will I give unto mine elect', and that in his very diffuse and obscure appendix to the Apocalypse, he has tried to break the dangerous doctrine of the ultimate salvation of sinners gently to his readers. But when the Arabic version of the Apocalypse is before us in the promised edition of MM. Griveau and Grébaut, we shall have better means of deciding.

E

APPENDIX

SECOND BOOK OF THE SIBYLLINE ORACLES, 190–338

It seems worth while to append here a translation of that portion of the Second Book which is most evidently taken from the Apocalypse of Peter. It may be remarked that Books I and II of the oracles really form but one composition, which is Christian and may be assigned to some time not early in the second century, or to the third. Many lines are borrowed from the older books, especially III and VIII.

After saying (l. 187) that Elias will descend on earth and do three great signs, it proceeds:

190 Woe unto all them that are found great with child in that day, and to them that give suck to infant children, and to them that dwell by the sea (the waves). Woe to them that shall behold that day. For a dark mist shall cover the boundless world, of the east and west, the south and north

And then shall a great river of flaming fire flow from heaven
and consume all places, the earth and the great ocean and
the grey sea, lakes and rivers and fountains, and merciless
200 Hades and the pole of heaven: but the lights of heaven shall
melt together in one and into a void (desolate) shape (?).
For the stars shall all fall from heaven into the sea (?), and
all souls of men shall gnash their teeth as they burn in the
river of brimstone and the rush of the fire in the blazing
plain, and ashes shall cover all things. And then shall all
the elements of the world be laid waste, air, earth, sea, light,
poles, days and nights, and no more shall the multitudes of
birds fly in the air nor swimming creatures any more swim
the sea; no ship shall sail with its cargo over the waves;
210 no straight-going oxen shall plough the tilled land; there
shall be no more sound of swift winds, but he shall fuse
all things together into one, and purge them clean.
214　　Now when the immortal angels of the undying God,
Barakiel, Ramiel, Uriel, Samiel, and Azael,[1] knowing all the
evil deeds that any hath wrought aforetime—then out of the
misty darkness they shall bring all the souls of men to
judgement, unto the seat of God the immortal, the great.
220 For he only is incorruptible, himself the Almighty, who shall
be the judge of mortal men. And then unto them of the
underworld shall the heavenly one give their souls and spirit
and speech; and their bones joined together, with all the
joints, and the flesh and sinews and veins, and skin also over
the flesh, and hair as before, and the bodies of the dwellers
upon earth shall be moved and arise in one day, joined
together in immortal fashion and breathing.
Then shall the great angel Uriel break the monstrous bars
framed of unyielding and unbroken adamant, of the brazen
230 gates of Hades, and cast them down straightway, and bring
forth to judgement all the sorrowful forms, yea, of the
ghosts of the ancient Titans, and of the giants, and all whom
the flood overtook. And all whom the wave of the sea hath
destroyed in the waters, and all whom beasts and creeping
things and fowls have feasted on: all these shall he bring
to the judgement seat; and again those whom flesh-devouring
fire hath consumed in the flames, them also shall he gather
and set before God's seat.
And when he shall overcome Fate and raise the dead, then
shall Adonai Sabaoth the high thunderer sit on his heavenly
240 throne, and set up the great pillar, and Christ himself, the
undying unto the undying, shall come in the clouds in glory
with the pure angels, and shall sit on the seat on the right
of the Great One, judging the life of the godly and the walk
of ungodly men.

[1] These names are from *Enoch*.

And Moses also the great, the friend of the Most High,
shall come, clad in flesh, and the great Abraham himself
shall come, and Isaac and Jacob, Jesus, Daniel, Elias,
Ambacum (Habakkuk), and Jonas, and they whom the
Hebrews slew: and all the Hebrews that were with (after?)
Jeremias shall be judged at the judgement seat, and he shall
250 destroy them, that they may receive a due reward and
expiate all that they did in their mortal life.

And then shall all men pass through a blazing river and
unquenchable flame, and the righteous shall be saved whole,
all of them, but the ungodly shall perish therein unto all
ages, even as many as wrought evil aforetime, and committed murders, and all that were privy thereto, liars,
thieves, deceivers, cruel destroyers of houses, gluttons,
marriers by stealth, shedders of evil rumours, sorely insolent,
260 lawless, idolaters: and all that forsook the great immortal
God and became blasphemers and harmers of the godly,
breakers of faith and destroyers of righteous men. And all
that look with guileful and shameless double faces—reverend
priests and deacons—[1] and judge unjustly, dealing per-
versely, obeying false rumours . . . more deadly than leopards
and wolves, and very evil: and all that are high-minded,
and usurers that heap up in their houses usury out of usury
270 and injure orphans and widows continually: and they that
give alms of unjust gain unto widows and orphans, and they
that when they give alms of their own toil, reproach them;
and they that have forsaken their parents in their old age and
not repaid them at all, nor recompensed them for their
nurture; yea, and they that have disobeyed and spoken
hard words against their parents: they also that have
received pledges and denied them, and servants that have
turned against their masters; and again they which have
280 defiled their flesh in lasciviousness, and have loosed the
girdle of virginity in secret union, and they that make the
child in the womb miscarry, and that cast out their offspring
against right: sorcerers also and sorceresses with these shall
the wrath of the heavenly and immortal God bring near unto
the pillar, all round about which the untiring river of fire
shall flow. And all of them shall the undying angels of the
immortal everlasting God chastise terribly with flaming
scourges, and shall bind them fast from above in fiery chains,
290 bonds unbreakable. And then shall they cast them down in
the darkness of night into Gehenna among the beasts of hell,
many and frightful, where is darkness without measure.

And when they have dealt out many torments unto all
whose heart was evil, thereafter out of the great river shall
a wheel of fire encompass them, because they devised wicked

---

[1] Something is lost or corrupt here.

works. And then shall they lament apart every one from
another in miserable fate, fathers and infant children, mothers
and sucklings weeping, nor shall they be sated with tears,
300 nor shall the voice of them that mourn piteously apart be
heard (?); but far under dark and squalid Tartarus shall
they cry in torment, and in no holy place shall they abide
and expiate threefold every evil deed that they have done,
burning in a great flame; and shall gnash their teeth, all of
them worn out with fierce thirst and hunger (*al.* force,
violence), and shall call death lovely and it shall flee from
them: for no more shall death nor night give them rest,
and oft-times shall they ·beseech in vain the Almighty God,
310 and then shall he openly turn away his face from them.
For he hath granted the limit of seven ages for repentance
unto men that err, by the hand of a pure virgin.
   But the residue which have cared for justice and good
deeds, yea, and godliness and righteous thoughts, shall angels
bear up and carry through the flaming river unto light, and
life without care, where is the immortal path of the great
God; and three fountains, of wine and honey and milk.
And the earth, common to all, not parted out with walls or
320 fences, shall then bring forth of her own accord much fruit,
and life and wealth shall be common and undistributed.
For there shall be no poor man, nor rich, nor tyrant, nor
slave, none great nor small any longer, no kings, no princes;
but all men shall be together in common. And no more
shall any man say 'night is come', nor 'the morrow',
nor 'it was yesterday'. He maketh no more of days, nor of
spring, nor winter, nor summer, nor autumn, neither marriage, nor death, nor selling, nor buying, nor set of sun, nor
rising. For God shall make one long day.
330   And unto them, the godly, shall the almighty and immortal
God grant another *boon*, when they shall ask it of him. He
shall grant them to save men out of the fierce fire and the
eternal gnashing of teeth : and this will he do, for he will gather
them again out of the everlasting flame and remove them
elsewhither, sending them for the sake of his people unto
another life eternal and immortal, in the Elysian plain
where are the long waves of the Acherusian lake exhaustless
338 and deep bosomed.
   Some artless iambic lines of uncertain date are appended here,
which show what was thought of the doctrine :

' Plainly false: for the fire will never cease to torment the damned.
I indeed could pray that it might be so, who am branded with
the deepest scars of transgressions which stand in need of utmost
mercy. But let Origen be ashamed of his lying words, who saith
that there is a term set to the torments.'

525

APOCALYPSE OF PAUL

Epiphanius tells us that the Caianites or Cainites had forged a book full of unspeakable matter in the name of Paul, which was also used by those who are called Gnostics, which they call the Anabaticon of Paul, basing it on the words of the apostle—that he was taken up into the third heaven. This has left no trace (*Heresy*, 38. 2).

St. Augustine laughs at the folly of some who had forged an Apocalypse of Paul, full of fables, and pretending to contain the unutterable things which the apostle had heard. This is, I doubt not, our book. (Aug. *on John, Tract* 98.) Sozomen, in his *Ecclesiastical History* (vii. 19), says: The book now circulated as the Apocalypse of Paul the apostle, which none of the ancients ever saw, is commended by most monks; but some contend that this book was found in the reign we write of (of Theodosius). For they say that by a Divine manifestation there was found underground at Tarsus of Cilicia, in Paul's house, a marble chest, and that in it was this book. However, when I inquired about this, a Cilician, a priest of the church of Tarsus, told me it was a lie. He was a man whose grey hairs showed him to be of considerable age, and he said that no such thing had happened in their city, and that he wondered whether the tale (*or*, the book) had not been made up by heretics.

Sozomen's story is that which appears in our book; and we need not doubt that this Apocalypse made its appearance in the last years of the fourth century.

It is condemned in the Gelasian Decree, and is mentioned with disapproval by various late church writers.

Though not an early book, it is made up very largely of early matter; and it had an immense vogue, especially in the West. Greek copies of it are rare, and the texts they contain are disfigured by many omissions. Of the Eastern versions—Syriac, Coptic, Ethiopic—the Syriac is the best. But possibly the full Latin version is superior to all other authorities. There are several abridged Latin texts, and from these were made the many versions which were current in almost every European language.

In an early canto of the *Inferno* (ii. 28) Dante mentions the visit of the 'Chosen Vessel' to Hell [1]—an undoubted allusion to the Apocalypse. And both in the Divine Comedy and in the hundreds of earlier mediaeval visions of the next world the influence of this book is perceptible, sometimes faintly, often very plainly indeed.

The reader will soon see for himself that *Paul* is a direct descendant of *Peter*, especially in his description of Hell-torments.[2] He will also see that the book is very badly put together; and that whole episodes,

[1] 'Andovvi poi lo Vas d'elezione,' &c.
[2] I have not marked the parallels with *Peter*: the reader cannot miss them; but I have adduced passages from *Elias* and *Zephaniah* which seem to be the sources of several episodes in *Paul*. Our texts of *Elias* and *Zephaniah* are not good; we have them only in Coptic, edited by Steindorff. Note, by the way, that what I (and most others) call *Zephaniah*, Steindorff too cautiously calls an 'anonymous Apocalypse'.

e.g. the visit to Paradise, are repeated. This means that the author is combining different sources in a very unintelligent way.

In the Greek, Latin, and Syriac the book is incomplete: it ends abruptly in a speech of Elijah. The Coptic version—only recently published—has a long continuation; part of this is, I think, original, but it tails off into matter which cannot be. This conclusion has even a third visit to Paradise! I give some particulars of it later.

The plan of the book is briefly this:

1, 2. Discovery of the revelation.
3–6. Appeal of creation to God against man.
7–10. The report of the angels to God about men.
11–18. Deaths and judgements of the righteous and the wicked.
19–30. First vision of Paradise.
31–44. Hell. Paul obtains rest on Sunday for the lost.
45–51. Second vision of Paradise.

The full Latin version is the basis of my translation: the Greek, Syriac, and Coptic are used where the Latin is corrupt.

Here beginneth the Vision of Saint Paul the Apostle.

But I will come to visions and revelations of the Lord. I knew a man in Christ fourteen years ago, whether in the body I know not, or whether out of the body I know not—God knoweth—that such an one was caught up unto the third heaven : and I knew such a man, whether in the body or out of the body I know not—God knoweth— that he was caught up into paradise and heard secret words which it is not lawful for men to utter. For such an one will I boast, but for myself I will boast nothing, save of mine infirmities.

1 *At what time was it made manifest ?* [1] *In the consulate of Theodosius Augustus the younger and Cynegius, a certain honourable man then dwelling at Tarsus, in the house which had been the house of Saint Paul, an angel appeared unto him by night and gave him a revelation, saying that he should break up the foundation of the house and publish that which he found ; but he thought this to be a lying vision.* 2 *But a third time the angel came, and scourged him and compelled him to break up the foundation. And he dug, and found a box of marble inscribed upon the sides : therein was the revelation of Saint Paul, and his shoes wherein he walked when he taught the word of God. But he feared to open that box, and brought it to the judge ; and the judge took it, sealed as it was with lead, and sent it to the emperor Theodosius, fearing that it might be somewhat strange ; and the emperor when he received it, opened it and found the revelation of Saint Paul. A copy thereof he sent to Jerusalem and the original he kept with him.* (Gr. reverses this: *he kept the copy and sent away the original.* It adds: *And there was written therein as followeth.*)

3 Now while I was in the body, wherein I was caught up unto the third heaven, the word of the Lord came unto me, saying: Speak unto this people: How long will ye transgress, and add

---

[1] *Syr.* puts the story of the discovery at the end of the book.

sin upon sin, and tempt the Lord that made you?[1] Saying that
ye are Abraham's children but doing the works of Satan (*so Gr.*;
Lat. Ye are the sons of God, doing the work of the devil), walking
in the confidence of God, boasting in your name only, but being
poor because of the matter of sin. Remember therefore and know
that the whole creation is subject unto God, but mankind only
sinneth. It hath dominion over the whole creation, and sinneth
more than the whole of nature. 4 For oftentimes hath the sun,
the great light, appealed unto the Lord, saying: O Lord God
Almighty, I look forth upon the ungodliness and unrighteousness
of men. Suffer me, and I will do unto them according to my
power, that they may know that thou art God alone. And there
came a voice unto it, saying: All these things do I know, for
mine eye seeth and mine ear heareth, but my long-suffering
beareth with them until they turn and repent. But if they
return not unto me, I will judge them all. 5 And sometimes the
moon and the stars have appealed unto the Lord, saying: O Lord
God Almighty, unto us hast thou given rule over the night; how
long shall we look upon the ungodliness and fornications and
murders which the children of men commit? suffer us to do
unto them according unto our powers, that they may know that
thou art God alone. And there came a voice unto them, saying:
I know all these things, and mine eye looketh upon them and
mine ear heareth, but my long-suffering beareth with them until
they turn and repent. But if they return not unto me, I will
judge them. 6 Oftentimes also the sea hath cried out, saying:
O Lord God Almighty, men have polluted thine holy name in
me: suffer me and I will arise and cover every wood and tree
and all the world, till I blot out all the children of men from
before thy face, that they may know that thou art God alone.
And again a voice came, saying: I know all, for mine eye seeth
all things, and mine ear heareth, but my long-suffering beareth
with them until they turn and repent. But if they return not,
I will judge them.

Sometimes also the waters have appealed against the children
of men, saying: O Lord God Almighty, the children of men have
all defiled thine holy name. And there came a voice, saying:
I know all things before they come to pass, for mine eye seeth
and mine ear heareth all things: but my long-suffering beareth
with them until they turn. And if not, I will judge. Often also
hath the earth cried out unto the Lord against the children of
men, saying: O Lord God Almighty, I suffer hurt more than all

[1] The Apocalypse of Elias is probably the source here. It begins:
The word of the Lord came unto me: Son of Man, say unto this
people: Wherefore do ye heap sin upon sin and provoke God the
Lord that made you? Love not the world, &c. . . . *After a few lines:*
For oftentimes hath the devil desired that the sun should not rise
upon the earth, &c.

thy creation, bearing the fornications, adulteries, murders, thefts, forswearings, sorceries, and witchcrafts of men, and all the evils that they do, so that the father riseth up against the son, and the son against the father, the stranger against the stranger, every one to defile his neighbour's wife. The father goeth up upon his son's bed, and the son likewise goeth up upon the couch of his father; and with all these evils have they that offer a sacrifice unto thy name polluted thine holy place. Therefore do I suffer hurt more than the whole creation, and I would not yield mine excellence and my fruits unto the children of men. Suffer me and I will destroy the excellence of my fruits. And there came a voice and said: I know all things, and there is none that can hide himself from his sin. And their ungodliness do I know; but my holiness suffereth them until they turn and repent. But if they return not unto me, I will judge them. 7 Behold *then* ye children of men. The creature is subject unto God; but mankind alone sinneth.

Therefore, ye children of men, bless ye the Lord God without ceasing at all hours and on all days; but especially when the sun setteth. For in that hour do all the angels go unto the Lord to worship him and to present the deeds of men which every man doeth from morning until evening, whether they be good or evil. And there is an angel that goeth forth rejoicing from the man in whom he dwelleth ⟨and another goeth with a sad countenance, *Gr.*⟩.

When therefore the sun is set, at the first hour of the night, in the same hour *goeth* the angel of every people and of every man and woman, which protect and keep them, because man is the image of God: and likewise at the hour of morning, which is the twelfth hour of the night, do all the angels of men and women go to meet God and present all the work which every man hath wrought, whether good or evil. And every day and night do the angels present unto God the account of all the deeds of mankind. Unto you, therefore, I say, O children of men, bless ye the Lord God without ceasing all the days of your life.

8 At the hour appointed, therefore, all the angels, every one rejoicing, come forth before God together to meet him and worship him at the hour that is set ; †and lo, suddenly at the *set* time there was a meeting,† and the angels came to worship in the presence of God, and the spirit came forth to meet them, and there was a voice, saying: Whence come ye, our angels, bringing burdens of news ? 9 They answered and said: We are come from them that have renounced the world for thy holy name's sake, wandering as strangers and in the caves of the rocks, and weeping every hour that they dwell on the earth, and hungering and thirsting for thy name's sake; with their loins girt, holding in their hands the incense of their heart, and praying and blessing at every hour, suffering anguish and subduing themselves,

weeping and lamenting more than all that dwell on the earth. And we that are their angels do mourn with them ; whither therefore it pleaseth thee, command us to go and minister †lest they do otherwise, but the poor† more than all that dwell on the earth. (The sense required as shown by *Gr.* is that the angels ask that these good men may continue in goodness.) And the voice of God came unto them, saying: Know ye that from henceforth my grace shall be established with you, and mine help, which is my dearly beloved Son, shall be with them, ruling them at all times; and he shall minister unto them and never forsake them, for their place is his habitation. 10 When, then, these angels departed, lo, there came other angels to worship in the presence of the majesty, to meet therewith, and they were weeping. And the spirit of God went forth to meet them, and the voice of God came, saying: Whence are ye come, our angels, bearing burdens, ministers of the news of the world? They answered and said in the presence of God: We are come from them which have called upon thy name; and the snares of the world have made them wretched, devising many excuses at all times, and not making so much as one pure prayer out of their whole heart all the time of their life. Wherefore then must we be with men that are sinners ? And the voice of God came unto them: Ye must minister unto them until they turn and repent; but if they return not unto me, I will judge them.

Know therefore, O children of men, that whatsoever is wrought by you, the angels tell it unto God, whether it be good or evil.

11 [*Syr.* Again, after these things, I saw one of the spiritual ones coming unto me, and he caught me up in the spirit, and carried me to the third heaven.]

And the angel answered and said unto me: Follow me, and I will show thee the place of the righteous where they are taken when they are dead. And thereafter will I take thee to the bottomless pit and show thee the souls of the sinners, into what manner of place they are taken when they are dead.

And I went after the angel, and he took me into heaven, and I looked upon the firmament, and saw there the powers; and there was forgetfulness which deceiveth and draweth unto itself the hearts of men, and the spirit of slander and the spirit of fornication and the spirit of wrath and the spirit of insolence, and there were the princes of wickedness. These things saw I beneath the firmament of the heaven.

And again I looked and saw angels without mercy, having no pity, whose countenances were full of fury, and their teeth sticking forth out of their mouth: their eyes shone like the morning star of the east, and out of the hairs of their head and out of their mouth went forth sparks of fire. And I asked the angel, saying: Who are these, Lord ? And the angel answered and said unto me: These are they which are appointed unto the souls of sinners

in the hour of necessity, even of them that have not believed that
they had the Lord for their helper and have not trusted in him.[1]

12 And I looked into the height and beheld other angels whose
faces shone like the sun, and their loins were girt with golden
girdles, holding palms in their hands, and the sign of God, clad in
raiment whereon was written the name of the Son of God, full of
all gentleness and mercy. And I asked the angel and said: Who
are these, Lord, that are of so great beauty and compassion?
And the angel answered and said unto me: These are the angels
of righteousness that are sent to bring the souls of the righteous
in the hour of necessity, even them that have believed that they
had the Lord for their helper. And I said unto him: Do the
righteous and the sinners of necessity meet [witnesses] when they
are dead?[2] And the angel answered and said unto me: The way
whereby all pass unto God is one: but the righteous having an
holy helper with them are not troubled when they go to appear
in the presence of God.

13 And I said unto the angel: I would see the souls of the
righteous and of the sinners as they depart out of the world.
And the angel answered and said unto me: Look down upon the
earth. And I looked down from heaven upon the earth and
beheld the whole world, and it was as nothing in my sight; and
I saw the children of men as though they were nought, and
failing utterly;[3] and I marvelled, and said unto the angel: Is
this the greatness of men? And the angel answered and said
unto me: This it is, and these are they that do hurt from morning
until evening. And I looked, and saw a great cloud of fire spread
over the whole world, and said unto the angel: What is this,
Lord? And he said to me: This is the unrighteousness that is
mingled †by the princes of sinners† (Gr. mingled with the
destruction of sinners; Syr. mingled with the prayers of the
sons of men).

---

[1] Apocalypse of Zephaniah (Steindorff's 'anonymous Apocalypse'):
I went with the angel of the Lord and looked before me and saw a
place through which passed thousand thousands and myriads of
myriads of angels, whose faces were as of panthers, and their teeth
stuck forth out of their mouth, and their eyes were bloodshot, and their
hair loose like women's hair, and burning scourges were in their hands.
(I feared and asked: Who are these? The angel answered:) These are
the ministers of the whole creation, which come unto the souls of the
ungodly and take them and lay them down here: they fly three days
with them in the air before they take them and cast them into their
everlasting torment.

[2] Probably the sense was: Must the righteous meet the sinners, or
their dreadful angels?

[3] Apocalypse of Zephaniah: I saw the whole earth . . . beneath,
like a drop of water (upon a bucket) that cometh up out of the well.
Our fragmentary text of the Apocalypse apparently begins with
a description of the death of a righteous man.

14 And I when I heard that sighed and wept, and said unto the angel: I would wait for the souls of the righteous and of the sinners, and see in what fashion they depart out of the body. And the angel answered and said unto me: Look again upon the earth. And I looked and saw the whole world: and men were as nought, and failing utterly ; and I looked and saw a certain man about to die; and the angel said to me: He whom thou seest is righteous. And again I looked and saw all his works that he had done for the name of God, and all his desires which he remembered and which he remembered not, all of them stood before his face in the hour of necessity. And I saw that the righteous man had grown *in righteousness*, and found rest and confidence: and before he departed out of the world there stood by him holy angels, and also evil ones: and I saw them all; but the evil ones found no abode in him, but the holy ones had power over his soul and ruled it until it went out of the body. And they stirred up the soul, saying: O soul, take knowledge of thy body whence thou art come out; for thou must needs return into the same body at the day of resurrection, to receive that which is promised unto all the righteous. They received therefore the soul out of the body, and straightway kissed it as one daily known of them, saying unto it: Be of good courage, for thou hast done the will of God while thou abodest on the earth. And there came to meet it the angel that watched it day by day, and he said unto it: Be of good courage, O soul: for I rejoice in thee because thou hast done the will of God on the earth; for I told unto God all thy works, how they stood. Likewise also the spirit came forth to meet it and said: O soul, fear not, neither be troubled, until thou come unto a place which thou never knewest ; but I will be thine helper, for I have found in thee a place of refreshment in the time when I dwelt in thee, when I was (thou wast ?) on the earth. And the spirit [thereof] strengthened it, and the angel thereof took it up and carried it into the heaven. †And the angel said† (*Syr.* And there went out to meet it wicked powers, those that are under heaven. And there reached it the spirit of error, and said): Whither runnest thou, O soul, and presumest to enter heaven ? stay and let us see if there be aught of ours in thee. And lo! we have found nothing in thee. I behold also the help of God, and thine angel; and the spirit rejoiceth with thee because thou didst the will of God upon earth. (*Syr. has more here.* There is a conflict between the good and evil angels. The spirit of error first laments. Then the spirit of the tempter and of fornication meet it and it escapes, and they lament. All the principalities and evil spirits come to meet it and find nothing, and gnash their teeth. The guardian angel bids them go back, 'Ye tempted this soul and it would not listen to you '. And the voice of many angels is heard rejoicing over the soul. *Probably this is original matter.*) And they brought it until it

did worship in the presence of God. And when they (it?) had ceased, forthwith Michael and all the host of the angels fell and worshipped the footstool of his feet and his gates, and said together unto the soul: This is the God of all, which made *thee* in his image and likeness. And the angel returned and declared, saying: Lord, remember his works; for this is the soul whereof I did report the works unto thee, Lord, doing according to thy judgement. And likewise the spirit said: I am the spirit of quickening that breathed upon it; for I had refreshment in it in the time when I dwelt therein, doing according to thy judgement. And the voice of God came, saying: Like as this *soul* hath not grieved me, neither will I grieve it, for like as it hath had mercy, I also will have mercy. Let it be delivered therefore unto Michael the angel of the covenant, and let him lead it into the paradise of rejoicing that it become fellow-heir with all the saints. And thereafter I heard the voices of thousands of thousands of angels and archangels and the cherubim and the four-and-twenty elders uttering hymns and glorifying the Lord and crying: Righteous art thou, O Lord, and just are thy judgements, and there is no respect of persons with thee, but thou rewardest every man according to thy judgement. And the angel answered and said unto me: Hast thou believed and known that whatsoever every one of you hath done, he beholdeth it at the hour of his necessity? And I said: Yea, Lord.

15 And he said unto me: Look down again upon the earth and wait for the soul of a wicked man going forth of the body, one that hath provoked the Lord day and night, saying: I know nought else in this world, I will eat and drink and enjoy the things that are in the world. For who is he that hath gone down into hell and come up and told us that there is a judgement there? And again I looked and saw all the despising of the sinner, and all that he did, and they stood together before him in the hour of necessity: and it came to pass in that hour when he was led out of his body to the judgement, that he (*MS*. I) said: It were better for me (*MS*. him) that I (he) had not been born. And after that the holy angels and the evil and the soul of the sinner came together, and the holy angels found no place in it. But the evil angels threatened (had power over) it, and when they brought it forth out of the body, the angels admonished it thrice, saying: O wretched soul, look upon thy flesh whence thou art come out; for thou must needs return into thy flesh at the day of resurrection to receive the due reward for thy sins and for thy wickedness.

16 And when they had brought it forth, the accustomed (i. e. guardian) angel went before it [1] and said unto it: O miserable soul, I am the angel that clave unto thee and day by day reported unto the Lord thine evil deeds, whatsoever thou wroughtest by night or day; and if it had been in my power I would not have

---

[1] Here the Coptic version begins.

ministered unto thee even one day; but of this I could do nothing, *for God* is merciful and a just judge, and he commanded us not to cease ministering unto *your* soul till ye should repent: but thou hast lost the time of repentance. I indeed am become a stranger unto thee and thou to me. Let us go then unto the just judge: I will not leave thee until I know that from this day I am become a stranger unto thee. (Here *Copt.* inserts a quite similar speech of the spirit to the soul, which may be original.) And the spirit confounded it, and the angel troubled it. When therefore they were come unto the principalities, and it would now go to enter into heaven, one burden (labour, suffering) was laid upon it after another:[1] error and forgetfulness and whispering met it, and the spirit of fornication and the rest of the powers, and said unto it: Whither goest thou, wretched soul, and darest to run forward into heaven? Stay, that we may see whether we have property of ours in thee, for we see not with thee an holy helper. (*Syr.* adds: And the angel answered and said: Know ye that it is a soul of the Lord, and he will not cast it aside, neither will I surrender the image of God into the hand of the wicked one. The Lord supported me all the days of the life of the soul, and he can support and help me: and I will not cast it off until it go up before the throne of God on high. When he shall see it, he hath power over it, and will send it whither he pleases.) And after that I heard voices in the height of the heavens, saying: Present this miserable soul unto God, that it may know that there is a God, whom it hath despised. When therefore it was entered into the heaven, all the angels, even thousands of thousands, saw it, and all cried out with one voice, saying: Woe unto thee, miserable soul, for thy works which thou diddest upon the earth; what answer wilt thou make unto God when thou drawest near to worship him? The angel which was with it answered and said: Weep with me, my dearly beloved, for I have found no rest in this soul. And the angels answered him and said: Let this soul be taken away out of our midst, for since it came in, the stench of it is passed upon us the angels. And thereafter it was presented, to worship in the presence of God; and the angel showed it the Lord God that made it after his own image and likeness. And its angel ran before it, saying: O Lord God Almighty, I am the angel of this soul, whose works I presented unto thee day and night, not doing according to thy judgement. And likewise the spirit said: I am the spirit which dwelt in it ever since it was made, and I know *it* in itself, and it followed not my will: judge it, Lord, according to thy judgement. And the voice of God came unto it and said: Where is thy fruit that thou hast yielded, worthy of those good things which thou hast received? did I put a

[1] Here Copt. has a long description of the powers of darkness which is certainly *not* original.

distance even of a day between thee and the righteous? did I not make the sun to rise upon thee even as upon the righteous? And it was silent, having nothing to answer; and again the voice came, saying: Just is the judgement of God, and there is no respect of persons with God, for whosoever hath done his mercy, he will have mercy on him, and whoso hath not had mercy, neither shall God have mercy on him. Let him therefore be delivered unto the angel Tartaruchus (*Gr.* Temeluchus) that is set over the torments, and let him cast him into the outer darkness, where is weeping and gnashing of teeth, and let him be there until the great day of judgement. And after that I heard the voice of the angels and archangels saying: Righteous art thou, O Lord, and just is thy judgement.

17 And again I beheld, and lo, a soul which was brought by two angels, weeping and saying: Have mercy on me, thou righteous God, O God the judge; for to-day it is seven days since I went forth out of my body, and I was delivered unto these two angels, and they have brought me unto those places which I had never seen. And God the righteous judge said unto it: What hast thou done? for thou hast never wrought mercy; therefore wast thou delivered unto such angels, which have no mercy, and because thou hast not done right, therefore neither have they dealt pitifully with thee in the hour of thy necessity. Confess therefore thy sins which thou hast committed when thou wert in the world. And it answered and said: Lord, I have not sinned. And the righteous Lord God was wroth with indignation when it said: I have not sinned; for it lied. And God said: Thinkest thou that thou art yet in the world? If every one of you there when he sinneth, hideth and concealeth his sin from his neighbour, yet here no thing is hidden, for when the souls come to worship before the throne, both the good works and the sins of every one are made manifest. And when the soul heard that, it held its peace, having no answer. And I heard the Lord God, the righteous judge, saying again: Come, thou angel of this soul, and stand in the midst. And the angel of the sinful soul came, having a writing in his hands, and said: These, Lord, that are in mine hands, are all the sins of this soul from its youth up unto this day, even from ten years from its birth: and if thou bid me, Lord, I can tell the acts thereof since it began to be fifteen years old.[1] And the Lord God the righteous judge said: I say unto thee, O angel, I desire not of thee the account since it began to be fifteen years old: but declare its sins of five years before that it died and came hither. And again God

[1] *Apocalypse of Zephaniah*: I looked and saw that a writing (the same word, *chirographum*) was in his hand: he began to open it, and when he had spread it out I read it in mine own language, and I found all my sins that I had committed, recorded by him, even those which I had committed from my childhood up unto this day.

the righteous judge said: For by myself I swear, and by mine holy angels and by my power, that if it had repented five years before it died, *even* for the walk (conversation) of one year, there should be forgetfulness of all the evil which it committed before, and it should have pardon and remission of sins: but now let it perish. And the angel of the sinful soul answered and said: Command, Lord, that (such and such an) angel to bring forth those (such and such) souls. 18 And in that same hour the souls were brought forth into the midst, and the soul of the sinner knew them. And the Lord said unto the soul of the sinner: I say unto thee, O soul, confess thy deeds which thou didst upon these souls whom thou seest, when they were in the world. And it answered and said: Lord, it is not yet a full year since I slew this one and shed its blood upon the earth, and with another I committed fornication; and not that only, but I did it much harm by taking away its substance. And the Lord God the righteous judge said: Knewest thou not that he that doth violence to another, if he that suffered violence die first, he is kept in this place until he that hurt him dieth, and then do both of them appear before the judge? and now hath every one received according as he did. And I heard a voice saying: Let that soul be delivered into the hands of Tartaruchus,[1] and he must be taken down into hell. Let him take him into the lower prison and let him be cast into torments and be left there until the great day of judgement. And again I heard thousands of thousands of angels singing an hymn unto the Lord and saying: Righteous art thou, O Lord, and just are thy judgements.

19 The angel answered and said unto me: Hast thou perceived all these things? And I said: Yea, Lord. And he said unto me: Follow me again, and I will take thee and show thee the places of the righteous. And I followed the angel and he took me up unto the third heaven and set me before the door of a gate; and I looked on it and saw, and the gate was of gold, and there were two pillars of gold full of golden letters; and the angel turned again to me and said: Blessed art thou if thou enterest in by these gates, for it is not permitted to any to enter save only to those that have kept goodness and pureness of their bodies in all things. And I asked the angel and said: Lord, tell me for what cause are these letters set upon these tables? The angel answered and said unto me: These are the names of the righteous that minister unto God with their whole heart, which dwell on the earth. And again I said: Lord, then are their names ⟨written while they are yet on the earth? And he said: Not only are their names written, but⟩[2] also their countenance and the likeness of them that serve God is in heaven, and they are

[1] So *Gr.*: *Lat.* (*Syr.*), Tartarus; *Copt.*, Temeluchus.
[2] Omitted in Latin by homoeoteleuton: supplied from Coptic; Syriac amplifies.

known unto the angels: for they know them that with their whole heart serve God before they depart out of the world.

20 And when I had entered within the gate of paradise there came to meet me an old man whose face shone like the sun, and he embraced me and said: Hail, Paul, dearly beloved of God. And he kissed me with a joyful countenance, *but* he wept, and I said unto him: Father (*Lat.* Brother), why weepest thou? And again sighing and weeping he said: Because we are vexed by men, and they grieve us sore; for many are the good things which the Lord hath prepared, and great are his promises, but many receive them not. And I asked the angel and said: Who is this, Lord? And he said unto me: This is Enoch the scribe of righteousness.

And I entered within that place and straightway I saw Elias,[1] and he came and saluted me with gladness and joy. And when he had seen me, he turned himself away and wept and said unto me: Paul, mayest thou receive *the reward of* thy labour which thou hast done among mankind. As for me, I have seen great and manifold good things which God hath prepared for all the righteous, and great are the promises of God, but the more part receive them not; yea hardly through much toil doth one and another enter into these places.

21 And the angel answered and said unto me: What things soever I now show thee here, and whatsoever thou hearest, reveal them not unto any upon earth. And he led me and showed me: and I heard there words which it is not lawful for a man to utter; and again he said: Yet again follow me and I will show thee that which thou must relate and tell openly.

And he brought me down from the third heaven, and led me into the second heaven, and again he led me to the firmament, and from the firmament he led me unto the gates of heaven. And the beginning of the foundation thereof was upon the river that watereth all the earth. And I asked the angel and said: Lord, what is this river of water? and he said unto me: This is the Ocean. And suddenly I came out of heaven, and perceived that it is the light of the heaven that shineth upon all the earth (*or*, all that land). And there the earth (*or*, land) was seven times brighter than silver. And I said: Lord, what is this place? and he said unto me: This is the land of promise. Hast thou not yet heard that which is written: Blessed are the meek, for they shall inherit the earth? The souls therefore of the righteous when they are gone forth of the body are sent for the time into this place. And I said unto the angel: Shall then this land be made manifest after (*Lat.* before) a time? The angel answered and said unto me: When Christ whom thou preachest cometh to reign, then by the decree of God the first earth shall be dissolved,

---

[1] *Lat.* has 'the sun', from confusing Helias with Helios. *Gr.* omits the paragraph.

and then shall this land of promise be shown and it shall be like dew or a cloud; and then shall the Lord Jesus Christ the eternal king be manifested and shall come with all his saints to dwell therein; and he shall reign over them a thousand years, and they shall eat of the good things which now I will show thee.

22 And I looked round about that land and saw a river flowing with milk and honey. And there were at the brink of the river trees planted, full of fruits: now every tree bare twelve fruits in the year, and they had various and divers fruits: and I saw the fashion (creation) of that place and all the work of God, and there I saw palm-trees of twenty cubits and others of ten cubits: and that land was seven times brighter than silver. And the trees were full of fruits from the root even to the upper branches. (*Lat.* is confused here. *Copt.* has: From the root of each tree up to its heart there were ten thousand branches with tens of thousands of clusters, [and there were ten thousand clusters on each branch,] and there were ten thousand dates in each cluster. And thus was it also with the vines. Every vine had ten thousand branches, and each branch had upon it ten thousand bunches of grapes, and every bunch had on it ten thousand grapes. And there were other trees there, myriads of myriads of them, and their fruit was in the same proportion.) And I said unto the angel: Wherefore doth every tree bring forth thousands of fruits? The angel answered and said unto me: Because the Lord God of his bounty giveth his gifts in abundance unto the worthy; for they also of their own will afflicted themselves when they were in the world, doing all things for his holy name's sake.

And again I said unto the angel: Lord, are these the only promises which the most holy Lord God promiseth? and he answered and said unto me: No; for there are greater by seven times than these. But I say unto thee, that when the righteous are gone forth out of the body *and* shall see the promises and the good things which God hath prepared for them, yet again they shall sigh and cry, saying: Wherefore did we utter a word out of our mouth to provoke our neighbour even for a day? And I asked again and said: Be these the only promises of God? And the angel answered and said unto me: These which now thou seest are for them that are married and keep the purity of their marriage, being continent. But unto the virgins, and unto them that hunger and thirst after righteousness and afflict themselves for the name of the Lord, God will give things seven-fold greater than these, which now I will show thee.

And after that he took me out of that place where I saw these things, and lo, a river, and the waters of it were white exceedingly, more than milk; and I said unto the angel: What is this? and he said to me: This is the lake Acherusa where is the city of Christ: but not every man is suffered to enter into that city:

for this is the way that leadeth unto God, and if any be a forni-
cator or ungodly, and turn and repent and bear fruits meet for
repentance, first when he cometh out of the body he is brought
and worshippeth God, and then by the commandment of the Lord
he is delivered unto Michael the angel, and he washeth him in
the lake Acherusa and so bringeth him in to the city of Christ
with them that have done no sin. And I marvelled and blessed
the Lord God for all the things which I saw.

23 And the angel answered and said unto me: Follow me,
and I will bring thee into the city of Christ. And he stood by
(upon) the lake Acherusa, and set me in a golden ship,[1] and angels
as it were three thousand sang an hymn before me until I came
even unto the city of Christ. And they that dwelt in the city of
Christ rejoiced greatly over me as I came unto them, and
I entered in and saw the city of Christ. And it was all of gold,
and twelve walls compassed it about, and there were twelve
towers within (a tower on each wall, Copt.; 12,000 towers, Syr.),
and every wall had a furlong between them (i. e. the walls were
a furlong apart, so Syr. ; Copt. the circumference of each was
100 furlongs) round about ; and I said unto the angel: Lord,
how much is one furlong ? The angel answered and said unto me:
It is as much as there is betwixt the Lord God and the men that
are on the earth, for the great city of Christ is alone.[2] And
there were twelve gates in the circuit of the city, of great beauty,
and four rivers that compassed it about. There was a river of
honey, and a river of milk, and a river of wine, and a river of oil.
And I said unto the angel: What are these rivers that compass
this city about ? And he saith to me: These are the four rivers
which flow abundantly for them that are in this land of promise,
whereof the names are these: the river of honey is called Phison,
and the river of milk Euphrates, and the river of oil Geon, and
the river of wine Tigris. Whereas therefore when the righteous
were in the world they used not their power over these things,
but hungered and afflicted themselves for the Lord God's sake,
therefore when they enter into this city, the Lord will give them
these things without number (?) and without all measure.

24 And I when I entered in by the gate saw before the doors
of the city trees great and high, having no fruits, but leaves only.
And I saw a few men scattered about in the midst of the trees,
and they mourned sore when they saw any man enter into the
city. And those trees did penance for them, humbling themselves
and bowing down, and again raising themselves up.

And I beheld it and wept with them, and I asked the angel

[1] Apocalypse of Zephaniah (beginning of the second fragment):
They took me by the hand and lifted me up into that ship and began
to sing before me, even thousand thousands and myriads of myriads
of angels.
[2] Not in Syr. or Copt.

and said: Lord, who are these that are not permitted to enter into the city of Christ? And he said unto me: These are they that did earnestly renounce *the world* day and night with fasting, but had an heart proud above other men, glorifying and praising themselves, and doing nought for their neighbours. For some they greeted friendly, but unto others they said not even ' Hail ', and unto whom they would they opened, and if they did any small thing for their neighbour they were puffed up. And I said: What then, Lord? their pride hath prevented them from entering into the city of Christ? And the angel answered and said unto me: The root of all evils is pride. Are they better than the Son of God who came unto the Jews in great humility? And I asked him and said: Wherefore is it then that the trees humble themselves and are again raised up? And the angel answered and said unto me: All the time that these spent upon earth (Of old time they were on the earth, *Copt.*) serving God (they served God): *but* because of the shame and reproaches of men they were ashamed (did blush) for a time and humbled themselves; but they were not grieved, neither did repent, to cease from this pride that was in them (and one day they bowed themselves because of the disgrace of man, for they cannot endure the pride that is in him, *Copt.*). This is the cause why the trees humble themselves and again are raised up. And I asked and said: For what cause are they let in unto the gates of the city? The angel answered and said unto me: Because of the great goodness of God, and because this is the entry of all his saints which do enter into this city. Therefore are they left in this place, that when Christ the eternal king entereth in with his saints, when he cometh in, all the righteous shall entreat for them; and then shall they enter into the city with them: yet none of them is able to have confidence such as they have that have humbled themselves, serving the Lord God all their life long.

25 But I went forward and the angel led me and brought me unto the river of honey, and I saw there Esaias and Jeremias and Ezekiel and Amos and Micheas and Zacharias, even the prophets lesser and greater, and they greeted me in the city. I said unto the angel: What is this path? and he said unto me: This is the path of the prophets: every one that hath grieved his soul and not done his own will for God's sake, when he is departed out of the world and hath been brought unto the Lord God and worshipped him, then by the commandment of God he is delivered unto Michael, and he bringeth him into the city unto this place of the prophets, and they greet him as their friend and neighbour, because he hath performed the will of God.

26 Again he led me where was the river of milk, and I saw in that place all the children whom the king Herod slew for the name of Christ, and they greeted me, and the angel said unto me: All they that keep chastity in cleanness, when they are gone out

of the body, after they worship the Lord God, are delivered unto Michael and brought unto the children: and they greet them, saying: They are our brothers and friends and members: among them shall they inherit the promises of God.

27 Again he took me and brought me to the north side of the city, and led me to where was the river of wine; and I saw there Abraham, Isaac, and Jacob, Lot and Job and other saints,[1] and they greeted me. And I asked and said: What is this place, Lord? The angel answered and said unto me: All they that are entertainers of strangers, when they are departed out of the world, first worship the Lord God, and *then* are delivered unto Michael and brought by this path into the city, and all the righteous greet him as a son and brother, and say unto him: Because thou hast kept kindliness and the entertainment of strangers, come thou and have an inheritance in the city of our Lord God. Every one of the righteous shall receive the good things of God in the city according to his deeds.

28 And again he took me to the river of oil on the east side of the city. And I saw there men rejoicing and singing psalms, and said: Who are these, Lord? and the angel said unto me: These are they that have devoted themselves unto God with their whole heart, and had in them no pride. For all that rejoice in the Lord God and sing praises to the Lord with their whole heart are brought here into this city.

29 And he took me into the midst of the city, by the twelve walls (to the twelfth wall, *Copt.*). Now there was in that place an higher wall; and I asked and said: Is there in the city of Christ a wall more excellent in honour than this place? And the angel answered and said unto me: The second is better than the first, and likewise the third than the second; for one excelleth the other even unto the twelfth wall. And I said: Wherefore, Lord, doth one excel another in glory? show me. And the angel answered and said unto me: All they that have in them even a little slandering or envy or pride, somewhat is taken away from his glory, even if he be in the city of Christ. Look thou behind thee.

And I turned myself and saw golden thrones set at the several gates, and upon them men having golden crowns and jewels: and I looked and saw within among the twelve men, thrones set in another order (row, fashion?), which appeared of much glory so that no man is able to declare the praise of them. And I asked the angel and said: Lord, who is upon the throne? And the angel answered and said unto me: These are the thrones of them that had goodness and understanding of heart and *yet* made themselves foolish for the Lord God's sake, knowing neither the

---

[1] *Apocalypse of Zephaniah*: (The angel) ran unto all the righteous that are there, Abraham, Isaac, Jacob, Enoch, Elias, and David. He conversed with them as a friend with a friend, who talk together.

Scriptures nor many psalms, but keeping in mind one chapter of the precepts of God they performed it with great diligence, and had a right intent before the Lord God; and for these great wonder shall take hold upon all the saints before the Lord God, who shall speak one with another, saying: Stay and behold the unlearned that know nothing [more], how they have earned such and so fair raiment and so great glory because of their innocency.

And I saw in the midst of the city an altar exceeding high. And there was one standing by the altar whose visage shone like the sun, and he held in his hands a psaltery and an harp and sang praises, saying: Alleluia. And his voice filled all the city. And when all that were upon the towers and the gates heard him, they answered: Alleluia, so that the foundations of the city were shaken. And I asked the angel and said: Who is this, Lord, that is of so great might? And the angel said unto me: This is David. This is the city of Jerusalem; and when Christ the king of eternity shall come in the fullness (confidence, freedom) of his kingdom, he shall again go before him to sing praises, and all the righteous together shall sing praises, answering: Alleluia. And I said: Lord, how is it that David only above the rest of the saints maketh (made) the beginning of singing praises? And the angel answered and said unto me: When (or, because) Christ the Son of God sitteth on the right hand of his Father, this David shall sing praises before him in the seventh heaven: and as it is done in the heavens, so likewise is it below: for without David it is not lawful to offer a sacrifice unto God: but it must needs be that David sing praises at the hour of the offering of the body and blood of Christ: as it is performed in heaven, so also is it upon earth. 30 And I said unto the angel: Lord, what is Alleluia? And the angel answered and said unto me: Thou dost examine and inquire of all things. And he said unto me: Alleluia is spoken in the Hebrew, that is the speech of God and of the angels: now the interpretation of Alleluia is this: *tecel . cat . marith . macha* (*Gr.* thĕbel marēmatha). And I said: Lord, what is *tecel cat marith macha*? And the angel answered and said unto me: This is *tecel cat marith macha*: Let us bless him all together. I asked the angel and said: Lord, do all they that say Alleluia bless God? And the angel answered and said unto me: So it is: and again, if any sing Alleluia, and they that are present sing not with him, they commit sin in that they sing not with him. And I said: Lord, doth a man likewise sin if he be doting or very aged? The angel answered and said unto me: Not so: but he that is able, and singeth not with him, know ye that such a one is a despiser of the word, for it would be proud and unworthy that he should not bless the Lord God his creator.

31 And when he had ceased speaking unto me, he led me out without the city through the midst of the trees and back from the place of the land of good things (or, men) and set me at the

river of milk and honey: and after that he led me unto the ocean that beareth the foundations of the heaven.

The angel answered and said unto me: Perceivest thou that thou goest hence? And I said: Yea, Lord. And he said unto me: Come, follow me, and I will show thee the souls of the ungodly and the sinners, that thou mayest know what manner of place *they have*. And I went with the angel and he took me by the way of the sunsetting, and I saw the beginning of the heaven, founded upon a great river of water, and I asked: What is this river of water? And he said unto me: This is the ocean which compasseth the whole earth about. And when I was come beyond (to the outside of) the ocean, I looked and there was no light in that place, but darkness and sorrow and sadness: and I sighed.[1]

And I saw there a river of fire burning with heat, and in it was a multitude of men and women sunk up to the knees, and other men up to the navel; others also up to the lips and others up to the hair: and I asked the angel and said: Lord, who are these in the river of fire? And the angel answered and said unto me: They are neither hot nor cold,[2] for they were not found either in the number of the righteous or in the number of the wicked; for they passed the time of their life upon the earth, spending some days in prayer, but other days in sins and fornications, until their death. And I asked and said: Who are these, Lord, that are sunk up to their knees in the fire? He answered and said unto me: These are they which when they are come out of the church occupy themselves in disputing with idle (alien) talk. But these that are sunk up to the navel are they who, when they have received the body and blood of Christ, go and commit fornication, and did not cease from their sins until they died; and they that are sunk up to their lips are they that slandered one another when they gathered in the church of God; but they that are sunk up to the eyebrows are they that beckon one to another, and privily devise evil against their neighbours.

32 And I saw on the north side a place of sundry and diverse torments, full of men and women, and a river of fire flowed down upon them. And I beheld and saw pits exceeding deep, and in them many souls together, and the depth of that place was as it were three thousand cubits; and I saw them groaning and weeping and saying: Have mercy on us, Lord. And no man had mercy on them. And I asked the angel and said: Who are these, Lord? And the angel answered and said unto me: These

---

[1] *Copt.* inserts an enumeration of several pits of torment: premature and not original.

[2] Something seems wanting in all the texts. These, who were neither hot nor cold, should not be in the river, but beside it. In fact, in the Ethiopic Apocalypse of the Virgin (see p. 564) which is copied from this, these souls do sit *beside* the river.

are they that trusted not in the Lord that they could have him for their helper. And I inquired and said: Lord, if these souls continue thus, thirty or forty generations *being cast* one upon another, if (unless?) they be cast down yet deeper, I trow the pits would not contain them. And he said to me: The abyss hath no measure: for beneath it there followeth also that which is beneath: and so it is that if a strong man took a stone and cast it into an exceeding deep well and after many hours (long time) it reacheth the earth, so also is the abyss. For when the souls are cast therein, hardly after five hundred years do they come at the bottom. 33 And I when I heard it, mourned and lamented for the race of men. The angel answered and said unto me: Wherefore mournest thou? art thou more merciful than God? for inasmuch as God is good and knoweth that there are torments, he beareth patiently with mankind, leaving every one to do his own will for the time that he dwelleth on the earth.

34 Yet again I looked upon the river of fire, and I saw there a man caught *by the throat* (*Copt.* an old man who was being dragged along, and they immersed him up to the knees. And the angel Aftemeloukhos came with a great fork of fire, &c. *Syr.* similar. Some sentences are lost in *Lat.*) by angels, keepers of hell (Tartaruchi), having in their hands an iron of three hooks wherewith they pierced the entrails of that old man. And I asked the angel and said: Lord, who is this old man upon whom such torments are inflicted? And the angel answered and said unto me: He whom thou seest was a priest who fulfilled not well his ministry, for when he was eating and drinking and whoring he offered the sacrifice unto the Lord at his holy altar.

35 And I saw not far off another old man whom four evil angels brought, running quickly, and they sank him up to his knees in the river of fire, and smote him with stones and wounded his face like a tempest, and suffered him not to say: Have mercy on me. And I asked the angel and he said unto me: He whom thou seest was a bishop, and he fulfilled not well his bishopric: for he received indeed a great name, but entered not into (walked not in) the holiness of him that gave him that name in his life; for he gave not righteous judgement, and had not compassion on widows and orphans: but now it is recompensed unto him according to his iniquity and his doings.

36 And I saw another man in the river of fire sunk up to the knees: and his hands were stretched out and bloody, and worms issued out of his mouth and his nostrils, and he was groaning and lamenting and crying out, and said: Have mercy on me for I suffer hurt more than the rest that are in this torment. And I asked: Who is this, Lord? And he said unto me: This whom thou seest was a deacon, who devoured the offerings and committed fornication and did not right in the sight of God: therefore without ceasing he payeth the penalty.

And I looked and saw beside him another man whom they
brought with haste and cast him into the river of fire, and he was
there up to the knees; and the angel that was over the torments
came, having a great razor, red-hot, and therewith he cut the
lips of that man and the tongue likewise. And I sighed and
wept and asked: Who is this man, Lord? And he said unto me:
This that thou seest was a reader and read unto the people: but
he kept not the commandments of God: now also he payeth his
own penalty.

37 And I saw another multitude of pits in the same place, and
in the midst thereof a river filled with a multitude of men and
women, and worms devoured them. But I wept and sighed and
asked the angel: Lord, who are these? And he said unto me:
These are they that extorted usury on usury and trusted in their
riches, not having hope in God, that he was their helper.

And after that I looked and saw a very strait place, and there
was as it were a wall, and round about it fire. And I saw within
it men and women gnawing their tongues, and asked: Who are
these, Lord? And he said unto me: These are they that mocked
at the word of God in the church, not attending thereto, but as
it were making nought of God and of his angels: therefore now
likewise do they pay the due penalty.

38 And I looked in and saw another pool (*Lat.* old man!)
beneath in the pit, and the appearance of it was like blood: and
I asked and said: Lord, what is this place? And he said unto
me: Into this pit do all the torments flow. And I saw men and
women sunk up to the lips, and asked: Who are these, Lord?
And he said unto me: These are the sorcerers which gave unto
men and women magical enchantments, and they found no rest
(i. e. did not cease?) until they died.

And again I saw men and women of a very black countenance
in a pit of fire, and I sighed and wept and asked: Who are these,
Lord? And he said unto me: These are whoremongers and
adulterers who, having wives of their own, committed adultery,
and likewise the women after the same sort committed adultery,
having their own husbands: therefore do they pay the penalty
without ceasing.

39 And I saw there girls clad in black raiment, and four fearful
angels holding in their hands red-hot chains, and they put them
upon their necks (heads) and led them away into darkness.
And again I wept and asked the angel: Who are these, Lord?
And he said unto me: These are they which being virgins defiled
their virginity, and their parents knew it not: wherefore without
ceasing they pay the due penalty.

And again I beheld there men and women with their hands
and feet off and naked, in a place of ice and snow, and worms
devoured them. And when I saw it I wept and asked: Who
are these, Lord? and he said unto me: These are they that

injured the fatherless and widows and the poor, and trusted not in the Lord: wherefore without ceasing they pay the due penalty.

And I looked and saw others hanging over a channel of water, and their tongues were exceeding dry, and many fruits were set in their sight, and they were not suffered to take of them. And I asked: Who are these, Lord? And he said unto me: These are they that brake the fast before the time appointed: therefore without ceasing do they pay this penalty.

And I saw other men and women hanged by their eyebrows and their hair, and a river of fire drew them, and I said: Who are these, Lord? And he said unto me: These are they that gave themselves not unto their own husbands and wives, but unto adulterers, and therefore without ceasing they pay the due penalty. (For this *Copt.* has: men and women hung head downwards, torches burning before their faces, serpents girt about them devouring them. These are the women that beautified themselves with paints and unguents and went to church to ensnare men. *Syr.* and *Gr.* omit.)

And I saw other men and women covered with dust, and their appearance was as blood, and they were in a pit of pitch and brimstone and borne down in a river of fire. And I asked: Who are these, Lord? And he said unto me: These are they that committed the wickedness of Sodom and Gomorrah, men with men, wherefore they pay the penalty without ceasing. (*Copt., Syr., Gr.* omit this paragraph.)

40 And I looked and saw men and women clad in white (bright) apparel, and their eyes were blind, and they were set in a pit, and I asked: Who are these, Lord? And he said unto me: These are they of the heathen that gave alms and knew not the Lord God; wherefore without ceasing they pay the due penalty.

And I looked and saw other men and women upon a spit of fire, and beasts tearing them, and they were not suffered to say: Lord, have mercy on us. And I saw the angel of the torments (Aftemeloukhos, *Copt.*) laying most fierce torments upon them and saying: Acknowledge the Son of God. For it was told you before, *but* when the scriptures of God were read unto you, ye paid no heed: wherefore the judgement of God is just, for your evil doings have taken hold upon you, and brought you into these torments. But I sighed and wept; and I inquired and said: Who are these men and women that are strangled in the fire and pay the penalty? And he answered me: These are the women which defiled the creation of God when they brought forth children from the womb, and these are the men that lay with them. But their children appealed unto the Lord God and unto the angels that are over the torments, saying: Avenge us of our parents: for they have defiled the creation of God. Having the name of God, but not observing his commandments, they gave us for food unto dogs and to be trampled on by swine, and others they cast into the river (*Copt.* adds: and did not permit us to grow up into righteous men and to serve God). But those children were delivered unto the angels of Tartarus (*Gr.* unto an angel) that they should bring them into a spacious place of mercy: but their fathers and mothers were haled (strangled) into everlasting torment.

And thereafter I saw men and women clad in rags full of pitch and brimstone of fire, and there were dragons twined about their necks and shoulders and feet, and angels having horns of fire constrained them and smote them and closed up their nostrils, saying unto them: Wherefore knew ye not the time wherein it was right for you to repent and serve God, and ye did not? And I asked: Who are these, Lord? And he said unto me: These are they that seemed to renounce the world (*Lat.* God), wearing our garb, but the snares of the world made them to be miserable: they showed no charity and had no pity upon the widows and fatherless: the stranger and pilgrim they did not take in, neither offered one oblation nor had pity on their neighbour: and their prayer went not up even one day pure unto the Lord God; but the many snares of the world held them back, and they were not able to do right in the sight of God. And the angels carried (*Lat.* surrounded) them about into the place of torments: and they that were in torments saw them and said unto them: We indeed when we lived in the world neglected God, and ye did so likewise. And we when we were in the world knew that we were sinners, but of you it was said: These are righteous and servants of God: now we know that ye were *only* called by the name of the Lord. Wherefore also they pay the due penalty.

And I sighed and wept and said: Woe unto men! woe unto the sinners! to what end were they born? And the angel answered and said unto me: Wherefore weepest thou? Art thou more merciful than the Lord God which is blessed for ever, who hath established the judgement and left every man of his own will to choose good or evil and to do as pleaseth him? Yet again I wept very sore, and he said unto me: Weepest thou, when as yet thou hast not seen the greater torments? Follow me, and thou shalt see sevenfold greater than these.

41 And he took me from the north side (to the west, *Syr.*) and set me over a well, and I found it sealed with seven seals. And the angel that was with me answered and said unto the angel of that place: Open the mouth of the well, that Paul the dearly beloved of God may behold; for power hath been given unto him to see all the torments of hell. And the angel said unto me: Stand afar off, that thou mayest be able to endure the stench of this place. When therefore the well was opened, straightway there arose out of it a stench hard and evil exceedingly, which surpassed all the torments: and I looked into the well and saw masses (lumps) of fire burning on every side,

and anguish, and there was straitness in the mouth of the pit so as to take but one man in. And the angel answered and said unto me: If any be cast into the well of the abyss, and it be sealed over him, there shall never be remembrance made of him in the presence of the Father and the Son and the Holy Ghost or of the holy angels. And I said: Who are they, Lord, that are cast into this well? And he said unto me: They are whosoever confesseth not that Christ is come in the flesh and that the Virgin Mary bare him, and whosoever *saith of* the bread and the cup of blessing of the Eucharist that it is not the body and blood of Christ.

42 And I looked from the north unto the west and saw there the worm that sleepeth not, and in that place was gnashing of teeth. And the worms were of the measure of one cubit, and on them were two heads; and I saw there men and women in cold and gnashing of teeth. And I asked and said: Lord, who are they that are in this place? And he said unto me: These are they which say that Christ rose not from the dead, and that this flesh riseth not again. And I inquired and said: Lord, is there no fire nor heat in this place? And he said unto me: In this place is nothing else but cold and snow. And again he said to me: Even if the sun (seven suns, *Copt.*) rose upon them, they would not be warmed, because of the excessive cold of this place, and the snow. And when I heard this I spread forth mine hands and wept and sighed, and again I said: It were better for us if we had not been born, all we that are sinners. 43 But when they that were in that place saw me weeping, with the angel, they also cried out and wept, saying: Lord God, have mercy upon us.

And after that I beheld the heaven open and Michael the archangel coming down out of heaven, and with him all the host of the angels; and they came even unto them that were set in torment. And they when they saw them wept again and cried out and said: Have mercy upon us, thou Michael, archangel, have mercy upon us and upon the race of men, for it is by thy prayers that the earth standeth. We have now seen the judgement and have known the Son of God. It was not possible for us to pray for this before we came into this place: for we heard that there was a judgement, before we departed out of the world, but the snares and the life of the world suffered us not to repent. And Michael answered and said: Hearken when Michael speaketh: I am he that stands in the presence of God alway. As the Lord liveth, before whose face I stand, I cease not for one day nor one night to pray continually for the race of men; and I indeed pray for them that are upon earth: but they cease not from committing wickednesses and fornication. And they bring not *forth* aught of good while they are upon earth; and ye have wasted in vanity the time wherein ye ought to have repented. But I have prayed alway, and now do I entreat that God would send dew and that rain may be sent upon the earth, and still pray I until the earth yield her fruits: and I say that if any man doeth but a little good I will strive for him and protect him until he escape the judgement of torment. Where then be your prayers? where be your repentances? ye have lost the time despicably. Yet now weep ye, and I will weep with you, and the angels that are with me, together with the dearly beloved Paul, if peradventure the merciful God will have pity and grant you refreshment. And they when they heard these words cried out and wept sore, and all said with one voice: Have mercy upon us, O Son of God. And I, Paul, sighed and said: O Lord God, have mercy upon thy creature, have mercy on the children of men, have mercy upon thine image.

44 I beheld and saw the heaven shake like unto a tree that is moved by the wind: and suddenly they cast themselves down upon their faces before the throne: and I saw the four-and-twenty elders and the four beasts worshipping God: and I saw the altar and the veil and the throne, and all of them were rejoicing, and the smoke of a sweet odour rose up beside the altar of the throne of God; and I heard a voice saying: For what cause do ye entreat me, our angels, and our ministers? And they cried out, saying: We entreat thee, beholding thy great goodness unto mankind. And thereafter I saw the Son of God coming down out of heaven, and on his head was a crown. And when they that were in torments saw him they all cried out with one voice, saying: Have mercy upon us, O exalted Son of God (*or*, Son of God Most High): thou art he that hast granted refreshment unto all that are in heaven and earth; have mercy upon us likewise: for since we beheld thee we have been refreshed. And there went forth a voice from the Son of God throughout all the torments, saying: What *good* works have ye done that ye should ask of me refreshment? My blood was shed for you, and not even so did ye repent: for your sake I bare a crown of thorns on mine head, for you I received buffets upon my cheeks, and not even so did ye repent. I asked for water when I hanged upon the cross, and they gave me vinegar mingled with gall: with a spear did they open my right side: for my name's sake have they slain my servants the prophets, and the righteous: and for all these things did I give you a place of repentance, and ye would not. Yet now because of Michael the archangel of my covenant and the angels that are with him, and because of Paul my dearly beloved whom I would not grieve, and because of your brethren that are in the world and do offer oblations, and because of your sons, for in them are my commandments,[1] and yet more because of mine own goodness: on that day whereon I rose from the dead I grant unto all you that are in torment refreshment for a day and a night for ever. And all they cried out and said: We bless thee, O Son of God, for that

---

[1] Among them are some that keep my commandments: so *Copt.*

thou hast granted us rest for a day and a night: for better unto us is the refreshment of one day than the whole time of our life wherein we were upon earth: and if we had known clearly that this *place* was appointed for them that sin, we should have done none other work whatsoever, neither traded nor done any wickedness. For what profit was our pride in the world? (*Copt.* What profit was it to us to be born into the world?) For this our pride is taken captive, which came up out of our mouth against our neighbour (*Copt.* our life is like the breath of our mouth): *and this* pain and our sore anguish and tears and the worms which are under us, these are worse unto us than the torments which we †suffer†. (This is hardly sense, but *Copt.* agrees; should it not have been 'these are worse than not to have been born'?) And as they thus spake, the angels of torment and the evil angels were wroth with them and said: How long have ye wept and sighed? for ye have had no mercy. For this is the judgement of God *on him* that hath not had mercy. Yet have ye received this great grace, even refreshment for the night and day of the Lord's day, because of Paul the dearly beloved of God who hath come down unto you.

45 And after these things the angel said unto me: Hast thou seen all these things? And I said: Yea, Lord. And he said unto me: Follow me, and I will bring thee into Paradise, that the righteous which are there may see thee: for, behold, they hope to see thee, and are ready to come and meet thee with joy and exultation. And I followed after the angel in the swiftness of the Holy Ghost, and he set me in Paradise and said unto me: This is Paradise, wherein Adam and his wife erred. And I entered into Paradise and saw the head of the waters, and the angel beckoned unto me and said to me: Behold, saith he, these waters: for this is the river Phison that compasseth about all the land of Evila, and this other is Geon that goeth about all the land of Egypt and Ethiopia, and this other is Tigris that is over against the Assyrians, and this other is Euphrates that watereth the land of Mesopotamia. And I entered in further and saw a tree planted, out of whose roots flowed waters, and out of it was the beginning of the four rivers, and the Spirit of God rested upon that tree, and when the spirit breathed the waters flowed forth: and I said: Lord, is this tree that which maketh the waters to flow? And he said unto me: Because in the beginning, before the heaven and the earth were made to appear, and all things were invisible, the Spirit of God moved (was borne) upon the waters; but since by the commandment of God the heaven and the earth appeared the spirit hath rested upon this tree; wherefore when the spirit breatheth, the waters flow out from the tree. And he took hold on mine hand and led me unto the tree of the knowledge of good and evil, and said: This is the tree whereby death entered into the world, and Adam

taking of it from his wife did eat, and death entered into the world. And he showed me another tree in the midst of Paradise, and saith unto me: This is the tree of life.

46 And as I yet looked upon the tree, I saw a virgin coming from afar off, and two hundred angels before her singing hymns: and I inquired and said: Lord, who is this that cometh in such glory? and he said unto me: This is Mary the virgin, the mother of the Lord. And she came near and saluted me, and said: Hail, Paul, dearly beloved of God and angels and men. For all the saints have besought my son Jesus who is my Lord, that thou shouldest come here in the body that they might see thee before thou didst depart out of the world. And the Lord said to them: Wait and be ye patient: yet a little while, and ye shall see him, and he shall be with you for ever. And again they all with one accord said unto him: Grieve us not, for we desire to see him while he is in the flesh, for by him hath thy name been greatly glorified in the world, and we have seen that he hath excelled (done away with) all the works whether of the lesser or the greater. For we inquire of them that come hither, saying: Who is he that guided you in the world? and they have told us: There is one in the world whose name is Paul; he declareth Christ, preaching him, and we believe that by the power and sweetness of his speech many have entered into the kingdom. Behold, all the righteous are behind me, coming to meet thee. But I say unto thee, Paul, that for this cause I come first to meet them that have performed the will of my son and my Lord Jesus Christ, even I come first to meet them and leave them not as strangers until they meet *with him* in peace.

47 While she was yet speaking I saw three men coming from afar, very beautiful, after the appearance of Christ, and their forms were shining, and their angels; and I asked: Who are these, Lord? And he answered: These are the fathers of the people, Abraham, Isaac, and Jacob. And they came near and greeted me, and said: Hail, Paul, dearly beloved of God and men: blessed is he that endureth violence for the Lord's sake. And Abraham answered me and said: This is my son Isaac, and Jacob my best beloved, and we knew the Lord and followed him. Blessed are all they that have believed thy word that they may inherit the kingdom of God by labour and self-sacrifice (renunciation) and sanctification and humility and charity and meekness and right faith in the Lord: and we also had devotion unto the Lord whom thou preachest, covenanting that we will come unto every soul of them that believe in him, and minister unto him as fathers minister unto their sons.

While they yet spake I saw twelve men coming from afar with honour, and I asked: Who are these, Lord? And he said: These are the patriarchs. And they came and saluted me and said:

Hail, Paul, dearly beloved of God and men. The Lord hath not grieved us, that we might see thee yet being in the body, before thou departedst out of the world. And every one of them signified his name unto me in order, from Ruben unto Benjamin; and Joseph said unto me: I am he that was sold; and I say unto thee, Paul, that *for* all that my brethren did unto me, in nothing did I deal evilly with them, not in all the labour which they laid upon me, nor did I hurt them in any thing (*Copt.* kept no evil thought against them) from morning until evening. Blessed is he that is hurt for the Lord's sake and hath endured, for the Lord will recompense him manifold more when he departeth out of the world.

48 While he yet spake I saw another coming from afar, beautiful, and his angels singing hymns, and I asked: Who is this, Lord, that is fair of countenance? And he said unto me: Dost thou not know him? And I said: No, Lord. And he said to me: This is Moses the lawgiver, unto whom God gave the law. And when he was nigh me, straightway he wept, and after that he greeted me; and I said unto him: Why weepest thou? for I have heard that thou excellest all men in meekness. And he answered, saying: I weep for them whom I planted with much labour, for they have borne no fruit, neither doth any of them do well. And I have seen all the sheep whom I fed that they are scattered and become as having no shepherd, and that all the labours which I have endured for the children of Israel are come to nought, and however great wonders I did in their midst [and] they understood not: and I marvel how the strangers and uncircumcised and idolaters are converted and entered into the promises of God, but Israel hath not entered in: and now I say unto thee, O brother Paul, that in that hour when the people hanged up Jesus whom thou preachest, God the Father of all, which gave me the law, and Michael and all the angels and archangels, and Abraham and Isaac and Jacob and all the righteous wept over the Son of God that was hanged on the cross. And in that hour all the saints waited upon me, looking on me and saying: Behold, Moses, what they of thy people have done unto the Son of God. Therefore blessed art thou, O Paul, and blessed is the generation and people that hath believed thy word.

49 While he yet spake there came other twelve and saw me and said: Art thou Paul that is glorified in heaven and upon earth? And I answered and said: Who are ye? The first answered and said: I am Esaias whose head Manasses cut with a saw of wood. And the second said likewise: I am Jeremias who was stoned by the children of Israel, and slain. And the third said: I am Ezechiel whom the children of Israel dragged by the feet over the stones in the mountain until they scattered my brains abroad: and all of us endured these labours, desiring

to save the children of Israel: and I say unto thee that after the toils which they laid upon me I would cast myself down upon my face before the Lord, praying for them and bowing my knees unto the second hour of the Lord's day, even until Michael came and raised me up from the earth. Blessed art thou, Paul, and blessed is the people that hath believed through thee.

And as they passed by, I saw another, fair of countenance, and asked: Who is this, Lord? [And when he saw me he was glad] and he said unto me: This is Lot, which was found righteous in Sodom. And he came near and greeted me and said: Blessed art thou, Paul, and blessed is the generation unto whom thou hast ministered. And I answered and said unto him: Art thou Lot, that wast found righteous in Sodom? And he said: I entertained angels in mine house as strangers, and when they of the city would have done them violence I offered them my two daughters, virgins, that had never known man, and gave them to them, saying: Use them as ye will, only do no ill unto these men, for therefore have they entered under the roof of mine house. Therefore ought we to have confidence, and know that whatsoever any man hath done, God recompenseth him manifold more when he cometh (they come) unto him. Blessed art thou, Paul, and blessed is the generation which hath believed thy word.

When therefore he had ceased speaking unto me, I saw another coming from afar off, very beautiful in the face, and smiling, and his angels singing hymns, and I said unto the angel that was with me: Hath, then, every one of the righteous an angel for his fellow? And he saith to me: Every one of the saints hath his own, that standeth by him and singeth hymns, and the one departeth not from the other. And I said: Who is this, Lord? And he said: This is Job. And he drew near and greeted me and said: Brother Paul, thou hast great praise with God and men. Now I am Job, which suffered much for the season of thirty years by the issue of a plague; and in the beginning the blains that came forth of my body were as grains of wheat; but on the third day they became like an ass's foot, and the worms that fell from them were four fingers long: and thrice the devil appeared unto me [1] and saith to me: Speak a word against the Lord, and die. *But* I said unto him: If thus be the will of God that I continue in the plague all the time of my life until I die, I will not rest from blessing the Lord God, and I shall receive the greater reward. For I know that the sufferings of this world are nought compared with the refreshment that is thereafter: wherefore blessed art thou, Paul, and blessed is the people which hath believed by thy means.

50 While he yet spake there came another crying out from

---

[1] It seems as if the author had read the Testament of Job (ed. by me in *Apocrypha Anecdota*, ii), in which are very similar details.

afar off and saying: Blessed art thou, Paul, and blessed am
I that have seen thee the beloved of the Lord. And I asked the
angel: Who is this, Lord? and he answered and said unto me:
This is Noe of the days of the flood. And straightway we greeted
one another, and he, rejoicing greatly, said unto me: Thou art
(or, Art thou) Paul the best beloved of God. And I asked him:
Who art thou? And he said: I am Noe that was in the days of
the flood: but I say unto thee, Paul, that I spent an hundred
years making the ark, not putting off the coat (tunic) which
I wore, and I shaved not the hair of mine head. Furthermore
I kept continence, not coming near mine own wife, and in those
hundred years the hair of mine head grew not in greatness,
neither was my raiment soiled. And I besought men at that
time, saying: Repent, for a flood of waters cometh upon you.
But they mocked me and derided my words; and again they said
unto me: This is the time of them that would play and sin as
much as they will, that have leave to fornicate not a little (Lat.
confused; other versions omit): for God looketh not on these
things, neither knoweth what is done of us men, and moreover
there is no flood of waters coming upon this world. And they
ceased not from their sins until God blotted out all flesh that
had the breath of life in it. But know thou that God loveth
one righteous man more than all the world of the wicked. Therefore blessed art thou, O Paul, and blessed is the people that hath
believed by thy means.

51 And I turned myself and saw other righteous ones coming
from afar off, and I asked the angel: Who are these, Lord? and
he answered me: These are Elias and Eliseus. And they greeted
me, and I said unto them: Who are ye? And one of them
answered and said: I am Elias the prophet of God. I am Elias that
prayed, and because of my word the heaven rained not for three
years and six months, because of the iniquities of men. Righteous
and true is God, who doeth the will of his servants; for oftentimes the angels besought the Lord for rain, and he said: Be
patient until my servant Elias pray and entreat for this, and I
will send rain upon the earth.

[Here the Greek, Latin, and Syriac texts end, save that the
Syriac adds thus much:

And he gave not, until I called upon him again; then he
gave unto them. But blessed art thou, O Paul, that thy generation
and those thou teachest are the sons of the kingdom. And
know thou, O Paul, that every man who believes through thee
hath a great blessing, and a blessing is reserved for him. Then
he departed from me.

And the angel who was with me led me forth, and said unto
me: Lo, unto thee is given this mystery and revelation: as
thou pleasest, make it known unto the sons of men.

And I, Paul, returned unto myself, and I knew all that I had seen: and in life I had not rest that I might reveal this mystery, but I wrote it and deposited it under the ground and the foundations of the house of a certain faithful man with whom I used to be in Tarsus a city of Cilicia. And when I was released from this life of time, and stood before my Lord, thus said he unto me: Paul, have we shown all these things unto thee that thou shouldst deposit them under the foundations of a house? Then send and disclose concerning this revelation, that men may read it and turn to the way of truth, that they also may not come to these bitter torments.

And thus was this revelation discovered. . . .

Then follows the history of the finding, which in the other texts is prefixed to the book.]

But this conclusion can hardly be the original one. The Coptic seems in part better. After the words 'rain upon the earth', it continues:

The sufferings which each endureth for God's sake will God requite unto him twofold. Blessed art thou, Paul, and blessed are the heathen who shall believe through thee. And whilst he was speaking, Enoch (here Enoch replaces Elisha) also came and saluted me and said unto me: The man who endureth suffering for God's sake, God will not afflict when he goeth out of the world.

Then there are similar meetings with Zacharias and John Baptist, and Abel. Zacharias says:

'I am he whom they killed when I was offering up the offering unto God: and when the angels came for the offering, they carried my body up to God, and no man found my body whither it had been taken.'

Then Adam, taller than the rest, appears. And this seems a suitable finale to the procession of saints.

After this Paul is carried into the third heaven. The angel who is with him changes in appearance and bursts into flames of fire, and a voice forbids Paul to reveal what he has seen.

There is a description of a mysterious vision of an altar with seven eagles of light on the right and seven on the left. And this is followed by more descriptions of Paradise—partly resembling a vision seen by one Siophanes, in the Book of Bartholomew (p. 185). Some sentences also are taken from, or at least found in, the Apocalypse of Zephaniah. The meek, the prophets, David, all figure again in this episode: last are the martyrs. The conclusion runs thus (in substance):

The angel of the Lord took me up and brought me to the Mount of Olives. I found the apostles assembled and told them all I had seen. They praised God and commanded us, that is me, Mark, and Timothy, to write the revelation. And while they were talking, Christ appeared from the chariot of the cherubim and spoke greetings to Peter, John, and especially

Paul. He promised blessings to those who should write or read the Apocalypse, and curses on those who should deride it. Peter and Paul should end their course on the fifth of Epiphi (29 June). He then bade a cloud take the apostles to the various countries allotted to them, and commanded them to preach the Gospel of the Kingdom. And a doxology follows.

I am disposed to think that nothing after the appearance of Adam in this version can be original. The rest is to a great extent, I think, a pasticcio from other Coptic apocrypha. It is quite possible, of course, that the original end of the Apocalypse was lost at an early date: but the supposition is probable that after the appearance of Adam a short conclusion followed in which Paul returned to earth. With so ill-proportioned and inartistic a book it is not perhaps worth while to spend much time on conjectural restoration. Yet another possibility should be pointed out. The climax of the Apocalypse is reached when the Sunday is granted as a day of rest from torment. Paul has seen Paradise and hell, and there is no more for him to do. Everything after ch. 44 is an otiose appendix.

And we do find in the Ethiopic Apocalypse of the Virgin, which copies that of Paul very literally, that the end comes at ch. 44, when the Virgin procures rest from Friday to Monday morning for the lost. The Greek Apocalypse—one form at least—ends when she has gained for them the days of Pentecost.

It may be the case, then, that the Apocalypse of Paul as first issued ended here, and that it was reissued with the appendix about Paradise (45–end). In the shorter Latin recensions there is no trace of anything after ch. 44: but this does not furnish a conclusive argument. More to the point would be the discovery of a copy of the full text ending with 44.

APOCALYPSE OF THOMAS

The emergence of this book has been recent. The Gelasian Decree condemns the book 'called the Revelation of Thomas' as apocryphal, and that was all that was known of it. In 1908 a quotation in the Berlin MS. (eighth–ninth century) of Jerome's Chronicle was noticed by Dr. Frick. At the eighteenth year of Tiberius, the manuscript has this note:

In a certain apocryphal book, said to be of Thomas the apostle, it is written that the Lord Jesus told him that from his ascension into heaven to his second advent *the time* comprised is nine jubilees.

This does not appear in any of the published texts. Already in 1907 F. Wilhelm had printed, in his *Deutsche Legenden und Legendare*, a text from a Munich MS. which attracted little attention, but was in fact the lost Apocalypse, or part of it.

In the same year E. Hauler showed that a leaf of a fifth-century palimpsest at Vienna—the same that contains a leaf of the Epistle of the Apostles (see p. 485)—was a fragment of this book. Professor E. von Dobschütz had, before this, begun making preparation for an

edition of the Apocalypse based on manuscripts at Munich and Rome,
which has not yet appeared.   In the *Journal of Theological Studies* for
1910 I printed the beginning of the book from a Verona MS. (of eighth
century).   Maffei had noticed this, and in 1755 Dionisi had printed
it in a forgotten volume.   In 1911 Dom Bihlmeyer printed another
'uninterpolated' text from Munich in the *Revue Bénédictine*.   Yet
more: in 1913 Max Förster (*Studien z. engl. Philol.: Der Vercelli-Codex*)
showed that the fifteenth sermon in the famous Anglo-Saxon MS.
at Vercelli is an Old English version of this Revelation; that a Hatton
MS. and the Blickling Homilies also contain matter drawn from it;
and that a shortened Latin form is to be found in a dialogue printed
by Suchier (*L'Enfant sage*, 1910, p. 272).   Lastly, there are quotations
from it in some odd—I think Irish—homilies in a Reichenau MS.
at Carlsruhe, printed by Dom de Bruyne as 'Apocryphes Priscillianistes'
in the *Revue Bénéd.*, 1907.

There is, then, a quantity of material which we shall look to Professor
Dobschütz to co-ordinate.   Latin appears to have been the original
language,[1] and the data of the fuller text point to the days of Arcadius
and Honorius.   How much earlier the shorter text may be it is not
easy to say: and I would not commit myself to the assertion that there
is not a Greek document at the back of that.

APOCALYPSE OF THOMAS

A. Verona fragment (eighth century) and Wilhelm's text (Munich Clm. 4585, ninth century).

Here beginneth the epistle of the Lord unto Thomas.

Hear thou, Thomas, the things which must come to pass in
the last times: there shall be famine and war and earthquakes
in divers places, snow and ice and great drought shall there be,
and many dissensions among the peoples, blasphemy, iniquity,
envy and villainy, indolence, pride and intemperance, so that
every man shall speak that which pleaseth him.   And my priests
shall not have peace among themselves, but shall sacrifice unto
me with deceitful mind: therefore will I not look upon them.
Then shall the priests behold the people departing from the
house of the Lord and turning unto the world (?) and setting up
(*or*, transgressing) landmarks in the house of God.   And they
shall claim (vindicate) for themselves many [things and] places
that were lost and that shall be subject unto Caesar (?) as also
they were aforetime: giving poll-taxes of (for) the cities, *even*
gold and silver,[2] and the chief men of the cities shall be condemned (*here Verona ends: Munich continues*), *and their substance*
brought into† the treasury of the kings, *and they* shall be filled.

[1] This is at least certain for the passage about Arcadius and
Honorius: H is not the eighth letter in the Greek alphabet!   But the
sentence, which is omitted in the Anglo-Saxon version, may be an
interpolation.

[2] The Anglo-Saxon renders: setting up gold and silver heads in
their cities.

For there shall be great disturbance throughout all the people, and death.[1] The house of the Lord shall be desolate, and their altars shall be abhorred, so that spiders weave their webs therein. *The place* of holiness shall be corrupted, the priesthood polluted, distress (agony) shall increase, virtue shall be overcome, joy perish, and gladness depart. In those days evil shall abound: there shall be respecters of persons, hymns shall cease out of the house of the Lord, truth shall be no more, covetousness shall abound among the priests; an upright *man* (*al.* an upright priesthood) shall not be found.

On a sudden there shall arise near the last time a king, a lover of the law, who shall hold rule not for long: he shall leave two sons. The first is named of the first letter (A, Arcadius), the second of the eighth (H, Honorius). The first shall die before the second (Arcadius died in 408; Honorius in 423).[2]

Thereafter shall arise two princes to oppress the nations, under whose hands there shall be a very great famine in the right-hand part of the east, so that nation shall rise up against nation and be driven out from their own borders.

Again another king shall arise, a crafty man (?), and shall command a golden image of Caesar (?) to be made (*al.* to be worshipped in the house of God), wherefore (?) martyrdoms shall abound. Then shall faith return unto the servants of the Lord, and holiness shall be multiplied and distress (agony) increase. The mountains [3] shall †be comforted† and shall drop down sweetness †of fire from the face†, that the number of the saints may be accomplished.

After a little space there shall arise a king out of the east, a lover of the law, who shall cause all good things and necessary to abound *in* the house of the Lord: he shall show mercy unto the widows and to the needy, and command a royal gift to be given unto the priests: in his days shall be abundance of all things.

And after that again a king shall arise in the south part of the world, and shall hold rule a little space: in whose days the treasury shall fail because of the wages of the Roman soldiers, †so that the substance of all the aged shall be commanded (to be taken) and given to the king to distribute†.

Thereafter shall be plenty of corn and wine and oil, but great dearness of money, so that the substance of gold and silver shall be given for corn, and there shall be great dearth.

At that time shall be very great rising (?) of the sea, so that no man shall tell news to any man. The kings of the earth and the princes and the captains shall be troubled, and no man shall

---

[1] The predictions in these paragraphs are very like those in the Testament of the Lord, i. 3–5.

[2] This paragraph is omitted in AS.

[3] This sentence omitted in AS.

speak freely (boldly). Grey hairs shall be seen upon boys, and the young (?) shall not give place unto the aged.

After that shall arise another king, a crafty man, who shall hold rule for a short space: in whose days there shall be all manner of evils, even the death of the race of men from the east even unto Babylon. And thereafter death and famine and sword in the land of Chanaan even unto (Rome?).[1] Then shall all the fountains of waters and wells boil over (?) and be turned into blood (or, into dust and blood). The heaven shall be moved, the stars shall fall upon the earth, the sun shall be cut in half like the moon, and the moon shall not give her light. There shall be great signs and wonders in those days when Antichrist draweth near. These are the signs unto them that dwell in the earth. In those days the *pains* of great travail shall come upon them. (*al.* In those days, when Antichrist now draweth near, these are the signs. *Woe* unto them that dwell on the earth; in those days great pains of travail shall come upon them.)[2] Woe unto them that build, for they shall not inhabit. Woe unto them that break up the fallow, for they shall labour without cause. Woe unto them that make marriages, for unto famine and need shall they beget sons. Woe unto them that join house to house or field to field, for all things shall be consumed with fire. Woe unto them that look not unto (?) themselves while time alloweth, for hereafter shall they be condemned for ever. Woe unto them that turn away from the poor when he asketh.

[Here is a break: the text goes on: For I am ⟨*the Son*⟩ of the high and powerful: I am the Father of all. (*al.* And know ye: I am the Father most high: I am the Father of all spirits.) This, as we shall see, is the beginning of the older (?) and shorter text, and of the Vienna fragment: only, in the latter, some words now unintelligible precede it: not the words, however, which are in Wilhelm's text. I will continue with Wilhelm.]

These are the seven signs ⟨before⟩ the ending of this world. There shall be in all the earth famine and great pestilences and much distress: then shall all men be led captive among all nations and shall fall by the edge of the sword.

On the first day of the judgement will be a great marvel (or, the beginning shall be). At the third hour of the day shall be a great and mighty voice in the firmament of the heaven, and a great cloud of blood coming down out of the north, and great thunderings and mighty lightnings shall follow that cloud, and there shall be a rain of blood upon all the earth. These are the signs of the first day (Monday *in the Anglo-Saxon, and so for the other days*).

And on the second day there shall be a great voice in the

[1] The manuscript has 'nona', ninth.
[2] Some of the following clauses are quoted (without acknowledgement) in the Irish (?) homily mentioned above.

firmament of the heaven, and the earth shall be moved out of its place: and the gates of heaven shall be opened in the firmament of heaven toward the east, and a great power shall be sent (belched) forth by the gates of heaven *and* shall cover all the heaven even until evening (*al.* and there shall be fears and tremblings in the world). These are the signs of the second day.

And on the third day, about the second hour, shall be a voice in heaven, and the abysses of the earth shall utter their voice from the four corners of the world. The first heaven shall be rolled up like a book and shall straightway vanish. *And* because of the smoke and stench of the brimstone of the abyss the days shall be darkened unto the tenth hour. Then shall all men say: I think that the end draweth near, that we shall perish.[1] These are the signs of the third day.

And on the fourth day at the first hour, the earth of the east shall speak, the abyss shall roar: then shall all the earth be moved by the strength of an earthquake. In that day shall all the idols of the heathen fall, and all the buildings of the earth. These are the signs of the fourth day.

And on the fifth day, at the sixth hour, there shall be great thunderings suddenly in the heaven, and the powers of light and the wheel of the sun shall be caught away, and there shall be great darkness over the world until evening, and the stars shall be turned away from their ministry. In that day all nations shall hate the world and despise the life of this world. These are the signs of the fifth day.

And on the sixth day there shall be signs in heaven. At the fourth hour the firmament of heaven shall be cloven from the east unto the west. *And* the angels of the heavens shall be looking forth upon the earth ⟨through⟩ the opening of the heavens. And all men shall see above the earth the host of the angels looking forth out of heaven. Then shall all men flee.

(*Here Wilhelm's text ends abruptly.*)

B. *Bihlmeyer's text, from Munich Clm.* 4563 (*eleventh to twelfth century, from Benedictbeuren*): *and the Vienna fragment.*

Hear thou, O Thomas, for I am the Son of God the Father, and I am the father of all spirits. Hear thou of me the signs which shall come to pass at the end of this world, when the end of the world shall be fulfilled (*Vienna*: that it pass away) before mine elect depart out of the world. I will tell thee that which shall come to pass openly unto men (*or,* will tell thee openly, &c.): *but* when these things shall be the princes of the angels know not, seeing it is now hidden from before them (*Vienna adds*: at what day the end shall be fulfilled, *and some defective clauses*).

[1] Here AS. has a long speech: 'Woe unto us wretched and sinful,' &c.: men lament that they were warned of these things and did not repent, but went on living in worldly delights.

Then shall there be in the world sharings (participations) between king and king, and in all the earth shall be great famine, great pestilences, and many distresses, and the sons of men shall be led captive among all nations and shall fall by the edge of the sword (and there shall be great commotion in the world: *Vienna omits*). Then after that when the hour of the end draweth nigh, there shall be for seven days great signs in heaven, and the powers of the heavens shall be moved.

Then shall there be on the first day the beginning: at the third hour of the day a great and mighty voice in the firmament of heaven and a bloody cloud coming up (down, *Vienna*) out of the north, and great thunderings and mighty lightnings shall follow it, and it shall cover the whole heaven, and there shall be a rain of blood upon all the earth. These are the signs of the first day.

And on the second day there shall be a great voice in the firmament of heaven, and the earth shall be moved out of its place, and the gates of heaven shall be opened in the firmament of heaven toward the east, and the (smoke of a great fire shall break forth through the gates of heaven and shall cover all the heaven until evening. In that day there shall be fears and great terrors in the world. These are the signs of the second day. *Vienna is defective here*).

But on the third day about the third hour shall be a great voice in heaven, and the abysses of the earth (*Vienna ends*) shall roar from the four corners of the world; the pinnacles (*so*) of the firmament of heaven shall be opened, and all the air shall be filled with pillars of smoke. There shall be a stench of brimstone, very evil, until the tenth hour, and men shall say: We think the time draweth nigh that we perish. These are the signs of the third day.

And on the fourth day at the first hour, from the land of the east the abyss shall melt (*so*) and roar. Then shall all the earth be shaken by the might of an earthquake. In that day shall the ornaments of the heathen fall, and all the buildings of the earth, before the might of the earthquake. These are the signs of the fourth day.

But on the fifth day at the sixth hour, suddenly there shall be a great thunder in heaven, and the powers of light and the wheel of the sun shall be caught away (*MS.* opened), and there shall be great darkness in the world until evening, and the air shall be gloomy (sad) without sun or moon, and the stars shall cease from their ministry. In that day shall all nations behold as in a mirror (?) (*or*, behold it as sackcloth) and shall despise the life of this world. These are the signs of the fifth day.

And on the sixth day at the fourth hour there shall be a great voice in heaven, and the firmament of the heaven shall be cloven from the east unto the west, and the angels of the heavens shall be looking forth upon the earth by the openings of the heavens, and all these that are on the earth shall behold the host of the angels looking forth out of heaven. Then shall all men flee unto the monuments (mountains?) and hide themselves from the face of the righteous angels, and say: Would that the earth would open and swallow us up! And such things shall come to pass as never were since this world was created.

Then shall they behold me coming from above in the light of my Father with the power and honour of the holy angels. Then at my coming shall the fence of fire of paradise be done away—because paradise is girt round about with fire. And this shall be that perpetual fire that shall consume the earth and all the elements of the world.

Then shall the spirits and souls of all men come forth from paradise and shall come upon all the earth: and every one of them shall go unto his own body, where it is laid up, and every one of them shall say: Here lieth my body. And when the great voice of those spirits shall be heard, then shall there be a great earthquake over all the world, and by the might thereof the mountains shall be cloven from above and the rocks from beneath. Then shall every spirit return into his own vessel, and the bodies of the saints which have fallen asleep shall arise.

Then shall their bodies be changed into the image and likeness and the honour of the holy angels, and into the power of the image of mine holy Father. Then shall they be clothed with the vesture of life eternal, out of the cloud of light which hath never been seen in this world; for that cloud cometh down out of the highest realm of the heaven from the power of my Father. And that cloud shall compass about with the beauty thereof all the spirits that have believed in me.

Then shall they be clothed, and shall be borne by the hands of the holy angels like as I have told you aforetime. Then also shall they be lifted up into the air upon a cloud of light, and shall go with me rejoicing unto heaven, and then shall they continue in the light and honour of my Father. Then shall there be unto them great gladness with my Father and before the holy angels. These are the signs of the sixth day.

And on the seventh day at the eighth hour there shall be voices in the four corners of the heaven. And all the air shall be shaken, and filled with holy angels, and they shall make war among them all the day long. And in that day shall mine elect be sought out by the holy angels from the destruction of the world. Then shall all men see that the hour of their destruction draweth near. These are the signs of the seventh day.

And when the seven days are passed by, on the eighth day at the sixth hour there shall be a sweet and tender voice in heaven from the east. Then shall that angel be revealed which hath power over the holy angels: and all the angels shall go forth with him, sitting upon chariots of the clouds of mine holy Father (so), rejoicing and running upon the air beneath the heaven to deliver the elect that have believed in me. And they shall rejoice that the destruction of this world hath come.

The words of the Saviour unto Thomas are ended, concerning the end of this world.

None of the Latin texts seem to be complete. But we see that Wilhelm's text is a blend of two sorts of Apocalypse—that akin to Daniel which, under the form of prophecy, describes events contemporary with the author and continues them into the future: and that which is more akin to John and describes the signs of the end.

Bihlmeyer's text has only the latter element, and as it agrees pretty closely with our oldest authority, the Vienna fragment (though in that, as I have said, something did precede Bihlmeyer's opening), I judge it to be the older of the two forms. The first part of Wilhelm's text with its clumsy indication of Arcadius and Honorius by means of their initials is much in the manner of the later Sibyllines, in which this particular trick is pushed to an absurd length, and used for quite imaginary personages as well as historic ones. In the second part Wilhelm's text departs widely from the Vienna fragment, and here again shows itself as probably inferior.

The Apocalypse, we see, was known in England in the ninth century at least: and I think it must probably be regarded as the ultimate parent of a little piece which is found in innumerable manuscripts and has often been printed: I mean Jerome on the Fifteen Signs of the last days before the judgement. The beginning of this states that Jerome found it 'in the annals of the Hebrews'. Its popularity was very great. Illustrations of the Fifteen Signs are occasionally to be found in manuscripts, and I have seen them on the alabaster tablets carved at Nottingham in the fourteenth and fifteenth centuries, but the best-known representation of them is in a window at All Saints', North Street, York, where they are accompanied by mottoes taken from the 'Prick of Conscience', which used to be attributed to Richard of Hampole.

The Anglo-Saxon version in the Vercelli Book (no. xv) begins thus:

We are told in this book how Saint Thomas the apostle of God asked our Lord when the time of Antichrist should be. Then the Lord spake unto him and said thus:

It behoveth that it be in the next days. Then shall be hunger and war, &c.:

The text conforms, generally speaking, to the longer recensions. The signs of the fifth day are omitted. The conclusion diverges from the Latin and tells how the Virgin, Michael, and Peter successively intercede with the Judge, and he forgives a third part of the sinners at the prayer of each. But not all are pardoned: for we then have the sentences: Venite benedicti and Discedite maledicti as in Matt. xxv.

Quite recently (in *Proc. R.I.A.*) the Rev. St. J. Seymour has pointed out the probable dependence of the *Saltair na Rann* (eleventh century) on our apocalypse in its description of the Signs of the End.

THE APOCALYPSE OF THE VIRGIN. A. GREEK

We have this in Greek in a great many texts. The oldest I have found was edited by me in 1893. A very brief summary of it will suffice, for it is a late and dreary production.

The Virgin at the Mount of Olives prays to be told about the torments of hell and the next world. Michael is sent. He takes her to the west: the earth opens and discloses the lost who did not worship the Trinity.

She sees a great darkness. At her prayer it is lifted and she sees souls tormented with boiling pitch. No one has yet interceded for them, neither Abraham, John Baptist, Moses, nor Paul. They are unbelievers.

They go to the south: there is a river of fire with souls immersed at various depths. Cursers of their parents. Causers of abortion. False swearers. A man hung by the feet and devoured by worms is a usurer. A woman hung by the ears, with serpents coming out of her mouth and biting her, is a backbiter and gossip.

They go (again!) to the west. In a cloud of fire lie those who lay late on Sunday. On fiery seats sit those who did not rise at the entry of the priest. On an iron tree hang blasphemers and slanderers. A man hung by hands and feet is the evil steward (*oeconomus*) of a church. Wicked priests, readers, bishops, widows of priests who married again, an ' archdeaconess ', covetous women, are severally described.

They go to the left-hand of paradise. In a river of pitch and fire are the Jews who crucified Jesus, those who denied baptism, those guilty of various impurities, sorcerers, murderers, they who strangle their children. In a lake of fire are bad Christians.

A great appeal of the Virgin follows, in which she entreats all the saints to intercede, with her, for the Christians. At last the Son appears, and grants the days of Pentecost as a season of rest to the lost.

In some texts a visit of the Virgin to paradise follows this ; but it is usually short and uninteresting. In one of the Eastern books on the Assumption (see p. 222) there is a very diffuse account of paradise as seen by the Virgin.

APOCALYPSE OF THE VIRGIN. B. ETHIOPIC

This is wholly different from the Greek. It was edited with a Latin version by Chaîne in 1909 (*Corpus Scriptt. Christ. Orient.* i. 7) with texts of the Protevangelium and a story of the Assumption.

The Apocalypse is almost wholly borrowed from that of Paul. Chaîne takes it to be a version from Arabic, and the Arabic he thinks was translated from Greek.

John is the narrator. The Virgin called him to listen to a
wonderful mystery which had been revealed to her: as she
prayed at Golgotha at noon on the sixth day of the week a cloud
came and took her into the third heaven. The Son appeared
and said that he would show her a great mystery. 'Look upon
the earth beneath.' (Here we have ch. 13 of *Paul*, and from this
point we continue with the text of *Paul* sometimes amplified
with quotations from the Bible.)

At *Paul* 31 we have the addition—doubtless correct—that the
souls who were neither hot nor cold sit beside the river of fire.
There are several variations and additions to the list of torments,
not worth specifying, but the section which corresponds to *Paul* 40
must be quoted (unpleasant as the topic is) on account of its
affinity with *Peter*.

Women are seen, bitten by serpents, dogs, lions, and leopards
of fire. They are nuns who violated the rule and slew their
children.

Often they caused their death before they were born. They
shed their blood on the ground, or killed them when born, or
their fathers gave poison to the mothers. 'But these children
cry out before the throne of my Father, and say: Lord, they
have not suffered us to grow up to do good or evil: the half
of us they gave to the dogs and cast the other half to the swine.
And when we heard the words of these children, I and my Father
and the Comforter were grieved, and I commanded Temliaqos
to set them in a beautiful abode. But for their fathers and
mothers this is their torment for ever.'

The Virgin says: If they repent wilt thou not forgive them?
Yes, if they do so from their heart. But as for their pastors
who did not admonish them, their part shall be with Eli and
Fola. Eli did not reprove his sons, Fola sold his daughters
for an ox.

I do not know who Fola was.

The Apocalypse ends with ch. 44 of Paul. There is no trace in it of
Paul 1–12 or 45–51.

REVELATION OF STEPHEN

The 'Revelation called of Stephen' is condemned, like that of
Thomas, in the Gelasian Decree. Sixtus Senensis, *Bibliotheca Sancta*
(1593), p. 115, says: 'The Apocalypse of Stephen the first martyr
who was one of the seven deacons of the apostles was prized by the
Manichaean heretics as Serapion witnesses.' Serapion of Thmuis, he
elsewhere says (p. 299), wrote a large and very notable work against
the Manichaeans in Greek 'which I have lately read'. Our texts of
Serapion contain no mention of the Apocalypse of Stephen. But no
Manichaean would have cared about the book which I am going to

speak of.[1] It has been usually guessed that the writing so described was the account of the finding of St. Stephen's body, the whereabouts of which was revealed by Gamaliel in a vision to Lucian. With Stephen were found the bodies of Gamaliel and his son Abibas, and of Nicodemus. Lucian's narrative was known to Augustine: it purports to be of the year 415, and there is little in it, as compared with similar 'inventions' of relics, which justifies its being solemnly condemned as apocryphal.

So says I. Franko, who in 1906 (*Zeitschr. f. Ntl. Wiss.*) published a Slavonic romance which, he says, is the real beginning of Lucian's narrative.

The substance of it is this:

Two years after the Ascension there was a contest about Jesus. Many learned men had assembled at Jerusalem from Ethiopia, the Thebaid, Alexandria, Jerusalem, Asia, Mauretania, and Babylon. There was a great clamour among them like thunder, lasting till the fourth hour.

Stephen, a learned man of the tribe of Benjamin, stood on a high place and addressed the assembly. Why this tumult? said he. Blessed is he who has not doubted concerning Jesus. Born of a pure virgin he filled the world with light. By Satan's contrivances Herod slew 14,000 (144,000) children. He spoke of the miracles of Jesus. Woe to the unbelievers when he shall come as judge, with angels, a fiery chariot, a mighty wind: the stars shall fall, the heavens open, the books be brought forward. The twelve angels who are set over every soul shall unveil the deeds of men. The sea shall move and give up what is in it. The mountains fall, all the surface of the earth becomes smooth. Great winged thrones are set. The Lord, and Christ, and the Holy Spirit take their seats. The Father bids Jesus sit on his right hand.

At this point the crowd cried out: Blasphemy! and took Stephen before Pilate.

Pilate stood on the steps and reproached them: You compelled me to crucify the Innocent; why rage against this man? Why gnash your teeth? Are ye yet foolish?

They led Stephen away. Caiaphas ordered him to be beaten till the blood ran. And he prayed: Lay not this sin to their charge. We saw how angels ministered to him.

[1] I must record one of the very rare errors of Fabricius here. He (*Cod. Apocr. N. T.*, i, p. 965) cites Sixtus Senensis as saying (on the authority of Serapion) that the Manichaeans so prized the Revelation of Stephen as to carry it in the skin of their thighs! This long puzzled me, and I could not find it in Sixtus. But at last I noticed that at the end of the article just preceding *Stephanus*, Victor Vitensis is quoted to this effect: The Manichaeans so honoured their teacher that they used to have these words inscribed on the skin of their thighs, '*Manichaeus, disciple of Christ Jesus*'. Perhaps some one has already explained this in print; if so, I have not seen it.

In the morning Pilate called his wife and two children: they baptized themselves and praised God.

Three thousand men now assembled and disputed with Stephen for three days and three nights. On the fourth day they took counsel and sent to Caesarea of Palestine for Saul of Tarsus, who had a commission to seize upon Christians. He took his place on the judgement seat and said: I wonder that thou, a wise man, and my kinsman, believest all this. None of the Sanhedrin have given up the Law. I have been through all Judaea, Galilee, Peraea, Damascus, and the city of the Jesitites to seek out believers.

Stephen lifted up his hands and said: Silence, persecutor! Recognize the Son of God. Thou makest me doubt of my own descent. But I see that thou shalt ere long drink of the same cup as I. What thou doest, do quickly. Saul rent his clothes and beat Stephen. Gamaliel, Saul's teacher, sprang forth and gave Saul a buffet, saying: Did I teach thee such conduct? know that what this man saith is acceptable and good.

Saul was yet more enraged, and looked fiercely on him, saying: I spare thine old age, but thou shalt reap a due reward for this. Gamaliel answered: I ask nothing better than to suffer with Christ. The elders rent their clothes, cast dust on their heads, and cried: Crucify the blasphemers.

Saul said: Guard them until the morrow. Next day he sat on the judgement seat and had them brought before him, and they were led away to be crucified. An angel came and cast away the cross, and Stephen's wounds were healed. Seven men came and poured molten lead into his mouth and pitch into his ears. They drove nails into his breast and feet, and he prayed for their forgiveness. Again an angel came down and healed him, and a great multitude believed.

Next day all assembled and took him out of the city to judge him. He mounted upon a stone and addressed them: How long will ye harden your hearts? The Law and the Prophets spake of Christ. In the first Law, and the second, and the other books it is written: When the year of the covenant cometh I will send my beloved angel, the good spirit of sonship, from a pure maiden, the fruit of truth, without ploughshare and without seed, and an image of sowing (?), and the fruit shall grow after the . . . of planting for ever from the word of my covenant, and signs shall come to pass. And Isaiah saith: Unto us a child is born, &c. And again: Behold, a virgin shall conceive, &c. And the prophet Nathan said: I saw one, a maiden and without touch of man, and a man child in her arms, and that was the Lord of the earth unto the end of the earth. And again the prophet Baruch saith: Christ the eternal appeareth as a stone from the mountain and breaketh in pieces the idol temples of the . . . David also said: Arise, O Lord, unto thy resting place,

&c. Understand then, O foolish ones, what the prophet saith: In this word shalt thou judge.

And he looked up to heaven and said: I see the heaven opened and the Son of man standing at the right hand of God.

Then they laid hands on him, saying: He blasphemeth! Gamaliel said: Wherein? This righteous man hath seen the Son saying to the Father: Lo, the Jews rage against me and cease not to ill-treat them that confess my name. And the Father said: Sit thou on my right hand until I make thine enemies thy footstool.

Then they bound Stephen and took him away to Alexander, the reader, who was a chief of the people, and of the troop in Tiberias.

In the fourth watch of the night, a light as of lightning shone round about him, and a voice said: Be strong. Thou art my first martyr, and thine hour is nigh. I will write the record of thee in the book of everlasting life.

The Jews took counsel and decreed that he should be stoned. There were with him Abibas, Nicodemus, Gamaliel, Pilate, his wife and two children, and a multitude of believers. Saul stood forth and beckoned, and said: It would have been better that this man should not be slain, because of his great wisdom: but forasmuch as he is an apostate, I condemn Stephen to be stoned. The people said: He shall be stoned: but those who stood in the front rank with staves looked on each other and durst not lay hands on him: for he was renowned among the people.

Saul was wroth, and stripped those servants of their garments and laid them on the table; and commanded the men to stone Stephen.

Stephen looked round and said: Saul, Saul, that which thou doest unto me to-day, that same will the Jews do unto thee to-morrow. And when thou sufferest, thou shalt think on me.

The people cast stones upon him so thickly that the light of the sun was darkened. Nicodemus and Gamaliel put their arms about him and shielded him, and were slain, and gave up their souls to Christ.

Stephen prayed, saying: Forgive them that stone us, for by their means we trust to enter into thy kingdom. And at the tenth hour he gave up the ghost. Then beautiful youths appeared, and fell upon the bodies and wept aloud: and the people beheld the souls borne up by angels into heaven, and saw the heavens open and the hosts coming to meet the souls. And the people mourned for three days and three nights.

Pilate took the bodies and put each one into a silver coffin with his name upon it: but Stephen's coffin was gilt: and he laid them in his secret sepulchre. But Stephen prayed: Let my body be buried in my land of Serasima in Kapogemala (Caphargamala) until the revealing, when the martyrs that follow me shall be gathered together. And an angel came and removed the bodies thither.

But Pilate rose early to burn incense before the bodies, and found them not; and rent his clothes, saying: Was I then not worthy to be thy servant? On the night following, Stephen appeared and said to him: Weep not. I prayed God to hide our bodies. In the time of our revealing one of thy seed shall find us after a vision, and thy desire shall be fulfilled, But build a house of prayer and celebrate our feast in the month of April. After seven months thou also shalt rest. And Pilate did so: and he died, and was buried at Kapartasala: and his wife also died in peace. But the holy martyrs appeared thrice to venerable and believing men, speaking to them, and revealing divine words: for after their death many believed.

One of Franko's two manuscripts omits all mention of Pilate, who is indeed not necessary to the story. The statements about him are quite irreconcilable with other legends, even those of the Eastern Church which take the favourable view of him.

Franko is clearly right in saying that this romance implies a continuation, and most likely right in holding that the Lucian-narrative implies a previous story. But the extravagance of the Slavonic text is such that one cannot but think it has been improved by the translator: and if Pilate could be gratuitously inserted—as I think he has been—by one redactor, others may equally well have been at work.

APPENDIX I.
UNKNOWN GOSPEL

In 1935 [Sir] Harold Idris Bell and T. C. Skeat published the following text as *Fragments of an Unknown Gospel*, which by reason of its extremely early date (not later than the middle of the second century) and its content is of unusual interest. It shows striking parallels, in language and matter, with both the Synoptic Gospels and St. John; but I believe its editors to have been right in their original conclusion that it 'is not a mere *réchauffé* of elements derived from the canonical Gospels'. The last incident which it describes might, I think, be based on one of Our Lord's parables about sowing—that of the seed growing secretly, or the mustard seed—but it is followed by an action, presumably miraculous, on the part of Jesus himself, which appears to emphasize the point of the foregoing saying; the addition at any rate is quite new. The editors successfully maintained most of their original supplements and interpretations against some objections and alternative suggestions made in 1936 by Professor Carl Schmidt. There is nothing to suggest that the fragments come from any of the uncanonical Gospels known to antiquity—for instance, the Gospel of the Egyptians, that according to the Hebrews, or the Gospel of St. Peter—or to connect it with any of the other fragments of uncanonical Gospels in the papyri; and there is no trace of heretical tendency in it. It is a much more convincing document than most extant apocrypha. In fragment 1 the text of the *recto* seems to follow naturally upon that of the *verso*; apart from this the editors are uncertain about the order in which the pieces of narrative are to be placed.

Fragment 1, verso

(And Jesus said) to the lawyers, (Punish?) every transgressor *and lawless person*, and not me ... what he doth, how doth he it? And turning unto the rulers of the people, he spake this saying: Search the scriptures, in which ye think ye have life; these are they which testify of me. Do not think that I came to accuse *you* to my father; there is one that accuseth you, even Moses, in whom ye trust. And when they said, We know that God spake unto Moses; but as for thee, we know not *whence thou art*; Jesus answering said unto them, Now is *your* unbelief accused. ...

Recto

... that they might draw (?) ... and having taken up stones with one accord might stone him; and *the rulers* laid hands on him that they might take him, and deliver him unto the multitude; and they *could* not take him, because the hour of his betrayal was not yet come; and the Lord himself going forth out of their hands conveyed himself away from *them*. And behold a leper came unto *him* and said, Jesu, master, *I* journeying with lepers, and eating with them in the inn, myself *took leprosy*; now if *thou wilt*, I am made clean. Then said the Lord unto him, I will; be thou clean. *And immediately* the leprosy departed from him. *And the Lord said unto him*, Go, *shew thyself* unto the *priests*. . . .

Fragment 2, recto

When they were come unto him, they by questioning tempted him, saying, Jesu, master, we know that thou art come *from God*; for those things which thou doest do testify above all the prophets; *tell* us *therefore*, is it lawful *to pay* unto the kings what is due unto the government? Shall we pay them, or not? Jesus knowing their mind, being moved with indignation said unto them, Why do ye with your mouth call me master, and ye hear not what I say? Well did Esaias prophesy of you, saying, This people honoureth me with their lips, but their heart is far from me; *teaching* the commandments *of men for doctrines*.

Verso

. . . having closed (it?) up in a secret (?) place (?) . . . it is subjected (?) obscurely . . . the weight thereof unweighed. . . . And when they were perplexed at *his* strange question, Jesus walked and stood *upon the* bank of the *river* Jordan, and stretching forth his right hand he (filled? it with seed?) and scattered (it) upon the . . . . And then . . . water; . . . and it (sprang up?) before them, and it brought forth fruit. . . .

Two more small fragments yield no connected sense.

APPENDIX II

ACTS OF PAUL

SINCE Dr. James's translation (pp. 270 ff.) was made, much more of this book, in the Greek version, has come to light. The largest addition is from the Hamburg papyrus codex, which was published by Carl Schmidt in 1936, and dated by him about A.D. 300. In it his previous conclusions, in outline and in detail, are generally confirmed. Here we have eleven fairly well-preserved pages, the first eight of which contain parts of the text which are not to be found in the Coptic manuscript, or are represented there in a very fragmentary state. After this two leaves (four pages) have been lost; when the text of the codex begins again we are well into the Martyrium, which it continues to the end. Most of the text of the eighth page is covered by three other Greek manuscripts: one, an Oxyrhynchus parchment leaf already published (late fourth century), and subsequently identified as belonging to the *Acts of Paul*; another, a Berlin papyrus, which a fragment at Michigan was found to join (probably end of third century); and a further small fragment from another Michigan papyrus (third or fourth century); most of these overlap, and the *verso* of the last was finally shown by Professor W. D. McHardy to overlap with, and be continued by the text of a leaf of Schmidt's Coptic manuscript believed by him to belong to another work, and translated separately by James on pp. 31 ff. of this book. The gap between the first eight and the last three pages of the Hamburg codex is thus partly filled and the amount still missing can be calculated. In his work on the Greek text Schmidt produces convincing evidence for the debt of its author to the *Acts of Peter* and on consideration of this would finally date its composition A.D. 180–90. The first page of the Hamburg text shows us Paul at Ephesus defending his cause before the governor, Hieronymus; it must have been preceded by some account of his preaching there and also (as Schmidt shows, from comparison with an Ethiopic *Letter of Pelagia* where the same material has evidently been used) of a journey previously made by him into the mountains and his meeting there with a huge lion, which at its own request he baptized. We meet the lion later in the story, which is from this point preserved in full; Nicephorus' condensed version of it is translated by James on p. 292, where the position of Paul's sojourn at Ephesus is still undetermined.[1] The new documents show the order of Paul's travels in the latter part of the *Acts* to have been: Ephesus, Philippi, Corinth, Rome.

In my translation I have adopted as many of the supplements and interpretations of Schmidt, and also of Kurfess (*Ztschr. f. ntl. Wiss.* xxxviii. 184 ff.) as seemed to me likely.[2] I owe several other suggestions to Prof. G. D. Kilpatrick. For further studies on the Acta Pauli, and smaller fragments of the Greek version, see: Oxyrhynchus Papyri, xiii. 1602; H. A. Saunders, *Harvard Theological Review*, xxxi. 73 ff.; G. D. Kilpatrick and C. H. Roberts, *J.T.S.* xlvii. 196 ff.; W. D. McHardy, *Expository Times*, lviii, no. 10, 279.

(The governor speaks:) . . . our (?) gods. Say, then, what are. . . . Paul said unto *him*, (Do what thou wilt?); for thou hast no power *over me save over* my body; thou shalt not kill my soul. But *hearken*, how thou must be saved, and taking all my (sayings?) to heart . . . (who?) hath fashioned the (sun?) and the earth and the stars and principalities and dominions and all good things in the world because of . . . *for* the use of men . . . they being carried away and enslaved . . . by (?) gold . . . and silver and precious stones . . . and adulteries and drunkenness. For having considered (?) they went (the ways?) that lead unto deception by reason of the things aforesaid, and were slain. Now therefore since the Lord will, that we should live in God because of the error in the world, *and not* die in (our) sins, he saveth through the chaste *men who* preach, that ye may repent and believe *that there is one God* and one Jesus Christ and there is none other; for your *gods are of brass* and stone and

---

[1] See also Nicetas of Paphlagonia, 'Panegyric on St. Paul', in *Orientalia Christiana*, xxiii (1931), 58–96.
[2] Cf. the review by Sir Harold Idris Bell in *J.T.S.* xxxviii (1938), 189–91 of Schmidt's edition of the Hamburg papyrus.

wood, being able neither to take food nor see nor hear nor even stand. Take a good resolution and be saved, lest *God* be wroth and consume ye with fire unquenchable, and *your* memorial perish. And when the governor heard these things . . . *in* the theatre with the multitude he said, Men of Ephesus, that this man hath spoken well, I know; but also that it is not yet time for ye to learn these things. What therefore ye will, determine. Then said some, Burn him by the. . . . But the goldsmiths said, To the beasts with the man. And there arose a great *tumult*; and Hieronymus when he had scourged him condemned him to the beasts. Now the brethren, since it was Pentecost, wept not, neither did they *bow* the knee, but they *stood* and prayed rejoicing. But after six days Hieronymus made an hunting show, so that all who beheld the greatness of the *wild beasts* were astonished. [*Page 2*] While Paul was bound . . . he turned not away from (his purpose? but) he prayed . . . (when) he heard the noise of the waggons and *the tumult* of them that did handle the beasts. And (a lion) came beside the wicket of the *stadium wherein* Paul was enclosed, and cried out mightily, so that all the *people* cried, The lion! For he roared fierce and furiously, *so that even Paul* left off praying, being afraid. And there was *a man named* Diophantus, a freedman of Hieronymus, whose wife was a disciple of Paul and sat by him night and day, *so that* Diophantus was jealous, and was instant for the beast fight. *And* Artemilla the wife of Hieronymus desired to hear Paul pray; and she said unto the wife of Diophantus, Eubula, (Let us go?) and hear the prayer of him who fighteth with the beasts. And she went and *told* Paul; and Paul being filled with joy said, Bring her. And she put on sadder raiment, and came away unto him with Eubula. But when Paul saw her, he groaned and said, Woman, thou ruler of this world, thou mistress of much gold, thou citizeness of much luxury, thou proud of thy raiment, sit down upon the ground and forget thy riches, thy beauty and thine ornaments; for these shall avail thee naught, if thou ask (?) not God who accounteth the things but dung, which are here marvellous (?), but freely granteth the wondrous things that are yonder. Gold perisheth, riches are consumed, raiment weareth out, beauty groweth old, great cities are changed, and the world is destroyed in fire through the wickedness of men. God only remaineth, and the adoption given through him in which it is necessary to be saved. And now, O Artemilla, hope in God and he shall deliver thee; hope in Christ and he shall give thee forgiveness of sins and shall set upon thee a crown of liberty, that thou mayest no more serve idols and the savour of sacrifice, but a living God and the father of Christ, whose glory is for ever and ever, Amen. And these things Artemilla having heard with Eubula, she prayed Paul that he would straightway baptize her in God.

And the fight with the wild beasts was (appointed) for the morrow. [*Page 3*] And Hieronymus heard through Diophantus that the women sat beside Paul night and day, and he was angered not a little with Artemilla and Eubula the freedwoman. And when he had supped, Hieronymus departed the earlier, that he might speedily accomplish the hunting show. But they said unto Paul, Wilt thou that we bring a smith, that thou mayest be loosed and baptize us in the sea? And Paul said unto them, I will it not; for I trust in God, who hath delivered the whole world out of bondage. And Paul cried unto God on the sabbath, as the Lord's day drew nigh, on the day when Paul was to fight with the beasts; and he said, O my God, Christ Jesus, who hast redeemed me out of so many evils, grant that before Artemilla and Eubula, that are thine own, the bonds be rent from off mine hands. And while Paul called witness upon these things, there entered in a youth exceeding fair and comely, and loosed the bonds of Paul, the youth smiling the while, and straightway departed. But because of the vision which befell Paul and the miraculous sign concerning the bonds, his grief at the beast fight vanished and he rejoiced and leapt as if in paradise, and taking Artemilla he went forth from the strait and *dark place where* the prisoners are guarded. And when they *were gone forth unknown to the* watchers and *were even* now in safety, *Paul* (called to witness?) his own God saying, The (gates are open? . . . bless?) thy dispensation . . . *that* Artemilla be initiated with the seal in the Lord; and *then the locked* gates flew open in the name of God . . . the guards were fallen into a deep sleep; and *straightway* came forth the matron and the blessed Paul with (Eubula) . . . the darkness . . . and a young man, like . . . of Paul, lightened not by a lamp (but) by the (sanctity?) of his person, went before them, so that they came nigh unto *the sea; and* the shining one stood over against (them?) . . . and *Paul when he had prayed* laid his hand upon Artemilla *and blessed the* water in the name of Christ Jesus, so that the *sea swelled exceedingly*; and *Artemilla* being seized with great fear well nigh swooned; (and Paul cried out?) and said, O thou who lightenest and shinest, *help, lest the* heathen say [*page 4*] that the captive Paul hath fled having slain Artemilla. And again the young man smiled; and the matron came to herself, and journeyed unto the house, as the day was already breaking. But as she (?) entered in, the guards being asleep, he brake bread, and brought water also and gave her to drink with a word, and sent her away to Hieronymus her husband; but he did supplicate. And early in the morning there was an outcry from the citizens, Let us go to the spectacle, let us go and see him that hath God, fighting with the beasts. But Hieronymus himself came thither, both because of the suspicion which he had toward his wife, and also because he

(Paul) had not fled; and he bade Diophantus and the other servants bring Paul into the stadium. And he (?) was haled forth, saying naught, but bowed down and groaning, that he was triumphed over by the city; and being led away straightway he was cast into the stadium; so that all were vexed at the grave mien of Paul. And Artemilla together with Eubula falling most perilously sick (with care) lest Paul should perish, Hieronymus was grieved not a little concerning his wife, but also because it was already noised abroad in the city, and he had not his wife with him. When therefore he was seated, the *chief huntsman* commanded that there be set loose against him a lion *taken in hunting* but a *little* while before, very fierce, so that the whole multitude . . . that *Paul* should be killed . . . but the *lion leapt down* out of the cage, *and did not roar while Paul* prayed. Moreover . . . out of the thornbrakes . . . *and* great wonder came upon *them all*, for he was exceedingly *great and mighty.* But Paul (persevered in his?) proper work of prayer *to Jesus Christ*, and rendered witness; *and* (?) *the lion*, when he had looked round *about him*, and fully shewn himself, came running *and lay down* beside the legs of Paul, like a docile lamb and *as it were* his *servant*; and when he had left off praying, even as one that awaketh out of *dreams* he spake unto Paul in human *speech, Grace* (?) *be with* thee. And Paul was not afraid but *himself said, Grace be with* thee, lion; and he laid his hand *upon him. And all the multitude* cried out, Away with the magician, away with the *sorcerer. But the lion* gazed at Paul and Paul *at the lion, and* Paul *perceived* that this *was the* lion [*page 5*] which had come and been baptized. And moved by faith Paul said, Lion, was it thou whom I baptized? And the lion answering spake unto Paul, saying, Yea. And again spake Paul unto him, saying, And how wast thou taken in hunting? And the lion spake with one (*sic*) voice, Even as thou, Paul. And Hieronymus sent in many wild beasts, so that Paul might be destroyed, and against the lion, archers that they might destroy him also; and out of a clear sky a hailstorm very thick and exceeding great did violently hurtle from heaven, so that many perished and all the rest fled. But neither Paul was touched, nor the lion, but the other wild beasts perished because of the hail, which was so heavy that Hieronymus' ear was struck and shorn off; and the multitude fleeing cried out, Save us, God, save us, thou God of the man who hath fought with the wild beasts. And Paul bade farewell to the lion, which spake no more; and he went forth from the stadium, and went down unto the harbour, and entered into the (?) ship bound for Macedonia; for many were they who sailed, (deeming) the city about to perish. Therefore went he with them as one of the fugitives; but the lion departed into the mountains as was his natural wont. Now Artemilla and Eubula mourned not a little, fasting and considering (?) what had befallen Paul. But when it was night there came (a youth?) plainly into the bedchamber where . . . Hieronymus had a running sore from his ear . . . Artemilla by reason of grief . . . (the youth drew near and) said unto them, Be not troubled (concerning Paul?) . . . *for in the* name of Christ Jesus and in the power *of the Almighty, Paul* his *servant* hath departed into Macedonia, *there also* to fulfil the dispensations *of the Lord;* but you . . . *great* astonishment possessed them. *But Hieronymus even now* grown sober in the night in his pains *said, O thou* God *who didst help the* man who fought with the beasts, save *me through* (?) *the youth* (?) that did come in a vision through *the locked* bedchamber. And he seeing them in fear *and* great . . . those who sat by, leaping up (?) . . . the physicians . . . a cry, By the will of Christ Jesus, . . . the ear. And it became whole, as the youth had charged them, (saying), Treat thyself with honey.

The Greek text, which does not insert the correspondence with the Corinthians here (see above, pp. 288 ff.), has no account of Paul's sojourn at Philippi. There is no certainty that it was described in the Coptic either; for there is no ground for the suggested supplement 'to Philippi' on p. 288, at the end of section VI, and the passage which begins VII has been wrongly restored by Schmidt; it belongs to the account of the visit to Corinth, which reads in the Greek as follows:

[*Page 6*] *From Philippi to Corinth*

And when Paul came unto Corinth from Philippi unto the house of Epiphanius there was joy; so that all our people rejoiced, and withal wept, when Paul told them what he had suffered in Philippi in the houses of labour, and in every place, what befell him, so that finally his tears flowed freely (?), and prayer was made without ceasing by all for Paul, and he accounted himself happy, that with such likemindedness they ordered his affairs every day in prayer to the Lord; and so the greatness of his joy was unsurpassable and the soul of Paul was exalted by reason of (?) the benevolence of the brethren, so that for forty days he taught the tale of his endurances, (namely), in whatsoever place each thing befell him and what great and wondrous works were vouchsafed unto him; so that at each declaration he did glorify the almighty God and Christ Jesus, who had found Paul well pleasing in every place. *But when* the days were fulfilled that Paul should be sent to Rome, there arose grief among the brethren (concerning) when they should see him again. And Paul being filled with the holy spirit said: Men and brethren, be diligent concerning fasting (?) and charity; for behold, I go away into a furnace of fire . . . I, and I prevail not if the Lord *afford me* not power. For David journeyed with Saul . . . *and* (though) angered, (spared?) Nabal, being persuaded by *the wife of* Nabal; for there was with him Christ Jesus, the God (?) . . . this precious fast.

(Here belong the Coptic fragments translated above, p. 293 (section IX). The text, now augmented by the Greek, is here retranslated.)

(And the grace of the Lord?) shall walk with (me? that I may fulfil?) *every* dispensation that shall come upon me . . . in patience. But they were sorrowful, and fasted. And Cleobius was in the spirit and said unto them, Brethren, it is necessary that Paul fulfil every dispensation and afterward go up unto the . . . of death . . . and (in?) much instruction and knowledge and sowing of the word; and that he being envied shall depart out of this world. But when the brethren and Paul (?) heard *these things* they lifted up their voice and said, O God of our Lord, the father of Christ, do thou help Paul thy servant *that* he may remain with us by reason of our weakness. And Paul was touched with compunction, and put away the fast with them; and as the offering was made by Paul . . . [*page 7*] (the bread divided?) of itself into parts . . . (asking?) what this *sign* might be (that they?) beheld . . . what . . . would say, but to him . . . would not. But the spirit came upon Myrte, so that she said unto them, Brethren, wherefore are ye *afraid* when ye behold this sign? For Paul the servant of the Lord shall save many in Rome, and shall feed many with the word, so that there shall be no numbering them; and he be manifest more than all the faithful; and thereafter mightily shall the glory of the Lord Christ Jesus come upon him, so that there shall be great grace in Rome. Thus straightway afterward was the spirit in Myrte stilled. And each one partook of the bread and they feasted (*Copt.* were in joy) after the custom of the fast, to the sound of the psalms of David, and songs; and Paul was glad. And on the morrow, when they had continued all night in the will of God, Paul said, Men and brethren, I shall sail on the day of the preparation, and I depart unto Rome, that I may not stay those things which are commanded and laid upon me; for unto this was I appointed. And they were exceedingly grieved when they heard these words; and all the brethren contributed according to their power, that Paul might be troubled in nothing save in that he was parting from the brethren. Now when he went up into the ship, while they all prayed, Artemon the captain of the ship was one that had been baptized by Paul; and he (greeted?) Paul (joyfully?), for that such great matters were entrusted unto him, (as if?) the Lord himself were entering into (the ship). But when the ship had set sail, Artemon partook with Paul in the *grace of God* to glorify the Lord Christ Jesus who made provision for Paul. And when they were upon the high sea, and there was silence, Paul being heavy by reason of his fasts and vigils fell asleep. And the Lord came unto him walking upon the sea, and he stirred Paul and said unto him, Arise, and see. And he awoke and said, Thou art my Lord Christ Jesus the king *of heaven.* But wherefore art thou thus (?) sad and downcast, Lord? If thou art pained, manifest it, Lord, for I am not a little anguished to see thee thus. And the Lord said, Paul, again am I about to be crucified. And Paul said, God forbid, Lord, that I should see this. But the Lord said unto Paul, Paul, depart, and go even unto Rome and exhort the brethren, that they continue in the calling which is unto the Father. And . . . *the Lord* . . . walking upon the sea, went before *him and* shewed. . . . And when the voyage was accomplished . . . Paul came out with great sadness; *and he saw* upon the harbour a man standing, who awaited Artemon *the* captain; and when he had seen him, saluted him. . . . [*Page 8*] And he said unto him, Claudius, behold *Paul the* beloved of the Lord, who is come here with me. *And then* Claudius embraced Paul and saluted him and without delay himself carried the (gear) from the ship unto his own home. And he rejoiced greatly, shewing also the things concerning him unto the brethren, so that straightway the house of Claudius was full of joy and thankfulness, for they saw how Paul put away his (look) of grief and taught the word of truth and spake: Men and soldiers of Christ, hear: how oft hath God delivered Israel from the hand of lawless men; and so long as they kept the things pertaining unto the Lord, he left them not. For he saved them out of the hand of Pharaoh, that was lawless, and Og, a king more unholy, and from Adar (Arad?) and the foreign peoples. And since they kept the things pertaining unto the Lord, he further gave unto them of the fruit of the loins, having promised them the land of Canaan, and subjected the foreign peoples unto them; and thereafter, what things he vouchsafed unto them in the desert and waterless place. Moreover he sent out prophets to preach our Lord Christ Jesus, who receiving according unto order and lot and due portion the spirit of Christ, having suffered affliction, were slain of the people. When therefore they departed from the living God according to their own lusts, they did lose their everlasting inheritance. And now, brethren, there doth impend a great trial; which having endured, we shall have access unto the Lord; and let us receive as a refuge and a shield of good will Jesus Christ who gave himself for us; if at least ye receive the word so as it is, that God hath for our sakes sent down a spirit of power at the last times into flesh, that is, into Mary the Galilaean according unto the word of prophecy, which was borne in the womb and made of her so that she gave birth and bore Jesus Christ our king out of Bethlehem of Judaea, who was brought up in Nazara, and having gone on to Jerusalem and all Judaea, taught: The kingdom of heaven is at hand; leave the darkness, receive the light, ye who did proceed (?) in the shadow of death; a light hath arisen unto you. And he did great and marvellous things; so that he chose out of the tribes twelve men whom having anointed (?) in understanding and faith he kept with himself, raising the dead, and healing diseases, and cleansing lepers, and healing the blind, [*end of page 8*] and curing the maimed, raising up the palsied, cleansing those possessed of devils; in general he went through all the (land) by . . . ministering and . . . of the river . . . *Israel*; for a woman . . . having an issue of blood . . . and . . . not . . . our Lord Jesus *Christ* . . . be led *into the* council (?) . . . go through . . . cemeteries . . . greatly by . . . the king of glory . . . the rest of the seed . . . the king of glory . . .

Remains of several more lines end the Berlin and Michigan papyrus. Little can have been lost after this before the beginning of the *verso* of the other Michigan fragment, whose text is continued on the leaf of the Heidelberg Coptic manuscript translated by James on p. 31.

. . . all the miracles (?) . . . for he maketh . . . works (And as they?) wondered, (and pondered these things?) in their hearts, he said unto them, &c.

Here, as McHardy observes, Jesus' own words are reported.

INDEX OF APOCRYPHAL WRITINGS MENTIONED

Laodiceans, Ep. to, **478.**
Lazarus, Revelation of, xxvi.
Lentulus, letter of, **477.**
Leucius : **xx.**
Acts of John, **228.**
Linus, Passions of Peter and Paul,
36, 470.
Longinus, Acts, 471.
Lucianus, Gospels acc. to, 22.
Luke, Acts, 471.
Lusa Apostolorum, 23.
ʹ
Marcellus, Passion of Peter and
Paul, 470.
Mark :
Acts, **471.**
Author of Apoc. of Paul (Coptic),
554.
Author of Life of John Baptist, xxv.
Mary Magdalene, Life of, 157
Mary, the Virgin :
Apocalypse, 555, 563 ; Gospel
(Gnostic), **xxii** ; Letters, 478 ;
questions of, 20.
Birth of (Gnostic), 19 ; narratives
of Birth, 38, **79** ; death (as-
sumption of), xix, 22, narra-
tives, **194.**
Syriac history of, 67, 80, 222.
Matthew :
Acts, **460, 466.**
Gospel of Pseudo-M., 38, **70.**
Matthias :
Acts, with Andrew, 453.
Gospel or Traditions of, 12, 22.
Mechtildis, revelation of, 150 n.
Melito (Ps.-) :
Narrative of Assumption, 209.
Acts of John, 257.
Mellitus, see Melito.
Memoria Apostolorum, 21.
Ministry of Jesus, Coptic narratives
of, **147.**

Nazarenes, Gospel of, see Gospel
acc. to the Hebrews.
Nicodemus, Gospel of (Acts of
Pilate), **94.**
[570.
Oxyrhynchus papyri, 25, 264, 325,
Passion, Gospels and Narratives of,
94.

Paul :
Acts, xviii, **xx,** 23, 270 (incl. Paul
and Thecla. 272), 470 ; of P. and
Andrew, 472.
Apocalypse (lost), 21 : (extant),
xxi, 525.
Epistles, **288, 478.**
Preaching of, **297.**
Peter :
Acts, **xx,** 22, **300,** 470, 472, 474 ;
of P. and Andrew, 458.
Apocalypse, xxi, 23, **505.**
Doctrine, 18.
Gospel, xix, 13, 22, **90** : **89.**
Preaching **16** : (Syriac), 18.
Teaching, 19.
Philip :
Acts, 22, **439,** 469.
Apocalypse, 505.
Gospel, 12.
Pilate :
Acts of, or Gospel of Nicodemus,
xix, Pt. I, **94** : Pt. II, 117.
Arabic Life of, 152.
Death of, 157.
Ethiopic fragment about, 151.
Letters to Claudius, 146 ; to Tibe-
rius, 153 ; to Herod, 155.
Paradosis of, 154 ; Reports of,
xix, 153.
Pistis Sophia, **xxiii,** 12, 31, 66.
Priesthood of Jesus, xxv.
Prochorus, Acts of John, 469.
Protevangelium, **38.**

Sangermanensis, Codex, addition
in, 33.
Seneca, letters to Paul, **480.**
Septuagint, 29 n., 47 n.
Sibylline Oracles II, 521.
Simon and Jude, Acts, 464.
Solomon, Testament of, 224.
Stephen, Revelation of, **564.**
Strasburg papyrus, **30.**

Thaddaeus, Acts, 471.
Thecla, see Acts.
Thomas :
Acts, **xx,** 23, 24, 364 : 468, 470.
Apocalypse, **xxi,** 555.
Gospel, 14, 22, 24, 49.
Tiberius, letter, 156 ; Healing of, 158

Titus :
    Acts by Zenas, 271, 272 n., 285,
    291, 471.
    Epistle of, 265–6, 303, 349.
    Twelve, Gospel of the, see Gospels.

Xanthippe and Polyxena, Acts, 471,
    475.

Zenaïs and Philonilla, Acts, 471.
Zenas, Acts of Titus, see Titus.

INDEX OF WRITERS CITED

I. ANCIENT AND MEDIAEVAL

II. MODERN [1]

[1] See also the Bibliography, pp. xxix–xxxi.

INDEX OF PROPER NAMES
I. PERSONS

II. PLACES

Thessalonica, **340**.
Thrace, 339.
Tiber, 306.
Tiberia, 203, 204.
Tiberias, lake, 9.

Tiberias, **566**.
Tyre, **284**.

Vienne, 158.

Warkan, 414.

INDEX OF SUBJECTS

Acherusian Lake, 185, 518, 524, 537–8.
Agape, 490.
Alleluia, 461 ; interpreted, 541.
Angelology, **175**.
Angels adore God at sunset, 528 ; report deeds of men, 528 ; meet souls at death, **531**.
Angels of punishment, 529.
Animals :
   men changed into, 68, 81.
   miracles with, 75, 451, 452, &c.
   speaking, 298, **313**, 383, **398**, 446, 452, 473.
Apocrypha :
   the word, xiii.
   lists of, 22.
Apostles :
   at death of Virgin, **194**.
   call of, 9.
   dispersion, 365.
Archangel baptized, 474.
Architect, 372.
Ascension of our Lord, 503, 519.
Assumption of the Virgin, **194**.
Ass :
   form of Jewish god, 19.
   speaking, 383.
   wild asses, **396**.

Baptism: [572.
   described, **375**, 388, 418, 423, 474, of our Lord, 5, 6, 9, 191.
   of the Fathers in Hades, 494.
Beasts, fights with, 278, 292, 313, 572.
Beetle, speaking, 473.
Bible, a great, 144.
   of Esdras, 145.
Birds of Hell, 517.
Bishop, priest, deacon, reader, punished, 543.
Bugs, 242.

Camel and needle's eye, 459.
Cannibals, **453**.
Canon, Canonicity, xvii.
Carpenter's craft described, 366.
Children, slayers and exposers of, punished, 391, 473, 506, 515, 545, 564.
Chronology of world's history, 145.
Church building, 446, 450, 466, 467.
Clay birds, miracle of, 49, 55, 76, 82, 171.
Commandments, Ten, used as charm, 111.
Creation :
   complaint against man, 527.
   silence of, at Nativity, 46.
Cross :
   set up in Hell, 139.
   sign of, 123, **139**, 339, 390, 496.
   the true cross, 221, &c.
   visions of, and explanation of, 92, **254**, **334**, 344, **359**, 450.

Death personified, 85, 182, 196.
   terrors of, 85, 269, 429, 450.
Deaths of righteous and sinners, 530.
Demoniacs, 81, 82, 285, 314, 338 sq. *and see* Devil.
Descent into Hell, **117**, 167, 183, 494.
Devil, described, 149, 174, 451, 468.
   creator, the world, 189.
   his fall, 178, 189.
   his progress through the universe, 188.
   describes his functions, 177, 379.
Devil :
   appears as soldier, 264, 461.
   as old man, 456.
   as serpent, 81, 82, 379.

PRINTED IN
GREAT BRITAIN
AT THE
UNIVERSITY PRESS
OXFORD
BY
CHARLES BATEY
PRINTER
TO THE
UNIVERSITY